41: *Afro-American Poets Since 1955*, edited by Trudier Harris and Thadious M. Davis (1985)

42: *American Writers for Children Before 1900*, edited by Glenn E. Estes (1985)

43: *American Newspaper Journalists, 1690-1872*, edited by Perry J. Ashley (1986)

44: *American Screenwriters*, Second Series, edited by Randall Clark, Robert E. Morsberger, and Stephen O. Lesser (1986)

45: *American Poets, 1880-1945*, First Series, edited by Peter Quartermain (1986)

46: *American Literary Publishing Houses, 1900-1980: Trade and Paperback*, edited by Peter Dzwonkoski (1986)

47: *American Historians, 1866-1912*, edited by Clyde N. Wilson (1986)

48: *American Poets, 1880-1945*, Second Series, edited by Peter Quartermain (1986)

49: *American Literary Publishing Houses, 1638-1899*, 2 parts, edited by Peter Dzwonkoski (1986)

50: *Afro-American Writers Before the Harlem Renaissance*, edited by Trudier Harris (1986)

51: *Afro-American Writers from the Harlem Renaissance to 1940*, edited by Trudier Harris (1987)

52: *American Writers for Children Since 1960: Fiction*, edited by Glenn E. Estes (1986)

53: *Canadian Writers Since 1960*, First Series, edited by W. H. New (1986)

54: *American Poets, 1880-1945*, Third Series, 2 parts, edited by Peter Quartermain (1987)

55: *Victorian Prose Writers Before 1867*, edited by William B. Thesing (1987)

56: *German Fiction Writers, 1914-1945*, edited by James Hardin (1987)

57: *Victorian Prose Writers After 1867*, edited by William B. Thesing (1987)

58: *Jacobean and Caroline Dramatists*, edited by Fredson Bowers (1987)

59: *American Literary Critics and Scholars, 1800-1850*, edited by John W. Rathbun and Monica M. Grecu (1987)

60: *Canadian Writers Since 1960*, Second Series, edited by W. H. New (1987)

61: *American Writers for Children Since 1960: Poets, Illustrators, and Nonfiction Authors*, edited by Glenn E. Estes (1987)

62: *Elizabethan Dramatists*, edited by Fredson Bowers (1987)

63: *Modern American Critics, 1920-1955*, edited by Gregory S. Jay (1988)

64: *American Literary Critics and Scholars, 1850-1880*, edited by John W. Rathbun and Monica M. Grecu (1988)

65: *French Novelists, 1900-1930*, edited by Catharine Savage Brosman (1988)

66: *German Fiction Writers, 1885-1913*, 2 parts, edited by James Hardin (1988)

67: *Modern American Critics Since 1955*, edited by Gregory S. Jay (1988)

68: *Canadian Writers, 1920-1959*, First Series, edited by W. H. New (1988)

69: *Contemporary German Fiction Writers*, First Series, edited by Wolfgang D. Elfe and James Hardin (1988)

70: *British Mystery Writers, 1860-1919*, edited by Bernard Benstock and Thomas F. Staley (1988)

71: *American Literary Critics and Scholars, 1880-1900*, edited by John W. Rathbun and Monica M. Grecu (1988)

72: *French Novelists, 1930-1960*, edited by Catharine Savage Brosman (1988)

73: *American Magazine Journalists, 1741-1850*, edited by Sam G. Riley (1988)

74: *American Short-Story Writers Before 1880*, edited by Bobby Ellen Kimbel, with the assistance of William E. Grant (1988)

75: *Contemporary German Fiction Writers*, Second Series, edited by Wolfgang D. Elfe and James Hardin (1988)

76: *Afro-American Writers, 1940-1955*, edited by Trudier Harris (1988)

77: *British Mystery Writers, 1920-1939*, edited by Bernard Benstock and Thomas F. Staley (1988)

78: *American Short-Story Writers, 1880-1910*, edited by Bobby Ellen Kimbel, with the assistance of William E. Grant (1988)

79: *American Magazine Journalists, 1850-1900*, edited by Sam G. Riley (1988)

(Continued on back endsheets)

Twentieth-Century Italian Poets
First Series

Dictionary of Literary Biography® • Volume One Hundred Fourteen

Twentieth-Century Italian Poets
First Series

Edited by
Giovanna Wedel De Stasio, Glauco Cambon, and
Antonio Illiano

A Bruccoli Clark Layman Book
Gale Research Inc.
Detroit, London

Printed in the United States of America

Published simultaneously in the United Kingdom
by Gale Research International Limited
(An affiliated company of Gale Research Inc.)

The paper used in this publication meets the minimum requirements
of American National Standard for Information Sciences—Permanence
Paper for Printed Library Materials, ANSI Z39.48-1984. ∞™

Library of Congress Catalog Card Number 92-44162
ISBN 0-8103-7591-5

Contents

Plan of the Series

. . . Almost the most prodigious asset of a country, and perhaps its most precious possession, is its native literary product—when that product is fine and noble and enduring.

Mark Twain*

The advisory board, the editors, and the publisher of the *Dictionary of Literary Biography* are joined in endorsing Mark Twain's declaration. The literature of a nation provides an inexhaustible resource of permanent worth. We intend to make literature and its creators better understood and more accessible to students and the reading public, while satisfying the standards of teachers and scholars.

To meet these requirements, *literary biography* has been construed in terms of the author's achievement. The most important thing about a writer is his writing. Accordingly, the entries in *DLB* are career biographies, tracing the development of the author's canon and the evolution of his reputation.

The purpose of *DLB* is not only to provide reliable information in a convenient format but also to place the figures in the larger perspective of literary history and to offer appraisals of their accomplishments by qualified scholars.

The publication plan for *DLB* resulted from two years of preparation. The project was proposed to Bruccoli Clark by Frederick C. Ruffner, president of the Gale Research Company, in November 1975. After specimen entries were prepared and typeset, an advisory board was formed to refine the entry format and develop the series rationale. In meetings held during 1976, the publisher, series editors, and advisory board approved the scheme for a comprehensive biographical dictionary of persons who contributed to North American literature. Editorial work on the first volume began in January 1977, and it was published in 1978. In order to make *DLB* more than a reference tool and to compile volumes that individually have claim to status as literary history, it was decided to organize volumes by topic, period, or genre. Each of these freestanding volumes provides a biographical-bibliographical guide and overview for a particular area of literature. We are convinced that this organization—as opposed to a single alphabet method—constitutes a valuable innovation in the presentation of reference material. The volume plan necessarily requires many decisions for the placement and treatment of authors who might properly be included in two or three volumes. In some instances a major figure will be included in separate volumes, but with different entries emphasizing the aspect of his career appropriate to each volume. Ernest Hemingway, for example, is represented in *American Writers in Paris, 1920-1939* by an entry focusing on his expatriate apprenticeship; he is also in *American Novelists, 1910-1945* with an entry surveying his entire career. Each volume includes a cumulative index of subject authors and articles. Comprehensive indexes to the entire series are planned.

With volume ten in 1982 it was decided to enlarge the scope of *DLB*. By the end of 1986 twenty-one volumes treating British literature had been published, and volumes for Commonwealth and Modern European literature were in progress. The series has been further augmented by the *DLB Yearbooks* (since 1981) which update published entries and add new entries to keep the *DLB* current with contemporary activity. There have also been *DLB Documentary Series* volumes which provide biographical and critical source materials for figures whose work is judged to have particular interest for students. One of these companion volumes is entirely devoted to Tennessee Williams.

We define literature as the *intellectual commerce of a nation:* not merely as belles lettres but as that ample and complex process by which ideas are generated, shaped, and transmitted. *DLB* entries are not limited to "creative writers" but extend to other figures who in their time and in their way influenced the mind of a people. Thus the series encompasses historians, journalists, publishers, and screenwriters. By this means

---

*From an unpublished section of Mark Twain's autobiography, copyright © by the Mark Twain Company

readers of *DLB* may be aided to perceive literature not as cult scripture in the keeping of intellectual high priests but firmly positioned at the center of a nation's life.

DLB includes the major writers appropriate to each volume and those standing in the ranks immediately behind them. Scholarly and critical counsel has been sought in deciding which minor figures to include and how full their entries should be. Wherever possible, useful references are made to figures who do not warrant separate entries.

Each *DLB* volume has a volume editor responsible for planning the volume, selecting the figures for inclusion, and assigning the entries. Volume editors are also responsible for preparing, where appropriate, appendices surveying the major periodicals and literary and intellectual movements for their volumes, as well as lists of further readings. Work on the series as a whole is coordinated at the Bruccoli Clark Layman editorial center in Columbia, South Carolina, where the editorial staff is responsible for accuracy of the published volumes.

One feature that distinguishes *DLB* is the illustration policy—its concern with the iconography of literature. Just as an author is influenced by his surroundings, so is the reader's understanding of the author enhanced by a knowledge of his environment. Therefore *DLB* volumes include not only drawings, paintings, and photographs of authors, often depicting them at various stages in their careers, but also illustrations of their families and places where they lived. Title pages are regularly reproduced in facsimile along with dust jackets for modern authors. The dust jackets are a special feature of *DLB* because they often document better than anything else the way in which an author's work was perceived in its own time. Specimens of the writers' manuscripts are included when feasible.

Samuel Johnson rightly decreed that "The chief glory of every people arises from its authors." The purpose of the *Dictionary of Literary Biography* is to compile literary history in the surest way available to us—by accurate and comprehensive treatment of the lives and work of those who contributed to it.

The *DLB* Advisory Board

Foreword

In structuring the two *Dictionary of Literary Biography* volumes on twentieth-century Italian poetry, of which *DLB 114* is the first, we grouped writers within two time frames, the first extending from the beginning of the century to the end of World War II, and the next covering the postwar era. The first volume includes significant poets who fall into the transitional age between the nineteenth and the twentieth centuries, including the Milanese Gian Pietro Lucini, who opened the way to symbolism in Italy, for example; Ada Negri, also from the Lombardy region, whose production was first driven by strong social interests and later inspired by religious feelings; and Ligurian Ceccardo Roccatagliata Ceccardi, who boldly experimented with analogy and synaesthesia, thus contributing to the renovation of modern Italian poetry.

The profound cultural and literary changes occurring in Italy between the mid nineteenth and early twentieth centuries were a reaction to the historical events that affected cultural developments all over Europe: from romantic idealism (inspired by nationalistic ferments) to the wars of the Risorgimento (Italy's national unification movement culminating in 1870); from belief in the so-called cult of freedom to the dominance of positivism (which insisted that experience, not speculation, is the basis of knowledge); from the explosion of industrialization to the eruption of individual and collective egotistic forces; from the rebellions of oppressed peoples to a renewed faith in Catholicism.

This complex historical and cultural process—also reflected in a variety of other ideological movements—affected poetic invention and experimentation. Generally, early-twentieth-century Italian poets reacted against the nineteenth-century high style and political rhetoric. They opposed the pompous aspects of the late nineteenth century, from Giosuè Carducci's historical verse to Gabriele D'Annunzio's aestheticism and artificiality. Yet, in many ways they were also influenced by their recent predecessors. Carducci was essentially a nineteenth-century poet, although he was initially sensitive to libertarian ideas and to the influence of the new mechanized society, and although he introduced metric and rhythmic innovations into his verse. More influential was the lexical, syntactical, and metrical legacy of Giovanni Pascoli and D'Annunzio, which may be found in most twentieth-century Italian verse. Pascoli revolutionized poetic language by introducing material traditionally believed to be antipoetic; he also attributed semantic value to phonic elements, utilizing (sometimes excessively) onomatopoeia and paronomasia. His poetic expression is alogical or prelogical. He makes use of analogy and musicality, as did French symbolist poets, who had developed new melodic possibilities by discarding syntactic and grammatical laws. The symbolists had attempted to express the ineffable by using words and rhythms in ways that evoked sensations and images rather than thought.

D'Annunzio, both in his prose and poetry, recalls the decadent atmosphere. He proved to be an artificer of hypnotically sonorous and dramatic effects, expressing strong emotions. With his aggressive vitality and fanatic heroism, he foreshadowed futuristic tensions; yet, in his "nocturnal" and "secret" poetic phase, he strenuously searched for the perfect word, the pliable, subtle, and deeply significant word, capable of illuminating the most mysterious aspects of the spirit. Therefore he devoted his poetic activity to prosodic, metric, phonosymbolic experimentation. Rightly, the poet Eugenio Montale stated that not to have learned anything from D'Annunzio would be a most negative sign for any poet who followed him.

In recent years the impact of the French symbolists and of their forerunner Charles-Pierre Baudelaire on twentieth-century Italian poetry has been studied and documented. Of particular interest is, for instance, Glauco Viazzi's anthology of poetry, *Dal simbolismo al Déco* (From Symbolism to Art Deco, 2 volumes, 1981), which analyzes the origins and development of the new poetry of this century by means of a wide sampling of major and minor writers. Early-twentieth-century Italian poets were influenced indirectly also by

Edgar Allan Poe, who had theorized that lyrical invention was an expression of an exceptional spiritual moment. The nineteenth-century Italian poet Giacomo Leopardi, whom Poe did not know, had formulated a similar theory in his private notebooks, which he called *Zibaldone di pensieri* (the last entry was made in 1832), and Leopardi's influence in the twentieth century has also been strongly felt; see, for example, the proceedings of the Third International Congress on Leopardi, held in 1972: *Leopardi e il Novecento* (Leopardi and the Twentieth Century, 1974).

During the first half of the twentieth century, European philosophical and ideological movements played an important role in the evolution of Italian poetry. Henri Bergson's philosophy of intuitionism; Sigmund Freud's postulation of the subconscious and his search for the irrational components of personality; the philosophy of existentialism; phenomenology; and the philosophy of contingentism all had a demonstrable impact. In Italy, Benedetto Croce's vindication of the autonomy of art (poetry in particular) as a form of intuitional knowledge (with intuition and expression thus coinciding) played a part in the revolution.

The *crepuscolari* (twilight poets), as the critic G. A. Borgese labeled them in 1910 to indicate the decline (evening) of nineteenth-century poetry, opened the way for new forms of poetic expression with stylistic innovations and the conviction that poetic practice was socially irrelevant. The *crepuscolari* adopted a colloquial tone of self-confession rather than heroic celebration and often preferred free verse to rigid traditional metrics. A recurrent topos in their verses is the pathological condition of the poet, which often reflects a dramatic reality, as some *crepuscolari* suffered and died of consumption. Such literary developments are symptomatic of the gradual decrease in popularity of the D'Annunzio-like vatic poets; they also coincide with postulations about the inability of people to exist within a society if they are deprived of solid traditional values. The incapacity to participate fully in life is translated by the *crepuscolari* into resigned melancholy, isolation, and escape to a dreamworld or the past.

A radical break with tradition was made possible by the futurists, led by Filippo Tommaso Marinetti, who adopted revolutionary means of expression and aimed at an objective kind of poetry. The futurists' free-word compositions, completely devoid of any syntactic or logical rules, are attempts to bring life into art, allowing an ulti-mate emancipation from traditional poetry. The futurists declared their intentions and goals in a series of manifestos; although they achieved considerable artistic results in the plastic arts, their poetry is often disappointing. During the early phase of futurism (1909-1912) the poets who contributed to *La Voce* (a Florentine journal founded by Giuseppe Prezzolini in 1908 and edited by him until 1914) also helped to modernize Italian culture. Some of these poets, such as Corrado Govoni and Aldo Palazzeschi, went through a stage of *crepuscolarismo* and futurism. Other *vociani*, such as Clemente Rèbora and Piero Jahier, showed a strong social and ethical commitment. Dino Campana and Arturo Onofri promoted, particularly during the final years of the journal (1914-1916), autobiographical confession, self-analysis, and the fusion of poetry and prose. From a stylistic point of view Edoardo Sanguineti defines these poets as the expressionists of Italy (in his introduction to *Poesia del Novecento*, 1969). This is especially true of Campana, who was influenced not only by Carducci and D'Annunzio; by American poets such as Poe and Walt Whitman; and by Arthur Rimbaud and Friedrich Nietzsche, but also by what Guillaume Apollinaire called "orphic cubism," a reference to Robert Delaunay's style of painting. Campana tried to render verbally the abstract and subjective quality of this style and borrowed its symbolic usage of vivid chromatism.

Among the other poets of *La Voce* Rèbora and Camillo Sbarbaro were extraordinarily innovative, even though their activity was not marked by the fanaticism and subversiveness of the futurists. Religious preoccupations, which were stimulated by philosophical idealism, colored their work. Sbarbaro's poetry seems pure and essential, yet full of tension. After the traumatic experience of World War I Rèbora's vigorous expressionistic style denotes emotions of anguish, uncertainty, angry dissent, and hope; his conversion to Catholicism in 1929, followed by a twenty-year period of poetic silence, influenced his final production.

Other Italian poets contributed in different ways to innovations in poetry: Umberto Saba avoided complacency, aiming at an "honest" poetry based on introspection and autobiography, and emblematically representative of the suffering and mystery of human existence. Vincenzo Cardarelli, in his journal *La Ronda* (1919-1923), expressed his debt to Leopardi's language and style; Cardarelli believed in strongly inspired yet emotionally detached verse. Onofri, originally influenced by Pascoli and D'Annunzio, and later by Rudolf Steiner's esoteric doctrines, invented a magical connection between physics and metaphysics through the use of analogy. Ungaretti assimilated the teachings of European avant-garde poetry—in particular that of the great French symbolists, from Rimbaud to Stéphane Mallarmé—but he also felt the necessity to go back to the well-known Italian poets of the past (such as Jacopone da Todi, Dante, and Petrarch). His spiritual and intellectual restlessness is a result of continuous experimentation and a constant yearning for the absolute. Ungaretti used the poetic word to suggest meanings which go beyond the direct object of reference; the mystical quality of his vocabulary after *L'Allegria* (1931) is clearly derived from Mallarmé.

Montale's poetic career, starting with *Ossi di seppia* (1925; translated as *The Bones of Cuttlefish*, 1983), reflects many of the historical and spiritual changes occurring during the twentieth century in Italy. His poetic persona objectifies emotion by means of penetrating imagery; his language is simple and dissonant. With Montale's *Satura*, published in 1962, a new poetic phase began: Montale reversed his focus from the absolute to the ephemeral, from sublimation to desecration, ironically manipulating words.

Salvatore Quasimodo, like other hermetic poets, such as Mario Luzi and Alfonso Gatto, learned from Ungaretti and Montale the suggestive power of the poetic word, while at the same time revealing a debt to D'Annunzio. In his early hermetic stage, Quasimodo aimed at the purity of the word, and he was stylistically influenced by his translations of Greek lyricists; later his poetry became socially committed—art was no longer designated the comforter of humanity. Instead its goal was to transform society.

Different criteria have been adopted to classify hermetic poets. In some anthologies Ungaretti, Montale, and Quasimodo are grouped together under this designation. In reality Ungaretti and Montale are prehermetics. Quasimodo is often, but not always, grouped with the first generation of hermetic poets. It should be kept in mind that hermeticism was never an organized school or a literary movement. Hermetic traits may be found in many poets who wrote during the Fascist regime. The obscurity of the hermetic style has been interpreted in political terms as a historical rejection of the regime and as a withdrawal into an ideal world of significant images

and sounds; philosophically in has also been viewed as the poets' ultimate attempt to preserve the integrity of conscience from the relativity and mutability of the phenomenal world. Regardless of these interpretations, the tendency toward a difficult and ambiguous style is not restricted to twentieth-century Italy.

DLB 114 also includes a selection of vernacular poets who expressed in a personal style the social changes undergone by Italy during the century. Industrialization and the development of mass communications, particularly after World War II, smothered Italy's regional culture, fostering national standardization in living and speaking. A reaction against this tendency favored a revival of regional identities and vernacular traditions. The relation between language and dialect is still at the center of lively critical debates; yet the use of dialect is no longer viewed as a shameful clinging to a pre-industrial past. Instead it is thought to facilitate spontaneous and immediate poetic expression.

The recent increase of interest in vernacular poetry is attested to by the publication of anthologies solely devoted to dialect poetry and by the inclusion of dialect verse in general anthologies of Italian poetry. *Poesia dialettale del Novecento* (Dialect Poetry of the Twentieth Century, 1952), edited by Mario Dell'Arco and Pier Paolo Pasolini, one of the earliest selections of vernacular poetry in Italy, is divided geographically. Pier Vincenzo Mengaldo includes vernacular poets in his *Poeti italiani del Novecento* (1978). Recent and well-documented samplers of vernacular poetry are *Le parole di legno* (Words Made of Wood), edited by Mario Chiesa and Giovanni Tesio in 1984; *Poesia in dialetto del Novecento italiano* (Dialect Poetry in the Italian Twentieth Century, 2 volumes, 1984); *Poeti dialettali del Novecento* (Dialect Poets of the Twentieth Century, 1987), edited by Franco Brevini; and *I poeti dialettali del ventesimo secolo* (The Dialect Poets of the Twentieth Century, 1987). H. Haller's bilingual anthology of Italian dialect poetry, translated for the English-speaking reader, deserves special acknowledgment: *The Hidden Italy* (1986) presents dialect poets of the eighteenth, nineteenth, and twentieth centuries in chapters according to region, from northern to southern Italy. Each chapter presents a series of poets in chronological order, preceded by a historical and linguistic description of the particular dialect. In his introduction to the anthology, Haller makes a distinction between dialect poetry and popular literature; as he points out, dialect poets are often well-educated writers, capable of writing also in standard Italian.

Throughout the evolution of Italian literature, dialect has played a significant role. Until the fourteenth century, dialects and the Italian language contended with one another. In the fifteenth and sixteenth centuries, dialect literature became an integral part of Italian literature, though it sometimes denoted rebellion. During the romantic period Carlo Porta, for example, opposed high traditional literature by presenting the humble and degraded reality of the poor, the "victims" of history. Similarly, the Roman G. G. Belli, in a different historical context, wished to fashion a literary "monument" to the people of his city by presenting the reality of his time, free of any conformism. Reacting to psychological and social interpretations of the use of dialect in poetry, Haller claims that the best vernacular poetry tends to be satirical, polemic, or mimetic. It is a conscious or subconscious reaction against official culture.

Today the use of dialect can work toward very different goals: toward realistic representation, as in the case of Virgilio Giotti's descriptions of Trieste; or toward a mythical representation, as in Pasolini's description of life in Friuli. Albino Pierro, a poet from the region of Lucania, after his publication of various collections of poetry written in Italian, chose to reinvent and adopt the ancient dialect of Tursi (almost unknown today). Particularly interesting for those readers who wish to approach the problem of the relations among dialect, literature, and poetry in the second half of the twentieth century in Italy is the collection of essays *I dialetti e l'Italia* (Dialects and Italy, 1981), edited by W. Della Monica and prefaced by B. Migliorini.

While twentieth-century Italian poetry is characterized by factionalism, with a profusion of literary schools and movements that were counterbalanced by those writers who resisted classification, poets of the period are united by a common theme—a sense of inertia and spiritual unrest articulated initially by the *crepuscolari*. The entries collected here describe the various voices that gave expression and artistic complexity to that theme.

—*Giovanna Wedel De Stasio, Glauco Cambon, and Alberto Frattini*

Acknowledgments

This book was produced by Bruccoli Clark Layman, Inc. Karen L. Rood is senior editor for the *Dictionary of Literary Biography* series. Antonio Illiano is the advisory editor for Italian volumes. Jack Turner was the in-house editor.

Production coordinator is James W. Hipp. Projects manager is Charles D. Brower. Photography editors are Edward Scott and Timothy C. Lundy. Layout and graphics supervisor is Penney L. Haughton. Copyediting supervisor is Bill Adams. Typesetting supervisor is Kathleen M. Flanagan. Systems manager is George F. Dodge. The production staff includes Rowena Betts, Teresa Chaney, Patricia Coate, Gail Crouch, Margaret McGinty Cureton, Bonita Dingle, Mary Scott Dye, Sarah A. Estes, Robert Fowler, Ellen McCracken, Kathy Lawler Merlette, John Myrick, Pamela D. Norton, Jean W. Ross, Laurrè Sinckler-Reeder, Thomasina Singleton, Maxine K. Smalls, Jennifer C. J. Turley, and Betsy L. Weinberg.

Walter W. Ross and Henry Cuningham did library research. They were assisted by the following librarians at the Thomas Cooper Library of the University of South Carolina: Jens Holley and the interlibrary-loan staff; reference librarians Gwen Baxter, Daniel Boice, Faye Chadwell, Jo Cottingham, Cathy Eckman, Rhonda Felder, Gary Geer, Jackie Kinder, Laurie Preston, Jean Rhyne, Carol Tobin, Virginia Weathers, and Connie Widney; circulation-department head Thomas Marcil; and acquisitions-searching supervisor David Haggard.

The editors are grateful for the generous assistance of Joe Siracusa and Alberto Frattini in preparing this volume for publication.

Twentieth-Century Italian Poets
First Series

Dictionary of Literary Biography

Sibilla Aleramo
(Rina Faccio)
(14 August 1876 - 13 January 1960)

Fiora A. Bassanese
University of Massachusetts—Boston

BOOKS: *Una donna* (Rome & Turin: STEN, 1906); translated by Mary Lansdale as *A Woman at Bay* (New York & London: Putnam's, 1908); translated by Rosalind Delmar as *A Woman* (London: Virago, 1979; Berkeley & Los Angeles: University of California Press, 1980);

Il passaggio (Milan: Treves, 1919);

Momenti (Florence: Bemporad, 1920);

Andando e stando (Florence: Bemporad, 1920);

Trasfigurazione (Florence: Bemporad, 1922);

Endimione (Rome: Stock, 1923);

Il mio primo amore (Rome: Terza Pagina, 1924);

Liriche (N.p., 1925);

Amo, dunque sono (Milan: Mondadori, 1927; revised, 1947);

Poesie (Milan: Mondadori, 1929);

Gioie d'occasione (Milan: Mondadori, 1930);

Il frustino (Milan: Mondadori, 1932);

Si alla terra: Nuove poesie (1928-1934) (Milan: Mondadori, 1935);

Orsa minore: Note di taccuino (Milan: Mondadori, 1938);

Dal mio Diario (1940-1944) (Rome: Tumminelli, 1945);

Selva d'amore (Milan: Mondadori, 1947);

Il mondo è adolescente (Milan: Milano-Sera, 1949);

Aiutatemi a dire: Nuove poesie (1948-1951) (Rome: Cultura Sociale, 1951);

Russia, alto paese (Rome: Italia-URSS, 1953);

Gioie d'occasione, e altre ancora (Milan: Mondadori, 1954);

Sibilla Aleramo

Luci della mia sera (Rome: Riuniti, 1956);

La donna e il femminismo: Scritti 1897-1910, edited by Bruna Conti (Rome: Editori Riuniti, 1978);

Diario di una donna: Inediti, 1945-1960, edited by Alba Morino (Milan: Fetrinelli, 1978);

Un amore insolito: Diario, 1940-1944, edited by Morino (Milan: Fetrinelli, 1979).

3

OTHER: Marie Madeleine de La Fayette, *La principessa di Cleves*, translated by Aleramo (Milan: Mondadori, 1935);

Le lettere di Alfred de Musset e George Sand, translated by Aleramo (Rome: La Bussola, 1945);

Le donne e la cultura, preface by Aleramo (Rome: Noi Donne, 1953);

Charles Vildrac, *Il pellegrino*, translated by Aleramo (Rome: Casini, 1953);

Beverly Allen, Muriel Kittel, and Keala Jane Jewell, eds., *The Defiant Muse: Italian Feminist Poems from the Middle Ages to the Present*, includes translations of three poems by Aleramo (New York: Feminist Press, 1986), pp. 44-47.

In the chronicles of modern Italian letters, Sibilla Aleramo appears with some frequency both in her own right and as an associate of other poets, artists, and intellectuals. Whether viewed as a celebrity, a curiosity, or a highbrow femme fatale, Aleramo was connected with scandal and women's emancipation as well as literature in her native Italy. In recent years there has been a resurgence of critical, biographical, and feminist studies on her and a reexamination of her works, particularly the novels and diaries. Aleramo's major lyric production is contained in two volumes: *Selva d'amore* (Woods [or Treasury] of Love, 1947) consists of poems written between 1912 and 1946, and *Luci della mia sera* (My Evening Lights, 1956) contains her later poems. But, as Aleramo declared, all her writing is essentially lyrical. Both the fictional works and poetry are used to project a self-image and achieve self-understanding and self-definition. There is also a remarkable consistency in her poetic voice through the decades and few stylistic variations from collection to collection. Having internalized certain romantic, decadent, and positivist attitudes, Aleramo kept her motifs constant through the years: autobiographical episodes are mythicized; youth, sensuality, natural beauty, and the pursuit of experience are exalted; and subtle emotional states and thoughts are explored. Stylistically she was neither an innovative nor a revolutionary writer. As Emilio Cecchi notes, Aleramo seems unaffected by the "cambiamenti e rinnovamenti stilistici e tecnici intervenuti con tanta abbondanza durante il secolo" (stylistic and technical changes and reawakenings that appeared with such abundance during the [twentieth] century). Aleramo's compositions originate in nineteenth-century prosody. Giovanni Pascoli and Gabriele D'Annunzio are more present than are the futurists and hermetics Aleramo knew personally. She was a poet by instinct, not training. Disinterested in theory, Aleramo saw verse as a means to self-expression, not as a mere technical craft. One of the few well-known modern women poets in Italy, Aleramo espoused innate gender differences and believed her work to be the product of a female spirit unlike the male in scope, contents, and means of expression. A poet of sensations, emotions, interludes, and symbolic natural images, she chose a direct, somewhat rhetorical, accessible, and uncomplicated lyric idiom. A romantic at heart, Aleramo believed that art and life were an indissoluble whole and that her works were an utterance of the soul. This belief constitutes both the strength of her verse and, at times, its major weakness.

Aleramo, an active feminist in the early years of the twentieth century, taught the migrant poor in the Agro Romano school, befriended the self-proclaimed cultural reformers of the journal *La Voce* in Florence, joined the futurists in Milan, met Auguste Rodin and Gabriele D'Annunzio in Paris, moved in the theatrical world of the 1920s, was present at the birth of influential periodicals, including *La Grande Illustrazione*, *Solaria*, *La Fiera Letteraria*, and *Mercurio*, and served the Communist cause in the post–World War II years. During her long life Aleramo encountered many of the leading cultural figures of the day. Her numerous friends and acquaintances included writers, critcs, artists, diplomats, actors, publishers, aristocrats, and millionaires, ranging from Maksim Gorky and Clemente Rebora to Eleonora Duse and Palmiro Togliatti. Her benefactors were as incongruous as the queen of Italy and the Soviet Union. Among her many lovers were intellectuals, an Olympic athlete, soldiers, musicians, and an assortment of poets, both brilliant and mediocre. This was an unexpected destiny for a largely self-taught provincial girl who gravitated to her rightful place among her peers.

Aleramo was born on 14 August 1876 as Rina Faccio, the first of four children of a Piedmontese science teacher, Ambrogio Faccio, and his wife. Many aspects of the poet's early life are depicted in her first novel, *Una donna* (1906; translated as *A Woman at Bay*, 1908): her childhood in Milan; the transfer of the family south to the Marches in 1888, where Ambrogio Faccio managed a glass factory; the mental decline and attempted suicide of her mother; a growing friendship between Aleramo and her father's clerk, Ulderico Pierangeli, which would lead to rape, then wedlock in 1893. As a child and young adolescent, Aleramo demonstrated a marked love for literature and a spirited intelligence, publishing pieces in regional newspapers even before her marriage at age sixteen. Her voracious readings, including the works of many European romantics and some Italian decadents, helped mold her character and literary taste. Later she would be drawn to Henrik Ibsen, whom she called the symbol of her conscience, and Friedrich Nietzsche, whose convictions served in shaping her worldview.

A loveless marriage in the provinces proved confining to Aleramo's spirit and intellectual development. Her situation was aggravated both by her abusive and possessive husband and her mother's final breakdown and institutionalization. The one bright spot was the birth of a son, Walter, in 1895, whom she adored. After an abortive affair the young wife found herself at the center of a local scandal, the first of many, and she attempted suicide in 1897. Even into old age she experienced severe depressions, fearing her mother's legacy of madness and contemplation of suicide.

Literally imprisoned at home, Aleramo turned to writing and meditating on her situation and its societal implications. More and more often her articles addressed serious public issues including the question of woman's rights. As she began to build a national reputation, she also began communicating with a variety of notable intellectuals and writing for political and feminist reviews, producing a steady stream of book reviews, literary critiques, sociological studies, and life-style commentaries. Until her death Aleramo would regularly contribute pieces to newspapers, magazines, and literary journals as she had done in her youth. By 1899 she was sufficiently well known to be offered the directorship of a new women's magazine in Milan. Aleramo accepted and moved with her family to Milan, where she worked at home at Pierangeli's insistence. Forced to resign because of editorial differences, her contacts nevertheless multiplied. Living in Milan was an electrifying experience that made her forced return to the provinces all the more devastating.

An intense intellectual life was not an adequate substitute for an intolerable marital situation in a suffocating environment. After painful soul-searching, Aleramo left her husband and son, whom she would not see again for decades,

to make her own way. As she often acknowledged it was the turning point in her life, but it left a void impossible to fill. Aleramo established a personal dogma of absolute liberty and individualism clearly borrowed from Nietzsche. In Rome she fell in love with the new director of the prestigious journal *Nuova Antologia*, Giovanni Cena. For seven years the relationship was an intense spiritual and physical bond, founded on shared thoughts and aspirations. They entertained artists and intellectuals such as Maria Montessori, Luigi Pirandello, and Gaetano Salvemini. Cena enjoyed his role as Pygmalion, taking over Aleramo's unstructured education, encouraging her to write her story. With the publication of *Una donna* in 1906, Rina Faccio became Sibilla Aleramo, a new identity for a new life. Immediately hailed as a second *Doll's House* by its advocates or criticized as an immoral tale of female degeneracy by its detractors, the autobiographical novel became an international cause célèbre. *Una donna* made Aleramo a European name, but it remained her only book for several years. In the meantime she metamorphosed into a social activist, working in a health clinic for the poor, creating schools for migrants in the Roman countryside, helping earthquake victims in 1908, and fighting for universal suffrage and woman's rights.

In 1910 Aleramo left Cena and began her odyssey in search of love and fulfillment. The years of cohabitation had shaped her intellectually, artistically, and ethically: "divenni libera amante, divenni scrittrice, imposi alla società la mia ribellione e la mia audacia" (I became a free lover, I became a writer, I imposed my rebellion and my daring on society). In a constant attempt to mold reality to suit her needs and dreams, Aleramo moved from place to place—Florence, Naples, Corsica, Paris, Milan, the Riviera, Capri, Sorrento, London, Assisi, Sardinia, Venice, Greece, even Moscow—and from luxurious hotels and spas to rundown furnished rooms. The sequence of travels was often determined by the vagaries of her liaisons. This "pilgrim of love," as one admirer defined her, was romantically involved with some of the most illustrious names in Italian culture. Among the most famous were the young Vincenzo Cardarelli; Giovanni Papini, for whom she wrote her first poem in 1912; futurist artist Umberto Boccioni; writer Giovanni Boine; visionary poet Dino Campana; and future Nobel laureate Salvatore Quasimodo. Her friend since the days of *La Voce*, Giuseppe Prezzolini would one day crudely, if privately, describe Aleramo as the "lavatoio sessuale della letteratura italiana" (sexual washtub of Italian literature). But for Aleramo herself each new rapport was an attempt—however illusory—at forging a perfect union that would give absolute meaning to her life.

Aleramo was producing her own mythic persona, re-creating herself in life and on paper in a series of autobiographical works that are her trademark. Her numerous affairs are an integral part of her image, that of a liberated woman whose own creativity is enlivened by the intensity of her emotional experiences. In this, too, she follows a Nietzschean precedent, formulating a female version of the individualistic, self-involved, and self-determined superman. After *Una donna* her entire prose production—novels, a play, sketches, essays—possesses a lyric tone deriving from its impressionistic or confessional character. Aleramo was self-absorbed, intense, and somewhat naive. As a poet, such self-absorption translated into a markedly subjective style. Aleramo quite consciously decided to cancel the boundaries between reality and art, as she would proclaim in a stanza from "Lunare" (Lunar; collected in *Poesie*, 1929), written in her fifties:

Per tutta la vita volli de' miei giorni
far cosa di luce, cosa d'amore;
ed essi posi avanti ogni mia arte,
e d'essi feci poesia perenne,

oh giorni, trascoloranti riviere,
giorni, miei duri diamanti!

(All my life, I wanted to make my days
things of light, things of love;
and I put them ahead of all my art,
and I made eternal poetry of them,

o days variegating rivers,
days, my hard diamonds!)

In 1913 a handful of poems by Aleramo was published in *La Grande Illustrazione*, an attractive review she directed briefly. Subsequently several pieces appeared in other magazines, but it was not until 1920 that her first volume of verse was published. *Momenti* was generally well received, possibly because of its essentially traditional character. Aleramo dedicated this first lyric collection to the myth of liberty, a freedom that extended to her versification. She favored the unconfining features of free verse, with marked

rhythms and sound repetitions rather than set rhyme schemes and meters. Many of her compositions are structured paratactically, stressing an internal, rather than semantic, logic and highlighting the use of analogy. The poem "O fiore" (O Flower) is representative:

Sul mare tanto azzurro che par bianco,
che par questo mio bianco stellato vestito,
tu viaggi verso l'isola, viaggi verso me,
giungerai che ancor non sarà sera,
o fiore, o colore, o ardore,
sul mare ancor tutto soave mi protenderò,
e t'avrò fra le braccia
che crederai proseguire con la dolce nave
ancora ancora in eternità d'azzurro.

(On the sea so azure it seems white,
it seems this white starlit dress of mine,
you travel towards the island, you travel towards
   me,
you'll arrive before evening comes,
o flower, o color, o ardor,
on the sea all gentle still I'll lean over,
and I'll have you in my arms
believing you're continuing on the sweet ship
still still in an azure eternity.)

The poem's melody is determined by the rhythm of the lines, based on sound and word repetitions, internal rhymes, and a masterful play of alliteration and assonance. The use of interjection and invocation are also typical. Aleramo would employ such techniques throughout her poetic career.

Individual freedom, personal candor, experimentation with alternative life-styles, emotional risk-taking, and a voluptuous desire to embrace all reality are at the core of Aleramo's search for self during her gypsy years, a stance synthesized in one of her preferred expressions: "dir sì alla vita" (to say yes to life). Not surprisingly she was often considered a female D'Annunzio, and during her first Parisian sojourn in 1913 and 1914 Aleramo met the legendary D'Annunzio, pursuing him by letter and telegram, as was her custom. The two established an immediate empathy. The psychological compatibility between Aleramo and D'Annunzio is self-evident, but the question of their literary rapport is more complex. Aleramo was intrigued by the man she called "il mago bianco" (the white sorcerer) and esteemed D'Annunzio's works, but she repeatedly rejected any critical attempt to categorize her as his imitator, a charge often leveled at both her prose and poetry. Instead she insisted that all her works

Dust jacket for the American edition of the second English translation of Aleramo's first book, an autobiographical novel

were offspring of her life—never "literature," by which she meant artifice and prevarication. Moreover they were signs of "la qualita del genio muliebre" (the quality of womanly genius). Nevertheless the young Aleramo had learned about the musical power of words and their phonic and symbolic effectiveness by reading D'Annunzio, a lesson she would translate into her own lyric voice, most notably in the long, autobiographical prose poem *Il passaggio* (1919) and the one-act dramatic poem *Endimione* (1923). Unlike D'Annunzio, Aleramo rejected art as aesthetic virtuosity or poetry as a refined game of words. She likewise shunned the darker tones of decadent literature prone to violence and perversity. But Aleramo did adopt the egoism, drive, sensuality, and Dionysian spirit typical of D'Annunzio's life and themes. Aleramo habitually cross-pollinated life and art. For example, several of her novels contain borrowings from epistolary exchanges; similarly her poetry has thematic, linguistic, and metaphorical ties with her prose, both fictional and

nonfictional. Aleramo's verse benefited from her grasp of D'Annunzio's lyric idiom, especially in the subtle depiction of states of being, identification with nature, and sensualism.

Issues of imitation and sources aside, in all her works Aleramo sought to personify what she termed an "autonoma spiritualità femminile" (autonomous feminine spirituality). She held a deepseated belief in innate gender differences that could and should be expressed artistically. Aleramo declared that women could only be true poets and find a fresh creative voice when they believed in themselves and in their otherness, which she considered a natural psychological as well as biological fact. And woman was most herself through love. In 1913 Umberto Boccioni pronounced Aleramo an "eterna dilettante di complicazioni amorose" (a never-ending dabbler in amorous complications): such erotic tension is at the heart of Aleramo's best poetry. Her lyrics are closely connected to the men and events of her love stories, often resulting in the creation of an amorous dialogue expressed through direct address and presupposing the existence of a real male interlocutor to receive the poetic message, as in the composition "O fiore." In both life and literature, Sibilla understood love sensually as passion and abandon. Uninhibited and unconcerned with conventional behavioral patterns, Aleramo's attitudes spilled into her poetry, resulting in unusually explicit erotic themes in a woman poet of her day. Her own femaleness is a constant motif, intentionally personal yet substantially universal, focused on the depiction of loving as an existential state. An early, well-known composition, "Dolce sangue" (Sweet Blood) typifies her vivid depiction of desire rendered subjectively in universal physical terms. The Italian original is effective because of the multiple meanings contained in much of the poem's lexicon, thereby veiling its erotic potential. Words such as *languire, vigore, gemere, delizia, grembo,* and *irrorare* concurrently offer chaste and sexual interpretative possibilities that are lost in the translation:

Dolce dolce sangue
  ne le vene mi langue.
  Oh vigor lontano,
    se vieni di delizia vi gemi!
Se vieni e mi premi,
  oh vigor lontano,
  se il grembo m'irrori che langue,
  dolce dolce sangue!

(Sweet sweet blood
  languishes in my veins.
  Oh distant vigor,
    if you come you'll moan with pleasure there!
If you come and crush me,
  Oh distant vigor,
  if you bedew my languishing womb,
  sweet, sweet blood!)

Again and again in letters and verse Aleramo offers herself as a vivifying life force, an incomparable boon for the beloved to contemplate and relish. Lyrically this theme is reiterated in multiple variations. "Nuda nel sole" (Naked in the Sun) presents woman metamorphosed into animist goddess. Sensuality, panic delectation, and communion with nature set the tone for the representation of the self as a generative force, as suggested by this excerpt:

Nuda nel sole ed immobile,
frammento di natura,
da te invasa da te riassorbita,
sei tu che mi divinizzi

o la mia divinità è che te crea,
artista, arte, spirito?

(Naked in the sun and motionless,
fragment of nature,
by you invaded by you reabsorbed,
do you render me divine
or does my divinity create you,
artist art spirit?)

"Nuda nel sole" contains one of Aleramo's central mythic motifs. The lyric protagonist embodies a prolific energy and a vital force; like Mother Earth she represents creation. Love and, consequently, art are generated through a transfigured erotic maternity that revivifies the beloved. In Aleramo's verse, eroticism and creativity are one.

During the early years of Fascism, Aleramo continued to produce autobiographical works and to attract lovers, one of whom—Tito Zaniboni—made an assassination attempt on Benito Mussolini in late 1925. Because of her connection to the failed assassin, Aleramo was arrested and jailed for two days, an experience immortalized in one of her most celebrated and longer meditative compositions, "Una notte in carcere" (A Night in Jail). Typically this encounter with persecution is rendered subjectively, the poem's calm cadences almost prosaic:

Giaceva la mia libertà
quella notte come in una tomba,
il bel mito giaceva
per amor del quale ho vissuto ardendo.
Lungi le spiagge le rose le selve.
E creatura nessuna in pena per me,
nessuno nella notte ad attendermi lungi.

(My freedom lay
that night as in a tomb,
[as] lay the beautiful myth
for love of which I lived in flames.
Far away beaches roses woods.
And not a soul anxious about me,
no one awaiting me in the night far away.)

That same year (1925), after more than a decade spent in temporary residences, Aleramo moved into a permanent home, a large attic room in Rome's via Margutta. Always in a precarious financial condition, by late 1928 she was destitute, notwithstanding a continued output of journalistic essays, literary translations, and fiction. Because her signature had appeared on the anti-Fascist Croce Manifesto, Aleramo was blacklisted by important well-paying publications such as the *Corriere della Sera*. Although she never became a Fascist stalwart, she did petition Mussolini, who received and rescued her with a modest subvention. In 1933, after the queen's intervention, the regime granted Aleramo a monthly pension, which allowed her to meet basic needs and continue writing.

The Mondadori company in Milan published Aleramo's second poetry collection, *Poesie*, in 1929; it comprises verse composed between 1912 and 1928, including the poems of *Momenti*. The new pieces continue key themes, tones and imagery introduced earlier. But the collection also demonstrates greater formal control, and on the whole *Poesie* found an admiring audience, receiving a monetary prize from the Accademia d'Italia. Within the autobiographical context of *Poesie* love remains Aleramo's preferred subject, always understood sensually, at times erotically, as in "Lembi nella sera" (Edges of the Evening), "Castitá" (Chastity), and "Fiamme" (Flames), in the last of which the speaker calls for the return of a distant lover, recalling his knowing hands, "mani che tutta mi predarono" (hands that pillaged all of me). Hands are one of Aleramo's repeated body images, appearing in titles such as "Nel cavo delle mie mani" (In the Hollow of My Hands) and the better known "Le mie mani" (My Hands), the latter poem containing this stanza:

Le mie mani,
ricordando che tu le trovasti belle,
io accorata le bacio,
mani, tu dicesti,
a scrivere condannate crudelmente,
mani fatte per più dolci opere,
per carezze lunghe,
dicesti, e fra le tue le tenevi
leggere tremanti,
or ricordando te
lontano
che le mani soltanto mi baciasti,
io la mia bocca piano accarezzo.

(My hands,
remembering that you found them beautiful,
I heartbrokenly kiss them,
hands, you said,
to writing cruelly condemned,
hands made for sweeter deeds,
for long caresses,
you said, and in your own you held them
light trembling,
now remembering you
far away

how you only kissed my hands,
my mouth slowly I caress.)

Hands are one of several images and metaphors Aleramo employs to define physicality, particularly her own sensuality and sexual desire/desirability. Other prominent emblems are also drawn from her body—blood, naked shoulders, and hair—and from an abundance of flowers, particularly roses. A common topos is fusion with nature, even an Ovidian metamorphosis of the self into plant, as in "Musica": "tutta e soltanto mi sento fiore" (I feel [I am] all and only flower). These are signs of the narcissism at the core of Aleramo's poetry. As she declared to Aldo Capasso in a 15 February 1931 letter: "credo . . . che tutta la mia vita e tutta la mia opera trovino nel libro delle liriche il loro specchio" (I believe . . . that my entire life and all my works are mirrored in the book of lyrics). Many Aleramo compositions clearly reflect their origins in reality, often containing biographical introductions or diary-like preliminaries (to borrow Rita Guerricchio's terms), meaning that the poems record actual events, as can easily be deduced from "Le mie mani."

In many of Aleramo's poems nature is the mirror reflecting the poet's inner life, a theme developed with multiple nuances. The motif's renditions vary from a Dionysian fusion with the natural universe (recalling some D'Annunzian verse) to impressionistic landscapes that merely hint at a state of being (bringing Giovanni Pascoli to mind). Significant recurring emblems are elemental—sun, flames, moon, sea, waves, wind, and earth. Aleramo's symbolism possesses none of the analogical opulence of the hermetic word. Some of Aleramo's lyrics on nature have been compared to Oriental verse, like the haiku, for their brevity and impressionistic characteristics. One such poem is "Isola" (Island), a mere two lines in length:

Ivi in conche d'ulivi i venti posano,
e ali chetamente radono le fronde.

(There in olive hallows the winds rest,
and wings quietly brush against the branches.)

Aleramo's theme of the vivifying (and feminine) force of nature is captured in the title of her next collection, *Si alla terra* (Yes to the Earth, 1935), and is woven throughout the volume. Reviewers immediately perceived a difference in the poetry—a reduction of self-involvement and a cor-

Aleramo circa 1959, the year before she died

responding expression of solidarity with others. There is also a growing sensitivity to the darker side of existence: fatigue, loss, sadness, and absence permeate many of these lyrics, including the love poems, such as "Fuoco" (Fire):

> Avvampi da anni la vita mia,
> pur non posso toccarti,
> pur non posso spiegarti,
> fuoco sei e mistero,
>
> da anni si consuma la vita mia
> dinanzi alla tua fiamma bianca,
> solo a guardarti, solo a guardarti,
> e mai di patire sono stanca.
>
> (For years you've set ablaze my life,
> yet I cannot touch you,
> yet I cannot explain you,
> you are fire and mystery,
>
> for years my life has consumed itself
> before your white flame,
> only gazing upon you, only gazing upon you,
> and never do I tire of pain.)

A living legend, Aleramo found herself facing physical decline, the loss of youth, and the prospect of loneliness. As always these existential realities became art, transforming her fear and dismay into melancholy and nostalgic lyrics. Yet even in the atmosphere of moral fatigue that exists in *Si alla terra*, Aleramo's emphatic personality interjects itself in opposition to the passage of time, the advance of old age, the inevitability of death, and the cruelty of humankind, proclaiming an unswerving faith in life and love, as in "Eternità," declaring her certainty in the promise of every new day, "come se in eterno / eroicamente si potesse crescere, / e migliori e più validi divenire" (as though we could eternally / grow in heroism / and become better and more strong).

Nearing sixty, Aleramo began her last passionate affair. Like previous lovers, Franco Matacotta was much younger than the woman whose attic home he shared for ten years. It was a difficult rapport and one in which Aleramo believed she was expressing selfless maternal affection as well as amorous ardor: "egli mi respirava e si nutriva di me, della mia anima, della mia esperienza enorme" (he breathed me and nourished himself on my soul, on my enormous experience). In the poems inspired by Matacotta there is a transference of identities between lover and beloved that is sexual and maternal as well as poetic, as evidenced in "Tu dissuggella il canto" (You Unseal the Song). The life tendered, characteristically represented through classic natural images, is art. Once again Aleramo offers herself as muse to the beloved, who in turn liberates her imprisoned lyric voice:

> Tu dissuggella il canto
> che da tanto le vene mi colma,
>
> tu che il giovine cuore
> alla mia voce antica sentisti tremare . . .
>
> (You unseal the song
> that's long filled my veins,
>
> you who felt your young heart
> tremble at my ancient voice . . .).

The last love poems dedicated to Matacotta, entitled "Imminente sera 1936-1942" (Imminent Evening), remained unpublished until 1947, when they were selected by Aleramo as part of the collection *Selva d'amore*. As Aleramo pointed out, the book's title is emblematic: *selva* refers not only to the volume's literary function as a treasury of the poet's best work but also to the figurative Dantesque meaning of a spiritual woods, or labyrinth. *Selva d'amore* was a critical and personal success, winning the 1948 Viareggio prize.

Aleramo's final infatuation was as all-consuming as her previous involvements had been, but it was not inspired by a man, nor was she as self-absorbed in her ardor. In 1946 she enrolled in the PCI, the Italian Communist party, in what was an emotional choice rather than a rational ideological conversion. Aleramo channeled her wanderlust and abilities into political action. Her activities intensified and, while maintaining a literary and feminist bent, ran the gamut of public lectures, poetry readings, journalistic writings, prize jury services, and participation in peace conferences, even an advice column in the Communist daily *L'Unita*. Throughout her seventies and into her eighties Aleramo would continue to travel, often at party request, sometimes venturing into Eastern block countries. Her friendships with the political and cultural elite of the PCI, especially its leader Palmiro Togliatti, and her intense activity on the party's behalf filled her last years. Aleramo's life had come full circle, returning to her youthful social activism and faith in human solidarity. Joining the PCI was a confirmation of her "visione antica di un mondo in cui ogni persona viva e operosa sara in grado di sentire l'esistenza e lo stesso lavoro sotto specie di poesia" (ancient vision of a world in which every living and industrious person will be able to experience life and work itself in the shape of poet-

ry). Her own poetry took on a different shape, adopting a sociopolitical content and a rhetorical cadence. Twelve poems make up *Aiutatemi a dire* (Help Me Speak, 1951), which Aleramo later integrated into the longer *Luci della mia sera* (My Evening Lights, 1956). Typical of Aleramo's final poems, the lengthy composition "Russia alto paese" (Russia High Country) sings the praises of the birthplace of her new credo, while "Aiutatemi a dire" (Help Me Speak) celebrates the proletariat, the feeling of community, and the power of work, in a hymn to Aleramo's newly discovered comrades:

> Ma non inerte attesa la nostra, oh dura passione
> oh masse di popolo per tutta la terra
> fra paludi fra roventi forni e giù nelle miniere,
> oh genti oppresse antiche e nuove,
> oh volontà ferma di redenzione, oh sollevamenti,
> oh fiere grida a prezzo di carcere e sangue . . .
>
> (But ours is no idle expectation, oh bitter passion
> oh masses of people throughout the earth
> amid marshes amid scorching ovens and down in
>   mines,
> oh oppressed peoples ancient and new,
> oh steady will of redemption, oh uprisings,
> oh undaunted cries dearly paid in prison and in
>   blood . . .).

Such poetry is an instrument for social renewal, political panegyric, and ideological communication with little autobiographical import. However, this verse also suffers from grandiloquence. Aleramo's standard devices are present, but they are taken to rhetorical extremes, such as repetitions and interjections. *Luci della mia sera* does possess a choral spirit that achieves a heroic, even epic, quality on occasion, notably in Aleramo's condemnation of war and exaltation of the proletariat at work. Although these political compositions received no critical acclaim, they did appeal to the comrades for whom they were written. Aleramo's proletarian audiences wrapped her in a warm embrace that lightened her spirit and eased her old age. Logically speaking, this empathy for the working class and group solidarity is directly opposed to the individualism Aleramo had espoused for decades. As Artal Mazzotti has perceptively noted, "la sfera del soggettivo [viene] trasferita in quella oggettiva della Rivoluzione" (the subjective sphere is transferred into the objective [sphere] of the Revolution). Actually the poet's affection for the millions of workers of the world is a transfer of her powerful potential for love from the one to the many. In a variation of her basic personality traits, the generative altruistic qualities expressed in the love lyrics come to fruition in the more receptive love for humanity. Nevertheless, the best lyric moments in *Luci della mia sera* come when Aleramo is personal rather than political, in keeping with her former inspiration, as in "Se dono. Vita, tu sei" (Life, If You Are a Gift).

> Se dono di remoti Iddii
> Vita, sei tu,
> perchè mai così ti consumiamo,
> oh non come frutto soave
> che sia fragranza delle primavere
> e noi consoli degli oscuri inverni
>
> (Life, if you are
> the gift of remote Gods,
> why do we consume you thus,
> oh not like sweet fruit
> that is the fragrance of springs
> and restores us after dark winters).

The final entries in the diaries Sibilla Aleramo religiously kept during the last decades of her life were registered only days before her death at eighty-three. To the end, she struggled with her inner demons in the endeavor to give words to life.

Letters:
Lettere, by Aleramo and Dino Campana, edited by Niccolo Gallo (Florence: Vallecchi, 1958);
Lettere d'amore a Lina, edited by A. Cenni (Rome: Savelli, 1982).

Interview:
Confessioni di scrittori (Interviste con se stessi), edited by L. Piccioni (Turin: Radio Italiana, 1951).

Biographies:
Piero Nardi, *Un capitolo della biografia di Sibilla* (Vicenza, Italy: Pozza, 1965);
Bruna Conti and Alba Morino, eds., *Sibilla Aleramo e il suo tempo: Vita raccontata e illustrata* (Milan: Feltrinelli, 1981);
Annarita Buttafuoco and Marina Zancan, eds., *Svelamento. Sibilla Aleramo: Una biografia intellettuale* (Milan: Feltrinelli, 1988).

References:
Vincenzo Cardarelli, *Lettere d'amore a Sibilla Aleramo*, edited by Gian Antonio Cibotto

and Bruno Blasi (Rome: Compton, 1974);
Emilio Cecchi, "Sibilla Aleramo incoronata," in his *Letteratura italiana del Novecento* (Milan: Mondadori, 1972), pp. 399-402;
Bruna Conti, Preface to Aleramo's *Selva d'amore* (Rome: Compton, 1980), pp. vii-xii;
Franco Contorbia, Lea Melandri, and Alba Morino, eds., *Sibilla Aleramo. coscienza e scrittura* (Milan: Feltrinelli, 1986);
Lino Delli Colli, "Sibilla Aleramo," in *Letteratura italiana contemporanea*, volume 1, edited by Gaetano Mariani and Mario Petrucciani (Rome: Lucarini, 1979), pp. 227-230;
Richard Drake, Introduction to *A Woman* (translation of Aleramo's *Una Donna*) (Berkeley & Los Angeles: University of California Press, 1980), pp. v-xxxvi;
Marina Federzoni, Isabella Pezzini, and Maria Pia Pozzato, *Sibilla Aleramo* (Florence: Nuova Ialia, 1980);
Massimo Grillandi, "La poesia di Sibilla Aleramo," *Letteratura*, 29 (March-June, 1965): 89- 95;
Rita Guerricchio, *Storia di Sibilla* (Pisa: Nistri-Lischi, 1974);
Keala Jane Jewell, *"Un furore d'autocreazione*: Women and Writing in Sibilla Aleramo," *Canadian Journal of Italian Studies*, 7 (1984): 148-162;
Olga Lombardi, "Sibilla Aleramo," in *Letteratura italiana: Il Novecento*, volume 1, edited by Gianni Grana (Milan: Marzorati, 1980), pp. 736-764;
Artal Mazzotti, "Sibilla Aleramo," in his *Letteratura italiana. Orientamenti culturali: I contemporanei* (Milan: Marzorati, 1963), pp. 211-235;
Lea Melandri, "La spudoratezza: Vita e opere di Sibilla Aleramo," *Memoria*, 8 (1983): 5-23;
Alba Morino, "Sibilla Aleramo: Autoritratto," in *Una donna un secolo*, edited by Sandra Petrignani (Rome: Ventaglio, 1986), pp. 43-55;
Salvatore Quasimodo, *A Sibilla*, edited by Giancarlo Vigorelli (Milan: Rizzoli, 1983);
Clemente Rebora, *Per veemente amore lucente: Lettere a Sibilla Aleramo*, edited by Anna Folli (Milan: Schweiwiller, 1986);
Claudio Rendina, Introduction to Aleramo's *Selva d'amore* (Rome: Compton, 1980), pp. xiii-xviii;
Sergio Solmi, Preface to Aleramo's *Luci della mia sera* (Rome: Riuniti, 1956).

Ignazio Buttitta

(19 September 1899 -   )

Emanuele Licastro
State University of New York at Buffalo

BOOKS: *Sintimintali* (Palermo: Sabbio, 1923);
Marabedda (Palermo: Trazzera, 1927);
Lu pani si chiama pani, with Italian translation by Salvatore Quasimodo (Rome: Cultura Sociale, 1954);
Lamentu pi la morti di Turiddu Carnivali (Palermo: Arti Grafiche, 1956);
La peddi nova (Milan: Feltrinelli, 1963);
Lu trenu di lu suli (Milan: Avanti, 1963);
La paglia bruciata (Milan: Feltrinelli, 1968);
Io faccio il poeta (Milan: Feltrinelli, 1972);
Il poeta in piazza (Milan: Feltrinelli, 1974);
Prime e nuovissime (Turin: Forma, 1983);
Pietre nere (Milan: Feltrinelli, 1983).

OTHER: Hermann W. Haller, ed. and trans., *The Hidden Italy: A Bilingual Edition of Italian Dialect Poetry*, includes twelve poems by Buttitta (Detroit: Wayne State University Press, 1986), pp. 508-539.

Ignazio Buttitta is the writer of the best-known poetry in the Sicilian dialect, and is known almost as well in Mexico, China, in the Caucasus as at the foot of Mount Etna. His is a Sicilian world molded by Sicilian language and rhythms; his best poetry, no matter how attached to regionalism in content and expression—or perhaps because of it—generates a particularly seductive music.

He was born to Provvidenza Raspante Buttitta and Pietro Buttitta in Bagheria, in the Sicilian province of Palermo, on 19 September 1899. He was sent to live with his wet nurse because there were already five children in his parents' house; in his poems his absent mother appears continually from his first collection to his last, at the beginning in a sentimental vein, later in a more detached yet more moving manner as the personal mother combines with Mother Sicily. Pier Paolo Pasolini thinks that Buttitta was "tormentato da una mancanza di amore materno che lo ha reso orfano e ossesso" (tormented by a lack of motherly love which has left him both orphaned and obsessed).

After elementary school—the only school he attended—Buttitta worked in his father's food store until military duty in World War I. His war experience traumatized him, and almost forty years later he still could not forget it, as reflected in "Littra a una mamma tedesca" (Letter to a German Mother) from *Lu pani si chiama pani* (Bread Is Called Bread, 1954):

> Mamma tedesca,
> ti scrivi ddu surdatu talianu
> chi t'ammazzò lu figghiu.
>
> Mmaliditta dda notti
> e l'acqui di lu Piavi
> e li cannuna e li bummi
> e li luci chi c'eranu;
> mmaliditti li stiddi
> e li prigheri e li vuci
> e lu chiantu e li lamenti
> e l'odiu, mmaliditti!
>
> Era accussi beddu to figghiu,
> mamma tedesca,
> lu vitti all'alba
> cu la facci bianca
> di picciriddu ancora addummisciutu.
>
> (German mother,
> the Italian soldier who killed your son
> is writing you.
>
> Cursed be that night
> and the waters of the Piave
> and the cannons and the bombs
> and the lights;
> cursed be the stars
> and the prayers and the voices
> and the crying and the mourning
> and the hate, cursed!
>
> So beautiful was your son,
> German mother,
> I saw him at dawn

with his white face
a child still asleep.)

When Buttitta returned from the war, he became interested in socialist politics and in the plight of the lower classes. He wrote for the Bagherian newspaper *La povera gente* (Poor People), publishing his first poems there, including "Primu maggiu" (May First). The newspaper organized demonstrations on May Day, 1922, demanding an eight-hour workday, and, according to the paper, Buttitta delivered an impassioned speech against war. In October he led a demonstration against the town taxes, and although he and the other organizers were detained for eleven days, the taxes were abolished. During this period Buttitta also published poems in the journals *Il Vespro Anarchico* (The Anarchic Vespers), published in Palermo, and *Fede!* (Faith!), published in Rome. Both magazines were anarchistic and anti-Fascist and were soon abolished.

In 1923 Buttitta published his first volume of poetry, *Sintimintali*, which emphasizes his concern for the poor, in such poems of social realism as "Lu scioperu" (The Strike) and "Pi li senza tettu" (For the Homeless), and also presents poems about his experience of sentimental love, including "Sintimintali," "T'amu," and "Primu amuri" (Sentimental, I Love You, and First Love).

In 1927, the year of his marriage to Angela Isaja, Buttitta cofounded *La trazzera* (Country Lane), a local magazine dedicated to the poetry of Sicilian-dialect writers. However, *La trazzera* lasted only one year because the Fascist government was trying to suppress every expression of localism and regionalism. Also in 1927 Buttitta published *Marabedda* (Beautiful Mary), a pastoral love poem in which the poet-shepherd implores Marabedda to love him. The tone of this volume is not lyrical but sentimental and conventional; it is his first attempt to change language into a personal instrument of metaphoric communication.

From 1928 through World War II Buttitta continued to write poetry, and some of his poems—anti-Fascist and in dialect—were distributed clandestinely. "Sariddu lu Bassanu" (Sariddu the Bassanu), composed in 1939, is the best known because Buttitta's friend the Sicilian painter Renato Guttuso recited it in Rome and finally published it, under a pseudonym, in 1944 in the second issue of the newly founded Roman magazine *Rinascita* (Rebirth; collected in *La peddi nova* [The New Skin, 1963]). The poem is a bitter satire molded on a catchy folkloric rhythm:

Sariddu lu Bassanu
fascista e talianu
è paisanu miu,
e mi nni vantu,
viva Diu!

Partiu pi la Spagna
e turnau cu na lasagna
longa di midagghi
a tanti tagghi
e lucenti, spirlucenti
comu fussiru pinnenti
nni lu pettu d'una fata . . .

(Sariddu the Bassanu
Fascist and Italian
is from my town,
and I am proud of it,
praise God!

He left for Spain
and came back with a long
lasagna of medals
of many sizes
shiny and resplendent
as if they were jewels
on the breast of a fairy . . .).

In 1943 Buttitta joined the local anti-Fascist partisans in Milan and, though he was arrested twice, survived the war. In the postwar period he moved his family to Milan, where he was in daily contact with his Sicilian friends Elio Vittorini and Salvatore Quasimodo. Through Guttuso, Buttitta also became friends with Carlo Levi and Massimo Bontempelli. In 1950 Buttitta returned to his native Bagheria, leaving it thereafter only to read his poems on national or international tours.

In 1954 he published *Lu pani si chiama pani* (Bread Is Called Bread), including an Italian translation by Quasimodo and drawings by Guttuso. The relevant note in this collection is of pain and of protest against the victimization of the oppressed. Buttitta sings of peace, brotherhood, and the redemption of the workers, whom he exhorts to think and struggle. In "Parru cu tia" (I Am Talking to You) Buttitta says the flag should be red, and the poem's last line reads, "russa era la tonaca di Cristu! russa!" (red was Christ's tunic! red!).

The beauty of the collection is in the violence of its lines, in the compelling strength of its language, and in the restlessness of its harmony. It is a beauty best perceived not in reading but in listening. In the preface to Buttitta's *La peddi nova* Carlo Levi states: "Tutta la poesia di Buttitta . . . è fatta per l'espressione orale, per essere detta o cantata. . . . È una poesia orale, che si appoggia sul metallo alto della voce, che ritrova la ricchezza di un dialetto che è una lingua, con tutti i suoi rapporti e interni significati" (All Buttitta's poetry . . . is made for oral expression, to be spoken or sung. . . . It is an oral poetry, which rests on the hard metal of the voice, and rediscovers the richness of a dialect, which is a language with all its relationships and internal meanings).

In *La peddi nova*, which was awarded the Carducci Prize, Buttitta's verse has become pensive and more reflective, and the immediate concerns of the feisty rabble-rouser of the preceding book are deepened and mellowed by a heartfelt awareness of the human community. In the title poem, he writes:

La storia di st'anni fucusi
ha zappatu cu l'ugna
dintra di mia,
e restu scantatu a taliari
l'omini tutti
mpinnuliati a un filu,
a un distinu sulu,
dintra na varca di pagghia c'affunna.

(The history of these fiery years
has dug with its nails
inside me,
and, frightened, I keep watching
humankind
hung by a thread,
on one destiny only,
inside a sinking straw boat.)

The poem concludes with these lines:

Nun campu cuntentu;
st'eredità di lacrimi
la portu comu un luttu
e vurrissi canciarla in odiu
e nun possu.

(I don't live happily;
this inheritance of tears
I carry like mourning
and I would change it into hate
and I can't.)

In this collection Buttitta, in the words of Giuseppe Cocchiara, is "un poeta che ama dialogare col mondo, con i suoi simili, ovunque essi si trovano, oppressi e oppressori, anche se le sue simpatie vanno agli oppressi" (a poet who loves to converse with the world, with his fellow-men, wherever they are, oppressed and oppressors, though his sympathies are with the oppressed).

With *La paglia bruciata* (The Burned Straw, 1968) Buttitta experiments for the first time with Italian, a special kind of Italian leavened with a Sicilian substratum. He also uses comedy and irony in his versification of ordinary facts, as well as an unexpected eroticism. *La paglia bruciata* is set in a surrealistic Sicily.

Buttitta's next book, *Io faccio il poeta* (I Am a Poet, 1972), which received the Viareggio Prize, contains all the concerns expressed in his preceding verse, but they are now wrought in less elaborate and more compelling images conveyed by a lucid dialect, a Sicilian that has become the language of his innermost desires. In "Lingua e dialettu" (Language and Dialect) Buttitta insists:

Un populu,
diventa poviru e servu,
quannu ci arrobbanu a lingua
addutata di patri:
è persu pi sempri.

Diventa poviru e servu,
quannu i paroli non figghianu paroli
e si mancianu tra d' iddi.
Mi nn' addugnu ora,
mentri accordu a chitarra du dialettu
ca perdi na corda lu jornu.

(A people,
becomes poor and servile,
when they steal the language
inherited from their fathers:
and it is lost forever.

It becomes poor and servile,
when words don't generate words
and they eat each other.
I realize it now,
as I am tuning up the guitar of the dialect
which is losing a string a day.)

One of the major activities of Buttitta's life in the 1970s and 1980s was his touring of other countries and the recital of his compositions. His volume *Il poeta in piazza* (The Poet in the Square, 1974) brings together poems and songs inspired by his longing to communicate with the public and by his poignant suspicion of the impossibility of being one with his listeners. "Il prologo," the introductory poem of the volume, is, as Fernando Gioviale expresses it, "una riflessione sulla somiglianza e sulla diversità del poeta: simile altri uomini, il poeta ne è poi radicalmente diverso, ed è questo il mistero . . . l'essere e voler essere simile agli altri, anzi uguale nel nome del solidarismo cristiano e socialista, e il ritrovarsi poi 'diverso,' più infelice . . . perché più capace di vedere e di soffrire anche per gli altri e insieme, inevitabilmente, più grande perché più creativo e durevole" (a reflection on the similarity and diversity of the poet: similar to other men, he is radically different, and this is the mystery . . . to be and to want to be similar to others, indeed equal in the name of Christian and socialist solidarity, and then yet finding himself "different," unhappier . . . because more capable of seeing and suffering also for others and yet, unavoidably, greater because more creative and more lasting). In "U pueta e a puisia" (The Poet and the Poetry), one of the last poems in the volume, Buttitta writes:

> Ora ca un cuntu nenti
> e a puisia non servi
> e sugnu aceddu spinnatu
> chi non vola
> non canta e non fa nidu
> io parru ancora a l'omini
> e restu un foddi chi ragiuna
> . . . .
> Un foddi ca non voli cridiri
> ca siddu i pueti non ci fussiru
> u munnu fussi u stissu,
> l'omini i stissi,
> e a vita un canciassi.
> Un foddi chi ragiuna
> e non voli moriri foddi.

> (Now that I don't count at all
> and poetry is no good for anything
> and I am a featherless bird
> that doesn't fly
> doesn't sing and doesn't build nests
> I still speak to the people
> and remain a madman who thinks
> . . . .
> A madman who doesn't want to believe
> that if poets didn't exist
> the world would be the same,
> people the same,
> and life wouldn't change.
> A madman who thinks
> and doesn't want to die mad.)

The anger and loneliness of *Il poeta in piazza* persists and becomes obsessive in Buttitta's last collection, *Pietre nere* (Black Stones, 1983). The beginning of the first poem, "I petri nivuri" (Black

Stones), is heavy with the "stones" of memory and existential despair:

> Sugnu cca
> sulu
> stanotti
> a scriviri e pinzari
> ca i ricordi i ricordi,
> na petra oggi e nautra dumani
> addiventanu muntagni
> e nni purtamu ncoddu sinu a morti . . .
> chi morti!

> (I am here
> alone
> tonight
> writing and thinking
> that memories, memories,
> one stone today and another tomorrow
> become mountains
> and we carry them on our shoulders until
>   death . . .
> what a death!)

These poems lack the feeling of community that compelled Buttitta to exhort, encourage, and cajole others to reflect on the unjust conditions of life and to change them. Buttitta no longer appears as a poet of the people but as a poet by himself: a solidarity poet with a mellifluous gift. His former call to arms is replaced by a call to existential questioning, as in "A natura è facciola" (Nature Is Fickle):

> E semu cca io e vuatri
> a taliarinni ni l'occhi
> nna facci
> pi sapiri cu semu
> cu siti
> e chi vinnimu a fari nno munnu
> si nascemu pi moriri:
> ci avita mai pinzatu? . . .

> (Here we are you and I
> looking into each other eyes
> at our faces
> to find out who we are
> who you are
> and why we came in this world
> if we were born to die:
> have you ever thought about it? . . .)

Before, people were the ideal center of his verses; now the "I" is the emanating force. Yet Buttitta's poetry continues to sing, no longer primarily inspired by the love of and sympathy for humanity but under the spell of life's mystery, as seen in "U misteru":

U misteru è puisia,
è u chiu granni sognu,
fa bella e ricca a vita
è dura di sempri;
e io ci campu dintra
filici di ci essiri
si sugnu cca all' arba
davanti u mari
a scriviri e pinzari
senza sapiri pirchì u fazzu,
cu mu fa fari,
e si servi fallu.

(Mystery is poetry,
and is the greatest dream,
it makes life beautiful and rich
and has lasted forever;
and I live inside it
happy to be in it
if I am here at dawn
before the sea
writing and thinking
without knowing why I do it,
who makes me do it,
and if it is worth doing.)

Buttitta, the former revolutionary ready to give his life, is enchanted by the mystery, and afraid of losing forever its sweetness. In his best and more enduring poetry he becomes the bard of the collective consciousness of laborers everywhere—not just Sicilian laborers—who through their struggle for survival and well-being express a first glimmer of the self-consciousness that in Buttitta's latest poems combines loss with anguish even as it inspires a personal and suprapersonal struggle against time and decay.

Interview:
Gianfranco Contini, "Intervista televisiva," in Buttitta's *Pietre nere* (Milan: Feltrinelli, 1983), pp. 7-8.

References:
Pietro Amato, "Ignazio Buttitta," in *I contemporanei*, volume 4 (Milan: Marzorati, 1976), pp. 365-379;

Giuseppe Cocchiara, "Ignazio Buttitta," in Buttitta's *La peddi nova* (Milan: Feltrinelli, 1963), pp. 199-200;

Gianfranco Contini, "Letter to Buttitta," in Buttitta's *Pietre nere* (Milan: Feltrinelli, 1983), p. 9;

Fernando Gioviale, "Il mestiere di poeta: Ignazio Buttitta," in *Operai di sogni: la poesia del Novecento in Sicilia* (Catania, Italy: Alfa Grafrica Sgroi, 1985), pp. 61-79;

Massimo Grillandi, "Ignazio Buttitta," *Belfagor*, 31, no. 2 (1976): 201-225;

Carlo Levi, Preface to Buttitta's *La peddi nova*, pp. 7-10;

V. Lombardo Toledano, *Nei mari di Ulisse—Ignazio Buttitta e la poesia popolare* (Mexico City: Universidad Obrera de Mexico, 1956);

Pier Paolo Pasolini, "Il poeta in piazza," in his *Scritti corsari* (Milan: Garzanti, 1975), pp. 224-229;

Marta Puglisi, Introduction to Buttitta's *Prime e nuovissime* (Turin: Forma, 1983), pp. 5-12;

Roberto Roversi, Preface to Buttitta's *La paglia bruciata* (Milan: Feltrinelli, 1968), pp. 7-12;

Leonardo Sciascia, Preface to Buttitta's *Io faccio il poeta* (Milan: Feltrinelli, 1972), pp. 7-10;

Sciascia, "La vera storia di Giuliano," in his *La corda pazza* (Turin: Einaudi, 1970), pp. 172-176;

Natale Tedesco, *Ignazio Buttitta e il mondo popolare siciliano* (Palermo: Flaccovio, 1965).

Dino Campana

(20 August 1885 - 1 March 1932)

Luigi Bonaffini
Brooklyn College

BOOKS: *Canti Orfici* (Marradi: Ravagli, 1914); translated by I. L. Salomon as *Orphic Songs* (New York: October House, 1968); revised and enlarged by Bino Binazzi as *Canti Orfici ed altre liriche* (Florence: Vallecchi, 1928); revised again as *Canti Orfici*, edited by Enrico Falqui (Florence: Vallecchi, 1941); enlarged again as *Canti Orfici e altri scritti*, edited by Falqui (Florence: Vallecchi, 1952; abridged, 1960); translated and edited by Luigi Bonaffini as *Orphic Songs and Other Poems* (New York: Lang, 1991);

Inediti, edited by Falqui (Florence: Vallecchi, 1942);

Taccuino, edited by Franco Matacotta (Fermo: Amici della Poesia, 1949);

Taccuinetto faentino, edited by Domenico De Robertis (Florence: Vallecchi, 1960):

Fascicolo marradese, edited by Federico Ravagli (Florence: Giunti-Bemporad Marzocco, 1972);

Il più lungo giorno, 2 volumes, edited by De Robertis (Florence: Vallecchi, 1973);

Opere e contributi, edited by Falqui (Florence: Vallecchi, 1973);

Taccuini (Pisa: Scuola Normale Superiore, 1990).

Interest in Dino Campana has been growing steadily, as evidenced by the proliferation of critical and biographical studies, to the extent that in 1989 alone four new editions of his *Canti Orfici* (1914; translated as *Orphic Songs*, 1968) were published, and there are those who are unabashedly calling Campana one of the greatest poets of the twentieth century. But even independently of the merits of his poetry, Campana would remain one of the most striking, dramatic, and exciting figures of Italian literature, and certainly one of the most disputed and controversial.

Canti Orfici is of great interest for its innovative use of language, for its imaginative syntactical patterns, for its free mixture of verse and prose, for the creation of new lexical and semantic relationships, for the original way Campana ap-

Drawing of Dino Campana (by permission of the Literary Estate of Dino Campana)

propriates preceding cultural experiences and uses them, and finally for the attention it has received from poets and critics alike. In its most controversial passages Campana's poetry exhibits all the elements of the most ground-breaking and avant-garde poetic language in modern Italian literature: irrational repetitions; illogical relative clauses; asyntactical, instinctive conjunctions; structures based on rhythmic, rather than semantic, nuclei; and a musical phrasing that is nonlinear, but which widens and spirals upward. For all these reasons, and because it occupies such a special place in Italian poetry, *Canti Orfici* is a fundamental text in twentieth-century Italian literature.

Dino Campana was born on 20 August 1885 in Marradi, Italy, near Faenza; he was the oldest son of an elementary-school teacher, Giovanni, and Francesca (Fanny) Luti Campana. He had three uncles who played a role in his life: Francesco, a public prosecutor in Florence; Torquato, another elementary-school teacher, who was appointed Campana's guardian when he was declared incompetent; and a third uncle who died in an insane asylum, and who is mentioned in Campana's admission documents at the asylum of San Salvi. According to Campana's biographer Sebastiano Vassalli, this family illness was Campana's curse—it provided a simple, hereditary explanation for his erratic behavior and was readily accepted, first by his fearful parents, then by the townspeople, and finally by the doctors who examined him.

Between 1891 and 1896 Campana attended elementary school in Marradi and was then sent to the Istituto Salesiano di Faenza to complete his secondary-school studies. In 1900 he registered for the first year of the *liceo* (high school) and commuted between Faenza and Marradi. This is the period in which, as stated by his father in a 1906 letter to the director of the insane asylum in Imola, Campana began to manifest signs of "impulsività brutale, morbosa, in famiglia e specialmente con la mamma" (brutal, morbid impulsiveness, with the family and especially toward his mother)—as quoted by Gabriel Cacho Millet in his *Dino Campana Fuorilegge* (Dino Campana Outlaw, 1985). Campana's father, stern and somewhat distant, but fair and caring, was clearly unable to mediate between him and his mother, who was becoming so increasingly intolerant and so obsessed with religious practices that she convinced herself, according to Vassalli, that she had begotten the Antichrist. Campana himself would later acknowledge that this period represented a decisive turning point in his life, the beginning of his compulsive wandering; as he told Carlo Pariani, the psychiatrist who often visited Campana in the asylum of Castel Pulci and wrote a well-known 1938 biography: "Dalla età di quindici anni, mi prese una forte nevrastenia, non potevo vivere in nessun posto. A quindici anni andai in collegio in Piemonte. Più tardi alla Università. Non riuscivo in chimica. E allora mi diedi un po' a scrivere e un po' al vagabondaggio" (From the age of fifteen, I was seized by a strong neurasthenia, I was unable to live anywhere. At fifteen I went to boarding school in Piedmont. Later to the university. I wasn't doing

well in chemistry. So I took to writing and to wandering).

Campana's father, urged by Campana's mother—who had always believed in the existence of hereditary flaws in the Campana family—decided to have Campana undergo a psychiatric examination, but the doctor did not make a negative diagnosis. In 1903 Campana was admitted to the Università di Bologna, where he registered in the school of sciences with a major in chemistry; in December of the same year, he entered the military academy at Modena, from which he was expelled after a few months for failure to pass the qualifying examination for the rank of sergeant. Having returned home, amid increasing tensions with his parents, between 1904 and 1905 Campana spent much of his time wandering alone in the mountains around Marradi and reading a great deal, especially Giosuè Carducci, Giovanni Pascoli, Gabriele D'Annunzio, and Friedrich Nietzsche. He also began to write literary articles—destined to remained unpublished. In 1905 he moved to Florence (where he probably stayed with his uncle Francesco) and attended the Università di Florence, but he did a lot of reading and little studying, and did not take a single examination. At the end of the year, he again registered at the Università di Bologna, while studying in Marradi under the supervision of his father and his uncle Torquato.

In May 1906 Campana suddenly began his long series of unpredictable "flights," first to Genoa and then to France, where the French police put him on a train back home because he did not have a passport. On 5 September Campana's father had him committed to an asylum in Imola for observation for "dementia praecox"—a term covering a wide variety of socially unacceptable behavior—which was strongly suspected; he was released on 31 October under his father's supervision and against the advice of the director, Dr. Angelo Brugia. Considering the short stay in the asylum and the 1906 letter from Campana's father to the director of the asylum—"egli ha la psiche esaltata, avvelenata, pervertita, non sente affetti e prende presto a noia luoghi e persone" (he has an excited, poisoned, perverted psyche, feels no affection and gets quickly bored with people and places)—Campana's biographers Millet and Vassalli conclude that the machine that was to crush his life, with the assistance of his family and Marradi's notables, had then been set in motion. From that time on Campana was officially

Francesca (Fanny), Dino, Manlio, and Giovanni Campana

"insane"; in November he was declared unfit for military service.

Sometime between 1907 and 1908 Campana, probably because his family decided to send the "psychopathic" son abroad, went to South America, where he worked at many different jobs: "Facevo qualche mestiere. Per esempio: temprare i ferri; tempravo una falce, una accetta. Si faceva per vivere. Facevo il suonatore di triangolo nella Marina argentina. Sono stato ad ammucchiare i terrapieni delle ferrovie in Argentina. Si dorme fuori nelle tende" (I worked at several jobs. For example: tempering tools; I would temper a sickle, an ax. In order to make a living. I was a triangle player in the Argentine navy. I was a doorman in a club in Buenos Aires. I had so many jobs. I worked on railway embankments in Argentina. We slept outdoors in tents)—as quoted by Pariani. Campana was also a miner, a fireman, a juggler, a gypsy, a pianist in brothels, a coal man on a steamship, and a worker at a rifle range.

In autumn 1908 Campana was back in Marradi, where he began to write the first nucleus of prose and poetry around which *Canti Orfici* would take shape. This is also a period characterized by intense study and by the voracious reading, while wandering on the mountains, of French, English, German, and Italian works. In April 1909, due to some disturbances caused by drunkenness, most probably a reaction to his status as "deranged" among the people of Marradi, Campana was committed to the asylum of San Salvi, from which he was released after a few days. There followed another brief trip to Paris, which, in conformity with a well-established pattern, would end in the insane asylum in Tournay, Belgium, but he soon returned to Marradi.

Campana spent the years from 1909 to 1911 in Marradi, Florence, and Bologna. In February 1912 he was in Genoa, where the police put him back on the train with travel orders. Finally he went back to the Università di Bologna and attended classes in the school year 1912-1913, passing the physics exam, but he still manifested extravagant behavior. These are the years in which Campana intensified his study of Nietzsche, in the original German, and completed his cultural development while publishing his first poems, "La Chimera," "Le cafard" (The Hypocrite), and "Dualismo," in the student paper *Il Papiro*. In 1913 Campana transferred to the Università di Genoa; the city held a particular fascination for him and often provides the background in *Canti*

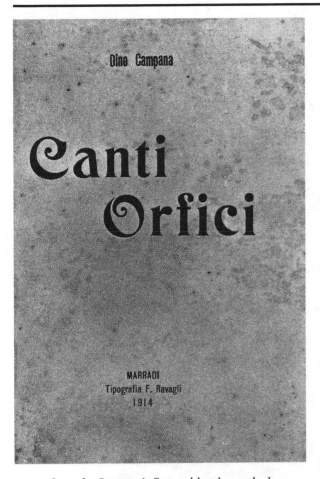

Cover for Campana's first and best-known book

Orfici. Genoa is the setting for the final, shattering epiphany at the end of the book. He discovered the journal *Lacerba* and the futurists and wrote a poem, "Traguardo" (Finish), dedicated to Filippo Tommaso Marinetti, the acknowledged leader of the movement, who nevertheless refused to publish Campana's work. Campana also sent some of his poems to *La Voce*, one of the most important and influential publications of the time, controlled by Giovanni Papini and Ardengo Soffici, who would eventually accept some of his verses. Forced to leave Genoa again after being interrogated by the police, Campana went back to Marradi, where in a few months he finished drafting his first major manuscript.

Campana gave his only copy of the manuscript, entitled *Il più lungo giorno* (The Longest Day, eventually published in 1973), to Papini, who read it and promised to publish it but then handed it over to Soffici. Soffici, in what became a cause célèbre in Italian letters, lost the manuscript while moving to a new house, as he would tell Campana when the young poet finally asked

him for it. In a rather baffling display of nonchalance, Soffici would much later say that he did not think it was very important, since Campana had not inquired about it for a long time.

However, this was a devastating experience for Campana and marked his complete break with contemporary Italian literature and literary institutions—the "Florentines" (Papini and Soffici) and *Lacerba* and *La Voce* in particular. Campana was therefore forced to rewrite the book, but it is unlikely that he did so totally from memory, since he almost certainly had notes and copies of at least some of the poems. Between December 1913 and January 1914 Campana worked on the manuscript, taking out some parts very decisively, adding others, and completely transforming some of the most important sections. The book, bearing the new title *Canti Orfici*, was published.

The loss of the original manuscript contributed considerably to Campana's legend, prompting more than one critic to consider the final product, *Canti Orfici*, somehow unfinished, not completely realized, a work in progress, while lamenting as a calamity the disappearance of *Il più lungo giorno*, whose supposed perfection *Canti Orfici* had not been able to recapture. All speculations, however, were put to rest in 1971, when Mario Luzi announced that the original manuscript had been found by Soffici's family. Everyone seems to agree, starting with Domenico De Robertis, who edited and published *Il più lungo giorno* in 1973, that *Canti Orfici*, far from paling in comparison, is in fact a decidedly superior work. It would be difficult to disagree with Neuro Bonifazi when he says that, while the loss of the original manuscript was undoubtedly a personal tragedy for the poet, it represented on the other hand a great fortune for Italian literature.

After the publication of *Canti Orfici* Campana appeared in Florence again, perhaps the only time in his life when he enjoyed some respect and consideration. He frequented the café Giubbe Rosse, talked to the artists, and visited art exhibits, and Papini and Soffici published in *Lacerba* three poems from *Canti Orfici*: "Sogno di prigione" (Prison Dream), "L'incontro di Regolo" (Meeting with Regolo), and "Piazza Sarzano." Campana also attended personally to the sale of his book, in a way that has become legendary. There are several eyewitness accounts, including Soffici's, of how Campana would sell his book among the customers of the café, but only after carefully sizing up each prospective buyer and

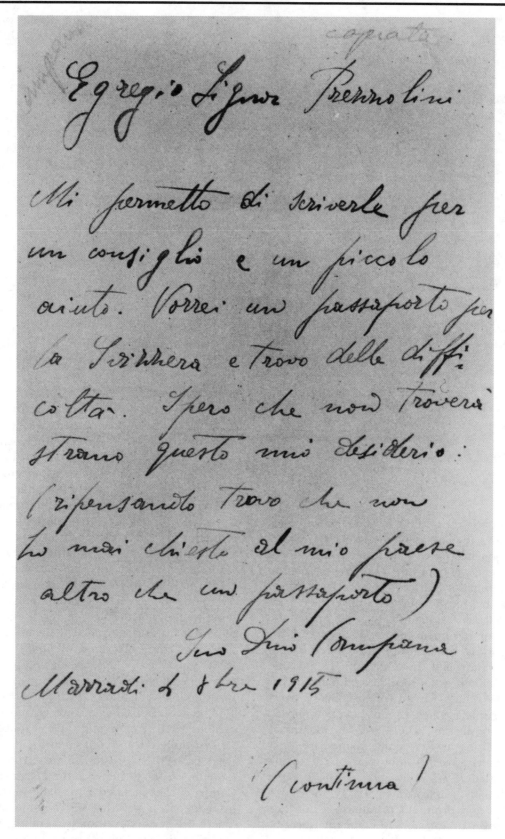

Letter to Giuseppe Prezzolini, 4 October 1915 (from Storia della letteratura, *volume 15, edited by Luciano Bertolini and Goffredo Dotti, 1965)*

then tearing out the pages he believed would not be understood. Soffici also says that Marinetti received just the cover of *Canti Orfici*, all the pages having been torn out by Campana.

With a characteristically iconoclastic, anti-bourgeois stance, deeply rooted in his painful condition as a social outcast, he had decided, on the eve of Italy's entrance into World War I against Germany, to dedicate *Canti Orfici* to the German emperor, using the subtitle "Die tragödie des Letzen germanen in Italien" (The Tragedy of the Last German in Italy). This caused quite a bit of consternation and attracted the attention of the police, so that Campana, to avoid further persecution, since he was normally under surveillance for being "demented" and just out of an asylum, erased the dedication from all the copies he had. But his polemical gesture, which had no political significance, was naturally misunderstood.

Again Campana ran away, to Pisa, Sardinia, and Turin (where he sold newspapers in the street), then to Switzerland looking for work. Back in Florence once more, when on 24 May 1915 Italy entered the war, he tried to enlist as a volunteer—a clear indication that the dedication to the kaiser was not politically motivated—but was rejected. After spending a month in a psychiatric hospital, suffering from strong headaches, insomnia, and a recurrent paralysis on his left side, Campana was becoming increasingly unstable and began to feel for the first time that poetry was abandoning him. During his frequent outbursts he would write to Papini and Soffici demanding that they return the lost manuscript and threatening to go after them with "un buon coltello" (a good knife).

In August 1916 he met the writer Sibilla Aleramo, with whom he began a stormy love affair. He alternated between periods of complete lucidity and moments of total alienation and fury. He was tormented by migraines and forms of delirium, and the relationship between the two lovers turned increasingly violent. Their separation, which took place in late January 1917, led to Campana's indulging in frequent bouts of drunkenness and strange and unpredictable behavior, often degenerating into fits of violence, which again landed him in prison and then in a psychiatric hospital. Finally on 12 January 1918, by order of the mayor of Lastra a Signa, where Campana was staying with his father, he was committed to the asylum of San Salvi, where he was diagnosed as suffering from the usual "dementia praecox." From there he was transferred to the

asylum of Castel Pulci, where he would remain until his death. As Pariani recalls, "nella permanenza ospedaliera dapprima diede indizi di allucinazioni uditive, espresse idee deliranti di grandezza e di persecuzione, ebbe scatti ingiustificati. Poscia prevalsero false percezioni acustiche cutanee muscolari viscerali, talvolta dolorose; fallacie rappresentative, ripetizioni sonore del pensiero. . . . Diceva di ricevere influssi elettrici magnetici medianici ipnotici; di produrne e di trasmetterne" (in the hospital at first he gave signs of auditory hallucinations, expressed delirious ideas of grandeur and persecution, had unjustified fits of temper. Later there prevailed false perceptions—acoustic cutaneous muscular visceral—at times painful; representational fallacies, verbalized repetitions of thought. . . . He said he was receiving electrical magnetic medianic hypnotic suggestions; that he was producing them and transmitting them).

In 1928 Vallecchi published the second edition of *Canti Orfici*, edited by Bino Binazzi, who made arbitrary modifications and additions. Campana, who received a copy in the hospital, perceived these changes made without his knowledge as the latest indignity against him and asked his brother, Manilo, to look for the original Marradi edition, so that the text of his poems would not be lost. Campana died of septicemia on 1 March 1932.

Perhaps no other poet has been so completely identified with one book as Campana, who repeatedly referred to *Canti Orfici* as the only justification of his life. There is, however, a rather large and complex body of preceding heterogeneous material: early poetry, fragments, rough drafts of both poetry and prose, and poems in various stages of development, all collected in his *Inediti* (Unpublished, 1942). There is also the recovered manuscript of *Il più lungo giorno* and the *Taccuinetto faentino* (Faenza Journal, 1960), a small notebook of preliminary notations and sketches. In *Inediti* one can find, as Bonifazi points out, the prehistory of Campana's poetry: the first decadent and symbolist European experiences, the influence of Charles-Pierre Baudelaire and the *scapigliati* (libertine poets), touches of sadism and vampirism, Emile Verhaeren and the post-symbolists, Giosuè Carducci, fashionable superman poses (via Nietzsche), a lot of *crepuscolarismo* (twilight poetry) and futurism, and some hooliganism. There are many passages that Campana would take up later in different form, so that the *quaderno* (notebook) is a valuable source for the

La notte mistica del amore e del dolore — Scorci bizantini
morti cinematografiche   «è solo il dolore è vero»

Cinematografia sentimentale.

L'amore.

I La notte mistica

Ricordo una vecchia città rossa di mura
e turrita; arsa sulla pianura sterminata
nell'Agosto torrido con il lontano refrigerio
di colline verdi e molli sullo sfondo —
Archi enormemente vuoti di ponti sul
fiume impaludato in magre stagnazioni
plumbee — Sagome nere di zingari mobili
e silenziose sulla riva — tra il barbaglio
lontano di un canneto lontane forme
ignude di adolescenti e il profilo e la
barba giudaica di un vecchio — E a un
tratto dal mezzo dell'acqua morta le
zingare e un canto — Dalla palude afona
una nenia primordiale monotona e
irritante — E del tempo fu sospeso il
corso.

Inconsciamente alzai gli occhi alla torre
barbara che dominava il viale

Page from the manuscript for Il più lungo giorno *(by permission of the Literary Estate of Dino Campana)*

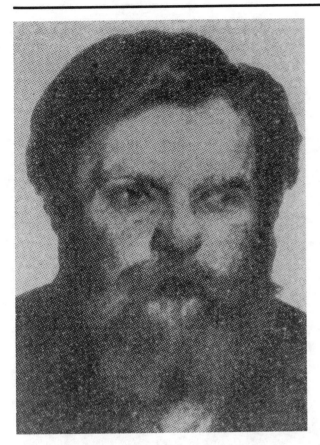

Dino Campana (portrait by G. Costetti; from G. A. Pellegrinetti, Un secolo di poesia, *1957)*

study of the variants, which show that he would work on the same passage with an almost obsessive insistence. And there are many passages that herald Campana's more mature work, as in "Oscar Wilde a San Miniato," with its almost surrealistic analogic intensity:

Ma bella come te, battello bruciato tra l'alto
Soffio glorioso del ricordo, gridai o città,
O sogno sublime di tendere in fiamme
I corpi alla chimera non saziata
Amarissimo brivido funebre davanti all'incendio
    sordo lunare.

(But beautiful as you, boat burnt in the high
Glorious breath of memory, I shouted o city,
O sublime dream to tender in flames
The bodies to the unsated chimera
Most bitter funereal shudder before the muted
    lunar blaze.)

Il più lungo giorno marks an intermediate stage, already displaying a powerful new voice and many of the stylistic innovations found in its subsequent reincarnation as *Canti Orfici.*

The section that opens *Canti Orfici,* entitled "La Notte" (Night), immediately shows his innovative use of language:

Ricordo una vecchia città, rossa di mura e turrita, arsa sulla pianura sterminata nell'Agosto torrido, con il lontano refrigerio di colline verdi e molli sullo sfondo. Archi enormemente vuoti di ponti sul fiume impaludato in magre stagnazioni plumbee: sagome nere di zingari mobili e silenziose sulla riva: tra il barbaglio lontano di un canneto lontane forme ignude di adolescenti e il profilo e la barba giudaica di un vecchio: e a un tratto dal mezzo dell'acqua morta le zingare e un canto, da la palude afona una nenia primordiale monotona e irritante: e del tempo fu sospeso il corso.

(I remember an old city, with red walls and towered, burnt on the endless plain in the torrid August, with the distant coolness of soft green hills in the background. Enormously empty bridge spans over the river mired in sparse leaden pools: black outlines of gypsies shifting and silent on the bank: amid the distant glare of a canebrake distant naked figures of adolescents and the profile and the Judaic beard of an old man: and suddenly from the midst of the dead water the gypsy women and a song, from the soundless marsh a primordial chant, monotonous and irritating: and time came to a standstill.)

With the very first word Campana introduces the fundamental theme of memory, which in *Canti Orfici* is a complex notion operating on several related levels of meaning and is inseparable from historical and metahistorical time, personal experience, and collective myth. The suspension of time at the end of the paragraph results from a redemptive memory, which transforms private occasions into mythical epiphanies, and aims at the abolition of chronological time through the recovery of an inner dimension beyond time and history (an important theme in subsequent modern poetry, as in the works of Giuseppe Ungaretti). Thus this Dantean "libro della memoria" (book of memory)—and there are many references to Dante's *Vita Nuova* in "La Notte"—is open to multiple levels of reading, as Fiorenza Ceragioli suggests. On the literal level Campana, in "La Notte," remembers episodes in the land of his youth, followed by a vision of a series of images from the past. "Il viaggio" (The Journey) is an episode set in Genoa, after which there is a return to the "scorci bizantini" (Byzantine perspectives) of Romagna. Dominant throughout is the theme

Pages 2 and 3 from an undated letter from Campana to Carlo Carrà (from Storia della letteratura, *volume 6, edited by Luigi Ferrante, 1965)*

con ironia ~~troppo~~ benigna e gentile
che nessun dominicano avrà
mai. L'Italia meridionale
vi Ieri, paese eminentemente
agricolo, ~~——~~ ha prodotto ~~——~~
~~troppi~~ contadini e questo ci
ha fatto molto male, quasi
quanto la coltura tedesca. In ~~una~~
~~quanto~~ teria di colture la colpa mi
sembra che sia specialmente dei
coltivatori.

~~————~~ Io che vivo in un
costante e fischiante paesetto toscà
uno ~~——~~ invidio ora ~~la~~ ~~————~~
~~Milano~~. Accetterei di andarla a costr-

of love in all its manifold manifestations, from animal lust—"Il suo corpo ambrato la sua bocca vorace i suoi ispidi neri capelli" (Her amber body her voracious mouth her bristly black hair)—to the unattainable ideal: "Amore, primavera del sogno sei sola sei sola che appari nel velo dei fumi di viola. Come una nuvola bianca, come una nuvola bianca presso al mio cuore, o resta o resta o resta!" (Love, spring of dream you are alone you are alone who appear in the veil of the purple haze. Like a white cloud, like a white cloud next to my heart, o stay o stay o stay!).

But "La Notte" is also a descent into the instinctual world of the unconscious: "Inconsciamente colui che io ero stato si trovava avviato verso la torre barbara, la mitica custode dei sogni dell'adolescenza" (Unconsciously he who I had been found himself moving toward the barbarous tower, the mythical guardian of the dreams of my youth). *Barbarous, mythical, savage* and *ancient* are obsessively recurring key concepts, always charged with strong positive connotations and belonging to the same semantic field expressing an essential primordial purity. In this netherworld, places and people take on an oneiric dimension (not only concerning Orphism and the vital Orpheus myth but also the descent into hell of Dante, whom Campana most probably considered one of the great exponents of the Orphic tradition, in the wake of Plato and Virgil). In this ambivalent realm—"tutto era arido e dolce nel panorama scheletrico del mondo" (everything was arid and sweet in the skeletal landscape of the world)—the figures encountered by the poet appear as the last incarnation of timeless presences perpetuating from generation to generation the eternal and unchanging story of passion and love, pleasure and pain. Finally there is an even deeper, barely fathomable region of being, reaching back in time to the most distant origin of man, which only the greatest artists have been able to reach with their imperishable creations, and which for a fleeting moment can become dimly perceptible through an intense visionary experience: "E allora figurazioni di un'antichissima libera vita, di enormi miti solari, di stragi di orgie si crearono davanti al mio spirito" (And then representations of a most ancient free life, of enormous solar myths, of massacres of orgies were created before my spirit). This is an important interpretive key to the recurrent surfacing of Michelangelo's *Night* and Dante's Francesca, two of the most important structural and thematic nuclei in the book.

The next section, a series of seven poems entitled "Notturni," takes up many of the themes of "La Notte"—hope, love, suffering—with the addition of another important element already implicit: death, seen as a liberating force, a bridge to infinity, as in "La speranza" (Hope): "Per l'amor dei poeti, porte / Aperte de la morte / su l'infinito" (For the love of poets, open / Doors of death / onto infinity); and therefore as a consoling, desirable presence, as in "Il canto della tenebra" (The Song of Darkness): "Non c'è di dolcezza che possa uguagliare la morte" (There is no sweetness that can equal death). The sense of alienation, the suffering, and the sacrificial blood shed by the poet (*sangue* [blood] and *sanguigno* [blood-red] are recurrent key words) are the main themes of "L'invetriata" (The Glass Window): "c'è / Nella stanza un odor di putredine: c'è / Nella stanza una piaga rossa languente" (there is / In the room a smell of putrefaction: there is / In the room a red stagnant wound). The poem in this section that Campana himself considered of the utmost significance is "La Chimera." The Chimera, a hauntingly complex, enigmatic projection/character appearing throughout Campana's work, represents not only the unreachable feminine ideal, but also the prefiguration of poetry itself, the ultimate aim of Campana's lifelong quest, so that the poem becomes in fact a passionate hymn to the poetic mission, the gaze of the nocturnal poet fixed intensely on the shadows of reality in search of a possible metaphysical opening, a sign from unknown distances suddenly showing the eternal forms of the objects of the world.

The following section, "La Verna" (the name of a mountain), is titled in *Il più lungo giorno* "Il mattino: il pellegrinaggio: le sorgenti" (the morning: the pilgrimage: the springs), a clear indication of the archetypal narrative structure of the book—based on the solar cycle and the alternation of darkness and light, and on the metaphor of the journey, which is central to *Canti Orfici*. "La Verna" represents, in the Orphic-Dantean iter of initiation, the reawakening of light after the oppressive darkness of hell—in other words a purgatorial ascent—and if Campana calls his walk on the mountains a pilgrimage, it is mainly because he feels Dante's presence: "Dante la sua poesia di movimento mi torna tutta in memoria. O pellegrino, o pellegrini che pensosi andate" (Dante his poetry of movement comes all to mind. O pilgrim, o pilgrims who walk so pensive). "La Verna" is, like

"La Notte," a journey toward origins, an initiatory journey that aims at the discovery of a temporal dimension in which past and present can coincide. The structure of "La Verna" is of interest because Campana constructs his pilgrimage on a series of ever-changing sceneries, conceived as vast backdrops, each profoundly different from the last and marked by a variety of elements running from the mystical to the grotesque; and because the spiritual itinerary also includes the lyrical recovery of everyday reality. Campana's climb—the verb *salire* (to climb) punctuates the various stages of the journey and expresses both physical and spiritual movement—is also a sacred quest that holds the promise of a "paese nuovo" (a new country); "un paesaggio promesso" (a promised landscape); an ancient castle seen in the distance, which is the symbol of both lost innocence and purity and of poetry itself; and "la poesia toscana" (Tuscan poetry), which once was the real purpose of the poet's search and whose characteristics are simplicity and austerity (as seen in the works of Dante and Michelangelo). "Ritorno," where the symbolic meaning of *salire* is made clear in the subtitle "SALGO (nello spazio, fuori del tempo)" (I CLIMB [into space, outside of time]), is an attempt to return to the beginning of things through a metaphysical history of nature (according to Bonifazi) and a cosmogonic theory of the origin of the elements, of things that are pure and sound:

L'acqua il vento
La sanità delle prime cose—
Il lavoro umano sull'elemento
Liquido—la natura che conduce
Strati di roccie su strati—il vento
Che scherza nella valle—ed ombra del vento
La nuvola—il lontano ammonimento
Del fiume nella valle—

(The water the wind
The soundness of first things—
Human toil on the liquid
Element—nature leading
Layers of rocks upon layers—the wind
Playing in the valley—and shadow of the wind
The cloud—the distant warning
Of the river in the valley—).

The image of human work is significant in that it denotes harmony between man and nature, as noted by Mario Luzi, when he says in *Dino Campana oggi* (Dino Campana Today, 1973) that Campana sets against the pattern of humanistic disillusionment a complete integration of man into the vicissitudes of the world, the continuity and omnipresence of all life. In this elemental symphony, "la tellurica melodia della Falterona" (the telluric melody of the Falterona), water is the primal element whose voice reverberates with the echo of undifferentiated oneness—"Nella voce dell'elemento noi udiamo tutto" (in the voice of the element we hear everything). It is the source, rising from the depths of the earth, the very essence of being in its roots and its immensity. But it is also the element for Campana that connects moments and places, memory and imagination, childhood and death, and the image of time itself.

A key stylistic device in all of Campana's work is the obsessive iteration, the constant intratextual and intertextual resurfacing of the same word or image, which Cesare Galimberti has likened to the Wagnerian leitmotiv; but Campana's reiteration, while preserving the more traditional musical function, also plays a marked structural role by effecting a process of identification across different places, times, and texts, which undermines the distinction between past and present and the concept of time as progression and sequentiality.

Canti Orfici is a constant revisiting of places and cities, especially those belonging to Campana's past—Bologna, Faenza, Florence, Genoa—each with its own unmistakable character, its own secret essence: "Se Firenze è l'immagine della musica, Faenza è l'immagine della danza latina" (If Florence is the image of music, Faenza is the image of Latin dance). Each is linked to a different experience, a different aspect of reality: in the poem "Firenze" (Florence) the great artistic tradition of the city and its high spiritual quality are set against the nightlife of its red-light district, while Bologna, in "Giornata di un nevrastenico" (The Day of a Neurasthenic), inspires scorn and derision in the almost surrealistic description of the people as small, leaping animals. But in "Scirocco" Campana presents Bologna as a fabled port toward the Orient, and its streets conjure "stilnovistic" apparitions: "Una figura giovine, gli occhi grigi, la bocca dalle linee rosee tenui, passò nella vastità luminosa del cielo. Sbiancava nel cielo fumoso la melodia dei suoi passi" (a young figure, with gray eyes, her mouth with soft rosy lines, went by in the luminous vastness of the sky. The melody of her steps paled in the hazy sky).

Campana is always pursuing a lyric ideal, a personal mode of expression, and, in trying to give it a definitive form, he constantly broadens and multiplies his experimental approach, attacks it from several angles, and starts over at every turn—as the host of variants, his proteiform style, and his iterative obsession amply indicate—but always in search of an absolute. This was the essential nature of Campana's work and his life. In other words poetry was for Campana the only nondeceptive absolute, which could be reached solely at the furthest limits of personal commitment. Finally it is poetry, against and beyond the failure of time and history, that justifies a senseless and dispersive life and totally defines it.

Campana's acute sense of alienation, his extreme, painful social eccentricity, is nowhere more clearly expressed than in the colophon at the end of *Canti Orfici*, a slightly modified quotation from Walt Whitman, to which Campana attributed a fundamental importance, as shown in a 1916 letter to Emilio Cecchi (in *Le mie lettere sono fatte per essere bruciate*, 1978): "Se vivo o morto lei si occuperà ancora di me la prego di non dimenticare le ultime parole *They were all torn and covered with the boy's blood* che sono le uniche importanti del libro" (If dead or alive you still show interest in me I beg you not to forget the last words in the book *They were all torn and covered with the boy's blood* which are the only important ones in the book). The image, as often is the case with Campana, is complex and multilayered, and it offers different levels of interpretation, from the personal (Campana's own role as sacrificial victim), to the mythical (Orpheus's fate at the hand of the Maenads and Dionysus's dismemberment by the Titans), to the deeper psychological and anthropological level of the *sparagmos*, the ritual tearing apart mentioned by Northrop Frye in his *Anatomy of Criticism* (1957). In any case it stands for a profound laceration affecting all aspects of expression and existence.

Campana did not have many followers and imitators, as for instance D'Annunzio did, because his experience was too intensely personal and unrepeatable, but Campana's voice has penetrated deeply into twentieth-century poetic consciousness, and its echo can be heard in the voices of numerous modern poets, among them Giuseppe Ungaretti, Vincenzo Cardarelli, Eugenio Montale, Piero Bigongiari, Alfonso Gatto, and Mario Luzi, as Silvio Ramat has shown (in *Dino Campana oggi*). Commenting on the irradiating power of *Canti Orfici*, he calls it the first complete book of our poetic experience. According to Ruggero Jacobbi, only in Campana and

with Campana does poetry show the full co-presence of word and image, and the dissolution of man into language, which is the supreme aspiration of the moderns and which has been attempted again and again in the different formulas of *lirica pura* (pure poetry), of Orphism, of *prosa d'arte*, and finally, more consistently, of hermeticism.

The critical evaluation of Campana, even after many years of close attention to his work and an ever-growing body of criticism, has yet to find a well-defined consensus, aside from the general acceptance of Campana as an authentic poet, and seems to oscillate between two principal positions: on one side are his designation as innovator and founder of modern Italian poetry; the abiding support and admiration of writers and critics connected with the Florentine hermetic movement (such as Luzi and Bigongiari); and the reassessment of Campana by Edoardo Sanguinetti in his *La poesia italiana del Novecento* (The Italian Poetry of the Twentieth Century, 1969), where Campana's greatness, as the foremost representative of expressionistic poetry in Italy, is proclaimed with conviction: "Ma Campana, finalmente, cioè uno dei pochi veramente grandi del nostro Novecento, trova qui la sua chiave legittima: è in lui, precisamente, che tutta la possibile tensione espressionistica del nostro Novecento ritrova il suo autentico protagonista. Per la prima volta, qui si tenta di misurare a quanto impeto d'anima il linguaggio sia capace di resistere, quanta intensità spirituale sia in grado di contenere, quale pressione, e anche proprio pressione morale, il verso spinto al limite riesca a arginare e sorreggere" (But finally Campana, namely one of the few truly great of our twentieth century, finds here his legitimate key: it is in him, precisely, that all the possible expressionistic tension of our twentieth century discovers its authentic protagonist. For the first time, there is here an attempt to measure how much vehemence of the soul language is capable of withstanding, how much spiritual intensity it is able to contain, how much pressure, even moral pressure, verse pushed to the limit can still check and sustain). For Sanguineti, Campana is the one who has brought this laceration within language to the breaking point, drawing the entire pathology of the collective poetic conscience into the alienation of his mind, the whirlwind of his images, his obsessive repetitions, and his outrageous rhythms. And Campana's greatness is inseparable from his extreme designs of cultural sabotage and his firm refusal to collaborate with literary institutions, and with all institutions in general.

On the other side there is a long series of tentative, reductive interpretations (by Giovanni Papini, Carlo Bo, Gianfranco Contini, and Pier Vincenzo Mengaldo) and some outright rejections, as by Umberto Saba: "era matto e solo matto" (he was crazy and only crazy)—quoted by Mengaldo in *Poeti italiani del Novecento*, 1978). Campana's turbulent, nomadic life; his well-known excesses and frequent detentions in prisons and asylums; his vehemently adversary stance with respect to literary institutions and movements; and his final, tragic internment in Castel Pulci—all inevitably elicited the creation of a public persona, the Rimbaudian bohemian, the "mad poet" of *Canti Orfici*. Campana's disconcertingly difficult language—the rupturing style of certain passages, which had no precedent or parallel in Italian letters, and was not in any way explainable in terms of preexisting models—if beyond the reach of critical exegesis, would then become accessible to a psychological interpretation.

Already in 1914 and 1915, the first critics to review Campana—Giuseppe de Robertis, Emilio Cecchi, and Giovanni Boine—notwithstanding their keen sensibility, discretion, and valuable stylistic analyses, by underscoring certain human aspects of the Campana "case," contributed unintentionally, and perhaps inevitably, to the formation of the enduring Campana myth. The legend of Campana, as Antonio Corsaro and Marcello Verdenelli have documented in their 1985 bibliography, exploded with devastating force, producing an enormous, overwhelming mass of newspaper articles that detail moments and aspects of Campana from every possible angle. Even the numerous biographies have shown a marked tendency to romanticize the figure of the poet. (A possible exception is Pariani's biography, the first of the series, which, whether or not it can persuade a modern reader, does take a rather neutral and objective stance and has produced a wealth of information utilized by subsequent researchers.) Corsaro and Verdenelli point out, however, that Campana from the very first was well known not for his extravagant behavior, but for the close, meaningful relationship with readers that that behavior instituted with *Canti Orfici*. After the legend gained momentum, those who wrote about him would remember the mad poet rejected and misunderstood for his unacceptable conduct by the ignorant townspeople and by the shortsighted Florentine culture. But that concept would be based on real intellectual interactions, with an essential role being played by a poetry that was not totally categorizable but which was being read over and over. Campana's legend was a strong preconditioning factor in the evaluation of his poetry. Already in August 1915 (in *Riviera Ligure*) Boine spoke of "allucinata febbre" (hallucinated fever), "lirica frenesia" (lyric frenzy), and "spasimo dell'inesprimibile" (agony of the inexpressible)—all terms that would become lasting features of Campana criticism. Sergio Solmi (*Fiera Letteraria*, 26 August 1928), who was the first to recognize the musical quality of *Canti Orfici*, spoke of thought coming apart in a "balbettio demente" (demented stuttering). Solmi was dealing with the fourth stanza of "Genova," the most expressly visionary passage in *Canti Orfici*, which has contributed more than any other to the miscomprehension of Campana's poetry. It exhibits all the elements of the most ground-breaking and avant-garde poetic language in modern Italian literature. The pertinent relationships in the construction of the stanza are not logical but musical and rhythmic, and they are sustained by a complex pattern of interthreaded iterations:

Quando,
Melodiosamente
D'alto sale, il vento come bianca finse una visione di
    Grazia
Come dalla vicenda infaticabile
Delle nuvole e de le stelle dentro del cielo serale
Dentro il vico marino in alto sale, . . .
Dentro il vico chè rosse in alto sale
Marino l'ali rosse dei fanali
Rabescavano l'ombra illanguidita, . . .
Che nel vico marino, in alto sale
Che bianca e lieve e querula salì!
"Come nell'ali rosse dei fanali
Bianca e rossa nell'ombra del fanale
Che bianca e lieve e tremula salì! . . ."

(When
Melodiously
From high salt, the wind fashioned like a white vision of Grace
As if from the tireless changing
Of the clouds and stars within the evening sky
Within the maritime alley in high salt, . . .
Within the maritime alley for red in high salt
The red wings of the streetlamps
Graced with arabesques the languishing shadow, . . .
That in the maritime alley, in high salt
That white and light and querulous it rose!

*"As in the red wings of the streetlamps
White and red in the shadow of the streetlamp
That white and light and tremulous it rose! . . ."*

Even Bo—in a 1939 essay that is perhaps the first balanced study of Campana's poetry and in which the critic underscores the visionary nature of that poetry—when confronted with "Genova" is forced to fall back on the "official" interpretation, and he writes that words seem to come to a standstill, "nel cerchio di un'insistenza disperata" (in the circle of a desperate insistence). That same year Contini, who defined Campana as "visivo" (visual), as opposed to visionary, spoke of the "fase magico-balbettata" (magical-stuttering phase) and the attempt to capture the ideal through "assurdità verbale" (verbal absurdity). Papini, who could not understand the interest generated by the poet, relegates him among other passing fads, reducing his more daring passages to "disordine mentale" (mental disorder). Giuseppe Raimondi also spoke of Campana's "balbettio verbale" (verbal stuttering) (*Il Mondo*, 25 April 1953). The word *balbettio*, with its implications of incompleteness and impotence, had become a prejudicial term, a conceptual filter inevitably applied to the fruition of Campana's poetry, which would be used again and again, even by critics of the stature of De Robertis and Marco Forti.

The first break with this restrictive critical orientation came only as late as 1953, with Parronchi's essay " 'Genova' e il senso dei colori nella poesia di Campana" ("Genova" and the Sense of Colors in Campana's Poetry), published in *Paragone* in December, in which the critic expresses the hope that as a result of his analysis the verb *balbettare* (to stutter) would no longer accompany the definition of even the most tormented of Campana's verses. Insisting on the formal consciousness of the poet and on the "effetto caleidoscopico del frazionamento dell'immagine" (the kaleidoscopic effect of splitting the image), Parronchi attempts to show how Campana's use of decomposition and fragmentation corresponds to the technical experimentation of contemporary figurative art, especially futurism and cubism, a fruitful suggestion exploited by later critics (such as Maura del Serra and Ceragioli). But the real turning point took place with Neuro Bonifazi's 1964 book, *Dino Campana*, one of the most intelligent and richest contributions of all Campana criticism, which not only examines the importance of Nietzsche (especially the Nietzsche

of *Thus Spake Zarathustra* [1883-1892] and *The Birth of Tragedy* [1872], with its Apollinian-Dionysiac duality) and the Orphic tradition (filtered through French symbolism), but undertakes as well a fundamental diachronic study of the variants of "Genova," demonstrating convincingly that the poem had gone through several "normal" phases lacking any logical-syntactical aberration of discourse. The *balbettio*, far from being an abnormality due to a mental disorder, is finally elevated to critical respectability as "il risultato di uno studio esigentissimo di stile" (the result of an extremely exacting study of style).

More strictly literary, adopting a methodology with structuralist tendencies, is *L'immagine aperta* (The Open Imagination, 1973), by Maura del Serra, for whom Campana is an avant-garde poet who effected a semantic, lyric, ideologic recovery of personal meaning in the Italian-European poetic tradition and heritage of the eighteenth century; he evokes a sense of an immediate and conscious attempt at total art, or rather at the dynamic conversion of the relationship (of Romantic origin) between art and life into the other relationship, both classical and modern, between knowledge and existence.

Ruggero Jacobbi, in *Invito alla lettura di Campana* (Invitation to the Literature of Campana, 1976), speaks of the power of Campana's voice in its dramatic certainty of being alone and of standing for a song that can at times be heard by common people, if they ever come out of the parameters of bourgeois life and emerge as nocturnal ghosts, apparitions marked by sarcasm, evil, and innocence. *Orfismo e poesia in Dino Campana* (1983), by Ida Li Vigni, presents Campana's Orphism as far from being a mere literary and cultural topos: it constitutes a process of symbolic resemanticization, which also affects the relationships between man and nature, and between erosive historical time and the regeneration of cyclical atemporality; it is a way of approaching not only the world and the depths of the self but, above all, poetry itself. It is a certain measure of the vitality of Campana's work that it has been able to generate so much attention, a critical discourse that continues to grow after almost eighty years, centering on the mystery of a text that is one of the shortest imaginable as justification of a lifetime, but whose infinity can still jar modern and postmodern sensibilities.

Letters:

Lettere: Dino Campana-Sibilla Aleramo, edited by Niccolo Gallo (Florence: Vallecchi, 1958);

Le mie lettere sono fatte per essere bruciate, edited by Gabriel Cacho Millet (Milan: All'Insegna del Pesce d'Oro, 1978);

Souvenir d'un pendu, edited by Millet (Naples: Scientifiche Italiane, 1985);

Epistolario (Milan: Lombardi, 1985).

Bibliography:

Antonio Corsaro and Marcello Verdenelli, *Bibliografia Campaniana (1914-1985)* (Ravenna, Italy: Longo, 1985).

Biographies:

Carlo Pariani, *Vite non romanzate di Dino Campana scrittore e di Evaristo Boncinelli scultore* (Florence: Vallecchi, 1938);

Federico Ravagli, *Dino Campana e i goliardi del suo tempo* (Florence: Marzocco, 1942);

Gino Gerola, *Dino Campana* (Florence: Sansoni, 1955);

Sebastiano Vassalli, *La notte della cometa* (Turin: Einaudi, 1984);

Gianni Turchetta, *Dino Campana: Biografia di un poeta* (Milan: Marcos & Marcos, 1985);

Gabriel Cacho Millet, *Dino Campana Fuorilegge* (Palermo: Novecento, 1985).

References:

Carlo Bo, "Dell'infrenabile notte," in his *Otto studi* (Florence: Vallecchi, 1939), pp. 105-125;

Luigi Bonaffini, *La poesia visionaria di Dino Campana* (Isernia: Marinelli, 1980);

Giovanni Bonalumi, *Cultura e poesia di Campana* (Florence: Vallecchi, 1953);

Neuro Bonifazi, *Dino Campana* (Rome: Dell'Ateneo, 1964);

Fiorenza Ceragioli, Introduction to Campana's *Canti Orfici* (Florence: Vallecchi, 1985);

Gianfranco Contini, "Dino Campana," in his *Esercizi di lettura* (Florence: Vallecchi, 1939);

Piero Cudini, ed., *Materiali per Dino Campana* (Lucca: Pacini Fazzi, 1986);

Dino Campana oggi (Florence: Vallecchi, 1973);

Enrico Falqui, *Per una cronistoria dei 'Canti Orfici'* (Florence: Vallecchi, 1960);

Teresa Ferri, *Dino Campana* (Rome: Bulzoni, 1985);

Cesare Galimberti, *Dino Campana* (Milan: Mursia, 1967);

Ruggero Jacobbi, *Invito alla lettura di Campana* (Milan: Mursia, 1976);

Pier Vincenzo Mengaldo, *Poeti italiani del Novecento* (Milan: Saggiatore, 1978);

Eugenio Montale, "Sulla poesia di Campana," *L'Italia che Scrive*, 9-10 (September-October 1942): 152-154;

Giovanni Papini, *Passato remoto* (Florence: Arco, 1948);

Alessandro Parronchi, " 'Genova' e il senso dei colori nella poesia di Campana," *Paragone*, 48 (December 1953): 13-34;

Edoardo Sanguinetti, *La poesia italiana del Novecento* (Turin: Einaudi, 1969);

Maura del Serra, *L'immagine aperta* (Florence: Nuova Italia, 1973);

Ida Li Vigni, *Orfismo e poesia in Dino Campana* (Genoa: Melangolo, 1983).

Vincenzo Cardarelli
(1 May 1887 - 15 June 1959)

Massimo Mandolini Pesaresi
Columbia University

BOOKS: *Prologhi* (Milan: Lombardo, 1916);
Viaggi nel tempo (Florence: Vallecchi, 1920);
Terra genitrice (Rome: Terza Pagina, 1924);
Favole e Memorie (Milan: Bottega di Poesia, 1925);
Il sole a picco (Bologna: Italiano, 1929);
Parole all'orecchio (Lanciano, Italy: Carabba, 1931);
Parliamo dell'Italia (Florence: Vallecchi, 1931);
Prologhi, viaggi, favole (Lanciano, Italy: Carabba, 1931);
Giorni in pièna (Rome: Novissima, 1934);
Poesie (Rome: Novissima, 1936; revised and enlarged edition, Milan: Mondadori, 1942; enlarged again, 1948);
Il cielo sulle città (Milan: Bompiani, 1939);
Rimorsi (Rome: Urbinati, 1944);
Lettere non spedite (Rome: Astrolabio, 1946);
Poesie nuove (Venice: Neri Pozza, 1946);
Astrid ovvero temporale d'estate (Rome: Concilium Lithographicum, 1947);
Solitario in Arcadia (Milan: Mondadori, 1947);
Villa Tarantola (Milan: Meridiana, 1948);
Il viaggiatore insocievole (Bologna: Cappelli, 1953);
Viaggio d'un poeta in Russia (Milan: Mondadori, 1954);
Opere complete, edited by Giuseppe Raimondi (Milan: Mondadori, 1962);
Invettiva e altre poesie disperse, edited by Bruno Blasi and Vanni Scheiwiller (Milan: All'Insegna del Pesce d'Oro, 1964);
La poltrona vuota, edited by G. A. Cibotto and Blasi (Milan: Rizzoli, 1969);
Lettera a un vecchio amico ed altri scritti, edited by Massimiliano Boni (Bologna: EDIM, 1970);
Lettere d'amore a Sibilla Aleramo, con appendice di poesie inedite, edited by Cibotto and Blasi (Rome: Newton Compton Italiana, 1974);
Così non si fece l'Italia (Bologna: Boni, 1980);
Opere, edited by Clelia Martignoni (Milan: Mondadori, 1981);
Lettere a un adolescente, edited by G. M. Masini (Milan: All'Insegna del Pesce d'Oro, 1983);
Pagine sparse (1904-1912): Giornali romani e fiorentini, edited by Martignoni (Rome: Bulzoni, 1988).

OTHER: "Inediti e varianti," edited by Benito Sablone, *Dimensioni*, 5-6 (December 1966).

Nazareno Caldarelli (who used the pen name Vincenzo Cardarelli) was born on 1 May 1887 in Tarquinia, Italy, and was the son of Giovanna Caldarelli Romagnoli and Antonio Romagnoli. After his mother and father went their separate ways (when he was too young to remember), Cardarelli knew a short idyll with his sweet and loving stepmother, who soon died. "Il mondo mi allevò" (The world raised me), he once said, referring to the following years of wandering from house to house in Tarquinia. In the bitterness of his childhood is to be found not only the origin of Cardarelli's ambivalent relationship to his loved-hated birthplace but also a certain harshness and sullenness of character. Prevented by his father from attending school past the fifth grade, Cardarelli, who, in his own words (in *Il sole a picco* [The Sun Sheer Above, 1929]), had "il bacillo della cultura e della letteratura nel sangue" (the bacillus of culture and literature in his blood), looked thereafter for an education in life and in the world. Later he was proud of his troubled career as a self-taught man. After his father's death in 1905, he went to Rome, where he did various jobs (bookkeeper, copyist, clerk in a metallurgical factory, and so on) and eventually started his apprenticeship as a journalist—in the socialist newspaper *Avanti!* and the reviews *Marzocco* and *La Voce*. His first literary essays (on Henrik Ibsen, Friedrich Hebbel, Torquato Tasso, and, in particular, Charles Pierre Péguy) were followed by the publication (in *Lirica*, December 1913) of six poems, significantly titled "I miei discorsi" (My Discourses). In these early lyrics Cardarelli reaches a perfection he rarely achieved afterward. Five of the six poems published in *Lirica* were collected, together with some fulgurant *poèmes en prose*, in Cardarelli's first book, *Prologhi* (1916).

In *Viaggi nel tempo* (Travels in Time, 1920) are gathered some prose pieces of the years 1916

Vincenzo Cardarelli

and 1917. Flashes from everyday life, such as "Voce di donna" (Voice of a Woman) and "Ritratto di dama spagnola" (Portrait of a Spanish Lady), can be contrasted with such amusing reflections as "Errori di don Giovanni" or the ambiguously Nietzschean fantasia "Un'uscita di Zarathustra" (Zarathustra Going Out). Cardarelli's desultory quest for an imagined past (adumbrated in the title *Viaggi nel tempo*) becomes an active re-creation of mythical origins in "Favole della Genesi" (Fables of Genesis) and "Fine di Sodoma" (End of Sodom), both composed in the years from 1919 to 1922 and published in *Prologhi, viaggi, favole* (Prologues, Travels, Fables, 1931).

In April 1919 Cardarelli founded, together with Riccardo Bacchelli, the journal *La Ronda*, in which a modern classicism (often labeled neoclassicism by some detractors) is championed against the experimentalism of avant-garde movements and the belated decadence of Giovanni Pascoli's and Gabriele D'Annunzio's epigones. In the pages of this short-lived review (1919-1922) Cardarelli's anti-Crocean perspective is first clearly expressed: far from being the product of intuition, art grows out of thought and ethos.

In 1926 Cardarelli started writing for *L'Italiano* (a journal founded in those days by Leo Longanesi in Bologna), in which were voiced populist and nationalist ideas supported by the Fascist regime. Collaboration in various periodicals, both journals and newspapers, was a constant element in his life, as well as the legendary frequenting of literary cafés: external signs of the uncertainties and vicissitudes of a saturnine author, who lived to a solitary and embittered old age, always carrying in himself the burden of an existential displacement exacerbated by the disquietude of his early childhood.

After a further exercise in the remembrance of his childhood, "Memorie della mia infanzia" (in *Prologhi, viaggi, favole*), Cardarelli reached a felicitous balance of pathos and irony in the mythical evocation of his Etruscan homeland and of other familiar landscapes in *Il sole a picco*. Reconciliation with life and the past seems to be the keynote of this work, which combines (as *Prologhi* does) poetry and prose. In *Il cielo sulle città* (The Sky on the Cities, 1939) the scope broadens from the native "Etruria" (in the section of that name) to "Aspetti di Roma," and from "Viaggio nelle Marche," his father's homeland crossed with Leopardian memories, to "Lombardia," a region no longer simply the dreamy locus of an early journey with his beloved stepmother. In *Viaggio d'un poeta in Russia* (published in 1954, but written in 1928 for the Roman newspaper *Tevere*), one hears the voice of the consummate columnist, who can capture a trace of old Russian finesse in the presentation of the graceful greeting of a woman without losing sight of the social and political landscape in a time (just before the expulsion of Leon Trotsky) so crucial for the destiny of the Soviet Union. The inexhaustible trope of the voyage finds a further dimension in *Il viaggiatore insocievole* (The Unsociable Traveler, 1953), in which the unrestricted curiosity of the author is shown. From the divagations on prehistoric Italy (such as "Italia preistorica" and "I Villanoviani") and the recurrent theme of the birthplace (as in "La Civita" and "Caratteri del mio municipio" [Characters of My Municipality]) to critical pieces on aesthetics ("Poesia pura" and "Le opere" [Works]) and the mythopoeia of "Fine di Cagliostro" (End of Cagliostro) and "Don Giovanni," the work is made up of memories, notes, and characters, significantly culminating in "La fortuna di Leopardi" (written in 1934), an epitome of Cardarelli's ideas about the true artist, in whom genius and humanity complement and enhance each other. A more coherent selection of Cardarelli's writings on art and aesthetics is *Solitario in Arcadia* (Solitary in Arcadia, 1947), which encompasses essays on such authors as Socrates, Ibsen, Blaise Pascal, Friedrich Nietzsche, Giacomo Leopardi, and Dante, and on general topics such as "Decadenza del genio" (Decadence of Genius), "La donna e l'arte" (Woman and Art), and "Allegoria."

Finally, *Lettere non spedite* (Letters that Were Never Sent, 1946) constitutes a genre of its own, in which Cardarelli continues his inner dialogue on the often painful synthesis of literature and life, which characterizes his deepest artistic vocation. Isolated in literature as well as in life—"una voce isolata" (an isolated voice) Eugenio Montale

called him—Cardarelli fought his artistic battle with the same obstinate courage with which he struggled through daily existence after, in 1906, he arrived in Rome with seven liras in his pocket. One may disagree with his stylistic (or, generally, aesthetic) choices, but the intensity of his convictions (their flavor of life) cannot be denied.

His sharp sense of extraneity, a reverberation of Cardarelli's experience of a shattered home, seems the primal ground for his Leopardian enthusiasm. His preference was for Leopardi's *Operette morali* (1827) and *Zibaldone* (1896), in which Leopardi's negative philosophy is most darkly expressed: in particular, the sense of a primordial and irreparable exclusion from the world (an attitude characterized as "Gnostic"). This sort of elective affinity, however, did not help (it may have hindered, instead) a deep understanding and creative elaboration of Leopardi's legacy. "La fortuna di Leopardi" is full of resentment against the endless misunderstanding and negligence that marked Leopardi's *Fortleben* (literary fortune). Cardarelli sets out to rescue the true image of Leopardi, too often disfigured by the triviality of superficial and biased judgments. In particular, the worn-out stereotype of Leopardi's incurable dejection is dispelled:

Che la segreta musa di Leopardi sia la vita, non la morte, è dimostrato trionfalmente da tutta l'opera sua. Occorre avere una tesi da sostenere o una cognizione molto imperfetta di quest'opera per mettere in dubbio la profonda carità di Leopardi verso l'esistenza, che ha, tra l'altro, il suo monumento nel dialogo di Plotino e Porfirio.

(That Leopardi's secret muse is life, not death, is triumphantly shown by his entire work. One must have a thesis to defend or a very imperfect knowledge of this work to doubt Leopardi's loving kindness toward existence, which has its monument, among others, in the dialogue of Plotinus and Porphyry.)

In a previous passage an ambivalent statement on Leopardi's destiny is directly relevant to Cardarelli's poetics:

E come la sua poesia fu di rimembranze, di commiati dal presente, così egli in letteratura non poteva essere il messia di nessuna religione nuova, ma piuttosto il restauratore dell'antica, non un Socrate, ma un Platone o, per meglio dire, il San Paolo del classicismo italiano.

Drawing of Cardarelli by C. E. Oppo (from Cardarelli's Terra genitrice, *1924)*

(And just as his poetry was poetry of remembrances, of leave-taking from the present, so he himself could not be in literature the messiah of any new religion, rather the restorer of the ancient one, not a Socrates, but a Plato or, better yet, the Saint Paul of Italian classicism.)

A few years before the composition of "La fortuna di Leopardi," Cardarelli wrote two essays, "Il nostro classicismo" (Our Classicism, 1929) and "Classicismo europeo" (European Classicism, 1930)—both collected in *Parliamo dell'Italia* (We Are Speaking of Italy, 1931). The former is a brief survey of the decadence of contemporary Italian literature and ends with the peculiar statement that "noi stimiamo di essere buoni filosofi concludendo che l'Italia di oggi non ha bisogno di filosofi, non ha bisogno di predicatori, e neppure di critici, ma di scrittori e di artisti" (we think that we are good philosophers by concluding that today's Italy does not need philosophers, does not need preachers, and not even critics, but writers and artists instead); the latter is even more peculiar and is disappointing, a narrow ti-

rade about the constitutional inability of northern European people to understand or even vaguely conceive of the classical ideal, which can grow and bloom only in the Italian clime: "Come non si può parlare di patria con un ebreo e di religione con un ateo, così credo che sia difficile intendersi su questa benedetta questione del classicismo con chiunque non sia nato in Italia" (As one cannot talk of homeland to a Jew and of religion to an atheist, so I think that it is difficult for anybody who was not born in Italy to understand this wretched old issue of classicism).

This crude rhetoric was certainly well attuned to the celebration of the resurgent Roman grandeur. Political contingencies apart, however, Cardarelli's argument is a weak repetition of Leopardi's polemic against Romanticism, stripped bare of its philosophical poignancy and reduced to a few picturesque commonplaces. The notion of classicism remains, therefore, less a theoretical statement than an indiscriminate attack. One can reasonably doubt that northern European literature at large was the real target of

Cardarelli, because such polemics are usually aimed at closer enemies. And in fact these neighbors, though unnamed, are alluded to in the crucial essay "Poesia pura" (1941; in *Il viaggiatore insociovole*). After the rather enigmatic definition of Italian lyrical poetry (from Petrarch to Leopardi) as anti-intellectual, Cardarelli fights against the so-called magic of the word (which Italian hermeticism had learned from French symbolism), in the name of the necessary conjunction of poetry and prose.

Cardarelli wants to defend himself from the accusation of being a "poeta discorsivo," and he does so first by quoting a celebrated passage of *Zibaldone* on prose as "nutrice del verso" (fostermother of verse), and later with a detailed description of his own style of poetic composition: "il discorrere è privilegio dell'uomo e perciò, in grado supremo, dei poeti di tutti i tempi e di tutte le nazioni, eccetto i cinesi" (discourse is a privilege of man and, therefore, in its highest degree, of poets of all times and of all nations, with the only exception of the Chinese). Such a solemn and engaging statement could be made the object of a wide debate, but the Pindaric flight of the argument is promptly curbed:

> E come discorrono questi poeti! Che divina eloquenza è la loro! Divina s'intende non in quanto differisca formalmente dall'eloquio comune, ma per la qualità degli affetti e dei sentimenti che chiama in causa. Ciò non esclude che Dante, Petrarca, Leopardi, siano, oltre che poeti sublimi, i più grandi retori, i più illustri oratori che l'Italia abbia avuti. Diciamoli senz'altro, in tutta l'estensione del termine, poeti civili.

> (And what a discourse is theirs! What a divine eloquence! Divine, of course, not insofar as it differs from common speech, but for the quality of affections and feelings it engages. That does not prevent Dante, Petrarch, and Leopardi from being not only sublime poets, but the greatest rhetoricians, the most illustrious orators Italy ever had. Let us call them, in the full extent of the term, civil poets.)

Cardarelli's argument becomes progressively obscure. How does one reconcile rhetoric with the advocation of a popular diction? What does it mean for Dante, Petrarch, and Leopardi to be civil poets? Poetry and prose actually appear less as separate domains than as ideal forms that may interact in a delicate (and difficult) balance for the best stylistic solution. Leopardi, in fact, emphasizes the importance of a poetic hue

in prose writing. Cardarelli presents an illuminating passage on the naturalistic concept of style as character: "Non è la ricchezza dei mezzi verbali che fa lo scrittore. E' il modo, è l'accento, è il tono. . . . Lo stile è un fatto naturale ed ereditario come il carattere" (It is not the wealth of verbal means that makes the writer. It is the mode, the accent, the tone. . . . Style is a natural and hereditary element like character). And in the name of stylistic rigor he ambiguously saves (or definitely damns) Friedrich Nietzsche as the supreme decadent who "non si curava troppo della solidità e consistenza delle idee, che pure costituivano tutto il suo capitale, ma degli effetti lirici e feerici ch'era capace di ricavarne" (did not take too many pains over the solidity and consistency of his own ideas, which, nevertheless, were all his capital, rather over the lyrical and fairy effects that he was able to win from them). Of Cardarelli's criticism, Emilio Cecchi says (in *Storia della letteratura italiana*):

> La verità sta in questo: che il Cardarelli era soprattutto un poeta, e forse in particolar modo un verace e talvolta grande poeta in prosa. Sistemi di idee critiche . . . per lui non avevano valore intrinseco, ma un valore pragmatistico, in quanto lo aiutavano al lavoro creativo.

> (The truth is that Cardarelli was above all a poet, and perhaps in particular a veracious and at times great prose poet. Systems of critical ideas . . . did not have any intrinsic value for him, but a pragmatic one, insofar as they helped him in his creative work.)

In Cardarelli's first collection, *Prologhi*, the oblique magic of time ("la obliqua magia del tempo" as he says in "Tempi immacolati" [Immaculate Time]) is the ever-elusive object of a painful quest and inspires some powerful images in which an impressive abstraction is often achieved by means of improbable predications, usually in the negative mode:

> Io faccio orge di tempo.
> Quante cose cominciate
> e rotte, nella mia vita!
> Quante offerte rifiutate!
> Le mie giornate sono
> frantumi di vari universi
> che non riescono a combaciare.
> La mia fatica è mortale.

> (I make orgies of time.
> How many things begun

and broken, in my life!
How many offers turned down!
My days are
splinters of various universes
which cannot fit.
My labor is mortal.)

Summer often becomes—as in "Saluto di stagione" (Season Greeting) and "Estiva" (Festival) —a favorite trope for the intimations of eternity enclosed in some breakage or suspension of the time flow. In his Nietzschean years, Cardarelli also discovered Arthur Rimbaud, whom he associated, in a letter to Cecchi of 1914 (in *Epistolario*, 1978), with Charles-Pierre Baudelaire as his spiritual fathers. In spite of this confession, dating from before Cardarelli's Leopardian conversion, it is difficult to find in Cardarelli's verses an echo of the lacerating tension of the French *maudits* (damned poets). The dry recitative "Incontro notturno" (Nocturnal Encounter), for example, inspired by a harmless nomadism, appears as a pale reflection of a profoundly "nocturnal" (in Rimbaud's sense) poetry. More recognizable is the presence of Baudelaire in Cardarelli's prose, in particular in "Autunno," in which the direct reference to the French poet's "Chant d'automne" nonetheless only shows lexical and syntactical reverberations.

The terse design, tinged with brave experimentalism, of these early Cardarelli poems grows thick with a rather conventional pathos when time is anthropomorphically represented as the withering of youth and the vanishing of illusions, as in "Parabola":

Anni di giovinezza grandi e pieni!
Mattini lenti, faticoso ascendere
di gioventù
. . . .
Giunti che siamo al sommo, vòlti all'ombra,
gli anni van giù rovinosi in pendio.

(Youthful years, large and full!
Slow mornings, wearing ascent
of youth
. . . .
Once we reached the summit, turned to darkness,
ruin the years down the slope.)

Leopardi was the reassuring persona that Cardarelli chose for himself, and the proselike rhythm of the earlier lyrics later acquires a smooth melodiousness. However, the graceful austerity of Leopardi's diction, when unsustained by his strength of thinking, reveals, like a worn-out fabric, a singsong Petrarcheanism. A comparison of the different versions of one poem may confirm this view.

In "Sera di Gavinana" (Evening at Gavinana; in *Il sole a picco*), for example, the fifty-three verses of the 1913 original manuscript were shrunk to thirty-four for publication. Such a condensation, however, does not involve a greater density: one has the impression of moving from a large block engraved with sharp features and broken edges to a balanced and polished statue. Lost is the impressionistic power of such images as "quel grigio campanile / che fora la verdissima selva" (that gray belltower / which pierces the overly green wood), or "scende la nube a valle a veleggiare" (the cloud goes down sailing in the valley); and the striking incipit "Odo rovesciarsi il camion come una valanga" (I hear the truck rolling down like an avalanche) is displaced and diluted in "il pulsare, il batter secco / ed alto del camion sullo stradone" (the pulsing, the sharp and high / beating of the truck on the country road). An almost surrealistic depiction is tamed in the form of a studiously musical idyll, reminiscent of some village sketches of Leopardi: "Sabato del villaggio" (Saturday Evening in the Village) and "Quiete dopo la tempesta" (The Calm after the Storm).

In the more personal realm of love's sorrows, Cardarelli's voice strives, successfully at times, after a more personal timbre, as in "Attesa" (Waiting; in *Giorni in pièna* [Overflowing Days, 1934]):

Quale un estivo temporale
s'annuncia e poi s'allontana,
così ti sei negata alla mia sete.

(As a summer storm
is heard and goes away,
likewise my thirst you eluded).

In "Amore," nevertheless, at the end of the two stanzas, a Leopardian echo resounds like a blunt refrain: "Amore e primavera vanno insieme" (Love and spring together fare), and "quel folle tuo amore ov'io non mordo / che sapore di morte" (your maddening love where I can bite / but a taste of death). Rare are the moments in which Leopardi's somber melody is well attuned to Cardarelli's dried anguish, but in "Alba" (Dawn) the opening distych—"Solo in te, alba, riposa / la mia morte affannosa" (In thee, alone, o dawn, reposes / my strenuous death)— acquires power from its closely resonant lines.

Cardarelli in Rome

The Leopardian theme of remembrance and of nostalgia for the irretrievable past often acquires a spatial dimension in the form of Cardarelli's longing for his hometown, Tarquinia. This place, frequently transfigured with the hues of mythical Etruria, has all the grievous ambivalence of Cardarelli's troubled origins. Such a burning matter cannot be easily handled, and originality is threatened by a facile pathos, which lingers in a naive idealization or gloomy remembering. In this dangerous ground, however, Cardarelli succeeds in dispelling the haunting presence of the abhorred Pascoli: Cardarelli's lament is never whiny or self-indulgent. Some of the best poems of his later period spring from this anguishing sense of exile (both in space and time). Exemplary is the lyric "Viaggio" (Journey; in *Poesie nuove*), in which departing is still a moving and persuasive metaphor for the endless vicissitudes of the poet's life, which is inexorably approaching the ultimate departure: "Nessun'arte imparai, niuna certezza / mi assiste / nel punto di salpare ormai per sempre" (No art I learned, no certainty / assists me / now that forever I shall sail).

The sense of a shattered home reaches its climax, perhaps, in the uncanny familiarity and intimacy of death. In "Alla morte" (To Death), a passionate prayer addressed to death, referred to as "sposa fedele" (faithful bride), Cardarelli is able to make a nonslavish variation on one of Leopardi's most astonishing poetic achievements: the image of death as secure repose and even loving tenderness. Cardarelli reaches a tension (enhanced by the terse staccato of the verses) that can be defined as sublime: a condition to which his poetry, with its deep austerity, always aspired. One might object, of course, to the belated nature of Cardarelli's sublime, too reminiscent of Leopardi's. Cardarelli simply could not forget in order to re-create, and he remained perpetually constrained by the idea that Leopardi's poetry was an unequaled example. Such a precept can be dangerous and paralyzing when one steps onto the metaphysical grounds of beginning and creating, which is, after all, what writing is about. Cardarelli always lingered on the threshold of sublimity; the rare times that he crossed it, his voice was pure and distinct.

Rare, too, are the descriptive passages in which the burden of pathos does not give a sententious gravity to the poem. Among the few exceptions are the merry opening of "Marzo" (in *Poesie nuove*, 1946)—"Oggi la primavera / è un vino effervescente. / Spumeggia il primo verde / sui grandi olmi fioriti a ciuffi" (Spring is today / like sparkling wine. / The first green froths / in tufts on the big blooming elms)—and the audacious metaphor (graced with D'Annunzian sensuality) "le prode rinverdite / son come carne d'adolescente" (the banks made green again / are like adolescent flesh) in "Primavera cittadina" (City Spring; in *Giorni in pièna*).

Letters:

Epistolario (1907-1929), edited by the Lions Club (Tarquinia, Italy: Grotte di Castro, 1978);

Epistolario II, edited by Bruno Blasi (Tarquinia, Italy: Centro Studi Cardarelliani, Lions Club, 1981);

Epistolario, 3 volumes, edited by Blasi (Rome: EBE, 1987).

Bibliography:

Clelia Martignoni, ed., "Bibliografia cardarelliana," in Cardarelli's *Opere* (Milan: Mondadori, 1981).

References:

Riccardo Bacchelli, "Vincenzo Cardarelli, *Viaggi nel tempo*," in his *Giorno per giorno dal 1912 al 1922: Entusiami e passioni letterarie* (Milan: Mondadori, 1966), pp. 241-246;

Piero Bigongiari, "Consuntivo cardarelliano," in *Poesia italiana del Novecento*, 2 volumes (Milan: Saggiatore, 1978), I: 250-266;

Bigongiari, "Gli 'indugi' di Cardarelli," in *Poesia italiana del Novecento* I: 230-245;

Carlo Bo, "Cardarelli," in *Storia della Letteratura italiana* (Milan: Garzanti, 1987), IX: 84-93;

Bollettino: Arte e Lettere, special Cardarelli issue, 4-5 (1947);

Emilio Cecchi, "Testimonianze classiche," in *Letteratura italiana del Novecento*, edited by Pietro Citati (Milan: Mondadori, 1972), pp. 737-754;

Cecchi, "Vincenzo Cardarelli," in *Storia della letteratura italiana*, IX: 318-327;

V. Coletti, "La finzione mitica di Vincenzo Cardarelli," in his *Momenti del linguaggio poetico novecentesco* (Genoa & San Salvatore Monferrato: Melangolo, 1978), pp. 62-95;

Gianfranco Contini, "Lettera da non spedire a Vincenzo Cardarelli," in his *Altri esercizî (1942-1971)* (Turin: Einaudi, 1972), pp. 137-144;

Contini, "La verità sul caso Cardarelli," in his *Esercizî di lettura sopra autori contemporanei con un'appendice su testi non contemporanei* (Turin: Einaudi, 1974), pp. 34-42;

Giuseppe De Robertis, "Vincenzo Cardarelli: *Poesie*," in his *Altro Novecento* (Florence: Monnier, 1962), pp. 184-190;

Carmine Di Biase, "Il classicismo moderno di Cardarelli," in his *La Ronda e l'impegno* (Naples: Liguori, 1971), pp. 209-277;

Di Biase, *Invito alla lettura di Cardarelli* (Milan: Mursia, 1975);

Enrico Falqui, "Il cielo sulle città," in his *Novecento letterario italiano, 3: Narratori e prosatori da D'Annunzio a C. E. Gadda* (Florence: Vallecchi, 1971), pp. 413-421;

Giansiro Ferrata, Preface to Cardarelli's *Poesie* (Milan: Mondadori, 1942);

Ferrata, ed., "Omaggio a Cardarelli," *Fiera Letteraria*, special issue, 21 (21 May 1950);

Franco Fortini, "La scansione di Vincenzo Cardarelli," in his *I poeti del Novecento* (Bari, Italy: Laterza, 1977), pp. 83-86;

Alfredo Gargiulo, "La conoscenza 'artistica,' " in *Letteratura italiana del Novecento* (Florence: Monnier, 1940), pp. 37-41;

Frederic Joseph Jones, "Vincenzo Cardarelli e l'ideale di un classicismo moderno," in his *La poesia italiana contemporanea (da Gozzano a Quasimodo)* (Messina & Florence: D'Anna, 1975), pp. 233-264;

Gilberto Lonardi, " 'Autunno': osservazioni sul Leopardi di Cardarelli," *Studi novecenteschi*, 9 (1982): 249-291;

Niva Lorenzini, "Il D'Annunzio di Cardarelli tra manierismo e memoria letteraria," *Lingua e stile*, 17 (1982): 473-485;

Mario Luzi, "La personalità e la poesia in Cardarelli," in his *L'inferno e il limbo* (Florence: Marzocco, 1949), pp. 87-95;

Oreste Macrí, "Poesie di Cardarelli," in his *Esemplari del sentimento poetico contemporaneo* (Florence: Vallecchi, 1941), pp. 265-283;

Clelia Martignoni, "Alle radici della prosa cardarelliana," *Letteratura italiana contemporanea*, 11 (1984): 161-186;

Martignoni, ed., *Assediato dal silenzio: Lettere a Giuseppe Raimondi* (Montebelluna, Italy: Amadeus, 1990);

Pier Vincenzo Mengaldo, "D'Annunzio e la lingua poetica del Novecento," in his *La tradizione del Novecento: Da D'Annunzio a Montale* (Milan: Feltrinelli, 1975);

Eugenio Montale, "Una voce isolata," in *Sulla poesia*, edited by Giorgio Zampa (Milan: Mondadori, 1976), pp. 307-310;

R. Negri, "Vociani e rondisti: Cardarelli," in his *Leopardi nella poesia italiana* (Florence: Monnier, 1970);

"Omaggio a Cardarelli," *Realismo Lirico*, special issue, 34 (July-August 1959);

Giovanni Papini, "Vincenzo Cardarelli," in "Lettres italiennes," *Mercure de France*, modern series 439 (1 October 1916);

Giuseppe Raimondi, Preface to Cardarelli's *Opere complete* (Milan: Mondadori, 1962);

Silvio Ramat, "La favola di Cardarelli: Cognizione e ricognizione," in his *I poeti del*

Novecento (Milan: Mursia, 1976), pp. 145-188;

Sergio Solmi, "Le poesie di Cardarelli," in his *Scrittori negli anni: Saggi e note sulla letteratura italiana del '900* (Milan: Saggiatore, 1963), pp. 202-207;

"Vincenzo Cardarelli nel cuore e nella memoria," *Fiera letteraria*, special issue, 26 (28 June 1959).

Eugenio Cirese
(21 February 1884 - 8 February 1955)

Luigi Bonaffini
Brooklyn College

BOOKS: *Sciure de fratta* (Campobasso, Italy, 1910);

Canti popolari e sonetti in dialetto molisano (Campobasso & Isernia, Italy: Colitti, 1910);

La guerra: Discurzi di cafuni (Campobasso, Italy: De Gaglia & Nebbia, 1912);

Ru cantone della fata: Storia de tiempe antiche (Pescara, Italy: Stabilimento Industriale, 1916);

Suspire e risatelle (Campobasso, Italy: Colitti, 1918);

Gente buona (Lanciano, Italy: Carabba, 1925);

Canzone d'atre tiempe (Pesaro, Italy: Federici, 1926);

La 'lettricità (Rome: Unione Arti Grafiche Abruzzesi, 1926);

Rugiade (Putaturo, Italy: Marsica, 1933);

Tempo d'allora: figure, storie e proverbi (Campobasso, Italy: Petrucciani, 1939);

Lucecabelle, edited by Mario dell'Arco (Rome: Bardi, 1951);

Poesie molisane, edited by Alberto Mario Cirese and Ferruccio Ulivi (Caltanissetta, Italy: Sciascia, 1955).

OTHER: "I disegni infantili," *Rivista di psicologia applicata* (May 1909);

Raccolta di canti popolari della provincia di Rieti, edited by Cirese (Rieti, Italy: Nobili, 1945);

Canti popolari del Molise, volume 1, edited by Cirese (Rieti, Italy: Nobili, 1953).

Eugenio Cirese has earned his place in the extremely varied landscape of Italian dialect literature as a notable poet. Critics and writers such as Pier Paolo Pasolini, Barberi Squarotti, Carlo Betocchi, and others consider him to have been the first important writer to use the dialect of Molise as a literary language with a keen awareness of the implications—personal, literary, social, ideological—inherent in such a choice. He instinctively recognized the dignity and latent power of this unwieldy, untested instrument, both mother tongue and sacred language, and he took it from the musical tradition of the popular song to the airy lightness and purity of his last poems. He was always convinced of the necessity to write in dialect. In 1953 Cirese wrote to Pasolini: "Il dialetto è una lingua. Perché possa essere mezzo di espressione poetica e trasformarsi in linguaggio e immagini è necessario possederla tutta; avere coscienza del suo contenuto di cultura e della sua umana forza espressiva. Nell'infanzia e nella prima giovinezza—o sia nel tempo più bello e più vivo d'interessi della mia vita—ho parlato, raccolto e cantato canzoni, gioito, pianto, *pensato* in dialetto. . . . Aggiungo che il dialetto è sempre stato il luogo del mio respiro: quando mi trovai a cantare l'amore, nato e patito sotto le finestre e sulle aie; ora che il ricordo giunge a farsi memoria tutto solo perchè tante cose ha lasciate per la via" (Dialect is a language. In order for it to become a means of poetic expression and to transform itself into a personal language and into images, it is necessary to possess it wholly; to be aware of its cultural content and its human expressive power. In my childhood and early youth—namely, during the best, most lively and interesting time of my life, I have spoken, I have collected and sung songs, I have rejoiced, I have wept, I have *thought* in dialect. . . . I add that dialect has always been the place of my breathing: when I happened to sing of love, born and endured beneath the windows and on the threshing floors; now that recollection becomes memory all alone because it has left so many things along the way).

Pasolini was the first to recognize three distinct phases, generally accepted by subsequent critics, in Cirese's poetic evolution: a melic phase, following in the tradition of the Neapolitan Salvatore Di Giacomo and the monody; a socialistic phase, in which Cirese expresses deeply felt participation in the life and suffering of his people; and finally, in his later years, a *squisita* (refined) phase, reflecting the search for an "essential" poetry, with its roots in the decadent and hermetic movements, responsive to the most important, decisive twentieth-century poetry, both in dialect and in standard Italian. Refusing to accept the supposedly subordinate status of dialect poetry, Cirese insisted on the universal nature of poetic language. He put to rest the question of whether his poetry belonged to Italian literature or to a regional literature with one, definitive reply: "Se è poesia, non può soffrire limiti né avere confini" (If it is poetry, it can have neither limits nor boundaries).

Complementing the image of Cirese the poet, and just as noteworthy, is that of Cirese the collector and editor of popular songs: his *Raccolta di canti popolari della provincia di Rieti* (Collection of Folk Songs from the Province of Rieti, 1945) and *Canti popolari del Molise* (Folk Songs from Molise, volume one, 1953) have won the praise of specialists and laymen alike.

Eugenio Cirese was born in Fossalto, Italy, a small town near Campobasso, in the mountainous region of Molise, on 21 February 1884. He spent an uneventful childhood with his parents, Luigi and Rosalina Bagnoli Cirese, his sister, and three brothers. His love for the moon, whose recurrent presence in his poetry has caused more than one critic to perceive an affinity with Giacomo Leopardi, has early origins. In the journal *Il Belli* (May 1953) Cirese wrote: "Mamma mi diceva che quando ero in fasce rimanevo incantato a guardare la luna e stendevo le mani per acchiapparla. Si può, perciò, stabilire che ho fatto l'acchiappalune da quando sono nato" (My mother used to tell me that when I was a babe in arms I would look spellbound at the moon and

would extend my hands to catch it. Therefore it can be said that since birth I have been a moon-catcher). After finishing elementary school he was sent to Velletri, where he obtained his teaching diploma, and for a brief time in Civitacampomarano he taught elementary school. Soon thereafter he moved with his family to Castropignano, where his brother Nicolino was employed as town clerk, and their house in Fossalto was closed forever. In Castropignano, which was to become Cirese's home, he devoted himself to teaching and began his long apprenticeship as a poet.

Cirese's early poetry is rooted in the culture of late romanticism, with a fondness for folk songs and popular traditions and a strong inclination to interpret the soul of the Molisan people. It is not by chance that one of his first books, *Canti popolari e sonetti in dialetto molisano* (Folk Songs and Sonnets in the Dialect of Molise, 1910), includes songs which were, as he writes in the preface to the book, "raccolte in mezzo al popolo" (gathered among the people) and transcribed "nella loro rustica, ma espressiva semplicità" (in their rough, but expressive simplicity), with the addition of a few sonnets "scritti nelle soste del pensiero" (written during the pauses of thought), an expression by Cirese of the dialect of Molise, "che ha, forse più di tanti altri d'Italia, spontaneità d'espressione e forza di sentimento" (which has, perhaps more than so many others in Italy, spontaneity of expression and strength of feeling). To the musical cadence of folk songs, the sonnets add realistic impressions of everyday life, with the exception of the last lullaby, "Duormi" (Sleep), which includes this couplet: "Duorme, bellezza me', duorme serene / nu suonne luonghe quant'a a la nuttata" (Sleep, my beauty, sleep serenely / a sleep as long as the whole night), a couplet that was to reappear, even as an epigraph, in subsequent collections by Cirese.

Also in 1910 Cirese published another small collection of poems, *Sciure de fratta* (Brushwood Flowers), which would soon be out of print but is included in the 1918 volume *Suspire e risatelle* (Sighs and Snickers). In 1912 he published another booklet, *La guerra: Discurzi di cafuni* (The War: Conversations among Peasants), which recorded the reactions of farmers to the Libyan war, alternating surges of nationalistic pride with memories of the fallen and including a poem about the anguished weeping of a mother for her son, faraway and wounded. These modest beginnings by Cirese attracted the attention of the distinguished linguist and philologist Francesco D'Ovidio, who, according to Luigi Biscardi, commented favorably on the "forme nuove" (new forms). Cirese replied, revealing his late-romantic roots, that he had taken them "con criteri esclusivi di arte, dal popolo, fonte naturale di forme e di concetti" (with criteria that excluded artfulness, from the people, natural source of forms and concepts). Somewhat ingenuously he was expressing his attitude toward the indissoluble bond between folk song and dialect poetry, a view that remained unaltered throughout his life, and which received lengthy treatment by him forty years later in the preface to his *Canti popolari del Molise*.

The young Cirese won a 1914 competition to become a school inspector, but due to reforms by Italy's minister of education, Giovanni Gentile, Cirese was forced to accept a position as principal in an elementary school in Teano. Meanwhile World War I began, and Cirese was called to serve in the army in Macerata, while his brothers Nicolino and Rocco were sent to the front. Cirese became a good friend of the journalist Raffaello Biordi and the poet Luigi Lodi, and wrote a patriotic poem, "La cuperta" (The Blanket; collected in *Suspire e risatelle*), which made him something of a celebrity among his friends and fellow soldiers. The superficial treatment of the patriotic theme in his poem is partly offset by his skillful handling of the disconsolate music of the verses:

> Se l'uocchie me z'allàchene de chiante,
> se me vuoglie addurmì,
> > làcreme e suonne i'gliótte che llu cante
> che prima de partì,
> > a mezzanotte me scegnètte 'n core . . .

> (If my eyes become flooded with weeping,
> if I want to fall asleep,
> > sleep and tears I swallow with the song
> that came into my heart,
> > at midnight before leaving . . .).

In 1916 Cirese published *Ru cantone della fata* (The Fairy's Rock), a short narrative poem written in octaves, which would be included later in *Rugiade* (Dews, 1933); the tale is based on the popular legend of a simple girl who chooses death rather than give in to the lustful advances of a tyrannical lord. The anonymous narrator is a simple, uneducated man, yet a bit too well acquainted with historical facts to be entirely believable. Cirese presents him as a sober storyteller,

however, and the poem has moments of dramatic efficacy, coupled with commonsense flashes of earthy wit. Nicola Scarano, in his introduction to the book, notes that "Cirese ha sentito la poesia della leggenda. . . . Anzi leggendo a voce alta par di sentire come una . . . nota mestamente carezzevole, della maniera di quella dei cantastorie" (Cirese sensed the poetry of legend. . . . In fact, reading out loud, one seems to hear something of a . . . sadly caressing note, in the manner of ballad singers).

After the war Cirese returned to his job as principal, this time in Avezzano, where he was able to collect in *Suspire e risatelle* the complete corpus of his early poems. The title itself, purposely unassuming, points to his twofold inspiration: the melic abandon of love songs and his keen observation of the attitude of the townspeople and farmers toward everyday events and extraordinary occurrences (the Libyan war and World War I). The ironic detachment of the man of culture does not, in Cirese's case, exclude his participation in common nationalistic feelings.

His *canzone appassionate*, the "passionate" love songs, echo popular airs and herald his later, more mature poems. In "Serenatella" (Little Serenade), for example, the bold opening, with its sudden dilation of space and its internalization of cosmic vastness, is reminiscent of the work of Leopardi, while the musical phrasing approaches the quality of Di Giacomo's best compositions:

> Iè notte e iè serene
> dentr'a ru core e n' ciele.
> Le stelle
> fermate
> vicine,
> a cocchia a cocchia
> o sole
> com'a pecurelle
> stanne pascenne
> l'aria de notte

> (It's night and it's clear
> within the heart and in the sky.
> The stars
> stopping
> near,
> two at a time
> or alone
> like little sheep
> are grazing
> the night air).

After this phase, which could be defined as philological and late romantic, Cirese's intellectual and cultural development took place under the aegis of the educational policy of Gentile, the minister of education, whose reforms envisioned greater freedom in the classroom and a more responsible approach toward teaching, based on experimentation and allowing the student's personality full expression. In keeping with these principles, Giuseppe Lombardo Radice, general director of elementary schools, tried to shift the focus of the teaching process from the teacher to the student, and the emphasis on abstract factual knowledge was replaced by a methodology stressing the needs and cultural background of the student. In order to understand and guide his pupils, a teacher had to be well acquainted with the environment and the culture in which they lived, and he had to strive to interpret that world for them. Even textbooks were required to reflect the life of the region in all its aspects, including the local dialect. In this climate Cirese, directly and actively involved in the everyday reality of the school system, published *Gente buona* (Good People, 1925), a primer for the schools of Molise. Written with undeniable skill and didactic effectiveness, it is a product of a personal and at the same time collective experience with the schools of the region. The book is patterned on the school calendar and is a compendium of useful information on the geography, industry, commerce, fairs, and holidays of the region, with a historical national calendar and short biographies of important regional figures. The result is a realistic picture of the social and economic life of the region, largely dependent on agriculture and, to a lesser degree, on handicraft—a faithful representation of the southern Italy of the time, which, however, does not try to conceal an underlying pride and satisfaction in the traditional values embodied by rural life.

In 1926 Cirese wrote the poem *Canzone d'atre tiempe* (Song of Other Times), which he set to music with his own melody, still faithful to the melic origins of his poetry. This song soon became quite popular and brought him wide recognition, eventually achieving the status of a widely circulated folk song. This was confirmed by Ferruccio Ulivi in his preface to *Lucecabelle* (Fireflies, 1951): " 'Canzune d'atre tiempe' . . . è salita al grado di canto popolare anonimo, e udii recitare ex abrupto da un dialettale dell'anima, Francesco Jovine, con un gusto che somigliava a protettiva tenerezza"

("Canzune d'atre tiempe" . . . has reached the level of an anonymous folk song, and I heard it being recited *ex abrupto* by the soul of dialect, Francesco Jovine, with a relish that resembled protective tenderness). It is ostensibly a poem about emigration, at the time a serious problem in the south, and it is the emigrant himself who tells his story, but with such intense melancholy that the reader immediately feels that the realistic theme is the substratum of a musically charged imagination:

> La via è lònga e sacce addó me porta:
> me porta a nu castielle affatturate
> 'ddó càmpene le gente senza sorta,
> 'ddó scorde ru dolore appena 'ntrate.
> Tu famme, core a core, cumpagnia,
> nen fa stutà la lampa pe la via.

> (The road is long and I know where it leads me:
> it leads me to a castle of enchantment
> where people without fortune make their home,
> where once inside you soon forget your torment.
> Close to my heart, always by my side remain,
> don't let the lamp die out along the way.)

There is no rebellion, no denunciation of poverty; there is instead the painful acceptance of the necessity imposed by a cruel and ineluctable destiny, modulated on a deeply melancholy melodic line that reaches notes of universal sorrow, set against an increasingly magical landscape, which holds the promise of final deliverance.

In 1933, marking the conclusion of the second phase of his poetic journey, Cirese published his second major volume of collected poems, *Rugiade*, which, in addition to unpublished material, contains many of the earlier poems, such as *Ru cantone della fata* and *La 'lettricità* (Electricity, 1926). Notably missing are the *canzone appassionate* of *Suspire e risatelle*. The poems in *Rugiade* are generally didactic, gnomic adaptations of popular legends or fables, or love songs echoing the catchy airs of folk songs, as in "Reninèlla" (Swallow):

> Sciurille verde:
> vularrisce vulà, ma nen t'azzärde,
> credènne sola sola ca te spierde.

> (Little green flower:
> You would like to fly, but you don't dare,
> thinking you'll get lost so all alone.)

In "Chitarra mèia" (My Guitar) there appears for the first time one of the recurrent themes of

Cirese's later poetry, the search for a lost world of innocence and purity:

> Famme, chitarra, ariturnà guaglione,
> famme turnà 'nnucente!
> Famme penzà, sunanne 'n tutte l'ore
> lu munne bielle e buone
>
> (Make me, guitar, a little boy once more,
> make me innocent again!
> Make me think, playing at all hours,
> the world is good and beautiful).

The real significance of *Rugiade*, however, rests in Cirese's abiding commitment to restore the cultural, historical, and geographic identity of his region, Molise, and to portray its people in all their complexity as members of an identifiable social and political system, against the background of historical events. This determination to rehabilitate personal and social history led Pasolini to speak of a "socialistic" phase in Cirese's poetry, rooted in the progressive movements of pre-Fascist Italy. This, however, would imply a pronounced sense of denunciation and class struggle, while Cirese's socialism is grounded in humanitarian empathy, not as a generalized concept but as the sorrowful personal experience of a sincere participant in the life of the people, particularly the people of Molise. His fundamental concern for human dignity is reflected in the verses that act as a preface to the last section of *Rugiade*, and which offer the key to the book's interpretation. The culture of the illiterate people, once recovered, can accept and assimilate even progress and novelty: "Nen fa lu superbiuse / liégge e pensa, / ca pure nu cafone / pò dà la 'ducazione" (Don't be so high and mighty / read and think, / because even a peasant / can teach you a few things). The attempt of the rural world to come to terms with new, unfamiliar concepts is reflected by differing lexical and semantic levels in *Rugiade*, a mixture of dialect and cultured speech. The result is stylistic tension, which at times becomes parodistic mimicry and betrays a subtle ambiguity, an underlying detachment and irony.

But Cirese's contributions to a redefinition of regional identity, as a collector of folk songs and as a dialect poet, are a real source of pride for him, and in his preface to *Rugiade* they are considered in the light of the cultural and political context of the time: "L'origine vera e profonda dello spirito e del carattere d'una regione è il dialetto, come l'origine dell'unità di coscienza d'una nazione è la lingua. Negare l'unità della lingua significa negare la Nazione, negare l'unità del dialetto significa negare la Regione, svuotare l'arte dialettale del suo contenuto e della sua funzione essenziale, che è quella di celebrare la regione col cuore e col linguaggio di tutti, di avanzare, con tutti, al possesso di nuovi valori" (The real, profound origin of the spirit and of the character of a region is the dialect, just as the origin of the unity of consciousness of a nation is the language. To deny the unity of the language means to deny the Nation, to deny the unity of dialect means to deny the Region, and to deprive dialect art of its essential content and function, which is to celebrate the region with the heart and language of all, to advance, with everyone, toward the attainment of new values).

Appointed school inspector in 1938, Cirese was sent to Campobasso, where the following year he published *Tempo d'allora* (Old Days), a collection of regional stories, vignettes, proverbs, and anecdotes, which again broke new ground by adapting the dialect to narrative prose, and he underscored once again in the preface the dialect's powers of adaptation and self-renewal: "A contatto della pulsante vita d'oggi e nel flusso irresistibile verso la lingua, accresce le sue possibiltà espressive. La prosa dialettale perciò è matura per le prove di capacità nel campo narrativo" (In contact with today's pulsating life and with the irresistible flow of language, it increases its expressive possibilities. Dialect prose is therefore ready to be tested in the narrative field).

In 1940 Cirese moved to Rieti, where he would live for the rest of his life, and there he began collecting the folk songs of the area of Sabinia, which would later appear, more than seven hundred of them, in *Raccolta di canti popolari della provincia di Rieti*, a work of considerable historical and documentary value but lacking philological acumen because of Cirese's inadequate knowledge of the dialects of that region.

His third major book of poems, *Lucecabelle*, generally considered his best and most mature work, came out in 1951, almost twenty years after *Rugiade*. The first section contains poems written between 1913 and 1932; others, previously unpublished, were written after 1944. While some of the earlier compositions are retained, the realistic poetry is completely eliminated. In the section called "La fatia" (meaning "weariness' as well as "toil"), the traditional realistic element—the ageless, interminable toil of the farmer in every season and in every possible condition—is subsumed and transcended, as Luigi Biscardi notes, in a desolate metaphor of the human condition:

> Ogge lu pane.
> Iere, lu recurdà.
> Demane, lu recumenzà.
> Ogge, iere, demane.
>
> (Today the bread.
> Yesterday, remembering.
> Tomorrow, starting all over.
> Today, yesterday, tomorrow.)

Emblematic of this eternal, metahistorical cycle of toil and misery and the stoical, uncompromising acceptance of universal suffering is Zì Minche (Uncle Menico) in the poem "Camina" (Walk), for which Cirese took second place in the Cattolica competition in 1951: "D'estate e dentr'a vierne, / sempre la stessa via, / isse la zappa e la fatia" (In summer and winter, / always the same road, / he, the hoe and the toil). The search for an essential language, already implicit in some of the earlier poems, in *Lucecabelle* produces verses of extreme semantic density, which attest to Cirese's lifelong preoccupation with finding the etymological unity underlying the various dialects of Molise—the original, irreducible, semantic core, still present and recoverable. Cirese's lexical sparseness and bareness demonstrate a neoromantic (and hermetic) search for Edenic innocence, for a remote *arké*, an inner dimension, beyond memory and history. In the somber and unrelentingly austere "Niente" (Nothing), for example, the process is clearly evident:

> Né fuoche nè liette nè pane
> né sciate de vocca
> né rima de cante
> né calle de core.
> Niente.
> —E tu? e tu? e quille?
> Niente.
> Finitoria de munne.
> L'uocchie sbauttite
> iè ssutte.
>
> (Neither fire nor bed nor bread
> nor breath from a mouth
> nor rhyme from a song
> nor warmth from a heart.
> Nothing.
> —And you? and you? and him?
> Nothing.

End of the world.
> The eyes, bewildered,
> are dry.)

Simple, familiar objects become the negative signs of a cosmic disintegration, a regression into nothingness. And in "E mo?" (And Now?) the presence of death is revealed through a threatening, nightmarish landscape, in the similarly relentless nominal progression of the polysyndeton:

> Nu ciele abbrevedite
> e nire come a la paura.
> E fridde e puzza e lóta,
> e sanghe e fame e arzura
> e tritteche de morte.
>
> (A shivering sky
> as black as fear.
> And cold and stench and mud,
> and blood and hunger and thirst
> and shuddering of death.)

Death is a pervasive element in *Lucecabelle*, as in "Repuote" (Funereal Lament) or the mournful " 'N eterne" (Forever), but the otherwise arid landscape, internal as well as external, is also inhabited by consolatory presences: the moon, the stars, the mountain, and the "fireflies" of the title poem, whose faint glow seems to reach the poet from a dimly perceived place of forgotten innocence or unattainable perfection: "Tu me fai crede che lu munne è buone, / i' pe te sacce come se sta 'n ciele" (You make me believe that the world is good, / thanks to you I know what it is like to be in heaven). Existentially defeated in life's journey toward death and tied only by a slender thread to a Christian acceptance of destiny, the poet seeks redemption in voices from the past, the lullabies and fables of his childhood, or in the openness of the sky. A few compositions— "Lucecabelle," "Vulà" (To Fly), and "L'astore" (The Hawk)—express this ethical and spiritual tension in a verbal lightness aiming at absolute purity.

In 1953, the year of his retirement, while concluding his long career as an educator, Cirese was finally able to publish the first volume of *Canti popolari del Molise* (the second volume was published in 1957 by Cirese's son, Alberto Mario Cirese), containing folk songs he had been collecting all his life. In the introduction Cirese touches on the complex reasons that had prompted him to collect the songs that had so enchanted him in his youth: "allora cominciai a raccogliere canti per imparare a cantarli: più tardi per riunirli e per cercare una voce mia nel linguaggio popolare" (then I began to collect songs to learn how to sing them: later to assemble them and to find my own voice in the language of the people). The book won the critical praise of Pasolini, who compared it to the two greatest collections of the past, the Tuscan folk songs of Niccolò Tommaseo and the Piedmontese songs of Costantino de Nigra, and Pasolini understood that implicit in Cirese's folk songs was a biography of the people of Molise. Aware of the importance of this work and of its implications for his evolution as a poet, Cirese called it "la più bella strofe della mia vita" (the most beautiful stanza of my life).

Also in 1953, his failing heart notwithstanding, Cirese founded the journal *La Lapa*, which he edited until his death and which was conceived—in keeping with his lifelong effort to reconstruct an authentic regional image, free of the old georgic and folkloric stereotypes—as "un luogo d'incontro di critici e storici del mondo 'illustre' con critici e storici del mondo che è stato detto dei 'semplici' " (a meeting place for critics and historians of the "illustrious" world, with critics and historians of the world of the so-called "simple" people). The declared objective of the publication would be to divulge "la coscienza della umanità del mondo popolare, fatta pur essa di pensiero, di patimento e di gioia" (the awareness of humanity of the popular world, also made of thought, suffering and joy).

Just before his death, on 8 February 1955, Cirese wrote to his friend Vann'Antò (Antonio di Giacomo): "Ma è tardi, caro Vann'Antò: anche se il cuore è sempre quello, la mano è stanca" (But it's late, dear Vann'Antò: even if the heart is still the same, the hand is weary). A few months after Cirese's death a new volume appeared in print, *Poesie molisane* (Songs of Molise), edited by Alberto Mario Cirese and Ferruccio Ulivi, which contained, in addition to the poems in *Lucecabelle*, two groups of new lyrics, one of which, "Nuove poesie" (New Poems), had already been approved for publication by the author, while the other, under the title "Varie" (Varia), consists of both finished and unfinished poems found among the poet's papers. In his last poems Cirese continues the process of sensitization of the word begun in *Lucecabelle*, filtering it and refining it even more, aiming at more intense and more subtle effects, as in the epigraphic terseness of "Salustre" (Lightning): "Éie mannate a spasse

la memoria, / iè festa" (I have sent memory out for a stroll, / it's a holiday). More than ever, death is an ever-present reality, accepted without pathos or anguish; in the doleful lines of "La svota" (The Turning Point), one of Cirese's last and most powerful poems, death's presence is felt even in the meter itself: "Z'affonna / com'a chiumme / pesante lu passe" (Like heavy lead / the step / sinks down).

Eugenio Cirese's first period, from the early poems to *Rugiade*, while steeped in the melic tradition of the folk song, through a self-limiting strategy of cultural meditation, is marked by the all-pervasive intention to restore an unbiased, objective image to his native region. The turmoil of World War I, the proliferation and reshuffling of cultural perspectives in its aftermath, the need to break the bounds of provincialism, and the physical separation from regional reality all had a hand in laying the groundwork for a new poetic direction for him. In *Lucecabelle* and "Nuove poesie" the innovations of twentieth-century poetry allowed Cirese to explore the original, mythical purity of his dialect, a confirmation of his long quest for the primal fullness of the word.

References:

Carlo Betocchi, "Un poeta sincero," *Sicilia del Popolo* (31 January 1956), pp. 3-4;

Luigi Biscardi, *La letteratura dialettale Molisana* (Isernia, Italy: Marinelli, 1983), pp. 57-79;

Mario Boselli, "Lucecabelle," *Belli*, 4 (April 1955): 1-4;

Giorgio Caproni, "Vive la sua terra fino ad assorbirne la storia," *Fiera Letteraria*, 10 (20 March 1955): 3;

Guiseppe Jovine, "La poesia dialettale Molisana," *Risveglio del Mezzogiornio*, 4 (July-August 1971): 8-13;

Eugenio Montale, "La musa dialettale," in his *Sulla poesia* (Milan: Mondadori, 1976), pp. 175-185;

Pier Paolo Pasolini, "I canti popolari del Molise," *Giovedì*, 2 (9 July 1954): 7;

Pasolini, "Poesia popolare e poesia d'avanguardia," *Paragone*, 64 (1955): 98-104;

Pasolini, "Un poeta in molisano," in his *Passione e ideologia* (Milan: Garzanti, 1960), pp. 304-308;

Giuseppe Petronio, "Un poeta in molisano," *L'Avanti* (3 December 1955);

Giosè Rimanelli, "Poesia dialettale molisana," *Fiera Letteraria* (17 February 1957);

Ferruccio Ulivi, Preface to Cirese's *Lucecabelle* (Rome: Bardi, 1951), pp. 5-11;

Ulivi, "La sua qualità umana," *Fiera Letteraria*, 10 (20 March 1955): 3.

Girolamo Comi
(23 November 1890 - 3 April 1968)

Maria Rosaria Vitti-Alexander
Nazareth College of Rochester

BOOKS: *Il lampadario* (Lausanne, Switzerland: Frankfurter, 1912);

Vedute di economia cosmica (Rome: Garroni, 1920);

Lettera a Giovanni Papini, poeta (Lucugnano, Italy: Tricase Raeli, 1921);

Riposi (festivi) (Rome: Garroni, 1921);

I rosai di qui (Rome: Garroni, 1921);

Smeraldi (Rome: Garroni, 1925);

Boschività sotterra (Rome: Garroni, 1927);

Cantico dell'Albero (Rome: Tempo della Fortuna, 1928);

Poesia, 1918-1928 (Rome: Tempo della Fortuna, 1929); enlarged as *Poesia, 1918-1938* (Rome: Modernissima, 1939);

Cantico del tempo e del seme (Rome: Tempo della Fortuna, 1930);

Nel grembo dei mattini (Rome: Tempo della Fortuna, 1931);

Poesia e conoscenza (Rome: Tempo della Fortuna, 1932);

Commento a qualche pensiero di Pascal (Lucugnano, Italy: L'Albero, 1932);

Cantico dell'argilla e del sangue (Rome: Tempo della Fortuna, 1933);

Necessità dello stato poetico. Tentativo di un diario essenziale (Rome: Tempo della Fortuna, 1934);

Adamo-Eva (Rome: Tempo della Fortuna, 1935);

Aristocrazia del cattolicesimo (Modena, Italy: Guanda, 1937);

Bolscevismo contro cristianesimo (Lucugnano, Italy: Salentina, 1938);

Spirito d'armonia, 1912-1952 (Lucugnano, Italy: L'Albero, 1954);

Canto per Eva (Lucugnano, Italy: L'Albero, 1955);

Sonetti e poesie, edited by Vittorio Vettori (Milan: Ceschina, 1960);

Fra lacrime e preghiere (1958-1965) (Rome: Società Edizioni Nuove, 1966);

Opera poetica, edited by Donato Valli (Ravenna, Italy: Longo, 1978).

OTHER: *Poesie di Arturo Onofri*, edited and annotated by Comi and Arnoldo Buccelli (Rome: Tumminelli, 1949).

Girolamo Comi's poetry began as a rebellion against the Enlightenment philosophy that exalted science and reason over art. Comi delighted in aesthetics and, later, in spirituality, and his poetry reflects these preferences. Nourished by the teachings of anthroposophic and theologic philosophy, and influenced by symbolist thinking, Comi developed a curiosity for the mysteries of creation and the scientific and rational laws that govern it. Later in his life, Comi's adoption of Catholic dogma compelled him to demonstrate the beauty of the universe, showing the greatness of its Creator, to whom Comi's poetry aspired. He used his poetry to sing the harmony and order of God's universe.

Throughout his long and eventful life, Comi never joined any literary movement and refused alignment with any specific school. From the beginning his poetry was a personal search for an understanding of man's place in the universe. The ever-changing conception of his poetics made his verses hard to classify, yet his poetry has remained important in Italian literature, reflecting this salient quest for understanding. Comi was a solitary poet, always searching for an understanding of the laws of the universe and the role that man plays in it, forever seeking guidance in the human search for the absolute.

Girolamo Comi was born in Casamassella, Italy, in the province of Lecce, on 23 November 1890 to Giuseppe and Costanza de Viti de Marco. He was the oldest of four children and was the nephew, on his mother's side, of the well-known economist Antonio De Viti de Marchi. From his father's family, Comi inherited the baronial title of Lucugnano. In his youth he was an undistinguished scholar and had little success at the Istituto Capece of Maglie and the Istituto Palmieri in Lecce.

After his father's death in 1908 his mother sent him to a private school in Ouchy, near Lausanne, Switzerland, with the hope that the new environment would stimulate and encourage his interest in formal studies. Comi's life in Switzerland included typical youthful adventures, and he had an ill-fated love affair with a married woman. This resulted in a quarrel with his family and the suspension of monthly support payments from his mother. Left to his own resources, Comi began supporting himself by giving private lessons in French and Italian.

Intellectually the move to Switzerland was a positive one for the young Comi. Having escaped the closed, backward environment of his little hometown, he was now exposed to the avant-garde movements of symbolism and futurism. Comi also came into contact with various religious credos, including the theories of Rudolf Steiner, the founder of anthroposophy, which aroused Comi's interest in the problems of the spirit and the place of man.

From 1912 to 1915 Comi alternated between Ouchy and Paris. These years were important in Comi's literary development, for they brought him into several prominent literary circles. He befriended Emile Verhaeren, Paul Claudel, Remy de Gourmont, and Paul Valéry, among other literati, and read the works of Charles-Pierre Baudelaire, Arthur Rimbaud, Stéphane Mallarmé, Paul Verlaine, and the Italian poets Giovanni Pascoli and Gabriele D'Annunzio.

On 22 May 1915, with the general mobilization of troops, Comi was drafted into the armed services in Chieti. Because of the discovery of some pacifist letters written to a friend in France, however, Comi was charged with defeatism and sentenced to six months in jail. In December 1915 his sentence was changed to military imprisonment, but through the intervention of his

uncle Antonio De Viti de Marchi, a Radical party deputy at the time, his penalty was commuted and he entered active combat on the Asiago Plateau. Comi was discharged before the end of the war, suffering from cerebral neurasthenia.

On 16 November 1918 Comi married Erminia de Marco, daughter of a wealthy farmer in Milan. The couple had a daughter, Miriam Stefania Giuseppina, on 7 October 1919.

In 1920 Comi took his family from Milan to Rome, and he again entered a circle of influential literary figures. Comi befriended Arturo Onofri, Nicola Moscardelli, and Ernesto Buonaiuti. With Onofri and Moscardelli, Comi founded and directed the publishing house Tempo della Fortuna. With Buonaiuti, Comi spent many hours discussing religious matters, including the problems of the spirit and tenets of Catholic dogma; these discussions culminated in his conversion to Catholicism in 1933.

At about this time Comi began to have marital problems. His difficulties with his wife would persist for many years thereafter and end in separation, as he spent more and more time away from Rome, usually in Lucugnano. His ineptitude in business, coupled with his strong opposition to the Fascist regime, worsened his already difficult financial situation. In 1946, after breaking with his wife, he left Rome to move to Lucugnano. This move coincided with the decision of several other writers and scholars to resurrect the Salento area as a cultural and economic center. The founding by Comi's group of the Accademia Salentina led to the creation of a publishing house, L'Albero, and to the opening of a library in Comi's house in Lucugnano to be used by researchers and students.

In 1965 Comi's wife died. Despite his financial difficulties, he refused an inheritance from her, and that same year he married his housekeeper, Tina Lambrini. On 9 March 1968 Comi was admitted to the Tricase hospital suffering from acute bronchitis, an intestinal blockage, and general toxicity associated with advanced arteriosclerosis. Comi died at home in Lucugnano on 3 April 1968.

The year 1933 remains perhaps the most important in Comi's life. It saw his conversion to Catholicism—the culmination of an arduous spiritual journey undertaken with Buonaiuti and of his assiduous readings of the works of Blaise Pascal. Comi regarded Pascal in some respects as a private teacher. Comi's readings of Dante, Saint

Thomas Aquinas, and Saint Paul had a similar influence.

In this new Christian light Comi began to understand his personal journey and the evolution of his poetics. In *Tentativo di un diario essenziale* (Attempt at an Essential Diary, published with *Necessità dello stato poetico* [Necessity of the Poetic State], 1934) Comi defines the first part of his poetic journey as "orgiastico culto dell'Io, posseduto e nutrito da . . . stati d'animo panteistici e panici" (an orgiastic cult of the "I," possessed and nourished by . . . pantheistic and sylvan states of the soul). He would later view his original expression of love for the earth and for earthly things as sinful, requiring redemption. For Comi, poetry provided the means for such redemption.

Though he started his poetic journey with a pagan, telluric religion, he ended with a deepfelt Catholic faith. His prose works *Poesia e conoscenza* (Poetry and Knowledge, 1932), *Necessità dello stato poetico*, and *Aristocrazia del cattolicesimo* (Aristocracy of Catholicism, 1937) represent Comi's final development and show most vividly this aspect of his literary and philosophical evolution.

Because of his religious conviction, Comi condemned modern art. He rejected poets such as Giacomo Leopardi, arguing that they negated the objective beauty of God-given nature. Comi even regarded poets such as Baudelaire and D'Annunzio as harmful to the young in their glorification of earthly love and beauty, bound only to the senses and flesh.

While living in Switzerland, Comi wrote his first collection of poems, *Il lampadario* (The Chandelier, 1912), which was reviewed favorably in *Mercure de France* (September-October 1912) by countryman Ricciotto Canudo. Canudo saw Comi's innovations at work and discerned a similarity between his poetics and those of the Roman group (whom Comi would meet eight years later).

The verses of *Il lampadario* reveal Comi's belief in the limited power of science and human progress. He always felt an uneasiness toward the dominance of rationalism, preferring instead the mysteries of the occult and the philosophies of the most knowledgeable French symbolist poets. In this first collection Comi's poetry has a sensual and languid atmosphere.

Poesia, 1918-1928, published in 1929, brings together *Il lampadario*, *I rosai di qui* (The Rosebushes of Here, 1921), *Smeraldi* (Emeralds, 1925),

and *Boschività sotterra* (Woody Undergrounds, 1927), and includes some additional unpublished material. Many critics (such as Arnaldo Bocelli and Oreste Macrì) have seen Comi's southern origin in these early works that sing the sensual triumph of light, colors, and the earth. For example, the central feature of the lyric "Immagine del Salento" (Image of Salento) is the harsh rays of Mezzogiorno, Italy:

> Cristalli di luce varia
> spaccano l'ozio dei suoli
> per fecondarlo di voli
> di cantici, d'aromi e d'aria
> e perché l'ansia del dire
> s'incanti nelle matrici
> rocciose delle radici
> e nel loro sordo fiorire.
>
> (Crystals of various light
> crack the idleness of soils
> to sew it with flights
> of hymns, aromas and air,
> and so that the eagerness of saying
> enchants itself in the rocky
> matrices of the roots
> and in their deaf blooming.)

In the poem "I rosai di qui" the clamorous clash of colors and smells reaches a climax:

> Rosai di qui: bionde selve
> d'aromi radiosi—consumo
> di luce, a ringhiere fulve . . .
>
> Orchestre di gialli voraci
> ospitate da spaziosità calde
> di mattinate felici . . .
>
> (Rosebushes of here: blond woods
> of radious aroma—consumption
> of light, to tawny railings . . .
>
> Orchestras of voracious yellow
> hosted by warm spaciousness
> of happy mornings . . .).

However, one must be aware that the sensual, sylvan inspiration of these early collections already reveals Comi's fascination with the mystical, spiritual participation of man in the universe, later to dominate Comi's verses.

Poesia was enlarged in a new edition in 1939, including *Cantico del tempo e del seme* (Song of Time and Seed, 1930), *Nel grembo dei mattini* (In the Womb of the Mornings, 1931), *Cantico dell'argilla e del sangue* (Song of Clay and Blood,

1933), and *Adamo-Eva* (Adam-Eve, 1935). The dominant theme of these poems is still Comi's yearning for total immersion in nature and his search for cosmic liberation, but what distinguishes this collection from the previous *Poesia* is that these sensual feelings have found resolution in Christian values in the later poems. The poet attempts to establish a rapport between his humanity and the reality of the cosmos. Poetry is viewed as a spiritual endeavor to discover God and his beauty: "Se la poesia non diventa mistica anzi religione armonica, profonda e categorica, riallacciata e saldata all tradizione e alla verità cristiane, essa permane un caso, un episodio (letterario, civile, culturale, ecc.)" (If poetry does not become mystic, better yet a harmonious, profound and categorical religion, bound and welded to traditional and Christian truth, poetry remains a case, an episode [literary, civic, cultural, etc.])—from *Aristocrazia del cattolicesimo*.

Such mysticism gives Comi's verses a new strength and harmony, as in "La grazia" (The Grace):

> Se Tu m'assisti il mio cuore diventa
> un grande bosco di pensieri vivi
> in cui regna e s'eterna la sementa
> dell'ansia antica dei morti e dei vivi.
>
> (If You assist me my heart becomes
> a big woods of live thoughts
> in which reigns and becomes eternal the seed
> of the ancient anguish of the dead and the living.)

In 1954 the collection *Spirito d'armonia* (Spirit of Harmony) earned Comi the Premio Chianciano. This anthology constitutes the final component of Comi's poetic writings through 1952 and is indispensable to an understanding of his poetic development. It demonstrates better than his other works the passage from the sensual, earthly vision of the world to a spiritual examination of it, followed by continuous movement toward the absolute and the transcendental. The poem "Conoscenza di Dio" (Knowledge of God) shows Comi's yearning to comprehend the universal architecture of the cosmos and to discover therein its Creator:

> Nella Tua gioventù che mai non muore
> sento la risonanza ed il calore
> dell'intensa armonia da cui derivo.
>
> ed alla quale voglio che ritorni
> —prima ch'io muoia e mentre ancora vivo—
> il respiro più ricco dei miei giorni.

> (In Your youth that never dies
> I hear the resonance and the warmth
> of the intense harmony from which I derive.
>
> and to which I wish to return
> —before I die and while still alive—
> the richest breath of my day.)

Another important aspect of *Spirito d'armonia* is found in Comi's presentation of rich woody landscapes, nymphs, water, and seeds, in a clash of colors and smells. The dominant sensual atmosphere that characterizes earlier verses is replaced by a feeling of the mystical beginning, of wonder over the dawn of the world. The frequent reappearance of Adam and Eve in the collection represents Comi's attempt to create a vision of mythical figures, prototypes of humanity, as in "Primo canto di Eva" (First Song for Eve):

> Io sono Eva sottomessa e indoma
> che ti tentai . . . E il nostro abbraccio, Adamo,
> è lievitato dell'aroma
> del dolce frutto che ti ha fatto umano . . .
>
> (I am Eve submissive and untamed
> who tempted you . . . And our embrace, Adam,
> is leavened by the aroma
> of the sweet fruit which made you human . . .);

and also in "Secondo canto di Eva" (Second Song for Eve):

> La mia estasi che dormiva aveva
> quasi un presentimento di languore
> . . . .
> scoccò l'insidia di un invito: Eva . . .
>
> L'albero si curvò a tal richiamo
> e il mio orgoglio fiorì . . . E cadde Adamo . . .
>
> (My ecstacy asleep had
> almost a foreboding of weakness
> . . . .
> darted the snare of an invitation: Eve . . .
>
> The tree bent at such a call
> and my pride blossomed . . . And Adam fell . . .).

The presentation of light is another element that can be used to trace the stages of Comi's poetic evolution. The light that seems to have a sensual life of its own and is a physical entity in the earlier poems becomes in these poems spiritual light, or spiritual reality, which manifests God's power, and demands that everything sing praise to him. Light and sun are now symbols of eternity, as in "Alla luce" (To Light):

> Invano tu m'inebri enormemente
> e vertebri i miei sensi e la mia mente,
> perché non so da dove cominciare
> ogni volta che ti voglio adorare.
>
> Invano, luce, sei quello che sei
> satura e colma d'incessanti dei
> perché non so, s'io voglia a te adeguarmi,
> come abbracciare le tue sacre carni.
>
> (In vain you inebriate me enormously
> and fill my senses and my mind,
> because I do not know where to begin
> every time I want to adore you.
>
> In vain, light, you are what you are
> saturated and full of unceasing gods,
> because I don't know, if I want to adapt myself to you,
> how to embrace your sacred flesh.)

The publication of the collection *Canto per Eva* (Song for Eve, 1955) shows another important step taken by Comi in his journey toward poetry as a spiritual instrument. In *Canto per Eva* Comi sings not of love for one Eve, but of love itself, a chain between the creator and creation itself. In the tradition of the angelic woman of the *Dolce Stil Nuovo* (Sweet New Style), readers are no longer immersed in earthly love, but lifted to a cosmic plane, as in the title poem ("Canto per Eva"):

> Creatura per cui ardo e m'abbandono
> come al richiamo della Luce-madre,
> più che gioia da consumare, cerco
> nella tua stessa carne il segno e il dono
> della fiamma nativa che riveli
> la nostra prima purezza che s'apre
> su itinerarii segreti di cieli
> intensi come il canto interiore
> dello spirito quando e solo Amore . . .
>
> (The being for whom I burn and give myself up
> as one does to the call of the mother of creation,
> more than the joy of consumption, I search
> in your flesh for the sign and the gift
> of the native flame so that it may reveal
> our first purity which opens
> upon secret itineraries of the heavens
> as intense as the inner song
> of the spirit . . .).

In "Canto per Eva," woman has a dual meaning. She is the fruit of terrestrial love but carries within herself the beauty and the eternal youth that man can find only in the celestial sphere. Through her beauty, man can reach the beauty of eternal life.

The last collection of Comi's poems published in his lifetime, *Fra lacrime e preghiere* (Among Tears and Prayers, 1966), represents the closing of his poetic circle. The title of this collection suggests its genesis: Comi's last years were difficult and sad. Living in absolute poverty, his health deteriorating, he was plagued with cardio-vascular disease and intestinal discomforts. But through these troubled years he seems to have freed himself from earthly ties and aspired to the world of the spirit. There is a strong sense in this collection of breaking away from earthly matter, from life itself—a definite passage from the physical to the metaphysical, for a final return to the maker—as in "Cristo":

> Se da te m'allontano, Amore, è per raggiungere
> un pò prima che gli occhi mi s'oscurino
> la fulgida sorgente
> degli spiriti puri.
>
> Se da te fuggo è perché la poesia
> in noi rinasca inesauribilmente
> immagine e realtà del paradiso intatto
> di cui qualche bagliore è come fermo
> sul ciglio di un paesaggio dell'eterno.
>
> (If I move away from you, Love, it is to reach
> a little before my eyes grow dim
> the bright source
> of the pure spirits.
>
> If from you I run away it is so that poetry
> may revive in us inexhaustibly
> the image and reality of the untouched paradise
> some ray of which is almost still
> on the edge of a landscape of eternity.)

"Cristo" closes the collection and recalls Dante's prayer to the Virgin in the last canto of the *Paradiso*: the poet sings of a departure, a breaking away from the earthly world of suffering.

Comi chose to have his tombstone adorned with one of Dante's verses, "La tua volontade è nostra pace" (Your will is our peace). These words reflect his own poetic evolution. From pantheistic earthly accents, Comi moved toward feelings of cosmic anguish. His thinking finally came to rest in a rarefied atmosphere of spiritual fulfillment. This evolution was driven by his search for *l'assoluto* (the absolute), a quest he maintained throughout his life and one which gave him the strength to remain an isolated poet, unwilling to compromise with the movements of his time.

References:

Giorgio Barberi Squarotti, *La cultura e la poesia italiana del dopoguerra* (Bologna: Cappelli, 1966), p. 116;

Arnaldo Bocelli, "Itinerario di una poesia," in his *Letteratura del Novecento* (Caltanissetta & Rome: Sciascia, 1977), pp. 264-269;

Bocelli, "Scrittori d'oggi," *Nuova Antologia*, 278 (16 August 1931): 534-536;

Oreste Macrì, "Girolamo Comi," in *Novecento. I Contemporanei*, volume 4 (Milan: Marzorati, 1979), pp. 3568-3596;

Macrì, "Verbo e tecnica nella poesia di Girolamo Comi," in his *Realtà del simbolo. Poeti e critici del Novecento italiano* (Florence: Vallecchi, 1968), pp. 37-71;

Pier Paolo Pasolini, "Una linea orfica," *Paragone*, 60 (December 1954): 82-87;

Gianni Pozzi, *La poesia italiana del Novecento. Da Gozzano agli Ermetici* (Turin: Einaudi, 1965), pp. 105-109;

Davide Puccini, "Girolamo Comi," in *Poesia italiana del Novecento*, edited by Piero Gelli and Gina Lagorio (Milan: Garzanti, 1980), pp. 339-342;

Michele Tondo, "Girolamo Comi," in *Novecento. I Contemporanei*, volume 3 (Milan: Marzorati, 1977), pp. 143-159;

Tondo, *Lettura di Girolamo Comi: Con antologia di testi* (Bari, Italy: Adda, 1973);

Donato Valli, *Girolamo Comi* (Lecce, Italy: Milella, 1978);

Valli, "Lingua e poesia in G. Comi," *Idea*, 19 (May 1963): 302-307;

Valli, "Valori lessicali e semantici nella poesia di G. Comi," *Letteratura*, 25 (January-April 1961): 34-54;

Aldo Vallone, *Aspetti della poesia italiana contemporanea* (Pisa: Nistri-Lischi, 1960).

Sergio Corazzini

(6 February 1886 - 17 June 1907)

Paolo Barlera
New York University

BOOKS: *Dolcezze* (Rome: Tipografia Operaia Romana Cooperativa, 1904);

L'amaro calice (Rome: T.O.R.C., 1905 [i.e., 1904]);

Le aureole (Rome: T.O.R.C., 1905);

Il traguardo (Naples, 1905);

Piccolo libro inutile, by Corazzini and Alberto Tarchiani (Rome: T.O.R.C., 1906);

Elegia (Rome: T.O.R.C., 1906);

Libro per la sera della domenica (Rome: T.O.R.C., 1906);

Liriche (Naples: Ricciardi, 1908; enlarged, 1922; enlarged again, 1959);

Poesie edite e inedite, edited by Stefano Jacomuzzi (Turin: Einaudi, 1968).

PLAY PRODUCTION: *Il traguardo*, Rome, Teatro Metastasio, 26 May 1905.

Sergio Corazzini was born in Rome on 6 February 1886. He attended school in the city and also at a boarding school in Spoleto (in the Umbria region), but his family's ill health and financial misfortunes forced him to quit the *ginnasio* (secondary school) and to start working for an insurance company. Shortly after, he started developing the first symptoms of tuberculosis, which eventually forced him to take hopeless trips to the healthier climate of Nocera (Umbria) and to a sanatorium in Nettuno, just outside Rome. In the spring of 1907 Corazzini returned to Rome, where he died on 17 June, at the age of twenty-one.

The apparent convergence of Corazzini's life and poetry has often led to hagiographic considerations, ranging from the myth of the young dying poet to the celebration of the purity of his sufferings. One fact, though, has to be taken into consideration: soon after his death Corazzini's friends and acquaintances decided to publish a posthumous collection of his poems. The publication—*Liriche* (1908), "a cura degli amici" (edited by his friends)—intentionally omitted several compositions and helped to create a romantic aura around the figure of the dead poet. The

Sergio Corazzini

two later Ricciardi editions added some, but not all, of the missing poems; only with the 1968 *Poesie edite e inedite* (Published and Unpublished Poems) was the full version of Corazzini's compositions made available.

Some of the romantic features of Corazzini's history were contributed by his friend Fausto M. Martini in the latter's novel *Si sbarca a New York* (Landing in New York), where actual episodes and conversations of their Roman circle are mixed with fictional elements. Corazzini's literary relevance, though, seems clearer through the reconstruction of his textual history rather than through these biographical accounts.

Corazzini's work has usually been labeled *crepuscolare* and considered, together with other "twilight poets," such as Corrado Govoni, Guido Gozzano, Marino Moretti, Aldo Palazzeschi, and the young Eugenio Montale, part of the literary movement that flourished in Italy between 1903 and 1920. Generally speaking, these writers can be associated with a "poetry of objects," as they took as their imagery small and forgotten objects, and places such as hospitals, convents, and enclosed gardens. Representations of such things are usually ruled by symbolic intentions and apparently characterized by their collocation in a twilight atmosphere, obviously related to the group's label.

The term *crepuscolare* was first used by Giuseppe Antonio Borgese in 1911 in his *La vita e il libro* (The Life and the Book) to denote the "fading" of the great sunny afternoon of Italian poetry; Gabriele D'Annunzio had been the main poet of that time. Despite the fact that the term and the concept were introduced after Corazzini's death, it seems improper, in order to approach his poetry, not to deal first with its position within *crepuscolarismo*. Literary critics have sometimes indulged in considering the *crepusculare* imagery as a specific component of the group's poetry, but the concept proves to be useful only to the extent of its interpretation within the daylight metaphor. While the full light of the afternoon can be ascribed to D'Annunzio and the auroral phase of poetry to Giovanni Pascoli, Corazzini's poetry of objects is qualified by the twilight: symbolic items emerge from darkness, and their story moves toward the end of the day, that is, the antiphrastic dead end of poetic expression.

In 1902 Rome the problem was probably not whether to be a *crepuscolare* or not, but rather whether to be *dannunziano* or not. The new fashionable names were those of the French symbolists Georges Rodenbach, Maurice Maeterlinck, and Francis Jammes, not to mention the earlier generation of Charles-Pierre Baudelaire and Arthur Rimbaud.

Despite the fact that D'Annunzio and, in a different perspective, Pascoli offered similar treatments of symbolism, those who wanted to say something new for Italian poetry seemed inclined to get rid of D'Annunzio's rhetorical pretension and Pascoli's mimetical harmony. But like young Hegelians, Corazzini, Govoni, and Gozzano could not help using—within their critical commitment against the masters—tokens of the masters' language: not only stylistic or lexical facets but also and foremost the very objects their poetry takes into consideration.

In sharing this linguistic and topical conservatism, the *crepuscolari* seemed also incapable of, or not interested in, dealing with the historical situation influenced by the new market-oriented attitudes of the arts and the weakness of the attempts of the Italian bourgeoisie to handle culture as well as politics. The other great Italian movement of the period, Filippo Tommaso Marinetti's futurism, was about to cause a serious change in the way art and society were viewed. In this respect Corazzini and the other *crepuscolari* seemed to look in an opposite direction, assigning to the investigation of new lyrical and rhythmical forms those cultural stimulations that would bring Marinetti to his iconoclastic formulations.

The "twilight" group's history, on the whole, appears to share the same enthusiastic inconsistency with the general turbulence of Italian culture at the turn of the century. As an example, the Florentine periodical *Leonardo*—between 1903 and 1908—introduced Italian intellectuals to many stimulating ideas, from those of Friedrich Nietzsche to those of Henri Bergson, and from pragmatism to mysticism. The influence of this cultural exposure on Corazzini's own repertoire resulted, though, in an almost complete lack of attention to social problems. Giovanni Papini and Giuseppe Prezzolini, in their articles in *Leonardo*, were developing a philosophical idea of self-consciousness as weltanschauung, whereas Corazzini turned his own consciousness to a glimpse at the idea of "pure poetry."

In this respect, the well-known crepuscular imagery paid its tribute to a French heritage (at least to Baudelaire and Victor Hugo). But its relationship with the Italian tradition also has to be explored, for the topoi of "death," "heart," and "soul" are at least as old as Italian literature itself. Accordingly—as Palazzeschi suggests in his introduction to Filippo Donini's *Vita e poesia di Sergio Corazzini* (Life and Poetry of Sergio Corazzini, 1949)—the spirit of the group's poetry seems to indicate a return to the mysticism of the *primitivi*.

The question somehow becomes more complicated as the "drama of the spirit" is joined by a "drama of the technique": the history of Italian rhythms finds here, in Govoni's and Corazzini's poetry, the debated break into free verse, which will set the stage for the remainder of contemporary Italian poetry. Since Giosuè Carducci the historical development of Italian meter has been a history of attempts to dig into the traditional forms in order to find new rhythmical solutions. There is a part in that development that belongs to the *crepuscolari*: Corazzini uses seven- and eleven-syllable verses and eventually forces the lines out of their metrical borders. The result was one of the first instances of free verse, although set in a uniform rhythm, where even the enjambments and the internal rhymes sound like repetitions within the same prosaical beat.

In 1902 Corazzini was sixteen; he spent his evenings with a circle of friends with whom he talked of life and poetry. Among these friends were Alberto Tarchiani, Martini, and, later on, also Govoni. Soon Corazzini became the "soul" of the group, carrying himself almost as a decadent or even dandyish figure, with an unusual concern for eccentric clothes and behavior; he often indulged in the pose of a *poète maudit* (doomed poet), as, for example, when he wrote to Palazzeschi (4 November 1905): "Quel poco che compongo è causa di una specie di delirio fittizio che provoco al mio cervello con delle strane bevande" (The little I write is caused by a sort of artificial delirium that I bring about to my brain with strange drinks). This period's milieu also marked the beginning of Corazzini's collaboration with a few Roman periodicals: *Rugantino*, *Marforio*, and *Fracassa*, all of them satirical—often against the Italian clergy—and champions of "romanesco," the dialect of Rome.

Corazzini's first poems are, then, in "romanesco." This shows not simply a willingness for a stylistic compromise, but also a familiarity with the roguish world of the bars of Rome, which he frequented despite his young age, often escorting his father. Soon he published more literary compositions, and after two years of his scattered though unusually refined presence in these periodicals, the first collection of seventeen poems was published—*Dolcezze* (The Sweetnesses, 1904). The choices for this edition probably constitute the first step toward Corazzini's textual history: why only these out of some fifty he had already written? Why this title, so close to Pascoli's homonym section in *Myricae* (1892), and why these subjects, so close to D'Annunzio's *Poema Paradisiaco* (1893)?

The title *Dolcezze* is reminiscent, of course, of the "Dolce Stil Nuovo" (Sweet New Style)—favored by Dante and Guido Cavalcanti. This is not surprising in view of Corazzini and his friends' interest in the poets of the Italian *Duecento* (thirteenth century). They would challenge each other with imitations of the earlier style. The book's dedication, "Per Alfredo Tusti—e per Sandro Benedetti—che più dolce fanno-la mia giovinezza" (To A. T.—and to S. B.—who make my youth sweeter), shows a privileged friendship among young poets. Moreover, Corazzini's compositions seem concerned with a fragmentation of the self and with the characterization of its elements—"Io" (I),"il mio cuore" (my heart), "la mia anima" (my soul)—as objects of the domain of the discourse. However, a great disparity with the poets of the Dolce Stil Nuovo has to be acknowledged in the thematic absence of women in Corazzini's *Dolcezze*. This is, apparently, a major factor in the selection of the lyrics for the book: only among the poems left out is it possible to find references to women and to eroticism: "Un bacio" (A Kiss, November 1902); "Amore e morte" (Love and Death, February 1903); "Lettere a una donna" (Letters to a Woman, July 1903); and "Sonetti all'amica" (Sonnets to his Lady-Friend, December 1903)—all collected in *Poesie edite e inedite*.

If Corazzini, as the last remarks suggest, is willing to assign from the very beginning a particular relevance to editing, concepts such as "sequence" and "position" are likely to reveal aspects of his poetic paradigm. The opening sonnet, "Il mio cuore," presents a metaphoric declaration of his poetic intentions:

Il mio cuore è una rossa
macchia di sangue dove
io bagno senza possa
la penna a dolci prove
eternamente mossa.

(My heart is a red
blood stain where
I dip with no end
my pen to sweet feats
eternally moved.)

The description of the writing activity is matched with the condition of having blood from the heart in order to continue writing: "questo sangue ardente / a un tratto mancherà / ... / ... e allora morirò" (This ardent blood / suddenly will lack / ... / ... and then I will die). Through the enjambments and the final truncated lines, this poem enjoys the security of perfectly enclosed metrical forms, reminiscent of the earliest

Italian tradition, as well as of the French Parnassians and symbolists.

The discourse around the pair "heart-death" also seems to follow the lines of more conspicuous allusions, especially to D'Annunzio, who is present in Corazzini's work mostly through the influence of *Poema Paradisiaco*, where the objects and the places, and the dialogues with the soul, seem to anticipate pivotal elements of *Dolcezze*.

What seemed to interest Corazzini to an even greater extent was the style of the French symbolists, and this concern is allegedly the key to a definition of Corazzini's overall lexicon. *Dolcezze* reveals Corazzini's work with adjectives, in order to engrave specific semantic areas such as emotion (with a high frequence of "sweet" and "sad") or color (mostly white and red). The target is a restricted lexical repertoire intentionally related to the symbolistic lyric genre. Jammes's *De l'Angelus de l'aube a l'Angelus du soir* (From the Dawn Angel to the Evening Angel, 1898), Maeterlinck's *Serres Chaudes* (Warm Greenhouses, 1889), and Rodenbach's *Le Regne du Silence* (The Kingdom of Silence, 1891) and *Bruges-la-morte* (Bruges-Death, 1892) seem the most immediate sources for Corazzini's first lyric production, providing the sweet and sad interiors of hospitals or churches, and the episodes of suffering or even death that characterize so much of Corazzini's early poetic landscape.

Corazzini uses liturgical imagery in an attempt to draw a parallel between the self and Christian icons, as in "La gabbia" (The Cage): "l'anima mia . . . / . . . continuamente si martira" (my soul . . . / . . . continuously martyrs herself). The focus on the concept of suffering leads the poet toward an almost penitential condition, similar to that of Petrarch's speaker in some of his canzones. On the other hand, the identification with liturgical characters or objects indicates a familiarity with catechistic attitudes, a religious predisposition most likely triggered by Corazzini's reading of poets such as Jammes or Jules Laforgue.

It is not difficult to see a continuity between the catechism classes Corazzini attended as a child and his passion for deserted churches, which he often visited and portrays in poems. This is also in line with the period's widespread rediscovery of mysticism in Italy: from the morbid religiosity of D'Annunzio's novels to Johannes Jörgensen's Franciscanism. *Dolcezze* is scattered with images such as "sangue ardente" (ardent blood), "cuor di Gesù tremante e puro" (Jesus'

heart, trembling and pure), "il suo cuor, trafitto, sanguinava" (his heart, stabbed, was bleeding)—images all familiar to educated Catholics. Yet this imagery can be connected not so much to evocative intention or psychological introspection but rather to a reflexive symbolism. The features of such a shift can be seen in "La Madonna e il suo lampioncello" (The Madonna and Her Little Lamp). The four movements of this sequence of triplets are based on an attempted communication between the Madonna and the "lampioncello," and they suggest that the traditional small light in front of the sacred image (to lighten darkness and in homage to the Virgin) bears a poetic resonance. Corazzini's lamp is unable, at first, to fulfill a call for light from the suffering lady; but once the lamp is lit by a pious hand, it is the Madonna who cannot fulfill the lamp's call. This final shortcoming seems to build a frustrating block in communication between the maternal-mystical figure and human light and poetry.

Corazzini's first book thus expresses the revelation of suffering as the condition for "sweet" poetry. The last poem, "Asfodeli"—asphodels are here considered as flowers sacred to the dead—seems to conclude the programmatic discourse started with "Il mio cuore" through the formulation of the connection between heart and death:

Madonna, se il cuore v'offersi,
. . . .
e se voi, con un magnifico atto,
lo accettaste insieme ai miei versi
. . . .
perché ieri lo faceste
sanguinare, lo faceste
lagrimare dolorosamente?

Tutte le sue gocce rosse
caddero a terra, mute,
. . . .
e come per incantamento
in ognuna fiorì un asfodelo

(Madonna, since I offered you my heart
. . . .
and since you, with a magnificient deed
accepted it, and with it my verse
. . . .
why yesterday did you make it
bleed, make it
cry with sorrow?

All its red drops
fell to the ground, silent,

. . . .
and as by enchantment
in each an asphodel bloomed).

In the fall of 1904 Corazzini published his second book, ten poems under the title *L'amaro calice* (The Bitter Cup). The use of *calice* evokes a liturgical presence, implying the dramatic experience of the biblical verse "if it be possible, let this cup pass from me" (Matthew 26:39) and the textual relevance of the Bible. As Corazzini later wrote in a letter to his friend Giuseppe Caruso (as quoted by Donini): "Avanti ogni cosa ti raccomando d'inspirarti sempre alla Bibia [*sic*]" (Before any other thing I recommend that you get inspiration from the Bible).

In *Dolcezze* Corazzini insists on situations that seem to make his youth sweeter; the second book takes a liturgical moment as its paradigm. If Corazzini's poetry had come from suffering, in *L'amaro calice* poetry becomes a bitter sacrifice. The opening sonnet, "Invito" (Invitation), concludes with two prophecies, characterized by the D'Annunzian topoi of the enclosed garden and of sisterly love: "non più rifioriranno i tuoi giardini / in questa vana primavera oscura" (never again will blossom your gardens / in this useless darkened spring); "vieni, sorella, il tuo martirio è il mio" (come, sister, your martyrdom is mine). These final lines seem to remark on how suffering no longer provides sweetness but rather martyrdom.

A similar victimized position of the self appears also in the following poem, "Rime del cuore morto" (Rhymes of the Dead Heart), where the uselessness of the love of the poet's heart is compared with Jesus' hagiographical image. Nonetheless, the poem's conclusion gives a symbolic qualification to the narrative and stifles any suspicion of an aesthetic or intellectual pose. Through the use of similes, the liturgical imagery of the host immediately finds an existential counterpart, thus suggesting a crisis of mystical and poetic communication: "[il mio cuore] fu come un'ostia . . . // le cui piccole parti infrante / non trovarono un cuore ove giacere" ([my heart] was like a host . . . // whose little broken parts / did not find a heart wherein to rest).

This particular structure offers a view of one of Corazzini's favorite textual strategies: the descriptive, yet symbolic, moment. The recurrence of descriptive metaphors can also be seen in one of his most praised poems: "Toblack." This composition, published earlier in the jour-

nal *Marforio* (27 October 1904), most likely dates back to the period of Corazzini's trip to health resorts in northern Italy, Toblack/Dobbiaco being one of them. In spite of the possibility of connection with elements of Govoni's *Armonie in grigio et in silenzio* (Harmonies in Gray and in Silence, 1903), "Toblack," with its own images of hospitals and funerals, reveals an originality that goes far beyond the simple biographical episode, and Corazzini shows his ability to distill other poets' concepts and adopt them for his own purposes. The narrative of "Toblack" leads to a final self-negation:

Anima, vano è questo lacrimare,
vani i sospiri, vane le parole
su quanto ancora in te viveva ieri

(Soul, useless is this crying,
useless the sighs, useless the words
on what still was alive in you yesterday).

The emblematic condition of the "bitter cup" continues in "La chiesa venne riconsacrata" (The Church Was Reconsecrated), where the apparent reconstruction of a suicide and several church scenes is inscribed in symbolism. In front of a red lamp—the relationship between light and poetry has already been seen—the death of a lonely usher in a deserted church appears "un macabro voto / improvvisamente sorto / fra il Cielo e l'Abisso" (a macabre vow / suddenly raised / between Heaven and the Abyss). The only "witness" to the suicide is a small *Libro delle massime eterne* (Book of the Eternal Maxims), which suggests, next to the European influence on Corazzini's work, the presence of a semantic model inspired by traditional Catholic prayers. On the one hand, images of meditation on death and suffering, of Jesus' heart and blood, and of Mary's heart with the seven swords denote a closeness to the decadent symbolists. On the other hand, the relevance of these kinds of prayers within *Dolcezze* and *L'amaro calice* can be linked to a project of "interior liturgy," whose tradition dates back at least to Saint Ignatius's *Spiritual Exercises* (1548).

The last poem in *L'amaro calice*, "L'isola dei morti" (The Island of the Dead), contains Baudelairian images such as "fetido museo" (fetid museum) and "sangue nerastro" (blackish blood), which characterize an opposition to the earlier "sweetness." The aim seems to be the characterization of an "odio inestinguibile" (inextinguishable haste) attributed to a source of light,

Mio diletto Marino, ora la no=
stra comunione è perfetta. Forse
l'anima, nel suo sogno quotidia=
no non aveva mai tanto imagi=
nato. Io ti parlo in un divino mo=
mento di oblio. E più la mia voce
sarà tenera più sarà vicina a mo=
rire. È questo il suo destino. Tu
sei stato triste nel passato, e perché
Era una tristezza dolce o amara? Che
cosa hai fatto in quei giorni d'esilio?
Ricordavi la Romagna lontanissima,
tutte le cose e le anime non presenti
(sono lontanissime) il mare e il
suo divino riso salmastro? (Io già

Page from a 4 December 1906 letter from Corazzini to Marino Moretti, a fellow crepuscolare, or "twilight poet" (from Storia della letteratura: Italiana, *volume 6, edited by Luigi Ferrante, 1965)*

the "tragico fanale della morte" (tragic gaslight of death). If the writing experience leads to a negative status where the poet can no longer reach the redeeming or healing properties of his activity, it is then a question of rejecting established cultural roles, something similar to what Baudelaire, in his *Spleen de Paris*, calls "perte d'aureole" (loss of aureole). Baudelaire's character, a poet, sees his "aureole" slipping from his head into the mud, so that poetry is denied its condition of "purity," whereas Corazzini approaches this kind of degradation as an isolation of the poetic effort, in view of its uselessness and bitterness.

Yet it is not the tradition of the Romantic poets of melancholy, who tried to state the autonomous adequacy of poetry to the sublime: the literary scene of those tears, in Italy, offered a transformation of that consciousness of tragedy, as in D'Annunzio's rhetorical dilatation or Pascoli's objectual reduction. Corazzini seemed to step aside, asking questions about the poetic medium and about his own aesthetic experience: what can poetry bring to the definition of identity of the subject? what is the influence of poetry on social relationships? In May 1905 Corazzini's only play, the one-act *Il traguardo* (The Goal), was performed in Rome. According to the reviews, it is a bad mix of D'Annunzio and Nietzsche, and it quickly failed.

Corazzini then returned to the medium of poetry: his next book was published in July of the same year, and the title, *Le aureole*, brings back in bold letters the Baudelairian question. The opening sonnet, "L'anima," focuses once again on the soul, but with the addition of a dialogic structure based on an indefinite "Thou":

Tu sai: l'anima ben vide cadere
tutte le foglie e in ogni foglia un puro
desiderio, fin che, in suo tormento,

le parve dolce figurarsi in nere
vesti, per sempre crocifissa al muro
di un lontano antichissimo convento.

(You know; the soul well saw all the leaves
falling and in each leaf a pure
desire, until, in her torment,

she felt sweet to picture herself dressed
in black, forever crucified on the wall
of a very ancient and faraway convent.)

Only when the soul feels comfortable in the convent is the self able to regain a new dignity.

The progress seems also to lead Corazzini to a conscious redefinition of his previously used images. Such is the case in "Il fanale" (The Gaslight), whose quatrains are scattered with many of the elements of his repertoire: "sacerdote-fanale" (priest-gaslight), "vetri malchiusi" (badly closed windows), "ospedale" (hospital), "piccolo cortile" (small courtyard), and "morire di tristezza" (to die of sadness). The narrative moment, though, is followed by a conclusive shift:

Cuor che ti duoli . . .
. . . non guardare, non udire, va'
dolce e solingo e la tua lampa rechi
luce a te solo e invano gli altri, ciechi,
implorino la buona carità.

(Grieving heart . . .
. . . do not look, do not listen, go
sweet and lonely and may your lamp bring
light to you only and may the others, blind,
in vain implore good charity.)

The last statement matches Baudelaire's brothel parable in *Spleen de Paris* and apparently aims at this solution: poetry gets back its aureole on condition of carrying its light for itself alone.

Corazzini's challenge to Baudelaire continues in "Spleen," another lyric from *Le aureole*, where "una di quelle canzoni / che non si cantano più" (one of those songs / that nobody sings anymore) is somehow opposite to what happens in Baudelaire's *Les fleurs du mal* (Flowers of Evil, 1857): "Des cloches tout a coup sautent avec furie" (Some church bells suddenly jump with fury). Corazzini's new attitudes, focused on poetry's possibilities for recovering an "aureolar" status, seem to put an end to his preoccupations with death and sadness.

"La finestra aperta sul mare" (The Window on the Sea) introduces in *Le aureole* a new kind of imagery: within the definite setting of free verse, an almost allegorical narrative replaces the usual procedure of key concepts as symbolic interpretations of narrative episodes. A "tower," its "pale blue lover" (the sea), and a shipwreck are the "characters" of this poem, along with Corazzini's old domain of objects. The conclusion matches old themes, through the tower's self-immolation in front of the "grigio albore dell'aurora" (dawn's gray albedo). The sea and aurora images, though similar to what one can find in Jammes (*De l'Angelus de l'aube a l'Angelus du soir*) or in Govoni (*Armonie in grigio et in silenzio*), suggest a deeper philosophical interest. The idea of a personal liturgy turns into a new possibility for the self to reach knowledge and expression through poetry. These points of view are not very far from those of Nietzsche's *Die fröhliche Wissenschaft* (The Gay Science, 1882), a copy of which remains—with a few other books—from Corazzini's library: the German philosopher was very fashionable in Italy in those years, thanks to D'Annunzio, Papini, and Prezzolini, and his works circulated among young intellectuals and poets.

In *Le aureole*, next to poems of a distinct Pascolian flavor such as "Il fanciullo" (The Child), "Alla serenità" (To Serenity), and "A la sorella" (To His Sister), one finds one long composition with a distinct philosophical flavor: "Dai 'Soliloqui di un pazzo'" (From "A Madman's Soliloquies"). Not only the linguistic unorthodoxies of a madman's monologue are conveyed but also the European motifs—via Baudelaire, Nietzsche and D'Annunzio—of the brothel and of the sunlight:

> Chi veste d'auree stole anche le immonde
> case che il fango d'un amplesso cinge?
> . . . .
> Ah, sei tu, sole, che le più profonde
> pupille ferme nell'eterna sfinge
> avvivi, anima orgiastica della luce?!
>
> (Who dresses with golden stoles even
> the dirty houses that the mud embraces?
> . . . .
> Ah, it is you, sun, who the deepest
> pupils, staring to the eternal sphynx,
> enliven, orgiastic soul of light?!).

The concluding sonnet, "Sonetto della desolazione" (Sonnet of Desolation), like the opening poem, characterizes the "soul" as an "invitation," but of a different kind. The dialectical momentum seems to lead, through a liturgical phrasing, to a more assertive attitude: "Ben è ora che di tutto si disperi / e che il rosario dei futuri giorni / ci conduca al più puro dei misteri" (It is now time to despair of everything / and for the rosary of future days / to lead us to the purest of mysteries).

The summer of 1905 saw positive reviews for *Le aureole*, and for Corazzini it was a period of vacation at Nocera Umbra, in search of some relief from his illness; it was also a time for meditation and, as some letters to friends show, for quasi-existentialist thoughts: Søren Kierkegaard's work made its first Italian appearance in 1907 in the pages of *Leonardo*, but anticipations of such ideas

were circulating in Italy before this date. Upon Corazzini's return to Rome, his literary circle of friends and acquaintances began working on a project for a periodical. The first issue of *Cronache latine* (a biweekly review of literature and art) was published in December 1905; the life of the journal was short (three issues) and not really effective in the Italian cultural scene. However, it contained hints of the group's literary and philosophical predilections, and it published two short essays by Corazzini, included in *Liriche* as "Poemetti in prosa."

The first of the two essays, "Soliloquio delle cose" (Soliloquy of Things), is reminiscent of Leopardian modalities, as the small objects of Corazzini's repertoire have their own voice. The second one, "Esortazione al fratello" (Exhortation to His Brother), seems to combine—according to the two epigraphs—Petrarchan epistolary attitudes with both the fashionable rediscovery of Franciscan spiritualism and Nietzschian philosophy. Corazzini's fusion of ideas can hardly be ascribed to a consistent philosophical system, but in his looking back on his work's development, the essay can be considered an attempt to charge with meaning the existential aspects of his being "with himself": "Non altra ombra godere se non quella generata dal prezioso lume della tua anima. E questo lume, assai dolce, sappia tu nutrire di olii non vani e curare affinché il suo raggio non sia parte di un tutto, ma un tutto, per se stesso. . . . E dovrai viverne fino a morire. . . . La tua tristizia sarà quella de l'uomo che sempre ritorna" (Do not enjoy any shadow except the one generated by the precious light of your soul. And this light, so sweet, shall you nourish not with oils, not vain ones, and cure so that its ray not be part of a whole, but a whole itself. . . . And from this light you shall live to the point of dying. . . . Your sadness will be the one of the ever-returning man).

In short, "Esortazione al fratello" sketches an *itinerarium*, not only prescriptive, for his brother, but also retrospective, for Corazzini's own poetry: "allora che l'anima si sarà cibata, divotamente dell'Ostia del silenzio . . . lo spasimo gaudioso vorrà tenerti tutto, in fino a che la morte non a te si figuri come il meraviglioso fiorir di un seme ignoto e divino" (once the soul has fed herself, devotedly with the Host of silence . . . the joyful spasm shall want to keep you entirely, until death shall appear to you as the beautiful blooming of an unknown and divine seed).

The end of the publication of *Cronache latine* was followed by a period of silence and by a second trip to Nocera Umbra; once again his return to Rome was followed by several projects, as Corazzini attended to the publication of three items: *Piccolo libro inutile* (Small Useless Book), *Elegia*, and *Libro per la sera della domenica* (Book for Sunday Evening)—all published in 1906. The three different volumes serve different purposes.

In *Piccolo libro inutile*, according to the title, the book and writing have become useless, just like all the small objects in the churches and hospitals. Once everything is in the silence of self-comprehension, it looks as if there is no need for a traditional poetic medium. The text thus offers a proposal for something that goes beyond the bridges between past and future or between suffering and heaven: poetry for the present. The most representative poem of the book is perhaps "Desolazione del povero poeta sentimentale" (Desolation of the Poor Sentimental Poet), based on eight aphoristic, free-verse episodes. These fragments offer a stigmatization of some of the earlier concepts, for example the refusal of a traditional rhetorical role and the decomposition of the subject in "self" and "thou": "Perché tu mi dici: poeta? / Io non sono un poeta. / Io non sono che un piccolo fanciullo che piange" (Why do you call me a poet? / I am not a poet / I am but a little child who cries).

Corazzini concludes *Piccolo libro inutile* by suggesting that his poetry is not "crepuscular" any more, but rather "auroral":

Chiudi tutte le porte
Noi veglieremo fino
all'alba originale,

fino a che un immortale
stella segni il cammino,
novizii, oltre la Morte!

(Shut every door
We shall be on the watch until
the original dawn,

until an immortal
star points to the walk,
novices, beyond Death!)

Probably in the beginning of the fall of 1906, *Elegia* was published—a single composition of eighty-three lines. Through a long scansion of ejambments and propositions that fill the whole stanza, *Elegia* resumes the *itinerarium* of

Corazzini's discourse about the "soul" and brings it toward an elegiac celebration of sorrow.

The objects come directly from the repertoire shared with the French symbolists, and with Govoni. The "tears," the old shabby furniture, the inclination to prayers, the melancholy of the holy days, ill children, and poor nuns with biscuits—all speak of a common semantic area that the writers of Italian literature—in the years preceding World War I—were willing to consider. In this respect Corazzini's narrative poem *Elegia* is one of the most clear and unaffected:

sarà come se tu cantassi una
preghiera incomprensibile, per lungo
volger di tempo, in fin che in una sera,
forse più dolce e triste, all'improvviso
t'avvenisse, così, senza sapere,
di comprenderla intera. . . .

canteremo le più vecchie canzoni
e sarà dolce non seguirne il senso.

(it will be like singing one
incomprehensible prayer, for a long
time, until one evening,
perhaps more sweet and sad, suddenly
you would happen, without realizing it,
to understand it completely. . . .

we will sing the oldest songs
and it will be sweet not to follow their sense.)

Toward the end of 1906 Corazzini entered the Nettuno sanatorium, in the vicinity of Rome, because of the critical condition of his health; in December the last book of his verse published in his lifetime, *Libro per la sera della domenica*, was released. The theme is widely derived, once again, from contemporary influences: Laforgue's "Dimanches" (Sundays; from *Des fleurs de bonne volonté* [Flowers of Good Will, 1890]) was spreading through the many "Sundays" of Govoni's and Moretti's works. The well-known "melancholy" of this day of the week can be easily seen in Corazzini's text, where objects and places fit with such a sentimental disposition; but the symbolic procedures that have characterized his poetry since the beginning ask for a more careful reading. If the "evening" of Sunday is the time after the morning and afternoon liturgy in the churches, a "book" for this particular time must be something that tries to set rules for a postritualistic moment; and poetry, with its words, images, and formulas, seems to have been—so far—Corazzini's "book" for an existential liturgy.

The ten lyrics of *Libro per la sera della domenica* can indeed be considered a shift from the style of the earlier collections, since they are almost all marked with the irony of the capitalized "moods," in the mode of allegorical characters revisited by Baudelaire: "Disperazione" (Desperation), "Speranza" (Hope), "Malinconia" (Melancholy), and "Tristezza" (Sadness). Moreover, poems such as "Dialogo di marionette" (A Puppets' Dialogue) or "Bando" (Sales Announcement) characterize a domain of discourse less interested in self-fragmented settings, and more in pseudorhetorical dialogues. The ironical tone of the compositions anticipates some of Gozzano's and Palazzeschi's poems and is reminiscent of visionary attitudes à la Rimbaud, as the first poem of the book, "Sera della domenica," shows: "Il Poeta, ebro di morte, / viene a patti / con la Disperazione" (The poet, inebriated with death, / comes to a pact / with Desperation). The "pact" is built as a climax, after a sequence of paratactic stanzas, each beginning with "Ora che" (Now that) and listing some of the images of previous episodes: Sunday happiness, convents, boarding schools, and brothels. Such a structure appears as a different type of dialectical progress, which suggests how the episodes have different consequences *now that* it is Sunday evening. Corazzini's intense experience with disease is likely to have a role in this change of scene: in the last lyric of the book, "Bando," he is almost willing to give up: "E non badate, Dio mio, non badate / troppo alla mia voce / piangevole" (Do not mind, my God, do not mind / too much my weeping / voice).

In Rome in the spring of 1907 Corazzini, now out of the sanatorium, was enthusiastically welcomed by his associates, and a poetry-reading benefit was organized in his honor, in order to collect money for his medical expenses. A short while later Corazzini, probably on his deathbed, wrote his last poems: "Il sentiero" (The Trail), published in *Rivista di Roma* in June 1907, and "La morte di Tantalo" (The Death of Tantalus), published posthumously in *Vita letteraria* on 28 June. Corazzini died eleven days before, committing his final thoughts to these two compositions, both collected in *Liriche*. The first one focuses its eight distichs on the symptomatic, but not strictly autobiographical, theme of the "pathway to death": "fin che le mie mani pure / non strinsero che rame oscure" (until my pure hands / grasped dark

branchlets). The second puts forth a symbolic narrative not easy to interpret: two lovers in a golden vineyard look for a divine cause in order to die, but one day—not finding one—they can drink the fresh water and eat the golden fruit throughout the night:

> O dolce mio amore,
> confessa al viandante
> che non abbiamo saputo morire
> negandoci il frutto saporoso
> . . . .
> E aggiungi che non morremo più
> e che andremo per la vita
> errando sempre.
>
> (My sweet love,
> confess to the wayfarer
> that we have not been able to die
> by denying ourselves the tasteful fruit
> . . . .
> And add that we will not die anymore
> and that we will go throughout life
> forever wandering.)

Undoubtedly this reversal of Tantalus's myth is unexpected in Corazzini's work; yet the images of the wayfarer and of the golden vineyard—another scriptural revival—suit his already tested philosophical attentions, enhancing the concept of "death by divine cause" in view of its unavailability, almost as an incompetence in the *ars moriendi* (art of death). The removal of the "divine cause"— that is the "fruit's negation"—transforms the human condition into a Nietzschian-flavored wandering through life.

After Corazzini's death the experience of the Roman group seemed at a dead point. The upcoming war would destroy much more than this group, bringing the definite end of what the "crepuscolari"—in a subdued tone—tried to deny: the Romantic idea of a poetry which is the depository of the "true word." After the war there was room for Giuseppe Ungaretti's reconstruction of the subject but also for Montale's ideal continuation of the crepuscular line, especially through his lexical treatment of daily objects. Corazzini's results were not always satisfactory, but his poetic experience seemed to set some of the fundamental premises for such developments of contemporary lyric poetry in Italy.

Bibliography:
Giuseppe Savoca, *Concordanza delle poesie di Sergio Corazzini* (Florence: Olschki, 1987).

Biography:

Filippo Donini, *Vita e poesia di Sergio Corazzini* (Turin: Da Silva: 1949).

References:

Giorgio Bàrberi Squarotti, *La poesia del Novecento* (Caltanissetta & Rome: Sciascia, 1985);

Aurelio Benevento, *Sergio Corazzini* (Naples: Loffredo, 1980);

Gianni Grana, ed., "Sergio Corazzini," in *Novecento: I Contemporanei*, volume 1 (Milan: Marzorati, 1979), pp. 825-854;

Stefano Jacomuzzi, *La poesia di Sergio Corazzini*, introduction to *Poesie edite e inedite* (Turin: Einaudi, 1968), pp. 5-30;

Jacomuzzi, *Sergio Corazzini* (Milan: Mursia, 1963);

François Livi, *Dai simbolisti ai crepuscolari* (Milan: Istituto di Propaganda Libraria, 1974);

Livi, *La parola crepuscolare* (Milan: Istituto di Propaganda Libraria, 1986);

Maria Carla Papini, *Corazzini* (Florence: Nuova Italia, 1978);

Giuseppe Petronio, *Poeti del secolo nostro: I crepuscolari* (Florence: Sansoni, 1937);

Edoardo Sanguineti, *Tra libertà e crepuscolarismo* (Milan: Mursia, 1961);

"Sergio Corazzini," *La Fiera Letteraria*, 9 (14 November 1954);

Sergio Solmi, "Sergio Corazzini e le origini della poesia contemporanea," introduction to *Liriche* (Naples: Ricciardi, 1959), pp. xix-xlii;

Natale Tedesco, *La condizione crepuscolare* (Florence: Nuova Italia, 1970);

Aldo Vallone, *I crepuscolari* (Palermo: Palumbo, 1973).

Libero De Libero

(10 September 1906 - 4 July 1981)

Romana Capek-Habeković
University of Michigan

BOOKS: *Solstizio* (Rome: Quaderni di Novissima, 1934);

Proverbi (Rome: Cometa, 1937);

Testa (Rome: Cometa, 1939);

Eclisse (Rome: Cometa, 1940);

Epigrammi 1938 (Milan: Scheiwiller, 1942);

Il libro del forestiero (Rome: Nuove Edizioni Italiane, 1945; enlarged edition, Milano: Mondadori, 1946);

Malumore (Rome: OET, 1945);

Banchetto (Milan: Mondadori, 1949);

Mafai (Rome: De Luca, 1949);

Amore e morte (Milan: Garzanti, 1951);

Camera oscura (Milan: Garzanti, 1952; revised edition, Milan: Mondadori, 1974);

Ascolta la Ciociaria (Rome: De Luca, 1953);

Valéry parente illustre (Milan: Scheiwiller, 1955);

Volti di Masaccio (Ivrea, Italy: Olivetti, 1956);

Mario Lattes (Milan: Milione, 1957);

Il Trionfo della Morte (Palermo: Flaccovio, 1958);

Il guanto nero (Venice: Sodalizio del Libro, 1959);

Gentilini (Milan: Riunione Adriatica di Sicurtà, n.d.);

Enotrio (Rome: Barcaccia, 1962);

Sinisgalli, poeta che disegna (Rome: Ferro di Cavallo, 1963);

Romanzo: 1934-1955 (Milan: Scheiwiller, 1965);

Madrigali (Luxembourg: Origine, 1967);

Racconti alla finestra (Milan: Bietti, 1969);

Sono uno di voi (Alpignano, Italy: Tallone, 1969);

Di brace in brace: 1956-1970 (Milan: Mondadori, 1971);

Scempio e lusinga: 1930-1956 (Milan: Mondadori, 1972);

Anna Claudi (Milan: Silvana, 1976);

Circostanze: 1971-1975 (Milan: Mondadori, 1976);

Mino Maccari (Milan: Scheiwiller, 1976);

Passaporto (Rome: L'Arco, 1976);

Poesie (Milan: Mondadori, 1980);

Roma 1935 (Rome: Cometa, 1981).

SELECTED PERIODICAL PUBLICATION—
UNCOLLECTED: "Hommage á Valery Larbaut," *Nouvelle Revue Française*, 57 (1 September 1957): 542-545.

A 1937 portrait of Libero De Libero by Carlo Levi (from Storia della letteratura, *volume 7, edited by Luigi Ferrante, 1965)*

Libero De Libero belongs to the generation of Italian poets who started to publish in the 1930s, the period of the second wave of hermetic writers. The language and style of hermeticism evolved around the complex, sophisticated, obscure, often abstract, and highly subjective images derived from strong personal emotions or the poets' perception of reality. The poets felt alienated from society and history, and found refuge in the search to discover new modes of expression. Poetic language was no longer a means of simple communication, a link between the poet and the reader, but rather an entity in itself, the main function of which was to try to express the inexpressible and to create new images estranged from reality. Historicity was neglected; both present and future were doubted. The past, the preferred time—with its memories, absences, and lost loves—and a hedonistic merging with a nature that consoles and understands were two of

the favorite foci of hermetic poets. This was the climate in which De Libero began to write.

From his first collection, *Solstizio* (Solstice, 1934), it was obvious to critics that De Libero was different from his contemporaries and that his poetry, although being in the center of hermeticism, had a new dimension added. De Libero continued to maintain and further develop his own style, puzzling those critics who tried to place him within certain literary currents or modes. Much of his poetry is based on memories of his youth spent in Ciociaria, in the region of Latium, his love for its arid, untamed landscape and people, and his feelings about World War II. Many of his poems focus on the love for a woman or the death of a loved one, as well as on such eternal subjects as life, death, pain, and joy. The characteristic that differentiates De Libero from the other poets of the 1930s is the imagery he employs to express emotions. The images spring from reality, from the animal and plant world. They are vivid and clear, simple yet complex in their expressiveness, and often shocking and tormenting. Naturalism, surrealism, and expressionism are the main sources of De Libero's poetic language.

De Libero was born to Francesco De Libero and Cesira Faiola De Libero in Fondi, in the Ciociaria area, on 10 September 1906. As reported by Elio Filippo Accrocca, he once described his childhood and early studies:

Nato a Fondi, in Ciociaria, nel 1906 e cresciuto in provincia, dentro una famiglia numerosa, sono stato il solito ragazzo nutrito con schiaffi fette di pane e libri d'ogni specie che, un giorno, scrive una poesia e se ne vergogna più che d'un grosso peccato, poi da giovane ci riprova e se ne vergogna di meno, ma da uomo ha continuato senza tanti scrupoli. Dopo essere stato un anno in un convento di frati missionari, frequentai gli studi classici tra Ferentino e Alatri, dove trovai professori d'ottima qualità e a uno di loro debbo il mio vero incontro con la poesia di Dante, Petrarca, Leopardi e Baudelaire: furono quelli gli anni del mio migliore noviziato, tra letture sistematiche e la scoperta dei poeti moderni che mi ubriacarono. Alla vita provinciale, traboccante di pollini e di visioni e di segreti allarmi, debbo le prime e scottanti vicende del sentimento.

(Born in Fondi, in Ciociaria, in 1906 and brought up in that province, I was one of a large family, the typical boy nourished with slaps, slices of bread, and all sorts of books, who one day writes a poem and is more ashamed of it than if he had committed some great sin. Later as a young man he tries again and is less ashamed, but he continues without many scruples. After having spent a year in a monastery of missionary monks, I did classical studies in Ferentino and Alatri, where I found excellent professors, to one of whom I owe my real encounter with the poetry of Dante, Petrarch, Leopardi, and Baudelaire: those were the years of my best apprenticeship, the systematic reading and discovery of the modern poets who intoxicated me. To provincial life, overflowing with pollen and visions and secret tumults, I owe my first important encounter with emotion).

After completing his studies in Ferentino and Alatri, De Libero went to Rome to study law in 1927. This was as valid a pretext as any, but the real reason he came to Rome was to leave the provincial atmosphere and to get involved in the mainstream.

In 1928, together with Luigi Diemoz, he founded *L'interplanetario*, a bimonthly. Although only eight numbers were published, he did come into contact with collaborators, who, among others, included Corrado Alvaro, Massimo Bontempelli, Alberto Moravia, Marcello Gallian, and Leonardo Sinisgalli.

The cultural atmosphere of the capital city was stimulating, and De Libero entered into Roman literary and artistic circles. His activity as an art critic led him to establish close friendships with some of the leading painters of the *Scuola Romana* (Roman School), such as Scipione (pseudonym for Luigi Bonichi) and Mario Mafai. From 1935 to 1938 De Libero was involved in the Roman gallery La Cometa, which organized many one-man exhibitions of the most important painters of that period. Cultural exchanges between writers and the painters took place there and in Villa Caffarelli, in the parlor of Countess Anne Letizia Pecci-Blunt, the founder of La Cometa, during the popular *Sabati della primavera* (The Spring Saturdays). De Libero was a regular participant in these exchanges.

He started to publish short stories and art criticism in various newspapers and magazines such as *Documento*, *Letteratura*, and *Fiera Letteraria*. The first critical approval of his poetry came in 1931, when Giovanni Battista Angioletti published two of his poems in *Italia Letteraria*. In 1934 Giuseppe Ungaretti and Rafaele Contu founded *Quaderni di Novissima*, which published, at Ungaretti's suggestion, De Libero's *Solstizio*. This brought him to the attention of a large public and gained him the support and recognition of critics and fellow writers. In 1941 De Libero began to teach art history at the Liceo Artistico in Rome.

Solstizio includes poetry written between 1930 and 1932. The Ciociaria he left behind is seen as a happy place. The landscape has the splendor of "arida luce" (arid light), under a sun that is "un'arida pietra" (an arid stone); in a valley where the river flows, olive trees and oranges grow, and the women work in the fields. There are a crowing rooster, partridges, crows, swallows, sparrows, and flocks of sheep. De Libero elevates humble creatures to the level of pure lyric. The images are simple and clear, based on the immediate perception of the real. Personifications are common devices of his style, which radiates with natural energy. Ciociaria is to him a sun-

Frontispiece for De Libero's 1959 novel

bitten land that gives life to stones and song to the birds; the land is dry and rough, yet gentle and giving, as in "Per un aprile" (For an April):

> Il sole è un'arida pietra
> stamane e per me si ripete
> il tempo di rondini
> novelle di altri paesi
> come acqua fresca alla mano.

> (The sun is an arid stone
> this morning and I experience again
> the time of the new swallows
> born in other countries,
> like fresh water on my hand.)

The collection *Proverbi*, which includes poems written from 1932 to 1934, was published in 1937, followed by *Testa* (Head, 1939), with verses from 1934 to 1936. In these two collections De Libero continues his voyage through the familiar landscape, through the contrast between opposites: hot-cold, summer-winter, white-black, sun-moon, night-day. The animal and the plant worlds are again part of his imagery, as in the poem "Cicala" (Cicada) from *Proverbi*: "Stagione immensa di pianura, / estate, / la cicala non vuole foresta, / sulla pietra è lamento di lunga / arsura (Immense season of the plain, / summer, / the cicada does not want the forest, / on the stone is the lament of a long / heat).

The second poem of *Testa*, "Elegia a Fondi" (Elegy to Fondi) further expresses De Libero's attachment to his native land. He returns not to seek comfort and peace but to nurture the familiar, to soak in the flavor of a nature that alone possesses things in their original essence. He perceives the wildness of the landscape as a natural chaos, which he orders within himself into happy or painful memories, into a nostalgic journey through his youth. He becomes one with nature, and this nature-soul interrelationship originates from his bonds with his native land, which he sees as a part of nature in its broadest sense. De Libero's search for images does not stop at those that ferment within the self and go no further than serving themselves, as in hermetic poetry; his images reveal his emotions, painful experiences, and past sufferings. *Testa* employs much imagery based on reality.

In the poem "Valle etrusca" (Etruscan Valley) the speaker deals with death. De Libero does not see it as a destructive force that annuls life. On the contrary, he perceives it as a part of life, as the end and the beginning of another cycle of neverending movement and continuing existence:

Della morte è ironico il vino
bevuto a sorsi di anni
e ogni seme sempre rimatura
per un cielo ignoto e fioco.
Quale uccello sinistro
il sole non è nominato
nella patria eterna dei morti.

(The irony of death is the wine
drunk in sips of the years
and every seed matures again
in an unknown and dim sky.
Like an ominous bird
the sun is not named
in the eternal homeland of the dead.)

The following two collections, *Eclisse* (Eclipse, 1940) and *Epigrammi 1938*, published in 1942, include the poetry written from 1936 to 1938 and are based on De Libero's experience of love. *Eclisse* embodies his emotions after the death of his beloved, whom he elevates post-mortem in the same way he does the sun and the moon, the mountains, and the rivers. De Libero and his beloved are drawn together by nature, merged with it, surrounded by forces comparable in strength to their feelings. Love for De Libero is not a celestial feeling embodied in one's soul but rather a terrestrial experience that finds its expression in a spontaneous unification with nature. Love for a woman is part of overall love for nature, and its glorification and invocation is a component of De Libero's communication with the material world. The poetic language of metaphors helps achieve this interaction of soul and nature, resulting in a vivid, familiar imagery expressing intense emotions, as in the poem "Eri la montagna che dice" (You Were the Mountain that Tells):

Eri la montagna che dice
la storia del giorno,
anche la notte tu eri
lenta all'aurora,

quasi un banchetto
ove non saziano i vini.
Ora la volpe è despota alla vigna,
la collina non vuole piú luna:
un triste paese la collina
ora che il nostro regno è decaduto.

(You were the mountain that tells
the story of the day,
you were also the night
slow in approaching dawn,
like a banquet
where the wines do not satisfy.
Now the fox is a despot in the vineyard,
the hill no longer wants the moon:
a sad place is the hill
now that our kingdom has fallen.)

De Libero's *Il libro del forestiero* (The Book of the Foreigner), which includes poems written from 1938 to 1942, was published in 1945. In this collection he tries to break away further from the hermetic tradition of the 1930s. His imagery still remains in the realm of the naturalistic, but his style acquires a narrative quality. The poems are tales of De Libero's youth spent in Ciociaria, narrated memories of familiar faces and the beloved woman, the history of an existence surrounded and protected by the known. There is a recognizable landscape, the tangible images of natural scenes from which a human figure emerges. The familiar house indicates "un mitico luogo della memoria" (a mythical place of the memory), as Gaetano Mariani describes it. Furthermore, it symbolizes well-defined boundaries, which offer a sense of security and abandon. As the mountains protect De Libero's valleys, so, too, the house shelters his soul. The places and things assume almost mythical proportions, with their secrets discovered, with the veil over them lifted, revealing the primal images stored in the poet's memory and heart.

The landscape of De Libero's Ciociaria assumes human qualities in the same way, as people naturally blend into it by recognizing the essence of things. Poems such as "Amici" (Friends), "Ritorno a Patrica" (The Return to Patrica), "Allodola" (Skylark), "Presso una pietra" (By a Stone), and "Un giorno a Formia" (One Day in Formia) express De Libero's relationship with his native land, a promised land of returns, not just to the physical reality of the land, but into the intimacy of the poet's psyche, too.

In *Banchetto* (Banquet, 1949), which includes poems dated from 1942 to 1945, De Libero extends his human experiences to a broader, more general and humanistic plane. His love for Ciociaria is transformed into a love for all of Italy, as in the poem "O mia patria in tutti i pensieri" (O My Country in All My Thoughts). New visions and perceptions of history change De Libero's poetry from one of pronounced lyric and subtle personal emotions into a poetry of social involvement. The human suffering during World War II urged him to look around himself rather than turn inwardly, as the hermetic poets had done. De Libero saw the horror of war, deaths, losses, and defeats, and this caused him to see himself as a part of humanity and no longer an individual looking for comfort in nature yet suffering in love. Sarcasm and irony express De Libero's negative feelings about the war. He sees it as a pointless conflict in which everybody loses. In the first part of *Banchetto*, entitled "O patria mia," his compassion has obviously been extended to the whole of Italy. The narrative quality in *Il libro del forestiero* is to be found in *Banchetto* as well. He feels the defeat of Italy, and the vertiginous motion common to many of his poems is even more pronounced in the latter collection.

The poem "Scende l'Italia" (Italy Descends) speaks of the country's downfall. In the long narrative poem "Settembre tedesco" (German September) De Libero describes the killing of a young boy, Claudio Bin, who was shot by a German guard: "fu ucciso col mitra perché rideva" (he was killed with the machine gun because he laughed). De Libero feels deeply the senselessness of the death of the child. His pain does not involve only a boy but the German soldier, who also has no control over events. In this way the poem shifts from a personal to a universal perspective. De Libero concludes that faith is a quality of lasting importance in human life. Claudio's death occupies an instant in history, like any other death. Realism is accentuated by the poem's being situated in a concrete time and place.

In the poem "Il morto soldato" (The Dead Soldier) De Libero lets the "io" (I) of the dead soldier speak. The soldier observes and describes his own senseless death. The surrealism and the grotesque qualities of this poem revolve around the image of the soldier's amputated hand that the poet compares to the last fruit falling from a branch. The poem culminates in two questions: "Dove si va? Per chi si muore?" (Where do we go? For whom are we dying?).

In the second part of the collection, "Versi neri" (Black Verses), the immediate experience of World War II takes De Libero back in history to 1920, when he lost someone close to him. This flashback results in a long poem, "Proprio un mattino d'aprile" (It Happened One Morning in April).

Ascolta la Ciociaria (Listen to Ciociaria), published in 1953, embraces the ominous feelings of belonging and the loyalty of De Libero to his motherland, which receives him back as a son. In this collection De Libero evokes Ciociaria and displays his love for it. He knows its geography in detail, is familiar with its animal and horticultural world, has followed its history, sees its present, loves its people, and participates in its everyday existence. De Libero also evokes Ciociaria in another poem of return, "Celeste creatura" (Celestial Creature), from the 1969 collection *Sono uno di voi* (I Am One of You). In this poem his native land resembles an open market, where everything has its place: farmers, young girls, old maids, mothers, births, deaths, and marriages; in unity with nature, they form an eternal natural circle.

Sono uno di voi contains poetry written from 1945 to 1956. It is divided into six parts, which offer a variety of themes: war, memories, familiar faces, and Ciociaria itself. The collection is based on the movement from the universal, that which belongs to the experience of all humanity, to De Libero's personal experience in his wartorn native land, and ultimately to his intimate pain. The style of the collection varies as well: from the initial dark, gloomy, violent imagery of the world that has been destroyed in the war—as in the poem "Per gli uccisi alle Fosse Ardeatine" (For Those Killed at the Fosse Ardeatine): "il mondo giace come un bambino ucciso" (the world lies like a murdered child)—to images from family life, as in the poem "Mio fratello e altre rondini" (My Brother and Other Swallows); to the landscape of his land that knows him as well as he knows every single part of it, as in "Lettera d'estate" (Summer Letter). The first part of the collection concentrates on a network of symbolic words and colors, such as *carcere* (prison), *grotte* (cave), *nero* (black), *requiem*, and *funerale*, which creates the atmosphere of hopelessness, the suffering of all humankind at war. De Libero achieves in those poems an interesting balance between grotesque images of dark and doom and natural images, which soften the

Page from the manuscript for De Libero's unpublished poem "Con l'autunno" (from Storia della letteratura, *volume 7, edited by Luigi Ferrante, 1965)*

impact of war's violence but do not lessen the intensity of the poet's vision.

In "Mio fratello e altre rondini" De Libero remembers his dead brother; the familiar figure appears in a picturesque setting, where nature vibrates in the initial verses and then becomes modulated, finally ending in the pain of death and loss. In the poem "Sono uno di voi" De Libero identifies himself with others who live the same existence and share the same experience. The common human need to belong gives the poem a universal meaning. "Sono uno di voi" ends with the conclusion that man's will is always overcome by chance: "la certezza d'essere ció che vogliamo / non muta verso al dado che decide" (the certainty to be what we want to be / does not change the throw of the dice that decides). De Libero's certainty and a sense of stability came from his returns to Ciociaria, which filled him with new strength.

De Libero's collection *Romanzo* (Novel) was published in 1965, and contains love poems written from 1934 to 1955, which appeared earlier in the separate collections or as parts of a larger collection, and the unpublished poems written from 1945 to 1955. Some of the poems were taken from *Solstizio*, *Proverbi*, and *Banchetto*. Also included are the complete *Eclisse* and *Il libro del forestiero*. *Romanzo* was awarded the Ibico Reggino prize for poetry in 1965.

In 1967 the Belgian literary magazine *Origine* published eight of De Libero's poems in a group entitled *Madrigali*, some of which had appeared at an earlier date, and for which De Libero was given the Vann'Antò award in 1968, under the auspices of the Università di Messina. The first two poems, "Per una ragazza virtuosa di giorno" (For a Girl Who Is Virtuous during the Day) and "Per una signora culturale" (For a Cultural Lady), are satirical, as were some of his earlier works. This satire alternates with the madrigal, creating an unusual amalgamation of verses, a juxtaposition between metaphorical and realistic images.

The five central madrigals focus on the theme of lost love. The dismal tone of these poems is created by contrasts: hope/desolation, flame/ashes, and so on.

Di brace in brace (From Embers to Embers) was published in 1971 and won the Viareggio prize the same year. It contains poems from the period 1956 to 1970. Existence in all its various forms is the unifying element of the poems— existence first in a personal sense, then in the sense of love that extends toward those close to us. The poet's recollection of people who are more alive in memory than in proximity, a major theme of De Libero's poetry, is evident in this collection as well. The poet is a traveler through space and time, noting any new meeting on a train or in the street. The remembrance of the past is part of his existential itinerary. The landscape is no longer located solely in Ciociaria. There are poems dedicated to England and Japan, for which he feels a deep affection. In spite of a past rich with lasting memories and present encounters that stimulate new interests, existence for De Libero is an instant, ending in ashes, as in "Conversazione notturna" (Night Conversation):

Passioni e desideri ho messo in gabbia
con la pica dei loro sogni,
sono arrivato dove ogni porta è sfinge
o tranello e Sesamo è vana preghiera.

(Passions and desires I put in the cage
with the magpie of their dreams,
I have come to where every door is a sphinx
or a trap and Sesame is an empty prayer.)

Scempio e lusinga (Havoc and Delusion, 1972) comprises poems written from 1930 to 1956 (*Solstizio*, *Proverbi*, *Testa*, *Eclisse*, *Il libro del forestiero*, *Banchetto*, and *Sono uno di voi*). The collection *Circostanze* (Circumstances) was published in 1976, and includes poetry written between 1971 and 1975. The verses flow, uninterrupted by punctuation, following their descendant course toward the final conclusion that life consists of pursuing shadows and ends in solitude, a life lived between escapes and returns. One is both free and a slave of oneself. The interplay between past and present and the consequently contrasting images are featured in the poetry of this collection. De Libero's last collection, *Poesie*, was published in 1980 and includes poetry from *Solstizio*, *Proverbi*, *Testa*, *Eclisse*, *Il libro del forestiero*, *Banchetto*, *Sono uno di voi*, *Di brace in brace*, and *Circostanze*.

De Libero's literary activity was not limited to poetry but was also extended to narrative. As a prose writer he tried to find new ways of expression, different from his poetic language, but the two often overlap. His narrative has its own merits regarding style and subject matter, which is often autobiographical, but his poetic flair cannot be overlooked. His prose works include the short stories in *Malumore* (1945), the novels *Amo-*

re e morte (Love and Death, 1951), *Camera oscura* (Dark Room, 1952), *Valéry parente illustre* (Valery the Famous Relative, 1955), *Il guanto nero* (Black Glove, 1959), and *Racconti alla finestra* (Stories at the Window, 1969).

Bibliography:

Giuseppe Apella and Vanni Scheiwiller, eds., *Un poeta come De Libero: Iconografia e bibliografia di L. De Libero* (Rome: Società Tipografica Italia, 1977).

References:

Elio Filippo Accrocca, *Ritratti su misura* (Venice: Sodalizio del Libro, 1960), pp. 155-157;

Enrico Falqui, "Per i madrigali di Libero de Libero," *Nuova Antologia*, 503 (June 1968): 212-216;

Oreste Macrì, *Caratteri e figure della poesia italiana contemporanea* (Florence: Vallecchi, 1956), pp. 233-252;

Giuliano Manacorda, *Letteratura italiana d'oggi 1965-1985* (Rome: Riuniti, 1987), pp. 44-46;

Gaetano Mariani, *Letteratura italiana: I contemporanei*, volume 3 (Milan: Marzorati, 1969), pp. 535-558;

Gianni Pozzi, *La poesia italiana del Novecento da Gozzano agli ermetici* (Turin: Einaudi, 1965), pp. 276-280;

Silvio Ramat, *Storia della poesia italiana del Novecento* (Milan: Mursia, 1976), pp. 432-435;

Sergio Solmi, *Scrittori negli anni* (Milan: Saggiatore, 1963), pp. 225-227.

Alfonso Gatto
(17 July 1909 - 8 March 1976)

Clara Orban
De Paul University

BOOKS: *Isola* (Naples: Libreria del '900, 1932);

Morto ai paesi (Modena: Guanda, 1937);

Poesie (Milan: Panorama, 1939); enlarged as *Poesie, 1929-1941* (Milan: Mondadori, 1961; enlarged, 1972);

Disegni di Ottone Rosai (Venice: Cavallino, 1939);

Luigi Broggini scultore (Milan: Milione, 1940);

Ottone Rosai (Florence: Vallecchi, 1941);

L'allodola (Milan: All'Insegna del Pesce D'Oro, 1943);

La spòsa bambina (Florence: Vallecchi, 1943; revised and enlarged, 1963);

Virgilio Guidi pittore (Milan: Milione, 1943);

Dodici opere di Virgilio Guidi (Milan: Milione, 1944);

La spiaggia dei poveri (Milan: Rosa & Ballo, 1944);

Amore della vita (Milan: Rosa & Ballo, 1944);

Il duello (Milan: Rosa & Ballo, 1944);

Il sigaro di fuoco (Milan: Bompiani, 1945);

Virgilio Guidi (Milan: Hoepli, 1947);

Il capo sulla neve (Milan: Milano-sera, 1947);

La coda di paglia (Milan: Milano-sera, 1949);

Nuove poesie, 1941-1949 (Milan: Mondadori, 1950);

La forza degli occhi: Poesie (1950-1953) (Milan: Mondadori, 1954);

Allegretto: Poesie inedite (Milan: Fuori Commercio delle Officine D'Arte Grafiche Lucini, 1957);

Disegni di Spreafico (Milan: Garzanti, 1958);

La madre e la morte (Galatina, Italy: Critone, 1959);

Osteria flegrea (Milan: Mondadori, 1962);

Carlomagno nella grotta (Milan: Mondadori, 1962);

Il vaporetto (Milan: Nuova Accademia, 1963);

La storia delle vittime: Poesie della Resistenza (Milan: Mondadori, 1966);

Cagli (Parma: Nuova STEP, 1967);

Mario Mostra di Sironi (Milan: Moneta, 1969);

Rime di viaggio per la terra dipinta (Milan: Mondadori, 1969);

Cézanne (Milan: Rizzoli, 1970);

Poesie d'amore: 1941-'49, 1960-'72 (Milan: Mondadori, 1973);

Le piscine lustrali di Sergio Vacchi (Bologna: Bora, 1974);

Alfonso Gatto circa 1963

Napoli N.N. (Florence: Vallecchi, 1974);

Le ore piccole (Salerno: Catalogo, 1975);

Lapide 1975 ed altre cose (Genoa: Giustiniani, 1976);

Desinenze, 1974-1976 (Milan: Mondadori, 1977).

OTHER: Giuseppe Marco Antonio Baretti, *Oga Magoga*, edited by Gatto (Milan: Muggiani, 1944).

In the varied panorama of styles and movements that characterize twentieth-century Italian literature, Alfonso Gatto cannot be firmly anchored to one movement because he was influenced by several. His poetry is, however, some of the finest from the years between the two world wars. His early poetry shows the influence of surrealism, and his sometimes dense language and imagery group him with the hermetic school of poetry. Ernestina Pellegrino sensed in his work "i toni di un certo crepuscolarismo . . . in quel-l'insistenza della 'sera,' ora 'armoniosa,' ora 'tranquilla' " (the tones of a certain crepuscularism in that insistence on "evening," which is at times "harmonious," at others "tranquil"). Gatto's lyric tone and subject matter are personal and varied, but he was not an innovator of forms, preferring to concentrate on typical Italian meter. In an autobiographical article published in *La Fiera letteraria*, he described his poetry: "le mie rime e il mio modo di usare metri tradizionali quali l'endecasillabo e il settenario, credo si hanno da interpretare nel valore di un 'canto' che supera e brucia ogni residuo tecnico, quasi a dare l'apertura e la durata della voce. Son rime di gravitazione" (my rhymes and my way of using traditional meter such as the hendecasyllable and the septenary, I believe must be interpreted as a 'song' that rises above and burns all technical residue, as if to give the voice an opening and make it durable. They are rhymes of gravitation). He purposely chose traditional meter to underscore content rather than form.

Alfonso Gatto was born on 17 July 1909 in Salerno into a Calabrian family of sailors and owners of small ships. His connection to the Italian South is evident in his poetic imagery, with its profusion of sunshine and warmth. After secondary school, in 1926, he enrolled in the Faculty of Letters of the University of Naples but did not finish his degree. He spent several years doing a variety of jobs, including those of book salesman and editor, before embarking on an important phase of his literary life. In 1934 he moved north to Milan, where he became a journalist, collaborating with Edoard Persico on the review *Casabella*, an avant-garde publication that defended new architecture. During this period of his life in Milan, Gatto was in contact with the nonconformist intellectuals of the Craja café, which was characterized by him as "Quasi una piccola stazione contemplativa da cui partire per l'Europa illuminata lontana per noi come un astro di Klee . . . (Almost like a small contemplative station from which to embark for enlightened Europe, as far from us as a Klee star . . .). Journalism was to remain a constant activity for Gatto, and he was alternately associated with several papers: *Ambrosiano; Settimana; Milano Sera*, of which he was coeditor; and *L'Unità*, the Communist daily for which he was a special correspondent.

His political conscience during these years was becoming ever more acute, and he was actively involved in the Resistance during the war. In 1936 he was incarcerated in San Vittore in Milan for his political views. The poet remembers these six months as a time of extreme introspection and reassessment of his life, solidifying his resolve to engage in public service, which led him to join the Communist party. Although he later left the party, he remained a dedicated activist.

During the Milanese years his first book of poetry, *Isola* (Island, 1932), was published and included poems from 1929 to 1932. Silvio Ramat (in *Dizionario critico della letteratura italiana*, volume two, 1986) characterized these prose and verse poems as "già contraddistinti da quella pienezza di melodie che sarà sempre specifica della sua arte" (already unique in that fullness of melody that will always be specific to his art). Melody and the musical aspects of poetry would continue to be central to Gatto's work. His poetry often concerns death, as contrasted to life in all its mutability. Poetry is the fixed point in this universe where time can stand still. The first and last poems of *Isola* vividly underscore these

Cover, designed by Gatto, for a collection of his World War II prose and poetry

themes. The first poem, "Poesia," speaks of the loneliness of the poet, who cannot find happiness, even briefly. The only opening in this closed circle of life is poetry, which both creates space for him and isolates him:

> In ogni gioia breve e netta scorgo il mio
>   pericolo.
> Circolo chiuso ad ogni essere è l'amore che lo
>   regge.
> Tendo a questo dubbio intero, a un divieto in cui
> cogliere il sospetto e la lusinga del mio
>   movimento.
> Universo che mi spazia e m'isola, poesia.
>
> (In every brief and spotless joy I discern my
>   peril.
> A closed circle to every being is the love that
>   supports it.
> I lean toward this whole doubt, to a prohibition
>   in which
> to gather the suspicion and the flattery of my
>   movement.
> Universe that gives me space and isolates me,
>   poetry.)

"Isola" on the other hand, the last poem of the collection, opens up the horizon before the reader who has made the journey through the poems:

> Or nella solitaria
> cadenza d'un approdo
> svanita la memoria
> al suo tepore effusa,
> esula bianca l'isola
> la brezza del mio cielo.

> (Now in the solitary
> cadence of a landing place
> the memory gone
> to its diffused tepidness,
> the white island lies outside
> the breeze of my sky.)

Isola spurred much critical discourse, including one of the first articles written on Gatto by Eugenio Montale (*Pegaso*, May 1933), who finds it to be an "espressione di un temperamento autentico ma ancora saturo di altrui esperienze, di altrui voci" (an expression of an authentic temperament, but still saturated with the experiences of others, with the voices of others). Gatto's ideas of the universe and the saving grace of poetry recall Giuseppe Ungaretti's poem "Mattino" (Morning): "m'illumino / d'immenso" (I illuminate myself / with immensity). Giuliano Manacorda in 1967 also saw in this first book by Gatto accents of Giovanni Pascoli. In terms of style, Gianfranco Contini says that Gatto's "immagini sono vertiginosamente analogiche, sia nelle singole metafore, sia soprattutto nelle loro connessioni" (images are dizzyingly analogical, be it in the single metaphors, be it above all in their connections). But this is in contrast to the regular syntax of these poems, which is relatively rich, with complex traditional rhythms. This modulation of syntax lends pathos to the sound of Gatto's poetic voice.

These poems were written during the years of surrealist influence. André Breton had inaugurated the movement in 1924 with the *Manifest du Surréalisme* and had refined his ideas in the second manifesto, published in 1930. Gatto's poetry shows a certain affinity to the core concerns of surrealism—perhaps most evident in the poem "Notte" (Night):

> Tremo l'esile vena per lontane
> arie di suono, mi lusingo in volto.
> Come alleviate toccano le vane
> solitudini il cielo vuoto, ascolto.

> (I tremble the thin vein in far
> zones of sound, I flatter myself to my face.
> As though relieved, the useless solitudes touch
> the empty sky, I listen.)

The atmosphere of dream worlds provides the central tone of the poem. Gatto's style, though never surrealist in its purest sense, is replete with surprising juxtaposed images and syntagms, similar to those found in Breton's and Paul Eluard's poetry. Contini suggests that Gatto's surrealism was different from others in that it "indulge di rado alla frase nominale e all'immediatezza in largo senso interiettiva e onomatopoeica" (rarely indulges in nominal phrases and, in a broad sense, in interjective and onomatopeic immediacy). Contini hypothesized that these instincts were extinguished in Italy in the futurist and *Lacerba* movements. Adriano Seroni sees in *Isola* an autobiography of sorts, where the poet desperately seeks a terra firma of reality, which he perhaps will not find.

In 1937 Gatto's second volume of poetry, *Morto ai paesi* (Dead in the Countries), was published. *Morto ai paesi*, which encompasses the poems from 1933 to 1937, presents an interconnection of voices and themes from other southern poets, such as Vincenzo Cardarelli and Salvatore Di Giacomo. Absence is death, a typical binomial ploy of the hermetic school. The poet's persona is more vivid; he is one who more confidently speaks out. The general vision of the world is more concrete than in *Isola*. Children are often topics of *Morto ai paesi*, but among the happier memories of childhood there is much sadness, as in this stanza of the title poem, where the poet encounters a happy child who dies:

> Il bambino festoso dove muore
> nel suo grido fa sera
> e nel silenzio trova bianco odore
> di madre, la leggera
> sembianza del suo volto.

> (where the festive child dies
> in his cry the night grows dark
> and in the silence he finds the white odor
> of mother, the light
> semblance of her face.)

There is another tender note in the poem "Alla mia bambina" (To My Little Girl), where Gatto recalls the vision of the daughter whose birth made him feel complete. Life and death are thus intertwined in *Morto ai paesi*, images of loss and of rebirth, of searching and longing.

Although Gatto never stopped writing poetry, in the years subsequent to *Morto ai paesi* he engaged in important literary criticism. In 1938 he joined Vasco Pratolini in codirecting the literary review *Campo di Marte* in Florence. This journal, which lasted until 1939, was one of the most hotly contested of its time. The notion of absence, which had until then remained within the scope of poetic imagery, took on overtones of political resistance. Ramat identifies another guideword of that generation—*attesa*—which means "waiting." Ramat points out that this word has a "valore schiettamente esistenziale" (an obvious existential value), which guarantees single-handedly the future of young people caught between the two wars, in the age of anxiety. *Campo di Marte* tried to reconcile popular traditions with the rather aristocratic tendencies of the hermetics. The name *Campo di Marte* refers to a peripheral area of Florence where workers lived, so by its title alone the authors sought to emphasize the geographic and physical union between the two socioeconomic classes (lower and upper).

Gatto produced several collections of poetry during this period. In 1939 *Poesie* was published. Here Gatto took a noticeably different turn from his Florentine colleagues whose poetry was dense with complex syntax and images. Gatto instead focused on personal inspiration and interconnections. *Poesie* shows a break with the spirit of isolation that characterizes *Isola*. The poet was moving toward reality.

These years also saw the publication of Gatto's first prose work, *La spòsa bambina* (The Childish Wife, 1943), a reflection on the grief of existence and on death seen through the eyes of children. He emphasized the South, which remained an important theme in his books. Of his beloved land, Gatto said: "Il nostro è stato sempre un paese distrutto" (ours has always been a country destroyed). However, as was the case in *Isola*, literature can give hope: "Io leggo questo libro e qualcosa di me è passato, che vive" (I read this book and something of me that has passed still lives). Gatto's South is a land from which people emigrate, a place of broken continuity, but one in which there is an eternal thread.

Other collections of prose and poetry from this period of Gatto's career are *La spiaggia dei poveri* (The Shores of the Poor, 1944) and *Amore della vita* (Love of Life, 1944). In the poem

"Amore di vita" he reaffirms the need to live, to embrace life under any circumstances:

> Tornerà, tornerà
> d'un balzo il cuore
> desto
> avrà parole?
> Chi amerà le cose, le luci, i vivi?
>
> I morti, i vinti, chi li desterà?
>
> (He will return, he will return
> with a leap of the heart
> roused
> will he have words?
> Who will love things, lights, the living?
>
> The dead, the vanquished, who will wake them?)

Il capo sulla neve (Head on the Snow, 1947) is made up of poems published clandestinely during the war. It was republished together with *Amore della vita*, "Giornale di due inverni" (Journal of Two Winters), and "La storia delle vittime" (The Story of the Victims) in the 1966 volume also titled *La storia delle vittime*, encompassing poetry from 1944 to 1965. These poems are all linked by a common theme of insurrection and the will to live even under the most horrid conditions, no doubt poems inspired by the anti-Fascist movements. In *Il capo sulla neve* "Anniversario," which many believe to be one of Gatto's greatest poems, is dedicated to those who died in the war:

> Oh, L'Europa gelata nel suo cuore
> mai più si scalderà: sola, coi morti
> che l'amano in eterno, sarà bianca
> senza confini, unita dalla neve.
>
> (Oh, heart-frozen Europe
> will never again be warm: alone with the dead
> that love it eternally, it will be white
> without borders, united by snow.)

After the war *Nuove poesie* (1950) and *La forza degli occhi* (The Strength of Eyes, 1954) indicated Gatto's continued interest in fusing autobiographical elements with moral and civic duties as affirmed by the Resistance. *Nuove poesie* collects the poems from 1941 to 1949, and *La forza degli occhi* those from 1950 to 1953. Soon after the liberation of Italy, Gatto had published a book of poetry for children, *Il sigaro di fuoco* (Cigar of Fire, 1945).

Gatto and his wife with their son, Leone, at their house in Milan

In 1962 Gatto published *Osteria flegrea* (Phlegraean Tavern), containing poems from 1954 to 1962, which are dedicated to a "serene contemplation of death." Many of these poems focus on his mother, who died on 3 November 1958. An entire section of *Osteria flegrea* is titled *La madre e la morte* (separately published in 1959). The scenes of his beloved South appear in some poems, but they are not the warm environs of the stereotypical South; rather, they are suspended in fog and in the cold wind of impending winter. For Gatto the South is a journey in space as well as time. He returned to his native land—the Phlegraean Fields being an area near Naples—and continued to write about death and the meaning of existence. In *Osteria flegrea* the season is autumn, the tone somber and withdrawn. Simultaneously with this collection, Gatto published perhaps his best prose work, *Carlomagno nella grotta* (Charlemagne in the Cave), a series of essays and stories, which also examines the South.

In the important 1966 collection, *La storia delle vittime*, Gatto reassesses his role in the Resistance and the very notion of resistance. As he says in the preface to that collection: "Che cosa è stata la Resistenza? 'Resistere' significa contrastare una forza che agisce contro di noi, che

minaccia di superarci e che ci invita a cedere. 'Resistere' significa durare al limite della nostra tenacia e della nostra pazienza fisica. È una prova che scegliamo nell'atto di essere, di convincimento interiore per una ragione ultima" (What was the Resistance? "To resist" means to fight a force that acts against us, that threatens to take us over and invites us to capitulate. To resist means to endure to the limits of our strength and of our physical patience. We choose it as a test of the act of being, driven by the inner conviction of an ultimate Reason). The symbol of this struggle to survive was, for Gatto, Hiroshima, remembered in his "Sei Agosto" (August Sixth):

Era un giorno del tempo, un mattino d'estate
e ventilava il mare aperto il suo rigoglio.
Diranno ancora "amate" i poeti di corte
e la fede che prospera più cieca dell'orgoglio?
Quel giorno a Hiroshima fu decisa la morte.
Ora, se parla l'uomo, quale voce credente
avrà la sua nel chiedere la fede che spergiura?
Quel giorno a Hiroshima tutto si ebbe in niente
del suo poter, l'empio mai fu così pietoso. . . ."

(It was a day in time, a summer morning
and the open sea fanned its vigor.
Will the court poets still tell us to "love,"
    encouraging
a faith that prospers more blind than pride?

A meeting of hermetic poets in 1958: Mario Luzi, Luigi Fallacara, Carlo Beteachi, Gatto, and Oreste Macrì

That day at Hiroshima, death was decided.
Now if man speaks, with what believing voice
will he be able to ask for the faith that perjures?
That day at Hiroshima everything became nothing
in its power, the impious was never so pitiful . . .).

Gatto was also an accomplished painter, and certain poems, such as "Natura morta" ("Still Life"), and his 1969 collection of poetry *Rime di viaggio per la terra dipinta* (Travel Poems Through the Painted Land) reflect this interest. In his introduction to the section as reprinted in the 1972 edition of *Poesie*, Gatto said, "qui, su queste pagine scritte, sulle altre per acqua trasparenti al segno e al colore, ancora di me si tramanda l'immagine che mi precede e mi aspetta" (here, on these written pages, on the others transparent to sign and color by water, the image which precedes and awaits me is passed on). These poems often have as their themes colors, painting, and the city of Venice, all seen as through a prism of forms and shades.

Gatto's last novel was *Napoli N.N.* (1974), a nostalgic look at his hometown from the perspective of one who has emigrated. It is a last look at his beloved South from the eyes of one who now wishes to sing the praises of his land.

Gatto died in an automobile accident in Orbetello (in the Grosseto region) in 1976 before he could prepare his last collection of poetry. In *Desinenze* (Ending), published posthumously in 1977, death returns as the final point of a voyage. These poems were dedicated to his friend Paolo Maria Minucci. Almost as an eerie foreboding of Gatto's death, the last poem of the collection, written the night before he was killed, is dedicated to death:

una striscia d'azzurro sull'argento
del cielo, alla mia gola con la mano
(stretto) senza più voce mi trovai col mento.

Non ricordavo il sonno, era passata
la notte sulla ghiaia dei miei denti.

(A blue stripe on the silver
sky, at my throat with my hand
[tight] without a voice I found myself with my chin.

I didn't remember sleep, the night had passed
on the pebbles of my teeth.)

Throughout his life, as well as being a poet, journalist, and literary critic, Gatto was an art critic. In 1939 he wrote an art monograph about the drawings of Ottone Rosai, a friend whose work Gatto often analyzed. He wrote about other modern artists as well, including Luigi Broggini, Virgilio Guidi, Mario Sironi, Sergio Vacchi, and Paul Cézanne, among others.

Gatto was awarded several literary prizes, including the Savini (1939), the Saint-Vincent (1948), the Marzotto (1954), the Bagutta (1956), the Rustichello da Pisa (1960), the Napoli (1960), the Elba (1962), and the Viareggio (1966). Alfonso Gatto added an unusual voice to the Italian literary landscape of the twentieth century. In his autobiographical article in *La Fiera letteraria*, he describes an artist as one who "medita l'estrema espressività delle cose, di tutte le cose, la loro identità diretta, plenaria, direi la loro natura squallida buona e sufficiente" (meditates on the extreme expressivity of things, of all things, on their direct, full identity, I would say in fact their very nature, squalid, good and sufficient). Gatto did this in all his literary and critical work.

Interview:

Ferdinando Camon, *Il mestiere di poeta* (Milan: Garzanti, 1982), pp. 81-99.

Biography:

Bortolo Pento, *Alfonso Gatto* (Florence: Nuova Italia, 1972).

References:

P. Borrero and F. D'Episcopo, eds., *Atti del convegno nazionale di studi su A. Gatto, Salerno-Mairore-Amalfi, 1978* (Galatina, Italy: Congedo, 1980);

Gianfranco Contini, *Storia della letteratura dell'Italia Unita, 1861-1968* (Florence: Sansoni, 1968), p. 919;

La Cultura italiana negli anni '30-'45: Omaggio ad Alfonso Gatto. Atti del convegno: Salerno, 21-24 aprile, 1980 (Naples: Scientifiche Italiane, 1984);

Giuseppe De Robertis, *Scrittori del Novecento* (Florence: Monnier, 1940), pp. 355-359;

Giansiro Ferrata, ed., *La Fiera Letteraria*, special Gatto issue, 10 (25 December 1955);

Franco Fortini, "Da Ungaretti agli Ermetici," in *La letteratura italiana: Storia e testi*, volume 9 (Bari, Italy: Laterza, 1976), pp. 299-349;

Oreste Macrì, *Esemplari del sentimento poetico contemporaneo* (Florence: Vallecchi, 1941), pp. 155-172;

Giuliano Manacorda, "Alfonso Gatto," *Belfagor*, 22 (1968): 325-347;

Manacorda, *Storia della letteratura italiana contemporanea (1940-1965)* (Rome: Riuniti, 1967);

Pier Vincenzo Mengaldo, *Poeti italiani del Novecento* (Milan: Mondadori, 1981), pp. 607-611;

Ernestina Pellegrino, *Poeti italiani del Novecento*, general editor Giorgio Luti (Rome: Nuova Italia Scientifica, 1985), pp. 85-88;

Adriano Seroni, *Ragioni critiche* (Florence: Vallecchi, 1944), pp. 111-121.

Virgilio Giotti
(Virgilio Schönbeck)
(15 January 1885 - 21 September 1957)

Fiora A. Bassanese
University of Massachusetts—Boston

BOOKS: *Piccolo canzoniere in dialetto triestino* (Florence: Gonnelli, 1914);

Il mio cuore e la mia casa (Trieste: Libreria Antica e Moderna, 1920);

Caprizzi, canzonete e storie (Florence: Solaria, 1928);

Liriche e idilli (Florence: Solaria, 1931);

Colori (Florence: Parenti, 1941); enlarged as *Colori: Tute quante le poesie* (Padua, Italy: Tre Venezie, 1943); revised as *Colori* (Milan & Naples: Ricciardi, 1957; enlarged edition, Milan: Longanesi, 1972);

Sera (Turin: De Silva, 1948);

Versi (Trieste: Zibaldone, 1953);

Appunti inutili (1946-1955) (Trieste: Zibaldone, 1959);

Racconti (Trieste: Svevo, 1977);

Poesie escluse, edited by Roberto Damiani (Trieste: Cassa di Risparmio, 1978);

Opere: Colori; Altre poesie; Prose, edited by Rinaldo Derossi, Elvio Guagnini, and Bruno Maier (Trieste: Lint, 1986).

Virgilio Giotti

In Italy, with its long tradition of fostering an official literary language, the poet who chose to compose in dialect invited limited diffusion, critical avoidance, and public silence. Such a fate befell Virgilio Giotti, whose extraordinary verse sings only in the idiom of his native city, Trieste. Giotti's dialect is a chosen *langage*, an instrument of efficient self-expression devoid of the folksy picturesqueness often associated with regional writers. In fact, the poet's language is not the local koine but a somewhat archaic, personalized, and rarified version of the "Triestino" dialect. As noted critic Gianfranco Contini has pointed out: "Giotti è forse il primo dialettale in cui il dialetto non abbia nulla di veramente vernacolo" (Perhaps Giotti is the first regional [writer] whose dialect is not at all vernacular). His verse is restrained, measured, and devoid of the superflu-

ous. Trieste's most celebrated dialect poet also composed in Italian, but these compositions never reach the succinctness and power of his dialect works, although Giotti's basic themes remain singularly consistent through the decades. His verse demonstrates an ability to absorb external currents without, in turn, being absorbed by them: there are traces of major Italian literary movements but no clear adherence to any one model.

Giotti produced relatively few works: his lyric output is condensed into two volumes—*Liriche e idilli* (Lyrics and Idylls, 1931) contains all the poems in Italian, whereas the far more acclaimed *Colori* (Colors, 1972 edition) has all those in dialect. *Colori* is an apt title that points to the visual nature of much of Giotti's poetry, with its emphasis on scenes, landscapes, figures, and sketches of popular life. Giotti's poems often center on the representation of patriarchal domestic life, which he imbues with a sense of timelessness and sanctity. Composed in a musical and seemingly facile tone, the poet's sketches, character studies, nature scenes, and depictions of familial and conjugal love manage to avoid banality and sentimentality because of Giotti's simple yet novel lexicon and his command of prosody. Indeed, familiar literary topics are revived due to the freshness of Giotti's expressive medium—dialect. Just as his language is personalized, so, too, his crystalline verse conceals a complex psychological matrix, filtered through an autobiographical core which personalizes even the most objective description. Giotti's inspiration springs from his paradoxical—and very modern—awareness that the joyful embrace of life coexists with the ever-present realization of death.

Born Virgilio Schönbeck on 15 January 1885, he was an unlikely candidate to become one of Italy's major dialect poets. Part of the lower middle class of Trieste, a city known for its lack of cultural tradition and literary interests, he was a prototypical Triestino of the Hapsburg era, when the city was the principal imperial seaport and an ethnic melting pot. His half-Austrian father, Riccardo, was a clerk who arrived in Trieste from Bohemia; his mother was Emilia Ghiotto, and her family was from the Veneto. The Schönbecks lived modestly but did not hamper their son's pronounced artistic talent, which was first directed to drawing and painting. He attended Industrial High School; his classmates there remembered his adolescent talent as a draftsman but recalled that he had no particular attraction for verse. In 1907 Giotti left Trieste to avoid military service in the Austrian army and resided briefly in Florence, then hub of the intellectual avant-garde in Italy, where he was a participant in the culturally active Triestino colony for a brief time. It was during this period that Giotti's love for poetry emerged. In 1909 the entire Schönbeck family moved to the Tuscan countryside, where Virgilio worked as a traveling sales representative throughout northern Italy and Switzerland, selling regional crafts and toys. For the rest of his life, the man who would become Trieste's most celebrated dialect poet spoke only in the Tus-

can of his youthful experience, never in the Triestino of his verse. As his good friend and fellow writer Giani Stuparich reminisced, Giotti's speech was vivid and visual—"era come se disegnasse e dipingesse, e tutti l'ascoltavano e 'vedevano'" (it was as though he drew and painted and everyone listened to him and "saw")—and never vernacular: "era il solo che in mezzo a noi parlasse in . . . una sobria lingua toscana" (he was the only one in our midst who spoke in an austere Tuscan tongue).

It was during this gypsy period that the young artist found his true vocation, not in brushes but in words. When his first volume was completed, he chose a pseudonym, Giotti, derived from his mother's maiden name, Ghiotto. *Piccolo canzoniere in dialetto triestino* (The Little Songbook in Triestino Dialect, 1914) was born in the Tuscan hills; in it Giotti's poetic universe is already clearly delineated: autobiographical elements coexist with character sketches, descriptions, anecdotes, and existential meditations. Stylistically there are distinct traces of the poems of Giovanni Pascoli and those of the *crepuscolari* (twilight poets) as well as elements of the confessional self-analysis favored by the group publishing in the journal *La Voce*. There is a melancholy tone, a diffusion of sadness, a humble cast of characters who immediately bring to mind the Pascolian lesson and its crepuscular variations. Giotti's subject matter is often alienation, the inability to communicate on a profound emotional level, or the regret of having dissipated possibilities. Even the romantic poems are permeated with the sense of loss or the tinge of illusion: loves that are lost or never were or could never be. Love is both a beacon and an illusion in these compositions—sought but not found, intuited but not experienced. Its depths can only be fathomed when love is viewed not as romance or passion but as the union of spirit and heart in serendipitous oneness. In other compositions a playful tone dominates the depiction of everyday scenes and characters drawn from the countryside, village life, and the streets: children, old maids, elderly peasants, young girls, and emblematic figures drawn from nature. Giotti generally manages to avoid overt sentimentality and pathetic self-pity. Due in large measure to the control he exerts over his verse, his taste for the everyday and the prosaic is never maudlin. While the tone of many of these compositions is colloquial, it is not unpoetic; rather, it brushes the rhythms of everyday speech without falling into the commonplace or the matter-of-factness of some crepuscular verse, owing to the vitality of the dialect employed. Giotti was a dedicated craftsman who polished and refined his compositions. Many handwritten and typed versions of the poems exist, verifying the artist's perfectionism.

The lyric persona that emerges from the *Piccolo canzoniere* does not resemble those found in Giotti's closest literary sources, possessing neither the sentimentality of Giovanni Pascoli nor the irony of Guido Gozzano. Instead it offers the image of a solitary meditative individual, caught in an alienated world while searching for a woman to give meaning and direction to his existence. This search for significance through love and family is self-aware and reflective: Giotti's works have an underlying intellectualism in contrast to the simplicity of his themes and language. The compositions are fraught with restlessness and emphasize the need for a meaning to life outside oneself, though one encounters estrangement, frustration, and death. The longed-for female becomes a life sign that consistently fails to satisfy the poet's need, thereby reinforcing the negative side of his psyche and checkmating his attempt at human participation. The poems of frustrated love point to the universal anguish of man facing his own mortality and attempting to block its inevitability in an embrace of all creation through union with the life force represented by the woman. Nevertheless, the hopes and dreams of love form a contrast to the series of poems presenting loves badly begun and badly ended. Positive and negative, dark and light meet in a verbal chiaroscuro, often expressed through the use of hues. There are a few basic colors that indicate the essentiality of Giotti's meanings. Manlio Dazzi has pointed out the extent of Giotti's use of color as sign: the joys of white and blue, the illuminating quality of pink, and the black of dead leaves and a sorrowful heart. "Felizità e Malinconia" (Happiness and Melancholy), one of the poems in *Poesie escluse* (Excluded Poems, 1978) eliminated from the final version of *Colori*, demonstrates the visual, the verbal, the life-affirming, and the painful in Giotti's artistic universe:

Xe la felizità
i oci; e lui el cuor
xe la malinconia.
I oci i xe del pitor, sua la felizità;
cuor e malinconia
xe invezi del poeta: i xe la mia poesia.

(Happiness is
the eyes; and the heart
it is melancholy.
Eyes are the painter's, happiness is his;
heart and melancholy
instead are the poet's: they are my poetry.)

In *Piccolo canzoniere* natural images are symbols of emotional states: swallows represent freedom and fellowship in contrast to the persona's loneliness: "El sambuco" (The Elder Tree) represents happy memories of childhood, while "L'usel bianco" (The White Bird) is the thought of death. Giotti's use of natural symbolism, color as meaning, and the themes of longing for love and its consequences—union and family—come together in "I zacinti" (The Hyacinths). Dominated by the delicate white and lilac of the flowers, the poem's colors tend to pallor, which is repeated in the woman's face, hands, and teeth, as well as in the room's floor and walls touched by pale sunlight; they are the colors of a fragile bond, as tenuous as the blossoms' perfume. The colors and essence of the hyacinths denote a love which is "un palido che lusi / che ardi, e un bon odor, una speranza" (a pallor that shines, / that burns, and a good smell, a hope) that fills his heart just as the flowers fill the room. As gossamer as the scent and shading of the flowers, the hope that imbues this poem, as it does many of the collection's compositions, is the joy of a loving family, a theme that will dominate Giotti's later volumes, represented by the dining table, locus of nourishment and communion:

'na casa mia e tua,
mèter insieme la tovàia,
mi e ti, su la tola,
con qualchidun che se alza
su le ponte d'i pie
pici e se sforza de 'rivar coi oci
su quel che parecemo.

(a house which is yours and mine,
putting the cloth together,
you and me, on the table,
with someone getting up
on tiny tiptoes
trying to see
what we are preparing.)

Apart from the color symbolism, natural emblems, and personal concerns expressed in many of the selections of this first collection, *Piccolo canzoniere* also introduces other themes and situations that would reappear throughout the poet's career. Ever a man of the people, Giotti the poet was also attracted to the lives, emotions, and environment of the working classes he knew well and lovingly called "crature de la vita" (creatures of life) and "cari esseri del mondo" (precious beings of the world). Common men and women, who inhabit the rooms, streets, and alleys of his daily experience, dominate Giotti's sketches. As Bruno Maier said in 1979, it was an "ideale solidarietà con il mondo umano e naturale" (ideal solidarity with the human and natural world). At times the lyrics of *Piccolo canzoniere* are vignettes; in one of the most well known, "I veci che 'speta la morte" (The Old Men Who Wait for Death), Giotti "draws" the portraits of immobile oldsters awaiting the inevitable with resignation, even indifference, while the sounds and images of life explode around them. This long composition is constructed along the opposing images of movement and inertia, youth and age, life and death. Ever present in Giotti's volumes, one discovers the seduction of death and an instinctive and developed sense of loss. Conjugal love, family life, and beauty coexist with a somber tendency to express the experience of suffering, existential pain, and death.

In Tuscany, Giotti met the woman who would fill his profound need for domestic tranquillity, family, and love. In 1911 Nina Stchekotoff, a Muscovite immigrant, entered his life. The two would soon live together and produce three children: Natalia, known as Tanda; Paolo; and Franco. The young family, including his mother, returned to Trieste after World War I, when the city ceased to be Austrian and became Italian. At first Giotti owned and ran a newspaper stand in a working-class neighborhood; later, he worked as a government clerk, while celebrating in dialect and Italian verse the bliss of his happy if unpretentious domestic life. The patriarchal myths that appear in *Piccolo canzoniere* continue to be prevalent in Giotti's later lyrics: the emblematic house-home-refuge; the exaltation of family; the joys of parenthood; and the companionship of spouses.

In peripheral Trieste, far from the intellectual centers and political upheavals of the 1920s and 1930s, Giotti's poetry took on an idyllic and musical character as suggested by the titles of his two collections in Italian: *Il mio cuore e la mia casa* (My Heart and My Home, 1920) and *Liriche e idilli*. The contentment of those years and the fondness for his subject is demonstrated linguistically by the prevalence of endearing diminutives

and a growing interest in metrical experimentation. In content the poems in Italian differ very little from those in dialect, stressing the emotive and the domestic, often in autobiographical terms. In *Il mio cuore e la mia casa* the personal and sentimental veins find expression in the icon of contentment, the house, which contains all love, warmth, and empathetic solidarity. Heart, home, family, and marital tenderness are a religion in themselves, forming a sacred tableau, as Giotti clearly notes in the ninth composition of *Liriche e idilli*: "Ci fu chi mi richiese s'io l'amavo / la mia casa. / Restai muto. Ma dentro / la mia risposta fu un grido" (Someone asked me if I loved it / my home. / I remained mute. But inside / my answer was a cry). In the same lyric, domestic objects such as the bed of conjugal love, the table of family unity, and the bookshelf lined with poetry assume the function of religious icons. On the whole, however, the verses in Italian do not equal the beauty of the ones in dialect: they do not sing. Instead, the length of the compositions, the habitual employment of speechlike meters and archaic Italian, and the repetition of limited themes occasionally border on the monotonous. Without the novel medium of the dialect, Giotti's contents and expression risk banality.

In the provincial atmosphere of his border city, Giotti was an active member of the small cultivated group that regularly met at a central café, including the writers Italo Svevo, Giani Stuparich, and Umberto Saba, as well as local sculptors, painters, philosophers, and intellectuals. Although lacking a formal education, Giotti had always been an attentive and far-reaching reader, whose interests included the ancients, French symbolists, Chinese and African-American poets, and nineteenth-century Russians, as well as traditional Italian literature. It was a quiet life, divided between his monotonous work as a clerk, the stimulating conversations of his friends, and the warmth of his loving home life. From the provinces, Giotti observed the significant Italian cultural movements of his day. Like many Triestini, he was not ignorant of avant-garde literary trends. Although he had not been personally involved in the Florentine Vociano movement while in Tuscany, Giotti favored its emphasis on confessional self-expression and was clearly influenced by its call for cultural renewal. He participated, albeit at a distance, in an innovative literary journal, *Solaria*. Its attached publishing house first published both *Liriche e idilli* and the earlier dialect collection

Caprizzi, canzonete e storie (Caprices, Popular Songs and Stories, 1928). Whereas Giotti was doubtlessly attracted to the *Solaria* writers' call for a humanistic art that could be contemporaneously dramatic and genuine, the journal's directors were attracted to Giotti's unusual subject matter, everyday situations, and narrative strategies, in keeping with the review's dislike of aestheticism, provincialism, and conventionality. Notwithstanding this assimilation of certain contemporary trends, it was to his own inner voice that Giotti listened most intently. On 23 July 1941, in a letter to his son, Giotti clearly states his case as an artist and as a man: "Sono sempre stato veramente l'uomo della misura e devo confessarlo, incline a contrastare alla corrente. Cosí fui anche antidannunziano e antiwagneriano" (I have always truly been a man of moderation and, I must confess, inclined to oppose the current. Therefore, I was also anti-Dannunzian and anti-Wagnerian). From its inception, Giotti's verse purposefully avoided the rhetorical eloquence of much Italian poetry. Nevertheless, his compositions are carefully wrought and concerned with the formal aspects of meter and technique.

Giotti composed primarily in the traditional meters of Italian prosody; the hendecasyllable and the shorter five- , seven- , and nine-syllable lines dominate. He paid particular attention to conventional lyric devices such as rhyme, repetition, alliteration, and assonance, while demonstrating a lifelong propensity for the employment of enjambment, often challenging standard syntactic and metric structures as his sentences range across lines and stanzas. To complement this use of enjambment, Giotti added caesuras and pauses, resulting in an original, innovative, and singular style. The later works, in particular, are considered avant-garde in their essential language, modernistic use of enjambment and musical lulls, and creation of symbols. However, it is the masterful adoption of dialect that separates Giotti from other major poets of his time. As Pier Paolo Pasolini recognized, Giotti reverted to Triestino as a language on the same level as Italian, seeing it as "una lingua reale viva (polemica rispetto alla fossilizzazione letteraria dell'italiano), e insieme assoluta, quasi inventata" (a true living tongue [polemical in regard to the literary fossilization of Italian], [which] at the same time, [is] ideal, almost invented). For Pasolini, Giotti's dialect is a poetic language more than a spoken tongue: externally it resembles the vernacular of the city, but, on a deeper level, it is the "idealiza-

tion" of Tuscan. Rarely used in verse or prose, Triestino had no history as a literary language; Giotti was the first to see its aesthetic potential— his dialect is easily distinguishable from the prosaic tones so typical of previous regional poetry. On the other hand, Giotti's verse in Italian was doubtlessly an attempt to reach a vaster public, for the poet was sadly aware that his ideal poetic idiom prevented him from obtaining a national audience.

A lifelong concern for proper prosody united Giotti and Trieste's most famous poet, his friend Umberto Saba. For a time in the 1920s Saba acted as Giotti's poetic adviser, editor, and sounding board. The Italian lyrics of *Il mio cuore e la mia casa* owe a great deal to the literary exchanges between the poets. In those years Giotti also gained some national recognition, resulting in professional friendships with such notable critics as Pietro Pancrazi, Mario Fubini, and Eugenio Montale. Like Saba, Giotti peoples his universe with familiar urban figures and cityscapes. Servants, street vendors, secretaries, clerks, workers, and children are expertly drawn. Similarly, the city fuses place (Trieste) and language (Triestino) into an inseparable whole. Trieste emerges as a character with its streets, sights, sea, and sky that are "colored" to suit the poet's pastel palette, especially in *Caprizzi, canzonete e storie*, which has occasionally been criticized for an excess of local color and sketches. One of the typical "stories" of the title concerns "La baba" (The Woman of the People), a character reflective of Giotti's marked affection for the common man and his depiction of life's difficult path. The "baba," a poor woman—"fia d'una venderigola de Ponte / Rosso ela la iera" (She was the daughter of a fruit vendor in the Ponte / Rosso market)—marries an abusive spendthrift, who burdens her with poverty and pregnancies until he is killed in the war. The widow's reactions are typical of the generous popular spirit Giotti admired and drew so well in words:

Le ga dito in contrada: "Un marì porco
de meno." Ela pian
la pianzeva, coi fioi 'torno le gambe,
disendo: "Pòaro can!"

(In the neighborhood they said: "One less pig
of a husband." She quietly
wept, her children gathered 'round her,
saying: "Poor devil!")

The widow's woes continue until she meets a mechanic, happily remarries, and has another baby, only to return to her market stall, having wed a second "baraba" (rogue). The narrative poem's conclusion is quintessential Giotti, its negativity mitigated by the final image of the protagonist, a life-giving Madonna figure, fondly embracing her child. The polarity of life and death, joy and suffering—standard Giottian themes—are humanized in the history of the "baba," its folk story giving way to a universal message of simple heroism and the affirmation of life, notwithstanding its inherent pain.

Due to Giotti's emphasis on traditional meters and rhyme, *Caprizzi, canzonete e storie* and the original *Colori* (1941) are far more musical than the somewhat prosaic *Piccolo canzoniere*. Yet all Giotti's collections are similarly peopled with humble souls, simple lives, suburban bars, quiet streets, and kinship with nature. Some compositions of this middle period of Giotti's life are more melodic and less narrative in character. There is an inclination toward lyric impressionism, which will persist throughout Giotti's later volumes. In "Inverno" (Winter, from *Caprizzi*), for example, melody, rhyme, color, symbolism, pauses, and the habit of associating images and states of mind come together:

> Dei purzitieri,
> ne le vetrine,
> xe verduline
> le ulive za;
>
> ghe xe le renghe
> bele de arzento;
> e sufia un vento
> indiavolà:
>
> cativo inverno
> ècote qua!
>
> (In the delicatessen
> windows,
> the olives are
> already greenish;
>
> the beautiful silver
> herrings are there,
> and a crazy wind
> is blowing:
>
> bad winter
> here you are!)

Another constant is Giotti's love for the natural world, reflected in poems dedicated to the seasons, the elements, or local landscapes. Like the compositions based on images of Trieste, these works abound in the use of color and design typical of this poet. In *Colori* colors are emblems of emotions and illustrations of the human condition. Giotti produces a refined chromatic scale in which shades are both visual and conceptual terms. The most banal of motifs—a flower, a tree, autumnal melancholy—is revitalized through the unusual medium of the dialect and Giotti's own ability to communicate a freshness and wonder that bring to mind Pascoli's poetic theory of the *fanciullino*, or child, who is able to renew life through an innate sense of wonder at all things. Among the poems dedicated to spring, the ones in the "Marzo" (March) series are replete with the positive hues associated with renewed life as embodied in ice-cream carts, flowers, even dreams: "Me la insognavo; e iera / quel sogno come un senso / del zeleste, del rosa / d'un ziel de primavera, / che se spècia par tera / ne l'aqua de la piova" (I dreamt of it; and that dream / was like a feeling / of blue, of pink / of a spring sky, / that's mirrored on earth / in rainwater). Yet even in the luminous context of *Colori* Giotti's pigments contain darker shades, in pieces dedicated to the passing of time, the coming of winter, the approach of old age and death, and even the decay of the mythic house. Another poem dedicated to "Marzo" and placed near the conclusion of the collection contrasts the appearance of two greening branches with the impossibility of renewing the past and recovering youth: "Ma a noi, quel che 'na volta / se ga sintì, godù, / nó pol dàrnelo piú / de novo nissun marzo" (But what we once / felt, enjoyed / can no longer be given to us / again by any March).

Giotti's idyllic period was destined to disappear. After the racial laws of the late 1930s were passed, the Fascist persecution of minorities and Jews eventually touched the poet. His *Mitteleuropean* surname (Schönbeck), which could be interpreted as Jewish, created difficulties for him as a civil servant. Consequently the family name was changed to an Italian semi-equivalent, Belli, that immediately brings to mind another great dialect poet, the Roman Giuseppe Belli. In the following decade, as war and destruction overran the world, the sorrowful elements innate in all Giotti's poetry prevailed, the destructive nature of time and the ubiquity of death gradually coming to dominate his poetic universe, often in emblematic terms. Notwithstanding his attraction to modest lives and quotidian events and his preference for subdued, even colloquial, linguistic registers, Giotti was drawn to the potential of *ermetismo*, or hermetic poetry, with its emphasis on the allusive power of the single word to evoke meaning without falling into the bombastic rhetoric of traditional verse and Fascist eloquence. Actually, through the use of dialect, Giotti was realizing a major goal of the hermetic program: the restoration and revivification of the power of the word. The word proposed by hermetic poets was to be cleansed of its historical baggage, made new again, and thereby capable of being magical and evocative while maintaining a direct rapport with the reality expressed. Similarly Giotti's impressionistic poems, notably those of the 1941 *Colori* and of *Sera* (Evening, 1948) and *Versi* (1953), reflect the poet's grasp of the hermetic renewal of prosody through the evocative power of words and the employment of analogy as an ideal lyric device. For example, "Utuno" (Autumn), from *Sera*, uses symbolism, implied analogy, powerfully simple vocabulary, fragmented syntax, and musicality reinforced by rhyme, alliteration, and assonance—as well as the emblematic use of the suggested colors red, black, and white—to evoke a desolate state of being:

No' più sul bianco, in tola,
i raspi de veludo
de la ùltima ua;
no' el vin novo bevudo
tra i viseti d'i fioi;

ma le làgrime longhe
de piova su le lastre,
ma el lamento del vento;
e l'inverno za in noi.

(No longer are the velvety bunches
of the last grapes
on the white table;
nor the new wine drunk amid
the children's little faces;

but the long tears
of rain on window panes,
but the lament of the wind;
and winter already in us.)

The national sorrow of the 1940s reached tragic personal proportions after both Giotti's sons were lost on the Russian front in late 1942. The death of Paolo Belli was confirmed years later, but the other son Franco's fate remains un-

known. The anguish suffered by the poet was deepened by his wife's severe depression: Nina could not accept the loss of her boys, and her pain was aggravated by their disappearance in her own homeland, Russia. As a result of aging and of these personal tragedies, a somewhat "new" Giotti emerges in both content and form. Always prone to raising the intimate aspects of his existence to the level of poetic symbol, he uses memory in his later poems as a formidable source of inspiration. These works are peopled by ghosts and apparitions in a universe decimated by loss. What was lost to death can only be recovered through memory and fantasy. Poems such as "El Paradiso" (Paradise), "La Casa" (Home), "Co' mia mama" (With My Mom), and "Ai mii fioi morti" (For My Dead Children)—all in *Sera*—are accompanied by a tone of regret and nostalgia for a past that cannot be recouped but draws the poet like a magnet. The dead return, not to haunt but to console in daydreams, recollections, and dreamscapes. In the later poems, the scales are tipped toward the dark shades of Giotti's paints; the lightness and simple joys of the earlier collections give way to the darkness of death and pain.

In *Sera* and *Versi* the surreal atmosphere also sounds a melancholy note. The escapist movement to the comfort of memory or the pleasures of fantasy is first seen in the collection *Sera*, the evening of the poet's life both biographically and figuratively. The contemplation of death that always accompanied Giotti's life draws ever closer, bringing with it the decay of body, will, and hope, tending to the dark hues of a cosmic pessimism suggested by some of the final works. Even the standard Giottian topoi of life are tinged with mortality, like the "Putela che dormi" (Little Girl Sleeping) in the trolley who is somewhere between sleep and death: "Col viseto de àngelo, / stanca, te dormi, sì, / piceta? O come tanti / te son morta ti?" (With your tiny angel's face, / are you sleeping, / little one? Or, like so many others, / are you dead too?) or the returning swallows "In zima de Montebello" (On Top of Montebello) that bring to mind a son who will not return. Although the brief collection *Versi* reprises some of the joyful elements typical of Giotti's work, it does so with a sense of wistfulness: the awareness of an old man loving life but nearing death. Love, spring, nature, sea, sky, children, and all humanity reappear as positive emblems but are contemplated at some distance. The poet and painter of "Davanti el mar" (In Front of the Sea) intently observe the water, hills, and sky on a blustery autumn day:

> E ghe sovien de bele antiche stòrie,
> e là viver i vedi ancora quel
> che no xe più, che pòlvere xe e ombre.

> (And they remember beautiful old stories,
> and there they still see living
> what is no longer, what is dust and shadows.)

Stylistically, these last works further amplify Giotti's tendency to essentialism in a reductive process that emphasizes the bare meanings of his signs while proposing universal significations beyond the personal. The vocabulary and simple metric lines achieve a semantic nudity, which is their strength. There is, in effect, an epigrammatic quality in Giotti's compositions that brings to mind the melodic succinctness of ancient lyrics, even in the more conversational rhythms of *Versi*. Moreover, there is a sense of closure in Giotti's opus that follows a natural cycle of birth, life, and death. The poet's myths come full circle: the desired home and family of *Piccolo canzoniere* become the reality of the middle works, only to dissolve in the late poems, inevitably, just as life promises death. In similar fashion the fantasy beloved becomes a loving wife, a young mother, a mature woman, a grandmother, and an old woman approaching her death—the "Vècia mòglie" (Old Wife) of *Versi*:

> La xe in leto, nel scuro, svea un poco;
> e la senti el respiro del marì
> che queto dormi, vècio anca lui 'desso.
> E la pensa: xe bel sintirse arente
> 'sto respiro de lui, sintir nel scuro
> ch'el xe là, no èsser soli ne la vita.
> La pensa: el scuro fa paura; forsi
> parchè morir xe andar 'n un grando scuro.
> 'Sto qua la pensa; e la scolta quel quieto
> respiro ancora, e no' la ga paura
> nò del scuro, nò de la vita, gnanca
> no del morir, quel che a tuti ghe 'riva.

> (She's in bed, in the dark, a bit awake;
> and she hears her husband's breathing.
> He's sleeping quietly, old himself now.
> And she thinks: it's nice to feel
> his breathing nearby, to feel he's there
> in the dark, not to feel alone in life.
> She thinks: darkness is frightening, perhaps
> because to die is to go into a great darkness.
> This is what she thinks; and again she listens to
>   that
> quiet breathing, and she's not afraid,

> not of darkness, not of life,
> not even of dying, which happens to everyone.)

In "Vècia mòglie," as in other poems, Virgilio Giotti re-creates his personal experiences, while transcending their ephemeral reality, to suggest a universal truth. The old woman lying in a dark room, as in a grave, finds solace in the mere fact of life—her husband's breathing— and in their companionship, a symbol of solidarity; she is an everyman figure facing her own humanity, both afraid and reconciled to her mortal essence. The modest, even banal, subjects of Giotti's production contain surprising depths beneath their unassuming surface. Like the old wife, Giotti himself found comfort and meaning in simple realities, threads that kept him joined to life notwithstanding its sorrows. An existence dedicated to the joys of family, nature, work, and art was paradoxically capped with recognition and frustration. Receiving Mario Fubini's endorsement, Giotti was awarded the prestigious prize of the Accademia dei Lincei in 1957, which represented the national recognition for which he had longed. But the poet did not live long enough to see the 1957 *Colori*, the anthology containing all his poems in dialect, issued by the prestigious Ricciardi publishing house. He died on 21 September 1957; *Colori* was published shortly thereafter. A few months later, his beloved wife, Nina, also died.

References:

Giuseppe Amoroso, "Virgilio Giotti," in *Letteratura italiana contemporanea*, volume 1, edited by Gaetano Mariani and Mario Petrucciani (Rome: Lucarini, 1979), pp. 411-414;

Giorgio Baroni, "Rilettura dei versi in dialetto di Virgilio Giotti," in his *Umberto Saba e dintorni: Appunti per una storia della letteratura giuliana* (Milan: Istituto Propaganda Libraria, 1984), pp. 117-131;

Mario Chiesa, "Memoria e sogno nella poesia di Giotti (con qualche altra nota)," *Giornale Storico della Letteratura Italiana*, 165, no. 529 (1988): 1-17;

Gianfranco Contini, "Virgilio Giotti," in his *Letteratura dell'Italia Unita (1861-1968)* (Florence: Sansoni, 1968), pp. 1039-1041;

Roberto Damiani, "Cap. V. Virgilio Giotti," in *Poeti dialettali triestini (1875-1980): Profilo storico-critico* (Trieste: Italo Svevo, 1981), pp. 81-110;

Manlio Dazzi, "Il mondo di Virgilio Giotti," *Letterature Moderne*, 7 (September-October 1957): 606-610;

Silvano Del Missier, "Virgilio Giotti poeta dialettale," *Pagine istriane*, 26-27 (September 1956): 29-34;

Rossana Esposito, *Virgilio Giotti* (Naples: Loffredo, 1982);

Franco Fido, "Introduzione alla lirica veneta del Novecento: Noventa, Marin e Giotti," *Italianist: Journal of Italian Studies*, 4 (1984): 35-53;

Mario Fubini, "Ricordo di Virgilio Giotti" and "*Sera* di Virgilio Giotti," in his *Saggi e ricordi* (Milan & Naples: Ricciardi, 1971), pp. 253-289;

Bruno Maier, "Postille autografe di Umberto Saba in una copia di *Il mio cuore e la mia casa* di Virgilio Giotti," "La poesia in dialetto triestino di Virgilio Giotti," "Virgilio Giotti poeta in lingua italiana," and "Gli *Appunti inutili* di Virgilio Giotti," in his *Saggi sulla letteratura triestina del Novecento* (Milan: Mursia, 1972), pp. 151-205;

Maier, "Virgilio Giotti," in *Letteratura italiana: Novecento: I Contemporanei*, volume 4 (Milan: Marzorati, 1979), pp. 3701-3713;

Pier Vincenzo Mengaldo, "Virgilio Giotti," in his *Poeti italiani del Novecento* (Milan: Mondadori, 1981), pp. 295-298;

Anna Modena, "Il percorso di un poeta: Virgilio Giotti," *Diverse Lingue*, 1 (1 February 1986): 9-18;

Eugenio Montale, "*Caprizzi, canzonete e storie* di Virgilio Giotti," in *Sulla poesia*, edited by G. Zampa (Milan: Mondadori, 1976), pp. 222-224;

Nicolò Nichea, "Virgilio Giotti," *Pagine Istriane*, 2 (May 1951): 44-52;

Pagine Istriane, special Giotti issue, 7, nos. 26-27 (1957);

Pietro Pancrazi, "Giotti poeta triestino," in *Ragguagli di Parnaso*, volume 3, edited by C. Galimberti (Milan & Naples: Ricciardi, 1967), pp. 177-183;

Pancrazi, "Virgilio Giotti poeta triestino," in his *Scrittori d'oggi* (Bari: Laterza, 1942), pp. 262-270;

Pier Paolo Pasolini, "La lingua della poesia," in his *Passione e ideologia (1948-1958)* (Milan: Garzanti, 1960), pp. 276-294;

Cesare Segre, "Giotti e l'inesprimibile," in *Letteratura italiana. Novecento: I Contemporanei*, pp. 3723-3729;

Giani Stuparich, *Trieste nei miei ricordi* (Milan: Garzanti, 1948).

Corrado Govoni
(29 October 1884 - 21 October 1965)

Joseph E. Germano
Buffalo State College

BOOKS: *Le fiale* (Florence: Lumachi, 1903);

Armonia in grigio et in silenzio (Florence: Lumachi, 1903);

Fuochi d'artifizio (Palermo: Ganguzza Lajosa, 1905);

Gli aborti; Le poesie d'Arlecchino; I cenci dell'anima (Ferrara: Taddei-Soati, 1907);

Poesie elettriche (Milan: Futuriste di Poesia, 1911);

Rarefazioni e parole in libertà (Milan: Futuriste di Poesia, 1915);

L'inaugurazione della primavera (Florence: Libreria della Voce, 1915);

Poesie scelte, 1903-1918 (Ferrara, Italy: Taddei, 1918; revised and enlarged, 1920);

La santa verde (Ferrara, Italy: Taddei, 1919);

Tre grani da seminare (Milan: Palmer, 1920);

Anche l'ombra è sole (Rome & Milan: Mondadori, 1921);

La terra contro il cielo (Rome & Milan: Mondadori, 1921);

Piccolo veleno color di rosa (Florence: Bemporad, 1921);

La strada sull'acqua (Milan: Treves, 1923);

Il quaderno dei sogni e delle stelle (Milan: Mondadori, 1924);

Brindisi alla notte (Milan: Bottega di Poesia, 1924);

La cicala e la formica (Milan: Bottega di Poesia, 1925);

Il volo d'amore (Milan: Mondadori, 1926);

Bomboniera (Rome: Sapientia, 1929);

La maschera che piange (Florence: Novissima, 1930);

Misirizzi (Florence: Vallecchi, 1930);

Il flauto magico (Rome: Tempo della Fortuna, 1932);

I racconti della ghiandaia (Lanciano, Italy: Carabba, 1932);

Canzoni a bocca chiusa (Florence: Vallecchi, 1938);

Poema di Mussolini (Rome: Cuggiani, 1938);

Le rovine del paradiso (Florence: Vallecchi, 1940);

Pellegrino d'amore (Milan: Mondadori, 1941);

Confessione davanti allo specchio (Brescia, Italy: Morcelliana, 1942);

Govonigiotto (Milan: S.T.E.L.I., 1943);

Corrado Govoni

La fossa carnala ardeatina (Rome: Movimento Comunista d'Italia, 1944);

Aladino (Milan: Mondadori, 1946);

L'Italia odia i poeti (Rome: Pagine Nuove, 1950);

Antologia poetica (1903-1953), edited by Giacinto Spagnoletti (Florence: Sansoni, 1953);

Patria d'alto volo (Siena, Italy: Maia, 1953);

Preghiera al trifoglio (Rome: Casini, 1953);

Manoscritto nella bottiglia (Milan: Mondadori, 1954);

Stradario della primavera (Venice: Neri Pozza, 1958);

Uomini sul delta (Milan: Ceschina, 1960);

Poesie, 1903-1959, edited by Giuseppe Ravegnani (Milan: Mondadori, 1961);

La ronda di notte, edited by Enrico Falqui (Milan: Ceschina, 1966);

Teatro (Rome: Bulzoni, 1984).

OTHER: Giacinto Spagnoletti, ed., *Poesia italiana contemporanea, 1909-1959*, includes poems and notes by Govoni (Parma, Italy: Guanda, 1959), pp. 33-49.

Corrado Govoni defies definition in spite of the fact that he has been identified as a member of both the *crepuscolari* (twilight poets) and Filippo Tommaso Marinetti's futurist movement. Govoni assimilated different poetics into his own particular brand of poetry, which includes a conflation of styles and influences that exemplify the nature of his eclecticism and his attempt to encompass all he liked and admired. It was he who first articulated those poetic elements that became indispensable to the *crepuscolari*, in a letter written to fellow poet Gian Pietro Lucini in 1904: "Ho sempre amato le cose tristi, la musica girovaga, i canti d'amore cantati dai vecchi nelle osterie, le preghiere delle suore, i mendicanti pittorescamente stracciati e malati, i convalescenti, gli autunni melanconici pieni di addii, le primavere nei collegi quasi timorose, le campagne magnetiche, le chiese dove piangono indifferentemente i ceri, le rose che si sfogliano sugli altarini nei canti delle vie deserte in cui cresce l'erba; tutte le cose tristi dell'amore, le cose tristi del lavoro, le cose tristi delle miserie . . . " (I have always loved sad things, strolling music, love songs sung by old men in the taverns, the nuns' prayers, the beggars colorfully ragged and sick, invalids, melancholy autumns full of farewells, the almost-timid springs in the private schools, the magnetic countryside, the churches where large candles cry with indifference, the roses shedding their petals on the little altars on the corners of deserted paths where the grass grows; all the sad things of love, the sad things of work, the sad things of trifles . . .).

These minutiae of daily life constitute the basis, for the most part, of the themes of the twilight poets, including Sergio Corazzini and Guido Gozzano, and especially Marino Moretti. Govoni's imaginativeness, his complex handling of previous influences, which become assimilated in his own work, and his quiet acceptance and adoption of varied subjects make him an important point of reference (it has been said that his opus is a veritable quarry) of European influences at the turn of the century. In his work are to be found strong reminiscences of nineteenth-century movements such as romanticism, Parnassianism, intimism, symbolism, and the individual voices of Stéphane Mallarmé, Jules Laforgue, Albrecht Rodenbach, and Francis Jammes. For these French and Flemish authors Govoni felt a particular affinity since they seemed to reflect the ideals he himself searched for (as quoted by Gualtiero Amici): "I decadenti sono i miei poeti prediletti perché io la poesia non la voglio né storica, politica, epica, ecc.; ma la considero soltanto raffinatezza e per me il poeta più sublime è colui che a lettura dei suoi versi mi fa provare maggiori sensazioni, colui che adopera immagini più nuove, più originali. A me la filosofia in versi garba poco, come ad esempio la poesia politica del Carducci" (The decadents are my favorite poets because I like my poetry neither historical, nor political, nor epic etc.; but I consider it only refinement, and for me the most sublime poet is he who, after reading his verses, makes me feel the most intense sensations, he who utilizes the newest and most original images. I have little sympathy for philosophy in verse, as for example the political poetry of [Giosuè] Carducci).

Govoni was born on 29 October 1884 in the small Italian town of Tamara in the Po River basin, near Ferrara, Romagna. For many generations his had been a family of well-to-do farmers and millers. It was inevitable, so it seemed, that Govoni would follow in his ancestors' footsteps were it not for a natural and compelling vocation felt from earliest childhood and an auspicious sojourn in a Ferrarese Salesian institute he entered in 1895 at age eleven. In Giacinto Spagnoletti's 1959 anthology, *Poesia italiana contemporanea, 1909-1959*, Govoni tells of his early years, which greatly affected his poetic formation: "Come senza dubbio tutte le vocazioni, essa ebbe origine da una circostanza assolutamente occasionale che per me fu quella della mia chiusura all'età di 11 anni in un collegio di Ferrara. Se fossi rimasto nel paese natio, e la massima punta dei miei studi pubblici si fosse arrestata alla terza elementare, molto probabilmente sarei diventato uno dei più grossi mugnai e fortunati agricoltori di tutto il Delta padano. . . . Così l'occasione mi ha fatto poeta. La lettura dei *Promessi sposi* e di poche cose permesse del Leopardi, nel corso ginnasiale del severo collegio salesiano, ha servito sicuramente ad aprire il misterioso germe di gusto artistico latente in me, e che non avrebbe forse mai avuto campo di svilupparsi e sarebbe rimasto eternamente infecondo come le gemme dormenti delle piante buone solo per gli innesti e a produrre foglie e spine" (As it is doubtless with all vocations, mine started from a purely fortuitous circumstance: it was my being placed in a private institute in Ferrara at age eleven. Had I stayed in my hometown, and had my highest level of public school education been limited to third grade, I would have most likely become one of the most prosperous millers and richest farmers of the Po River basin. . . . Thus, instead, circumstances made me a poet. The perusal of the *Betrothed* and the few things by [Giacomo] Leopardi that were allowed in the junior high curriculum of the strict Salesian Institute, surely served to develop in me the mysterious germ of my latent artistic talent, and which would have never perhaps had the opportunity to develop, and would have remained eternally barren like the dormant buds of those plants good only for grafting and for producing leaves and thorns).

However, at times, Govoni voiced his regrets at having left Tamara and what, by all indications, would have been a comfortable existence. In moments of bitterness and disappointment he even arrived at the fatalistic conclusion that his sufferings were perhaps the result of a punishment from a mysterious higher source for having betrayed his roots and the sacred trust of a way of life he helped destroy—by abandoning his place of birth and by selling his inherited land. This sense of guilt assumed more tragic proportions when his first-born son, Aladino, a fighter in the Italian Resistance, was murdered at the infamous "Fosse Ardeatine" (Ardeatine mass graves) on 24 March 1944. Two years later the grief-stricken poet dedicated *Aladino*, an entire volume of poems, to the memory of his son.

Govoni's first important encounter with the Italian literati of his era was with Giovanni Papini in Florence in 1903, when the aspiring poet from Ferrara visited the latter for the purpose of showing him his first book manuscript. Papini interceded favorably, and Govoni's first volume of poetry, *Le fiale* (The Phials), was published by Lumachi, Papini's publisher, in 1903, with illustrations by Adolfo De Karolis. Soon after *Le fiale*, in the same year, Lumachi published Govoni's second book, *Armonia in grigio et in silenzio* (Harmony in Gray and in Silence). His innate eclecticism afforded him the ability to collaborate with a variety of literary journals, some of which espoused diametrically opposed ideologies. For example, during what came to be known as his futur-

ist period, 1911-1915 (1911 is the year of his futurist book of poems *Poesie elettriche* [Electric Poems]), Govoni published in Mario Novaro's *Riviera Ligure*, where Giovanni Boine, Clemente Rèbora, and Camillo Sbarbaro published regularly, and in the Neapolitan *Diana*, an exponent of the hermetic movement. By 1914 his participation in the futurist movement was significant enough to spur him to sell his family land in Tamara and to move to Milan, the center for the futurists. The futurist period helped Govoni relinquish some outdated metrical, grammatical, and stylistic forms. Nevertheless, he remained faithful to his own particular tendencies, which never fully adhered to any school or movement. His familiarity with the anti-D'Annunzian Lucini, author of *Revolverate* (Pistol Shots, 1909), was perhaps based on the fact that in many ways Lucini and Govoni were kindred spirits. First of all, Govoni's fascination with Lucini consisted in the latter's special role in establishing cultural links during the beginning years of the twentieth century. While maintaining the utmost integrity in his ideological stances, Lucini managed to foster and implement some of the most innovative stylistic experimentations of his time. He also exposed to public scrutiny, and challenged, those traditional institutions that tended to stifle new voices and prevent any kind of cultural rebirth.

In 1917 Govoni was inducted into the military service; at the end of the war he tried several uneventful occupations, each of which he soon grew weary, before deciding to go to Rome to work for the S.I.A.E. (the Italian labor union of authors and publishers). From 1928 until 1943 he was secretary of the union. He then was assigned the inconsequential position of records keeper in a ministerial office where he spent many years in anonymity until his retirement. He spent the last years of his life in poor health in a very modest house in Lido dei Pini di Tor San Lorenzo, near Rome. Govoni died in Anzio on 21 October 1965. Eugenio Montale sadly recounted (in the newspaper *Corriere della Sera*, 22 October 1965) that, a few months before dying, Govoni had written him requesting his help in saving his eyesight; unfortunately, he died before Montale was able to reply.

Although it is impossible to identify the exact point when a break took place between the poetic modes of the nineteenth and twentieth centuries, it would not be totally incorrect (at least not chronologically) to mention Govoni's *Fiale* as the author's *adieu de rigueur* (obliged farewell) to

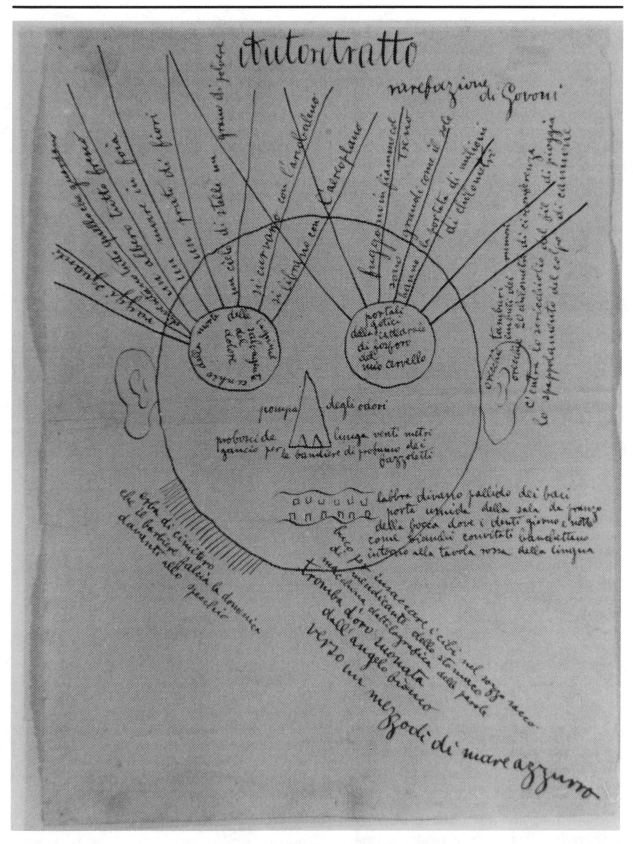

A self-portrait by Govoni (Fondazione Primo Conti Collection)

his most immediate antecedents (Parnassians, symbolists, Gabriele D'Annunzio, Giovanni Pascoli, and others) and as the first concrete evidence of a break with the past in twentieth-century Italian poetry. Govoni became the example to follow for several years. By 1907 Govoni had already introduced a new type of verse (that no longer contained the preciosity and loftiness of his decadent predecessors) by altering the meter and even the traditional musicality expected in a hendecasyllable (as in *Fiale*). All this experimentation is a prefiguration of the free verse of *Armonia in grigio et in silenzio* and *Fuochi d'artifizio* (Fireworks, 1905).

Govoni's innovation becomes especially manifest if compared with D'Annunzio's *Poema paradisiaco* (Paradisiacal Poem). D'Annunzio's impeccable technique is even parodied (most likely unintentionally) by Govoni, who leaves behind the purely technical considerations for a more open, prosaic representation that, in a few years, was to be transformed with the mediation of Corazzini and Gozzano into the Morettian *poesia-prosa* or *prosa-poesia*. The break with the past seems complete.

The elegant and luxurious sonnets of *Le fiale* are characterized by their detailed craftsmanship, exotic images, difficult and rare rhymes, and unusual lexicon interspersed with archaic vocabulary. They represent a tour de force of Govoni's poetic bravura in his ability to resolve difficult problems in meter, rhythm, and rhyme. The poet is self-conscious of these procedures and gloats over his own ingenious solutions. The direct antecedents of these images and structures are obvious: Parnassians, symbolists, and D'Annunzio. However, under the surface and hidden within this poetic opulence are to be found the innovative elements that give significance to *Le fiale*: a certain realism not found in Govoni's decadent antecedents, the very simple image (typical of the twilight poets) next to the D'Annunzian bombastic expression, the unusual and even rare internal accentuation of some hendecasyllables (verses that read more like prose), the long enumerations, and the lack of synthesis, which would abound in future Govoni poetry. All of these elements constitute the beginning of the break from his poetic mentors: while Govoni is paying homage to them by emulating them, he is clearly showing off innovations that are his own. The following quatrain from "Alito di

ventaglio" (Fan's Breeze) exemplifies both the imitations and the innovations:

> Presso un canale una bambina triste
> dagli occhi a mandorla, fiori di loto,
> soavemente sfilza dal suo koto
> dei suoni come grani d'ametiste.

> (Near a canal a sad little girl
> with almond eyes, lotus flowers,
> gently unravels from her koto
> sounds like beads of amethyst.)

Armonia in grigio et in silenzio takes up again many elements of *Le fiale* and develops them to a point at which D'Annunzio, the symbolists, and other influences (so much a part of *Le fiale*) are now distant and secondary to other preoccupations, mainly to typical twilight themes. The love for the countryside, which in Govoni is felt with utmost sincerity, devotion, and profound yearning (he grew up in that atmosphere), continually surfaces throughout his entire opus. Poem 10 of *Armonia* exemplifies this particular theme and atmosphere:

> La strada è tutta erbosa
> come una strada di campagna;
> vicino, un'acqua stagna
> con una barchetta corrosa.

> Vi passano dei pescatori
> la sera e la mattina,
> qualche scalza bambina
> con dei mazzi di agresti fiori.

> (The street is very grassy
> like a countryside path;
> nearby, a pond
> with a corroded boat.

> Fishermen pass by
> evening and morning,
> some barefoot little girls
> with bunches of wildflowers.)

In this poem Govoni's style becomes more spontaneous and achieves a certain internal and formal freedom of expression; it is also a sort of declaration of freedom from *Le fiale*. In fact, it should be surprising that *Le fiale* and *Armonia* are both from 1903, considering the gulf between these two works in terms of themes, technique, and tone. The poet is close to the objects he describes because they are within the sphere of his experience, they are real, and they are loved by him.

The new language he uses is in consonance with a new poetic stance, one that is more personal.

In *Fuochi d'artifizio* Govoni continues the themes of *Armonia* and carries out a further expansion of themes and interests. The big difference between the two works is not formal but concerns Govoni's temperament: in *Fuochi d'artifizio* he gives vent to an unprecedented eclecticism and fantasy. He also recalls a remote past with the genuine memory of a child, the so-called *fanciullismo pascoliano* (Pascolian childlike state), which in Govoni is not an imitation *ad litteram*, but a generalized aesthetic imitation without the intention to reproduce Pascoli. In "La cucina di campagna" (Country Kitchen), for example, the "child" remembers the details of a certain scene:

> Fido sotto la tavola rosicchia
> il catriosso di un'anatra. Adelina picchia
> il mao perche à pisciato contro l'uscio,
> e che strisciando e miagolando si rannicchia
> dentro il canile, come una lumaca nel suo guscio.
>
> (Fido under the table gnaws
> the carcass of a duck. Adelina hits
> the kitty for having urinated against the door,
> and crawling and meowing he crouches
> inside the dog-house, like a snail in his shell.)

In the poem "Fuori di moda" (Out of Fashion) the furniture in an old abandoned palace is described in its decadent state, suggesting a past that has left nothing to future generations that might be called functional or useful:

> Oh le camere di palazzi antichi inabitati,
> sempre chiuse con la loro mobilia rococò,
> come vecchie che portano ori disusati,
> letti di mogano a traforo, alti comò
>
> sostenuti da grandi zampe animalesche
> e che ànno sui coperchi lucidi a mosaico
> delle argentee pendole settecentesche
> con dei quadranti adorni d'un disegno arcaico. . . .
> . . . .
> Si trovan anche della tabacchiere pornografiche
> sature di tabacco, qualche ricamato fazzoletto
> che scuotendolo s'anima di menta, delle prove
>   fotografiche,
> dei ventagli di avorio e un recipiente di belletto.
>
> (Oh the rooms of the old abandoned palaces,
> always shut with their rococo furniture,
> like old women wearing old-fashioned jewelry,
> mahogany beds with frets, tall chests of drawers

> sustained by great animalesque paws,
> and on their shiny mosaic tops
> some eighteenth-century silver pendulum clocks
> their dials adorned with an archaic design. . . .
> . . . .
> There also are pornographic snuffboxes
> full of tobacco, some embroidered kerchiefs
> which, shaken, smell of mint, some photographs,
> some ivory fans and a makeup kit.)

Gli aborti (The Abortions, 1907) is a daring title indeed for those times. Together with a series of sonnets dedicated to flowers, laughter, and even macabre themes such as the suicide of two lovers, are found the themes of the twilight poets and the simple daily pleasures derived from such seemingly banal things as spring Sundays and white doves on rooftops. The sonnet "Il riso" (The Laughter) illustrates Govoni's unbridled fantasy and poetic ability to tackle any subject in an unconventional fashion:

> Grottesca maschera della pazzia,
> riso, stecchito piccolo folletto
> penna e ossa come il cuculo, belletto
> dell'anima rugosa. Frenesia.
>
> (Grotesque mask of madness,
> laughter, dried up little elf
> feathers and bones like a cuckoo,
> makeup of wrinkled souls. Frenzy.)

The twilight themes are evident in the poem "Le dolcezze" (The Sweetnesses):

> Le domeniche azzurre della primavera.
> La neve sulle case come una parrucca bianca.
> Le passeggiate degli amanti lungo il canale.
> Fare il pane la mattina di domenica.
> La pioggia di marzo che batte sui tegoli grigi.
>
> (The sky-blue Sundays of spring.
> The snow on top of the houses like a white wig.
> The lovers' walks along the canal.
> Making bread on Sunday mornings.
> The rain in March that beats on the gray rooftops.)

Poesie elettriche is considered part of Govoni's futurist experience. This was one of two volumes of Govoni's poetry—the other being *Rarefazioni e parole in libertà* (Rarefactions and Words in Freedom, 1915)—published by Marinetti's company. Most critics do not see much futurism in *Poesie elettriche*, and in spite of a format that visually suggests strong ties with the futurist movement, *Rarefazioni e parole in libertà* is considered an exercise that is inconsistent with Govoni's other works. The contents of these two works, all futuristic claims aside, are basically the typical imagistic, all-encompassing, "torrential" Govoni, impossible to grasp and to place into a neat codification. Govoni's poems show the torrential nature noted by Lionello Fiume in 1918 and a modernity of expression unparalleled by his peers. All the attempts made to call *Poesie elettriche* a futurist book inevitably must collapse at the sight of the poem Govoni composed for Corazzini, a fellow twilight poet and friend, who died at the young age of twenty-one, "In morte di Sergio Corazzini" (In Memory of Sergio Corazzini):

> O dolce amico, è l'ora
> che tu mantenga la promessa.
> A che indugi? Perché tardi ancora?
> La neve se n'è di già andata.
> Qua e là, sui tetti,
> brillò l'ultimo bianco,
> nido d'emigrate cicogne.
> Il frumento diffonde
> la sua verde speranza di pane
> pei campi; e le viole
> come lacrime azzurre di sereno
> odoran lungo i fossi fra le foglie secche.
> Oh dolce dopo tanto freddo e tanta morte
> sedersi al sole sulle porte,
> sentir quella carezza luminosa
> fluire sulla fonte pura
> lungo le mani pallide!

> (Oh my sweet friend, it's time
> that you keep your promise.
> Why hesitate? Why do you still delay?
> The snow is gone already.
> On the rooftops here and there
> shone the last white,
> nest of emigrant cranes.
> The wheat is spreading
> its green hope of bread
> throughout the fields; the violets
> like blue tears from a clear sky
> smell along the ditches amidst the dry leaves.
> How sweet, after much cold and death,
> to sit under the sun on the thresholds,
> to feel that luminous caress
> flowing pure on one's forehead
> along one's pallid hands!)

In *Rarefazioni e parole in libertà* Govoni attempted to present his verses in full futuristic regalia. Govoni's interpretation of futurism had little or nothing to do with Marinetti's solemn document "Fondazione e Manifesto del Futurismo" (The Founding and Manifesto of Futurism), first published in French in the Parisian *Figaro* on 20 February 1909, and then in Italian in the literary journal *Poesia*, February-March 1909. Govoni continued to make use of his imagination and fantasy and devised certain concoctions that visually suggested a futurist matrix; closer scrutiny, however, reveals that he was able to invent *ideogrammi* (ideograms) that seem to have amused the author as much as they amuse the reader, since there is no explainable depth or ideology. The poem "Anima" (Soul) is a litany of images, unusual, to be sure, but not very different from other poems Govoni composed before or after 1915:

> Oh quel verde di menta glaciale!
> Oh quel rosso recidivo!
> Oh quell'azzurro tonico dell'anima!
> Nella sua bara di cristallo blu,
> piccola come una bomboniera,
> piccola come una scatola di cerini,
> piccola come una tabacchiera,
> giace il cadaverino impube dell'anima
> simile a quei puttini di sapone roseo
> che si vendono nelle fiere.
> Un pettine d'ambra pieno di rose?

> (Oh that green of glacial mint!
> Oh that recidivous red!
> Oh that blue tonic of the soul!
> In his blue crystal coffin,
> tiny as a bonbonnière,
> tiny as a matchbox,
> tiny as a snuffbox,
> lies the soul's little corpse
> similar to those tiny cupids of pink soap
> that are sold at the fairs.
> An amber comb full of roses?)

L'inaugurazione della primavera (The Inauguration of Spring, 1915) received widespread critical accolades and, by general consensus, was soon called his very best work. With this book Govoni enters a Postimpressionistic period. No longer trying to fit within the futurist group, he exhibits his most lyrical, elegiacal, and creative poems, but they are controlled, in spite of the eclectic nature of his inspirations. The countryside and the city are treated in the long poems "Casa paterna" (Paternal Home) and "Io e Milano" (I and Milan). "La città morta" (The Dead City) is a salient example of Govoni's new tone:

> Non più cieli d'un blu gendarme!
> Non più prati d'un verde bandiera!
> Amo errare lontano con le nuvole.
> Odio la primavera.

E questo sole atroce che ti fa
pallida come un astro,
è così trasparente, di giorno in giorno sempre più,
ch'io vedo continuamente
arder l'anima tua
attraverso il tuo corpo innocente,
come fiamma attraverso l'alabastro.

Oh, così fine e lieve sei
e tanto divorata dalla luce,
ch'io quasi ti perderei
se non fosse quell'ombra fonda dei tuoi occhi
che verso di te mi conduce!

(No more police-blue skies!
No more flag-green lawns!
I love to wander far with the clouds.
I hate spring.

And this atrocious sky that turns you
as pale as a star,
and so transparent, more so from day to day,
that I continuously see
your soul burn
through your innocent body,
like a flame through alabaster.

Oh, so fine and light you are
and so devoured by the light,
that I would almost lose you
if it weren't for your eyes' deep shadow
that leads me toward you!)

Govoni in 1954

After *L'inaugurazione della primavera* Govoni did not produce his next book of new poetry until 1924 (an unusual hiatus in his career). From 1924 until 1943 Govoni consistently published poetry that addressed what were basically the same themes of *L'inaugurazione* but in a more polished language: *Il quaderno dei sogni e delle stelle* (The Notebook of the Dreams and the Stars, 1924), *Brindisi alla notte* (A Toast to the Night, 1924), *Il flauto magico* (The Magic Flute, 1932), *Canzoni a bocca chiusa* (Songs with One's Mouth Shut, 1938), *Pellegrino d'amore* (Pilgrim of Love, 1941), and *Govonigiotto* ("Young-Man-Govoni," 1943). These books confirm once again the well-known Govonian repertoire without significant surprises, although *Canzoni a bocca chiusa* suggests interesting variations with strong musicality, as in the poems "Prateria," "Sottomarino," "Specchio di Venezia," and "Suona chitarra mia" (Prairie, Submarine, Mirror of Venice, and Play, My Guitar). These poems, for the first time, reveal an existential vein in Govoni's poetry never before expressed; it is perhaps an almost mystical acceptance of one's fate in life.

At a time when Govoni had reached what seemed to be a poetic balance in both content and form, a tragedy suddenly caused him immeasurable grief. The death of his son Aladino (1944) found profound poetic expression in *Aladino*, where a father's grief is transformed into moving elegies. Endless reminiscences with his son always at the center provide profound insights. A harmless trick the poet and his wife played a long time ago on their three-year-old child, through the poet's memory, becomes an occasion to grieve, in poem number 6:

A Milano piccino di tre anni,
correvi sempre avanti, quasi ansioso
di conoscere il mondo. E noi, per giuoco,
un dì ci nascondemmo. I pianti e strilli,
trovandoti poi solo e abbandonato.
Per farci perdonare, ti coprimmo
dei più teneri baci, divertiti;
tu, di dolci schiaffini sopra gli occhi
e sulla bocca, singhiozzando: "Brutti!"
Ora il crudele giuoco lo fai tu,
dietro i vestiti e i poveri ossicini,
dove ti sei nascosto a noi, per sempre.
Senza te, il nostro piangere ed urlare
non sarebbero più di alcun conforto,
durassero l'intera eternità.

(As a child, in Milan, three years old,
almost anxious you'd run ahead
to find the world. And we, in jest,
one day we hid. What tears and cries
finding yourself abandoned and alone.
So that you might forgive us, we lavished
upon you kisses most tender, still bemused;
you slapped our eyes and mouths
harmlessly, sobbing: "Naughty!"
And now it's you who play that cruel game,
under your clothes and your poor little bones,
where you did hide yourself from us, forever.
Without you here, our cries and our tears
would never comfort us in any way
were they to last eternally.)

In poem 15 even the night Aladino was born is seen through a negative perception by Govoni's presenting the falling snow as black snow (a prophetic element, even if by hindsight): "La notte che nascesti, nevicava: / dai vetri ci sembrò una neve nera" (The night when you were born the snow was falling: / and through the glass to us the snow seemed black). The sound of music, which before this tragedy would have summoned happier sensations, now throws the poet into an abyss of grief, as in poem 65:

Quando sento suonare un organetto
mi si annebbia la vista anche di dentro
e il cuore mi si spezza dallo strazio:
il mio triste passato di dolore
è chiamato a raccolta da quel suono.

(When I hear a concertina playing
my eyesight grows foggy from inside,
my heart is torn apart:
and my grief-laden past
is summoned to roll call by that tune.)

Preghiera al trifoglio (Prayer to the Clover, 1953) reintroduces Govoni's love for nature: flowers, plants, and birds. However, these themes are seen through the experience of immense grief and become vehicles for exorcizing that grief. The title of *Manoscritto nella bottiglia* (Manuscript in the Bottle, 1954) suggests a final message from its author. Spagnoletti, in his *Letteratura italiana del nostro secolo* (1985), states that Govoni's message "è quello stesso del neorealismo, celebrato singolarmente da Govoni con una sorta di furia pedagogica: il suo allievo è sempre l'angelo, al quale non dovranno più interessare le tristi anime delle beghine, ma quelle di tutti i poveri sopravissuti agli orrori del secondo conflitto mondiale, che non vogliono più

subire altre sopraffazioni" (is similar to that of neorealism, singularly celebrated by Govoni with a sort of pedagogic fury: his disciple is always the angel, who will no longer be interested in the sad souls of bigoted women, but in those of all the poor people who survived the horrors of World War II, and who do not want to suffer other indignities).

In Giuseppe Ravegnani's 1961 anthology of Govoni's poetry there is a poem titled "Povertà" (Poverty), which is part of an unpublished collection of poetry under the title "I canti del puro folle" (The Songs of a Completely Mad Man). The following lines give an insight into the poet's view of himself vis-à-vis the world, and his view is the pessimistic and, at times, cynical outlook of a man about to die who will cry his grief until the end:

Anche se vi nascondo
la mia pena segreta
sono il vecchio più ricco del mondo:
ho un tesoro più grande dell'amore:
ho il dolore.
Non mi chiamate più povero;
se volete chiamatemi pazzo,
chiamatemi poeta . . .

(Even if I hide from you
my secret sorrow
I am the richest old man in the world:
I have a greater treasure than love:
I have grief.
No longer call me poor;
if you wish, call me mad,
call me a poet . . .).

In his *Scrittori e artisti* (1959) Giovanni Papini stated that for Govoni "la poesia è un bisogno naturale e quotidiano come il bere e il dormire" (poetry is a natural and daily need as are drinking and sleeping). During his long poetic career perhaps Govoni's most important contribution was that of opening new paths to other poets unselfishly; his poetry, rich with innovations and new themes, provided new ideas to countless poets, some of them major poets of this century. Govoni's contributions would be easy to find even in the work of such personalities as Giuseppe Ungaretti, Eugenio Montale, and Dino Campana, to say nothing of his colleagues of the twilight movement. Many of his poems, from those in *Le fiale* of 1903 to those of *Manoscritto nella bottiglia* of 1954, have achieved the importance of milestones for the influence they have exercised on other twentieth-century poets. Although Govoni participated in most major poetic schools or groups, such as those of the twilight poets and futurism, always with enthusiasm and exuberance, his particular mind-set was such that he was never assimilated by any movement. His poetic works constitute an unusual phenomenon in the world of Italian letters, a phenomenon that Niccolò Sigillino has called "govonismo" (Govonism).

References:

Gualtiero Amici, "Corrado Govoni, 'bambino illuminato,' " in his *Teoria e spazio del Novecento e altri saggi* (Milan: Laboratorio della Arti, 1971), pp. 41-48;

Carlo Bo, "Govoni, Martini e Moretti," in *Storia della letteratura italiana: Il Novecento*, volume 9 (Milan: Garzanti, 1969), pp. 277-282;

Arnaldo Bocelli, "Panorama letterario del Novecento," in *Letteratura del Novecento* (Caltanissetta & Rome: Sciascia, 1977), pp. 11-30;

Fausto Curi, *Corrado Govoni* (Milan: Mursia, 1964);

Lionello Fiume, *Corrado Govoni* (Ferrara: Taddei, 1918);

Alfredo Gargiulo, "Gozzano, Govoni," in his *Letteratura italiana del Novecento* (Florence: Monnier, 1958), pp. 273-278;

Elio Gioanola, "Futurismo e Marinetti," in his *Storia letteraria del Novecento in Italia* (Turin: SEI, 1976), pp. 67-75;

Giuliano Manacorda, *Storia della letteratura italiana tra le due guerre 1919-1943* (Rome: Riuniti, 1980);

Gaetano Mariani, *Poesia e tecnica nella lirica del Novecento* (Padua: Liviana, 1958), pp. 194-195;

Ettore Mazzali, "Corrado Govoni," in *Letteratura italiana: I contemporanei*, volume 1 (Milan: Marzorati, 1963), pp. 565-576;

Pietro Pancrazi, "Il flauto magico di Govoni," in his *Scrittori d'oggi* (Bari, Italy: Laterza, 1946), pp. 172-178;

Giovanni Papini, "Govoni," in his *Scrittori e artisti* (Milan: Mondadori, 1959), pp. 905-913;

Jean Pierrot, *The Decadent Imagination, 1880-1900*, translated by Derek Coltman (Chicago & London: University of Chicago Press, 1981);

Adriano Seroni, *Il decadentismo* (Palermo: Palumbo, 1964);

Niccolò Sigillino, "Govoni," in his *Parnaso contemporaneo* (Rome: SELI, 1940), pp. 99-125;

Giacinto Spagnoletti, "Govoni," in his *Letteratura italiana del nostro secolo* (Milan: Mondadori, 1985), pp. 192-202.

Guido Gozzano
(19 December 1883 - 9 August 1916)

Anthony Julian Tamburri
Purdue University

BOOKS: *La via del rifugio* (Turin: Streglio, 1907);
I colloqui: Liriche di Guido Gozzano (Milan: Treves, 1911);
I tre talismani (Ostiglia, Italy: La Scolastica editrice, 1914);
La principessa si sposa: Fiabe (Milan: Treves, 1917);
Verso la cuna del mondo: Lettere dall'India (1912-1913) (Milan: Treves, 1918);
L'altare del passato (Milan: Treves, 1918; revised and enlarged, 1930);
L'ultima traccia (Milan: Treves, 1919);
Primavere romantiche (Appia-Rivarolo, Italy: Arti Grafiche Canavesane, 1924);
I primi e gli ultimi colloqui (Milan: Treves, 1925);
Opere, di Guido Gozzano, 5 volumes, edited by P. Schinetti (Milan: Treves, 1935-1937);
Opere, edited by Carlo Calcaterra and Alberto De Marchi (Milan: Garzanti, 1948; revised, 1953; revised and enlarged, 1956);
La fiaccola dei desideri: Fiabe (Milan: Garzanti, 1951);
Lettere d'amore di Guido Gozzano e Amalia Guglielminetti, edited by Spartaco Asciamprener (Milan: Garzanti, 1951);
Le poesie (Milan: Garzanti, 1960);
Fiabe (Milan: Garzanti, 1961);
Poesie e prose, edited by Marchi (Milan: Garzanti, 1961);
La moneta seminata e altri scritti, edited by Franco Antonicelli (Milan: All'Insegna del Pesce d'Oro/Scheiwiller, 1968);
Lettere a Carlo Vallini; con altri inediti, edited by Giorgio De Rienzo (Turin: Centro Studi Piemontesi, 1972);
Poesie, edited by Edoardo Sanguineti (Turin: Einaudi, 1973);
I colloqui e prose, edited by Marziano Guglielminetti (Milan: Mondadori, 1974);
Cara Torino (Turin: Viglongo, 1975);
Poesie, edited by Giorgio Bàrberi Squarotti (Milan: Rizzoli, 1977);
Guido Gozzano: Tutte le poesie, edited by Andrea Rocca (Milan: Mondadori, 1980);
I sandali della diva: Tutte le novelle, edited by Giuliana Nuvoli (Milan: Serra & Riva, 1983);
Opere di Guido Gozzano, edited by Giusi Baldissone (Turin: UTET, 1983);
Un Natale a Ceylon e altri racconti indiani, edited by Piero Cudini (Milan: Garzanti, 1984).

Editions in English: *The Man I Pretend to Be: The Colloquies and Selected Poems of Guido Gozzano*, translated and edited by Michael Palma (Princeton, N.J.: Princeton University Press, 1981);
Guido Gozzano: The Colloquies and Selected Letters, translated by J. G. Nichols (New York: Carcanet, 1987).

OTHER: Antonio Stäuble, ed., "Un manoscritto di Gozzano e l'elaborazione della poesia 'Convito,'" *Lettere Italiane*, 22 (April-June 1970): 248-252;
Franco Contorbia, ed., "Un inedito di Guido Gozzano: Guerra di Spetri," *Lettore di Provincia*, 1 (December 1970): 14-24;
Marziano Guglielminetti, ed., "Gozzano recensore-Guido Gozzano: Recensioni (1907-1908)," includes literary reviews by Gozzano, *Lettere italiane*, 23 (July-September 1971): 401-430;
Mariarosa Masoero, ed., "Guido Gozzano: Quaderno petrarchesco," includes previously unpublished material by Gozzano, in *Petrarca e il petrarchismo*, edited by Marziano Guglielminetti and Masoero (Turin: Giappichelli, 1975), pp. 173-197;
Franco Contorbia, ed., "Lettere di Gozzano a Moretti (1907-1914)," in *Atti del Convegno di Studio-Cesenatico 1975-Marino Moretti*, edited by G. Calisei (Milan: Saggiatore, 1977), pp. 107-22;
Andrea Rocca, ed., "Fra le carte di Guido Gozzano: Materiali autografi per 'I Colloqui,'" *Studi di filologia italiana*, 35, no. 4 (1977): 395-471;

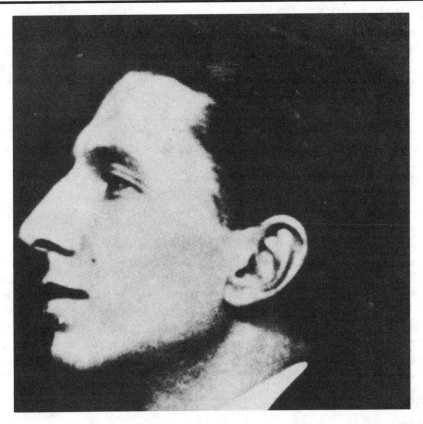

Guido Gozzano

Rocca, ed., "Gozzano debuttante: Cinque sonetti e una prosa," *Lettere Italiane*, 30 (July-September 1978): 371-387;

Guglielminetti and Masoero, eds., "Spogli danteschi e petrarcheschi di Guido Gozzano," *Otto-Novecento*, 4, no. 2 (1982): 169-258.

Guido Gozzano died at thirty-two, having completed only two collections of poetry—*La via del rifugio* (The Road to Shelter, 1907) and *I colloqui* (The Colloquies, 1911); many of his works, poetry and prose, remained uncollected. *La via del rifugio*, while still tied to an Italian/D'Annunzian tradition on the one hand and a foreign (mostly French/Belgian) tradition on the other (Maurice Maeterlinck, Paul Verlaine, Jules Laforgue), also indicates a certain independence. Gozzano borrowed heavily from other poets, at times paraphrasing, at times lifting entire verses. Yet he managed to manipulate, with irony, his constant borrowings and adapt them according to his own worldview and notions of poetry.

Gozzano was born on 19 December 1883 in Turin to an upper-middle-class family. His father, Fausto Gozzano, was an engineer; his mother, Diodata, daughter of the senator Massimo Mautino, was an actress. Gozzano attended the Liceo Cavour, the Istituto Ricaldone, and the Collegio Nazionale di Savigliano, from which he finally graduated with moderate success. In 1904 he enrolled in the Facoltà di Giurisprudenza in Turin, but he abandoned his law studies in order to become a writer. During law school Gozzano had met Arturo Graf, whose university seminars he attended. The relationship with Graf was one factor that influenced his decision to deviate from his initial plan of a legal career. It was also during this time that he suffered his first bout with tuberculosis, a malady that eventually took his life.

Highly sentimentalized, much of Gozzano's early poetry is reminiscent of that of Gabriele D'Annunzio, especially the early D'Annunzio of, for instance, *La Chimera* (The Chimera) and *Il Poema Paradisiaco* (The Paradisiacal Poem). Gozzano's cold, distant woman of "La preraffaellita" recalls D'Annunzio's "Due Beatrici, II" in *La Chimera*; his "Vas voluptatis" recalls the D'Annunzian "Vas spiritualis" (*La Chimera*) and "Vas mysterii" (*Il Poema Paradisiaco*). In a similar manner "Il Castello di Agliè" evokes the theme of the abandoned gardens in D'Annunzio's *Il Poema Paradisiaco*, with specific reference to "Climene," "La statua, I," and "La statua, II."

To a certain degree *La via del rifugio* can be considered poetry of recollection. The poems hark back to the world of the previous generation both in content and form, although some— "La via del refugio," "L'analfabeta" (The Illiterate), and "L'amica di nonna Speranza" (The Girlfriend of Grandma Speranza), for instance— overturn seemingly fixed, aesthetic notions of the nineteenth century and stand out for their opposing force. That is, one notices a radical reduction of the linguistic and thematic levels in his poetry, especially when compared to the celebratory and symbolic characteristics of Giovanni Pascoli and D'Annunzio. With other early Gozzano poems, these serve to introduce the irony that would later aid Gozzano in desacralizing his entire literary inheritance. The following quatrain from "La via del rifugio" underscores Gozzano's reluctance to consider himself part of the artistic community; he refers to himself not as poet but as a living thing called "guidogozzano": "Ma dunque esisto! O strano! / vive tra il Tutto e il Niente / questa cosa vivente / detta guidogozzano" (But then I exist! How strange! / between All and Nothing lives / this living thing / called guidogozzano).

In 1907, in addition to publishing his first collection of poetry, he suffered a life-threatening attack of tuberculosis, which left him pondering his future. He also met Amalia Guglielminetti, with whom he immediately established a close relationship that lasted until his death.

Gozzano's second collection, *I colloqui*, was successful with the public and the critics. Divided into three sections, the collection, in Gozzano's words, offers "una sintesi della prima giovinezza— dell'autore—un riflesso pallido del *suo* dramma interiore" (a synthesis of early youth—the author's—a pale reflection of *his* interior drama). The first section, "Il giovanile errore" (The Youthful Error), tells of the sentimental and hedonistic pleasures of the poet-protagonist's alter ego, the "fratello muto" (mute brother); "Il gioco del silenzio" (The Game of Silence) and "Invernale" (Winter) have been considered the best compositions in this section. Alberto De Marchi, in the introduction to Gozzano's 1961 collection *Poesie e prose*, says he considers the first poem a masterpiece for its "creazione lirica e la rapidità dei trapassi ove la fantasia si muove tra lucenti smaltature, leggera e felice in un sorgivo incanto" (lyrical creation and the swiftness of transitions as

the imagination moves along shining surfaces, light and gay in a spontaneous enchantment).

Section 2, "Alle soglie" (On the Threshold), recounts the poet's somber encounters with death. In the opening poem, "Alle soglie," death appears as a "Signora vestita di nulla e che non ha forma" (Woman dressed of nothing and without form), yet everything she touches is transformed. More skeptical than before, the poet here comes to terms with his malady and with his inevitable early demise.

Death also figures as the central theme of "Il più atto" (The Fittest), "Salvezza" (Salvation), and "Paolo e Virginia" (Paul and Virginia), this last poem the most significant of the three. Inspired by Bernardin de Saint-Pierre's seventeenth-century novel, *Paul et Virginie*, Gozzano combines the tragedy of Virginia's death and Paolo's inability to love again with the death (his rejection) of his own literary heritage, as suggested by the phrase, "la retorica dei tempi" (The rhetoric of the times). This expression appears in two parts of the poem: for along with Virginia die also the poet and the past, the "retorica dei tempi" and the time of tender feelings, of virtue, and of simple ideals. The poem ends on a strong Leopardian note:

> —Virginia! O sogni miei!
> Virginia!—E ti chiamai, con occhi fissi . . .
> —Virginia! Amore che ritorni e sei
> la Morte! Amore . . . Morte . . .—E più non dissi.
>
> (—Virginia! Oh my dreams!
> Virginia!—And I called you,
>   with my eyes fixed . . .
> —Virginia! Love you return and you're now
> Death! Love . . . Death . . .—And I said
>   no more.)

The protagonist is reborn through this tragedy as one who is unable to love and, consequently, unable to write: "Ah! Se potessi / amare, canterei si novamente!" (Ah! If I could only love, how I would sing again!). But he is reborn with his "sogno . . . distrutto" (dream . . . destroyed). This and three other poems of this section ("La signorina Felicita, ovvero La Felicità" [Miss Felicita, or Felicity], "L'amica di nonna Speranza," and "Cocotte") do not present a "colloquio personale con la morte." Yet it is also true that all the poems in "Alle soglie" are thematically homogeneous. Thus one may see in Paolo a metaphor for the poet, whose own dream had been destroyed. In addition, his own sense of his inability to write

Gozzano and his mother, Diodata, in the garden of Meleto, the family's country house in Aglié

can surely be implied by his writing a poem dependent on a novel of the seventeenth century. Gozzano does not, as he did not in his previous collection, find satisfaction and solace in writing verse according to the exigencies of his immediate predecessors and many contemporaries. In this context, "La signorina Felicita, ovvero La Felicità" figures as Gozzano's manifesto in verse, in which he makes his well-known declaration, "Io mi vergogno, / sí, mi vergogno d'essere un poeta" (I am ashamed, / yes indeed, I am ashamed of being a poet), categorically disassociating himself from the contemporary literary world. His is a total rejection of that world on all levels, and in "La signorina Felicita, ovvero La Felicità," Gozzano rejects all aspects of his cultural environment. The figure of the beautiful woman, object of man's desire, is transformed by Gozzano into one who roasts coffee, mends linen, and is "innebriata" (intoxicated) by his words. Gozzano's Felicita is unattractive—"Sei quasi brutta" (You're almost ugly)—and of simple intellectual background. In this poem, Gozzano fur-

ther divests established turn-of-the-century culture of its honor and privileges. His well-known, irreverent rhyming of "Nietzsche" with "camicie" (shirts) underscores, for instance, his disdain for Friedrich Nietzsche's notion of the overman:

> Tu non fai versi. Tagli le camicie
> per tuo padre. Hai fatta la seconda
> classe, t'han detto che la Terra è tonda,
> ma tu non credi . . . E non mediti Nietzsche . . .

> (You don't write poetry. You mend your father's
> shirts. You finished the second grade,
> they told you the Earth is round
> but you don't believe it . . . And you don't read
>   Nietzsche . . .).

In "Paolo e Virginia" Gozzano laments the loss of a time of tender and simple feelings. In like manner, "La signorina Felicita, ovvero La Felicità" harks back to a similar type of uncomplicated life. He offers a portrait of a middle-class provincial way of life through the narrator's reminiscence of previous visits spent with Felicita. He shifts his attention from a general description of her and her house, to her father. In shifting back to Felicita once more, he speaks of her homeliness and peasant-type dress, the sight of which once comforted him during his past visits. The narrator continues his recollection of these happier times in his detailed description of Felicita's house, the objects therein, and the surrounding garden, where they had spent much time together. But the poem ends on a sad note, as the narrator concludes it with a description of his final departure. Yet, despite the apparently sad, final farewell in this rhapsodic reminiscence, it nevertheless seems fitting that Gozzano followed this poem with a reprint of "L'amica di nonna Speranza," another example of an "idealized 'time tunnel,'" as Erasmo Gabriele Gerato labeled it. In "L'amica di nonna Speranza," the poet again reverts to an uncomplicated moment in the time of the "buone cose di pessimo gusto" (good things of the worst taste); it is a call for happier, past times, evoking 1850 and a girl named Carlotta, Grandma Speranza's friend, as the only one the poet-protagonist could possibly love. It is significant, then, that she does not replicate the homeliness of Felicita, nor is she one of the "donne rifatte sui romanzi" (women weaned on literature); she is portrayed as looking up at the sky, with her "l'indice al labbro, secondo l'atteggiamento romantico" (finger to her lip, in a romantic manner).

As in "Paolo e Virginia," "La signorina Felicita, ovvero La Felicità," and "L'amica di nonna Speranza," recollection is the underlying factor in "Cocotte," the closing poem of section 2. The "cocotte," or prostitute, so termed by the poet-protagonist's mother, appears as a mysterious figure from long ago to whom the adult poet-protagonist is strongly attracted. More than the mysterious female she seems to represent (another past, potential beloved), on a greater scale her presence as a positive love object is more symbolic of the poet-protagonist's life trajectory—more specifically, where it did not lead. Like all the female characters in Gozzano's verse, among them Carlotta, Graziella—of "Le due strade" (The Two Roads)—and Felicita, the cocotte draws the poet away from his troubled present moment into a past happier time:

Oggi ho bisogno
del tuo passato! Tí farò bella
Come Carlotta, come Graziella,
Come tutte le donne del mio sogno!

(Today I need
your past! I will make you beautiful
like Carlotta, like Graziella,
like all the women of my dream!)

Indeed none of the female characters revered in Gozanno's poetry correspond to the "donne rifatte sui romanzi": nor, however, are they accessible to the poet-protagonist, ill-fated that he is to nourish his dream of abandonment and regret: "Il mio sogno è nutrito d'abbandono, / di rimpianto . . ." (My dream is nourished with abandonment, / with regret . . .). Further still, they do not represent mere love objects. Together with their respective surroundings and ways of life, they all contribute to the poet's recollection and yearning for a way of life he did not lead. They recall for the narrator those things that might have been but never were: "Non amo che le cose / che potevano essere ma non sono / state . . ." (I only love those things / which could have been but never / were . . .).

Gozzano successfully passes over the *soglie* (threshold) with "Il reduce" (The Survivor), section 3 of *I colloqui*. In it Gozzano celebrates the conquering of every physical and moral dilemma, as he, content, resigns himself to life as it is. The reappearance of the female reflects part of his resignation. "Una risorta" (Another Resurrected), and "L'onesto rifiuto" (The Honest Refusal) close the final chapter on the poet-protagonist's inability to love. Whereas, before, such inability seemed inexplicably tied to an urgency beyond the poet-protagonist's control, here, conversely, he admits his own inability: he has never been able to love. Symbolically, then, it is appropriate that two of the women characters in this final chapter are but shadows of the women they were, and they appear at an advanced age, no longer the beauties of long ago; it is also significant that the poet-protagonist refuses to accommodate the third, a lovely, seemingly young woman. The first two women underscore his lost love opportunities in the past, whereas his present "rifiuto onesto" (honest refusal) of the young, third woman originates from his "arido . . . cuore" (arid heart) and his ever-present inability to fall in love: "Non posso amare, Illusa! Non ho amato mai!" (I cannot love, you fool! I've never loved!).

"Totò Merùmeni," "In casa del sopravissuto" (In the House of the Survivor), and the final "I colloqui" are fundamental to Gozzano's ars poetica. They underscore his disdain for the literary tradition of his times, as they express his

decision not to extol any longer the Nietzschean rebellion against the positivistic bourgeoisie. Representative of Gozzano himself, Totò is a polemical
figure vis-à-vis the literary/philosophical notions
of the beginning of the century. Having deviated
from the Italian poetic tradition represented by
D'Annunzio and Pascoli, this once "Frivolo . . .
mondano . . . vent'anni appena . . ." (Frivolous
. . . worldly . . . / just twenty-years-old) man—
once also an "anima ribelle" (rebellious spirit) à
la Nietzsche—is now a self-exile: "Totò scelse
l'esilio" (Totò chose exile), no longer in concert
with Arthur Schopenhauer and Nietzsche. Totò
"non è cattivo. E' il *buono* che derideva il Nietzsche" (is not bad. He is the good man Nietzsche
mocked). Totò now "quasi è felice. Alterna
l'indagine e la rima. / . . . / Totò opra in disparte,
sorride, e meglio aspetta" (is almost happy. He alternates research and rhyme. / . . . / Totò works
apart, he smiles and waits for better things), as
he with "il cuore in pace" (his heart at peace) is
transformed into the "fanciullo . . . tenero e
antico" (boy . . . gentle and of long ago) who abandons the "pagina ribelle" (rebellious page).

In "Pioggia d'agosto" (August Rain) Gozzano alludes to future verse writing: "con altra
voce tornerò poeta" (with another voice I shall return as poet). An amateur entomologist, Gozzano
had intended to focus his next collection of poetry on butterflies and appropriately call it "Le
farfalle." His stylistic intentions were to emulate
an eighteenth-century Arcadian poem about butterflies in an ironic manner with borrowings
from Maeterlinck. But this collection remained incomplete because of Gozzano's premature death
and perhaps, also, because of his own disenchantment with the project.

"Ketty" (date of composition unknown, first
published in the *Opere* volume *I Colloqui*, 1935)
and "Risveglio sul Picco d'Adamo" (Waking up
on Adam's Peak, published in *Apritium*, October-
November, 1913) are two of the poems Gozzano
saved from his trip to India in 1912. Indeed, as
he wrote in a 1916 letter (quoted by Giorgio
Bàrberi Squarotti), except for the "poemetto di
Ketty, l'agile ragazza americana, tutto il resto è
per il cestino: la pornografia di raro diventa arte,
forse mai. Io non sono tagliato per le spirituali
sconcezze letterarie. Ho letto il poemetto di Ketty
a [Carlo] Chiaves e a mia madre. Ne sono
entusiasti" (poem for Ketty, the agile American
girl, everything else is for the trash can: pornography rarely becomes art, perhaps never. I'm not
cut out for emotional obscenities of a literary

type. I read the poem to Chiaves and to my
mother. They liked it). The poem's fascination
lies in its presentation of enticing qualities of the
young female in its evocation and emulation of
Gozzano's earlier writings, be it the subject matter of this "vergine folle da gli error prudenti"
(foolish virgin of prudent errors) or the melancholy tone reminiscent of earlier love poems. In
his encounter with Ketty, the poet-protagonist is
attracted to her, as she, sitting cheerfully at his
side, smokes, whistles, and spits, freshening him
with her saliva. Different from other women in
Gozzano's poetry, Ketty possesses a "virile
franchezza" (manly frankness) that attracts the
poet-protagonist. Betrothed to her boxer cousin
in the United States, she, alone in Italy, "prima
delle nozze, in tempo ancora / esplora il mondo
ignota che le avanza / e qualche amico esplora
che l'esplora" (in the time before her wedding / explores the unknown world before her / and some
friends she explores who explore her). Yet, while
allowing the poet-protagonist to pull her close,
she remains indifferent to his desires, and while
extolling her cousin's virtues, she defends her vir-
ginity.

Throughout his poetry, Gozzano makes reference to verse writing and, especially in "Totò
Merùmeni," offers what many have perceived to
be a self-portrait. In considering the notion of
the self-portrait in Gozzano's poetry, one gains
greater insight into his rejection of traditional
turn-of-the-century poetics. In a 28 June 1907 letter to Giulio De Frenzi (quoted by Edoardo
Sanguineti in 1966) Gozzano wrote that he was suffering from "sintomi che fanno passare la voglia
di cantare le *cose non serie*: sdegno dei retori [è]
unica mia delizia! Cantare le *cose serie*? Temo che
non siano il mio forte" (symptoms that squelch
the desire to sing of *things not serious*: disdain for
the rhetoricians is my only delight! Sing of *serious things*? I am afraid they are not my forte).
Juxtaposed to "cose non serie" the "cose serie"
may be an allusion to traditional poetic invention. As Sanguineti states, Gozzano "ribadirà
programmaticamente, e con grande forza polemica . . . la propia seria poetica di lirico frivolo" (will programmatically confirm, with great
polemical force . . . his own poetics of the frivolous lyric poet). In Gozzano's poetry this is often
represented by his persistent paraphrasing and
borrowing from other poets. His constant borrowings serve to set up certain contradictions and ex-
aggerations; they also aid in the interpretation of
Gozzano's verbal irony. Such interpretation

brings into play both linguistic and cultural/ideological notions of the ironist and his or her reader.

Ezra Pound once stated that "The ironist is one who suggests that the reader think, and this process being unnatural to the majority of mankind, the way of the ironical is beset with snares and with furze-bushes" (*Poetry*, November 1917). Considering Gozzano's poetry from 1904 to 1911 as a whole, and from the perspective of irony, the reader's task then is to think and rethink in order to grasp the ironic. Consequently one may speak of a game that Gozzano plays while writing verse: a game of the "cose non serie" juxtaposed to the "cose serie," which affords him the possibility to communicate his dissatisfaction with the times. A major way in which Gozzano succeeds is through the series of self-portraits he offers, a series that, on a greater scale, becomes one portrait.

Like many of his contemporaries—Marino Moretti, Sergio Corazzini, and Aldo Palazzeschi—Gozzano refused to take part in traditional poetic invention, represented in Italy at that time by poets such as Giosuè Carducci, Pascoli, and D'Annunzio. Well known is the quasi-proverbial quatrain of Gozzano's "L'altro" (The Other, 1907), where he blatantly states that God, "invece che far[lo] gozzano / un po' scimunito, ma greggio, / far[lo] gabrieldannunziano: / sarebbe stato ben peggio!" (instead of making him gozzano / a little foolish, but unrefined, / could have made him gabrieldannunziano: / it would have been much worse). Yet Gozzano prepares his reader for what is to come in his earliest of poems. His rejection is evident in "A Massimo Bontempelli" (1904), where he confesses to have abandoned the ways of tradition. He describes himself as weakened by the "veleno dell' 'altro evangelista' " (poison of the other evangelist), deceived by both the art and life of the times: "Mia puerizia, illusa dal ridevole / artificio dei suoni e dagli affanni / di un sogno esasperante e miserevole" (My childhood, fooled by the laughable / artifice of sounds and by the difficult breathing / of an exacerbating and miserable dream). So that his dream is not the exacerbating and miserable one of Andrea Sperelli (the protagonist of D'Annunzio's novel *Il Piacere* [1889] whose way of life Gozzano rejects), he offers himself to nature. In so doing, he creates an image which anticipates that of "La via del rifugio." The closing lines of "A Massimo Bontempelli"—"le mie smorte / membra distenderò" (my pale / limbs I'll

spread wide)—foreshadow those which close "La via del rifugio": "socchiudo gli occhi, sto / supino sui trifoglio" (I half-close my eyes, and I lie / on my back on the clover).

In concert with the spirit of "A Massimo Bontempelli," "La via del rifugio" also addresses poetic invention. It opens with the nursery rhyme of hide-and-seek the narrator's nieces are playing—cheerful verses interspersed with his own philosophical queries. At one point, as noted earlier, he refers to himself as "questa cosa vivente / detta guidogozzano!" (this living thing / called guidogazzano). And as the closing of the former poem anticipated that of the latter, "La via del rifugio" offers imagery similar to what would later appear in "L'altro." In both cases Gozzano presents proper names in lower cases ("guidogozzano," "gozzano," and "gabrieldannunziano"), which, when coupled with "questa cosa vivente," endorse the devaluation of both poetry and the image of the poet. "La via del rifugio" represents not so much a refuge from life as it does an escape from the poetic tradition and system of fin-de-siècle life. In this poem, one also finds clear evidence of his desire to escape: "Oh la carezza / dell'erba! Non agogno / che la virtù del sogno: / l'inconsapevolezza" (Oh the caress / of the grass! I long only / for the virtue of dreams: / ignorance). One finds an analogous situation in "L'analfabeta," where the illiterate is not so much the old man who cannot read, but the poet-narrator himself, as he would like to be: "Ah! Vorrei ben non sapere / leggere, o Vecchio, le parole altrui! / Berrei, inconscio di sapori scaltri, / un puro vino dentro il mio bicchiere" (Ah! I would like not to know, / how to read, oh Old One, others' words! / I would drink, unaware of shrewd flavors, a pure wine from my glass).

Of the numerous self-portraits Gozzano offers, "Totò Merùmeni" clearly stands in the foreground. On the one hand, Totò is a product of his times. A man of much culture and good taste in literature, and with a disdainful temperament, he is also the "gelido sofista" (cold sophist) who has no capacity for feelings; he thus represents "il vero figlio del tempo nostro" (the true child of our time). Exactly who this *figlio* is becomes clearer once one looks not only within but also outside of this poem.

Totò stands in opposition to the "uomo d'altri tempi" (man of other times), who belongs to the overly sentimental Romantic age to which Gozzano alludes at the end of "La signorina

Illustration by G. Brunelleschi for Gozzano's poem "Il richiamo" (The Call; from Lettura, *June 1909)*

Felicita." Totò is one who truly understands the life of the spirit and, as such, chooses to stand alone and work apart. Waiting, thus, for better things to come along, Totò's parched soul is capable of only, at best, a slender spray of consoling verses: namely, a type of new poetry that Edoardo Sanguineti considers a bridge from Giacomo Leopardi to Eugenio Montale, as symbolized in the figure of the "anima arsa" (scorched spirit).

Gozzano's "sdegno dei retori" (disdain for the rhetoricians) is most explicit in "In casa del sopravissuto" and "Pioggia d'agosto." In the first poem—an apparent continuation of Totò's portrait—the survivor symbolizes both love and death; that is, the spiritual and physical. Here, as is not the case in most earlier poems, Gozzano articulates his rebellion more explicitly through his choice of vocabulary. The survivor figures as an "anima rebelle" (rebellious spirit) who, staring at his portrait, contemplates his past self as ridiculous and mad. And recovering more and more from his disillusioned dream of art, he, too, like Totò, is "quasi felice" (almost happy), as the final image is that of a sneering veteran who "fissa a lungo la fotografia / di quel sé stesso già cosí lontano. / 'Un po' malato . . . frivolo . . . mondano . . .'" (stares for a long time at the picture / of himself already so far away. / A bit sick . . . frivolous . . . worldly). The figure of the poet, rebelling from the maladies and the superficiality of his times, was already present in "A

Massimo Bontempelli." Analogous also is the use of *ribelle* in unison with health, which is set up as a contrast to the atmosphere of the times, as expressed in the "veleno dell'altro evangelista' " (poison of the other evangelist).

One might consider "Pioggia d'agosto" the last of a triptych dedicated to Totò's portrait as "il vero figlio del tempo nostro" (the true son of our times). Here the poet-protagonist's disdain for the rhetoricians reaches its peak, where he clearly expresses his philosophical and formalistic abhorrence of the nineteenth-century legacy, evident in Gozzano's juxtaposition of the "fede alta" (high faith) to the "parole . . . nauseose" (nauseating words):

E' tempo che una fede alta ti scuota,
ti levi sopra te, nell'Ideale!
Guarda gli amici, ognun palpita quale
demagogo, credente, patriota . . .

Guarda gli amici. Ognuno già ripose
la varia fede nelle varie scuole.
Tu non credi e sogghigni. Or quali cose
darai per meta all'anima che duole?
La Patria? Dio? l'Umanità? Parole
che i retori t'han fatto nauseose! . . .

Lotte brutali d'appetiti avversi
dove l'anima putre e non s'appaga . . .

(It's time that a noble faith shake you,
that you rise above yourself, into the Ideal!

Look at your friends, each one quivers as
demagogue, believer, patriot . . .

Look at your friends. Each one has already placed
his different faith in the different schools.
You do not believe and you sneer. Now what things
will you set as a goal for the soul that pains?
Country? God? Humanity? Words
that the rhetoricians rendered nauseating to
    you! . . .

Brutal struggles of adverse desires
for which the soul rots and is not
    fulfilled . . .).

In fact, midway through these allegations, one
finds characteristics similar to those already apparent in "Totò Merùmeni" and "In casa del sopravissuto." His friends' "varia fede" is in opposition to the initial "fede alta." While the first two
poems, as counterpoints to tradition, end on an
unspecific note, "Pioggia d'agosto" concludes
with a firm declaration of a future ars poetica:
"con altra voce tornerò poeta!" (with another
voice I shall return as a poet!)

Bibliographies:

Andrea Rocca, ed., "Bibliografia," in *Guido
    Gozzano: Tutte le poesie* (Milan: Mondadori,
    1980), pp. 3-39;

Mariarosa Masoero, *Catalogo dei manoscritti di
    Guido Gozzano* (Florence: Olschki, 1984).

Biographies:

Henriette Martin, *Guido Gozzano (1883-1916)*
    (Paris: Presses Universitaires de France,
    1968);

Giorgio De Rienzo, *Guido Gozzano: Vita di
    rispettabile bugiardo* (Milan: Rizzoli, 1983).

References:

Lina Angioletti, *Guido Gozzano* (Milan: Mursia,
    1975);

Franco Antonicelli, *Capitoli gozzaniani: Scritti editi
    e inediti*, edited by Michele Mari (Florence:
    Olschki, 1982);

Giorgio Bàrberi Squarotti, ed., Introduction to
    Gozzano's *Poesie* (Milan: Rizzoli, 1977), pp.
    7-21;

Carlo Calcaterra, *Con Guido Gozzano e altri poeti* (Bo-
    logna: Zanichelli, 1944);

Angela Casella, *Le fonti del linguaggio poetico di
    Gozzano* (Florence: Nuova Italia, 1982);

Franco Contorbia, *Il sofista subalpino: Tra le carte
    di Gozzano* (Cuneo, Italy: Arciere, 1980);

Gigliola De Donato, *Lo spazio poetico di Guido
    Gozzano* (Bari, Italy: Adriatica, 1982);

Alberto De Marchi, ed., Introduction to Goz-
    zano's *Poesie e prose* (Milan: Garzanti, 1961),
    pp. 7-20;

Giorgio De Rienzo, "Gozzano e la critica
    (1916-1966)," in his *Camerana, Cena e altri
    studi piemontesi* (Bologna: Cappelli, 1977),
    pp. 203-237;

Aldo De Toma, " 'Le non godute' e altre note
    gozzaniane," *Lettere Italiane*, 37 (January-
    March 1985): 83-108;

Erasmo Gabriele Gerato, *Guido Gustavo Gozzano:
    A Literary Interpretation* (Potomac, Md., Stu-
    dia Humanitatis, 1983);

Marziano Guglielminetti, "Guido Gozzano," in
    *Novecento: Gli scrittori e la cultura letteraria
    nella società italiana*, volume 1 (Milan: Mar-
    zorati, 1987), pp. 593-633;

Guido Gozzano: I giorni, le opere (Florence:
    Olschki, 1985);

François Livi, *La parola crepuscolare: Corazzini,
    Gozzano, Moretti* (Milan: Istituo Propaganda
    Libraria, 1986);

Antonio Piromalli, *Ideologia e arte in Guido
    Gozzano* (Florence: Nuova Italia, 1972);

Bruno Porcelli, *Gozzano: Originalità e plagi* (Bolo-
    gna: Pàtron, 1974);

Gianni Pozzi, "Guido Gozzano," in *La poesia
    italiana del Novecento* (Turin: Einaudi, 1967),
    pp. 27-37;

Edoardo Sanguineti, *Guido Gozzano: Indagini e
    letture* (Turin: Einaudi, 1966);

Sanguineti, *Tra libertà e crepuscolarismo* (Turin:
    Mursia, 1977);

Giuseppe Savoca, *Concordanza dei "Colloqui"* (Cata-
    nia, Italy: University of Catania, 1970);

Savoca, *Concordanza di tutte le poesie di Guido
    Gozzano: Testo, Concordanza, Lista di frequenza,
    Indici* (Florence: Olschki, 1984);

Antonio Stäuble, *Sincerità e artificio in Gozzano* (Ra-
    venna, Italy: Longo, 1972);

Giovanna Wedel De Stasio, "Il crepuscolarismo e
    la poetica del rifiuto," *Gradiva*, new series 4,
    no. 2 (1988): 24-32.

Piero Jahier

(11 April 1884 - 19 November 1966)

Joseph E. Germano
Buffalo State College

BOOKS: *Fruzzicano* (Florence: Claudiana, 1904);

Resultanze in merito alla vita e al carattere di Gino Bianchi (Florence: Libreria della Voce, 1915);

Con me e con gli Alpini (Florence: Libreria della Voce, 1919; revised edition, Turin: Einaudi, 1943);

Ragazzo (Rome: Libreria della Voce, 1919);

Ragazzo e prime poesie (Florence: Vallecchi, 1939; revised, 1943);

Arte alpina (Milan: All'Insegna del Pesce d'Oro/Scheiwiller, 1958; revised edition, Florence: Vallecchi, 1961);

Qualche poesia, edited by Vanni Scheiwiller (Milan: All'Insegna del Pesce d'Oro/Scheiwiller, 1962);

Con Claudel, edited by Scheiwiller (Milan: All'Insegna del Pesce d'Oro/Scheiwiller, 1964);

1918: L'Astico, giornale della trincea, edited by Mario Isnenghi (Padua, Italy: Rinoceronte, 1964);

Poesie (Florence: Vallecchi, 1964);

Opere (Florence: Vallecchi, 1964);

Poesie in versi e in prosa, edited by Paolo Briganti (Turin: Einaudi, 1981);

Con me, edited by Ottavio Cecchi and Enrico Ghidetti (Rome: Riuniti, 1983).

OTHER: *Canti di soldati*, edited by Jahier, music by Vittorio Gui (Milan: Sonzogno, 1919);

Giacinto Spagnoletti, ed., *Poesia italiana contemporanea, 1909-1959*, includes poems and notes by Jahier (Parma, Italy: Guanda, 1959), pp. 75-87.

TRANSLATIONS: Daniel Halevy, *Il castigo della democrazia* (Florence: Libreria della Voce, 1911);

John Calvin, *La religione individuale* (Lanciano, Italy: Carabba, 1912);

Pierre-Joseph Proudhon, *La guerra e la pace* (Lanciano, Italy: Carabba, 1912);

Piero Jahier

Paul Claudel, *Arte poetica*; *Conoscenza del tempo*; *Trattato della conoscenza del mondo e di se stesso* (Milan: Milanese, 1913);

Claudel, *Crisi meridiana* (Rome: Libreria della Voce, 1920);

Lin Yu-T'ang, *Importanza di vivere* (Milan: Bompiani, 1940);

Yu-T'ang, *Momento a Pechino* (Milan: Bompiani, 1941);

Yu-T'ang, *Il mio paese e il mio popolo* (Milan: Bompiani, 1941);

Robert Louis Stevenson, *L'isola del tesoro* (Turin: Einaudi, 1943);

Murasaki Scikibu, *La signora della barca e Il ponte dei sogni* (Milan: Bompiani, 1944);

Joseph Conrad, *Racconti di mare e di costa* (Turin: Einaudi, 1946);

Scikibu, *La storia di Ghengi* (Turin: Einaudi, 1947);

Conrad, *Gioventù e altri racconti* (Milan: Bompiani, 1949);

Conrad, *Appunti di vita e di letteratura*, translated by Jahier and M. L. Rissler Stoneman (Turin: Einaudi, 1950);

Wilkie Collins, *La pietra lunare*, translated by Jahier and Stoneman (Turin: Einaudi, 1953);

Conrad, *Lo specchio del mare*, translated by Jahier and Stoneman (Turin: Einaudi, 1953);

Graham Greene, *La fine dell'avventura*, translated by Jahier and Stoneman (Milan: Mondadori, 1953);

Molière, *Il borghese gentiluomo* (Turin: Einaudi, 1953);

Yu-T'ang, *La saggezza dell'America* (Milan: Bompiani, 1954);

Yu-T'ang, *Una vedova, Una monaca, Una cortigiana e Altre famose novelle cinesi* (Milan: Bompiani, 1955);

Yu-T'ang, *L'imperatrice Wu* (Milan: Bompiani, 1955);

Thomas Hardy, *Via dalla pazza folla* (Milan: Garzanti, 1955);

Chin P'ing Mei, translated by Jahier and Stoneman (Turin: Einaudi, 1955);

Greene, *Una pistola in vendita* (Turin: Einaudi, 1956);

Greene, *Il tranquillo americano*, translated by Jahier and Stoneman (Milan: Mondadori, 1957);

Yu-T'ang, *L'isola inaspettata*, translated by Jahier and Stoneman (Milan: Bompiani, 1957);

Greene, *Saggi cattolici* (Milan: Garzanti, 1958);

G. Bibby, *Le navi dei Vichinghi* (Turin: Einaudi, 1960).

The literary rigor Piero Jahier imposed on himself as a writer seems to be an artistic manifestation of a profoundly moral and deeply religious *forma mentis* firmly rooted in him since childhood. His was a temperament of uncompromising integrity, which he persevered to maintain uncontaminated throughout his life, at times at the expense of his own personal safety. His style and themes betray his strong moral temperament and the Protestant concept of good and evil. The biographical element becomes inter- connected with the author's inspiration: in Jahier's work one finds the most salient example of the conflation of lyricism and naturalism.

Jahier was born in Genoa on 11 April 1884. His father, Pier Enrico Jahier, was an evangelical minister of Waldensian origin, while his mother, Giuseppina Danti Jahier, a convert to Protestantism, was Florentine. His parents had met in the church of the Darbist Brothers in Florence while his father was employed as a librarian in the household of Count Piero Guicciardini. After marrying, Jahier's parents moved to Genoa, and in 1889 they left for Susa, a small town in the Alps, where his father practiced his ministry. In 1897, unable to overcome the guilt of an adulterous relationship, his father committed suicide, leaving behind his widow with six children of whom Piero Jahier at age thirteen was the eldest. This tragedy was to condition Jahier's life in various ways. His father's suicide was to be recounted by Jahier in the chapter "La morte del padre" (The Father's Death) in *Ragazzo* (Boy, 1919), a work of prose interspersed with verse that exploits fully the expressive possibilities of both genres in rapid exchanges alternating poetry and prose. The stylistic upheaval of this clash achieves a remarkable lyrical pathos and reflects artistically the human tragedy and upheaval of an abandoned family. Elio Gioanola, in his *Storia letteraria del Novecento in Italia* (1976), suggests that, in Freudian terms, Jahier sublimates his father's suicide and the strong sense of sin of puritan Calvinism in his own uncompromising social moralism and his instinctive and unselfish dedication to others.

To this concept, one might add that it is not, perhaps, sheer coincidence that Jahier chose to translate Paul Claudel's *Partage de midi* (Break of Noon, translated into Italian as *Crisi meridiana* [1920], meaning Crisis at Noon). *Partage de midi* is biographical and was written in the aftermath of Claudel's own crisis due to an adulterous relationship. Claudel wanted to exorcise and expel from his system the remorse he harbored inside. Jahier must have been touched by the parallel events between Claudel's text and his own father's tragedy.

Soon after 1897 the Jahier family moved to Florence, where Piero Jahier attended the *liceo*, and in 1902 he registered at the same Waldensian School of Theology where his father had received his religious training. After two years Jahier had serious doubts about his vocation and left the school. Instead he found employment with the Adriatic Railroad Company; however, he studied without interruption and received two university degrees: a law degree from the University of Urbino in 1911 and a degree in modern literature, with a specialization in French literature, from the University of Turin in 1913.

In 1909 Jahier had written Giuseppe Prezzolini and offered his services to help the cause of the journal *La Voce*, in its second year of publication. The offer was accepted, and in 1909 Jahier began his collaboration with a series of essays on religion and the Waldensians in Italy. They are not creative texts, but they provide a profound insight into Jahier's background and particular moralism. Jahier also began to translate foreign authors' works. His first choices include a selection of John Calvin's writings titled *The Individual Religion* (translated in 1912). In 1911, in addition to collaborating with articles, Jahier joined *La Voce* on a full-time basis as cashier, manager of its bookstore, and administrator of the journal until 1913. In 1913 and 1914 Jahier translated Paul Claudel's *Arte Poetica*, wrote for the journal *Riviera Ligure*, and continued to contribute to *La Voce*. Considering the original political intentions of *La Voce*, especially those concerning the moral and cultural renewal of the nation, Jahier exemplifies *ad litteram* these aspirations. It is he who is most closely and almost exclusively identified with *La Voce*.

In 1914 Charles Péguy, the French poet, died on the battlefield. Jahier began to write against German imperialism, and in 1915 he volunteered as a lieutenant in the Alpine corps. That same year Jahier published his *Resultanze in merito alla vita e al carattere di Gino Bianchi* (Outcome Concerning the Life and Character of Gino Bianchi), a work of prose that contains the well-known poem "Ballata dell'uomo più libero" (Ballad of the Most Liberated Man). From 14 February to 10 November 1918 Jahier edited *L'Astico*, the only newspaper edited, printed, and published in the trenches; in addition to the soldiers' participation, the work of well-known critics such as Emilio Cecchi appeared in it.

After World War I Jahier was encouraged by Prezzolini to become editor of another newspaper, *Il nuovo contadino*, with the express intention to create a vehicle of communication between different social classes, and to help veterans become reintegrated into society. When it became clear to Jahier that the newspaper was being exploited by the rich landowners, he promptly resigned. In 1919 he published *Con me e con gli Alpini* (With

Me and the Alpine Brigade), a lyrical diary of his war years.

Having left the newspaper, he returned to his job with the railroads and became active in a cultural club that promoted democratic ideals and political awareness on the part of the average citizen. This activity was diametrically opposed to the events taking place in Italy at this time. The Fascist movement was creating disturbances that led to the march on Fiume. Jahier refused to be a card-carrying member of the Fascist party. Because of his past experience as editor of *L'Astico* and *Il nuovo contadino*, Jahier was well-known to Benito Mussolini, who invited him to Milan in 1921. Jahier flatly refused his offer to become the editor of the Fascist newspaper *Il popolo d'Italia*, and from that day on Jahier was constantly and mercilessly persecuted by the Fascists. Although he was blacklisted and his personal notes were frequently confiscated, Jahier was not deterred and became an active member of the anti-Fascist group "Italia Libera." He was also active in the publication of the newspaper *Non Mollare*, whose leaders were anti-Fascists. In 1924 Jahier was attacked and beaten by Fascists when he attempted to pay homage to the murdered Giacomo Matteotti in the Florentine cemetery of Porte Sante. In 1927 Jahier was transferred against his will to Bologna, where for quite some time, before being joined by his family, he lived alone in a room in Via dell'Osservanza, the same room Giovanni Pascoli had occupied years before. Jahier became active in the resistance movement in Bologna. In 1939 he published *Ragazzo e prime poesie* (Boy and First Poems) and *Importanza di vivere* (published in 1940), the Italian version of the Chinese essayist Lin Yu-T'ang's *The Importance of Living*. Jahier's wife died in 1945, and he returned to Florence to his house he had built himself years before with Prezzolini's help. Jahier's activity as a translator intensified as he was translating works by Joseph Conrad, Wilkie Collins, Molière, Graham Greene, and others.

In Giacinto Spagnoletti's 1959 anthology, *Poesia Italiana contemporanea 1909-1959*, Jahier describes his most personal feelings concerning his poetic vocation: "Fu nell'adolescenza che sentii, con assoluta certezza, di non essere tanto chiamato ad agire, nella vita, quanto ad esprimere. Ma con altrettanta certezza sentii che non avrei potuto esprimermi se non avessi avuto il coraggio di essere, anzitutto, un uomo comune che si guadagna il pane vendendo qualsiasi merce, all'infuori della poesia. . . . Ritenevo che

A 2 June 1909 letter from Jahier to Giuseppe Prezzolini (from Storia della letteratura: Italiana, *volume 6, edited by Luigi Ferrante, 1965)*

in una società savia, ogni uomo avrebbe dovuto iniziare la vita nella posizione di povero, per poter imparare a esser giusto" (It was during my adolescence when I felt, with absolute certainty, that my mission in life was not to act, but to express. But with similar certainty I felt that I would not have been able to express myself had I not had the courage to be, above all, a common man who makes a living by selling any kind of merchandise, other than poetry.... I believed that in a just society, each man should have begun his life as a poor man, in order to be able to learn to be just).

Justice, in fact, became an intrinsic part of Jahier's life and literary mission. Jahier begins with a strict observance of one's duties and a strong sense of ethics and morality: to feel that each moment is crucial because it affects one's total existence and the welfare of others and to know that everything man does has the substance of a rite. In one of his most successful poems, "Ballata dell'uomo più libero," Jahier wishes that man be given the dignity and freedom to stand alone and follow his destiny unhindered; at the same time, the poet offers himself as a sacrificial lamb, in order to set right any social imbalance that may have created injustices and victims. The first three lines and the last nine lines illustrate this concept:

> Chi è salito più in alto?
>   Perché io voglio scendere
>   quanto è salito
> . . . .
> Rendetemi, dunque, il mio peso
>   perché non barcolli
>   perché non perda piede
>   sul sentiero segnato
>   Se siamo miseri,
> se siamo deboli, se siamo stremati
>   abbiam diritto al più acuto
>   grido di gioia
>   disperato

> (Who has climbed the highest?
> Because I wish to descend
>   as much as he has climbed
> . . . .
> Give me back, then, my burden
>   so that I stagger not
> so that I lose not my footing
>   on the marked path
>   If we are wretched,
> if we are weak, if we are exhausted
>   we have the right to the shrillest
>   desperate cry
>   of joy).

Jahier was a witness to social injustices and established a personal dialogue with those who suffered; thus the poet carried out what he called the "fatica d'Adamo" (Adam's labor). The poem "Canto del camminatore" (The Walker's Song, in *Resultanze*) may very well be the song of a modern-day Adam trapped in a nightmarish, polluted, unfeeling, urban ghetto:

> Come ho potuto allogarmi, giornaliero a scrivania, io che lavoro camminando come un cavallo, e partorisco all'aperto come la pecora!

> Abbastanza di quest'aria respiro-respirato; e nuvole prigioniere di tetti.—Vedo batter l'ombra delle loro grandi ali, affogata nei casamenti.

> Come la pianta acquatica mi allevo intombato in acque di solitudine e di tristezza penosamente sforzandomi di portare alla luce il mio fiore.

> (How could I chain myself to a desk, I who work walking like a horse, and give birth in the open like sheep!

> Enough of this exhaled-breath air; and clouds prisoners of rooftops.—I see the flashing shadow of their large wings, suffocated in the tenement-houses.

> Like the aquatic plant I grow entombed in waters of solitude and sadness painfully striving to bring to light my flower.)

Jahier's firsthand experiences in the trenches as a lieutenant of the Alpine Brigade are recounted in what many consider his finest work, *Con me e con gli Alpini*. Written between 1915 and 1917, it was first published in the journal *Riviera Ligure* on 1 January 1918, then published as a book the next year. Poetry and prose become intertwined and give lyrical depth to Jahier's moralism and critical musings. Some of the poems are hymns or march songs and have the simple musicality of popular songs (in 1919 Jahier edited *Canti di soldati* [Soldiers' Songs], set to music by Vittorio Gui). Still, the poet's social moralism and strong sense of duty permeate even the simplest poems and songs. Jahier goes one step further: what had been an individual ethic becomes a search for a collective ethic confirmed by the generous and emotional cooperation between Jahier and his troops. The opening poem, "Dichiarazione" (Declaration; first intro-

Italo Calvino and Jahier at the award ceremony for the Viareggio Prize, 1957

duced in the 1943 Einaudi edition), is an exposition of the poet's reasons for waging war and his pride in being with such simple and good people:

> Altri morirà per la Storia d'Italia volentieri
> e forse qualcuno per risolvere in qualche modo la
>   vita.
>   Ma io per far compagnia a questo popolo digiuno
>   che non sa perché va a morire
>   popolo che muore in guerra perché "mi vuol
>   bene"
>   "per me" nei suoi sessanta uomini comandati
>   siccome è il giorno che tocca a morire.
>
>   Altri morirà per le medaglie e per le ovazioni
>   ma io per questo popolo illetterato
>   che non prepara guerre perché di miseria ha
>   campato
>   la miseria che non fa guerre, ma semmai
>   rivoluzioni.
>
>   (Others will die willingly for the History of
>   Italy
> and some perhaps to somehow resolve their life.
>   But I to keep company to these hungry people

who ignore why they die
people who die in war because "they love me"
  "for me" with sixty men under orders
  as on the day when one must die.

  Others will die for the medals and the ovations
    but I for these illiterate people
who don't create wars because they have lived in poverty
  poverty doesn't wage war, but if anything revolutions.)

The poet's appreciation for his troops' devotion to him and their duties is seen in his humility, privately expressed, alone at night in the poem "Silenzio" (Silence); the poet seems embarrassed, but is moved, by the salutes and respect he receives during the day from his soldiers, whom he considers and treats as equals:

> Tutto il giorno questo scansarsi reverente,
>   tutto il giorno questi lunghi saluti:
>   tre passi prima la mano alla visiera,
> quattro passi durante lo sguardo fitto in cuore.
>   E chi sono io, superiore?
>   Questi saluti chi li ha meritati?
>   Ma la sera, giornata finita,
>   traversando i cortili annerati
>   son io che sull'attenti, rigido,
>   la mano alla tesa
>   tutti e ciascuno
>   per questa notte e questa vita
>   vi saluto, miei soldati.
>
> (All day long this reverent side-stepping,
>   all day long these long salutes:
>   three steps ahead the hand on the visor,
> four steps during the heart-fixed stare.
>   And who am I, superior?
>   Who has deserved these salutes?
>   But at night, the day gone by,
>   crossing the darkened courtyards
>   it is I who at attention, rigid
>   my hand on the visor
>   all and each one
>   for this night and for this life
>   salute you, my soldiers.)

The performance of one's duties and one's dedication to others were for Jahier, the man and the poet, lifelong aspirations. In assessing Jahier's poetry in 1969, Emilio Cecchi stated: "La poesia diventa un'arte di attiva aspirazione verso l'ordine e la felicità delle buone opere, Poesia d'una vita con compiti immediati ed esatti, dentro uno spazio ben preciso e senza imprevisti, e nella quale si ha da rendere stretto conto del pane mangiato, con compenso e la soddisfazione che i compiti, la respònsabilità e il rendiconto hanno assoluto valore e certezza" (Poetry becomes an art of active aspiration toward the order and happiness of good deeds, the poetry of a life with immediate and exact duties, within a very precise space without surprises, and in which one must be accountable for the bread one eats, with the reward and satisfaction that duties, responsibility and accountability have absolute value and certainty).

Jahier did make himself accountable at no small personal sacrifice. The very few books he wrote up to 1919 (before the two decades of Fascism during which he literally stopped writing) are a testament to his integrity, both as a man and as a writer, consistent with the philosophy in *La Voce* regarding literature as autobiography. It is the same intellectual integrity innate in Cesare Pavese, who, like Jahier, resisted the temptation to trivialize his art by compromising his principles. Their intransigence could not be understood, nor quietly accepted, in an age of Fascist oppression and corruption. Jahier's poetic experimentations are to be considered important also for their seminal value in the development of twentieth-century Italian poetry. His total rejection of the false, purely decorative word and his ability to stay away from the many fashionable groups, such as the *crepuscolari* (twilight poets) and futurists, were due to the consistent direction his poetry followed. This was possible perhaps because his poetry was an antiliterary, avantgarde expression originating not from any polemical stance but from a particular *forma mentis* that innately rejected traditional syntax, logic, and grammar. These tools were alien to Jahier's expressive needs; he fashioned a style in accord with the ideas he set out to convey. His was a stylistic renewal in Italian letters that came from within: Jahier's poetry represents a fusion of his moral and poetic expressions in his quest for truth and the spiritual and social improvement of the human condition.

Letters:

Henri Giordan, *Paul Claudel en Italie*, includes correspondence between Claudel and Jahier (Paris: Klincksieck, 1975).

References:

Aurelio Benevento, *Studi su Piero Jahier* (Florence: Monnier, 1972);

Carlo Bo, "La poesia del frammento: Sbarbaro e Jahier," in *Storia della letteratura italiana: Il Novecento*, volume 9 (Milan: Garzanti, 1976), pp. 282-294;

Paolo Briganti, *Jahier* (Florence: Nuova Italia, 1976);

Giulio Cattaneo, "Le realtà sacre di Jahier," in his *Esperienze intellettuali del primo Novecento* (Milan: Mondadori, 1968), pp. 87-102;

Emilio Cecchi, "Piero Jahier," in *Storia della letteratura italiana: Il Novecento*, volume 9 (Milan: Garzanti, 1969), pp. 513-517;

Paul Claudel, *Partage de midi* (Paris: Gallimard, 1949);

Maura Del Serra, *L'uomo comune: Claudellismo e passione ascetica in Jahier* (Bologna: Pàtron, 1986);

Enrico Falqui, "Piero Jahier dalle *Resultanze* alle *Poesie*," in his *Novecento letterario* (Florence: Vallecchi, 1968), pp. 141-156;

Romeo Forni, *L'uomo dai capelli di lana bianca* (Milan: Todariana, 1972);

Elio Gioanola, "Piero Jahier," in his *Storia letteraria del Novecento in Italia* (Turin: SEI, 1976), pp. 105-109;

Alberto Giordano, *Invito alla lettura di Jahier* (Milan: Mursia, 1973);

Paolo Gonnelli, "Piero Jahier," in *Letteratura italiana: I contemporanei*, volume 1 (Milan: Marzorati, 1963), pp. 531-545;

Klaus Kaemper, *Piero Jahier (1884-1966): Ein patriarchalischer Avantgardist* (Nuremberg, Germany: Carl, 1974);

Romano Luperini, "Piero Jahier," in his *Gli esordi e l'esperienza della "Voce"* (Rome & Bari, Italy: Laterza, 1976), pp. 90-103;

Rodolfo Macchioni Jodi, "Sanità di Jahier," in his *Scrittori e critici del Novecento* (Ravenna, Italy: Longo, 1968), pp. 15-34;

Bortolo Pento, "Piero Jahier: Impegno novecentesco," in his *Poesia contemporanea* (Milan: Marzorati, 1964), pp. 108-113;

Antonio Testa, *Piero Jahier* (Milan: Mursia, 1970);

Rosita Tordi, "Piero Jahier," in *Letteratura italiana contemporanea*, edited by Gaetano Mariani and Mario Petrucciani (Rome: Lucarini, 1979), pp. 695-712.

Gian Pietro Lucini
(30 September 1867 - 13 July 1914)

Giovanni Sinicropi
University of Connecticut

BOOKS: *Il libro delle Figurazioni Ideali* (Milan: Galli, 1894);

Gian Pietro da Core; Storia della Evoluzione della Idea (Milan: Galli, 1895; revised edition, published with *Spirito ribelle*, edited by Carlo Cordiè, Milan: Longanesi, 1974);

Il libro delle Imagini Terrene (Milan: Galli, 1898);

La Nenia al Bimbo di un Çi-devant (N.p., 1898);

Il Sermone al Delfino (N.p., 1898);

Il Monologo di Rosaura (Milan: Esercenti, 1898);

Il Monologo di Florindo (Milan: Esercenti, 1898);

L'Intermezzo della Arlecchinata (Milan: Esercenti, 1898);

I Monologhi di Pierrot (Milan: Esercenti, 1898);

Per una vecchia croce di ferro (Milan: Esercenti, 1899);

La Ballata di Carmen Monarchia, Corifea di Cafè-Chantant (N.p., 1900);

La Prima Ora della Academia (Milan: Sandron, 1902);

Elogio di Varazze (Varazze, Italy: Botta, 1907);

Ai Mani gloriosi di Giosué Carducci (Varazze, Italy: Botta, 1907);

Ragion Poetica e programma del Verso Libero (Milan: Poesia, 1908);

Carme di Angoscia e di Speranza (Varazze, Italy: Botta, 1909);

Revolverate (Milan: Poesia, 1909); revised by Edoardo Sanguineti as *Revolverate e Nuove Revolverate* (Turin: Einaudi, 1975);

La Solita Canzone del Melibeo (Milan: Futuriste di Poesia, 1910);

L'Ora Topica di Carlo Dossi (Varese, Italy: Nicola, 1911); revised edition, edited by Terenzio Grandi: (Milan, Ceschina, 1973);

Giosuè Carducci (Milan: Aliprandi, 1911);

Le Nottole ed i Vasi: Traduzioni e Note di G. P. Lucini e di F. M. D'Arca-Santa [pseudonym of Lucini] (Ancona, Italy: Puccini, 1912);

Il Tempio della Gloria, by Lucini and Innocenzo Cappa (Ancona, Italy: Puccini & Figli, 1913);

Filosofi ultimi: Rassegna a volo d'aquila del "Melibeo," controllata da G. P. Lucini (Rome: Libreria Politica Moderna, 1913);

Antidannunziana: D'Annunzio al vaglio della critica (Milan: Lombardo, 1914);

Poesie scelte (Milano: Lombardo, 1917);

Scritti scelti, edited by Mario Puccini (Lanciano, Italy: Carabba, 1917);

La piccola Chelidonio, edited by Carlo Linati (Milan: Bottega di Poesia, 1922);

La gnosi del Melibeo, ossia i suoi Filosofici Svaghi, edited by Grandi (Turin: L'Impronta, 1930); revised edition, edited by G. Battista Nazzaro (Rome: Espansione, 1979);

Parade; Seguito da un Dialogo Notturno tra il Passante e la Passante, edited by Grandi (Milan: All'Insegna del Pesce d'Oro, 1967);

Le Antitesi e le Perversità, edited by Glauco Viazzi (Parma, Italy: Guanda, 1970);

Il Verso libero-Proposta, edited by Marta Bruscia (Urbino, Italy: Argalìa, 1971);

Prose e canzoni amare, edited by Isabella Ghidetti (Florence: Vallecchi, 1971);

Libri e cose scritte, edited by Viazzi (Naples: Guida, 1971);

Per una poetica del Simbolismo, edited by Viazzi (Naples, Guida, 1971);

Scritti critici, edited by Luciana Martinelli (Bari, Italy: De Donato, 1971);

I Drami delle Maschere, edited by Viazzi (Parma: Guanda, 1973);

Marinetti, Futurismo, Futuristi, edited by Mario Artioli (Bologna: Boni, 1975);

Esperienze d'amore del Melibeo (Alpignano, Italy: Tallone, 1976).

OTHER: *Appunti Stendhaliani*, edited by Lucini and Alberto Lambruso (Saluzzo, Italy: Bovo & Baccolo, 1903);

"Inediti e Documenti," *Il Verri*, 33-34 (October 1970).

Gian Pietro Lucini possessed a highly personal and original voice manifested in the development of Italian poetry at the onset of the twentieth century. Some aspects of his work were assimilated into *scapigliatura* (free-and-easy style) and symbolism, others, more conspicuously, into futurism. However, confronted by Lucini's strong personality and manifold interests, the reader soon realizes that the label, any label, is more a convenience than a reality. Recognizing his affinity to the symbolists, he went his own way, maintaining a good distance from the pack; Lucini jealously guarded his independence and freedom. The repeated attempts on the part of futurists to co-opt him into the movement were met with misgivings at first and, after the publication of the *Manifesto Futurista* (1909), with fierce hostility, as seen in his *Marinetti, Futurismo, Futuristi* (1975).

On the other hand, the physical infirmities that plagued him from the age of nine allowed Lucini no close participation with any of the literary groups. He traveled little, mostly in search of sun and clean air; his contacts were mostly epistolary. His presence was, however, strongly felt in a large sector of twentieth-century Italian avant-garde movements. Not only futurists but even, more recently, the "neo-avanguardia" of the 1960s recognized in him their inspiration. With Lucini, in fact, one sees the beginning of a deformation of poetic institutions that affects not only the structures of expression but the institutionalized view of reality, and the structures of content as well. Such deformation had an extraordinary impact on the development of twentieth-century literature, and not only in Italy.

Lucini was born in Milan into a prosperous family of ancient lineage on 30 September 1867. At the age of nine he developed a particularly insidious case of tuberculosis of the bone, which progressively weakened him: in 1909 one of his legs had to be amputated; the other was expected to be amputated in 1914, but death, caused by pneumonia, came sooner. Probably in order to alleviate his sufferings, his father, an affluent banker, had a villa built in Breglia, high in the mountains above Menaggio, on Lake Como, where Lucini spent an increasing amount of time, especially after completing his studies in Milan, Genoa, and Pavia, where, in 1882, he obtained a degree in law. He traveled briefly to Nice, Rome, Naples, and Venice, and now and then took longer sojourns in Varazze on the Riviera, or in Dosso Pisani. He endured his infirmities with unfailing courage and without self-indulgence, turning them into an urgency for laborious activity, with the help of Giuditta Cattaneo, whom he married

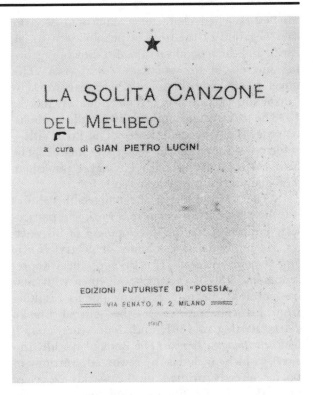

Cover for Lucini's 1910 book, a prose narrative that incorporates poems and dramatized sections

in 1896 against the ungenerous opposition of his parents. He never had the love of his mother: a somber recounting of this loveless relationship is contained in the most poignant of his poems, "Lai della Borghesuccia," (The Lai of a Petty Bourgeoise; in *Revolverate e Nuove Revolverate* [Gunshots and New Gunshots], 1975). His attitude toward his father, whom he judged severely, is more ambiguous. In 1895 he undertook the only business venture in his life, as a partner in the Galli Publishing House, an arrangement that ended two and a half years later in disappointment and financial disaster.

Lucini's literary activity began with a long poem, "Il Galileo," written in 1887 and never published. A year later his novella, *Spirito ribelle* (Rebellious Spirit), based on the struggle by Lombard farmers for better working conditions and inspired by the strikes and incidents of 1884 and 1885, was published in installments in a weekly journal devoted to agricultural problems. Immediately following publication, he completely reworked the story and characters and published it in 1895 as a full-length novel, *Gian Pietro da Core*. The metamorphosis from the first to the second version marks Lucini's break from naturalism and naive socialism (he would later call one of his best-sketched characters, Manicozzo il Savio, the "negation of the present possibility of socialism"), and the second version also shows his growing interest in the poetics of symbolism. This novel is the only organically narrative work by Lucini still extant. It is certain, however, that by 1898 he had written another novel in the symbolistic style, "La Villa delle Rose" (The Rose Villa—referred to also as "La lotta per amare" [The Struggle for Love]), which was never published. The manuscript is now apparently lost.

The last decade of the nineteenth century was the most prolific in Lucini's work and particularly important for the development of his poetics. He published two volumes of poetry: *Il libro delle Figurazioni Ideali* (The Book of Ideal Representations, 1894), in which, together with new compositions, he gathers many poems resulting from his collaboration in the journal *Cronica d'Arte*, starting in 1891; and, four years later, *Il libro delle Imagini Terrene* (The Book of Worldly Images), which includes a reworked version of poems already printed in the weekly *Domenica Letteraria*. The poetics inspiring the two collections is avowedly symbolistic, echoing the modes of the English Pre-Raphaelites, French, and Italian poets of the period, and especially Gabriele D'Annunzio, whom Lucini soon came to loathe for the rest of his life. He faithfully adhered to the prosodic meter of the traditional canon.

However, it appears that before 1890 Lucini was already experimenting with free prosodic forms in "Armonie sinfoniche" (Symphonic Harmonies), a work started in 1888, reworked in 1892, and a second time in 1895. It remained unpublished except for two poems in "versi liberi" (free verse) printed by *Cronica d'Arte* in 1892. The most significant outcome of such experimentations is represented by *I Drami delle Maschere* (The Dramas of Masks, 1973), a series of dramatized long poems composed between 1893 and 1897 and published individually beginning in 1898. The poems are structured according to the "verso libero" technique. Lucini makes no attempt to break the canonical structure of the minimal prosodic units, which, at this stage at least, he retains. He was bent, however, on freeing the minimal prosodic unit from bonds imposed by the institutionalized metrical scheme. Lucini goes beyond traditional polymetric experimentations (as in Francesco Redi's dithyrambic *Bacco in Toscana* [Bacchus in Tuscany], or Giuseppe Giusti's and Carlo Porta's satyric compositions). Lucini's content is no longer forcibly formed according to the laws of a metrical scheme, but, on the contrary, it subordinates all metrical elements (including rhyme) to its expressive necessities. In a drastic reduction of the rhetorical level of poetic form, prosodic and sonant elements underline subtle chords and correspondences. The result is a closer adherence between content and expression, a poetic form supple enough to follow all the intricate meanderings of thought. As he says in *I Drami delle Maschere*, "amo le idee a sciame, incatenate pecchie d'oro, / al sonoro timpano del comporre" (I love ideas in swarms, chains of gilded honeybees, / on the sonorous drum of composing). Lucini was honest enough always to aim at truth: "forse la Verità ama nuda e sovrana / un pozzo d'acqua limpida, stringendo in mano uno specchio d'argento" (perhaps Truth naked and sovereign loves / a well of limpid water, clasping a silver mirror in her hand).

Poetic dramatization implies a space divided into two dimensions: inner and outer. In Lucini's poetic drama it is the character's inner dimension that reveals the outer dimension, allowing the poetry to become theater. The subject is alone on a sceneless stage (years before James Joyce or Samuel Beckett), telling of what ought to be and is not. Being is negative; what ought to be is the negation of the negative. The mask can only be, rather than symbol or allegory, an enigma, the figure that hides truth at the dark bottom of its well; and its word can only be irony.

I Drami delle Maschere represents an extremely important step in the development of Lucini's poetics. During the same period he published several other pieces on symbolism and its techniques.

Irony became open sarcasm when Lucini realized that the refusal of reality must involve the negation of the sociopolitical organization in its entirety. His political interest was already only too clear in his first narrative work, *Spirito ribelle*. By the end of the century, his republicanism and socialism, nurtured in his youth by Giuseppe Mazzini, Giuseppe Garibaldi, and Giosuè Carducci, became more radically intransigent as he saw that his political ideals were better reflected by individual anarchism. With his usual penchant for enigmatic contradiction, he repeatedly defined himself as "an aristocratic anarchist" or "an aristocratic revolutionary." Preferred targets of his bitterly vehement polemics were the strongholds of bourgeois institutions and their hypocrisies, the old evils of civil and religious autocracy, militarism, and its natural counterpart, imperialism. In this climate he wrote some of his most poignant ballads, *La Nenia al Bimbo* (The Lullaby for the Child, 1898), inspired by the bloody repressions of 1894 in Sicily; *Il Sermone al Delfino* (Sermon for the Prince, also 1898)—with regard to Vittorio Emanuele III, then crown prince—after the repressions of 1898 in Milan; and especially *La Ballata di Carmen Monarchia, Corifea di Cafè-Chantant* (1900), an allegory of Italy at the onset of the century. A little later, the same inclination produced *Elogio di Varazze* (Eulogy for Varazze, 1907), similar in mood to Giacomo Leopardi's *Ginestra* (1836). More somber and less controlled, *Carme di Angoscia e di Speranza* (Poem of Anguish and Hope, 1909) was inspired by the tragic earthquake of 1908 that leveled Reggio and Messina.

By this time Lucini's symbolistic poetics, which had reached theoretical maturity, culminated in *Ragion Poetica e programma del Verso Libero* (Poetics and Program on Free Verse, 1908), offering a detailed, if not cogent, panoramic view of the development of Italian (and European) literature in the nineteenth century. This work serves as a manifesto for his symbolism: "SIMBOL-ISMO, il nostro, è la negazione d'ogni e qualunque scuola in quanto obblighi una disciplina, è arte libera. Quella che procede anche per *riflessi*, cioè che adopera dei simboli, o sia delle immagini, per rappresentare le idee, valendosi di secrete concordanze soggettive, il cui valore completo e complesso sfugge alla analisi critica, ma è *sentito*. Il simbolismo è l'arte dei sensi. E l'effervescenza dell'anima nuova, che non si accontenta di vivere nel vecchio modo, ma vuol vivere forte, libera, egoarchica, anarchica" (Our SYMBOLISM, the negation of any and whatever school imposing a discipline, is free art. An art that also proceeds by *reflexes* or uses symbols, that is to say images, in order to represent ideas by means of secret subjective concordances, whose full and complex value escapes critical analysis and can only be *felt*. Symbolism is the art of the senses. It is the effervescence of a new soul, no longer content to live in the old modes, but wanting to live strong, free, egoarchic, anarchic).

Thus conceived, symbolism shifts from poetics to aesthetics, becoming identified with poetry itself: "E pure il simbolismo è antico come la letteratura, sempre insorgente a rinascenza. Grido del ribelle contro la consuetudine, è l'arte vera di fronte allo stampo ed alla fotografia; donde, al nostro giudizio, ciascun poeta ed artista, che abbia cominciato *un suo modo, è simbolista*. Ed i Geni, i quali produssero a loro somiglianza, grandissime ed immortali personificazioni, sono tali: essi inventarono, li altri ricalcarono sopra i loro dettagli di tecnica, già trascolorita, impropria e putrida nelle mani delli imitatori" (And yet symbolism is as old as literature, always resurgent. Cry of the rebel against custom, it represents authentic art against the mold and photography. Therefore, in our opinion, any poet or artist, who has ever begun *his own poetic mode, is a symbolist*. Poetic geniuses who produced great and immortal personification in their image and likeness are symbolists; they invented, others followed, tracing over the details of their technique, soon discolored, inappropriate and putrified in the hands of imitators).

In 1905 a group of artists under the leadership of Filippo Tommaso Marinetti launched a new journal, *Poesia*, in which Lucini, attracted by its enthusiastic program, collaborated assiduously. His friendship with Marinetti, based on mutual admiration, grew stronger in the following years, during and beyond the 1909 publication of the *Manifesto Futurista*. *Poesia*, in the meantime, had begun to publish, in separate volumes, works of the new poets, and among those works the most important of Lucini's collections, *Revolverate*, a few months after the *Manifesto*; Lucini's book includes a "Futurist" preface by Marinetti. The collection's title was originally "Canzoni amare" (Bitter Songs). The new title came after a jocose suggestion by one of Lucini's friends, the painter Carlo Agazzi, during a convivial gathering at Marinetti's home.

Revolverate collects poems written between 1901 and 1908. Poems of the same intonation written after that date formed a new collection, *Nuove Revolverate*, which remained unpublished until 1975, when it was combined with the first one. In the two collections the technique of *verso libero*, so successfully practiced in *I Drami delle Maschere* and the ballads, is exploited to its limits. At times the deformation of metric institutions strikes at the very heart of prosodic structure—the tonic rhythm, which is wittingly destroyed, as in these lines from *Revolverate*:

Ma indovinare i fatti e le persone; raccoglier
     nuvole ingannatrici,
in un lungo lavoro di supposizione, foggiare la
     mente,
perché senta, ed, a stento, intorno a sé,
qualche cosa di tiepido, di vivo? Vegetare
     l'equivoco.

(But guessing the facts and the persons; gather-
     ing deceiving clouds,

in a long work of supposition, shaping the mind,
so that it feels, and, barely, around itself,
something warm, alive? Vegetating the equivo-
cal.)

At times the internal structure of the syntagma or lexeme is parodistically subverted. By emphasizing the automatism of prosody and syntax, institutional meaning is destroyed and then reconstructed as meaningful nonsense with surrealistic overtones:

Molti dell'Imbecilli son canuti: sono i piú astuti.
Altri Imbecilli tirano al grigio: hanno il cuor
   ligio alle galere.
Altri ancora son calvi: son li spavaldi della
   menzogna.

(Many Imbeciles are gray-haired: they are the
   most astute.
Other Imbeciles are rather grizzled: their hearts
   are faithful to the jails.
Still others are bald: they are the enforcers of
   the lie.)

Irony ("l'ironia bianca e rossa come una ferita che s'incancreni" [irony, white and red as a gangrenous wound]) drills its sarcasm directly into the logical structures of hypocritical language, which is exposed as a linguistic covering, stretched over a malformed social reality. No wonder, then, that futurist and other avant-gardes saw in Lucini their precursor and inspiration. In fact many of Lucini's formulas, many of his constructive modalities, were taken over by futurists. This was a gross misunderstanding on the part of the futurists, as Lucini hastened to tell Marinetti immediately after receiving from him a copy of the *Manifesto*. Lucini was frightened by their program's blind iconoclasm, by the exaltation of the "hygienic" necessity of war, of crude physicality, their scornful contempt for women and the meek, their reveling in the grief of human existence, their provocative violence.

Marinetti tried in vain to coax him into acknowledging the affinities of his poetics to that of futurism or, at least, to abandon his polemical attitude. Instead Lucini became more and more relentless, and in 1912 he published "Come ho sorpassato il Futurismo" (How I Left Futurism Behind), in Giuseppe Prezzolini's *La Voce*, in which in unequivocal terms Lucini disassociated himself from the group.

In 1910 *Poesia* published another important work by Lucini, *La Solita Canzone del Melibeo* (The

Usual Song of Melibeo), where the prose narrative sustains the framework, while poems and dramatized sections are included. The intonation is more intimately autobiographical, evoking three love stories featuring three different women. In 1911 Lucini published *L'Ora Topica di Carlo Dossi* (The Topical Hour of Carlo Dossi), devoted to the writer and novelist Alberto Pisani (Carlo Dossi), who had died the year before and had been a friend of Lucini.

In 1912 Lucini completed and published *Le Nottole ed i Vasi*—a series of prose narratives inspired by classical and modern stylists—which he had begun at least ten years before and reworked at different times. The text is accompanied by philological and pseudophilological notes displaying heavy and, at times, uncontrolled erudition. A year later he coauthored with Innocenzo Cappa *Il Tempio della Gloria* (The Temple of Glory), a cumbersome drama dealing with the social situation in Russia around 1905. This book includes, as an appendix, a study of Maksim Gorky and the revolution. That same year, *Filosofi ultimi* (Latest Philosophers), a series of essays by Lucini on recent philosophers (Benedetto Croce, Henri Bergson, William James, and others) and on the crisis in systematic philosophy was published.

The last book published by Lucini before his death was *Antidannunziana: D'Annunzio al vaglio della critica* (Against D'Annunzio: D'Annunzio Evaluated by the Critics, 1914), which he intended to follow with a second volume, "D'Annunzio al vaglio dell'humorismo" (D'Annunzio Evaluated through Humor), which remains unpublished. Lucini's reaction against the poet whose overpowering presence filled the literary scene between the two centuries is virulently negative and polemical, even though Lucini had initially admired him.

Among the works published posthumously, a special place is held by *La piccola Chelidonio* (The Little Chelidonio, 1922), a kind of precious epistolary novel, in the style of some of the stories included in *Le Nottole ed i Vasi*. Also of interest is *Le Antitesi e le Perversità* (Antitheses and Depravities, 1970), a collection of poems that add little to Lucini's poetic achievements.

Lucini is undoubtedly one of the most influential Italian poets of the twentieth century, signaling a new dawn in Italian poetic history. To him goes a great part of the credit for the renovation of Italian poetic language. Caught between D'Annunzian literary triumphs and militaristic ventures on the one hand, and futurist and Fascist revelries on the other, his poetic and ideological experimentations seemed doomed to defeat or obscurity. He was, however, well remembered during the 1960s, in the wake of renewed interest in avant-garde movements, when a group of young critics equipped with sharper analytical tools resurrected his reputation and placed Lucini once again at the forefront of critical poetic inquiry.

Bibliographies:

Bibliography, in Lucini's *Le Antitesi e le Perversità*, edited by Glauco Viazzi (Parma, Italy: Guanda, 1970), pp. lxxxiii-xcv;

Bibliography, in Lucini's *Prose e canzoni amare*, edited by Isabella Ghidetti (Florence: Vallecchi, 1971), pp. 545-551.

References:

Carlo Cordiè, "Appunti su Gian Pietro Lucini e la Russia," *Filologia e Letteratura*, 14, no. 1 (1968): 37-38;

Cordiè, "*Gian Pietro da Core* e la società italiana di fine Ottocento," *Siculorum Gimnasium* (University of Catania, July-December 1964);

Cordié, "Testimonianze letterarie sulla fucilazione di F. Ferrer," *Siculorum Gimnasium* (January 1966);

C. Costa, "La poetica del bimbo perverso," *Quindici*, 2-3 (1968);

Graal, special Lucini issue (September 1967);

Anatoly Lunaciarskij, "Futuristi," in his *La rivoluzione proletaria e la cultura borghese* (Milan: Mazzotta, 1972), pp. 127-134;

Giorgio Luti, "Il caso Lucini," preface to *Prose e canzoni amare*, edited by Isabella Ghidetti (Florence: Vallecchi, 1971);

C. Maraini, "Beltramelli fra Gorki e Lucini," *Nuova Antologia* (September 1965);

La Martinella di Milano, special Lucini issues (September 1954 and September 1964);

C. Martini, "G. P. Lucini," *Rassegna di Cultura e Vita Scolastica*, 18 (November-December 1964);

Pier Vincenzo Mengaldo, "Lucini," in his *La tradizione del Novecento (da D'Annunzio a Montale)* (Milan: Feltrinelli, 1975), pp. 110-112;

Il Pensiero Mazziniano, special Lucini issues, 10 (15 July 1954), and 14 (15 July 1959);

Simonetta Petruzzi, "Un poeta erudito fra *scapigliati* e futuristi: G. P. Lucini," *Nuova Antologia*, 492 (September 1964): 109-115;

A. Pinchera, "L'influsso della metrica classica sulla metrica italiana (da Pascoli ai 'novissimi')," *Studi Urbinati*, 1 (1966): 92-127;

La Provincia di Como, special Lucini issue (25 July 1964);

Silvio Ramat, "Genio, maschera, trasparenza all'origine del sistema novecentesco," *Forum Italicum*, 5 (1971): 3-32;

A. U. Tarabori, *Gian Pietro Lucini* (Milan: Caddeo, 1922);

M. Verdone, "Gian Pietro Lucini," *Ausonia* (July-August 1967);

Il Verri, special Lucini/futurism double issue, 33-34 (October 1970);

Glauco Viazzi, "Lucini e il dialetto," *La Martinella di Milano*, 23, nos. 3-4 (1969): 109-114;

Viazzi, "G. P. Lucini critico," *Il Ponte*, 16 (1970), no. 1: 111-126; no. 2: 270-286;

La Voce Repubblicana, special Lucini issues (13 July 1954 and 8 August 1964).

Filippo Tommaso Marinetti

(22 December 1876 - 2 December 1944)

Andrea Guiati
Buffalo State College

BOOKS: *La Conquête des Etoiles* (Paris: La Plume, 1902; enlarged edition, Paris: Sansot, 1908); translated into Italian by Decio Cinti as *La conquista delle stelle* (Milan: Sonzogno, 1920);

D'Annunzio intimo (Milan: Verde & Azzurro, 1903);

La Momie sanglante (Milan: Verde & Azzurro, 1904);

Destruction (Paris: Vanier, 1904); translated as *Distruzione* (Milan: Poesia, 1911);

Le roi Bombance (Paris: Société du Mercure de France, 1905); translated as *Re Baldoria* (Milan: Fratelli Treves, 1910);

La Ville Charnelle (Paris: Sansot, 1908);

Les Dieux s'en vont, D'Annunzio reste (Paris: Sansot, 1908);

Enquête internationale sur le vers libre et Manifeste du Futurisme (Milan: Poesia, 1909);

Poupées électriques (Paris: Sansot, 1909);

I manifesti del futurismo (Milan: Istituto Editoriale Italiano, 1909);

Tuons le clair de lune! (Milan: Poesia, 1909);

Mafarka le futuriste (Paris: Sansot, 1909); translated by Cinti as *Mafarka il futurista* (Milan: Poesia, 1910);

Le Futurisme (Paris: Sansot, 1911);

Uccidiamo il chiaro di luna (Milan: Poesia, 1911);

La bataille de Tripoli (26 octobre 1911), vécue et chantée (Milan: Poesia, 1912); translated as *La battaglia di Tripoli (26 ottobre 1911), vissuta e cantata da F. T. Marinetti* (Milan: Poesia, 1912);

Le monoplan du Pape (Paris: Sansot, 1912); translated by Cinti as *L'aeroplano del Papa* (Milan: Poesia, 1914);

Zang Tumb Tumb; Adrianopoli: Ottobre 1912; Parole in libertà (Milan: Cavanna/Poesia, 1914);

Manifesti del Futurismo, by Marinetti and others (Florence: Lacerba, 1914);

Guerra sola igiene del mondo (Milan: Poesia, 1915);

Il Teatro futurista sintetico, by Marinetti, Emilio Settimelli, and Bruno Corra (Milan: Istituto Editoriale Italiano, 1915; revised edition, Piacenza, Italy: Costantino, 1921; revised again, Naples: CLET, 1941);

Poesie scelte (Milan: Istituto Editoriale Italiano, 1916);

Come si seducono le donne (Florence: Centomila Copie, 1916; enlarged edition, Florence: Casciano/Cappeli, 1918);

Noi futuristi (Milan: Quintieri, 1917);

L'isola dei baci (Milan: Lombardo, 1918);

Scelta di poesie e parole in libertà (Milan: Istituto Editoriale Italiano, 1918);

Democrazia futurista: Dinamismo politico (Milan: Facchi, 1919);

8 anime in una bomba (Milan: Poesia, 1919);

Un ventre di Donna, by Marinetti and Enif Robert (Milan: Facchi, 1919);

Les mots en liberté futuristes (Milan: Poesia, 1919);

Come si seducono le donne e si tradiscono gli uomini (Milan: Sonzogno, 1920);

Elettricità sessuale (Milan: Facchi, 1920);

Al di là del comunismo, Il cittadino eroico, Scuole di coraggio, Gli artisti al potere, Le case del genio, La vita festa (Milan: La Testa di Ferro, 1920);

L'alcova d'acciaio (Milan: Vitagliano, 1921);

Lussuria velocità (Milan: Modernissima, 1921);

Gli amori futuristi (Cremona, Italy: Ghelfi, 1922);

Il tamburo di fuoco (Milan: Sonzogno, 1922);

Enrico Caviglia (Piacenza, Italy: Porta, 1922);

Gli Indomabili (Piacenza, Italy: Poesia, 1922);

Futurismo e Fascismo (Foligno, Italy: Campitelli, 1924);

Umberto Boccioni (Milan: Bottega di Poesia, 1924);

Prigionieri e Vulcani (Milan: Vecchi, 1927);

Scatole d'amore in conserva, by Marinetti and Carlo A. Petrucci (Rome: Arte Fauno, 1927);

Primo dizionario aereo italiano, by Marinetti and F. Azari (Milan: Morreale, 1929);

Marinetti e il futurismo (Rome & Milan: Augustea, 1929);

Novelle colle labbra tinte: Simultaneità e programmi di vita con varianti a scelta (Milan: Mondadori, 1930);

Filippo Tommaso Marinetti

Futurismo e noventismo (Milan: Galleria Pesaro, 1930);

Il club dei simpatici (Palermo: Hodierna, 1931);

Spagna veloce e toro futurista; Teoria delle parole in libertà (Milan: Morreale, 1931);

Il paesaggio e l'estetica futurista della macchina (Florence: Nemi, 1931);

La cucina futurista (Milan: Sonzogno, 1932);

Parole in libertà futuriste tattili-termiche, olfattive, edited by Tullio d'Albisola (Zinola, Savona, Italy: Lito-Latta, 1932);

Poemi simultanei futuristi (La Spezia, Italy: Casa d'Arte, 1933);

Il fascino dell'Egitto (Verona, Italy: Mondadori, 1933);

Antonio Sant'Elia, by Marinetti and M. Del Bello (Rome: Libro Periodico, 1933);

L'aeropoema del Golfo della Spezia (Milan: Mondadori, 1935);

L'originalità napoletana del poeta Salvatore Di

Giacomo (Naples: Casella, 1936);

Notari, scrittore nuovo (Milan: Società Anonima Notari, 1936);

Il poema Africano della Divisione "XXVIII Ottobre" (Milan: Mondadori, 1937);

Il poema del vestito di latte (Milan: Esperia, 1937);

Il poema di Torre Viscosa (Milan: Ufficio di Propaganda della Snia Viscosa, 1938);

Patriottismo insetticida (Milan: Mondadori, 1939);

Il poema dei Sansepolcristi (Milan: Popolo d'Italia, 1939);

Il poema non umano deí tecnicismi (Milan: Mondadori, 1940);

Canto eroi e macchine della guerra Mussoliniana (Milan: Mondadori, 1942);

L'esercito italiano, poesia armata (Rome: Cenacolo, 1942);

Lo riprenderemo (Wir nehmen es uns wieder) (Rome: CLET, 1943);

L'Aeropoema di Cozzarini primo eroe dell'esercito

Cover for the first of Marinetti's books to be published in Italy, an essay on a poet who inspired the futurists

repubblicano (Milan: Erre, 1944);

Quarto d'ora di poesia della X Mas (Milan: Mondadori, 1945);

Teatro, 3 volumes, edited by Giovanni Calendoli (Rome: Bianco, 1960);

Teoria e invenzione futurista, edited by Luciano De Maria (Milan: Mondadori, 1968);

Il teatro della sorpresa, by Marinetti and Francesco Cangiullo (Livorno, Italy: Belforte, 1968);

Lettere ruggenti, edited by Giovanni Lugaresi (Milan: Quaderni dell' Osservatore, 1969);

La grande Milano tradizionale e futurista, edited by De Maria (Milan: Mondadori, 1969);

Poesie a Beny, translated (from the French) by Vera Drisdo (Turin: Einaudi, 1971);

Collaudi futuristi, edited by G. Viazzi (Naples: Guida, 1977);

Il fascino dell'Egitto (Milan: Mondadori, 1981);

Scritti francesi, edited by Pasquale A. Jannini (Milan: Mondadori, 1983).

Editions in English: *Poems by Marinetti*, translated by Anne Simon (Boston: Poet Lore, 1916);

Marinetti: Selected Writings, translated by R. W. Flint and Arthur A. Coppotelli (New York:

Farrar, Straus & Giroux, 1972; London: Secker & Warburg, 1972).

SELECTED PERIODICAL PUBLICATIONS—
UNCOLLECTED: "Les Vieux Marins," *Anthologie-Revue* (Paris), 12 (20 September 1898);

"Il tattilismo," *Comoedia* (Milan, 1921);

"La tecnica della nuova poesia," *Rassegna Nazionale* (April 1937);

"L'arte tipografica di guerra e dopoguerra," by Marinetti, Alfredo Trimarco, Luigi Scrivo, and Piero Bellanova, *Graphicus*, 32 (May 1942).

Futurism first appeared in 1909, at the same time as the *crepuscolari* (twilight poets) movement, but it was clear that the sensibilities of the groups were diametrically opposed. However, both movements were characterized by their reactionary poetic representations. The *crepuscolari* chose to withdraw into a literary world of quiet villages, people of the provinces, and their uneventful everyday routines. They used a simple rhetorical lexicon and simple images that recall classical poetic language. The futurists, on the other hand, chose to destroy all tradition. Under the guidance of Filippo Tommaso Marinetti they produced shocking literary manifestos and publicized their ideas through all possible channels, including conferences, literary journals, and extravagant dinners. As R. W. Flint says in his introduction to *Marinetti: Selected Writings* (1972), Marinetti "was everywhere at once, thanks to the railroads, organizing, orating, propagandizing, staging exhibitions and theatrical 'evenings' of music, recitation, and riot; clowning, providing a screen of systematically irrational uproar behind which his friends for the most part enjoyed themselves immensely."

The main initial source of Italian futurism was Marinetti's French cultural and educational background. In fact the foundations of his artistic theory can be easily linked to the ferments of the Bâteau Lavoir, to such avant-garde French poets as Charles-Pierre Baudelaire, Stéphane Mallarmé, Paul Valéry, Alfred Jarry, and Guillaume Apollinaire.

Futurism was conceived by its Franco-Italian-Egyptian father (Marinetti) as a revolutionary movement that was going to affect every aspect of life. But it ended in a sterile literary program, a poetic theory without much poetry. Its bombastic simultaneity and radical symbolism, expressed through words, pictures, and sound, however, not only enjoyed three decades of success but also paved the road to the poetry of Giuseppe Ungaretti, Eugenio Montale, and other Italian hermetic poets.

Futurism, like *crepuscolarismo*, used as a springboard the heroic exasperation and exaltation in the poetry of Gabriele D'Annunzio. Futurism's objective was to become the immediate, aggressive expression of the modern world, a dynamic, accelerating world. Time equals speed was the fulcrum of Marinetti's revolutionary theory. He destroyed syntax, eliminating from the free-verse style all the qualifiers, using verbs in the infinitive, in order to achieve the illusion of eternal motion: the motion of the words keeps turning, never defining temporally the sentence-verse. This idea first appeared in "Distruzione della sintassi, immaginazione senza fili, parole in libertà" (Destruction of Syntax, Imagination without Strings, Words-in-Freedom), Marinetti's manifesto of 1913, collected in *Manifesti del Futurismo* (1914).

Marinetti was born in Alexandria, Egypt, on 22 December 1876 and died in Bellagio, Italy, on 2 December 1944. He was the second son of Enrico Marinetti, a young lawyer from Voghera, Italy, and Amalia Grolli Marinetti, daughter of a professor of Italian literature. The young Marinetti inherited his artistic sensitivity from his mother and his large fortune from his entrepreneurial father. In 1888 Marinetti entered the French Jesuit school Saint François Xavier, where he received a solid French cultural background. The Jesuit school had a reputation for having high standards and a rigid curriculum. Marinetti enjoyed furthering his schoolmates' education with extracurricular material; however, one day he was caught and consequently expelled for bringing to school and discussing Emile Zola's novels.

Marinetti was at Xavier until 1893; in those years he founded a small literary journal named *Le Papyrus*. He finished his baccalaureate in Paris. In 1894 the family left Alexandria and moved to Milan, into a flat, in Via Senato 2, overlooking the Naviglio River. The five years between 1894 and 1899 were busy ones for Marinetti: to make his father happy, both he and his brother Leone enrolled at the University of Pavia to study law. A few years later Leone, already afflicted with severe forms of rheumatism and arthritis, died. Marinetti joined the editorial staff of the Italian-French journal *Anthologie-Revue*, directed by Edward Sansot-Orland, Roger Le Brun, and Renzo Ermes Ceschina. In the issue of 20 September 1898 Marinetti published a free-verse French poem, "Les Vieux Marins" (The Old Sailors), which received the winning prize in the "Samedis Populaires" contest, directed by Catulle Mendès and Gustave Kahn. Sarah Bernhardt recited the poem to the audience at the ceremony. On 14 July 1899 the young poet received his "Dottorato in Legge" (Law Degree) from the University of Genoa, to which he had transferred, defending a dissertation on "La corona nel governo parlamentare" (The Crown in Parliamentary Government).

In 1900 Marinetti made a final commitment to literature. In France he began to cooperate in *La Vogue, La Plume,* and *La Revue Blanche*; he also began to recite, in public, French Romantic poetry and symbolist poetry. Among his preferred poets were Baudelaire, Mallarmé, Valéry, Paul Verlaine, Arthur Rimbaud, Victor Hugo, and Emile Verhaeren. He met regularly with such Italian intellectuals as Carlo Botta and Luigi

Marinetti in his motorcar, circa 1908. In La Ville Charnelle, *published that year, he refers to cars as gods.*

Capuana. Marinetti's French background is clear, from his first writings and recitations, just as it is clear that the path to futurism was influenced by French decadents and symbolists.

Italy's political and literary condition then was without a doubt one of Marinetti's inspirations. Futurism was, whether intentionally or otherwise, a literary, cultural, and political revolution. Marinetti, very quickly, had come to grasp the Italian style of government; his approach compared to that of the *crepuscolari* and was sharp and severe. While the *crepuscolari* reaction was quiet, the futurists' presence was loud and intimidating.

The years between 1897, when Marinetti had started to publish in the Franco-Italian journal *Anthologie-Revue*, and 1909, when he published his first futurist manifesto in the French newspaper *Le Figaro*, constitute his prefuturistic years. It is in these years especially that one can find evidence of Marinetti's French educational background, as seen, for example, in his extensive use of the French language.

The poems "L'échanson" (The Cupbearer) and "Les Vieux Marins" reveal Marinetti's affin-

ity with decadentism and symbolism. These verses are dominated by images brightly colored with red and yellow, counterbalanced by other sets of green and blue. In both these poems there is metaphysical irony, a form of irony that Marinetti had seen in the verses of the unusual French symbolist Jules Laforgue. Nature is the main focus of young Marinetti: in "L'échanson" there are trees, wind, "et la lune, très pale, émerge au creux des plaines" (and the moon, very pale, emerges over the empty plains). These images are fairly common in Marinetti's early poetry, proving that futurism was not a thought-out poetic ideology, but rather a sudden strike of genius, a bombastic idea that Marinetti put into practice. He had recognized a world about to explode and took advantage of it. He exchanged country settings with quiet evenings and moonlit nights for a good look at the city and the factories that were blossoming as fast as spring flowers. Naturally a poetic theory, like most new theories, is not easily welcomed. Marinetti, therefore, proceeded programmatically to destroy the past. This attitude explains the long essay *Uccidiamo il chiaro di luna* (Let's Murder the Moonshine), first published in

April 1909 in *Poesia*, the journal he directed (the essay was separately published in 1911): "Per ora, ci accontentiamo di far saltare in aria tutte le tradizioni, come ponti fradici!" (For the moment we are content with blowing up all the traditions, like rotten bridges! [translation by Flint and Arthur A. Coppotelli]).

In 1904 Marinetti had published *La Momie sanglante* (The Bloody Mummy). It is a late-Romantic echo, a representation of the resurrection of a mummy. Aside from its obvious Egyptian imagery, worth mentioning is the sensual tone used by Marinetti when speaking of death, a reality the futurists were to defy fearlessly.

Destruction (1904) can be seen as a continuation of *La Conquête des Etoiles* (Let's Conquer the Stars, 1902), elaborating further on the captivating theme of a war between the armies of the seas against those of continents, cities, and women. After conquering them, the seas would continue to expand their boundaries by attacking the skies and the stars. Most images are visual, characterized for the most part by the poet's aggressive tone.

La Ville Charnelle (The Carnal City), published in 1908, expands on the same themes. The most notable development is the glorification of a technological world:

> Dieu véhément d'une race d'acier,
> Automobile ivre d'espace,
> qui piétines d'angoisse,
> le mors aux dents stridentes!

> (Vehement god of a steel race,
> Car intoxicated by space,
> that tramples with anguish,
> jaws of strident teeth!)

In general the poetry written by Marinetti in French, between 1898 and 1908, can be called prefuturistic. Marinetti, still strongly influenced by the French symbolists, nonetheless employs analogies, metaphors, and poetic structures that show an early trace of the theory that was going to shake the artistic and cultural establishments of Italy and many of its neighboring countries.

The first futurist manifesto appeared in *Le Figaro* on 20 February 1909. It proclaimed freedom: freedom for the poets, because, according to Marinetti, literature had exalted a pensive immobility. The futurists wanted to get rid of all established forms, so they concentrated on creating new ones. The idea of speed was at the center of it all—no more dipping into the past, the dangerous graveyard of museums, libraries, and academies. The job of the futurist poet was to sing of the future and its infinities: arsenals and shipyards, railroad stations, factories, bridges, steamers, locomotives, and planes. The futurists idealized beauty and youth: the oldest of them was thirty.

Only two months after the publication of his first manifesto, Marinetti published the first version of *Uccidiamo il chiaro di luna*. The first paragraph lists the names of the futurist artists that had joined Marinetti; among them are painters, poets, and musicians. The change proposed by the futurists was warlike; they constantly searched for obstacles to conquer. The language used was insolent and offensive: he calls those who do not agree with him cowards. Neither the tone nor the message would change. The strategies used by Marinetti show how much he had been affected by Jarry, a young French intellectual, who was eccentric, alcoholic, extravagant, arrogant, and bombastic. Yet Jarry had positive qualities too: he was efficient, expedient, and, above all, charismatic. Marinetti followed Jarry's example in many ways. He conquered the Italy of his time by using well a new marketing method: advertising. He reached successfully the young and the old, the rich and the poor; he literally forced himself upon everyone, even by throwing punches when necessary. He was a madman, perhaps, but a very convincing one. Marinetti personified Friedrich Nietzsche's superman and embraced what the German philosopher had called "prometheic atheism." This philosophy presupposes God's death; God is replaced by a supernatural creature, a superman. It shows the continuity between romanticism and futurism. Marinetti's work that best exemplifies this aspect is *La Conquête des Etoiles*.

On 27 April 1910 Marinetti published "Contro Venezia passatista" (Against Past-Loving Venice); a few months later futurists dropped copies of this publication from the top of Venice's clock tower (8 July 1910). The content is almost identical to that of *Uccidiamo il chiaro di luna*. Marinetti made an improvised speech while the leaflets were being dropped by his friends.

On 11 May 1912 Marinetti published the "Manifesto tecnico della letteratura futurista" (Technical Manifesto of Futurist Literature; republished with *Zang Tumb Tumb*, 1914)—a list of do's and don't's, a foretaste of the message of later groups such as the dadaists, the absurdists, and most of all the surrealists. Destroy syntax, he

Cover for the journal that includes Marinetti's "Uccidiamo il chiaro di luna," his second futurist manifesto

advised; use the verb in the infinitive; give every noun substance; abolish punctuation; use an ever-vaster gradation of analogies; abolish adjectives and adverbs in order to accentuate continuity; render the successive motion of an object by a chain of analogies; destroy the literary "I"; and pursue a lyrical obsession with matter. Literature should be enriched by sound, smell, and weight, and ugliness should be introduced into literature. Clearly Marinetti proceeded from free verse to what he called "parole in libertà" (words in freedom).

Le monoplan du Pape (The Pope's Monoplane) was published in 1912, followed by the Italian version in 1914. It is a novel in free-verse style, one of Marinetti's experiments falling between symbolism and futurism. The protagonist attempts a revolutionary act by boldly kidnapping the pope during a war. Marinetti had already indicated theoretically that the Vatican had to be removed from the face of the modern world. The pope, in the eyes of Marinetti, was nothing more than a tyrant monopolizing human feelings and ideals. The hero plunges into a he-

roic mission in order to restore an upside-down world, a world of past-lovers, sedentary men incapable of action. In his plane, fast-moving and high in the skies, he represents the future-lovers, men devoted to constant destruction, creation, reconstruction, doomed to start over and over again. Moreover, the war is a new myth, replacing the pagan and the Christian myths.

Zang Tumb Tumb is the best example of words in freedom. With this long poem—an epic—Marinetti successfully transformed the theories of his manifestos into a complex artistic creation. The theme throughout the poem is the Balkanic war of 1912-1913. On the question of war Marinetti, influenced by Nietzsche and Charles Darwin, introduces a profound thought: war is identified with the fundamental laws of life. "Umanità e necessità di lottare divengono sinonimi" (Humanity and the necessity to fight become synonymous), according to Luciano De Maria (*Introduzione a F. T. Marinetti*, 1968).

Futurism became a fashion of the political and cultural arena of the Italy of that time, but as an artistic ideology its impact can still be felt

Cover for Marinetti's futurist epic in which war is presented as a basic part of nature

reader would read about the train, hear its sounds, feel its presence, be taken for a ride, and enjoy its tremendous speed simultaneously:

> treno treno treno treno TREN TRON
> TRON TRON (ponte di ferro:
>   TATATLUUUUN-
> TLIN) SSSSSSSIIII SSIISSII SSIISSSSSSIIII
>   treno treno febbre del mio
> treno express-express-expressssssss press
> press-press-press-press-press-press-press
> press-press-pressss punzecchiato dal sale
>
>   (train train train train TREN TRON
> TRON TRON (iron bridge:
>   TATATLUUUUN-
> TLIN) SSSSSSSIII SSIISSII SSIISSSSSSSSIIII
>   train train fever of my
> train express-express-expressssssss press
> press-press-press-press-press-press-press
> press-press-pressss stung by the sea salt) [.]

Marinetti certainly embraces the idea of simultaneity, which was to become one of futurism's important aspects. The growth from absolute objectivism to relative subjectivism is clear. Marinetti's poetry can best be appreciated if heard and seen simultaneously, rather than read, which is what Marinetti intended. Also, it must be noted that the cooperation of the reader is needed for this poetry to come to life. Marinetti's poetry was intended for intellectuals; in fact it was supposed to reeducate them, to instill in them a new sensorial-auditorial-visual-intuitive primeval state, one of the few links he shared with the *crepuscolari*.

After *Zang Tumb Tumb* Marinetti spent almost twenty years (1912-1931) translating with Decio Cinti his French writings into Italian, producing manifestos, novels, short stories, and plays and lecturing around Europe. His active political involvement had ended in 1920 when he left the "Fasci Italiani di Combattimento." Before returning to poetry, Marinetti wrote the "Manifesto dell'Aeropoesia" (Aerialpoetry Manifesto) in 1929; its theory was then applied to *Spagna veloce e toro futurista* (Fast Spain and Futurist Bull), published in 1931. The poem presents two antitheses: "Vento Burbero" (Surly Wind) symbolizes the past, and a fast car represents the future. The car travels along a seven-hundred-kilometer stretch from Barcelona to Madrid, carrying the poet. No matter how hard the "whiiiisling wiiiind" blows, it has no chance against "Marinetti, el dios de la velocidad" (Marinetti, the god of speed) and the power of the "automobile

today. One may disagree with it, but one cannot ignore it.

Zang Tumb Tumb often describes the dynamic molecular structure of an explosion, as already onomatopoeically suggested by the title. The combination of images, in a Bergsonian way, produces matter, which replaces the traditional psychological literary "I": "The lyrical obsession with matter was to protect it from the anthropomorphic emotions with which romantic poets and pantheists had endowed it. The life of massed molecules and whirling electrons would form the modern poet's imagination" (Caroline Tisdall and Angelo Bozzolla, *Futurism*, 1978). It follows that, compared to the romantic "I," matter for the futurists would have no feelings whatsoever.

Zang Tumb Tumb offers a sample of visual poetry, along with typographic possibilities and onomatopoeic combinations pushed to extremes. Marinetti's inventiveness is geared toward a phonetic reproduction of realistic sounds in order to join intuition to logical intelligence. His expectations for the following verses were that the

F. T. MARINETTI
DELL'ACCADEMIA D'ITALIA

SPAGNA VELOCE
E
TORO FUTURISTA

EDITORE MORREALE MILANO

Frontispiece for a long poem that exemplifies Marinetti's concept of aeropoesia *(aerial poetry), in which technology conquers nature*

civilizzatissima" (very civilized car), which rapidly covers the distance in spite of the resistance: "vvvvvv rrrrrrrr vvvvvv." Although the mechanical world will conquer nature, the new semigod is a supreme being.

The metaphors and analogies are effective but not as free as they are in *Zang Tumb Tumb*. Marinetti describes a corrida in Madrid (during which the poet sympathizes with the animal, "pobre toro" (poor bull). The speaking bull, which can be heard only by the poet-narrator, says: "Vi faccio dunque tanta paura? Siete la spavalda spensierata e mordente Gioventù che sogna nei suoi agili voli di baciare due stelle con una bocca sola, nello stesso, istante!" (Do I scare you so much then? You are the swaggering, happy-go-lucky and devouring youth who dreams in his nimble flights to kiss two stars with only one mouth!)

In 1933 Marinetti published four new poems in *Poemi simultanei futuristi* (Simultaneous Futuristic Poems); the first poem is dedicated to

his daughter Luce. Since the infant was born on 20 September 1933, the same day the "bersaglieri" (an elite army unit) entered Rome through Porta Pia, the poet attempts to blend the two events, as if Luce were the outcome of the military action. Nonetheless, the two events remain antithetical; the synthesis of the two realities is not achieved, in spite of the metaphor of the third verse:

La vampa bersaglieresca tutta guance affocate
    dalle trombe

gonfia d'oro veloce le cupole
calde mammelle puntate contro il cielo,
palloni con in cresta mitragliatrici a croci.

(The bersaglieri's flame all cheeks inflamed by
    trumpets

inflates with quick gold the cupolas
warm breasts pointing to the sky,
balloons topped with crosslike machine guns.)

L'aeropoema del Golfo della Spezia (The Aerial Poem of the Gulf of La Spezia) was published in 1935. Marinetti again applies the theory of simultaneity, already applied to the futurist theater, and in substance the difference between words in freedom and aerial poetry is minimal. In a way Marinetti takes a step backward, by reinstating logical verb tenses:

Di collera sussulta tremolando e pigolando sospesa
sotto il piano centrale dell'apparecchio la grassa
covata di bombe da 250 chili tritolo accanto
al lungo serbatoio nebbiogeno gonfio d'amara
    filosofia.

(Angrily jumps shaking and peeping suspended
under the central compartment of the plane the
    rich
covey of bombs of 250 kilograms of T.N.T. next
to the long hazy tank swelling with bitter philoso-
    phy.)

But he clearly continues to conceive of war positively, as one can see from the metaphor: bombs are seen as birds' eggs, and a connecting verb is *peeping*. The poem is composed of six individual simultaneities, for the most part independent from one another, as if readers were witnessing six episodes of a movie. Often there are geometric metaphors and repetitions, along with some baroque echoes.

In 1937 Marinetti published *Il poema Africano della Divisione "XXVIII Ottobre"* (The African Poem of the "XXVIII October" Division). The theme of a man seemingly belonging to two countries is the most important element of this poem (Marinetti, one could say, belonged to three: Italy, France, and his native Egypt):

Chi mi chiama chi mi chiama sei tu mamma con
　la tua voce bagnata di lagrime tu che sulla
　　spiaggia
di Ramleh nativa mi supplicavi di non nuotare
　lontano bambino.

(Who's calling me who's calling me is that you
　mother with
your voice soaked with tears you who on the beach
　of
native Ramleh used to beseech me not to swim far
　out child.)

With the exception of the images representing the themes and the memories the poet has of all the sounds, smells, colors, and events of his native country, the poem offers nothing new. It is a description of an African war, as one should expect from Marinetti. The images are as real and as direct as can be, a long series of onomatopoeic warlike episodes assailing the reader at such speed that he seemingly has no time to think, much less react. Yet a new *chanson de geste* (song of war) is born, though the emphasis is denuded of all human feelings, only to concentrate on the exaltation of imperialistic war, the only hero worthy of praise, according to Marinetti.

The same year (1937), he published *Il poema del vestito di latte* (The Poem about the Milk Dress), a work that follows in the footsteps of its immediate predecessor:

Con una tempestosa precipitante ferraglia una
　sonadriglia di aeroplani
o forbicioni aerei ci soffitta di battaglie
　facendo
sì che gambe all'aria le loro ombre a lingua
　lunga
lecchino acrobaticamente il latteo Altare della
　Patria.

(With a tempestuous precipitating ironware a
　squadron of airplanes
or aerial scissors garrets us with battles in such
　a way
that upside down their shadows with long tongues
lick acrobatically the milky Altar of the
　Country.)

The images of gluttony are used to solidify Marinetti's intention to find once again a primeval state, symbolized by a childish image of gluttony. The poem ends with an address to aerial poets, aerial painters, aerial sculptors, aerial musicians, and futurists to sing glorious poems.

In 1938 Marinetti published the manifesto "Poesia dei Tecnicismi" (Poetry of Technical Words), followed by *Il poema di Torre Viscosa* (The Poem of Torre Viscosa). At its best the poem offers a polyphonic "happening," experimenting with new sounds and technical applications:

Ma continuare continuerebbero senza fine
　continuino
　　　　　　　　　　　　　　continuino
le vostre gare di saluti inchini moine cerimoniose
　e le
　　　　　　　　　　　　　　svenevoli
leggiadrie di donne molto bruciavano si svestono
　con pudori
　　　　　　　　　　　　e levigate
spudoratezze di brilli queste soavi canne d'amore

(But to continue they would continue without
　end continue
　　　　　　　　　　　　　　continue
your competition of greeting bows ceremonial
　affectations
　　　　　　　　　　　　and the decadent
attitude of women burned a lot they undress
　with
　　　　　　　　　　　decency and polished
shamelessnesses of lushes these sweet reeds of
　love).

Not only for its new theoretical applications and innovations, but also for its contemplative natural state, most critics contend that this poem is inhuman because the focus is not on man; yet Marinetti is criticizing old-fashioned man and his behavior. A new man, the futurist, deistic man, now exists, which explains the use of such language. Marinetti is mythologizing futurism. *Il poema non umano dei tecnicismi* (The Nonhuman Poem of Technical Words) was published in 1940. The poem is symbolic of futurist poetry; with the arrival of machines the world has discovered a new god, velocity. Moreover, says Marinetti in the introduction to the poem, machines will make man's work less individualistic, since the use of machines will render it more automatic. True, but the other side of what Marinetti was idealizing is that machines have created unemployment. Therefore, Marinetti's ideals, when related to economics and politics, have remained utopias.

Benedetta and Filippo Tommaso Marinetti with their daughters (from left), Ala, Vittoria, and Luce, 1936
(photograph by Luxardo)

Nonetheless, Marinetti pioneered a movement in which writers such as Paolo Volponi later succeeded in achieving a poetic dimension.

In 1942 Marinetti published *Canto eroi e macchine della guerra Mussoliniana* (I Sing of Men and Machines of the Mussolinian War). It is an apologetic poem intended to glorify Italy's autarchy. The poet strives to fulfill his theory of a poetry open to new themes, new heroes, and new styles: his theme is war; the heroes are Benito Mussolini, Italo Balbo, and the Fascist army; and the style has not changed much from the other aerial poems. The poem describes the events, then announces its hero: "Il più grande annuncia col pungere lo zenit che il Duce entra solennemente a Tripoli" (The older announces by pricking the zenith that the Duce enters solemnly in Tripoli). The same can be said for *L'Aeropoema di Cozzarini primo eroe dell'esercito repubblicano* (The Aerial Poem of Cozzarini, First Hero of the Republican Army), published in 1944.

Quarto d'ora di poesia della X Mas (Quarter of an Hour of the Poetry of the X Mas) was published in January 1945, only a month after Marinetti's death. The preface was written by Benedetta Cappa, Marinetti's wife; the last two phrases read as follows: "Marinetti il tuo sangue ha seminato i campi del cielo il 2 gennaio, per i fiori della primavera italiana L'hai promessa con questo poema ai soldati della nostra Italia Repubblicana" (Marinetti, your blood has seeded the fields of the sky on 2 January, for the flowers of the Italian spring you promised with this poem to the soldiers of our Republican Italy). The poem introduces yet another of Marinetti's contradictions: the former anarchic, imperialistic defender is now fighting for a Republican Italy. The subject of the poem is the Russian war in which Marinetti had fought, even though he was tired and old. In one of the verses is the explanation of Marinetti's attitude:

voi becchini cocciuti nello sforzo di seppellire
primavere entusiaste di gloria ditemi siete
   soddisfatti
d'aver potuto cacciare in fondo al vostro letamaio
ideologico la fragile e deliziosa Italia ferita
   che non muore

(you stubborn gravediggers in the effort to
bury enthusiastic springs of glory tell me are you

Marinetti in his study, 1938, the year in which he published the manifesto "Poesia dei Tecnicismi"

satisfied to have been able to hide in the bottom
   of
your ideologic dunghill the fragile and delicious
   Italy
wounded but not
   dying).

    In 1971 Einaudi published *Poesie a Beny* (Poems to Beny), verses written by Marinetti between 1920 and 1932. For the most part these poems deal with love and the difficulties that arise in a relationship as time goes by. Marinetti attempted to point out some time-related fundamental stages. The images are enlarged, as though seen through a microscope.

    Filippo Tommaso Marinetti, born in Egypt and educated in France and Italy, proved to be a precursor of modern art. He intelligently realized the social, economic, and ideological changes that were taking place in Italy during his lifetime. He threw himself into the Italian intellectual scene and founded futurism: a movement that revolutionized Italian and European art. Marinetti was indeed a great theoretician and a poetic innovator; however, he was not a great poet. The numerous contradictions to be found in his manifestos and poetic productions are to be expected. When one attempts, as he did, to change drastically every artistic form, these are unavoidable. Nevertheless, Marinetti, as fast as a racing car and as powerful as a tank, proceeded to free Italian artists from the long-sedentary traditional residue of the late nineteenth century and to lead them into the twentieth century.

Letters:

Carteggio futurista, edited by Luciano Folgore (Rome: Officina, 1987).

References:

Giovanni Antonucci, *Lo spettacolo futurista in Italia* (Rome: Studium, 1974);

Guido Ballo, "Marinetti e Boccioni," in *Présence de F. T. Marinetti* (Lausanne, Switzerland: L'Age de l'Homme, 1982), pp. 61-66;

Fortunato Bellonzi, *Saggio sulla poesia di Marinetti* (Urbino, Italy: Argalia, 1943);

Mirko Bevilacqua, *Passaggi novecenteschi: Da Marinetti a Benjamin* (Florence: Sansoni, 1985);

Walter Binni, "Crepuscolari e Futuristi," in his *La poetica del decadentismo* (Florence: Sansoni, 1961), pp. 127-148;

Massimo Bontempelli, *Analogie in "900"* (Florence: Vallecchi, 1974);

Sandro Briosi, *Marinetti* (Florence: Nuova Italia, 1969);

Briosi, *Marinetti e il futurismo* (Lecce: Milella, 1986);

Maurizio Calvesi, *Le due avanguardie* (Milan: Lerici, 1966);

Fausto Curi, "Una stilistica della materia: F. T. Marinetti e le 'parole in libertà,' " in *Présence de F. T. Marinetti*, pp. 26-48;

Luciano De Maria, *Introduzione a F. T. Marinetti: Teoria ed invenzione futurista* (Milan: Mondadori, 1968);

De Maria, *Per conoscere Marinetti e il futurismo* (Milan: Mondadori, 1973);

Robert Dombroski, *Il futurismo tra movimento e utopia* (Naples: Guida, 1984);

Enrico Falqui, *Futurismo e Novecentismo* (Turin: Rai, 1953);

Francesco Flora, *Dal romanticismo al futurismo* (Piacenza, Italy: Porta, 1921);

Mario Isnenghi, *Il mito della grande guerra da Marinetti a Malaparte* (Bari, Italy: Laterza, 1970);

Sergio Lambiase and Gian Battista Nazzaro, *Marinetti e i futuristi* (Milan: Mursia, 1978);

Giovanni Lista, "Marinetti et les anarchosyndacalistes," in *Présence de F. T. Marinetti*, pp. 67-85;

Lista, *Marinetti et le futurisme* (Lausanne, Switzerland: L'Age de l'Homme, 1977);

Lista, *Marinetti, Poètes d'aujourd'hui* (Paris: Seghers, 1976);

Gaetano Mariani, *Il primo Marinetti* (Florence: Monnier, 1970);

Marianne W. Martin, *Futurist Art and Theory* (Oxford: Clarendon Press, 1968);

Luigi Paglia, *Invito alla lettura di Filippo Tommaso Marinetti* (Milan: Mursia, 1987);

Tullio Panteo, *Il poeta Marinetti* (Milan: Mursia, 1908);

Marzio Pinottini, *L'estetica del futurismo—Revisioni storiografiche* (Rome: Bulzoni, 1979);

Ugo Piscopo, "Marinetti prefuturista," in *Présence de F. T. Marinetti*, pp. 141-155;

Piscopo, *Questioni e aspetti del futurismo* (Naples: Ferraro, 1976);

Antonio Saccone, *Marinetti e il futurismo* (Naples: Liguori, 1985);

Claudia Salaris, *Storia del futurismo* (Rome: Riuniti, 1985);

Roberto Tessari, *Il mito della macchina* (Milan: Mursia, 1973);

Caroline Tisdall and Angelo Bozzolla, *Futurism* (New York & Toronto: Oxford University Press, 1978);

Rosa Trillo Clough, *Futurism* (New York: Philosophical Library, 1961);

Mario Verdone, *Cinema e letteratura* (Rome: Bianco e Nero, 1968);

Jean Weisgerber, "Le saut dans l'avenir du temps des avants-gardes: la conception de Marinetti et la discontinuité," in *Présence de F. T. Marinetti*, pp. 115-124.

Eugenio Montale

(12 October 1896 - 12 September 1981)

Rebecca West
University of Chicago

BOOKS: *Ossi di seppia* (Turin: Gobetti, 1925; enlarged edition, Turin: Fratelli Ribet, 1928); translated by Antonino Mazza as *The Bones of Cuttlefish* (Oakville, Ont. & New York: Mosaic, 1983);

La casa dei doganieri e altri versi (Florence: Vallecchi, 1932);

Le occasioni (Turin: Einaudi, 1939; enlarged, 1940); translated by William Arrowsmith as *The Occasions* (New York & London: Norton, 1987);

Finisterre (Lugano, Switzerland: Collana di Lugano, 1943);

La bufera e altro (Venice: Neri Pozza, 1956); translated by Charles Wright as *The Storm and Other Poems* (Oberlin, Ohio: Oberlin College, 1978); also translated by Arrowsmith, as *The Storm and Other Things* (New York & London: Norton, 1985);

Farfalla di Dinard (Venice: Neri Pozza, 1956); translated by G. Singh as *The Butterfly of Dinard* (London: London Magazine, 1970; Lexington: University Press of Kentucky, 1971);

Satura (Verona: Bodoni, 1962); enlarged as *Satura: 1962-1970* (Milan: Mondadori, 1971); partially translated by Singh in his *New Poems: A Selection from "Satura" and "Diario del '71 e del '72"* (New York: New Directions, 1976);

Accordi e pastelli (Milan: Strenna per Gli Amici/Scheiwiller, 1962);

Celebrazione di Italo Svevo (Trieste: Circolo della Cultura delle Arti, 1963);

Xenia (San Severino Marche, Italy: Bellabarba, 1966);

Auto da fé (Milan: Saggiatore, 1966);

Il colpevole (Milan: Scheiwiller, 1966);

Lettere Italo Svevo (Bari, Italy: De Donato, 1966);

Fuori di casa (Milan & Naples: Ricciardi, 1969);

Diario del '71 (Milan: Scheiwiller, 1971); enlarged as *Diario del '71 e del '72* (Milan: Mondadori, 1973); partially translated by Singh in his *New Poems: A Selection from "Satura" and "Diario del '71 e del '72"*;

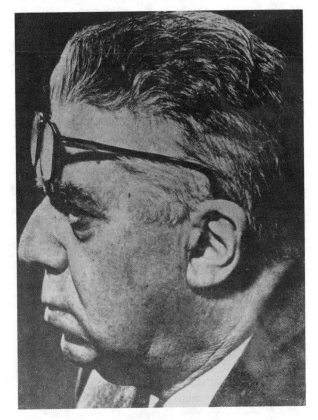

Eugenio Montale

La poesia non esiste (Milan: All'Insegna del Pesce d'Oro/Scheiwiller, 1971);

Seconda maniera di Marmeladov (Milan: Scheiwiller, 1971);

Il poeta: Diario (Verona: Bodoni, 1972);

Nel nostro tempo (Milan: Rizzoli, 1972); translated by Alastair Hamilton as *Poet in Our Time* (London: Boyars, 1976; New York: Urizen, 1976);

Mottetti, with a translation by Lawrence Kart (San Francisco: Grabhorn Hoyem, 1973; London: Agenda, 1977; Milan: Adelphi, 1988);

Trentadue variazioni (Milan: Lucini, 1973);

E ancora possibile la poesia? (Stockholm & Rome: Italica, 1975);

Otto poesie (Milan: Scheiwiller, 1975);

Sulla poesia, edited by Giorgio Zampa (Milan: Mondadori, 1976);

Tutte le poesie (Milan: Mondadori, 1977; enlarged, 1984);

Quaderno di quattro anni (Milan: Mondadori, 1977); translated by Singh as *It Depends: A Poet's Notebook* (New York: New Directions, 1980);

Montale premio Nobel, by Montale, Giovanni Arpino, and others (Bologna: Boni, 1977);

Montale commenta Montale, edited by Lorenzo Greco (Parma, Italy: Pratiche, 1980);

L'Opera in versi, edited by Rosanna Bettarini and Gianfranco Contini (Turin: Einaudi, 1980 [i.e., 1981]);

Prime alla Scala, edited by Gianfranca Lavezzi (Milan: Mondadori, 1981);

Lettere a Salvatore Quasimodo, edited by Sebastiano Grasso (Milan: Bompiani, 1981);

Quaderno genovese, edited by Laura Barile (Milan: Mondadori, 1983);

Poesie inedite, 6 volumes, continuing (Lugano, Switzerland & New York: Fondazione Schlesinger, 1986-   );

Il carteggio Einaudi-Montale per "Le occasioni" (1938-39), edited by Carla Sacchi (Turin: Einaudi, 1988).

Editions in English: *Poems*, translated by Edwin Morgan (Reading, U.K.: University of Reading, 1959);

Poesie/Poems, translated by George Kay (Edinburgh: Edinburgh University Press, 1964); abridged as *Selected Poems* (Harmondsworth, U.K. & Baltimore: Penguin, 1969);

Selected Poems, translated by Ben Belitt and others (New York: New Directions, 1966);

Provisional Conclusions: A Selection, translated by Edith Farnsworth (Chicago: Regnery, 1970);

Selected Essays, translated by G. Singh, with an introduction by Montale (Manchester, U.K.: Carcanet, 1978);

The Second Life of Art: Selected Essays, translated and edited by Jonathan Galassi (New York: Ecco, 1982);

Otherwise: Last and First Poems, translated by Galassi (New York: Random House/Vintage, 1984).

TRANSLATIONS: John Steinbeck, *La battaglia* (Milan: Bompiani, 1940);

Narratori spagnoli, edited by Carlo Bo (Milan: Bompiani, 1941);

Teatro elisabettiano, edited by Alfredo Obertello (Milan: Bompiani, 1941);

Dorothy Parker, *Il mio mondo è qui* (Milan: Bompiani, 1941);

Teatro spagnolo, edited by Elio Vittorini (Milan: Bompiani, 1941);

Americana, edited by Vittorini (Milan: Bompiani, 1942);

Herman Melville, *La storia di Billy Budd* (Milan: Bompiani, 1942);

Eugene O'Neill, *Strano interludio* (Rome: Teatro dell'Università, 1943);

Poeti antichi e moderni tradotti dai lirici nuovi, edited by Luciano Anceschi and Domenico Porzio (Milan: Balcone, 1945);

Steinbeck, *Al dio sconosciuto* (Milan: Mondadori, 1946);

Nathaniel Hawthorne, *Il volto di pietra* (Milan: Bompiani, 1947);

Quaderno di traduzioni (Milan: Meridiana, 1948);

William Shakespeare, *Amleto, principe di Danimarca* (Milan: Cederna, 1949);

Shakespeare, *Teatro*, edited by Mario Praz (Florence: Sansoni, 1949);

Miguel De Cervantes, *Il cordovano* (Milan: Suvini-Zerboni, 1949);

Omar De Carlo, *Proserpina e lo straniero* (Milan: Ricordi, 1952);

Iconografia italiana di Ezra Pound, edited by Vanni Scheiwiller (Milan: Scheiwiller, 1956);

Angus Wilson, *La cicuta e dopo* (Milan: Garzanti, 1956);

Teatro francese del Grande Secolo, edited by Giovanni Macchia (Turin: ERI, 1960);

Manuel de Falla, *Atlantida* (Milan: Ricordi, 1961);

W. H. Hudson, *La vita della foresta*, edited by Maria Antonietta Grignani (Turin: Einaudi, 1987).

Eugenio Montale, winner of the Nobel Prize in literature in 1975, is regarded as one of the dominant voices of modernism, not only within the context of Italian letters but also internationally. His poetry, from the first publications in the 1920s to his complete works (*L'Opera in versi*) that appeared in 1981, is a touchstone for all those who seek to understand the potential and achievement of twentieth-century verse. He is one of the strongest voices of Italian poetry; however, his work is characterized by understatement, existential and philosophical diffidence, and a quiet dedication to his craft rather than a declaration of art's hegemony and an assertion of unassailable truths.

The power of Montale's verse lies, somewhat paradoxically, in its continual declaration of

Montale in the garden of his family's villa in Monterosso, 1920

the powerlessness of either art or the human race ever to know itself fully. He believed, nonetheless, in the necessity of seeking knowledge, as well as the importance of the ethical dimension in both art and life, a dimension called simply "decenza quotidiana" (daily decency) in "Visita a Fadin" (Visit to Fadin), a prose poem in *La bufera e altro* (1956; translated as *The Storm and Other Poems*, 1978). A strict separation between the immanent and the transcendent was unacceptable to Montale. Instead he emphasized their inevitable oneness, as well as the equally inevitable contradictions that result.

Montale completely absorbed the Italian lyric tradition, from Dante to Petrarch to Giacomo Leopardi, and including Montale's immediate precursors: the *crepuscolari* (twilight poets) and futurists. His poetry further reveals the extraordinary importance of certain antimodels, especially Gabriele D'Annunzio and Benedetto Croce, whose art and philosophy, respectively, dominated Montale's formative years. Although,

like T. S. Eliot—to whom his work has often been compared—Montale can be seen ultimately as a philosophical poet, he himself refused this label, insisting that he sought not to promote ideas but rather to seek knowledge, however partial, of individual as well as collective truths about the human condition. He was, then, a metaphysical poet, whose art probes and questions both personal and collective historical experience as well as the eternal questions of the meaning of existence, the role of love, and the place of humankind. Like all great poets, Montale goes beyond precursors and contemporaries alike, creating an unmistakably original tonality that is capable of intense lyricism as well as the most antirhetorical and even dissonant music.

Montale was always stubbornly laconic about the intimate details of his life. In a 1978 interview with Enzo Biagi he suggested that, if life is a labyrinth, he passed through its many twisting paths without sustaining any real harm. He was born on 12 October 1896 in Genoa and spent his childhood and early adult years there and in the Cinque Terre, a rugged coastal area south of the city, where his family had a summer residence. That Ligurian coast, with its then-unspoiled beauty, and the Mediterranean Sea spreading out beneath the rocky cliffs figure prominently in his first collection of poetry, *Ossi di seppia* (1925; translated as *The Bones of Cuttlefish*, 1983). Writing many years later of the spiritual essence of landscape, he noted in the prose poem "Dov'era il tennis" (Where The Tennis Court Was; in *La bufera e altro*) that each individual has "il *suo* paesaggio, immutabile" (*his own* immutable landscape), which is always internalized: "è curioso che l'ordine fisico sia così lento a filtrare in noi e poi così impossibile a scancellarsi" (it is curious how the physical order is so slow in filtering into us and then so impossible to erase). From the beginning of his career Montale endowed the physical with a metaphysical dimension. The sea and shores of the region of Liguria became emblematic of an abstract rather than concrete reality. His goal is never merely to describe but rather to seek out the correlations between landscapes and certain emotions and states of mind. For example, in the suite of poems entitled "Mediterraneo," in *Ossi di seppia*, the sea is portrayed as a "father" whose natural power and limitless mutability are in contrast to the "son's" self-conscious entrapment in words and in the predestined, inevitable boundaries of human space and time.

In 1915 Montale decided to dedicate himself to the study of bel canto, but his musical career was cut short by the death of his maestro, Ernesto Sivori, in 1916. In a fictionalized autobiographical story, "Nella chiave di 'fa'" (In the Key of "F"), in the collection of prose pieces *Farfalla di Dinard* (1956; translated as *The Butterfly of Dinard*, 1970), Montale recounts his experience with Sivori. The young aspirant was especially impressed by his teacher's insistence that a successful singer needs, even more than a good voice, a certain "fire," which Montale was never sure he possessed. Upon the death of Sivori, he wrote that "l'incanto, se non il canto" (the magic, if not song itself) was finished for him. Nonetheless, music remained of paramount importance to Montale, permeating both his art and life. Some of his first poems were in fact attempts at imitating the music of Claude Debussy, and Montale's love for and knowledge of opera were legendary. When in the 1950s he was hired as music critic for the Milanese newspaper *Corriere d'Informazione*, he assiduously attended opening nights at La Scala, scarcely missing a performance. His reviews of those performances as well as other pieces dedicated to musical subjects are collected in *Prime alla Scala* (Opening Nights at La Scala, 1981), an invaluable source of information for those interested in understanding better the role played by music in Montale's daily life.

Beyond his personal attachment to music, which led him to entertain close friends by giving private "concerts" from time to time, when they could enjoy his rich baritone, and beyond his professional commitment as a music critic, music, within Montale's poetry, is not only incidental or thematic but functions as a constitutive element of his poetics and subsequent verse. In his "Intenzioni (Intervista immaginaria)" (Intentions [Imaginary Interview]), first published in 1946 and now included in *Sulla poesia* (On Poetry, 1976), the poet describes the importance of his early musical training, which through experience rather than intuition led him to see the "fondamentale unità delle varie arti" (fundamental unity of the diverse arts). He further writes that he came to understand that "esiste un problema d'impostazione anche fuori del canto, in ogni opera umana" (there exists a problem of pitch even outside of singing, in every human enterprise) and that, when he wrote the poems that would form his first book, he obeyed "un bisogno di espressione musicale" (a need for musical expression), engaging in a search that was

"istintiva, non programmatica" (instinctual and unprogrammatic). The "voice" he sought was neither mellifluous nor melodic; rather, he wished to act upon "l'eloquenza della nostra vecchia lingua aulica" (the eloquence of our old noble language) by "torcere il collo" (twisting its neck), even "a rischio di una contraeloquenza" (at the risk of a counter-eloquence). Many years later, in his Nobel Prize acceptance speech, *E ancora possibile la poesia?* (Is Poetry Still Possible?, 1975), Montale again emphasized what for him is the indissoluble tie between music and poetry:

> Se considero la poesia come un oggetto ritengo ch'essa sia nata dalla necessità di aggiungere un suono vocale (parola) al martellamento delle prime musiche tribali. Solo molto più tardi parola e musica poterono scriversi in qualche modo e differenziarsi. Appare la poesia scritta, ma la comune parentela con la musica si fa sentire.

> (If I consider poetry as an object I think that it was born from the necessity of joining a vocal sound [the word] to the beat of the first tribal music. Only much later could word and music be written in some way and thus be differentiated. Written poetry appears, but its common parentage with music is still felt.)

The sonorities of poetry—its aural potentialities—were for Montale the salient characteristic of an art that is also profoundly allied to the other arts. He also insisted throughout his career on the importance of prose to poetic invention, writing in "Intenzioni" that "naturalmente il grande semenzaio d'ogni trovata poetica è nel campo della prosa" (naturally the great seedbed of every poetic intention is in the field of prose), an assertion that might first appear to counter his emphasis on the constitutive role of music in poetic creation and elaboration. However, the "musical, instinctual, and unprogrammatic" origins of Montale's verse, and the resultant tonalities, remain a major source of its power.

After the early training in bel canto, Montale began to experiment in verse with futurist and symbolist models. The first poem described by him as "tout entier à sa proie attaché," a poem, that is, which hit its mark beyond imitation or exercise, was the 1916 composition "Meriggiare" (To Noon), later included in his first collection. In it one sees many of the thematic and formal components that will inform much of his future poetry. The observing pres-

Page from the manuscript for "Barche sulla Marna" (collected in Le occasioni*), written by Montale in the 1930s (by permission of the Estate of Eugenio Montale)*

ence, "pallido e assorto" (pale and intent), is depersonalized through the consistent use of infinitives "to listen"; "to observe"; "to feel"), which creates a static, suspended, meditative space from which a kind of detached consciousness registers the details of the natural world around it. That world is harsh and dry under the noonday sun, filled with the chattering of blackbirds, the rustling of snakes, the endless circling of red ants, and the tremulous creaking of cicadas. From near the scorching garden wall, the observer can make out the far-off undulations of the sea. The indifference and pitilessness of nature—a Leopardian theme carried over into much of Montale's early verse—are magisterially re-created in the first three stanzas. In the fourth and final stanza, the observer's emotional reaction is recorded: "sentire con triste meraviglia / com'è tutta la vita e il suo travaglio / in questo seguitare una muraglia / che ha in cima cocci aguzzi di bottiglia" (to feel with sad amazement / how all of life and its anguish is / in this following along a wall / that is edged with sharp glass shards).

The movement from the physical world to the spiritual and mental interiority of the speaker was to become a mainstay of Montale's early verse. The garden wall ("muro d'orto") announces two lexical leitmotifs: the garden, most often called "orto" (vegetable garden) rather than the more lush decorative "giardino" of tradition; and the wall. Both motifs are endowed in later poems with the symbolic force of emblems of enclosure, imprisonment, and predestination. In contrast, the sea is a liberating presence representing constant change, potency, and existential freedom. These meanings are, however, implicit at this early stage of Montale's writing; they were to emerge more directly as the first collection took shape. The rich and antimelodic lexicon of "Meriggiare"—apparent in terms such as "cocci aguzzi" that seek to capture the harshness, both natural and spiritual, of this world—reveals the young Montale's debt to Dante's plurilingualism (he even borrows the Dantesque rhyme "serpi"/"sterpi" from the wood-of-the-suicides episode of *The Inferno*), as well as his search for sound/sense equivalencies. But Montale avoids easy fluidity by using hyperrhyme ("veccia"/"si'intrecciano"), assonance and consonance ("abbaglia"—"meraviglia"—"travaglio"—"muraglia"—"bottiglia"), and rough consonantal sounds ("serpi"/"sterpi"; "scricchi"/"picchi"). The poem was an accomplished debut for the twenty-year-old poet. His thematic and stylistic pitch was to be developed and enriched, but not drastically departed from,

through all the poems included in the collection *Ossi di seppia*.

In 1917 war intervened, and from 1917 to 1919 Montale served as a soldier, mostly in the Trentino region and in and around Genoa. Unlike his contemporary Giuseppe Ungaretti, whose early poetry was heavily conditioned by his wartime experiences, Montale did not incorporate many direct personal or collective references to those difficult times into his subsequent poetry. There is no doubt, however, that the war was a watershed for all Italian intellectuals and artists, for some of whom the destruction of the old order was cause for rejoicing, and for others a cause for increased disorientation and somber reflection on what the future might bring. Already assailed by a sense of perennial maladjustment—a metaphysical rather than simply personal or social condition—Montale did not rush headlong and joyfully into the unknown future but instead kept his distance from the many "isms" of the avant-garde, who proclaimed sure victory for newness and modernity.

After the war Montale returned to his family home and continued to frequent the literary circles of Genoa and Turin, where he had already begun to develop friendships. He was an autodidact (he never studied for a university degree), immersing himself in readings of philosophy, Italian classics, and an eclectic selection of foreign writers. In 1922 he met the antifascist intellectual Piero Gobetti, who was to publish *Ossi di seppia* in 1925. One of the most important influences on the diffident young poet, Gobetti's open anti-D'Annunzianism as well as his informed interest in the increasingly potent intellectual hegemony of Crocean idealism fed strongly into Montale's own development.

As Jared Becker has recently argued, much of Montale's overall production can be seen as a fundamental and continuous coming to terms with these two powerful presences in twentieth-century Italian culture: D'Annunzio's vitalism, his Nietzschean will to power and embrace of the concept of the "superman," and his political activism were all profoundly antithetical to Montale, while Crocean idealism, which emphasized the separation of art from practical activity and privileged the aesthetic over the political or social, appealed to Montale's basic disbelief in the ability of humankind to counter the inexorable and humanly indifferent forces that condition experience. Many years later Montale would acknowledge the necessity for any poet of his generation of "passing through" D'Annunzio, just as he would distance himself from many aspects of Crocean thought. Nonetheless, these two figures loomed large in his early formation.

The publication of *Ossi di seppia* established Montale as a poet worthy of serious critical attention. The attention given Montale by renowned and respected critics such as Gianfranco Contini, Alfredo Gargiulo, and, later, Pier Vincenzo Mengaldo and Glauco Cambon, among many others in Italy and elsewhere, has not abated. The first collection was not universally acclaimed, but for the most part contemporary critics praised it as an event of lasting importance, which presented an authentically new voice. The young poet's muted yet powerful "counter-eloquence" and what Gargiulo, in his introduction to the expanded second edition (1928), called a "corrosione critica dell'esistenza" (scathing critical corrosion of existence) met with widespread approval, especially at that moment in Italian culture, when Fascist bombast proliferated and the spiritual malaise of many was being smothered by declarations of certainty, prosperity, and optimism.

Montale once wrote in a letter to his friend P. Gadda Conti (subsequently published in the journal *Letteratura* in 1966) that his essential poetic motifs (and motives: both meanings are contained in the original *motivi*) were three: "paesaggio" (landscape); "amore" (love); and "evasione" (escape). All three are prominently present in *Ossi di seppia*. The harsh terrain of the Ligurian coast and the Mediterranean below; the Proustian "intermittences of the heart" created by beloveds, whom Montale called "fantasmi che *frequentano* le varie poesie" (ghosts who *frequent* the various poems); and the constant search for an escape from "la catena ferrea della necessità" (the iron chain of necessity), what he also called "il miracolo laico" (the lay miracle)—all these inform the poems of *Ossi di seppia*. There is a compelling directness to the poetic voice, which often speaks in the imperative to an unnamed interlocutor, the "tu," or intimate "you," that soon becomes a salient characteristic of Montale's poetry. Many opening lines call out with strong immediacy: "Ascoltami" (Listen to me); "Non chiederci la parola" (Don't ask of us the word); "Portami il girasole" (Bring me the sunflower); "Arremba su la strinata proda" (Board the cardboard ships).

After the success of his first published collection of verse, Montale wished to escape the somewhat provincial atmosphere of Genoa. He had be-

Montale in 1938 (portrait by Renato Guttuso; Galleria Nazionale d'Arte Moderna, Rome)

come better known among critics and writers not only with the appearance of *Ossi di seppia* but also with his "Omaggio a Italo Svevo" (Homage to Italo Svevo), which was published in the journal *L'Esame* in 1925 and aroused widespread interest in the hitherto ignored Triestine. Finally, in 1927, Montale was offered a position as a copywriter for Bemporad Casa Editrice in Florence, where he was to live and work for more than a decade. In 1929 he became director of the Vieusseux Research Library, a distinguished institution that drew many critics and writers to its doors. The poet's Florentine years were filled with journalistic and other literary activities. He often wrote for *Solaria*, a prominent literary journal, and frequented two cafés—the Giubbe Rosse and the Antico Fattore—that functioned as meeting places for primarily antifascist artists, writers, and intellectuals. In 1931 the Antico Fattore established a literary prize to be awarded by the nonwriters of the group; Montale won it for his "La casa dei doganieri" (The Customs

House), subsequently published in the small collection *La casa dei doganieri e altri versi* (1932). In "Intenzioni" Montale wrote of his years in Florence:

> Fino a trent'anni non avevo conosciuto quasi nessuno, ora vedevo anche troppa gente, ma la mia solitudine non era minore di quella del tempo degli *Ossi di seppia*. Cercai di vivere a Firenze col distacco di uno straniero, di un Browning; ma non avevo fatto i conti coi lanzi della podesteria feudale da cui dipendevo.

> (Until I was thirty I had scarcely known anyone; now I actually saw too many people, but my solitude was not less than that of the period of *Ossi di seppia*. I tried to live in Florence with the detachment of a foreigner, of a Browning; but I had not taken into account the "mercenaries" of the feudal regime on which I depended.)

The poet is certainly referring to his experience with the Fascist government that relieved him of his post as the Vieusseux's director in 1938 because he was not a party member. A fictionalized version of this episode is recounted in *Il colpevole* (The Guilty One), a story in *Farfalla di Dinard* that was separately published in 1966.

In spite of his solitary existence, Montale had two encounters during his Florentine period that were to be of lasting importance in both his life and art. Drusilla Tanzi, then the wife of the art critic Matteo Marangoni, was to become Montale's lifelong companion and, shortly before her death in 1963, his wife; and Irma Brandeis, an American Dante scholar, was to become his "Beatrice," the source of inspiration for his poetic beloved called Clizia. When Brandeis returned definitively to America, at least in part because of the highly inhospitable environment in Europe for Jews, Montale contemplated following her there and made some attempts to secure a teaching post at Smith College and the University of Chicago, but he abandoned these plans and was to remain in Italy for the remainder of his life. These women—and many others—appear frequently in his verse as persistent "ghosts" or tenacious symbols of strength. Tanzi, known in life as "Mosca," or "Fly," because of her enormous bespectacled eyes, is commemorated after her death in the series of poems called *Xenia*, included in *Satura* (Miscellany, 1962) and separately published in 1966, while Clizia is already present, although unnamed, in some of the love poems of *Le occasioni* (1939; trans-

lated as *The Occasions*, 1987) and will emerge as a named presence in *La bufera e altro*, where she is literally an angel of transcendental power and clear-sightedness. Some of Montale's latest poems, written on the eve of his death, are addressed to her. These women, immortalized in Montale's poetry, served him well: Tanzi materially supported and encouraged the professionally unsettled poet, and Brandeis was one of the first to translate and speak of his work in America (in the *Quarterly Review of Literature*, 1962).

The second major collection of Montale's poetry, *Le occasioni*, includes the poems of the 1932 volume and many new poems. As in the case of *Ossi di seppia*, where the title is indicative of the marine ambience informing the verse as well as of its honed-down, unrhetorical, plain, and "bleached" language, the second title is "pregnante di intelligenza autocritica" (pregnant with autocritical intelligence), according to Contini. In Italian, "occasions" signify not just occurrences or casual events but also rare moments of illumination and epiphany, literally "opportunities" that the poet then re-creates in brief lyrical flashes. The poems of this period (1928-1940) are generally thought of as Montale's most hermetic, both in terms of their extreme thematic privacy and their formal compression. Not all contemporary critics were pleased with what Guido Almansi and Bruce Merry called (in the title of their study) the "private language of poetry," which took precedence in this phase of Montale's career. The poet himself insisted that he never embraced hermeticism as a program or a school, that he never willfully sought obscurity. Rather, in "Intenzioni," he states that he continued his unprogrammatic "lotta per scavare un'altra dimensione nel nostro pesante linguaggio polisillabico, che mi pareva rifiutarsi a un'esperienza come la mia" (battle to dig out another dimension from our heavy polysyllabic language, which seemed to me to refuse an experience like mine). Nonetheless Montale was accused of obscurantism by more than one critic, and he has continued to be rather inaccurately labeled a member of the hermetic school, along with Ungaretti, Salvatore Quasimodo, and others for whom this tag is more appropriate.

The central series of the collection—*Mottetti* (Motets, translated and separately published in 1973)—is made up of twenty short love poems written to and of a beloved woman who is now absent from the speaker's life. Montale explained years later that in fact there were several diverse

Montale circa 1963

sources of inspiration for the various lyrics, but that nonetheless the section has the unity of a "romanzetto autobiografico" (autobiographical novelette). The importance of Dante and of "stilnovism" (the sweet new style) is evident; in "Intenzioni" Montale writes of "la Selvaggia o la Mandetta o la Delia (la chiami come vuole) dei *Mottetti*" (the Selvaggia or the Mandetta or the Delia [call her what you will] of the *Mottetti*), thus alluding, with the first two names, to the emblematic names of the beloved ladies of Cino da Pistoia and Guido Cavalcanti, both typically included with Dante as poets of the stilnovistic school. In a note to the poem "Iride" (Iris), in *La bufera e altro*, Montale identifies the lady of the *Mottetti* with Clizia, a name he explicitly connects to a Dantesque source in his epigraph to "La primavera hitleriana" (Hitler Spring), another poem in *La bufera*. The epigraph—"Né quella ch'a veder lo sol si gira" (Nor she who turns to see the sun)—is a line attributed, although with some doubt, to a poem by Dante in which Clizia is the mythic lady enamored of Apollo and transformed by the sun god into a sunflower. The importance of the literary rather than actual identity of the beloved is underscored by Montale in

his essay on Dante (included in *Sulla poesia*) when he writes of the feminine presences in Dante's work as stylistic adventures. Similarly the many women of Montale's poetry, from Clizia to the later Volpe (Vixen) and Annetta-Arletta, all live their authentic lives as poetry, no matter what the actual autobiographical details may be.

After his dismissal from the Vieusseux, Montale lived on translations and journalistic writing, and he continued to write poetry. During the dark years of World War II he led a relatively quiet, if troubled, existence in Florence, for although he was not an active participant in the armed struggle against Fascism, he was by no means indifferent to the events affecting not only Italy but the whole world. A short story titled *La poesia non esiste* (Poetry Does Not Exist), later included in *Farfalla di Dinard* and separately published in 1971, was originally published in *Corriere della Sera* in 1946. Set in the winter of 1944, it recounts an evening in the home of the autobiographical first-person narrator, who has opened his doors to those Italians being sought by the Germans for their partisan activities. The setting serves as a frame to the dialogue that ensues between the host and a young German soldier; the immediate contingencies of a threatening reality are strongly evoked while the conversation speaks of more literary and abstract concerns—the life of poetry—ostensibly remote from and yet deeply related to the political and social upheavals of the war. The German, whose unannounced arrival throws the household into a crisis of fear, turns out to have come for the sole purpose of bringing the host some poems of Friedrich Hölderlin, promised several years back in the course of their brief correspondence but never delivered until this most inopportune moment. As they settle in over a glass of wine—the host sweating all the while for fear that his hidden guests will be discovered—the German begins to expostulate on Western literary culture, finally reaching the summary conclusion that "poetry does not exist." Upon the soldier's departure, the narrator goes into a darkened room where the partisans have been hiding to give them the all-clear signal. One of them asks what the German had to say, and the narrator answers, "dice che la poesia non esiste" (he says that poetry does not exist). The response is an "ah," accompanied by the snores of another partisan, who is sleeping "in un lettuccio strettissimo" (in a very narrow old bed).

This little story reveals Montale's belief in the importance of daily decency. There are no grand gestures, no clearly defined heroes or villains. The narrator is neither a hero nor a coward but rather a man capable of seeing the limitations of both life and art, action and contemplation. The self-portrait that emerges from this story, told with a light touch and no small dose of irony, as is true of most of Montale's prose, is consonant with the poet's self-description as expressed in "Intenzioni": "Ho vissuto il mio tempo col minimum di vigliaccheria ch'era consentito alle mie deboli forze, ma c'è chi ha fatto di più, molto di più, anche se non ha pubblicato libri" (I have lived my time with the minimum of cowardice that was allowed to my weak powers, but there are those who did more, much more, even if they did not publish books). Montale was to be severely criticized for his lack of *engagement* and his presumed "ivory-towerism" both during the war and after, yet it is clear that such sweeping judgment is not only too easy but ultimately highly unfair. His contribution to culture, although never explicitly or strongly political in nature, was nonetheless far from detached from the deeper ethical and metaphysical questions that ideally condition political action; and his

quiet commitment to certain principles of fairness, justice, and decency cannot be dismissed as incidental or inferior to more ostentatious shows of social and political concern for the destiny of humankind.

In 1943 Montale published a short collection of verse titled *Finisterre*, smuggled out of Italy by Contini and printed in Switzerland. The volume was unpublishable in Italy, prefaced as it was by an epigraph from Théodore-Agrippa d'Aubigné that made clear the poet's appraisal of the crumbling Fascist regime: "Les princes n'ont point d'yeux pour voir ces grands merveilles; leur mains ne servent plus qu'à nous persécuter" (The princes have no eyes with which to see these great marvels; their hands now serve only to persecute us). Montale was very active as a translator during this period, and some of his versions of the works of T. S. Eliot, W. B. Yeats, William Shakespeare, and other poets is available in *Quaderno di traduzioni* (Translation Notebook), published in 1948. Recently a translation of William Henry Hudson's *Green Mansions* (1904) done by Montale in the mid 1940s and retrieved by him from the 1966 Florentine flood but never published, was acquired along with other autograph materials of the poet by the University of Pavia and finally printed in 1987, edited by Maria Antonietta Grignani.

During the mid 1940s Montale was approaching fifty years of age and was still without a fixed post or means of earning a stable living. As a hobby he took up painting, using wine, coffee grounds, toothpaste, and cigarette ashes to blend his colors, averse as always to more "noble" raw materials. (This dislike for expensive tools extended to his writing as well; rather than use good paper, he would write many of his poems on bus tickets and candy wrappers, only to find that they disappeared into the garbage.) Two of his whimsical watercolors serve as covers to his prose collections *Farfalla di Dinard* and *Fuori di casa* (Away From Home, 1969), the latter a series of travel sketches recounting his meetings with certain well-known personages and his impressions of foreign lands. But, as amusing as painting was, Montale needed a job; finally in 1946 he was hired by the Milanese newspaper *Corriere della Sera* as a part-time theater critic.

Montale's Milanese period, which was to last until the end of his life, began in 1948 when he was taken on as a full-time contributor to the *Corriere*, thanks to a well-known "occasion." The poet happened to be in the chief editor's office

Montale, Giuseppe Ungaretti, and Salvatore Quasimodo (photograph by Giovanneti)

one day when notice of Mahatma Gandhi's death was received. The editor needed a cover story immediately, and Montale complied, supposedly sitting down then and there and pounding out a piece so pleasing to the boss that he was hired on the spot. He wrote many of the prose pieces now included in *Farfalla di Dinard* as stories for the *terza pagina*, or cultural page, of the newspaper; he also did most of his traveling during this period on various assignments for the paper, including his ninety-hour sole visit to the United States (to New York City), recounted in *Fuori di casa*. His association with the newspaper continued actively well into the 1960s. In 1955 he became music critic, and for the next twelve years he is reputed never to have missed an opening night at La Scala. On official documents Montale listed his occupation as "giornalista" (journalist), and although he often denigrated that trade, calling it a "lucha por los garbanzos" (a grind for grub), he, in fact, spoke equally often of the importance of constant, disciplined writing to the development of his poetry, as well as the conditioning effect of prose creation on his lyric output.

The year 1956 saw the appearance of Montale's third major collection of verse, *La bufera e altro*, which includes the earlier *Finisterre*

as its opening section. *La bufera* contains some of the most powerful and accomplished poems of Montale's entire production, from the title poem to "Gli orecchini" (The Earrings), to the "Silvae" series at the collection's center and the two openly autobiographical poems, "Piccolo testamento" (Little Testament) and "Il sogno del prigioniero" (The Prisoner's Dream), that form the final section, "Conclusioni provvisorie" (Provisional Conclusions). Clizia is squarely at the heart of the volume; she is, in the poet's own words in "Intenzioni," more than a woman, transformed now into an "angelo" (angel) or a "procellaria" (stormy petrel), a messenger of hope and strength from beyond the strife of the war-torn world below. She is good incarnated, however, and Montale emphasizes the importance of her materialized and concrete being that is best recognized by "l'uomo che meglio conosce le affinità che legano Dio alle creature incarnate, non già lo sciocco spiritualista o il rigido e astratto monofisita" (those who know best the affinities that tie God to incarnate beings, not by the silly spiritualist or the rigid and abstract Monophysite). One of the poems of the "Silvae" series, "Iride," is pointed to by the poet himself as "terribilmente in chiave" (terribly essential) to an understanding of Clizia's salvific role as one who "sconta per tutti" (expiates for everyone). Montale writes that the poem was translated from a dream and is one of the few that might legitimately be called "obscure," given its oneiric origins. The beloved Clizia, called Iride in this poem, returns to earth in order to carry on her work, which is a form of divine work; she is so radically transformed as to be herself no longer: "Ma se ritorni non sei tu, è mutata / la tua storia terrena" (But if you return you are not you, your earthly history is transformed). In the midst of the terrible "bufera," or storm of war and its aftermath, Clizia provides a rare vision of strength, moral direction, and hope.

The *La bufera* collection is by no means restricted to poems of and to Clizia, however. There is the earthy feminine figure called Volpe, sung about in the series of "Madrigali privati" (Private Madrigals) immediately following the "Silvae"; there are also poems to the poet's mother, father, and other beloved dead who haunt him more and more assiduously. The thematic variety is matched by stylistic virtuosity, as Montale experiments with the sonnet form, the madrigal, and the prose poem, which points up the deep connection between prose and poetry that emerges more vividly in his collections that follow. From the relative obscurity of *Finisterre* to the fairly open autobiographical thrust of the final "Provisional Conclusions," this collection embodies an intense and rich period of Montale's creative life. If the public had nothing but the poems of *La bufera e altro*, readers would still be able to count Montale as one of the great poets of this century.

The decades after the publication of *La bufera e altro* were filled with public recognition of Montale's work. In 1961 he was awarded honorary degrees from the Universities of Rome, Milan, and Cambridge; in 1967 he was named Senator for Life (an honorific membership in the Italian Senate); and in 1975 he received the Nobel Prize in literature. Yet in 1963 Montale's wife died, and, as the 1960s progressed, he became less and less involved in the social and literary circles of Milanese society in which he had formerly moved.

Italian culture and society both had been radically transformed in the postwar years, and poets were following new directions and seeking forms of expression totally unrelated to Montale's generation. The so-called neoavant-garde sought to sweep away ancient and more recent

tradition alike, and Montale was in danger of becoming a sort of living relic. The surprise was enormous, therefore, when he published a hefty collection of new verse in 1971 under the title of *Satura: 1962-1970* (partially translated in *New Poems*, 1976), and surprise modulated into something like astonishment when this was followed by others, including *Diario del '71 e del '72* (Diary of '71 and '72) in 1973 and *Quaderno di quattro anni* (Notebook of Four Years) in 1977 (translated as *It Depends: A Poet's Notebook*, 1980). Thus began the "second season" of Montale. Nor, as it turns out, was this the end of the poet's productivity: the critical edition of his complete works (*L'Opera in versi*), edited by Contini and Rosanna Bettarini and published by Einaudi in 1980, contains another entirely new collection, "Altri versi" (Other Verses); and many poems, left in the care of Annalisa Cima, herself a poet and the close friend and inspiration of Montale in his final years, are currently being published yearly in small, elegant editions of six poems each (in the series *Poesie inedite*), at the poet's express wish. The "unprolific" poet whose production seemed destined to consist of three collections was a writer of great productivity in his old age; more significantly, the Montale of the post-*Bufera* years is "new," and the later poetry held surprises for those who thought they knew Montale's range and pitch.

Returning to the musical analogy with which he sought to explain the beginnings of his career in poetry, Montale stated in a 1973 interview with Cima that he wished to "suonare il pianoforte in un'altra maniera, più discreta, più silenziosa" (play the piano in another manner, more discreet, more silent). He further commented that "i primi tre libri sono scritti in frac, gli altri in pigiama, o diciamo in abito da passeggio" and "sono cambiati l'accento, la voce, l'intonazione" (the first three books are written in tails [a tuxedo], the others in pajamas, or let's say in afternoon clothes. . . . The accent, voice, and intonation are changed). The voice is indeed changed, singing in a lower and much less lyrical register. The post-*Bufera* poems are more prosaic, both in theme and style, more allied to everyday speech and current events. Yet it is also true that Montale retains themes, motifs, and characters from his earlier verse. The result is a layering effect as the "high" period is incorporated into the new "low" period. Many of the late poems are satirical and epigrammatic, ironic self-portraits, or comic and even sardonic commentaries on contemporary society. The people who were part of the poet's daily existence—Mosca Tanzi, his faithful housekeeper Gina, old friends such as the editor Bobi Bazlen, and various unnamed members of the intimate domestic circle—all populate the poems, as real presences in his life, but there are also "ghosts" whose absence through death has paradoxically intensified their visitations, which occurred often during Montale's sleepless nights. Another beloved, Annetta-Arletta, whose presence had been submerged and barely hinted at in earlier poems, emerges as one of the most tenacious of Montale's ghosts. The titles of these late collections are indicative of their eclectic and occasional nature: *Satura*, which according to Montale himself means "miscellany"; *Diario* (Diary); and *Quaderno* (Notebook).

Yet the books are far from casually thrown together; the poet assiduously noted the date of composition of each poem. They are ordered not chronologically but by a self-conscious structuring principle: the poems are intended to be read in relation to each other, in order that thematic and stylistic echoes reverberate. Montale himself commented in a 1971 radio interview that "sarebbe un errore leggere una sola poesia e cercare di anatomizzarla, perché c'è sempre un richiamo da un suono all'altro, non solo, ma anche da una poesia all'altra" (it would be a mistake to read one poem only and to seek to dissect it, because there is always a cross-reference from one sound to another, not only internally, but also from one poem to another). The ostensible "artlessness" of casual verse is belied by a careful reading of these artfully constructed volumes.

There are thematic centers to which Montale returns time and again in these late poems. Among the most evident are poetry in general and his own past poetry in particular; the meaning of individual, social, and transcendental experience; and the relation between art and politics or between aesthetics and ideology. True to his early conviction that artistic and political spheres should remain separate (a conviction partly conditioned by Crocean thought), and true to his refusal to privilege the poet's role (a refusal strongly conditioned by his early anti-D'Annunzianism), Montale adamantly continues to favor the eccentric (in its etymological sense of that which is not "in the center") and the unknowable qualities of human experience. Love matters not because it is a source of ultimate clarity or escape from the vicissitudes of individual solitude, but because it is one of the ways by which we recognize most strongly the uniqueness and mystery of ourselves and others. Poetry matters because, as Montale commented in his Nobel Prize acceptance speech, it is "una entità di cui si sa assai poco" (an entity about which we know quite little). Poetry's tenacious survival through the social, cultural, and spiritual upheavals of human history, its "resistenza," or obdurate endurance, is, for Montale, its ultimate meaning and worth. Perhaps beyond particular meanings of a thematic or ideological nature, then, his own last outpouring of poetry should be read as the old poet's own "endurance" in art.

Montale died on 12 September 1981, exactly a month before his eighty-fifth birthday. His long life was relatively uneventful on the surface, but his poetry is deeply reflective of the eventfulness and complexity of his inner life where he absorbed the trials, the lessons, and the continuing search for answers that characterize human experience. His is undeniably a modern voice, attuned to the times in which he lived and wrote, but it is also a voice with a timeless pitch, expressing poetry's transcendent music. Unable to offer concrete solutions to existential and spiritual dilemmas, Montale's poetry nonetheless retains an abiding power in its formal beauty, its incisive, deeply intelligent consciousness and conscience, and its commitment to the importance of the individual and to that which is unrepeatable in life and in art. Eugenio Montale's achievement is best measured not against that of his immediate predecessors or contemporaries but within the select company of those few poets whose art endures and will continue to endure.

Interviews:

Annalisa Cima, *Incontro Montale* (Milan: Scheiwiller, 1973);

Cima, "Le reazioni di Montale," in *Eugenio Montale: Profilo di un autore*, edited by Cima and Cesare Segre (Milan: Rizzoli, 1977), pp. 192-201;

Enzo Biagi, *Dicono di lei* (Milan: Rizzoli, 1978);

Lorenzo Greco, *Montale commenta Montale* (Parma: Pratiche, 1980).

Bibliographies:

Rosanna Pettinelli and Amedeo Quondam Giovanni Maria, "Bibliografia montaliana (1925-1966)," *Rassegna della letteratura italiana*, 70 (May-December 1966): 377-391;

Laura Barile, *Bibliografia montaliana* (Milan: Mondadori, 1977).

Biography:

Giulio Nascimbeni, *Montale* (Milan: Longanesi, 1969); revised and enlarged as *Montale: Biografia di un poeta* (Milan: Longanesi, 1986).

References:

Guido Almansi and Bruce Merry, *Eugenio Montale: The Private Language of Poetry* (Edinburgh: Edinburgh University Press, 1977);

Atti del Convegno Internazionale: La Poesia di Eugenio Montale (Milan: Librex, 1983);

Atti del Convegno Internazionale tenuto a Genova 1982: La poesia di Eugenio Montale (Florence: Monnier, 1984);

Silvio D'Arco Avalle, *Tre saggi su Montale* (Turin: Einaudi, 1972);

Jared Becker, *Eugenio Montale* (Boston: Twayne, 1986);

Gian Paolo Biasin, *Il vento di Debussy: La poesia di Montale nella cultura del Novecento* (Bologna: Mulino, 1985);

Glauco Cambon, *Eugenio Montale's Poetry: A Dream in Reason's Presence* (Princeton: Princeton University Press, 1982);

Umberto Carpi, *Montale dopo il fascismo: dalla "Bufera" a "Satura"* (Padua, Italy: Liviana, 1971);

Joseph Cary, *Three Modern Italian Poets: Saba, Ungaretti, Montale* (New York: New York University Press / London: University of London Press, 1969);

Annalisa Cima and Cesare Segre, eds., *Eugenio Montale: Profilo di un autore* (Milan: Rizzoli, 1977);

Gianfranco Contini, *Una lunga fedeltà: Scritti su Eugenio Montale* (Turin: Einaudi, 1974);

Franco Contorbia, ed., *Eugenio Montale: Immagini di una vita* (Milan: Librex, 1985);

Maria Corti, "Montale negli Stati Uniti," *Autografo*, 12 (1987): 11-27;

Marco Forti, *Eugenio Montale: La poesia, la prosa di fantasia e d'invenzione* (Milan: Mursia, 1973-1974);

Forti, ed., *Per conoscere Montale* (Milan: Mondadori, 1976);

Emerico Giachery, "Metamorfosi dell'orto," *Atti e Memorie dell'Arcadia*, third series 7 (1977): 35-60;

Maria Antonietta Grignani, *Prologhi ed epiloghi: Sulla poesia di Eugenio Montale, con una prosa inedita* (Ravenna, Italy: Longo, 1987);

Claire Huffman, *Montale and the Occasions of Poetry* (Princeton: Princeton University Press, 1983);

Angelo Jacomuzzi, *La poesia di Montale: Dagli "Ossi" ai "Diari"* (Turin: Einaudi, 1978);

Letture montaliane in occasione dell'ottantesimo compleanno del Poeta (Genoa: Bozzi, 1977);

Romano Luperini, *Montale o l'identità negata* (Naples: Liguori, 1984);

Luperini, *Storia di Montale* (Bari, Italy: Laterza, 1986);

Pequod, special Montale issue, 2 (Winter 1977);

Arshi Pipa, *Montale and Dante* (Minneapolis: University of Minnesota Press, 1969);

I Poeti a Montale (Genoa: Provincia di Genova, 1976);

Quarterly Review of Literature, special Montale issue, 11, no. 4 (1962);

Silvio Ramat, *Montale* (Florence: Vallecchi, 1965);

Ramat, ed., *Omaggio a Montale* (Milan: Mondadori, 1966);

Luciano Rebay, "I diaspori di Montale," *Italica*, 46 (1969): 33-53;

Rebay, "La rete a strascico di Montale," *Forum Italicum*, 3 (1971): 329-350;

Rebay, "Sull' 'autobiografismo' di Montale," in *Innovazioni tematiche espressive e linguistiche della letteratura italiana del Novecento* (Florence: Olschki, 1976);

Giuseppe Savoca, *Concordanza di tutte le poesie di Eugenio Montale* (Florence: Olschki, 1987);

G. Singh, *Eugenio Montale: A Critical Study of His Poetry, Prose, and Criticism* (New Haven: Yale University Press, 1973);

Rebecca West, *Eugenio Montale: Poet on the Edge* (Cambridge: Harvard University Press, 1981).

Papers:

Autografi di Montale, edited by Maria Corti and Maria Antonietta Grignani (Turin: Einaudi, 1976), is a catalogue of the manuscript holdings at the University of Pavia's Fondo di Autori Contemporanei; the collection includes poems and letters.

Marino Moretti

(18 July 1885 - 6 July 1979)

Andrea Guiati
Buffalo State College

BOOKS: *Le primavere* (Florence: Elzeviriana, 1902);

La sorgente della pace (Florence: Ducci, 1903);

Il poema di un'armonia (Florence: Ducci, 1903);

Fraternità (Milan: Sandron, 1906);

Il paese degli equivoci (Milan: Sandron, 1907; revised edition, Milan: Treves, 1921);

Sentimento (Milan: Sandron, 1908; revised and enlarged, 1912; revised again, 1924);

La serenata delle zanzare (Turin: Streglio, 1908);

I lestofanti (Milan: Sandron, 1909; revised edition, Milan: Treves, 1921);

Ah, Ah, Ah! (Palermo: Sandron, 1910);

Poesie scritte col lapis (Naples: Ricciardi, 1910; revised edition, Milan: Mondadori, 1949);

Leonardo da Vinci, by Moretti and Francesco Cazzamini Mussi (Milan: Baldini & Castoldi, 1910);

Gli Allighieri, by Moretti and Mussi (Milan: Baldini & Castoldi, 1911);

Frate Sole, by Moretti and Mussi (Milan: Baldini & Castoldi, 1911);

Poesie di tutti i giorni (Naples: Ricciardi, 1911);

I poemetti di Marino (Rome: Nazionale, 1913);

I pesci fuor d'acqua (Milan: Treves, 1914);

Il giardino dei frutti (Naples: Ricciardi, 1916);

Il sole del sabato (Milan: Treves, 1916);

La bandiera alla finestra (Milan: Treves, 1917);

Guenda (Milan: Treves, 1918; revised edition, Milan: Mondadori, 1944);

Adamo ed Eva (Milan: Sonzogno, 1919);

Conoscere il mondo (Milan: Treves, 1919);

Poesie: 1905-1914 (Milan: Treves, 1919);

Personaggi secondari (Milan: Treves, 1920);

L'Isola dell'amore (Milan: Treves, 1920);

Cinque novelle (Rome: Simpaticissima/Formìggini, 1920);

Una settimana in Paradiso (Rome: Mondadori, 1921);

La voce di Dio (Milan: Treves, 1921; revised, 1931);

Né bella né brutta (Milan: Treves, 1921; revised edition, Milan: Mondadori, 1944);

I due fanciulli (Milan: Treves, 1922); revised as *Il*

Marino Moretti

pudore (Verona: Mondadori, 1950);

I puri di cuore (Rome & Milan: Mondadori, 1923);

Mia madre (Milan: Treves, 1924; revised edition, Turin: SEI, 1945; revised again, 1956);

Il romanzo della mamma (Milan: Treves, 1924; revised edition, Milan: Mondadori, 1944);

La vera grandezza (Milan: Treves, 1925);

Il segno della croce (Milan: Treves, 1926; revised edition, Milan: Mondadori, 1945);

Le capinere (Milan: Mondadori, 1926);

149

Le più belle pagine di Emilio Praga, Igino Ugo Tarchetti e Arrigo Boito (Milan: Treves, 1926);

Allegretto quasi allegro: Variazione su un unico tema (Milan: Treves, 1927);

Il trono dei poveri (Milan: Treves, 1928; revised edition, Milan: Mondadori, 1946);

Il tempo felice: Ricordi d'infanzia e d'altre stagioni (Milan: Treves, 1929); revised as *Il tempo migliore* (Milan: Mondadori, 1953);

La casa del Santo Sangue (Milan: Mondadori, 1930);

Via Laura: Il libro dei sorprendenti vent'anni (Milan: Treves, 1931; revised and enlarged edition, Milan: Mondadori, 1944);

Sorprese del buon Dio (Verona: Mondadori, 1932);

Fantasie olandesi (Milan: Treves, 1932);

L'Andreana (Milan: Mondadori, 1935; revised, 1954);

Parole e musica (Florence: Vallecchi, 1936);

Novelle per Urbino (Urbino, Italy: Istituto d'Arte del Libro, 1937);

Anna degli elefanti (Milan: Mondadori, 1937; revised, 1963);

Scrivere non è necessario: Umori e segreti di uno scrittore qualunque (Milan: Mondadori, 1938);

Pane in desco: Pensieri immagini di uno che sente l'erba crescere (Milan: Mondadori, 1940);

La vedova Fioravanti (Milan: Mondadori, 1942);

L'odore del pane (Brescia, Italy: Morcelliana, 1942);

Cento novelle (Turin: SEI, 1943);

I coniugi Allori (Milan: Mondadori, 1946; revised, 1959);

Il fiocco verde (Milan: Mondadori, 1948; revised, 1956);

I grilli di Pazzo Pazzi (Milan: Mondadori, 1951);

Il ciuchino (Turin: SEI, 1953);

Doctor Mellifluus (Milan: Mondadori, 1954);

Uomini soli (Milan: Mondadori, 1954);

Cinquanta novelle (Turin: SEI, 1954);

1945 (Milan: Mondadori, 1956);

La camera degli sposi (Milan: Mondadori, 1958);

Tutte le novelle (Milan: Mondadori, 1959);

Lingua madre: Grammatica, by Moretti and Domenico Consonni (Turin: SEI, 1959); revised as *Nuova grammatica* (Turin: SEI, 1973);

Il libro dei miei amici (Milan: Mondadori, 1960);

Romanzi della mia terra (Verona: Mondadori, 1961);

Tutti i ricordi (Milan: Mondadori, 1962);

Romanzi dal primo all'ultimo (Milan: Mondadori, 1965);

Il canto di Arione, edited by Walter Mauro (Milan: Mondadori, 1966);

Tutte le poesie, edited by Geno Pampaloni (Milan: Mondadori, 1966);

Racconti scelti (Milan: Mondadori, 1967);

Romanzi dell'amorino (Milan: Mondadori, 1968);

L'ultima estate (Milan: Mondadori, 1969);

Tre anni e un giorno (Milan: Mondadori, 1971);

Le poverazze: Diario a due voci (Milan: Mondadori, 1973);

Diario senza le date (Milan: Mondadori, 1974);

Marino Moretti in Verso e in Prosa, edited by Pampaloni (Milan: Mondadori, 1979).

OTHER: *Guy de Maupassant: Una vita*, translated by Moretti (Milan: Mondadori, 1931);

Alfredo Panzini: La cicuta, i gigli e le rose, edited by Moretti (Milan: Mondadori, 1950).

Marino Moretti came from a family of fishermen, but his mother was an elementary-school teacher, from the Marche region. Moretti was born on 18 July 1885 in Cesenatico. On many occasions he was to write of roots, intelligently and ironically, depicting himself as inferior. A good example can be found in a statement by Moretti in the newspaper *Resto del Carlino* on 30 October 1955:

> Conterranei e concittadini, gente volgare e ostinata, lasciatemi tutti i vostri difetti, lasciate che mi fermentino dentro. Pur con questa voce melata, con questo sorriso d'angelo, con quest'aria dolcemente distratta, che piace ancora alle damigelle, io, non rinunzio a uno solo dei vostri difetti.

> (Fellow countrymen and fellow citizens, crude and stubborn people, leave me all your faults, let them ferment in me. Even with this honeyed voice, this angelic smile, this slightly absent-minded look, still loved by the damsels, I will not renounce a single one of your faults.)

Moretti was educated first in his mother's classes in Cesenatico, then attended high school in Ravenna and Bologna. After high school he enrolled in the Florentine acting school directed by Luigi Rasi. Moretti was to be a poor actor but an excellent secretary to Rasi, who recognized his elegant writing skills. It was in Florence that Moretti met Aldo Palazzeschi; the two of them had so much in common, they became inseparable friends. They had the same dreams and interests; they followed, even though from aside, the

Moretti circa 1907 (photograph by Nunes Vais)

developments of such literary journals as *Leonardo, Lacerba, Hermes, Cronache Letterarie*, and *La Voce*. It was obvious that the two young men were captivated more by Italian letters than by acting.

Moretti was a quiet man, avoiding the limelight all his life, yet in 1925 he signed Benedetto Croce's "Manifesto dell'antifascista." During World War I he served the Italian Army as a field medic, then was a journalist in Rome, where he met and worked with Federigo Tozzi.

In 1932 Moretti was nominated for the Corriere della Sera/Accademia d'Italia Prize, but the Fascist party, at the very last minute, awarded it to another writer. Later on, when Benito Mussolini wanted to recognize a non-Fascist author with the same prize, once again Moretti was the chosen one; to many it appeared to be a political statement. Nonetheless Moretti never claimed the prize. In 1948 he shared the Premio Fila with Francesco Flora. Four years later, in 1952, the Accademia Lincei awarded Moretti's prose a prize, thereby astonishing Italian intellectuals: for the first time in its history the Accademia had recognized a nonscientist.

In 1955 he won the Premio Napoli for his best-known novel, *La vedova Fioravanti* (Fioravanti's Widow, 1942), and in 1969 he was awarded the Premio Viareggio, Italy's most prestigious literary prize. This provincial poet, during his long and productive life, was able to collect quite a few literary prizes in spite of his aloof attitudes. Also he took a strong stand by signing Croce's manifesto, yet Moretti is almost never mentioned among the political intellectuals of his time, always overshadowed by his own "absent" participation and by more powerful personalities such as Gabriele D'Annunzio.

The poetry of Marino Moretti is that of the *crepuscolari* (twilight writers), who portrayed common feelings. These poets were the bridge between the exasperation of tonality in the D'Annunzian *Poema Paradisiaco*, the poetics of the *fanciullino*, and the existential and hermetic tones of modern and contemporary poetry. They also constituted a reaction to the heroic affirmation of the "I," the omniscient, godlike poetic first person of the romantic period.

In 1906 Moretti published his *Fraternità*; these poems were written between 1902 and 1904. Many of them represent an autobiographical confession, a metaphysical representation of concepts re-created through a simple rhetorical lexicon in order to portray the human inability to comprehend earthly existence:

> Chiede un bambino alla sua bella mamma:
> "Che vorràdire l'M della mano?"
> Ecco lo stringe forte al petto e piano
> gli dice: MAMMA.
>
> (A child asks his fair mother:
> "What does the *M* on my hand mean?"
> She holds him tight to her breast and softly
> says: MAMMA.)

Yet the child grows very quickly and experiences his independence. He asks another woman the same question he had asked his mother, and he is told the *M* stands for "MALIA" (enchantment). He outgrows his adolescent years and reaches maturity, only to hear a wise man say that the *M* on the palm of his hand stands for "MALE" (evil). The boy becomes an old man himself, and even though he is still uncertain about the future, he holds a truth: there is no need to ask anybody else; the *M* on his hand stands for "MORTE" (death). Moretti has taken a childish story and carefully crafted it into a simple philosophy of life. His choice of morphemes reminds one of

Giovanni Pascoli and echoes the classics, but the poem is very modern. Young and disillusioned, the speaker searches within for comfort and for answers to unveil the meaning of human existence, only to find looming death. This poem presents a well-established form, aesthetically enhanced by a mournful condition and emblematic of a clear pre-existential topos.

In *Fraternità* Moretti discloses his poetics, his longing for simple images, while at the same time he stresses the idea that poetry should be an expression of dreams and feelings written just as the soul evokes them. Most early critics, and some of the later ones (including Francesco Casnati, Geno Pampaloni, and Claudio Toscani), find romantic reminiscences in this idea. However, Moretti also imposes an anti-D'Annunzian voice. Moretti's lexicon comes from a spoken language, while D'Annunzio's lexicon is that of a higher station, a sublime choice, when compared to Moretti's everyday language. The poem "Così" (Thus) shows Moretti's sensitive representation of an abstract concept:

"Marino, è difficile scriver
così come fai, con le rime?
e forse di là dall'oceano
la gente si esprime
così?"

"È facile, cara, assai facile
finché si è tentati a provarlo.
Comprendi? Ma io scrivo, o mia piccola,
così come parlo,
così.

È facile, cara, assai facile
finché si è un poeta che vive
di sogni e di palpiti e un'anima
che parla e che scrive
così."

("Marino, is it difficult to write
as you do, in rhymes?
and maybe beyond the ocean
people express themselves
thus?"

"It's easy, my darling, very easy
as long as one is tempted to try it.
Do you understand? But I write, my little dear,
as I speak,
thus.

It's easy, my darling, very easy
as long as one is a poet that lives
of dreams and of throbs and a soul

that speaks and writes
thus.")

Doubtless Sergio Corazzini, Guido Gozzano, and Corrado Govoni were the twentieth-century poets who exerted the greatest influence on Moretti. Nevertheless, in Moretti one can sense the constant recurrence of a weak spiritual condition, a quiet, yet desperate cry for a literary identity, a new *persona poetica*. His depressive theme—E così tetro, / d'altronde, avere un gran secolo dietro / e un gran secolo innanzi, è così triste" (It's so gloomy, / besides, to have a great century behind / and a great century ahead, it's so sad) —suggests an effort to move away from the romantic period and to depict ironically its sadness. Modesty is the unveiling key to the ironic mode of these verses.

The so-called twilight poets felt alienated from the political and cultural problems of their era: instead of reaching out, they looked for answers within, only to find a silent, intimate world. Moretti was one of them, since his poems seem to represent a longing to revere small towns and rural villages, nestled in a remote and nostalgic countryside. He also felt a strong desire, more than the other *crepuscolari* poets, to re-create an idyllic existence, a timeless past of innocence, where the wave of the verse distills eternally, in a world of "real dreams."

Between 1906 and 1907 Moretti wrote the poems of *La serenata delle zanzare* (The Mosquito's Serenade), published in 1908. An example of their idealization of life, from "Il fiume" (The River), follows:

È così bello addormentarsi come
le donne dei romanzi d'appendice;
piangere e dire: "Sono un infelice,"
poi scompigliarsi gli abiti e le chiome.

(It's so nice to fall asleep
like the women of romances;
to cry and say: "I am a wretch,"
then mess up one's clothes and hair.)

Today critics have a much better picture of the *crepuscolari* poets. Their passive reaction to life was a counteraction to the active participation of the bourgeoisie and its intellectuals. These solitary poetic voices were to impose their ideologies through a new phenomenon, absenteeism, or escapism.

The opening poem of *Poesie scritte col lapis* (Poems Written with a Pencil, 1910) could be

Page from the manuscript for "Dopo D'Annunzio, oltre Pascoli," a 1962 autobiographical essay by Moretti, collected in his
Tutti i ricordi *(from* Storia della letteratura: Italiana, *volume 6, edited by Luigi Ferrante, 1965)*

considered a manifesto of Moretti's first poetic phase, which is indicative of the condition of all *crepuscolari* poets. It has been said that their poetry expressed a radical refusal of life. Such a refusal became systematized for these poets, and it was directed against the exaltation of life by D'Annunzio and the upcoming Fascist regime. In short, the *crepuscolari* refused only a certain kind of life. Moretti did not preach for an alternative: his verses reveal his determination to degrade the optimistic Nietzschean superhero, admired by D'Annunzio, the superman who will manipulate his future at any cost. For Moretti, time goes by so fast that one has no time to talk about his past, as he always has to struggle with his present. With this concept at the base of his poetry, Moretti could overturn the D'Annunzian utopic optimism and more realistically say:

> Si discorre d'avvenire,
> si rammemora il passato?
> Chi è vivo deve morire,
> chi è morto è bell'e spacciato.

> (Are we speaking of the future
> and remembering the past?
> Those who live right now must die,
> those who are dead are dead and gone.)

Moretti's pessimism was so deeply rooted that he reproached the poets who sang about their ideal women and blue skies when they should have paid more attention to social welfare. Therefore Moretti confirmed his belief in the engagement of art in improving existence. His indirect approach to the problems of the first half of the twentieth century, what has been called "absence," is in reality a subtle "presence." This is the ironic tone that Pampaloni calls "Il giuoco della verità" (the game of truth) in *Marino Moretti in Verso e in Prosa* (1979).

One of Moretti's intentions is certainly his willingness to recover the original value of words, of culture, and of self-esteem, for the most part focusing on Pascoli and the classical tradition. In many instances Moretti's subdued verse is a sort of bitter confession of a biographical nature. Many of his poems recapture a nostalgic youth, as in "La signora Lalla" (Mrs. Lalla)—from *Poesie scritte col lapis*—in which the poet remembers his school days:

> Ma sì, prendiamo la cartella scura,
> il calamaio in forma di barchetta,

> i pennini, la gomma, la cannetta,
> la storia sacra e il libro di lettura.

> (Yes, let's take our dark schoolbag,
> our boatlike inkwell,
> our pen nibs, our eraser, our pen-nib handle,
> our sacred history book and our spelling book.

He also accomplishes this in "Che è che vaga nell'aria?" (What's Roving in the Air?), remembering a day at the park:

> Non parlare, anima mia
> prima che venga una stella
> giriamo la manovella
> d'un organo di Barberia.

> (Do not speak, soul of mine,
> before a star appears
> let's turn the crank
> of an organ from Barberia.)

With the following poem, "Andiamo via" (Let's Go Away), he expands on the same theme:

> Lasciamo quel che ci è caro
> al suo posto, come sia,
> e andiamo andiamo via
> col povero zampognaro.

> (Let's leave what is dear to us
> in its place, as it is,
> and let's go away let's go away
> with the poor bagpipe player.)

Moretti's poetry is often a sensitive reaction to the events that were taking place within the first decade of the century. He saw humankind's inability to cope with the fast pace of modern life and, like the other *crepuscolari*, he preferred to rediscover the countryside and the provinces. Therefore, by ignoring the immediacy of their history and the limelight of the front page, these poets were fighting a silent war. Their strategy was ingenious and systematic. They did not officially form a school, but they had the impact of a school.

The positivists acclaimed the Fascist party, the war, and the African campaign, while Moretti chose to sing about a day at the local barbershop:

> Tutti occupati avanti le specchiere
> i seggioloni comodi e io mi metto
> a seder sul divano e aspetto: aspetto
> che sia libero un posto e un parrucchiere.

(All taken facing the mirrors
the comfortable big chairs and I sit down
on the sofa and I wait: I wait
for an empty seat and a free hairdresser.)

Moretti preferred to write about an everyday event, rather than the war or a glorious political personality. The *crepuscolari* ignored heroic and historical subjects, and by doing so they made a strong statement. Their poetic ideals are now recognized to be closely linked to modern and contemporary poetry.

I poemetti di Marino (Marino's Little Poems, 1913) is dominated by poems dealing with monks. It appears that the poet wants to find once again an example of a simple moral life, as in the life of Saint Francis of Assisi:

Tutte le cose dal buon Dio create
cantava con inchini e con sorrisi
il fraticello che aveva nome Frate
Francesco ed era di là su: d'Assisi.

(All things created by the good Lord
he praised with bows and smiles
the little friar whose name was Friar
Francis and he came from up above: from Assisi.)

Friar Francis's ideal is well in tune with Moretti's poetic attitude:

e costui dice qualcosa
che stupisce in verità:
"Le più bella e gaia sposa,
la più ricca? Povertà!"

(and that man says something
that is really amazing:
"The most beautiful and joyful bride,
the richest? Poverty!")

This collection offers a fine sample of Moretti's religious themes.

In 1916 Moretti published *Il giardino dei frutti* (The Garden of Fruits), which ends the first phase of Moretti's "twilight" period. In constant search for truth, the poet, wandering through a series of everyday events, finds himself caught between art and life, as in "La sera dopo" (The Evening After):

Nulla: se in questa nostra ombra romita
sento che tutto è inutilmente come
se fosse una parola o un nome
breve, di quattro lettere, la v-i-t-a.

(Nothing: if in this lonely shadow of ours
I feel that everything exists needlessly as

if it were a word or a short
noun, of four letters, l-i-f-e.)

This inextricable thematic element differentiates Moretti from the other *crepuscolari*. He constantly reaches for the unseizable antithesis life poetry. The "I" is consequently divided between the two. Finally his "Io non ho nulla da dire" (I have nothing to say) is not an admission of lack of inspiration or of ideology; on the contrary, it is an ironic and strong ideological statement. It is the poet's only possible way out of that antithetical division, as sharply identified by Pampaloni in *Marino Moretti in Verso e in Prosa*.

Moretti's poetry sings of the common, everyday life of the provincial antihero. The days of the D'Annunzian myths, heroes, and glittering golden colors were slowly fading into a period of disillusionment. The *crepuscolari* found their definition in the brilliant and sensitive criticism of Giuseppe Antonio Borgese and their themes in the critical condition of contemporary man. The tone of this first phase of Moretti's poetry already contains the desperate existential cry that was to dominate twentieth-century poetry.

Between 1915 and 1969 Moretti published many short stories and novels, and revised his verses. His return to poetry came in 1969 with *L'ultima estate* (The Last Summer). After more than fifty years Moretti's poetic form and central themes matured, moving away from the created sorrows of his "twilight" period. This volume marks Moretti's second phase, the one Pietro Pancrazi defines as "unita di visione, di stile, di contenuto" (unity of vision, of style, of content). The poetry's historical dimension is ambivalent: "Io son fatto così: / Sei tu moderno? Sì! / Sei proprio d'oggi? No!" (I am like that: / Are you modern? Yes! / Are you really of today? No!). His search for truth is constantly subject to the test of time: "Ed, anche, io resto fuori / del tempo, della stessa vita mia, / come se me ne fossi andato via / là dove tutto è spento e lazzi e onori" (And, too, I remain outside / of time, and of my own life, / as if I had gone away / there where everything is lifeless, both jests and honors).

Moretti has risen above his *crepuscolarismo*, as seen in "La verità dell'arte" (The Truth of Art):

Si può, non più orgogliosi
ma neppure sommessi,
dirla anche a se stessi
la verità, la propria verità,

155

quella che avverti quando sei nato.
Lungi dal chiasso, dalla verità
da cui sciamo una voga adulatrice
come in versi si dice
meglio la verità.

(One can, no longer proud,
but neither submissive,
tell even to oneself
the truth, one's own truth,
the one you feel when you are born.
Far from the uproar, from the truth
from which we ski a flattering path
as the poet says:
truth is better.)

Two years later Moretti published *Tre anni e un giorno* (Three Years and a Day, 1971), in which his poetic refuge is a kind of intellectual solitude. He seems proud of himself and his poetry. To Casnati, who called him a layman, he replies: "laico, sì laico della misericordia, ed è cosa felice / ... laico, io sarei pur sempre un cittadino, / Casnati, sì, della Città di Dio" (layman, yes layman of forgiveness, and it is a positive thing / ... layman, I would be always a citizen, / Casnati, yes, of the City of God).

The poet of absence became the poet of presence in his *Le poverazze* (The Mollusks, 1973). The invented social and psychological sorrows of the early period have become realities, influencing his poems more intimately. As Pampaloni says in *Marino Moretti in Verso e in Prosa*, this is the beginning of Moretti's third phase: "L'antico 'non avere nulla da dire' si rivela per ciò che era, il destino di 'dire'" (The ancient "I have nothing to say" reveals itself for what it was, the destiny of "saying"). Moretti was attempting a "vertical" dimension, preferring the intimate journey of the soul to the everyday anecdotes that characterized his earlier poetry: "Chi mi ha fatto così. Dio o la madre? / È un'altra cosa questa ch'io non so" (Who made me so. God or my mother? / This is something else I don't know).

The last literary work by Moretti published in his lifetime was *Diario senza le date* (Diary without Dates, 1974). Once again the truthfulness of the "I" is the only muse the poet admires or follows. Moretti sees his last chance to redeem himself and to open his wounded, tired heart. He confesses how in the past he lied about his sadness, only to write poems:

Come fioriva la parola "triste"
nei versi giovanili, ed ero allegro!
Ora ben so ch'io fui come poeta,

e più ancor nella vita,
scarsamente sincero;
e la parola che più spesso insiste
nella pagina stanca, anzi sgradita,
fa sì ch'io scioccamente la ripeta,
ma non potrei più dire "sono triste"
se lo sono davvero.

(How the word *sad* bloomed
in my youthful poems, and I was happy!
Now I know well that I, as a poet,
and more so in life,
was hardly sincere;
and the word that more often remains,
on the tired page, or rather unpleasant page,
forces me to foolishly repeat it
but I could no longer say "I am sad"
if I really am so.)

Letters:

Carteggio, 1907-1943, by Moretti and Mario Novaro, edited by Claudio Toscani (Milan: IPL, 1981);

Carteggio, 1914-1936, by Moretti and Alfredo Panzini (Rimini, Italy: Panozzo, 1986).

Interview:

Claudio Toscani, "Marino Moretti," in his *La voce e il testo* (Milan: IPL, 1985), pp. 133-148.

Biographies:

Francesco Cazzamini Mussi, *Marino Moretti* (Florence: Vallecchi, 1931);

Francesco Casnati, *Marino Moretti* (Milan: PL, 1952);

Italo Cinti, *Marino Moretti* (Bologna: Tamari, 1966);

Tonia Fiorino, *Moretti in diacronia* (Naples: Liguori, 1974);

Claudio Toscani, *Marino Moretti* (Florence: Nuova Italia, 1975).

References:

Antonio Altomonte and others, *Moretti 90* (Milan: Quaderni dell'Osservatore, 1975);

Sergio Antonielli, "I nuovi versi di Marino Moretti," in his *Letteratura del disagio* (Milan: Comunità, 1984), pp. 159-168;

Giorgio Barberi Squarotti, "Il grado zero di Moretti," in his *Poesia e ideologia borghese* (Naples: Liguori, 1976), pp. 170-187;

Piero Bigongiari, "Moretti tra il sole e la morte," in *Poesia italiana del Novecento* (Milan: Saggiatore, 1978), pp. 45-62;

Walter Binni, "Crepuscolari e Futuristi," in his *La poetica del decadentismo* (Florence: Sansoni, 1961), pp. 127-148;

Marino Biondi, *Uno scrittore nel secolo, Marino Moretti: I libri, i manoscritti, i luoghi e gli amici* (Rimini, Italy: Maggioli, 1983);

Giuseppe Antonio Borgese, *La vita e il libro* (Turin: Bocca, 1913);

Giorgio Calisesi, ed., *Atti del convegno su Marino Moretti* (Milan: Saggiatore, 1977);

Enrico Falqui, "Revisioni di Moretti: la condizione di superstite," in *Novecento: I contemporanei*, edited by Gianni Grana (Milan: Marzorati, 1979), III: 2841-2852;

Marziano Guglielminetti, "Marino Moretti," in his *La "scuola della ironia": Gozzano e i viciniori* (Florence: Olschki, 1984), pp. 61-89;

Anna Nazzoli and Jole Soldateschi, "Marino Moretti," in their *I crepuscolari* (Florence: La Nuova Italia, 1978), pp. 51-65;

Geno Pampaloni, "Il giuoco della verità," in *Marino Moretti in Verso e in Prosa*, edited by Pampaloni (Milan: Mondadori, 1979), pp. xi-xxxv;

Pampaloni, Introduction to Moretti's *Tutte le poesie*, edited by Pampaloni (Milan: Mondadori, 1966), pp. xi-xxvi;

Ottavo Panaro, "Marino Moretti," in his *I poeti crepuscolari* (Livorno, Italy: Favillini, 1962), pp. 99-111;

Pietro Pancrazi, "Marino Moretti si confessa," in his *Scrittori d'oggi* (Bari, Italy: Laterza, 1953), VI: 32-38;

Giuseppe Petronio, *Poeti del nostro secolo: I crepuscolari* (Florence: Sansoni, 1937), pp. 60-82;

Ines Scaramucci, "Bilancio spirituale del mondo narrativo di Moretti," in her *Studi sul Novecento: Prospettive e itinerari* (Milan: PL, 1968), pp. 231-254;

Giacinto Spagnoletti, "Con i crepuscolari," in his *Il verso è tutto* (Lanciano, Italy: Carabba, 1979), pp. 115-140;

Giuseppe Zaccaria, *Invito alla lettura di Marino Moretti* (Milan: Mursia, 1981).

Ada Negri

(3 February 1870 - 11 January 1945)

Natalia Costa-Zalessow
San Francisco State University

BOOKS: *Fatalità* (Milan: Treves, 1892); translated by A. M. von Blomberg as *Fate* (Boston: Copeland & Day, 1898);

Tempeste (Milan: Treves, 1895);

Maternità (Milan: Treves, 1904);

Dal profondo (Milan: Treves, 1910);

Esilio (Milan: Treves, 1914);

Le solitarie (Milan: Treves, 1917; revised edition, Milan: Mondadori, 1945);

Orazioni (Milan: Treves, 1918);

Il libro di Mara (Milan: Treves, 1919; revised edition, Milan: Mondadori, 1934);

Stella mattutina (Rome & Milan: Mondadori, 1921; revised, 1940); translated by Anne Day as *Morning Star* (New York: MacMillan, 1930);

Finestre alte (Rome & Milan: Mondadori, 1923);

I canti dell'isola (Milan: Mondadori, 1925);

Le strade (Milan: Mondadori, 1926);

Sorelle (Milan: Mondadori, 1929);

Vespertina (Milan: Mondadori, 1930);

Di giorno in giorno (Milan: Mondadori, 1932);

Il dono (Milan: Mondadori, 1936);

Erba sul sagrato (Milan: Mondadori, 1939);

Fons amoris (Milan: Mondadori, 1946);

Oltre (Milan: Mondadori, 1947);

Tutte le opere di Ada Negri, 2 volumes, edited by Bianca Scalfi and Egidio Bianchetti (Milan: Mondadori, 1948, 1954);

Santa Caterina da Siena (Rome: Cateriniane, 1961);

Opere scelte, edited by Elena Cazzulani and Gilberto Coletto (Lodi: Lodigraf, 1988).

OTHER: D. Mauro Pea, *Ada Negri*, includes previously unpublished poems by Negri (Bergamo: Cattaneo, 1960), pp. 212-240.

Ada Negri's poetry underwent a gradual but steady evolution of style and content. Having gained immediate popularity with her early socialistic, humanitarian themes, through the use of a highly rhetorical language that evoked compassion for the daily miseries of the late-nineteenth-century working class, Negri turned to more personal aspects. She explored her intimate feelings as a woman: as mother to her daughter and as a lonely and misunderstood wife who broke her marriage bonds and found fulfillment only in a late-blooming love that reconciled her with life. These deeply felt experiences changed her way of writing. From the declamatory, hurried style of her social poems, she moved to a more refined language, indicative not only of a better understanding of the world's ills but also of a more profound knowledge of literary elegance as practiced by the so-called decadent poets. Most, and by far the best, of her poems are autobiographical. The pain, sensual pleasures, and thoughts of death she experienced gush forth in the form of a delirium, pivoting around her personal problems as a woman. She achieved artistic self-discipline in maturity, when she found peace in a subdued religious resignation that permitted her to look at the world in a more philosophical way. She conceived her art as a mission and pointed out the sufferings of the poor, of the destitute, of the old, and, above all, of women, especially mothers. Her early works, translated into Spanish, influenced Latin-American women writers such as Alfonsina Storni.

Negri was born in the town of Lodi, Lombardy, near Milan, on 3 February 1870. Her father, Giuseppe Negri, had left his native village, Massalengo, to make a living as a cabby in Milan. He was a fun-loving man who spent his money easily with his friends in taverns, and when he died of typhus fever in 1871, his wife, Vittoria Cornalba, found herself penniless. She decided to return to Lodi, where her mother and brother lived. Annibale, Ada's brother, went to live with his uncle, a teacher who, with his wife, kept a boardinghouse for young pupils. Ada, together with her mother, moved in with Grandmother Giuseppina Panni Cornalba, concierge at the palace belonging to the Cingia family. Vittoria found a job as weaver in the local textile factory, where she had to work thirteen-hour days for mea-

Ada Negri

ger pay. Ada grew up helping her grandmother, when not playing with the Cingia girls, whom she tried to outdo in all games.

Conscious of social differences since her earliest childhood, Negri felt humiliated by her family's position and strove to do well in school. With the encouragement of her relatives she enrolled in the local Scuola Normale Femminile in 1881 in order to become a teacher. She completed her studies in July 1887, but had to wait until her eighteenth birthday to receive her diploma and elementary-school credentials. After a temporary job as substitute teacher in a girls' boarding school in Codogno, she was sent to Motta Visconti, halfway between Abbiategrasso and Pavia, and here she found herself facing a large class of unruly peasant children, whom, in spite of her initial fears, she managed to tame by using unorthodox pedagogical methods, such as rewards of freshly baked sweet rolls from the bak-

ery of her landlord's daughter. The latter had become one of her friends, among whom she enjoyed the liberty of village life, living in direct contact with nature, and roaming through fields and woods in her free time. It was from Motta Visconti that Ada regularly sent out her poems to various Lombard newspapers, gaining the attention of Raffaello Barbiera, editor of the Milanese periodical *Illustrazione Popolare*, who liked her moralizing style and published her work. As a result Sofia Bisi Albini, an established writer, visited Negri in Motta Visconti and wrote an article in 1891 for the newspaper *Corriere della Sera* on the schoolteacher-turned-poet. Encouraged by Barbiera, Emilio Treves decided that the novelty of a rural poetess with her themes of rebellion and call for social justice was appealing and he published in 1892 Negri's first collection of poems, *Fatalità* (translated as *Fate*, 1898). In spite of its stylistic imperfections and simplistic ap-

159

proach, the book went rapidly through repeated editions, not only making the author a heroine of the socialists but also gaining her a ministerial transfer to the girls' upper school Gaetana Agnesi in Milan. This was followed in 1894 by Negri's being awarded the Giannina Milli Prize, bestowed on women prominent in literature and education.

Stunned by such success, Negri produced a second, similar collection of poems, *Tempeste* (Tempests, 1895), also popular with readers. But her compositions were criticized by prominent literary figures such as Benedetto Croce and Luigi Pirandello for the poems' defective metric form, lack of imagination, hurried generalizations, and no sign of improvement. Indeed her first two volumes of verse abound in clichés: her poor people are always blond, unless she speaks about gypsies; the men are always wide shouldered, so their women can lean on them; the upper classes are condemned for their refined food, neckties, and jewelry; and the working class is glorified for its manual labor. She cleverly imitates the rapid style of the late-nineteenth-century poets, especially Lorenzo Stecchetti and Giosuè Carducci. In later life Negri herself condemned her early poetic production, putting the blame on insufficient literary preparation. Where she tried to describe generic masses she rarely succeeded, but when she expressed a deeply felt personal pain she was more poetic. Knowing her personal experiences helps one understand her works. D. Mauro Pea with his *Ada Negri* (1960) produced the best and most systematic study of the many autobiographical elements in her prose and poetry. For example an accident in which her mother hurt her hand in the factory prompted in *Fatalità* the poem "Mano nell'ingranaggio" (The Hand in the Wheelwork), where, through poetic exaggeration, the hand gets cut off by the monstrous machine. The composition is powerful, but the repeated line "povera donna bionda e mutilata" (the poor mutilated blond woman) becomes tedious. On the other hand, Negri's personal yearning for peace and love is much better expressed, as in "Te solo" (Thee Alone), where triple repetition occurs with a variant at the end of each verse: "Ho bisogno di pianto. // Ho bisogno di pace. // Ho bisogno d'amore" (I need tears. // I need peace. // I need love).

The longed-for love did come, in Milan, where Negri met Ettore Patrizi, an engineer active in the socialist movement, who went to California and founded the Italian newspaper *L'Italia* in San Francisco. Two of the poems singled out by Pirandello as the best of *Tempeste* were inspired by Patrizi's love. In "Piccola mano" (Little Hand) the poet addresses her hand, which once wrote daring verses without fear, but now:

> Per lui, per lui ne l'anima inspirata
> or palpitan gli alati inni supremi. . . .
> E tu intanto, manina innamorata,
> entro le sue timidamente tremi.
>
> (For him, for him in my inspired soul
> my winged hymns now palpitate. . . .
> While you my little enamored hand
> timidly tremble in his hands.)

Unfortunately Negri's happiness was short lived. Ettore stopped writing, and she feared the worst, as seen in "È malato" (He Is Sick):

> E malato, è malato, e a sé mi chiama
> forse, laggiù, su l'inclemente suolo.
> Il tetro annuncio il mar passò di volo,
> e mi s'infisse in cor come una lama.
>
> (He is sick, he is sick and he is calling me,
> perhaps, to his side down there on the harsh
>   terrain.
> The gloomy news flew over the sea
> and struck my heart like a blade.)

Reality, however, was quite different: the young man had met another woman, who was to become his wife. Negri tried to forget him and in 1896 married Giovanni Garlanda, a wealthy industrialist, with whom she had two daughters, Bianca and Vittoria.

Three other poems from *Tempeste* were praised by Pirandello and are not autobiographical. In "Canto notturno" (Nocturnal Song) there is a melancholy affinity between the poet and a woman's voice singing at a distance. "All'asilo notturno" (Overnight Shelter) is the story of a homeless mother who, along with her sick baby, is given a bed in a shelter and dreams that the place is her own, only to be rudely awakened by the dawn. She rushes out into the street in search of her daily bread and enviously stares at the busy city with its factories: she has no job.

Particularly effective is the "finale stupendo" (marvelous conclusion), as Pirandello called it, of "I grandi" (The Great), where the meek, hungry, and oppressed are admired for not hating; the starving for not stealing; the mistreated for not killing; the forlorn for believing in God; and the dying for being able to love.

Postcard from Negri to her longtime friend Grazia Deledda, also a writer (from Dizionario universale della letteratura contemporanea, *volume 3, edited by Alberto Mondadori, 1961)*

This is not revolutionary socialism but rather Christian resignation.

Negri's marriage to the modest Garlanda, from Valle Mosso, northwest of Milan, co-owner with his two brothers of a textile factory, proved a failure from the very beginning. Living in Valle Mosso, neither of the spouses was willing to accept the other's way of living or thinking: he clung to his bourgeois traditions, expecting her to reform; she felt isolated and unloved, especially by her mother-in-law, who saw no need for a woman poet in her family. Therefore, Negri concentrated all her attention on her daughter Bianca, born in 1898, who succeeded in bringing the parents together for a while. (Their second daughter lived only a month.) But new problems arose when the family moved to Milan. Negri resumed her former literary and political associations and became active on behalf of the poor; Garlanda was jealous of her fame and liberty and tried to restrict her. In addition her brother, Annibale, who had never completed his studies, died of tuberculosis in 1903 at the age of thirty-

five, after having drifted from job to job, the last of which had been secured for him by Negri. These facts are the basis of her 1904 collection of poems Maternità (Maternity), which contains some compositions of a social nature, such as "Funerale durante lo sciopero" (Funeral During the Strike) and "Redenzione" (Redemption), among others, but an evolution is evident, for the central theme is that of motherhood. Stylistically the work is more refined, reflecting new influences—those of Gabriele D'Annunzio and Giovanni Pascoli—though everything is seen from the personal point of view of a mother trembling over her child and communicating with her. In "Acquazzone" (Shower) the speaker embraces her daughter, drenched by the rain, and reflects that, as the days pass, her little one will have to face more serious storms to come, but without mother's help. "In memoria" (In Memory) and "Piccola tomba" (Little Tomb) both reflect a mother's grief. Why did the baby die? Did life seem so terrible? Who will visit the tomb of the little one who died, perhaps because of its mother's illness? The father is rarely mentioned.

Negri's personal unhappiness is also evident in the nostalgic evocation of the past in such poems as "Ritorno a Motta Visconti" (Return to Motta Visconti), one of the best descriptive compositions of *Maternità*. In the poems of *Dal profondo* (From Depth, 1910), themes of doubt concerning her profession and marriage recur: she feels cheated by life, which gave her neither love nor peace. She is more miserable than the caged eagle of "Aquila reale" (King Eagle), for she created her prison herself. There would be a way out through suicide, as she intimates in "Il segno della croce" (The Sign of the Cross), but she has a daughter who still needs her:

> V'è un modo, per fuggir l'affanno atroce.
> Ma tu mi tieni col tuo dolce laccio,
> tu che non puoi dormir s'io non ti traccio
> in fronte, a sera, il segno della Croce.

> (There is a way to escape the terrible anguish.
> But you hold me back with your sweet snare,
> you who cannot sleep if I don't make
> the sign of the Cross on your forehead in the evening.)

At the same time the poet realizes in "Passione" (Passion) that Bianca, one day, will become independent. In the poem "Suor Nazarena" (Sister Nazarena) Negri describes the suffering she has wanted to confess to her friend during a visit at the convent, but she is disarmed at the complete serenity and candor of the nun, who unknowingly calms her by a gift of roses and by the invitation to return soon. The contrast of the two women is the contrast of secular and spiritual life. As an escape, Negri frequently returns to childhood memories, as in "Il giardino dell'adolescente" (The Adolescent's Garden), or "La stanza e il balcone" (The Room and Balcony). In "L'errante" (The Wanderer) she describes a woman, forever traveling, who left her home and buried her past. Negri did the same in 1913. She separated from her husband and went to live in Zurich, Switzerland. Appropriately her next book has the title of *Esilio* (Exile, 1914); in it she rejoices over her new-won liberty but at the same time is afraid she has taken the wrong step. Especially in "Parole non dette" (Words not Said) she effectively describes the problem of lack of communication or incapacity on her part to say the right words to her husband. She continuously examines her own rebellion and concludes that it all happened because the right man did not cross her path, as seen in "A colui che non è venuto" (To Him Who

Drawing of Negri by Enrico Sacchetti

Did Not Come) and in "Confessione" (Confession), which approaches autoanalysis. She repeatedly implores God to give her strength in her solitary journey, while she herself shows compassion toward all who suffer. Her only comfort is her daughter's cheerfulness and intelligence, together with the ever-present memory of Lodi.

While in Switzerland, Negri started writing short stories for various Italian literary periodicals, which, upon returning to Milan in 1915, she included with some new ones in *Le solitarie* (Solitary Women, 1917). These eighteen stories, which narrate in a rapid and concise prose the lonely existence and intimate drama of eighteen tormented women, were considered by some critics as superior to Negri's poetry for their realistic presentation of something new: women in need of creating their own reasons for living.

During World War I, Ada did her utmost to help the wounded and was glad to see her daughter join the Italian Red Cross. The destruction and death caused by the war awoke in her a new desire to live and love. The poems of *Il libro di Mara* (Mara's Book, 1919) are her most personal ones, constituting an unabashed confession of her late-blooming passion (cut short by death in 1917) for the "right one" who had finally come. Her liaison with a building constructor, who was to die of Spanish influenza, lasted less than a year but was intense. She made use of free verse to pour forth her rapture, which she considered an immersion into universal life, a perfect fusion of man and woman, where the male figure retains a primitive domineering position and the woman enjoys being dominated. Such a rapport was readily accepted by Negri, yet the modern reader will find her descriptions rather theatrical and her desperation after his death—which is poetically attributed to a fall from the scaffolds of a house he was building—somewhat melodramatic. However, this type of intimate erotic confession on the part of a woman was new in modern Italy: it was shocking to Croce, but it was praised by Michele Scherillo and Attilio Momigliano as a new contribution to love poetry. Even if it ended tragically, this love helped Negri overcome her restlessness: her short happiness had been such that she felt fulfilled and at peace with herself.

After this time Negri wrote with a more subdued tone. She was able to look at her past with detachment, as is evident from *Stella mattutina* (1921; translated as *Morning Star*, 1930), an autobiographical novel written in the third person, in which she describes her childhood and school years in Lodi. The collection of short stories *Finestre alte* (High Windows, 1923) seems to show her moving away from D'Annunzio's influence, even if that is not the case with her poems of *I canti dell'isola* (Songs of the Island, 1925), dealing mainly with Capri, which she visited in 1923. For her it was a hallucinating, sun-bathed, fragrant, and sensuous time in nature. While the visual sensations are feverishly rendered in her poems, the same places are described with greater realism in her prose in *Le strade* (Roads, 1926), a series of travel impressions and encounters. Yet *I canti dell'isola* also contains compositions on her traditional themes of maternal and filial bonds. Her thoughts go to her faraway daughter, now nursing her own baby; or Negri thinks of her dead mother.

Sorelle (Sisters, 1929) contains stories and portraits of women. Negri tends to assume the part of a well-observing, precise chronicler, capturing passions, weaknesses, and physical and psychic torments of young girls, mothers, and old women, all of whom are fighting their own battles, unassisted and unappreciated by others. Many stories contain scattered autobiographical references. Her subsequent books of prose, including *Di giorno in giorno* (From Day to Day, 1932), *Erba sul sagrato* (Grass on the Church Square, 1939), and the posthumous *Oltre* (Beyond, 1947), are sketches of places visited or encounters with various people, from the famed actress Eleonora Duse to the child next door, though *Oltre* in-

cludes five short stories and the lives of two women saints: Saint Catherine of Siena and Saint Thérèse of Lisieux. (Negri's *Santa Caterina da Siena* was published separately in 1961.)

With the three volumes of poetry of her maturity, *Vespertina* (Evening Star, 1930), *Il dono* (The Gift, 1936), which earned her the Firenze Prize, and the posthumous *Fons amoris* (Fountain of Love, 1946), Negri achieved greater artistic refinement. Influenced by the vogue of a return to the style of Giacomo Leopardi, combined with the existential stress on prosaism, she used a simpler style and chose her words without attempting a striking effect. The result is a series of limpid poetic images within a naturally flowing discourse rendered in blank verse. The dominant themes are the loss of youth, since the flowers of returning springs seem to belong to the younger generations, and the approach of death, which she contemplates with melancholy and religious resignation. In the process of gradual detachment from the world, loneliness becomes inevitable. The only consolation of old age is memories, accompanied by the necessity to accept equally the bad and the good as part of life.

Among the compositions rendered in the form of a prayer is "Pensiero d'autunno" (Autumn Thought), which concludes *Vespertina*:

> Fammi uguale, Signore, a quelle foglie
> moribonde che vedo oggi nel sole
> tremar dell'olmo sul più alto ramo.
> Tremano, sì, ma non di pena: è tanto
> limpido il sole, e dolce il distaccarsi
> dal ramo per congiungersi alla terra.
> S'accendono alla luce ultima, cuori
> pronti all'offerta; e l'agonia, per esse,
> ha la clemenza d'una mite aurora.
> Fa ch'io mi stacchi dal più alto ramo
> di mia vita, così, senza lamento,
> penetrata di Te come del sole.

> (O Lord, make me equal to those dying leaves
> that I see today trembling in the sun
> on the highest branch of the elm.
> They tremble, indeed, but not from pain:
> the sun is so limpid and the fall
> from the branch to join the earth is so sweet.
> Hearts ready for the offering flare up
> in the last light and agony for them
> has the clemency of a mild dawn.
> Let me thus fall from the highest branch
> of my life, without lament,
> permeated by You as by the sun.)

Ada Negri

Negri's new spirituality permitted her to celebrate the gifts of life—a blooming flower, the song of a bird, even death—with a calm contemplation. Her religiosity, however, is not always orthodox, as seen in the last poem of *Fons amoris*, where she implores God not to send her soul after her death to the faraway celestial regions, but to leave it among the people tilling the soil, so that she may lead them to him. Her last thought goes to the day when universal peace and love, not hate, will govern the world:

Giorno verrà, dal pianto dei millenni,
che amor vinca sull'odio, amor sol regni
nelle case degli uomini. Non può
non fiorire quell'alba: in ogni goccia
del sangue ond'è la terra intrisa e lorda
sta la virtù che la prepara, all 'ombra
dolente del travaglio d'ogni stirpe.

(A day will come, from the lamentation of
  millennia,
when love will triumph over hate, love alone will
  reign
in the houses of men. That dawn
cannot but shine: in each drop of blood

that soaked and dirtied the earth,
lies the virtue that is preparing it
in the aching shadow of the afflictions of every
  race.)

These words were written during World War II, which she witnessed almost to the end; she died on 11 January 1945 in Milan.

Unfortunately, the most frequently republished and translated volume of her verses remains *Fatalità*. It made her famous for the wrong reasons. She was branded "the red maiden" and her work was included in the index of prohibited books in 1893 by the Catholic church. Socialists subsequently accused her of having betrayed the political cause by moving on to other themes. Benito Mussolini, who met her through their mutual friend Margherita Sarfatti, liked her socialist tendencies and wrote a highly favorable review of *Stella mattutina* for the Fascist newspaper *Il Popolo d'Italia* (9 July 1921). This review was reproduced as a preface in a later reprint of *Stella*. Once in power, Mussolini singled Negri out by proposing her for the Nobel Prize in literature in 1926, which was given, however, to Grazia

Deledda. To make up for this disappointment, he had the Mussolini Prize bestowed on her in 1931, which made her a heroine of the Fascist regime and opened the doors for articles, books, and conferences on her works, as well as the awarding of the Grande medaglia d'oro (Gold Medal) for poetry in 1938 by the Ministero dell'Educazione Nazionale. To top it all Mussolini insisted that she be made a member of the Reale Accademia d'Italia (Royal Academy of Italy), instituted by the Fascist regime. Negri thus became in 1940 the first and only woman to be so distinguished. As a consequence, after the war she was not much read, even though she had not been politically active. Few postwar anthologies include her poems. Critics now eagerly point out her shortcomings, literary derivations, and lack of originality, with only a few defending her. Vincenzo L. Fraticelli, in his *Incontri con Ada Negri*, credits her with having written "la preghiera più religiosa, che si sia avuta dopo il Manzoni" (the most religious prayer that we have had since [Alessandro] Manzoni)—alluding to her poem "Padre, se mai questa preghiera giunga" (Father, if Ever This Prayer Reaches). But perhaps her true merit is that of having, in all her books, explored motherhood and the various sentiments—love, fear, doubt, hope, and resignation—that tie mothers to their offspring (good and bad, living and dead) in a matriarchal type of bond at all social levels.

Biography:

Simonetta Grilli, *Ada Negri: La vita e l'opera* (Milan: Gastaldi, 1953).

References:

Salvatore Comes, *Ada Negri da un tempo all'altro* (Milan: Mondadori, 1970);

Benedetto Croce, "Ada Negri," in his *La letteratura della nuova Italia* (Bari, Laterza, 1956), II: pp. 343-364; and "L'ultima Ada Negri," VI: 289-299;

Vincenzo L. Fraticelli, *Incontri con Ada Negri* (Naples: Conte, 1954);

Daniele Mattalìa, "Ada Negri," in *Orientamenti culturali—Letteratura italiana: I contemporanei* (Milan: Marzorati, 1963), I: 105-135;

Attilio Momigliano, *Impressioni d'un lettore contemporaneo* (Milan: Mondadori, 1928), pp. 104-111;

D. Mauro Pea, *Ada Negri* (Bergamo: Cattaneo, 1960);

Luigi Maria Personè, "Ada Negri," in his *Scrittori italiani moderni e contemporanei: Saggi critici* (Florence: Olschki, 1968), pp. 123-140;

Luigi Pirandello, "Sulle *Tempeste* di Ada Negri," in his *Saggi, poesie, scritti varii*, edited by Manlio Lo Vecchio-Musti (Milan: Mondadori, 1960), pp. 925-929;

Nino Podenzani, *Il libro di Ada Negri* (Milan: Ceschina, 1969);

Michele Scherillo, "Ada Negri," *Nuova Antologia* (16 September 1927): 167-182;

Giovanni Titta Rosa, "Ada Negri," in his *Second Ottocento* (Milan: Garzanti, 1947), pp. 221-234.

Mario Novaro

(25 September 1868 - 9 August 1944)

Pietro Frassica
Princeton University

BOOKS: *Lettera a Simirenko* (Turin: Roux, 1890);

Die Philosophie des Nicolaus Malebranche (Berlin: Mayer & Muller, 1893);

La teoria della causalità in Malebranche (Rome: Rendiconti della Regia. Accademia dei Lincei, 1893);

Il partito socialista in Germania (Turin: Partito Socialista dei Lavoratori Italiani, Comitato Regionale Piemontese, 1894);

Il concetto di infinito e il problema cosmologico (Rome: Baldi, 1895);

Murmuri ed echi (Naples: Ricciardi, 1912; revised and enlarged, 1941); revised again, edited by Giuseppe Cassinelli (Milan: All'Insegna del Pesce d'Oro, 1975);

La Riviera Ligure (Genoa: Sagep, 1984).

OTHER: Nicolaus Malebranche, *Pensieri metafisici*, 2 volumes, translated and edited by Novaro (Lanciano, Italy: Carabba, 1910, 1932);

Ciuang Ze, Acque d'autunno, translated and edited, with an introduction, by Novaro (Lanciano, Italy: Carabba, 1922);

"Inediti," *Fiera letteraria*, 2 (2 October 1947): 4;

Luciano Anceschi and Sergio Antonielli, eds., *Lirica del Novecento*, includes poems by Novaro (Florence: Vallecchi, 1961), pp. 107-112;

Piero Gelli and Gina Lagorio, eds., *Poesia italiana del Novecento*, includes poems by Novaro (Milan: Garzanti, 1980), I: 14-23.

Mario Novaro in 1900

Mario Novaro was the brother of the better-known Angiolo Silvio Novaro, who enjoyed fame disproportionate to his literary talent in the years between World Wars I and II; his reputation was due mostly to his contributions in children's literature. Mario, instead, was a poet whose value has yet to be fully recognized. In order to rectify this situation, an important congress was convened at Oneglia, Imperia, Italy, in 1987. The conference ultimately uncovered the profundity of Novaro's intellect and poetry. Similarly the 1975 edition of

Murmuri ed echi (Murmurings and Echoes, 1912), the only volume of poems and prose poems produced by Novaro, gave definitive form to his poetic production. The collection represents virtually his entire career in poetry because Novaro reworked and polished the compositions almost uninterruptedly right up to the time of his death in 1944. He devoted much time to refining the poems' lexicon, phrasing, and punctuation, as well as to reducing or reshaping the texts, which he judged rather harshly. As a result, the collec-

166

tion represents a stylistic testing ground to which Novaro returned repeatedly, motivated by a desire to achieve formal purity in the poems and prose poems, where even biographical details undergo a metaphysical transformation, assuming as they do the subtle connotative power of poetic fragments, as in these lines from the title poem:

La casa alla marina,
dove tuo padre sempre
ricordava trascorsi,
con tua madre e con voi, piccoli bimbi,
gli anni suoi più lieti:
riso suono perpetuo di mare,
così soave, anche inavvertita,
frangia alla vita!

(In the seaside home,
where your father always
recalled the happiest days of his life,
spent with your mother and you, young children:
laughter the perpetual sound of the sea,
so gentle, even imperceptible,
fringe of existence!)

Born in Diano Marina on 25 September 1868, Novaro was the son of Augustino Novaro and Paolina Sasso Novaro. After graduating from high school in Oneglia, he spent the fall semester of the academic year 1889-1890 at the University of Berlin. The winter semester found him instead in Vienna, where he remained until the winter semester of the next academic year. Finally he settled in Berlin and obtained his doctoral degree in philosophy in 1893 with a thesis on Nicolaus Malebranche, which was published in German. In 1895 he earned a second degree at the University of Turin. Meanwhile in 1890 he had published *Lettera a Simirenko* (A Letter to Simirenko)—A. J. Simirenko was a university friend of his. The text reveals Novaro's preoccupation with the great themes of Western metaphysics (noteworthy is the persistence with which he reverts to citing his favorite writer, Giordano Bruno), as well as his fascination with the Ligurian landscape. These elements were to assume central importance in his poetry. In 1893 he published *La teoria della causalità in Malebranche* (The Theory of Causality in Malebranche); in 1894 *Il partito socialista in Germania* (The Socialist Party in Germany), which was originally attributed by some to his brother Angiolo; and in 1895 *Il concetto di infinito e il problema cosmologico* (The Concept of Infinity and the Cosmological Problem). These works are the fruits of that philosophical

and political system of knowledge (German socialism) Novaro had acquired in Berlin. Furthermore, his conversion to socialism, which began in his homeland and matured during his stay in Berlin, made it logical for him to accept an appointment as aldermanic representative for the newly formed Socialist party, once he returned to Oneglia. Other factors in this political decision were his intellectual ties with the Socialists of Turin and his acquaintance with Gustavo Sacerdote, a Piedmontese Jew who was, at that time, a Berlin correspondent for Italian Socialist newspapers.

In 1898, following a brief period of teaching in the high school at Oneglia, he and his brothers (Angiolo, Eugenio, and Enrico) assumed administrative control of the family olive-oil business, owned by their mother. As Italo Svevo was doing during those same years on the other side of the Italian peninsula, Novaro continued to cultivate his interest in literature and culture while he engaged in commercial activities. He wrote *Murmuri ed echi*; he also translated and edited the *Pensieri metafisici* (Metaphysical Thoughts) of Malebranche (two volumes, 1910, 1932), as well as the *Acque d'autunno* (Waters of Autumn) of the Chinese philosopher Ciuang Ze (1922).

From 1899 to 1919 Novaro acted as managing editor and a writer of *La Riviera Ligure*, the magazine born as an advertising bulletin for the family commercial enterprise but soon acting as a forum for the new poetic tendencies of certain groups that began to develop around magazines and periodicals. This was due to Novaro's willingness to invite contributions from aspiring writers in addition to submissions from well-established authors. For this reason the Italian poetry of the early twentieth century is greatly indebted to magazines such as Novaro's, as it is to the general atmosphere of active experimentation that characterized the century's first twenty years. *La Riviera Ligure* began in 1895. Since it was initially tied to a particular industry, its chief purpose was to publicize the olive-oil-producing facilities of the Sassos and Novaros. However, the dialogue with the reading public was destined to increase. The firm promoted culture, and its commercial expectations grew along with its literary ambitions. When Novaro became the magazine's editor, his personal tastes and aspirations caused *La Riviera Ligure* to surpass the regional boundaries of Liguria and reach a national audience. A refined sponsor of new talent, a capable promoter, and a man knowledgeable about the ideologies of his day,

Novaro was responsible for the magazine acquiring an increasingly literary orientation and format, to the point where it became an interpreter and initiator of literary trends, both narrative and poetic; and the olive-oil business's profits enabled the magazine to remunerate its contributors handsomely. For twenty years *La Riviera Ligure* served as a vehicle for the voices of writers and literary critics of the new Italy—voices that were destined to remain significant in the context of twentieth-century Italian literature. The publishing of *La Riviera Ligure* concluded in 1919. World War I had intervened, seriously affecting the lives and careers of magazine collaborators and taking the lives of Cellino and Jacopo Novaro—the sons of Mario and Angiolo Silvio respectively. The scars left by the war were deep, and Novaro came to realize that an era had ended as he prepared to print the final issue of *La Riviera Ligure*.

From that period on Novaro would express himself essentially through revising the words and thoughts of the only volume of poetry he would produce, *Murmuri ed echi*. The process, as has already been noted, spanned more than thirty years. Perhaps the reasons for the many revisions are to be found in the author's firm conviction that words are severely limited in their capacity to convey the anxiety experienced by the self as it contemplates the cosmos. However, it is certain that behind this meticulous textual editing lies an intellectual journey that unfolds in the form of passionate or disillusioned inquiries and quintessential juxtapositions (nature/God, soul/world, spirit/matter, finitude/infinity, real/ideal), which constitute Novaro's cultural heritage and which permit him to approach poetry as a form of mystical escapism.

Even in the performance of day-to-day business transactions, Novaro continued to seek out the hidden meaning of the life of man, of his love and his suffering. As Fausto Montanari has argued in "Ritratto di Mario Novaro" (Portrait of Mario Novaro, in *Mario Novaro tra poesia e cultura*, 1988), "La letteratura poetica e narrativa doveva essere la filosofia quotidiana ('conosci te stesso') che facesse sentire il mistero del vivere umano come limite delle passioni ferine e come partecipazione alla vita che fluisce senza fine di famiglia in famiglia, di secolo in secolo . . ." (Poetry and narrative had to be [for him] the philosophy of daily living ["know thyself"] which enables us to feel the mystery of human existence, in terms of the limits of our animal passions and in terms of our participation in a life that flows without

end from generation to generation, century after century . . .).

In other words, for Novaro real poetry resides in truth—that is, in the contemplation of the universe: meditation allows us to establish a rapport with the world. Furthermore, these would appear to be the premises adopted by a young Novaro fascinated (during the years spent in Berlin and Vienna) more by the problematical nature of the universe and of infinity than by rhetorical devices. In this sense, Bruno's ideas in those years exerted an almost magical influence on Novaro's personality and constituted the basis for the lengthy activity he devoted in equal measure to philosophical, literary, and pragmatic issues. Similarly Novaro's artistic evolution could not be fully understood if one failed to consider that, in addition to being knowledgeable about Western philosophy, he had seriously studied Chinese thought, in particular the relationship between the pragmatism of *Wu-wei* (Do Not Act)—the concept of teaching without words, which is the basis of the *Tao te ching* (the ancient Book of Life and Virtue)—and Ciuang Ze's book that Novaro translated. In all probability such a background explains the need to conceive of a free poetry in which rhetorical devices are considered insufficient to modify the substance of an idea. Novaro gave fuller form to his thoughts on poetic discourse upon his 1893 return as a youth from Germany to Italy, in the context of textual revisions on his poems. Edoardo Villa, in "L'apprendistato di un poeta" (The Apprenticeship of a Poet, in *Mario Novaro tra poesia e cultura*), has summarized in the following way Novaro's cultural evolution from the "European" years to the time of his involvement in *La Riviera Ligure*: "Elementi diversi vi concorrono: da un lato le nuove esperienze culturali sulla linea di una scoperta religiosità, dall'altro le esigenze della quotidianità (la famiglia, la società olearia, la direzione di "Riviera") per una visione meno astratta del reale" (Various factors are involved here: on the one hand, the new cultural experiences on the road to discovering religion, on the other hand, the demands of daily living [the family, the olive-oil industry, and the management of *(La) Riviera (Ligure)*] give rise to a less abstract vision of reality).

The experience of lengthy philosophical study had the result of producing an acute awareness of human limitations: it is not in humankind's purview to know the essence of the universe. One can only contemplate the cosmos and immerse oneself in nature; one can intuit its mysterious voices and try to express them in poetic discourse, as occurs in the poem "Murmuri ed echi":

> E ài tu provato la gioia
> di un sereno oblioso abbandono
> ti sei dissolto nel mare dell'essere
> senz'altro chiedere che di ammirare
> e perderti tutto nell'estasi?
>
> (And have you experienced the joy
> of a serene, oblivious solitude
> have you dissolved into the sea of being
> asking nothing but to be allowed to admire
> and lose yourself entirely in the ecstasy?)

Meditation always prevails over descriptive or naturalistic language. What counts most is the succession of thoughts concerning existential or philosophical problems proper to man. Of course, landscape is also present in the form of elements such as the sky, sea, trees, and flowers, but physical nature appears largely as a function of the poet's keen determination to capture all of the visible world, all of life and nature, in order to find a new perspective from which to view phenomena and situations. It is this comprehensiveness of view that allows man to think of himself as a microcosmic model of the universe. As one can see in Novaro's "Libeccio" (Southwest Wind), the text mirrors the scope of material reality:

> Libeccio furioso sfrenato
> tu che pieghi durevolmente gli ulivi
> che pur nella calma
> a te seconde stendan le braccia:
> tu vento che l'onde volgi maggiori,
> che i moli oltrepassino gonfie
> spumeggiando in tumulto,
> belle e tremende a vedere:
> libeccio, tu che soffi che soffi a gran voce
> coprendo la voce del mare
> (oh come tu amando lo sferzi!
> fin qui sulle colle gli spruzzi ne sperdi!)
> bruciando, rapendo
> pur le foglie de' lecci tenaci,
> strinando i pini
> e alle palme le chiome di serpi
> che per te sibilano
> e urlano col mare a gara:
> non mi sdegnare!
> poi che sempre sempre io ti amai . . .
>
> (Impetuous, unbridled southwest wind,
> you, who forcefully bend the olive trees
> which even in the calm willingly

> extend toward you their branches:
> you, wind, that causes the waves to billow,
> as swollen they sweep over the moorings
> seething in frenzied whirl,
> beautiful and inspiring to behold,
> southwest wind, you blow and blow loudly
> with a voice that silences the sea
> [oh, how lovingly you lash at it!
> until it casts its spray upon the hills]
> searing, scorching
> even the leaves of the clinging willows,
> scorching the pines
> and the palm trees' leafy branches
> which whistle on your account
> and shriek in rivalry with the sea:
> do not disdain me!
> for I have always loved you . . .).

Thus Novaro establishes a relationship between a state of mind and the wind. It is apparent that the poet gives absolute primacy to his own internal experience, which is reflected in nature.

There is little doubt that in the poetry and prose of Mario Novaro the primary component is reflection. However, beyond the search for a solution to the problematical relationship between the self and the universe or between nature and culture, one senses his desire to alleviate the torment suggested by the interaction of imagery and moralistic or philosophical statements. It is, in effect, an attempt to fuse descriptions of landscape and rationalization; in this process, the landscape is converted into a symbolic locus that articulates an ethic not dissimilar to the one enunciated by other authors of Ligurian origin (including Camillo Sbarbaro, Engenio Montale, and Angelo Barile). Nevertheless, in Novaro's work one finds an unusual philosophy and an equally unusual ethical vision of language, with respect to those found generally in the Italian literature of the period in question. It is probably for this reason that, despite various approaches attempted, critics find considerable difficulty in positioning Novaro satisfactorily among the poets of the twentieth century without diminishing his value. Occasionally, due to the simultaneous presence of various types of experimentation, Novaro's work runs the risk of appearing not to have a focus; on the other hand, this same diversity—also seen in the works of some of his contemporaries, such as Giuseppe Ungaretti and Giovanni Pascoli (whose own work contains echoes of Giacomo Leopardi)—assumes particular importance in the context of Italian poetry of the first decades of this century. At the same time, it is somewhat removed from the more conspicuous poetic forms proposed by the "crepuscolari" (twilight poets), the futurists, and by Gabriele D'Annunzio.

Letters:

Carteggio 1907-1943, by Novaro and Marino Moretti, edited by Claudio Toscani (Milan: IPL, 1981);

Lettere a Mario Novaro, by Novaro and Giovanni Boine (Bologna: Boni, 1987).

References:

Gianfranco Amoretti, "La poesia di Mario Novaro," *Resine*, new series 12 (April-June 1982): 3-14;

Carlo Bo, "Mario Novaro," in *Letteratura italiana contemporanea*, edited by Gaetano Mariani and Mario Petrucciani (Rome: Lucarini, 1979), I: 831-834;

Bo, "La poesia di Mario Novaro," *Corriere del Popolo*, 23 June 1946;

Pino Boero, ed., *Lettere a "La Riviera Ligure,"* 2 volumes: volume 1, 1900-1905 (Rome: Storia e Letteratura, 1980); volume 2, 1906-1909 (Turin, Meynier, 1987);

Giovanni Boine, "Mario Novaro," *Voce*, 26 September 1912, p. 901;

Giovanni Cattanei, "Mario Novaro," in his *La Liguria e la poesia italiana del Novecento* (Milan: Silva, 1966), pp. 98-108;

Gaetano Mariani, "Mario Novaro," in his *Poesia e tecnica nella lirica del Novecento* (Padua, Italy: Liviana, 1958), pp. 97-110;

Mario Novaro tra poesia e cultura (Florence: Monnier, 1988);

Giuseppe Angelo Peritore, "Mario Novaro," in his *Alcuni studi* (Imola, Italy: Galeati, 1961), pp. 71-83;

Claudio Toscani, "L'ombra di Pascoli tra Moretti e Novaro," *Otto/Novecento*, 1, no. 1 (1977): 116-122.

Papers:

Fondazione Mario Novaro in Genoa has letters by and to Novaro and also holds original issues of *La Riviera Ligure*.

Giacomo Noventa
(31 March 1898 - 4 July 1960)

Elena Urgnani
Wheaton College

BOOKS: *Versi e poesie* (Milan: Edizioni di comunità, 1956; enlarged edition, Milan: Mondadori, 1960; enlarged and revised, 1975);

Il vescovo di Prato (Milan: Saggiatore, 1958);

Nulla di nuovo (Milan: Saggiatore, 1960);

Il re e il poeta (Milan: Scheiwiller, 1960);

Il grande amore in "Uomini e no" di Elio Vittorini e in altri uomini e libri (Milan: All'Insegna del Pesce d'Oro, 1960);

Renato Guttuso, Gott mit Uns, by Noventa and Antonello Trombadori (Milan: Saggiatore, 1960);

Versi e poesie di Emilio Sarpi, edited by Vanni Scheiwiller (Milan: Scheiwiller, 1963);

I calzoni di Beethoven (Milan: Saggiatore, 1965);

Tre parole sulla Resistenza (Milan: All'Insegna del Pesce d'Oro, 1965; enlarged edition, Florence: Vallecchi, 1973);

C'era una volta, edited by Scheiwiller (Milan: Scheiwiller, 1966);

Portème via . . . (Milan: All'Insegna del Pesce d'Oro, 1968);

Caffè Greco, edited by Franca Noventa (Florence: Vallecchi, 1969);

Storia di una eresia, edited by Franca Noventa (Milan: Rusconi, 1971);

Hyde Park (Milan: All'Insegna del Pesce d'Oro, 1972);

Opere complete, 4 volumes, edited by Franco Manfriani (Venice: Marsilio, 1986-1989).

OTHER: *La fiala* [play], *Situazione*, 18-19 (February 1961).

Giacomo Noventa

Giacomo Noventa is the pseudonym that Giacomo Ca'Zorzi, scion of an aristocratic Venetian family, chose out of modesty or perhaps unwillingness to flaunt his patrician heritage. He began to use it with his first publication, an article in the Florentine magazine *Solaria* (May-June 1934), "A proposito di un traduttore di Heine" (About One of [Heinrich] Heine's Translators). His family, patrician landowners, including his parents—Antonio and Emilia Ceresa Ca'Zorci—had noble roots in the small village of Noventa di Piave, Italy, where he was born and where the large paternal villa was located, in the flatland crossed by the Piave River. He received a Catholic, patrician education, of which he was always proud and from which he was able to derive his moral values: a code of friendship and honor that was the natural inheritance of his aristocratic background. His life was an uninterrupted succession of various tensions, inspired by idealistic feelings of nobility, an antidemagogic passion, and a polemic attitude toward hermeticism.

Noventa attended the Universitè di Torino (Turin), where he received his law degree in

1923, with a dissertation on the philosophy of law that had a significant title: "Come abbia ragione da un punto di vista giuridico chi sostiene la sovranità del Papa, chi la nega, chi pur ammettendola, attribuisce al Papa una sovranità *sui generis*" (About the Pope's Sovereignty, How Those Who Maintain It, Those Who Deny It, Those Who Admit It Even if Partially, Are Right). In Turin he studied with such well-known economists as Luigi Einaudi and Gaetano Mosca, and he made friends with such important literati as Giacomo Debenedetti, Mario Soldati, Piero Gobetti, Eugenio Montale, and Umberto Saba.

After graduation he spent a short time in Rome, attempting to practice penal law. It was his first and only attempt, since he had little patience for a normal bourgeois profession. In Rome he became a member of the Partito Liberale (Liberal party), but resigned after eight days, since his friend Count Camillo Benso di Cavour did not take the same membership. He returned to Turin in 1925, where he joined the Partito Socialisto; but his deeply rooted traditionalism, as well as his antimaterialism, did not allow him to fit in. It was difficult for him both to get along with others and to renounce them.

For about ten years (from 1926 to 1936) he simply traveled around Europe, alternating periods of intense study with periods of passionate loves and friendships; he was in Paris, then in Savoy, attracted by this ancient francophone province, so different from his native Veneto region. He also studied the ancient Corsican dialect during one of his trips to the island; later he visited Brussels and Grenoble. He felt that living abroad enhanced his appetite for knowledge and was much more intellectually challenging than living at home. In 1929 he published in the magazine *La Libra* the poem "Il castogallo" (The Elegant Cock), which he had written together with Mario Soldati; he also composed his first song in the Venetian dialect, "Senza schei ambassadori . . ." (Without Money as Ambassador . . .), including these lines:

> Mi no' gèro che un putèlo,
> Tì ti-géri apéna fìa;
> Ma d'un baso un garanghèlo
> Se façeva, Lina mia.
>
> Ah, se podéssimo riscominziar . . .
>
> (I was no more than a boy,
> You were just a girl;

> But out of a kiss we could
> make a party, my Lina.
>
> Oh, if we could just start all over . . .).

The choice of the Venetian dialect was not motivated by ignorance of standard Italian or narrowness of horizons; on the contrary, it is a sophisticated choice. Noventa's native dialect is that illustrious Venetian language (a mixture of the popular dialect and Italian) spoken by his social class: the land-owning, well-educated Venetian aristocracy who lived in the region because of its people's attachment to the land and respect for tradition. It was a class proud of its Italian culture but not forgetful of having formerly been part of a large middle-European empire. In several poems, Noventa attempts to explain the reason for his choice of dialect over the Italian language. One such self-explanation is in the poem "Mi me son fato . . ." (I've Made Myself . . . ; collected in *Versi e poesie*, 1956):

> Mi me son fato 'na lengua mia
> Del venezian, de l'italian:
> Ga' sti diritti la poesia,
> Che vien dai lioghi che regna Pan.
>
> La ghe n'a' altri, no' tuti credo,
> Se ben par ela se pol morir:
> No' tuto quelo che penso e vedo
> Vol i me versi spiegar e dir . . .
>
> (I've made myself my own language
> From the Venetian, from the Italian:
> Poetry has these kinds of rights,
> It comes from Pan's kingdom.
>
> It also has other rights, not all of them, I believe,
> Since people can die for it:
> My verses cannot explain
> Everything I think and see . . .).

In "Nei momenti che 'l cuor" (In Those Moments When My Heart . . . ; in *Versi e poesie di Emilio Sarpi*, 1963) he writes:

> Nei momenti che 'l cuor me se rompe
> Mi no' canto che in Venessian
> De una lengua le "splendide pompe"
> Lasso a chi fa mestier d'italian
>
> No' gh' è lengua che valga el dialeto
> Che una madre nascendo ne insegna
> Ah! L'artista xe' ben povareto
> Che a le prime parole no' impegna
>
> Le so piu' vere canzon

(In those moments when my heart breaks
I only sing in Venetian
I leave to those who proclaim themselves Italian
The "splendid pompousness" of a language

There is no language worth the dialect
That a mother teaches her child
Ah! He is a very poor artist
Who does not trust his first words

With his most true songs).

From 1930 to 1932 Noventa lived in Germany during another formative stage; he studied for three semesters in Heidelberg and Marburg an der Lahn, where he learned German so well that he began to compose a poem in that language. Later he traveled to Vienna and stayed there for a few months, but in the summer of 1932 he was in Madrid. Intermittently he traveled back and forth to Italy: to Turin, Noventa di Piave, and Venice.

On 16 April 1933, in Turin, he married Franca Reynaud, a former university colleague he first met in 1923 (they were to have two sons, Alberto and Antonio, and a daughter, Emilia). The couple went to Paris later in 1933, where they became acquainted with Carlo Rosselli, Aldo Garosci, Carlo Levi, and Lionello Venturi. In the autumn the Noventas visited London, where he studied English, but in the summer of 1934 they were back in Italy, in Meana, where he met Benedetto Croce, who was vacationing there. Noventa was starting to develop a passion for philosophy.

Some of his poems in Venetian were already known to his friends in literary circles, but he was shy about his works. He did not want to publish them, and it was only at his wife's insistence that he continued to write them. In the meantime he started writing what he thought would become his masterpiece: a philosophical work entitled "Principio di una scienza nuova" (Principle of a New Science), published in *Nulla di nuovo* (Nothing New, 1960). The first chapter appeared in the journal *Solaria* in March 1935. In May his troubles with the political authorities flared again (he had been stopped by Turin police in 1932): like many other Italian intellectuals who contributed to *Cultura*, he was suspected of being anti-Fascist, was arrested, and was kept in prison for about a month. Later he was released but forbid-

den to reside in Piedmont or travel abroad. He took up residence in Florence.

In 1936, after a failed attempt to write a movie script together with Soldati, he founded in Florence the magazine *Riforma Letteraria* (1936-1938). This was a central episode in his life as a militant critic. He was the editor in chief and almost the only journalist, but he had the opportunity to show the public some of his most beautiful poems under the pseudonym Emilio Sarpi, a poet who, Noventa claimed, died in London in 1933 during one of his deepest crises. From 1936 on, Noventa would be both a political and religious writer, and not merely a poet anymore. In *Riforma Letteraria* he published excerpts of his major works, such as "Principio di una scienza nuova," "Manifesti del classicismo" (both collected in *Nulla di nuovo*), and *I calzoni di Beethoven* (Beethoven's Trousers, 1965), and took a position on some of the most important philosophical problems of his time. He thought that Italy was betrayed and misrepresented by its political and cultural leading class, and that it was more and more in need of a new, great, and heroic interpretation of its vitality. He also thought that Fascists and anti-Fascists were making mistakes that were analogous and complementary, in response to which he proposed a return to classicism and Catholicism. Because of this he was accused of ambiguity by the anti-Fascists, and of trying politically to corrupt youth by the Fascists.

Noventa's *Riforma Letteraria* happened to be noticed by some hermetic writers and derived its success from the scandal it raised, but the ideas of Noventa were not fully understood. His reformist ideas were directed against the liberal and democratic cultural establishment, who he felt had gotten too far from the common people and the eternal truths of Catholicism. Only some of the youngest critics, such as Franco Fortini or Geno Pampaloni, fascinated as they were by Noventa's anticonformism, gave him their unconditional sympathy.

However, it is precisely his refusal of ideologies and his battle against all kinds of dogmatism that place him among the moderns. But Pier Paolo Pasolini is critical of Noventa: "È una libertà, però, quella di Noventa, che minaccia di degradare, nei casi meno rilevanti, in una sorta di gratuità, e nella stravaganza in quelli più tipici: una stravaganza linguistica coincidente con quella del suo pensiero, con la sua posizione politica." (His is a sort of freedom, which seems to degrade into gratuity, into a linguistic extravagance that coincides with his political and philosophical extravagance). Noventa's psychological ambiguities always coincide linguistically, though, with some shadowy moods, and one can say that he sometimes operates at the edge of irrationality.

One consistent harmonizing theme in his work is love, which coincides with the joy of life. The poem " 'Sta canzon" (This Song), for example, is dedicated to a child:

> 'Sta canzòn
> Me xe' vignùa da tì:
>
> Cèa, come tì
> Lisiera, come tì.
> E fùssela! . . .
> Come ti', bela;
>
> Senza savér par chi.
>
> (This song
> Has come from you:
>
> Little, like you
> Light, like you.
> And I wish it were! . . .
> Like you, beautiful;
>
> Not knowing for whom.)

In another poem, "In t'un prà, perso par sempre" (In a Meadow, Lost Forever), the poet's love song becomes almost physical, with malicious allusiveness:

> In t'un prà, perso par sempre
> Mi morivo de ssé.
>
> Xé passada una donéta,
> La so broca de aqua in man,
> Cofà una qualunque.
> "Dove xéla la fontana,
> Regineta, ché gò ssé?"
>
> La me gà vardà un momento,
> La ga' messo zo' la broca,
> Par sentarse viçin.
>
> (In a meadow, lost forever
> I was dying of thirst.
>
> A little woman came by,
> With a jug of water in her hand,
> Like anybody.
> "Where is the fountain,
> Little Queen, since I am thirsty?"

> She stared at me for a moment,
> She put down the pitcher,
> To sit down closer.)

At other times love gives place to religious feelings, as in the poem "El saor del pan" (The Taste of Bread) dedicated to Noventa's wife, or in the lyric "Gh'è nei to grandi oci de ebrea" (There Is in Your Large Jewish Eyes):

> Gh'è nei to grandi—Oci de ebrea
> Come una luse—Che me consuma;
> Nó ti-ssì bèla—Ma nei to oci
> Mi me vergogno—De aver vardà.
> . . . .
> Vero xe' forse—Che in tuti i santi
> Gh'è un fià de l'ànema—Del servidor,
> Ma forse, proprio—Par questo, i santi
> Nó se pardona—Nel mondo amor . . .
>
> (There is in your large—Jewish eyes
> Something like a light—That consumes me;
> You are not beautiful—But in your eyes
> I am ashamed—To have looked.
> . . . .
> Maybe it's true—That in all saints
> There is a bit—Of a servant's soul
> But maybe—For this reason the saints
> Do not allow themselves—Any love in the world . . .).

Fortini states that this is the most successful (and the most celebrated) of Noventa's love poems. He also argues that Noventa's language is only superficially dialectal. Fortini claims that the syntactic structures of Noventa's lyrics, as well as their themes, have little to do with the traditional, affective repertory of dialects. Noventa's is a language that has as an antithetical point of reference the sublime language of Giuseppe Ungaretti's modernism and hermeticism. Noventa's cultural references are not hidden, but rather emphasized by his dialectal frame.

Civil and political passion is also a strong theme in Noventa's poetry. Sometimes it takes the form of a satirical patriotic hymn, as in "Soldi, soldi . . ." (Money, Money . . .):

> Soldi, soldi, vegna i soldi,
> Mi vùi venderme e comprar,
> Comprar tanto vin che basti
> 'Na nazion a imbriagar.
>
> Cantarò co' lori i beve,
> Bevarò se i cantarà,
> Imbriago vùi scoltarli,
> Imbriaghi i scoltarà.

Ghè dirò 'na paroleta,
Che ghe resti dopo el vin,
Fioi de troie, i vostri fioi,
Gavarà 'l vostro destin.

(Money, money, let the money come,
I want to sell myself and buy,
Buy so much wine that it should be enough
To make a nation drunk.

I will sing while they drink,
I will drink if they will sing,
Drunk I want to listen to them,
Drunk they will listen to me.

I will tell them a little word,
That will stay with them after the wine,
Sons of bitches, your children,
Will have your destiny.)

At other times political passion emerges through an affectionate portrait Noventa draws of a political personality whom he could really meet or has met, as in "Piero Gobetti," the poem he wrote in Paris in July 1933, following a visit to Gobetti's tomb:

Piero Gobetti—I te gà fato
Un altro articolo—De propaganda:
Dei to compagni—La prima banda
Te gà tradìo—Ma questi qua,
Che al çimitero—Te gà trovà:
Te loda solo—Par dirse grandi,
E te lassa là.

Megio, Gobetti—I to primi amiçi!
Ti xe' par lori—Una spina in cuor,
Almanco . . . —Ma questi qua,
Che al çimitero—Te gà trovà,
No' te tradisse,—No' te continua,
Morti, co' un morto—I gà da far.

(Piero Gobetti—They made for you
Another article—For propaganda:
The first bunch—Of your pals
Has betrayed you—But these here,
Whom you found—At the cemetery:
They only compliment you—To make themselves
    more important,
And there they leave you.

Much better, Gobetti—Your first friends!
You are for them—A thorn in the side,
At least . . . —But these here,
Whom you found—At the cemetery,
They do not betray,—They do not continue you,
Dead, with a corpse—They deal.)

Gobetti had been a charismatic leader of the Italian Liberal party and founded the magazines *La Rivoluzione Liberale* and *Il Baretti*. He died in Paris at the age of twenty-five from injuries sustained during a beating by Fascists. His liberalism was different from the tradition of Italian liberalism, which is often reactionary and right wing. Noventa was also a nontraditional Catholic, a nontraditional socialist, and a nontraditional liberal; it is difficult to understand him without considering his philosophical works. Though he had a liberal mind, he felt, like Gobetti, the inadequacy of idealism. He also felt the necessity to go beyond the barrier of his national culture, and he tried to provide a global answer to the fundamental problems of his century. He denied that freedom could be identified with a history of individualism, and he valued acts of love, faith, revolt, and reflection. He also forecast the intervention of a super-individual Soul, who would mediate between human conscience and the reality of the new century.

Noventa's Catholic faith, though taking its premise from Vincenzo Gioberti's positions (from his call for national primacy, for example), was nevertheless quite modern. Noventa had, from his youth, been influenced by Jacques Maritain's thoughts. For Noventa clericalism was without any doubt the negation of Catholicism, and he was keen on a dialogue with the Reformed church. All of Noventa's accusations against idealism, antifascism, and "aristocratic literature" come from his premises of religious solidarity with life. There is in the background of Noventa's poetry a polemic revolt against hermetic solitude, which, he felt, built between people and the world a space populated by obscure and artificial forms. His values were friendship, loyalty, poetry, and love; his target was solitude, and the pride of solitude, in thought, in the social order, and in literature. His most important philosophical points of reference are Croce, Giovanni Gentile, Gobetti, Goffredo Pareto, and Henri Bergson.

In 1939, while he was trying to move the headquarters of his magazine *Riforma Letteraria* to Milan, he was arrested again and forbidden to reside in any city that was the seat of a university. He was able to get away for a while, but in September, in Florence, he avoided another arrest only by hiding in a friend's house. He later hid in Cortona, then in Rome, where he attended meetings with other artists, some of whom were politically active Communists.

At the end of World War II, in Venice, he found himself again close to the Liberal party; he founded a newspaper (once again he was almost the only writer, editor, and subeditor): *La Gazzetta del Nord* (1946-1947). In those pages he repeatedly defined himself as a liberal Catholic, but as usual it was a temporary label.

In 1947 he was in Turin again, calling himself a socialist Catholic. He contributed to magazines such as *Mondo Nuovo* and *L'Italia Socialista*. Later he founded two other periodicals: *Il Socialista Moderno* (1949-1950) and *Il Giornale dei Socialisti* (1951). He also actively participated in political life, always maintaining his independence. His weapons were paradox, sarcasm, elegance, and keenness.

He hoped for the unification of the different socialist groups, and the organizational, political, and theoretical independence of communism, which should have been grounded on a universal principle of brotherhood. His Catholic faith was anticlerical, and his theoretical sympathy went to philosophers such as Gioberti or Maritain; however, Noventa's personal synthesis of socialism, patriotism, and liberalism was not easily accepted. In 1953 he ran for parliament as a member of the Partito di Unità Popolare, but he was not elected. This defeat led to his withdrawal from political life.

Only in 1956 did he finally decide to publish his poetry, and *Versi e poesie* obtained the prestigious Viareggio prize. The encouragement he derived from that success pushed him toward the publication of another book, a theoretical work on Catholicism: *Il vescovo di Prato* (The Bishop of Prato, 1958), a fictitious dialogue whose protagonists are Emilio Sarpi (his old pseudonym) and Mario Soldati. In the spring of 1960 he republished his theoretical essays, under the title *Nulla di nuovo*. He also wrote a comedy, *La fiala* (The Vial, *Situazione*, February 1961), which has never been staged. Noventa died on 4 July 1960 of a brain tumor. He is regarded by new generations as an independent religious thinker and poet.

References:

Domenico Astengo, "Giacomo Noventa," in his *La poesia dialettale* (Turin: Marietti, 1976), pp. 191-195;

Franco Fortini, "Giacomo Noventa," in his *I poeti del novecento* (Bari, Italy: Laterza, 1977), pp. 122-129;

Fortini, "Giacomo Noventa e la poesia," *Il Ponte*, 8/9 (1956): 1393-1404;

Fortini, "Noventa e la poesia contemporanea," in *Novecento, I contemporanei*, edited by Gianni Grana (Milan: Marzorati, 1979), IV: 3776-3786;

Franco Manfriani, Preface to Giacomo Noventa's *Versi e poesie* (Venice: Marsilio, 1986), pp. xi-lxv;

Geno Pampaloni, "Giacomo Noventa," in *Novecento, I contemporanei*, pp. 3761-3765;

Pier Paolo Pasolini, *Passione e ideologia* (Milan: Garzanti, 1960), pp. 111-114;

Giovanni Raboni, "Giacomo Noventa," in *Novecento, I contemporanei*, pp. 3790-3792;

Claudio Varese, "Giacomo Noventa," *Nuova Antologia*, 1 (1957): 273-275.

Arturo Onofri

(15 September 1885 - 25 December 1928)

Douglas Radcliff-Umstead

BOOKS: *Liriche* (Rome: Vita Letteraria, 1907; revised edition, Naples: Ricciardi, 1914); revised again, edited by Enrico Falqui (Milan: Garzanti, 1948);

Poemi tragici (Rome: Società Editrice Laziale, 1908);

Canti delle oasi (Rome: Tusculana, 1909);

Disamore (Rome: Dell'Autore, 1912);

Orchestrine (Naples: Diana, 1917);

Arioso (Rome: Bragaglia, 1921);

Le trombe d'argento (Lanciano, Italy: Carabba, 1924);

Il Tristano di Riccardo Wagner (Milan: Bottega di Poesia, 1924);

Nuovo rinascimento come arte dell'Io (Bari, Italy: Laterza, 1925);

Terrestrità del sole (Florence: Vallecchi, 1927);

Vincere il drago! (Turin: Ribet, 1928);

Simili a melodie rapprese in mondo (Rome: Tempio della Fortuna, 1929);

Zolla ritorna cosmo (Turin: Buratti, 1930);

Suoni del Gral (Rome: Tempio della Fortuna, 1932);

Aprirsi fiore (Turin: Gambino, 1935);

Poesie, edited by Arnaldo Bocelli and Girolamo Comi (Rome: Tumminelli, 1949);

Letture poetiche del Pascoli, edited by Comi (Lucugnano, Italy: L'Albero, 1953);

Poesie d'amore, edited by Vittov Vettori (Milan: Ceschina, 1959);

Poesie scelte, edited by Franco Floreanini (Parma, Italy: Guanda, 1960);

Poesie edite e inedite, 1900-1914, edited by Anna Dolfi (Ravenna, Italy: Longo, 1982).

OTHER: Rudolph Steiner, *La scienza occulta nelle sue linee generali*, preface by Onofri (Bari, Italy: Terza, 1924);

Laura Lepri, "Onofri edito e inedito," includes poems by Onofri, *Studi Novecenteschi*, 11 (June 1984): 55-70.

Although Arturo Onofri remains an isolated figure in the history of Italian poetry, he

Arturo Onofri, 1916

properly belongs in the international ranks of the modernists who, like Ezra Pound with his technique of "superposition," endeavored to communicate experience by reflecting on a series of visual pictures. Throughout his brief but extremely productive writing career, Onofri attempted to create a visionary, contemplative form of poetry that would express the disorder and complexity of human life, while he also sought a sense of eternal truth beyond the chaos of everyday life. He eventually saw his role as that of a prophet who must point out a realm of spiritual significance that could redeem the wearisome cycles of reincarnated existences. His poetry of multifaceted images was to serve as a means of illumination for humankind, to free them from an attachment to the imprisoning material world so they could know the joyousness of eternity. For Onofri all art, and especially poetry, should serve as a form of prayer.

Born on 15 September 1885 in Rome to an upper-middle-class family, Onofri grew up in the fin de siècle culture of the capital, with its pretensions to rival the sophisticated societies of Paris, London, Berlin, and St. Petersburg while actually retaining much of the provincialism of the pre-unification era. While his father, Vincenzo, was of long-standing Roman background, his mother, Beatrice Shreider Onofri, was of Polish origin. During late summer and early fall the family would vacation at Castel Gandolfo. Onofri shared with the youth of his generation a fascination with Nietzschean philosophy, Wagnerian music, and French symbolism as all were transformed and interpreted through the writings of Gabriele D'Annunzio, the electrifying influence of that period.

A D'Annunzian spirit of celebration pervades Onofri's first collection of verses, *Liriche* (1907), which opens with its own version of D'Annunzio's *Laus Vitae* (1903) in the hymn "O Vita, o Vita!"—hailing life as the magnificent dream of the infinite and the longing for unchangeable perfection in a universe fulfilling its potential greatness. Just as D'Annunzio's volume of poems *Elettra* (1903) salutes military and artistic heroes such as Dante, Giuseppe Garibaldi, Giuseppe Verdi, and Victor Hugo for their daring achievements, Onofri's *Liriche* features poems in honor of Maksim Gorky and the intrepid polar explorer the duke of Abruzzi, who inspired the youth of Italy to conquer physical and spiritual frontiers. Onofri exalts an activism that transcends a mere affirmation of human will for self-aggrandizement and instead seeks a way to mystic illustriousness. An elegy for the deceased Giosuè Carducci proclaims his immortality and feats that forever will inspire Italians to throw off the chains of slavery. Along with verses exhorting warfare and deeds of undying glory there occur twilight and nocturnal poems such as "Notte di Venezia" (Night in Venice), which suggests the amorous stillness of nighttime across the Venetian lagoon. A tenderness reminiscent of the poems of Giovanni Pascoli characterizes "La Canzone dei passeri" (The Song of the Sparrows) in the contrast between the free flight of the friendly birds and the sadness of the lyricist in

the earthbound cage of his daily life. In the sonnet "Dall'Antro" the image of a cavern appears as one not of refuge but of confinement. In his initial volume, Onofri creates a vocabulary and an imagery of the fertile earth (*terra*), the consoling sky (*cielo*), the tremulous sea (*mare*), and the promising universe (*cosmo*), as opposed to the restrictive cavern or lair (*antro, tana*) that will persist throughout all his poetic writings to communicate a longing to discover cosmic harmony away from tormenting existence.

With his *Poemi tragici* of 1908 he juxtaposes a transcendent drive toward self-actualization in "Interludio propulsivo" to the frustrating limitations of heroic endeavor in "Interludio spasmodico": while in the first poem the human soul triumphantly establishes an aspiration for every day, in the second lyric a twilight soul cannot awaken the weary poet from his torpor in a world that seems timeworn. Throughout the volume the speakers listen to the musical voice of nature that speaks of solitude and humility. At times Onofri expresses a form of socialism as he identifies with the masses toiling in the fields, where their labor builds a rapport with the earth. Hope for regeneration arises again from his fascination with the Hindu doctrine of metempsychosis, as reflected in the verses of "Il cipresso," where he declares his desire to be buried near his beloved cypress tree in order to enter its spirit and know eternal life:

E rivivrò in una vita, più bella,
di foglie e di bacche. Sarà in un arbusto
trafuso il mio fiore carnale.

(And I shall live again in a more beautiful life,
of leaves and berries. My carnal flower
will be transfused into a bush.)

The earth in which the poet will be interred can act as regenerative lymph for the soul's transmigration: the more deeply the tree sends its roots into the earth, the higher it will lift up into the sky. That tree, continually pointing upward, appears not as a sign of graveyard mourning but of the soul's eternal ascent toward fulfillment in the cosmos.

As a poet who returns again and again to certain archetypal images, Onofri, in *Poemi tragici*, pictures in "La falena" (The Moth) the quest of the human soul for self-consummation and completion as the flight of a moth toward a flame burning within an oil lamp. Repeatedly Onofri was to focus on a cocoon or chrysalis as the image of

Onofri (center) surrounded by friends, circa 1907

the material confines from which the soul must struggle to free itself and realize its heaven-designated potential. Like the poets of the *crepuscolar* school (twilight poets), Onofri poses the oxymoron of gaining eternal life in experiencing death, for after the "I" of the poem lifts the glass cover of the lamp for the moth to enter the flame, the insect will perish. The Alexandrine verses of "La falena" run to fifteen or sixteen syllables and anticipate the rhythmic prose of some of his later volumes of lyrical reflections.

In several of the poems in *Poemi tragici*, such as "Ebe" (Hebe [Greek goddess of youth]), "Ai confini" (At the Frontiers), "Il sonno del pilota" (The Pilot's Sleep), "Il ritorno" (The Return), and "I vinti" (The Vanquished), Onofri views a sea journey in terms of the myth of the human desire to be elevated toward a divine, Olympian plane. The marine imagery serves as a ritualistic invitation for the soul to fuse with the eternal universe. The seafaring poet acts as a *vate* (prophet) with a lyre who sings of the promises of an often-mysterious world. The journey of the ship of human experience reflects his vision of a palingenetic nature. Frequently the poems recap-

ture the rocking of waves against the ship to suggest the eternal rhythms of the universe, where the heroic soul will alone find liberation from the chimerical experiences of its odyssey.

The second volume of Onofri's verses, of course, points to the tragic condition of humans as creatures imprisoned in materiality, and his third volume, *Canti delle oasi* (Songs of Oases, 1909), marks an instant of pause to take refuge away from the desert of life. More than in any of his other books of verse, Onofri stresses an overall symphonic structure to demonstrate a coherent vision of human experience. The volume opens with a prelude, "Sinfonia claustrale" (Cloistered Symphony), and then presents twenty-one "Poemi del sole" (Poems of the Sun). Four lyrics make up the third movement of "Lacustri" (Lakeland Poems). The fourth division, "Momenti varii," acts like an adagio singing of nocturnal, elegiacal moments of reflection: a series of nine prayers expresses Onofri's desire to know a calm life, to find a woman to love, and to be transformed into the life of plants. An autumnal envoi to a Leopardesque Silvia closes the collection with the melancholy falling of petals and leaves. The entire movement of the volume is from the honeyed sweetness of springtime to the dolorous retreat of fall. In the "Sinfonia claustrale" he expresses his hope to make of key words a vocabulary of small mirrors to reflect the sun's brilliance to be held in a shrine of creativity. The solar radiance, as shown in the first extended section, may serve as a source of illuminating salvation, permitting his anguish to know a moment of peace when he can recall the naiveté of a child's delight before the sights and sounds of nature. Onofri comes closest in spirit to the twilight-school poet Guido Gozzano in the impressionistic attention to minute details of somewhat faded but still charming items of furnishing and decor, no longer fashionable articles of clothing, white cottages atop green hills, and fragrances that awaken the dream of romance.

Once again sea imagery pervades many of the poems, as the emblem of oblivion. The eternal movement of the waves inspires Onofri to compose songs of sweet surrender before the titanic forces of nature. A poem such as "I naviganti" (The Sailors) brings to mind Charles-Pierre Baudelaire's "Le Voyage" (1857) and Arthur Rimbaud's "Le Bateau ivre" (The Drunken Boat, 1871): Baudelaire looks back on a sea voyage to issue a challenge to plunge to the depths of an abyss to discover the unknown, while Rimbaud imagines an intoxicatingly wild journey beyond the bounds of civilization. Onofri's sailors are on a poetic adventure searching for a remote archipelago that will take them back to the glories of the Age of Gold in a lost Eden where the lotus invites forgetfulness of homeland and the Dionysiac dance renews the chorus of fatal tragedy. Although the sea can wash over the ship in eternal closure, the linking motion of the rising and falling waves makes possible a renascence of hope for the languishing souls of life's voyagers.

Adoration of women also provides a leitmotiv for *Canti delle oasi*. A frank sensuality, not D'Annunzio's panic sensuality, characterizes the twelfth solar poem, addressed to Silvia and taking delight in the naked display of her carnal beauty at the time of nature's reawakening and blossoming in the spring. Rather than being an invitation to pure eroticism, the poems to the beloved are a magical re-creation of shared moments of passion though the lovers are fated for separation. As in Stéphane Mallarmé's sonnet "Tristesse d'Eté" (Summer Sadness, 1885), the lakeland poems of Onofri intensify the languor and veiled sorrow of consummated desire, where

all that remains is a dreamlike memory of reciprocated emotions. Along with the symbol of the lady as beloved object of sensual yearning there also occurs the image of the woman as sister, particularly in the poem "A mia sorella non nata" (To My Unborn Sister), where the speaker sees her as the redeeming figure of purity. To all the poisonous tumult of his mind and body she alone can offer peace and restoration, but that dream is in vain since his destiny is to remain cut off from the luminous celestial sphere that she occupies in her innocence. A sense of loss then comes to prevail as he acknowledges the impossibility of his salvation. In both types of poems on the feminine presence an atmosphere of worship predominates to express the impulse to love and admiration.

Since neither the memory of carnal loveliness nor the symbol of female purity can rescue the poet from imprisoning weaknesses of will, the section of prayers ("Momenti varii") communicates his yearning to know a higher plane of existence than this life of travail. The invocation, "Per confondersi con la natura" (To Be Fused with Nature), speaks of his longing to break the narrow bonds in the dark lair of his present condition and to be fused into the immense life of nature. He is prepared to leave behind every semblance of human form to be reborn in a branch trembling in the morning breeze. Onofri has here reached a stage in his poetic career in which he has clearly defined a spiritual goal. The rest of his life was to be spent in discovering the means to achieve that mystical fusion with maternal nature.

From 1910 to 1916 Onofri became actively involved in writing for avant-garde journals and popular periodicals. He founded with Umberto Fracchia the journal *Lirica*, which ran from January 1912 to the end of 1913 and featured writings by Antonio Baldini and Vincenzo Cardarelli, among the promising young authors of the day. Though an extremely reserved person with a distaste for the petty politics of literary and artistic coteries, Onofri still decided to speak out on the controversies raging among creative Italians, including the call to arms of the futurists to demolish all the monuments of Italian art in order to bring the nation into the dynamic spirit of modern times, and the challenges of form and content offered by French symbolists and their immediate followers. According to Onofri a critic had to be a poet who would take up a literary work not as a finished piece but as a process in the making. Throughout 1913 the periodical *Il Popolo Romano* published reviews of his on Mallarmé, D'Annunzio as journalist, Walter Pater, Paul Claudel, André Gide, and Gustave Flaubert. Onofri was particularly drawn to the journal *La Voce* under the directorship of Giuseppe De Robertis from December 1914 to December 1916. For *La Voce* he produced in spring and summer of 1916 a series of essays on Pascoli's poetic volume *Myricae* (Tamerisks, 1891) that would eventually be gathered together in 1953 as *Letture poetiche del Pascoli* (Poetic Readings of Pascoli); Onofri analyzed every single poem as he expressed his admiration for Pascoli for being the first to free Italian poetry from narrow academic norms. At the time of these critical and editorial activities Onofri also succeeded in publishing the excessively D'Annunzian narrative *Disamore* (Mislove, 1912) and a thoroughly revised version of *Liriche* in 1914.

Scattered poems of Onofri's kept appearing during this time on the pages of *Nuova Antologia*, *Lirica*, and *La Voce*. Inspired by the book *Les grands initiés* (1901), by Edouard Schuré, he became fascinated with the destinies of boldly innovative individuals, such as Prometheus and Rama, who transcended their original situations to acquire divine attributes. His lengthy terza-rima poem "Prométeo" (*Nuova Antologia*, 7 June 1910) has three divisions that each end in a different one-line coda: part 1 includes dawn reflections on the mountain where Prometheus is chained and the arrival of the eagle to devour his heart (not the liver, as Onofri prefers the more "noble" organ); part 2 is the memory of a confrontation with Zeus; in part 3 night thoughts occur as the heart grows back. Even in his imprisonment (a metaphor for the human condition) Prometheus, the son of a Titan, is a superior being whose cries echo like thunder. The central section recalls a visit from Zeus, who offered to unchain Prometheus and allow him to enter Olympus. But the Titan refused the offer of clemency from a divinity he considered a false god whose bestial passions resembled the brute drives of wild animals. Prometheus was seeking a sublimely numinous identity for himself and the humans who had benefited from his gift of fire. His torture would serve as a rite of purification from every base instinct. By analogy, according to Onofri, humans should emulate his self-surpassing example to turn the banishment and suffering of their earthly existence into a time of preparation to be elevated to godliness.

Onofri's mythopoetic work continued with a poem in quatrains, "La morte di Rama" (Rama's Death, *Nuova Antologia*, 16 June 1911), whose title character is the epic hero, priest-king, warrior, and guardian of peace seen at the moment of dying after having completed his life's mission of leading the Celtic tribes to their promised land in the Indus River Valley of India. With death comes the lifting of the veil of illusion. Rama's future is to participate in the divinity of Vishnu, the preserver god who provides for the welfare of humankind by vanquishing evil, as Rama did in opposing the human immolations practiced by the Druidic priesthood of his homeland, from which he delivered his people. Twice in this poem Onofri uses a term that will be of paramount importance for his later anthroposophic verses: *verbo* (the supreme word), as in line 8—"Verbo santo" (holy word)—and line 69—"Verbo solare" (the word of solar brilliance). All persons must heed the sacred word to free themselves of destructive inclinations and enter the promised land of the divineness that dwells within them. This feeling for life as a sacrifice for future deification is open not only to a mythic Titan rebel like Prometheus or a legendary leader like Rama but to every self-transcending individual, such as Michelangelo, as expressed in the free-verse poem "Preghiera nella Cappella Sistina" (Prayer in the Sistine Chapel, *Lirica*, February 1912), where the verses run from seven to seventeen syllables as the intensity of this hymn to creativity swells to seraphic rapture. Michelangelo appears as a clairvoyant whose paintings reveal messages of spiritual redemption. In these poems to Prometheus, Rama, and Michelangelo, Onofri goes beyond the glory-seeking heroism of his earliest verses, as is evident from a comparison with the scene in the Sistine Chapel in D'Annunzio's *Laus vitae*, where the paintings serve to inspire the poetic narrator in his resolve to be a superhuman hero of domineering greatness. Onofri's trinity sacrificed themselves so that all of humanity might recognize and achieve the divinity that was inherent in them.

Already Onofri's poems of his middle period were beginning to show a desire to break from the mold of traditional meter and rhyme. He had before him the example of the French symbolists and *vers-libristes*, such as Jules Laforgue. In April 1912 Onofri took a critical position with the essay "La libertá del verso," in his journal *Lirica*, where he declared that technique is not an aesthetic fact in and for itself since a work of art contains its own laws and raison d'être. The controversy over free verse had started in Italy with Giampietro Lucini's *Ragion poetica e programma del verso libero* (Poetic Doctrine and the Program for Free Verse, 1908) and continued with the arguments of the futurist leader Filippo Tommaso Marinetti, who eventually rejected free verse for *parole in libertà* (words free of syntactic rules of order). For Onofri every verse was perfectly free as it responded like music to the intrinsic expression of an inner motivation. Poetic form as meter, stanza, and outer structure, such as a sonnet or canzone, had to find justification from the writer's inspiration because the true poet created lyrically. Following Mallarmé's beliefs on pure poetry, Onofri affirmed that every verse arose as a rhythmical and expressive unity and not as the result of academic norms. Onofri's lyrical principle recognized the melodious soul of poetic emotion and expression. According to him verse forms such as tercets and hendecasyllables had to be destroyed consciously in order to be reconstituted spontaneously as poetic expressions; artistic discipline still prevailed with free verse, not imposed externally but as imaginative lyrical patterning.

Like most of the literary theorists of that period, Onofri was also attempting to determine the exact nature of poetic expression, whether in free verse or traditional forms. Many Italian critics agreed with the observation of Edgar Allan Poe that the only genuine poem had to be brief, dismissing lengthy poems such as ancient epics as collections of intense moments of inspiration bolstered by nonpoetic structural material. That minimalist attitude also found expression in the aesthetic philosopher Benedetto Croce's distinction between poetry and nonpoetry, reducing authentic poetry to instants of flashing intuition. Onofri joined the minimalists of *La Voce* with an essay published there on 15 June 1915, "Tendenze" (Tendencies), where he upheld the idea of a poetry of pure images unconnected with each other. He called for an absolutely free type of poetry that could take lyric flight. Such poetic expression would lose that pompous solemnity that in the past smothered inspiration. At a given moment and in a given way true poetry would arise as the total creation of the world. A poet would exist as the agent of creative activity, in a perpetual becoming that is opened toward the chaos of life, which could inspire him with the aesthetic emotion of the supreme word (*verbo*). This poetry of in-

tensely creative moments would no longer require verse meter or strophic structuring. Following the model of the Italian translation of Rimbaud's *Illuminations* (1886) by the futurist Ardengo Soffici in 1911, Onofri in "Tendenze" was basically arguing for a poetry in the form of prose fragments.

Onofri was also facing a personal crisis of creative disintegration. Unlike many of his contemporaries at the outbreak of World War I, he did not call for Italy's entry into the hostilities, since he recognized the disastrous consequences of such a course of action. After Italy declared war on the central powers, Onofri took a clerical position with the Italian Red Cross and remained in that capacity for the rest of his life. The period of the war years was one of agonizing soul-searching for him, as he attempted to discover a poetic mode that would be a liberating experience away from the destructive circumstances of the present world situation. In his quest for a purifying vision, he recalled how Rimbaud had demanded the hallucination of the word, and in *Orchestrine* (Little Orchestras, 1917) Onofri presents brief prose fragments infused with hallucinatory spirit, which exhibit the explosive energy of neutrinos, as described in physics, moving in free flight. The centrifugal movement of these poetic monads, some as brief as a single line, results from a technique of impressionism aimed at presenting cosmic visions. In place of harmonious organization are flashing insights of hidden realities, as in "Vendemmia" (Vintage), "Cattedrale" (Cathedral), "Scrittoio" (Desk), "Animali," "Campagna" (Countryside), "Sera sul fiume" (Evening on the River), and "Settembre." With its very title, this work abandons the vast symphonic structure of a volume such as *Canti delle oasi* but retains the verbal instrumentation of word-music.

A poem such as "Tramonto" (Sunset) works by analogy, associating the visual image of buildings in the winter sunset with the metallic quality of the coppery color reflected on them as their slanting cornices shine like lowered lances in the crystal-clear cold of the air; Onofri forces readers to behold novel formations of imagery that represent the waning of the inanimate into a timeless transparency. A scene such as that in "Tramonto" suggests the broken and reconstituted facets of cubist paintings. Across the seemingly chaotic succession of coruscating passages there emerge certain basic themes: lost childhood; the vulgarization of modern industrial society (an attitude that places Onofri in direct opposition to the futurists); and nature struggling to retain its lyrical beauty. With the unchecked spread of cities, nature has been grotesquely mechanized and rendered artificial, like cardboard and papier-mâché assemblages. The deformation of a polluted world compelled Onofri to produce deadened still-life visions that often read like parodies ("the electric stove of the sunset"), which belie his alienation. At times Onofri takes refuge in an eroticism where sexual desire is reduced to crude animal hunger (as in "Animali"). But along with the verbal violence of bestial desire, love can lead away from alienation, as seen in "Mattino d'Orvieto" (Morning in Orvieto), where the radiant vision of a smiling blond awakens the narrator and stirs a restoring sense of marvel. From *Orchestrine* with its various nonmusical concerts, Onofri had to find a way back to spiritual recovery.

Marriage in 1916 to Bice Sinibaldi and the subsequent birth of two sons, Fabrizio and Giorgio, did restore Onofri to serenity. He almost totally withdrew from active participation in literary controversies. His sole period of writing full-time for a journal occurred for a few months in 1922 with reviews and articles for the Roman *Le Cronache d'Italia*. By 1921 he had issued a volume that marked his reconciliation with the world of lyrical inspiration: *Arioso* (Airy), a collection of verse and prose fragments transfused with the airy lightness of regained harmony of soul. Titles such as "Alba" (Dawn), "Arabesco," "Una farfalla" (A Butterfly), and "Nel bosco" (In the Woods) might at first cause one to think of the distorted visions of the preceding volume, but a sense of relief immediately transpires in the poems. Nearly narrative prose fragments alternate with free-verse poems modeled after the brief lines of Claudel's poetry. Pictures of loving domestic life describe maternal devotion and the spontaneous joy of infants in a world they are discovering for the first time. The springtime awakening of March resembles a child capriciously smiling after a time of tears. A memory of the narrator's childhood delight on finishing school in June as if overcoming an obstacle (in "L'Ostacolo") makes him think of a tiny seed buried in the dark ground but struggling to draw nourishment from that obstructing soil until the day the plant can push itself to the surface and enjoy the warmth of sunlight. Such is the spirit of personal and cosmic renewal that suffuses the volume. Toward the close, in "Salmo di Primavera" (Springtime Psalm), religious mysti-

cism reaffirms the spirituality of the universe: the first melodies of spring proclaim the miracle of rebirth.

In an effort to fashion a poetry of ecstatic contemplation, Onofri turned to the music of Richard Wagner for inspiration. After his death in 1883 Wagner had become a cult figure among avant-garde artists. The French journal *La Revue Wagnérienne* published on 8 January 1886 an issue of sonnets by eight different poets paying homage to the German composer, including Mallarmé and Paul Verlaine. Mallarmé called Wagner a god radiating a sacredness. In his *Letter on Music* (1858) Wagner had stated that poetry should substitute for the conventional meaning of words and return language to its primeval and sensual signification. D'Annunzio also fell under Wagner's sway, writing in the preface to his novel *Il trionfo della morte* (The Triumph of Death, 1894) that he wanted to accomplish the mimetic re-creation of natural sensations through a musical language that would be orchestrated like a Wagnerian music drama. The poetry of nocturnal mystery and the *Liebestod* (Love-death) in *Tristan und Isolde* (1857-1859) became the subject of Onofri's study *Il Tristano di Riccardo Wagner* (1924), where he looks to the composer to define poetic musicality. In his introduction to the book, Onofri distinguishes two spiritual traditions: the paganizing cult of Johann Joachim Winckelmann and Johann Wolfgang von Goethe as opposed to the romantic Christianity running from Novalis to Wagner. Unlike Friedrich Nietzsche, Onofri did not regard *Parsifal* (1882) as a betrayal of the spirit of tragedy but as the natural crowning glory of redemptive power as realized by Wagner at the end of his career. For Onofri the poetics to be learned from Wagner was a lyricism that would be the fusion of music with the sublime emotions of death in life and life in death, as achieved in *Tristan und Isolde*. Onofri interpreted Tristan's fate in Christian terms as the passionate yearning for the afterlife. From Wagner also came the technique of the leitmotiv, which would permeate the final cycle of Onofri's anthroposophic poems.

Along with Wagner as a source of mystical and lyrical inspiration, Onofri sought in the writings of Rudolf Steiner the spiritual solace to give his poetry a transcendent direction. Steiner, first the leader of the German section of the Theosophical Society and later founder of the International Anthroposophic Society, expressed in books such as *Christianity as Mystical Fact* (1902)

Drawing of Onofri by L. Cecchi-Pieraccini (from Dizionario universale della letteratura contemporanea, *volume 3, edited by Arnoldo Mondadori, 1961)*

his belief that all artistic creation manifested the cosmic activity of the human soul-life to which every individual was destined. Humankind would be the meeting point for all the forces of the universe as people came to recognize the Christ-principle in their souls. Italian interest in Steiner's views came about partly because of his commentary on the Gospel of St. John, which exerted a major influence on spiritual reawakening in the first two decades of the twentieth century by concentrating on the Logos (the word, *verbo*) that was made incarnate. Beginning in 1918 Onofri frequented the Roman salon of Emmelina de Renzis, the first translator in Italian of Steiner's religious writings. Onofri's longtime interest in the relationship between human life and plant life found agreement in Steiner, who asserted an unbroken evolutionary line across the mineral, plant, and animal realms to culminate in the triumph of the spiritual element in the cos-

mos. Nature would be redeemed through the activity of persons who acknowledged the world's reality as development toward the divine. Onofri felt he was discovering in Steiner's theories the way to eventual spiritual liberation, the means to escape that dark cavern of materiality that had figured in his earliest poems. He came to see religion as a dynamic process revealing the unity of all things and creatures. He accepted Steiner's evolutionary view of the movement from matter to pure spirituality: physical body, ethereal body, astral body, ego, spiritual self, vital spirit, and the man-spirit. An essential part of the Steinerian doctrine was belief in reincarnation, since humans ascended in stages of succeeding incarnations until the time of reawakening to the spiritual world as the one true world. For Onofri the mediator of the entire cycle leading humans back to the redeeming light of the word was the cosmic Christ.

Steiner's influence led Onofri to attempt a theory of art as spiritual activity in the treatise *Nuovo rinascimento come arte dell'Io* (The New Renascence as Art of the Ego, 1925). Premodern art, as in the *Odyssey* and the *Divine Comedy*, served as a channel between God and humankind, where poets such as Homer and Dante drew external inspiration from the culture of their respective eras. Modern art must be self-conscious, and the poet must find in himself a divine essence without relying on exterior cultural tradition in order to know the joining of the physical world with the spiritual realm. The activity of the modern poet must culminate in purification and the soul's liberation. Onofri disagrees with Rimbaud's position in the *Lettre du voyant* (The Seer's Letter, 1871), which declares that the poet becomes a seer through an intense disordering of all his senses. Instead, Onofri asserts that in place of the irrational as the essence of art an ultrarational element should arise from the inner consciousness. A poet could act as seer by creating a literature of images revealing the spiritual reality of the cosmos; poetic language would function like a magical formula to evoke the sacred essence of the world. Poets must work through the magic of their language to uncover divine mysteries. The poet's task would be an act of love toward humankind and the entire physical universe of plants and animals. All of Onofri's poetical writings in the final phase of his career indeed arise from that loving gesture to bring others to spiritual liberation.

Already in 1924 he had published his first volume of anthroposophic revelations: *Le trombe d'argento* (Silver Trumpets), a series of rhythmic prose passages resounding like thunder blasts. Onofri's apocalyptic message assumes the tones of biblical rhetoric, for, by evoking the word of God, language becomes a divine sword to break open the prison of earthly life to free humankind for their flight to heaven. A tremor of redemption pervades this text of Steinerian inspiration as it calls readers to the portals of mystical elation. A nearly Manichaean dualism characterizes the volume's descriptions of the battle between good (heaven, sun, dawn, angels, butterflies, flames) and evil (darkness, night, lair, cocoon, cold, desert), leading to the soul's victorious ascension to celestial spheres. Earthly love appears as a manifestation of an earlier existence when souls were united in a single thought of heavenly glory. Onofri's symbolism of the sea as guardian of the memory of previous ages coincides in *Le trombe d'argento* with Steiner's reworking of the myths of Atlantis and Lemuria to create a cataclysmic vision of the destruction by flood and fire of those two ancient kingdoms, as a necessary stage in the cycles moving toward the triumph of the immaterial world. Onofri echoes Rimbaud's *Lettre du voyant* in a section entitled "Io è un altro" (The "I" Is Another), except that here humanity has reached the anxious moment of the encounter with the celestial "I" of the universe. As beggars of the spirit people must turn in their poverty of soul to Christ's redemptive charity. Many of the brief passages read like intense charismatic sermons, such as the rapturous "Salmo di Primavera" (Psalm of Spring), where springtime figures as the earth's rite of renewal for an eternal season, so that in the greening of trees all might be reborn to divine light. But since eloquence does not always arise from authentic poetic inspiration, Onofri's monotonously ecstatic and repetitious sermonettes only occasionally succeed in achieving verbal radiance and mystic enlightenment.

Steinerian and Wagnerian strains come together in Onofri's final, massive project: the six-volume cycle, nearly twenty thousand verses, of *Terrestrità del sole* (Terrestriality of the Sun). The volumes run in the following manner: *Terrestrità del sole* (1927) is the epic of heavenly light; *Vincere il drago!* (Conquering the Dragon!, 1928) concerns the abnegation required to overcome the forces of evil preventing one from attaining one's spiritual destiny; *Zolla ritorna cosmo* (A Clod of Soil Comes Back as the Universe, 1930) reveals how Christ's blood will redeem the very soil to

make it an element of the divine world; *Suoni del Gral* (Sounds of the Grail, 1932) addresses the new knights of the Holy Grail, who in responding to the melodies of Wagner's *Parsifal* will uncover the mystery of the Resurrection; *Aprirsi fiore* (The Flower's Opening, 1935) is on spiritual rebirth through divine grace; and *Simili a melodie rapprese in mondo* (Like Melodies Crystallized in the World, 1929) concerns the glories of a harmonious universe. Actually this final volume is the last section of *Aprirsi fiore* that Onofri's widow and closest friends managed to publish soon after his death. In Onofri's lifetime only the first two volumes were published.

Particularly significant in this project is his return to traditional meters and strophic forms such as the sonnet, with frequent use of rhyme. In *Simili a melodie rapprese in mondo* there are thirty-three poems in blank-verse hendecasyllables. Like other modern poets, such as Ungaretti a few decades later, Onofri moved from experimentalism to the discipline of regular meter and stanza structure, to communicate in rigorous fashion his message of Christian pantheism. Direct metaphors, rather than similes expressed with the term *come* (as, like), prevail to create an impression of concreteness for the heavenly visions. Assuming the role of priest and prophet, Onofri employs words as agents of revelation, coining new terms, such as *smiracola* (unmakes miracles); combining words, as in *sempre-inizio* (always-beginning), *ultra-orchestrale*, and *sorgere-estasi* (arising-ecstasy); and introducing foreign terms such as *gulf-stream*. Enjambment often occurs to represent the dynamism of the solar process in defeating darkness for the victory of divine light. One influence of futurism is the use of the verb in the infinitive form, as revelation seems to require asyntactical construction. Onofri also develops a modern *dolce stilnovo* (sweet new style) around the eternal feminine, which symbolizes an unending springtime of hope, a magical presence, and the source of human spirituality, as he associates the individual loving woman with universal forces such as the sea, heavens, and fertile plains. Just as Steiner had intended in the art form of eurythmy, intended to create a "visible speech" in dance and mime, so Onofri designs a "visible music" for the omnipotent word to resound like a Wagnerian music drama. To convey the sense of totality of the entire cycle of volumes, the individual poems do not bear titles but merely numbers, like one musical opus playing after another. At their weakest the six texts of

Terrestrità del sole fall into rhetorical bombast in the attempt to persuade rather than enchant. But again and again the passages soar to sublime heights to express religious faith as empowering experience.

Onofri's death took place on Christmas Day, 1928. His subsequent critical fortune has been one of a poet manqué who permitted the promise of his early verse to be led astray into anthroposophic propaganda, when otherwise he might have been ranked with the great hermetic poets Giuseppe Ungaretti and Eugenio Montale. The critic Franco Lanza has divided Onofri's writings into two periods: the first ending with *Orchestrine* and the second closing with the *Terrestrità* cycle, with *Arioso* being a work of transition. On close examination his work falls into three stages: the early collections through *Canti delle oasi*; the years of critical essays and experimental poems in avantgarde reviews, culminating with the crisis of *Orchestrine*; and the time of poetic and spiritual reintegration starting with *Arioso* and concluding with the six-volume cycle. But continuities in theme and diction can be seen in all of his writing. Unfortunately most of his works after 1921 are available only in editions that are difficult to obtain. Although Onofri, like most of the poets of his generation, was open to the influence of French symbolists and decadents, literary critics in France have failed to take serious notice of his writings. Among critics in the English language the sole, scant appreciation of Onofri has been for him as a writer of prose-poem fragments. But through the comprehensive studies of recent Italian writers, such as Susetta Salucci, Franco Lanza, and Anna Dolfi, the works of Arturo Onofri are beginning to receive the proper evaluation they deserve for their originality and enduring importance.

Biography:

Anna Dolfi, *Arturo Onofri* (Florence: Nuova Italia, 1976).

References:

Luciano Anceschi, *Lirici nuovi* (Milan: Mursia, 1964), pp. 135-152;

Carlo Bo, "Arturo Onofri," in *Storia della letteratura italiana: Il Novecento*, 9 volumes (Milan: Garzanti, 1969), IX: 354-359;

Arnaldo Bocelli, "Arturo Onofri," in *Letteratura italiana: I contemporanei*, 6 volumes edited by Gianni Grana (Milan: Marzorati, 1979), I: 691-705;

Rosanna Caira, "Motivi crepuscolari nella poesia di Onofri," *Galleria*, 26 (January 1976): 51-62;

Emilio Cecchi, ed., *Letteratura italiana del Novecento*, 2 volumes (Milan: Mondadori, 1972), II: 710-726;

Mario Fittoni, *La visione del mondo di Arturo Onofri* (Florence: D'Anna, 1973);

Francesco Flora, *La poesia ermetica* (Bari, Italy: Laterza, 1936);

Flora, *Saggi di poetica moderna* (Messina, Italy: D'Amico, 1949), pp. 187-197;

Ruggero Jacobbi, "Per un ritratto di Onofri," *Forum Italicum*, 10 (Spring 1976): 178-187;

Franco Lanza, *Arturo Onofri* (Milan: Mursia, 1973);

Giorgio Luti, ed., "Arturo Onofri," in his *Poeti italiani del Novecento* (Rome: NIS, 1985), pp. 154-157;

Adele Luzzatto, *Rimbaud, Onofri, Valéry* (Genoa: Emiliano degli Orfini, 1933);

Gaetano Mariani, *Poesia e tecnica nella lirica del Novecento* (Padua, Italy: Liviana, 1958), pp. 196-200;

Giorgio Petrocchi, *Poesia e tecnica narrativa* (Milan: Mursia, 1962), pp. 50-59;

Gianni Pozzi, *La poesia italiana del Novecento* (Turin: Einaudi, 1965), pp. 96-104;

Silvio Ramat, *L'ermetismo* (Florence: Nuova Italia, 1969);

Ramat, "La poesia di Onofri equivalente simbolico dell'infinito," in *Storia della poesia italiana del Novecento* (Milan: Mursia, 1976), pp. 242-253;

Susetta Salucci, *Arturo Onofri* (Florence: Nuova Italia, 1972);

Donato Valli, "Il misticismo della forma: il primo Onofri," in his *Anarchia e misticismo nella poesia italiana del primo Novecento* (Lecce, Italy: Milella, 1973), pp. 143-235;

Alfio Vecchio, "Arturo Onofri nella critica recente," *Cultura e Scuola*, 24 (January 1985): 49-60.

Aldo Palazzeschi
(2 February 1885 - 8 August 1974)

Anthony Julian Tamburri
Purdue University

BOOKS: *I cavalli bianchi* (Florence: Cesare Blanc, 1905);

Lanterna (Florence: Aldino, 1907);

:riflessi (Florence: Cesare Blanc, 1908);

Poemi (Florence: Cesare Blanc, 1909); enlarged as *Poesie* (Florence: Vallecchi, 1925; enlarged edition, Milan: Preda, 1930; enlarged again, Milan: Mondadori, 1971);

L'Incendiario; Col rapporto sulla vittoria futurista di Trieste (Milan: Futuriste di "Poesia," 1910); revised as *L'Incendiario* (Milan: Futuriste di "Poesia," 1913);

Il codice di Perelà: Romanzo futurista (Milan: Futuriste di "Poesia," 1911); revised as *Perelà, uomo di fumo* (Florence: Vallecchi, 1954); translated by Peter M. Riccio as *Perelà, the Man of Smoke* (New York: Vanni, 1936);

Due imperi . . . mancati (Florence: Vallecchi, 1920);

Il re bello (Florence: Vallecchi, 1921);

La Piramide: Scherzo di cattivo genere e fuor di luogo (Florence: Vallecchi, 1926);

Stampe dell'800 (Milan-Rome: Treves-Treccani-Tumminelli, 1932; enlarged edition, Florence: Vallecchi, 1957);

Sorelle Materassi (Florence: Vallecchi, 1934, enlarged, 1943); translated by Angus Davidson as *The Sisters Materassi* (Garden City, N.Y.: Doubleday, 1953); also published as *Materassi Sisters* (London: Secker & Warburg, 1953);

Il palio dei buffi (Florence: Vallecchi, 1937);

Romanzi straordinari (Florence: Vallecchi, 1943);

Nell'aria di Parigi (Rome: Cultura Moderna, 1945);

Tre imperi . . . mancati (Florence: Vallecchi, 1945);

Difetti 1905 (Milan: Garzanti, 1947);

I fratelli Cuccoli (Florence: Vallecchi, 1948);

Bestie del 900 (Florence: Vallecchi, 1951);

Roma (Florence: Vallecchi, 1953); translated by Mihaly Csikszentmihalyi (Chicago: Regnery, 1965);

Viaggio sentimentale (Milan: All'Insegna del Pesce d'Oro/Scheiwiller, 1955);

Scherzi di gioventù (Milan: Ricciardi, 1956);

Tutte le novelle (Milan: Mondadori, 1957);

Opere giovanili (Milan: Mondadori, 1958);

Vita militare (Padova, Italy: Rebellato, 1959);

I romanzi della maturità (Milan: Mondadori, 1960);

Il piacere della memoria (Milan: Mondadori, 1964);

Schizzi italofrancesi (Milan: All'Insegna del Pesce d'Oro/Scheiwiller, 1966);

Il buffo integrale (Milan: Mondadori, 1966);

Ieri oggi e . . . non domani (Florence: Vallecchi, 1967);

Il Doge (Milan: Mondadori, 1967);

Cuor mio (Milan: Mondadori, 1968);

Stefanino (Milan: Mondadori, 1969);

La passeggiata (Milan: M'arte, 1971);

Storia di un'amicizia (Milan: Mondadori, 1971);

Via delle cento stelle (Milan: Mondadori, 1972);

Piazza della libertà e altre poesie (Milan: M'arte, 1977);

Sotto il magico orologio (Lecce, Italy: Manni, 1987);

Interrogatorio della contessa Maria (Milan: Mondadori, 1988).

OTHER: *Le piu belle pagine di Giuseppe Giusti*, edited by Palazzeschi (Milan: Treves, 1922);

Alphonse Daudet, *Tartarino*, translated by Palazzeschi (Milan: Mondadori, 1932);

Francesco Donini, *Vita e poesia di Sergio Corazzini*, introduction by Palazzeschi (Turin: De Silva, 1949);

G. Tibalducci, *I prati dell'oltre*, preface by Palazzeschi (Bologna: Cappelli, 1951);

F. T. Marinetti, *Teoria e invenzione futurista*, preface by Palazzeschi (Milan: Mondadori, 1968);

Gianfranco Bruno, ed., *L'opera completa di Boccioni*, preface by Palazzeschi (Milan: Rizzoli, 1969).

SELECTED PERIODICAL PUBLICATIONS—
UNCOLLECTED: "Il controdolore, manifesto futurista," *Lacerba*, 2 (15 January 1914): 17-21;

Aldo Palazzeschi

"Futurismo e Marinettismo," by Palazzeschi, Giovanni Papini, and Ardengo Soffici, *Lacerba*, 3 (14 February 1915): 49-51;

"Marinettismo," *Lacerba*, 3 (13 March 1915): 88;

"Primavera," *Lacerba*, 3 (20 March 1915): 93-95;

"Piazza della libertà," *Caffè*, 2 (June 1972): 3-7;

"Goliardica," *Verri*, 5 (March 1974): 14-17;

"Gente," *Galleria*, 2-4 (March-August 1974): 59;

"I contrari," "Ipocrisia," and "La Poesia," *Gradiva*, new series 3, no. 4 (1986): 47-61;

"Poesia," *Gradiva*, new series 4, no. 1 (1987): 89.

Aldo Palazzeschi (nom de plume of Aldo Giurlani) began his literary career in search of a new mode of literary expression. Two literary/art movements, *crepuscolarismo* (twilight poetry) and *futurismo*, provided the tolerant atmosphere necessary for experimentation and innovation. *Crepuscolarismo* served chiefly as a springboard from which Palazzeschi could desacralize contemporary, social, and literary canons through irony.

Futurismo, in turn, allowed him to continue his battle against literary conventions and eventually develop his own mode of poetic and prose expression.

Born on 2 February 1885 in Florence into a well-respected, middle-class family, Palazzeschi was the son of Alberto and Amalia Martinelli Guirlani, who owned and operated a clothing store together. Palazzeschi earned a diploma in accounting in 1902. He divided part of his youth between Florence and Paris, where he first came into contact with the European avant-garde. Never intending to follow in his father's footsteps as a businessman, Palazzeschi dedicated himself to acting, but, soon after, he turned to literature. His early years of verse writing constitute a difficult period to categorize. For the most part, it was a time of experimentation that eventually led him to the poetics of the *saltimbanco/ incendiario* (clown/arsonist). Certain *crepuscolare* motifs are nonetheless present in Palazzeschi's early poetry, as one may also find expressions of strong personal feelings. Yet a sense of dejection or sadness, or of a longing for the return of happier times, is virtually nonexistent. *Experimentation* thus seems a better term for his early poetry; he selected what appeared the best of various methods and styles, and he mixed the many themes and images according to their efficacy and applicability to the realization of his own poetic invention and utopianism. All this is an obvious sign of the times—proof of a crisis; a sense of alienation and peculiarity on the part of the modern individual—which for Palazzeschi meant the possibility to change and deviate from the norm, to seek what he needed wherever he could find it.

"Chi sono?" (Who Am I?; in *Poemi*, 1909) is the first explicit manifestation in verse of Palazzeschi's *ars poetica*; it contains the imagistic foundation of his literary philosophy, found in *follìa* (folly), *malinconìa* (melancholy), *nostalgìa*, and the figure of the *saltimbanco*. The most important elements are *follìa* and the *saltimbanco*, recurring images throughout most of Palazzeschi's lyric production. While *malinconìa* and *nostalgìa* were fundamental to the poetry of the contemporary movement *crepuscolarismo*, in this poem they are parenthetically situated between *follìa* and the *saltimbanco*, two elements in concert with one another, and characteristic of the avant-garde. In Palazzeschi's poetry, the artist does not necessarily search for a remedy or solution (an absolute); instead, he emphasizes deviation. The clown becomes an instrument of upheaval so that the artist may turn the world upside down in order to show its absurdities, and eventually to rediscover and redefine old values. The *saltimbanco*, therefore, while keenly aware of himself and his situation, refutes the laws of society and of nature, thereby creating chaos from which to create his own world sui generis.

Palazzeschi's intent of questioning the status of art is implicit in the structure of the poem, which consists of a series of five questions, the first three of which are resolved negatively; each represents a different art form: poetry, painting, and music. The result is a refusal to accept the entire cultural inheritance at the beginning of the century. In fact, as did Sergio Corazzini and Guido Gozzano, Palazzeschi rids himself of the traditional label of poet. But in his case, he also downplays major components of the *crepuscolare* movement: *malinconìa* and *nostalgìa*. With this rejection Palazzeschi surpasses his contemporaries

in refuting tradition. In the place of introspection he introduces *follìa* as the end product of poetry. It is a folly manifested both thematically and stylistically: for folly implies nonsense and irrationality, and in light of all that had preceded Palazzeschi, his poetry could only be considered irrational and eccentric in meaning, and frivolous in style. Thus in "Chi sono?" Palazzeschi demonstrates his awareness of the change taking place in individual thought processes at the beginning of the twentieth century. The final two questions lead to the definition of his new role. In his fourth answer some have perceived an ambiguity: "lente / dinanzi al ... cuore / per farlo vedere alla gente" (lens / over my ... heart / to show it to the world). While it is true that an initial impression may be that of introspective poetry, it is also possible to consider the statement a prelude to his self-definition: a simple expression of candor as he bestows upon himself the label of *saltimbanco*. "Chi sono?" thus marks the resolution of his literary dilemma: away with the old in order to rebuild anew, thus leading to the upsetting of reality, and, specifically, Palazzeschi's break from social and cultural standardization.

Palazzeschi's move away from traditional verse, however, did not take place only after 1909; even his earliest compositions signal a turn in another direction. Among many, Georges Güntert considers him one of the authentic innovators and places Palazzeschi spiritually close to Luigi Pirandello. Regarding the tone and atmosphere of Palazzeschi's initial poetry, Güntert speaks in terms of a climate of weary monotony, a suspension of time frequent in poems of this period. The majority of these poems, especially those of *I cavalli bianchi* (The White Horses, 1905), appears devoid of any emotion, be it on the part of the poet-protagonist or the characters within. This suspension of time and emotion is rendered by the constant use of similar words and phrases. Thus any sense of emotional or physical dramaticity is lacking, actions and colors are mollified, and many times one is left with an image seemingly devoid of any inherent meaning. Such opacity or lack of communication is a technique Palazzeschi employed often and with great efficacy in many of his lyrical and prose compositions during these early years of his career. And while it is true that at this point the violent dynamics of the *incendiario* and the tomfoolery of the *saltimbanco* have yet to be developed, Palazzeschi is, nevertheless, already well on his way toward the acquisition of an *ars poetica* that de-

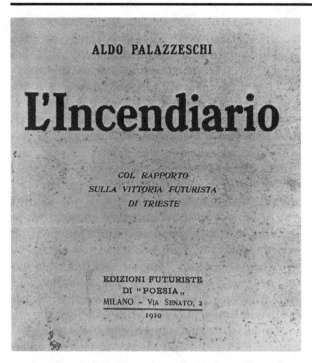

Cover for the collection of poetry that marked Palazzeschi's absolute break from conventional moral and aesthetic values

viates from the traditional canon.

The softened tone of this early poetry, due to its lack of dramaticity and its *monotonia*, anticipates the fixity of the metaphysical object, apparent not only in "I prati di Gesù" (Jesus' Meadows; in *Poemi*), as Piero Bigongiari has demonstrated, but also in earlier poems such as "Le fanciulle bianche" (The White Young Girls), "Ara Mara Amara," and "Oro doro odoro dodoro" (*I cavalli bianchi*). One finds simple, realistic images in enigmatic, inexplicable situations. In "Le fanciulle bianche," for example, if readers try to resolve the problem of whom or what the "gente" (people) or the "fanciulle bianche" represent, they find themselves hard-pressed for an answer. The same is also true for "Il passo de le Nazarene" (The Nazarenes' Walk; in *Lanterna*, 1907), which is constructed around a continuous to-and-fro of two groups of nuns.

These are just a few of the many poems Palazzeschi wrote during this period, poems that emanate an aura of ambiguity if not inscrutability, especially when the reader attempts to ground them interpretatively according to previously gathered intertextual knowledge as he is confronted with unfamiliar codes and images. Short scenes taken from reality are presented to the reader within a suspended state of time and action. It is precisely this state of animation that im-

plants an aura of inscrutability into many of these early compositions. They are common descriptions of normal events whose element of surprise lies in the fact that there is not any surprise. The poet simply presents the images, whereas it is the reader's task to form an impression. It is an efficacious attempt, and early realization, of negative, nonsense verse writing: an upheaval of tradition representative of the beginning of the twentieth century. In fact, with regard to Palazzeschi's later moment of conscious decision to move away from traditional poetics ("Chi sono?"), it is important to keep in mind that the notion of art in general at the turn of the century was questioned by many.

The crystallization of Palazzeschi's antiestablishment philosophy is ultimately realized with the inception and subsequent publication of *L'Incendiario* (1910), a contemptuous, rebellious stance against traditional values and mores. Nothing, in fact, is spared from his ridicule and sarcasm, which proves to be more pungent than ever before. The collection opens with the homonymous treatise in verse of his unorthodox philosophy, which encompasses both social and cultural aspects of life.

The *incendiario* figures as the poet's new messiah, whose task is to reeducate the "sciame insidioso / di piccoli vigliacchi" (insidious swarm / of little cowards) and "riscaldare / la gelida carcassa / di questo vecchio mondo" (warm up / the frozen carcass / of this old world). Consequently, the figure of the *homo dolens* (sad man), which had dominated much of the cultural scene to date, is replaced by the *homo ludens* (playful man). The metamorphosis on both a social and literary level culminates in this collection of poetry; more specifically in the poems "L'Incendiario" and "E lasciatemi divertire" (And let me enjoy myself). In the first poem Palazzeschi unveils the rudiments of his *ars poetica*. Accordingly the semantic aspect of verse writing is no longer the major element of poetic invention; the act itself takes on greater importance. The only sentiments implied are those of joy and laughter, at the expense of overstepping the boundaries of convention: "Àn tutte le cose la polizia, / anche la poesia" (Everything has a police force / even poetry). Thus, the *incendiario*, exemplar par excellence of Palazzeschi's new individual, "quando l'ànno interrogato, / à risposto ridendo / che brucia per divertimento" (when they interrogated him, / answered laughing / that he burns for fun). Again, the emphasis is placed on the act rather than the product thereof.

The *saltimbanco* now takes on characteristics of the *incendiario*. Thus, Palazzeschi's first steps away from tradition are now closer to completion as the incendiary quality adds to the realization of total diversion from tradition. And though there may seem to be moments of hesitation in accepting this new role—"un povero incendiario che non può bruciare, / ... / da povero incendiario mancato" (a poor incendiary that cannot burn, / ... / as a failed incendiary)—Palazzeschi can finally declare himself "poeta" and "incendiario da poesia" (an incendiary of poetry), but in a very particular sense:

Là sopra il mio banco ove nacque,
il mio libro, come benedizione
io brucio il primo esemplare,
e guardo avido quella fiamma,
e godo, e mi ravvivo,
e sento salirmi il calore alla testa
come se bruciasse il mio cervello.

(There over my desk where my book
was born, like a blessing
I burn the first copy,
and I look eager at that flame,
and I am delighted. And I revive,
and I feel the heat going to my head
as if my brain burned.)

The *incendiario* represents the lighthearted individuals capable of change and therefore enjoying life. Those instead who are incapable of change experience little joy and merriment as they are overshadowed by their fear. Precisely because *fuoco* (fire) represents destruction of the old (tradition) in order to build anew, metaphorically speaking it is the creation of a new type of poetry.

"E lasciatemi divertire" is Palazzeschi's explicit denouncement of traditional poetics. The opening stanza's nonsensical onomatopoeia clearly signals his break from tradition:

Tri tri tri
fru fru fru
ihu ihu ihu
uhi uhi uhi!
Il poeta si diverte,
pazzamente,
smisuratamente!
Non lo state a insolentire,
lasciatelo divertire
poveretto,

queste piccole corbellerie
sono il suo diletto.

(Tri Tri Tri
Fru fru fru
ihu ihu ihu
uhi uhi uhi!
The poet's having fun,
madly,
excessively!
Don't insult him so,
let him have his fun
poor thing,
these foolish little words
are his delight.)

Echoed here is a major element introduced in "Chi sono?": exaggerated, absurd, unbecoming conduct or action. Palazzeschi divests poetry of its honor and privileges, reducing it to mere "diletto [di] piccole corbellerie" (delight of silly little things); the poem thus becomes the realization of the commentary, as traditional poetry has lost all of its value and meaning for Palazzeschi. His only inheritance from the past is the "spazzatura / delle altre poesie" (rubbish-heap of other poems). Thus poetry is garbage, and, as is evident in "L'Incendiario," the act of writing verse itself has significance and not necessarily any logical, coherent message communicated therein.

Curiosity is aroused by a comparison between Palazzeschi's *ars poetica* and that of the futurists. In Palazzeschi's literary production one does not find the basic cult images of futurism: speed, the automobile, or the large metropolis, for example. Instead he concentrates much more on the individual and the ability to survive according to whim and fancy, while at the same time rejecting traditional codes and a logical thought process. Indeed Palazzeschi himself had proclaimed his adhesion to futurism in 1909 in a letter to Filippo Tommaso Marinetti. However, it is not far-fetched to read into his verses a hesitation at a total commitment to the futurist mode, both stylistically and philosophically, in light of the basic differences between the two poetics in question. Palazzeschi seems to denounce the standardization of an entire set of new rules espoused by Marinetti in his early manifestos. In the final stanza of "L'Incendiario" Palazzeschi concludes this literary treatise not with a sneering grin but a roaring laugh: "Ahahahahahah / Ahahahahahah / Ahahahahahah." Well aware of the cultural crisis evolving around him,

Poster advertising a concert and reading by futurists

Palazzeschi scorns and derides the seriousness so long associated with literature, all of which becomes threatened and challenged by a new generation of writers.

In 1913 Palazzeschi underscored his break from Italian poetic tradition in the poem "Addio" (Farewell; in *L'Incendiario*, revised edition). By 1914 he was completely independent, having also cut his ties with the futurists in a 28

April article in *La Voce*: "Da oggi in poi non ho più nulla a che fare con il movimento futurista. Se F. T. Marinetti si servisse del mio nome per il suo movimento lo farebbe abusivamente" (From today on I have nothing more to do with the futurist movement. If F. T. Marinetti were to use my name for his movement he would do so abusively). This break is also evident in his change of style in certain later poems. "Boccanera" (1915) is one of the most significant of this period. Palazzeschi reintroduces the *saltimbanco/incendiario*. However, while in the previous poems the fire figure conveys a strong, explicitly antisocial message, at this point he has evolved into a passive revolutionary no longer desirous of direct confrontation, leaving tomfoolery and merriment as the poet's only goal. Metaphorically speaking, such is the case with Boccanera the fire-eater, who no longer resembles the previous *incendiario*. More clownlike, he remains alone, similar to Palazzeschi with his new poetry, having now overstepped the boundaries of both traditional poetics and futurism: "M'ànno lasciato solo alla 4a stazione del *nulla*" (They abandoned me all alone at the 4th station of *nothingness*). The poem thus represents Palazzeschi's poetry; likewise, the protagonist Boccanera "tutta la vita à mangiato il fuoco" (all his life has eaten fire), just as Palazzeschi had informed much of his literary production with the fire motif. Finally, it is here that his *divertimento*—both amusement and deviation—finds its culmination. He has momentarily realized an ideal combination: the deformation of both theme (with nonsense) and style (with grammatical fragmentation). Having thus achieved it, Palazzeschi decided to still his poetic voice.

After a prolific period of poetic production from 1905 to 1915, Palazzeschi virtually retired from verse writing. In 1938 Palazzeschi's mother died; two years later his father succumbed to a long illness. Distraught by his losses—the only child, and of a significantly small extended family—Palazzeschi moved to Rome in 1941, where, except for vacations to Florence, Venice, and occasionally Paris, he spent the rest of his life. The only volume of new poetry to appear between 1915 and 1968 was *Viaggio sentimentale* (Sentimental Journey, 1955), a relatively unknown collection, much of which was later included in *Cuor mio* (My Heart, 1968).

In his preface to *Cuor mio* Palazzeschi spoke of a "nuovo abito" (new suit) for his poetry: "Per un lunghissimo periodo non scrissi più poesie . . . ; ci detti dentro a costruirmi una prosa, compito assai diverso e ben più laborioso di scrivere in versi, preparando alla mia poesia un nuovo abito" (for a very long time I didn't write poetry anymore . . . ; I applied myself to constructing a prose style, a task much different and much more laborious than writing in verse, while preparing for my poetry a new suit). This new *abito* consists of a much more subdued poetry, stylistically tending toward the prosaic and the matter-of-fact. For the most part, the shocking qualities of his earlier poetry are lacking: vulgarly described deformities are no longer employed; the pungent sarcasm and ridicule are all but nonexistent; and the highly animated dialogues of his earlier poetry have fallen by the wayside. One of the few salient resemblances in style is his use of free-verse form.

"Dove sono?" (Where Am I?), one of the most significant poems of *Cuor mio*, reiterates much of Palazzeschi's philosophy of *controdolore* (countergrief), which permeates his early literary production. It recalls various concepts of his early poetry and manifestos: the motifs of *follìa* and the *saltimbanco*; the emphasis he placed on *diversità dell'uomo* (human diversity) and the *gusto dell'opposto* (desire for opposites). Despite the enormous difference in length, "Dove sono?" proves to be a companion piece to "Chi sono?"; however, in "Dove sono?" the emphasis is directed toward the poet-protagonist's surroundings. Considering the world a giant stage upon which everyone is, or can be, both actor and spectator, Palazzeschi employs a technique similar to that of "Chi sono?" Then, he questioned his possible role as artist; now, he continuously questions his whereabouts. In "Chi sono?" the traditional cultural titles poet, painter, and musician were rejected and subsequently replaced by the artist-acrobat. In "Dove sono?" the societal institutions—church, school, courts, and jail—are cast aside and replaced by the theater, where the poet-protagonist admits to experiencing his "unica gioia" (only joy). His joy is nourished by a variety of human characteristics: the physical, cerebral, and emotional qualities of the individual, represented by the shows, subject matter, and feelings.

In a note in *Viaggio sentimentale* Palazzeschi referred to the eventual publication of *Cuor mio* as his *saluto*; more than a farewell, though, it is his retrospective appraisal and approval of a modus vivendi based on both *follìa* and *saggezza* (wisdom). The volume serves as a panegyric of his unorthodox philosophy of life, which always called for joy conquering grief, and instinct over reason.

These and other themes found in his early compositions permeate his final complete edition of poetry published in his lifetime, *Via delle cento stelle* (Street of a Hundred Stars, 1972). Notwithstanding the few moments of seemingly anguished spiritual crisis, a call for an active spiritual involvement is present throughout this collection, manifested primarily by the desire to experience opposing and divergent forces. "Insanabili contradizioni" (Incurable contradictions) recalls Palazzeschi's 1955 note, where he spoke of *follìa* and *saggezza*. Here he slightly alters the two into the oxymoron *saggezza-stoltezza* (wisdom-foolishness), the one quality a necessary complement of the other for comprising the whole. "Insanabili contradizioni" underscores this notion:

> Mi piace la gente *saggia*
> per la qual *l'ammirazione*
> è sconfinata
> da parte mia;
> non esente però
> da un vago e inesplicabile senso
> di *freddezza*, di *perplessità*,
> e non di rado di *malinconìa*.
> E al tempo stesso . . .
> . . . .
> mi piace la *stoltezza*,
> sì,
> trovo *adorabile* la gente *stolta*,
> e mi attira,
> perchè essa pure dà *sapore* e *colore* alla vita,
> provocando dentro a me
> *calore* e *allegria*.
>
> (I like *wise* people
> for whom *admiration*
> is unlimited
> on my part;
> not exempt however
> from a vague and inexplicable sense
> of *coldness*, of *perplexity*,
> and not rarely of *melancholy*.
> And at the same time . . .
> . . . .
> I like *foolishness*,
> yes,
> I find *foolish* people *adorable*,
> and they attract me,
> because they also give *gusto* and *color* to life,
> provoking within me
> *heat* and *happiness*.)

Thus, the seemingly contradictory *serietà-allegria* (seriousness-happiness), prevalent in his early compositions, is reiterated, in a slightly modified way, in *saggezza-follìa* (wisdom-folly). One finds a constant variation of the *controdolore* theme of *dolore-gioia* (grief-joy).

Palazzeschi's love of life celebrated a carpe diem theme, which modifies the enjoyment of pleasure for the moment to the enjoyment of all things at hand. It is a philosophy that reasserts the simultaneity and diversity of intellect and emotion while minimizing the validity of tradition and convention. It accentuates the present and affords the individual the privilege of singularity within a social structure that would otherwise demand conformity. With this collection Palazzeschi draws closer to the end of his long and prolific literary career, reflective of a way of life based on the dialectics of divergence and antagonism, maintaining his freedom and individuality as a craftsman and person.

Many of Palazzeschi's poems were the expression of his *spirito*. As a result, therefore, one can easily discern a continuum from "Chi sono?" and "E lasciatemi divertire" to the bulk of the compositions in *Via delle cento stelle*. In tracing a line of consistency and interdependency among Palazzeschi's poetic compositions, one also finds here a companion piece to the previous two interrogatives, "Chi sono?" and "Dove sono?"—in *Via delle cento stelle* Palazzeschi completes the final design of a triptych with the poem "Dove andavo?" (Where Was I Going?), which signals an end to a long and productive career:

> Dove andavo?
> Chi lo sa.
> A costruire qualche nuova menzogna?
> No,
> alla ricerca della verità.
>
> (Where was I going?
> Who knows.
> To build some new lie?
> No,
> in search of truth.)

Palazzeschi left the unpublished poem "Poesia" among his papers. It presents his notion of the institution of poetry: from its regal throne poetry had become a "soggetto da marciapiede / una bagascia / una squaldrina" (streetwalker / a floozy / a tart)—no longer in possession of "la parola che risuona" (the word that rings out). In the best of cases,

> Ti parla con l'eloquio da maestro di buon senso
> o ti dice delle cose per le quali

Drawing of Palazzeschi by Anselmo Bucci (from the 1930 edition of Palazzeschi's Poesie)

> non basta un professore
> di matematica a decifrarla.
>
> (It speaks to you with the teacher's style of good sense
> or it tells you things that
> a professor of mathematics
> could not decipher.)

While certain changes in style occurred over the years, Palazzeschi's disdain for social and literary norms and conventions sounded a continual ideological chord. His novel, *Stefanino* (1969), for example, exemplifies the Palazzeschian scornful derision of society already evident in *Il codice di Perelà* (Perelà's Code, 1911). Similar disdain in his early verse for both social and literary norms is also apparent in his later poetry: *Cuor mio* and *Via delle cento stelle*, for example, echo the content and tone of his early poems. His craft as poet and his philosophy of life can be defined by seemingly contradictory binomials: *serietà-allegria*; *saggezza-follìa*; *realtà-fantasia*. His was a philosophy whose dialectic of opposing and divergent forces carries with it the belief in the possibility of all things being realized through a constant spiritual involvement. This, in turn, leads to a total freedom of thought by which the individual—artist and person—is in complete control of his own destiny.

Letters:

Carteggio Palazzeschi-Marinetti, edited by Paolo Prestigiacomo (Milan: Mondadori, 1978);

Lettere all'amico avvocato (Rome: Cometa, 1981).

Bibliographies:

Stefano Giovanardi, ed., *La critica e Palazzeschi* (Bologna: Cappelli, 1975);

Siro Ferroni, "Nota bibliografica," in *Palazzeschi oggi: Atti del convegno, Firenze 6/8 Novembre 1976*, edited by Lanfranco Caretti (Milan: Saggiatore, 1978), pp. 339-365;

Anna Grazia D'Oria, *Bibliografia degli scritti di Aldo Palazzeschi* (Rome: Storia e Letteratura, 1982).

Biographies:

Giacinto Spagnoletti, *Palazzeschi* (Milan: Longanesi, 1971);

Valentino Brosio, *Ritratto segreto di Aldo Palazzeschi* (Turin: Piazza, 1985).

References:

Luciano Anceschi and Luciano De Maria, eds., "Palazzeschi: inediti," *Verri*, 5 (1974): 1-77;

Anceschi and De Maria, eds., "Palazzeschi," *Verri*, 6 (1974): 1-99;

Piero Bigongiari, "Il 'correlativo soggettivo' di Palazzeschi," *Approdo letterario*, 77-78 (1977): 75-96;

Lanfranco Caretti, ed., *Palazzeschi oggi: Atti del convegno, Firenze 6/8 novembre 1976* (Milan: Saggiatore, 1978);

Gianfranco Contini, "Palazzeschi: il congedo poetico," *Paragone*, 322 (1976): 3-15;

Fausto Curi, "Edipo, Empedocle e il saltimbanco," *Verri*, 6 (1974): 58-140;

De Maria, *Palazzeschi e l'avanguardia* (Milan: Scheiwiller, 1976);

Guido Guglielmi, *L'udienza del poeta: Saggi su Palazzeschi e il futurismo* (Turin: Einaudi, 1979);

Georges Güntert, "Palazzeschi e la giocondità," *Paragone*, 262 (1971): 62-88;

Giuseppe Impellizzeri, "Palazzeschi, poeta futurista," *Trimestre*, 11 (1978): 67-91;

Laure Lepri, *Il funàmbolo incosciente: Aldo Palazzeschi, 1905-1914* (Florence: Olschki, 1991);

François Livi, "Palazzeschi e l'esorcismo futurista," *Italianistica*, 8, no. 2 (1979): 252-274;

Francesco Paolo Memmo, *Invito alla lettura di Aldo Palazzeschi* (Milan: Mursia, 1976);

Mario Miccinesi, *Palazzeschi* (Florence: Nuova Italia, 1972);

Michele Picchi, ed., *Galleria*, special Palazzeschi triple issue, 2-4 (March-August 1974);

Piero Pieri, *Ritratto del saltimbanco da giovane. Palazzeschi: 1905-1914* (Bologna: Pátron, 1980);

Paolo Prestigiacomo, "Palazzeschi e il futurismo," *Ponte* (October 1979): 1194-1216;

Giorgio Pullini, *Aldo Palazzeschi* (Milan: Mursia, 1972);

Giuseppe Savoca, *Eco e Narciso: La ripetizione nel primo Palazzeschi* (Palermo: Flaccovio, 1979);

Ruggero Stefanini, " 'Poesia' di Aldo Palazzeschi," *Gradiva*, new series 4, no. 1 (1987): 89-95;

Anthony J. Tamburri, "Aldo Palazzeschi's Later Poetry: A Continuation," *Italiana*, 1 (1988): 307-320;

Tamburri, *Of Saltimbanchi and Incendiari: Aldo Palazzeschi and Avant-Gardism in Italy* (Madison, N.J.: Fairleigh Dickinson University Press, 1990);

Tamburri and Luigi Fontanella, eds., "Homage to Aldo Palazzeschi," *Gradiva*, new series 3, no. 4 (1986): 9-61.

Papers:

The Fondo Palazzeschi is at the Facoltà di Lettere e di Filosofia of the Università degli Studi di Firenze (Florence). It contains his own manuscripts and books, and his private library of books, magazines, and journals.

Sandro Penna
(12 January 1906 - 21 January 1977)

Jack Shreve
Allegany Community College

BOOKS: *Poesie* (Florence: Parenti, 1938; enlarged edition, Milan: Garzanti, 1957); enlarged again as *Tutte le poesie* (Milan: Garzanti, 1970);

Appunti (Milan: Meridiana, 1950);

Arrivo al mare (Rome: De Luca, 1955);

Una strana gioia di vivere (Milan: All'Insegna del Pesce d'Oro/Scheiwiller, 1956);

Croce e delizia (Milan: Longanesi, 1958);

Un pò di febbre (Milan: Garzanti, 1973);

Poesie (Milan: Garzanti, 1973);

L'Ombra e la luce (Milan: Scheiwiller, 1975);

Stranezze (Milan: Garzanti, 1976);

Il viaggiatore insonne (Genoa: San Marco dei Giustiniani, 1977);

Il rombo immenso (Milan: Scheiwiller, 1978);

Confuso sogno, edited by Elio Pecora (Milan: Garzanti, 1980); translated in part by George Scrivani as *Confused Dream* (New York: Hanuman, 1988);

This Strange Joy: Selected Poems of Sandro Penna, a bilingual edition, translated by W. S. Di Piero (Columbus: Ohio State University Press, 1982);

Peccato di gola (Milan: Scheiwiller, 1989).

TRANSLATIONS: Prosper Mérimée, *Carmen e altri racconti*, translated by Penna and Natalia Ginzburg (Turin: Einaudi, 1943);

Paul Claudel, *Presenza e profezia*, translated by Penna (Rome: Comunità, 1947).

Sandro Penna

Together with Constantine Cavafy and Luis Cernuda, Sandro Penna is one of the twentieth century's finest poets on the subject of homosexual love. His homoerotic lyrics, dreamy and delicately unpornographic, are a supple blend of melancholy and exhilaration in the classical tradition; they re-create the tension between the real and the imaginative world of erotic experience. From the hermetic tradition, in whose hour of glory Penna emerged on the literary scene, he internalized the urgent personal tone of voice dear to its practitioners as well as their love of the epi-

gram and the allusiveness of clarified imagery. Like the hermetic poets, Penna spurned the proverbial *aulicità* (courtly elegance) of long centuries of Italian literary history in a commitment to avoid preciosity; but, unlike them, he did not rejoice in the exalted notion of metaphor, taking the stuff of his poetry from the humble substance of his everyday life instead of from rarified intellectualizing. At its best the poetry of Penna, with its highly synthesizing epigrammatic format and distilled, quintessential imagery, has the ease and coherence of enduring art.

Penna was born in Perugia on 12 January 1906, the first child of Armando Penna, an Umbrian shopkeeper, and Angela Antonione Satta, who was born in Lazio of a family originally from Sardinia. At the time of Sandro's birth, his father was twenty-three years of age and his mother, who inherited a cash dowry that she herself administered, was twenty.

Because of chronic bronchitis, Sandro Penna did not enter school until he was eight. During his childhood there were frequent family quarrels, with his mother blaming his father for mismanagement of funds and for infidelities to her. After years of irregular studies at the Istituto Tecnico di Perugia, Penna managed to get a diploma in accounting in 1925. Later he worked as a clerk in a bookstore in Milan, and then in 1929 he moved with his mother to Rome, where he did a variety of odd jobs and made his home for the rest of his life.

Penna became an avid reader. During these years he read closely the works of Giacomo Leopardi, and became familiar with the writings of Friedrich Hölderlin, Friedrich Nietzsche, and Arthur Rimbaud, whom he characterized in an interview as "un Leopardi più felice, sensuale, meno umano e mitico" (a happier, more sensual Leopardi, less human and less of a legend). When Penna read from Leopardi's *Pensieri LXXIX* (1845), "Il giovane non acquista mai l'arte del vivere ... finchè dura in lui la vemenza dei desiderii" (The young man can never learn the art of living ... as long as desires burn in him), he knew for certain that he would never attain that art of living, for desires were very much a part of him. He wanted to free himself from the enslaving power of his passions, which he called "voli epilettici dell'anima" (epileptic fits of the soul), but he knew that he could not, and so, instead, he learned to turn his desires into poems. Furthermore, in Leopardi's *Zibaldone* (1845), Penna found intellectual support for the pederasty that he knew was destined to be a major part of his life.

He also read Edgar Allan Poe, Oscar Wilde, and Charles-Pierre Baudelaire, but in the poem "C'è ora nel mio cuore adolescente" (There Is Now in My Adolescent Heart), written in 1927 and collected in *Confuso sogno* (1980; translated in part as *Confused Dream*, 1988), he called the three writers "magnifici tormentatori / di chiusi uragani di passione" (magnificent tormentors / of pent-up hurricanes of passion) and abjured their noxious decadence for the ecstatic nature-worship of Gabriele D'Annunzio. Penna savored not so much D'Annunzio's pagan delight in the rich potential of vocabulary but his other pagan delight in the richness of the potential of nature. From D'Annunzio, Penna learned to love sun-

light and the wide-open, luminous spaces that serve to distract the poetic sensibility from the narrowness of grief. Penna tried to read Alessandro Manzoni but abandoned the attempt, preferring to spend his time on Jack London, whose *Martin Eden* (1909) he found "full of great and virile poetry."

Through the efforts of a psychologist both poets consulted, Penna in 1932 was able to meet Umberto Saba, to whom he had been mailing copies of his poems under a pseudonym. Upon meeting Penna in person, Saba was immediately enthusiastic about his poetry and helped him publish two poems in the 20 November 1932 issue of *L'Italia Letteraria*: "La vita ... è ricordarsi di un risveglio" (Life ... Is Remembering an Awakening) and "Sotto il cielo di aprile la mia pace" (Under the April Sky the Peace I Feel)—both collected in *Poesie* (1938). Through Saba's contacts, Penna was able to meet Eugenio Montale, who liked Penna and became for a time his literary mentor.

In the first months of 1936 the editors of *Solaria*, which that same year would cease publication, discussed putting together a volume of Penna's verse. When Penna requested the assistance of Montale in the endeavor, Montale said the plan was useless since most of the better poems were liable to be censored. In a historical context Montale's reservations do not seem unreasonable during the last, most intense years of the Benito Mussolini regime. Later even an old friend of Penna's such as Elsa Morante, herself the author of novels dealing frankly with the issue of homosexuality, advised against publishing material that was too explicit.

The attempt to publish a volume of Penna's poetry in 1936 failed, yet when *Poesie* was finally published by Parenti in 1938, the critical reception was enthusiastic, and Penna rode the crest of the wave by contributing more and more poems to literary journals and magazines (especially *Paragone*), and his second slender volume of poetry, *Appunti* (Notes), was published in 1950.

Penna's work, unusual for its evenness and its lack of an evolving ideology, generated within Italy a substantial amount of criticism, which itself makes interesting study. First there is the criticism from the hermetic period that views Penna as an ingenuous and uncontaminated poet of ancient Greek or "alexandrine" purity and delicately overlooks the patently homosexual source of his inspiration. In 1950 Piero Bigongiari made his well-known pronouncement that the poetry of Penna was like a flower without a visible stem.

There are also those who see Penna as a forerunner of postwar realism. Pier Paolo Pasolini, though an admirer of Penna and his work, especially questioned the innocence of Penna's inspiration, seeking to probe its opacities for the humiliations of the poet's implied life, and identified in Penna a protest against social conformity. What had been called the mysticism of Penna, he labeled instead "narcissism," and Penna's sorrow-saturated persona he analyzed as stemming from the trauma of Penna's exclusion from normal society.

While subsequent critics tend to agree with Pasolini's identification of the narcissism of Penna, many have reacted violently to Pasolini's interpretation of Penna's sorrow as the product of the trauma of being an outsider. Giulio Di Fonzo, in particular, attributes this view to the Catholic prejudices and sense of guilt that characteristically weighed down Pasolini's own homosexuality, and Di Fonzo suggests, after citing Penna's denial that his life could be documented in terms of his poetry, that Penna was thinking of Pasolini when he wrote the following lines in *Stranezze* (Oddities, 1976):

> Oh il triste fatto della vita mia.
> La musa mia segreta, tutta mia,
> ancor prima ch'io fossi un pò lodato,
> altri, per troppo amor forse, ha sporcato.

> (Oh the sad fact about my life.
> My secret muse, all mine,
> even before I was a little praised,
> others, out of too much love perhaps, have tainted her.)

Yet Pasolini's admiration for Penna was reciprocated (Penna honored Pasolini by incorporating lines from the latter's poetry into his own work, and the two men often enjoyed exchanging stories of homosexual escapades); and Penna's alleged trauma from being different may not be as off-target as some critics think. Penna's attitude toward his homosexuality is at times defensive, and he does speak in his poems of his obsession with young men in terms of its being an actual problem. This is not to say, however, that his concern about being different is obsessive enough to have been the major motivating force responsible for his poetry. Perhaps the best solution to this critical dilemma comes from Penna's own lines in *Stranezze*:

> Arso completamente dalla vita
> io vivo in essa felice e dissolto.

> La mia pena d'amore non ascolto
> più di quanto non curi la ferita.

> (Burned completely by life
> I live in it happy and resolved.
> My pain of love I don't listen to
> any more than I treat the wound.)

A third school of criticism looks beyond the confines of Italian literary history to situate Penna in a wider, cosmic tradition, seeking analogues in Japanese haiku or Indonesian pantoum, for example, and stressing the Oriental rather than the Occidental nature of his poetry. Di Fonzo especially stresses the pantheism and immanentism of Penna's psychology.

A fourth criticism emphasizes the historical uniqueness of Penna without resorting to groping for mythical or non-Western analogues. For some, Penna is simply a nonhermetic poet who happened to share his era with the hermetic poets. He is not a born anomaly, but rather a poet who managed somehow to remain impervious to the predetermined ideas of his contemporaries. Although Penna is so often called an outsider or an island within twentieth-century Italian poetry, Edoardo Sanguineti, G. A. Pellegrinetti, and other anthologists have nonetheless classed him as a hermetic poet in their collections, no doubt on the strength of his epigrammatic sententiousness alone.

A typical Penna poem is an epigram or a taut, pared-down description of an intense moment in the manner of a Joycean epiphany, characteristically involving a young boy who either is beautiful or demonstrates some other form of allure. An example of the first epigrammatic type is in *Tutte le poesie* (All the Poetry, the 1970 edition of *Poesie*):

> Oh nella notte il cane
> che abbaia di lontano.
> Di giorno è solo il cane
> che ti lecca la mano.

> (Oh at night the dog
> that barks in the distance.
> In daylight he is only the dog
> that licks your hand.)

A typical poem of the second, more personal type is in *This Strange Joy* (1982):

> Quando la luce piange sulle strade
> vorrei in silenzio un fanciullo abbracciare.

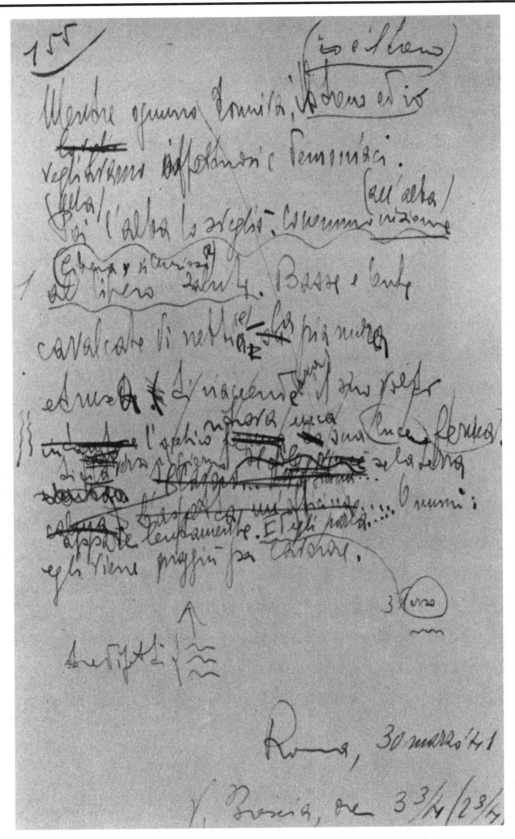

Page from the first draft for "Mentre orguno dormiva . . . " (30 March 1941). The final version was collected in the 1957 edition of Penna's Poesie *(from* Storia della letteratura, *volume 7, edited by Luigi Ferrante, 1965).*

(When light weeps on the streets
I want to hug a boy in silence.)

Penna was a poet demonstratively in love with life; he wished he could even go to sleep amid the sweet roar of life. He saw his mission as a bystander—as he says in *This Strange Joy*—"unir parole ad uomini" (joining words to men) to create poetry that "non sarà / un giuoco leggero / fatto con parole delicate e / malate" (won't be / a breezy game / made of fragile / sickly words). Penna described himself as "intriso di una strana gioia di vivere" (permeated with a strange joy of living). This joy—or *enthusiasmus*, as Pasolini called it, invoking the etymological sense of the word—Penna referred to as strange because, despite all adversity, he was always able to confront the enigma of sorrow with euphoria.

Despite Penna's great concern for love and its perception through the senses, there is rarely any mention in his verse of satiety or dissipation. His brimming vitality overrides the dangers of dissipation, and even when he speaks of *ebbrezza* (drunkenness), it conveys the meaning of rapture rather than commonplace inebriation. Even the unbridled image of himself as a *lupo impazzito* (crazed wolf) who goes sniffing the hot shadows in search of companions does not lead to a statement of remorse or guilt for his excesses. Impelled by his insatiable love of life even when others are sleeping—the title of Penna's last book of verse published in his lifetime, *Il viaggiatore insonne* (The Sleepless Traveler, 1977), is a fitting epithet for the poet himself—and moving as if in a dream, he took long walks through Roman streets to lose himself in the loving contemplation of the faces of passersby. His poetry always seems *in itinere*, on the track of some unattainable essence.

The word *oneiric* is often used by critics to describe Penna's perception of reality, and *sogno* and *sonno* are indeed key words for him, as in *This Strange Joy*: "Nel sonno incerto sogno ancora un poco" (In my fitful sleep I'll dream a little longer). A vignette of the "tenera grazia" (soft grace) of a tough-looking baker's boy is savored as a lovely memory "da sgranar a sera" (to be plucked at night). In one instance, in *Una strana gioia di vivere* (A Strange Joy for Life, 1956), Penna's voice even intervenes in his own poem to caution the reader that what is being described is not necessarily what is happening:

Io vedevo alle svolte nel sole apparire
un nudo corpo di fanciullo, ma badate

ho detto io vedevo apparire—chè il fanciullo
nudo non c'era.

(I saw appear at the crossroads in the sun
a nude body of a boy, but note
I said I saw him appear—there really
wasn't a nude boy there.)

One consistent feature of his two- , three- , and four-line vignettes of beautiful boys is the characterlessness of the boys themselves. Penna's idealized boys seldom have personalities or even faces. Instead, what forms the substance of the poetic observation are gestures or attributes, generic and impersonal as the blue and white of a sailor's uniform, the self-assured lighting of a cigarette, the red poppies in someone's eyes, the voice of a young worker singing in an empty room, or a young boy urinating against a spindly tree.

In a 1964 interview Penna said he was sometimes sorry he had not sought to extract from his solitude and from his reading "un certo nutrimento" (a certain nourishment), and he proceeded to express his admiration for Mario Luzi and the wise tone of meditation in his poetry. If the philosophical meditation in Luzi's work makes conspicuous its absence in Penna's, then the same is true of Luzi's deep faith in God. Addressing the ashen dawn in the poem "Città" (City), Penna writes "Io sono senza dio" (I am without God). Although Penna refers to the gods or the god of love and even speaks of a bad god who, with a single gesture, petrified an entire landscape that seemed to share the poet's pain, the God of Christianity is not invoked. Penna's consciousness of his own melancholy takes the place of what in other poets has been called religiosity, and Penna finds it in the eyes of the boys he dreams and writes about.

Although the typical age of Penna's boys appears to be about twelve or thirteen years, when it is still possible to find reasonably angelic innocence, sometimes the fantasy of nude men, nude workers, or nude soldiers inspires a poem. Despite Cesare Garboli's insistence that Penna was a pederast rather than a homosexual, lines such as "Sulla riva del fiume ancora brillano / nudi corpi di uomini lontani" (Bodies of naked men in the distance / are shining on the riverbank), from *This Strange Joy*, presumably imply interest in adults as well as boys. His fascination with the nude bodies of men is reminiscent of a similar tendency in Walt Whitman, yet Whitman did not share

Penna's fascination with *fanciulli* (boys). Also unlike Whitman, who made every attempt to democratize his attraction for men by restating the same desire in reference to women, Penna rarely wrote about women at all, and when he did, it was not to communicate desire. Women are usually mentioned as a backdrop or in consideration of their role as competition, as in this line from *Tutte le poesie*: "Cosa sanno le donne della tua bellezza" (What do women know about your beauty). Saba characterized Penna as a singer of frustrated motherhood, referring to his loving and seemingly unlascivious vignettes of young boys; on at least one occasion, in the remarkable poem "Donna in Tram" (Woman in a Streetcar), also from *Tutte le poesie*, Penna does identify sympathetically with the role of a young mother. As a woman on a public conveyance tries to caress her son, he ignores her, preferring to stare in fascination out the window. It then becomes clear that the boy resembles someone else who was more interested in the outside world than in the woman: the child's father who abandoned her.

The boys in Penna's poetic world are sometimes adorned with cats, kittens, or dogs; are compared to young animals for their unstudied grace; or are portrayed in some other sort of natural setting. One boy in a harvest setting wears an apron heavy with fruit. Light, which is often intense enough to be called dazzling, typically surrounds Penna's idealized boy.

On the other hand, in Penna's simplified world, where boys are luminous, angelic, and sleek as young animals, Penna as their pursuer is an unsavory figure, and he consistently uses images of unloved animals such as *mosca* (fly), *ramarro* (green lizard), or *lucertola* (lizard) to symbolize himself. Thus the poet is the fly caught in honey, or the helpless lizard crushed between idle boyish hands for fun.

To those who might complain about the monotony of Penna's subject matter, he offers the following quatrain in *This Strange Joy*, not without its ironic self-deprecating humor:

Sempre fanciulli nelle mie poesie!
Ma io non so parlare d'altre cose.
Le altre cose son tutte noiose.
Io non posso cantarvi Opere Pie.

(Always boys in my poems!
But I can't talk about anything else.
Everything else bores me.
I can't sing you Salvation Army songs.)

The language of Penna demonstrates a basic, colloquial diction and a simple, unconvoluted syntax. Nonetheless, literary archaisms such as *ei* for *égli* (he) or the attachment of the reflexive pronoun to the conjugated form of the verb, as in *muovonsi* (they move), are deftly used by Penna to isolate images and endow them with an attention-getting halo of emphasis. Another archaism dear to Penna is the poetic dative of Leopardi, suggestive of vastness, as in Penna's line "un ultimo gabbiano alla tempesta" (a last gull in the storm).

Penna's nouns are ordinary and crepuscular in flavor (some bring to mind Giovanni Pascoli) and are often followed by a pair of adjectives, as in "La veneta piazzetta, / antica e mesta . . . (The little Venetian square, / old and mournful . . .). These adjectives sometimes serve a mitigating function that verges on oxymoron: "orinatoi" (public urinals) are "freschi" (fresh); "il bel sogno sportivo" (the beautiful athletic dream) is "reale" (real); "ingenue bugie" (ingenuous lies) are "luminose" (bright); and the smell of poverty is "casto e gentile" (chaste and gentle).

Adjectives of color are important, and a chromatic antithesis is clearly discernible. While *nero*, *grigio*, *livido*, and *opaco* (black, gray, purple, and opaque) are attributes of Penna's own doleful world, *bianco*, *azzurro*, *oro*, and *limpido* (white, azure, gold, and clear) customarily accompany the boys who enlighten the poet's drab loneliness. Some critics have explained this heightened sensitivity to color as deriving from his friendship with the Postimpressionistic painter Filippo De Pisis, who was also a poet.

Another poetic recourse dear to Penna was repetition—of rhymes, alliteration, words, and entire lines. The concept of repetition in the cyclical pattern of life is also found thematically in Penna's work. Penna was confident that nothing is lost in death: in death one lives again in others, or so Penna posits in *Stranezze*:

Tu morirai fanciullo ed io ugualmente.
Ma più belli di te ragazzi ancora
dormiranno nel sole in riva al mare.
Ma non saremo che noi stessi ancora.

(You will die, boy, and I will, too.
But more beautiful boys than you will yet
sleep in the sun on the seashore.
But they will be only ourselves once again.)

World War II came and went without making much of an impression on Penna's verse. He continued to reside in wartime Rome, the Rome of the Cave Ardeatine massacre (1944), while many of his friends fled to the Latium or Campanian countryside. Moreover he seems to have had partisan friends, for he was once seen near the Campo de' Fiori, nonchalantly distributing partisan leaflets without seeming to realize the risks involved.

He worked on translations of two volumes from the French (*Carmen e altri racconti*, by Prosper Mérimée [1943], and *Presenza e profezia*, by Paul Claudel [1947]) and afterward managed to support himself by buying and selling prepared foodstuffs, such as hams, marmalade, and *pastine glutinate* (glutinized fine pasta), as well as soap. Later, his painter friends gave him paintings that he collected, traded, and sold. He always managed to live in *ozio beato* (happy idleness) due above all to the generous and providential nature of his mother, who survived until 1964.

In the spring of 1956 the Milanese publisher Scheiwiller accepted thirty of Penna's poems and published *Una strana gioia di vivere*. Interest in Penna's literary reputation was rekindled when Pasolini reviewed the slim volume in *Paragone* in April 1956. Within a year Penna's newly collected *Poesie* (1957) was published by Garzanti. This volume combines the contents of his first poetry books with more than a hundred unpublished poems.

In 1957, after the committee's long and bitter struggle to reach a decision, *Poesie* won the Premio Viareggio, which was shared with Pasolini's *Le cenere di Gramsci* and Alberto Mondadori's *Quasi una vicenda*. Although some journalistic vitriol was spent on Pasolini's book, the bulk of the backlash was aimed at Penna. His victory was condemned as a triumph for the Left, pornography, and the forces of immorality; the judges who supported him, Giuseppe De Robertis, Giorgio Caproni, and Leone Piccioni, were singled out for special reproach.

Poesie was followed in 1958 by *Croce e delizia* (Trouble and Delight), which contains forty-three previously unpublished poems in which critics discerned a somewhat more funereal Penna. Nonetheless, since Penna was always arbitrary about offering up his poems for publication, they are extremely difficult to date, and inferring tendencies from his specific collections is risky. For example, Penna's volume of prose pieces, *Un pò di febbre* (A Little Fever)—useful because it sheds light on many of the individual vignettes limned in the poems and interesting because of Penna's

descriptions of various Italian cities such as Perugia, Rome, and Milan—had been written over thirty years before it was published in 1973.

Ill health plagued Penna during the last decade of his life; he lost his teeth to pyorrhea and suffered from chronic insomnia. He took some joy from his German shepherd dog, but this loving animal was eventually taken from him. His sixth-floor apartment in the building he had always inhabited was cluttered and depressing. In 1974 Natalia Ginzburg and Goffredo Parise raised ten million lire to help ease his situation, but it reportedly made little difference in his standard of living.

Although Penna was never interested in discussing literary theory, cared nothing for literary society, and did not consistently cultivate and maintain literary friendships, in his old age he became fond of giving interviews to popular magazines and sometimes made some startling evaluations about his contemporaries (for example, that Salvatore Quasimodo wrote only one good poem).

In June 1975 Penna was persuaded to offer for publication a selection of his oldest poems, and these were published posthumously in 1980 with the title *Confuso sogno*. Also in 1975 Penna gave Giorgio Devoto thirteen of what he considered his most beautiful poems for a Genoese edition. They appeared two years later in a small volume called *Il viaggiatore insonne*, with admiring commentaries by Natalia Ginzburg and Giovanni Raboni.

Ginzburg marveled at how unfrenetic Penna had always been about the publication of his work. She attributed the lack of career-oriented drive to Penna's indifference to time as it is generally perceived. This was an enduring characteristic of Penna as a writer. When publication of his poetry was first considered in the 1930s, Penna was undisturbed by the inevitable delay. He wanted his poetry to be enjoyed by like-minded readers, and if the times were not favorable to reaching that type of reader, then he preferred to sit back and wait patiently until the prevailing mood did become more favorable.

In 1976 Garboli persuaded Penna to publish 119 of his poems written between 1957 and 1976; this volume was given the title *Stranezze*. Although Penna was immediately sorry that he had released this particular group of poems, he changed his mind when *Stranezze* won the Premio Bagutta. Ginzburg and Garboli went to Milan to receive the prize for him only one week before his death. He died in his sleep in Rome on 21 January 1977 of heart failure, caused by what authorities deemed an overdose of sleeping pills.

During Penna's lifetime, selections from his poetry were translated into French, Swedish, and English. In the years since Penna's death many book-length analyses of his work have been published in Italy, and there is no indication that this fascination is likely to cease—a fitting tribute to a poet who, standing apart from the crowd in order to see it better, knew how to encapsulate tantalizingly in one line an entire mood or scene.

Interviews:

Elio Filippo Accrocca, "Sandro Penna" in *Ritratti su misura di scrittori italiani* (Venice: Sodalizio del Libro, 1960), pp. 324-235;

Giacinto Spagnoletti, ed., *Poesia italiana contemporanea* (Parma: Guanda, 1964), pp. 483-484;

Vittorio Masselli and Gian Antonio Cibotto, "Intervista con Penna," in *Antologia popolare di poeti italiani del Novecento* (Florence: Vallecchi, 1967);

Dante Matelli, "Chi son? Sono un poeta. E come vivo? Boh," *Tempo*, 47 (27 November 1976).

Biographies:

Giulio Di Fonzo, *Sandro Penna: La luce e il silenzio* (Rome: Dell'Ateneo, 1981);

Gualtiero De Santi, *Sandro Penna* (Florence: Nuova Italia, 1982).

References:

Piero Bigongiari, "Per una sistemazione poetica,"

Paragone, 1, no. 10 (October 1950);

Maria Grazia Boccolini, *Sandro Penna: Il cosmo, il fanciullo, il kouros e il cinema dell'Eros* (Rome: Cooperativa Editrice il Ventaglio, 1985);

James Anthony Cascaito, *Lieto disonore: The Poetry of Sandro Penna*, Ph.D. dissertation, Columbia University, 1981;

W. S. Di Piero, Foreword to *This Strange Joy: Selected Poems of Sandro Penna* (Columbus: Ohio State University Press, 1982), pp. xv-xix;

Robert S. Dombroski, "The Undisciplined Eros of Sandro Penna," *Books Abroad*, 47 (Spring 1973): 304-306;

Cesare Garboli, *Penna Papers* (Milan: Garzanti, 1984);

Garboli, Postface to Penna's *Stranezze* (Milan: Garzanti, 1976), pp. 127-135.

Antonio Iacopetta, *Sandro Penna: Il fanciullo con lo specchio* (Rome: Bonacci, 1983);

Pier Paolo Pasolini, "Una strana gioia di vivere," *Paragone*, 7 (April 1956); revised in *Passione e ideologia* (Milan: Garzanti, 1960), pp. 385-403;

Elio Pecora, *Sandro Penna: Una cheta follia* (Milan: Frassinelli, 1984);

Gianni Pozzi, *La poesia italiana del Novecento: Da Gozzano agli Ermetici*, third edition (Turin: Einaudi, 1970), pp. 319-326;

Giovanni Raboni, "Sandro Penna," in *Novecento: I contemporanei*, volume 9, edited by Gianni Grana (Milan: Marzorati, 1979), pp. 8415-8448.

Lucio Piccolo
(27 October 1903 - 26 May 1969)

Maria Rosaria Vitti-Alexander
Nazareth College of Rochester

BOOKS: *Canti barocchi e altre liriche* (Milan: Mondadori, 1956);

Gioco a nascondere; Canti barocchi e altre liriche (Milan: Mondadori, 1960; enlarged, 1967);

Plumelia (Milan: All'Insegna del Pesce d'Oro/ Scheiwiller, 1967);

La seta, edited by Giovanna Musolino and Giovanni Gaglio (Milan: All'Insegna del Pesce d'Oro/Scheiwiller, 1984).

Edition in English: *Collected Poems*, translated and edited by Brian Swann and Ruth Feldman (Princeton: Princeton University Press, 1972).

SELECTED PERIODICAL PUBLICATIONS—
UNCOLLECTED: "L'esequie della luna," *Nuovi Argomenti*, 7-8 (July-December 1967): 152-167;

"Five Poems," translated by Charles Tomlinson, *Agenda* (London), 6 (Autumn-Winter 1968): 68-74.

Lucio Piccolo

Lucio Piccolo's first verses were almost immediately labeled archaic, as critics found them difficult to understand and accept, since they were outside the well-established 1950s currents of hermeticism, neorealism, and postfuturism. From the first years of publication, Piccolo's poetry was regarded as unclassifiable. Although these were the years that saw the end of neorealism as a movement, there persisted a need to understand the relation between poetry and reality. Piccolo's difficult verses seemed to offer no immediate connection to the contemporary world. His first poems evoke a world of past beauty and reawakened a taste for the delicate, intricate images of antiquity, while his later verses convey an existential, metaphysical anguish not found among Italian poetic currents of the time. All are presented in such a refined, baroque style as to evoke the charge that the works are anachronistic.

Piccolo's reclusive, somewhat uneventful life seemed to underscore the public's general feeling of incomprehension about his poetry. Baron Lucio Piccolo was born on 27 October 1903 in Palermo to Giuseppe Piccolo and the former Teresa Tasca Filangeri, members of an aristocratic family. Among his close relatives was the well-known Prince Giuseppe Tomasi di Lampedusa, author of the novel *Il Gattopardo* (The Leopard, 1958). Lampedusa and Piccolo were also kindred souls in their perusal of books. In the 1920s and the 1930s they kept abreast of the literary milieu of Europe, without participating directly.

Piccolo studied at the Liceo Garibaldi (Garibaldi High School), but, after receiving his diploma, he abandoned formal studies completely. Having no interest in a *laurea* (university degree), Piccolo spent his life studying various subjects of interest to him, including philosophy, astronomy, and mathematics. He was also a musicologist and composer, and while still in his youth he composed a magnificat. His love of music shows in his verses, for Piccolo's poetry continually explores the musical quality of words. In a September 1964 letter quoted by Vittoria Bradshaw in *From Pure Silence to Impure Dialogue* (1971), Piccolo wrote: "I try to transpose on the page the elements of perspective effects. I am very responsive to musical stimuli while writing a poem. All my poems are composed like symphonies. . . ."

Piccolo's vast knowledge of many disciplines was recognized by all those who came to know him well. Piccolo read in several foreign languages, among them Greek, Spanish, French, English, and Arabic, and read most of the great masterpieces in the original. He was familiar with most of the poetic works from antiquity to the present. He was a student of philosophy, a scholar of Greek, an accomplished musicologist, and known among his peers as a truly erudite man. In introducing Piccolo to the public at a literary conference at San Pellegrino Terme in 1954, Eugenio Montale expressed his embarrassment at having to present an older, more knowledgeable writer than he had expected, one who, in his words, was "a savant so learned and well-informed . . . who has read 'tous les livres' in the solitude of his estate at Capo d'Orlando, but follows no school" (preface to Piccolo's *Canti barocchi e altre liriche* [Baroque Songs and Other Lyrics, 1956]).

Piccolo lived with his family in Palermo but frequently visited Capo d'Orlando (in the province of Messina). After his father's death in 1933, and in the midst of the ensuing financial difficulties, he moved to Capo d'Orlando permanently, where he lived with other family members in a villa situated on a large family estate. His villa soon became a meeting place for friends and family, a setting for readings and lively discussions. Other members of the family found the opportunity to bring their varied interests to bear on the group. His brother Casimiro was a student of parapsychology, painting, and photography, and his sister Agata studied botany.

Piccolo traveled infrequently. His few trips abroad took him to France and England, but his usual visits were to Palermo and the town of Messina, where he bought almost all his books. With Maria Paterniti, Piccolo had a son, Giuseppe, born on 24 June 1960. On 26 May 1969 Piccolo was found dead in his bathroom, having suffered a cerebral embolism. He was buried in a chapel in Capo d'Orlando constructed by the Fondazione Piccolo.

Piccolo was already in his fifties when he was discovered by Montale. Piccolo owed his literary emergence in large measure to Montale's favorable response to his first volume of poetry, *Canti barocchi e altre liriche*. In 1954 Montale received a small package in the mail, a gift of Piccolo's verses, accompanied by a letter. In this letter Piccolo introduced himself as a poet who wanted

> rievocare e fissare un mondo singolare siciliano, anzi più precisamente palermitano, che si trova adesso sulla soglia della propria scomparsa senza avere avuto la ventura di essere fermato da un'espressione d'arte. E ciò, s'intende, non per una mia programmatica scelta di un soggetto, ma per una interiore, insistente esigenza di espressione lirica. Intendo parlare di quel mondo di chiese barocche, di vecchi conventi, di anime adeguate a questi luoghi, qui trascorse senza lasciar traccia. Ho tentato non quasi di rievocarlo ma di dar di esso un'interpretazione su ricordi d'infanzia.

> (to evoke and fix a particular Sicilian world, or, more specifically, the world of Palermo, which is now on the verge of disappearing without having the good fortune to be preserved in any art form. And this, of course, is not because of deliberate choice of a subject but because of an insistent inner need for lyric expression. I mean to speak of that world of baroque churches, of old convents, of souls suited to these places, who spent their lives here without leaving a trace. I have tried not so much to recall as to interpret it from my childhood memories [quoted by Natale Tedesco in his *Lucio Piccolo: La figura e l'opera*, 1986; translation by Brian Swann and Ruth Feldman in *Collected Poems*, 1972].)

Montale was immediately attracted by Piccolo's verses, admitting he "was struck by the afflatus, a rapture that made me think of the better pages of Dino Campana. . . . I found myself thinking vaguely . . . of Dylan Thomas. . . . Still a distant echo of D'Annunzio came to me. . . . But how far we are here from anything Parnassian and D'Annunzian, and how lean, intense, and sharpened is the diction!" (preface to *Canti barocchi*). When Montale was asked if he could present a new writer at the conference in 1954, he immediately thought of Piccolo. Montale presented Piccolo as "a very unusual man, a man forever in flight, . . . a man whom the crisis of our time has hurled outside time."

The themes are varied in *Canti barocchi*, which can be called a poetic fable, recounting humankind's first contact with the world and the first knowledge of sin and suffering, as well as a meditation on time and the ruin it brings. The poems are rich in baroque figures, in images of fruit, flowers, and colors. The images whirl without pause in an opulent crescendo of visual, olfactory, and other sensory stimuli. Trees, flowers, bushes, fruits—all take on lives of their own, one image following another, always in an intricate abundance of colorful canvases, as in "Oratorio in Valverde," where everything lives perennially:

> Ferma il volo Aurora opulenta
> di frutto, di fiore,
> . . . .
> diffondi ancora tremore
> di conchiglie, di luci marine,
> . . . .
> e sono albicocche in festoni,
> pesche, ciliege, viticci attorti,
> orgoglio fragrante degli orti.
>
> (Cease your flight Aurora opulent
> with fruit, with flower,
> . . . .
> spread again tremor
> of seashells, of marine lights,
> . . . .
> and there are festoons of apricots,
> peaches, cherries, twining tendrils,
> the orchards' fragrant pride
> —translation by Swann and Feldman.)

Another baroque constant in Piccolo's poetry is the combination of single nouns, adjectives, and verbs, as in "La Meridiana" (The Sundial):

> Guarda l'acqua inesplicabile:
>   contrafforte, torre, soglio
> di granito, piuma, ramo, ala, pupilla
> tutto spezza, scioglie, immilla . . .
>
> (Regard water the undecipherable:
>   buttress, tower, granite
> throne, feather, branch, wing, pupil,
> it fragments, dissolves everything, multiplies it a
>   thousand fold . . .
> —translation by Swann and Feldman.)

But more important in poems such as "La Meridiana" is the rendering of the clash between the eternal and the ephemeral, a collision that reaches sensory high notes, as in a musical symphony: "Ma se il fugace è sgomento / l'eterno è terrore" (But if fleeting is dismay / forever is ter-

ror). It is in poems such as this that Piccolo's twentieth-century consciousness is brought into focus; the artist's existential interrogation of human purpose is created in seventeenth-century style.

Perhaps Piccolo is best noted for his second collection, *Gioco a nascondere* (Hide and Seek; published with *Canti barocchi* in 1960), which takes its name from the first poem of the collection. These poems embrace all his essential themes, in a style reminiscent of a past world of baroque churches and old convents, seen through childhood memories. The protagonists are images of hidden places, which whirl up and down, in and out of secluded areas and forbidden alcoves. This game of hide and seek recalls, in its stunning visual sensations, the chapter titled "Donnafugata" in Lampedusa's *Il Gattopardo*. On the subject of the striking similarity between the two, Piccolo said: "I do not find anything so peculiar in the analogy of atmosphere between my work and Lampedusa's, for obvious reasons. . . . Now, 'Donnafugata' is actually the palace of the Cutò family, common ancestors on our mothers' side. . . . The first draft of 'Gioco a nascondere' was in prose, and I read it to Lampedusa long before he started working on *Il Gattopardo*" (quoted by Bradshaw). Gioacchino Lanza Tomasi has recalled that the Piccolo family liked to reminisce with Lampedusa about Santa Margherita, the place that became Donnafugata in his novel.

Therefore, Piccolo's baroque inventions were not only literary creations; they also had a physical, tangible origin. Piccolo's own childhood and adolescence had been spent among castles and baroque residences that eventually entered the fantasy world of his literary production. Throughout *Gioco a nascondere* Piccolo writes of his obsessive interest in the hidden qualities of things, of the obscure and mysterious world of inanimate objects, and of his attempts to penetrate that world. The lyrics are interposed with prose, creating a harmonious composition similar to a symphony. In the poem "Gioco a nascondere" the speaker seeks to distinguish appearance from reality and continues in search of the absolute:

> Se noi siamo figure
> di specchio che un soffio conduce
> senza spessore né suono
> pure il mondo dintorno
> non è fermo ma scorrente parete
> dipinta, ingannevole gioco,
> . . . .
> Cerca

una sua fase il tempo, e se uno specchio
si svela ci riflette
come fummo o saremo; volti
trascorrono, cui diedero un contorno
l'ansia, l'ignoto . . .

(If we are mirror-images
a breath blows
without substance or sound
the world around us
is not stable either but a fleeting
painted wall, deceitful game,
. . . .
Time
seeks its own phase, and if a mirror
is unveiled it reflects us
as we were or will be; faces
flit by, their contour fixed
by anxiety, the unknown . . .
—translation by Swann and Feldman.)

Plumelia, published in 1967, includes meditations on the mysteries of the "other" world, on sin and spiritual punishment, and on death and the passing of everything. *Plumelia* is perhaps Piccolo's richest baroque poetry, with much of its vocabulary and metaphors originating in the seventeenth century. His culture and his love for a past that was rich with majestic structure moved Piccolo to search for rare metaphors and lexicons, to re-create a past world, as in "I sobborghi," "Le tre figure," and "L'andito" (The Suburbs, The Three Figures, and The Passage). In "L'andito" the light through the small, secluded vestibule brings with it baroque images of a time past and voices of people and events that follow one another, leaving no lingering traces behind. The sun's rays are the only regular recurrence in the vestibule:

E i giorni vanno,
ma se la vita
dimentica e trasvola
ogni anno in questo tempo
espiatorio il sole
reclino chiama la preghiera,
dell'andito ignorato
fa l'oratorio in fiamme.

(And the days go by,
but if life
forgets and every year
flies quickly in this expiatory
time, the recumbent
sun evokes prayer,
makes of the neglected corridor
a flaming oratory
—translation by Swann and Feldman.)

La seta (Silk, 1984), published posthumously, comprises thirty-two poems never before published. A calm, quiet voice emerges from this late collection that speaks with certitude of objects and events, as in "Scendevano un tempo" (They Descended upon a Time):

Scendevano un tempo dai sentieri
delle montagne con lenta andatura
le grandi mule, le mule bianche
. . . .
Ma oggi un respiro che varia
le tempre della luce m'ha detto
che dalla china dei monti le bianche
mule sempre scendono, sempre l'aria
di giugno che schiuma i canneti
scuote su la sabbia dei greti
tremula piuma di fonti.

(They would descend upon a time
from mountains' paths with slow gait
the big mules, the white mules
. . . .
But today a breath that changes
the tempering of light told me
that from the top of the mountains the white
mules will always descend, always the air
of June that skims the cane fields
shakes on the gravel-bed's beach
a tremulous feather of springs.)

A sense of the natural world filtering through the mind of the poet dominates the poems of this last collection, creating forms that take on a universal representation.

Piccolo sought in his poetry to wrest from the ghostly specter of time the frail and fleeting qualities of the self. Of Piccolo's verses, Montale said, "his poetry is just on the brink of individuality; suspended in antecedent fact or in post factum, it would lose all its worth if it became the manner—and the career—of an oneiric and surrealistic poet" (preface to *Canti barocchi*). It is the pervasive timelessness in Piccolo's works, his continual attempt to arrest, even if for a moment, the unfolding of events, that explains the still-vibrant interest in his poetry.

Biography:
Natale Tedesco, *Lucio Piccolo: La figura e l'opera* (Marina di Patti, Italy: Pungitopo, 1986).

References:
Vittoria Bradshaw, *From Pure Silence to Impure Dia-*

logue: *A Survey of Post-War Italian Poetry* (New York: Las Américas, 1971), pp. 256-281;

Alberto Frattini, *Poeti italiani tra primo e secondo Novecento* (Milan: IPL, 1967), pp. 320-323;

Melo Freni, "Lucio Piccolo e la Feldman," *Fiera Letteraria*, 44 (12 December 1971): 5;

Giovanni Gaglio, "Lucio Piccolo," in *Poesia Italiana—il Novecento*, edited by Piero Gelli and Gina Lagorio (Milan: Garzanti, 1980), pp. 499-503;

Gioacchino Lanza Tomasi, "Donnafugata non c'è più," *Fiera Letteraria*, 6 (8 February 1968): 5;

Luciana Lombardo Frezza, "Un poeta siciliano," *Belfagor*, 3 (May 1959): 353-357;

Mario Luzi, "Tre poeti: Vigolo, Piccolo e Solmi," *Fiera Letteraria*, 20 (16 May 1968): 23;

Gianluigi Paganelli, "Il poeta di Calanovella," *Belfagor*, 3 (May 1959): 350-353;

Giovanni Raboni, "Due note," *Paragone*, new series 38 (April 1968): 141-142;

Leonardo Sciascia, "Le 'soledades' di Lucio Piccolo," in his *La corda pazza* (Turin: Einaudi, 1970), pp. 127-183;

Natale Tedesco, *La condizione crepuscolare* (Florence: Nuova Italia, 1971), pp. 273-284;

Tedesco, "Dimora fisica e morale del 'barocco' di Lucio Piccolo," in his *Testimonianze siciliane* (Caltanissetta & Rome: Sciascia, 1970), pp. 227-236;

Giuseppe Zagarrio, *Sicilia e poesia contemporanea* (Caltanissetta & Rome: Sciascia, 1964), pp. 121-126.

Salvatore Quasimodo

(20 August 1901 - 14 June 1968)

Stelio Cro

McMaster University

BOOKS: *Acque e terre* (Florence: Solaria, 1930);

Oboe sommerso (Genoa: Circoli, 1932);

Odore di eucalyptus, ed altri versi (Florence: Antico Fattore, 1933);

Erato e Apollion (Milan: Scheiwiller, 1935);

Poesie (Milan: Primi Piani, 1938);

Ed è subito sera (Milan: Mondadori, 1942);

Con il piede straniero sopra il cuore (Milan: Costume, 1946);

Giorno dopo giorno (Milan: Mondadori, 1947);

La vita non è sogno (Milan: Mondadori, 1949);

Billy Budd [libretto based on the story by Herman Melville] (Milan: Suvini Zerboni, 1949);

Il falso e vero verde (Milan: Schwarz, 1954); enlarged as *Il falso e vero verde; Con un discorso sulla poesia* (Milan: Mondadori, 1956);

La terra impareggiabile (Milan: Mondadori, 1958; enlarged, 1962);

Poesie scelte, edited by Roberto Sanesi (Parma, Italy: Guanda, 1959);

Petrarca e il sentimento della solitudine (Milan: All'Insegna del Pesce d'Oro/Scheiwiller, 1959);

Tutte le poesie (Milan: Mondadori, 1960; enlarged, 1962; enlarged and edited by Gilberto Finzi, 1984); translated by Jack Bevan as *Complete Poems* (London: Anvil, 1983; New York: Schocken, 1984);

Il poeta e il politico e altri saggi (Milan: Schwartz, 1960); translated by Thomas G. Bergin and Sergio Pacifici as *The Poet and the Politician, and Other Essays* (Carbondale: Southern Illinois University Press, 1964);

Orfeo Anno Domini MCMXLVII (Milan: Curci, 1960);

Scritti sul teatro (Milan: Mondadori, 1961);

Nove poesie (Verona: Riva, 1963);

L'amore di Galatea (Palermo: Teátro Massimo, 1964);

Anita Ekberg, edited by Sennuccio Benelli (Milan: Lerici, 1965);

Salvatore Quasimodo

Dare e avere (Milan: Mondadori, 1966); translated by Edith Farnsworth as *To Give and to Have, and Other Poems* (Chicago: Regnery, 1969); translated by Bevan as *Debit and Credit* (London: Anvil, 1972);

Salvatore Quasimodo: Premio Nobel per la letteratura 1959 (Milan: Fabbri, 1968);

Un anno (Genoa: Immordino, 1968);

Le opere, edited by Guido di Pino (Turin: Unione Tipografica, 1968);

Birolli, X. Bueno, Cantatore, De Chirico, Elsa D'Albisola, Fabbri Manzù, Marino C., Mastroianni, Migneco, Rossello, Rossi, Sassu, Sotilis, Usellini, Tamburi visti (Milan: Trentadue, 1969);

Poesie e discorsi sulla poesia, edited by Finzi (Milan: Mondadori, 1971; revised and enlarged, 1973);

A colpo omicida e altri scritti, edited by Finzi (Milan: Mondadori, 1977);

Bacia la soglia della tua casa (Siracusa, Sicily: Schittino, 1981);

A Sibilla, edited by Giancarlo Vigorelli (Milan: Rizzoli, 1983);

Tra Quasimodo e Vittorini, edited by Rosa Quasimodo (Acireale, Italy: Lunarionuovo, 1984);

Il poeta a teatro (Milan: Spirali, 1984);

Le Medaglie di Francesco Messina (Milan: Scheiwiller, 1986).

Editions in English: *Selected Writings*, translated and edited by Allen Mandelbaum (New York: Farrar, Straus & Cudahi, 1960);

Poems, translated by G. H. McWilliam and others (Dublin: Italian Institute of Culture, 1963);

Selected Poems, translated by Jack Bevan (Harmondsworth, U.K.: Penguin, 1965).

OTHER: *Lirici minori del XIII e XIV secolo*, edited by Quasimodo and Luciano Anceschi (Milan: Conchiglia, 1941);

Lirica d'amore italiana, edited by Quasimodo (Milan: Schwartz, 1957; republished, 2 volumes, Milan: Garzanti, 1974);

Poesia italiana del dopoguerra, edited by Quasimodo (Milan: Schwartz, 1958);

Milano in inchiostro di china, edited, with an introduction, by Quasimodo (Milan: Scheiwiller/ Amilcare Pizzi, 1963);

Opera grafica di Aligi Sassu incisa dal 1929 al 1962, edited, with an introduction, by Quasimodo (Milan: Luigi De Tullio, 1963);

Mastroianni—Il ritratto, edited, with an introduction, by Quasimodo (Biella, Italy: Rosso, 1964);

L'opera completa di Michelangelo pittore, edited, with an introduction, by Quasimodo (Milan: Rizzoli, 1966);

Hesiod, *Le opere e i giorni*, introduction by Quasimodo (Rome: Edizioni dell'Elefante, 1966);

Gli inediti di Migneco, edited, with an introduction, by Quasimodo (Milan: SEDA, 1967);

Boris Lovet-Lorski: The Language of Time, introduction by Quasimodo (Syracuse, N.Y.: Syracuse University Art School, 1967);

Giorgio De Chirico, includes an essay by Quasimodo (Naples: Marotta, 1968).

TRANSLATIONS: *Lirici greci* (Milan: Corrente, 1940);

Virgil, *Il fiore delle Georgiche* (Milan: Gentile, 1944);

Catullus, *Veronensis Carmina* (Milan: Uomo, 1945);

Homer, *Dall'Odissea* (Milan: Rosa & Ballo, 1945);

John Ruskin, *La Bibbia di Amiens* (Milan: Bompiani, 1946);

Sophocles, *Edipo re* (Milan: Bompiani, 1946);

William Shakespeare, *Romeo e Giulietta* (Milan: Mondadori, 1948);

Aeschylus, *Le Coefore* (Milan: Bompiani, 1949);

Il Vangelo secondo Giovanni (Milan: Gentile, 1950);

Shakespeare, *Macbeth* (Turin: Einaudi, 1952);

Shakespeare, *Riccardo III* (Milan: Piccolo Teatro, 1952);

Pablo Neruda, *Poesie* (Turin: Einaudi, 1952);

Sophocles, *Elettra* (Milan: Mondadori, 1954);

Catullus, *Canti* (Milan: Mondadori, 1955);

Shakespeare, *La tempesta* (Turin: Einaudi, 1956);

Fiore dell'antologia Palatina, edited and translated by Quasimodo (Bologna: Guanda, 1957);

Molière, *Tartufo* (Milan: Bompiani, 1958);

E. E. Cummings, *Poesie scelte* (Milan: All'Insegna del Pesce d'Oro/Scheiwiller, 1958);

Shakespeare, *Otello* (Milan: Mondadori, 1958);

Ovid, *Dalle Metamorfosi*, edited and translated by Quasimodo (Milan: All'Insegna del Pesce d'Oro/Scheiwiller, 1959);

Euripides, *Ecuba* (Urbino, Italy: Argalìa, 1962);

Conrad Aiken, *Mutevoli pensieri* (Milan: All'Insegna del Pesce d'Oro/Scheiwiller, 1963);

Shakespeare, *Antonio e Cleopatra* (Milan: Mondadori, 1966);

Euripides, *Eracle* (Milan: Mondadori, 1966);

Tudor Arghezi, *Poesie*, edited and translated by Quasimodo (Milan: Mondadori, 1966);

Pericle Patocchi, *Chemin de Croix* (Lugano, Switzerland: Topi, 1967);

Y. Lecomte, *Il gioco degli astragali*, edited and translated by Quasimodo (Milan: Moneta, 1968);

Dall'Antologia Palatina, edited and translated by Quasimodo (Milan: Mondadori, 1968);

Homer, *Iliade—Episodi scelti*, edited and translated by Quasimodo (Milan: Mondadori, 1968);

Leonidas, *Leonida di Taranto*, edited and translated by Quasimodo (Manduria, Italy: Lacaita, 1969);

Paul Eluard, *Donner à voir*, edited and translated by Quasimodo (Milan: Mondadori, 1970).

Born on 20 August 1901 in Modica, near Siracusa, Sicily, to Gaetano Quasimodo, a station master, and his wife, Clotilde Ragusa, Salvatore Quasimodo, the 1959 Nobel Prize winner for literature, followed irregular studies: elementary school in Gela, in the Messina region; vocational school in Palermo; and finally, in 1919, engineering school at the Politecnico in Rome. Soon he abandoned his studies, due to financial stringencies. In order to support Bice Donetti, with whom he began to live in 1922 and whom he married in 1925, he worked at several jobs: as a technical designer for a builder; a store clerk; a maintainance technician for a large department store in the capital; and with the Italian army engineering corps. As an army worker he was transferred to Reggio Calabria, where in 1928 he decided to compose verses, an activity that increasingly occupied his attention. His first compositions were shared with his friend Salvatore Pugliatti and his brother-in-law Elio Vittorini, the latter of whom resided in Florence. Quasimodo moved to Florence in 1929 at Vittorini's invitation, and there, the following year, he published three poems in the journal *Solaria* and, in the same year, his first book of verses, *Acque e terre* (Waters and Lands). This book signaled the appearance on the Italian poetic scene of a young, yet mature, hermetic poet. The influence of Giuseppe Ungaretti is evident from the first fragment of this collection: "Ed è subito sera" (And Suddenly It's Evening)—which became the title poem of a book in 1942:

Ognuno sta solo sul cuor della terra
trafitto da un raggio di sole:
ed è subito sera

(Each one stands alone in the center of the earth
pierced by a ray of sun:
and suddenly it's evening).

This first book also defines the first period of Quasimodo's poetry, which was heavily influenced by hermeticism, a movement recognized in Italian poetry since 1925, the year of publication of *Poeti d'oggi*, the first anthology of Italian hermetic poets, prepared by Giovanni Papini and Pietro Pancrazi. Quasimodo's first phase also includes *Oboe sommerso* (Sunken Oboe, 1932), *Erato e Apollion* (1935), and *Poesie* (1938). Hermeticism became the most important Italian poetic school between the two world wars and includes, besides Quasimodo, the works of Ungaretti and Eugenio Montale. Its poetic process is based on analogy and associative images, and it conveys pessimistic meditations on the human condition. Yet, in spite of the death of illusions, the poet typically believes in poetic beauty. Therefore critics have seen in Quasimodo a tension between a world of despair, anguish, and solitude, and a mythical paradise lost, the golden island of his childhood,

Portrait of Tristan Tzara and Quasimodo by Aligi Sassu (from Storia della letteratura, *volume 7, edited by Luigi Ferrante, 1965)*

which is enshrined in Greek mythology and ancient primitive traditions, and is intertwined with the sea and rocks of the Sicilian landscape. "Vento a Tindari" (Wind at Tindari) perhaps best expresses this tension:

Tindari, mite ti so
fra larghi colli pensile sull'acque
dell'isole dolci del dio,
oggi m'assali
e ti chini in cuore.

(Tindari, I know how pleasant
you hang on the waters between the wide hills
of the sweet islands of the god,
today you assail me
and lean into my heart.)

The vagary of the landscape, with the metaphysical implications, reminds one of Giacomo Leopardi's "L'infinito" (1819). The fear of alienation from his native land compels Quasimodo to conjure up archetypes of the Sicilian landscape:

Salgo vertici aerei precipizi,
assorto al vento dei pini,
e la brigata che lieve m'accompagna

s'allontana nell'aria,
onda di suoni e amore,
e tu mi prendi
da cui male mi trassi
e paure d'ombre e di silenzi,
rifugi di dolcezze un tempo assidue
e morte d'anima

(I climb up vertical aerial peaks,
caught in the wind of the pines,
while my lighthearted company
moves further away in the air,
like a wave of sound and love,
and you take me
you whom I left unwillingly
and fears of shadows and of silences,
shelters of sweetnesses once assiduous
and death of the soul).

The elegance and clarity of this composition owes much to a twofold influence: the Greek poetess Sappho, and Leopardi, who deeply influenced Quasimodo throughout his poetic career but especially during the hermetic period.

In 1938 Quasimodo left his engineering job with the army because Arnoldo Mondadori hired him as drama editor for the weekly *Tempo*. Then, in 1941, he moved to Milan to become professor of Italian literature at the Conservatory Giuseppe Verdi. In Milan he met several writers, artists, critics, musicians, and intellectuals, such as Arturo Martini, Giuseppe Cantatore, Aligi Sassu, Leonardo Sinisgalli, Luigi Rognoni, Arturo Tofanelli, Edoardo Persico, and Mario Novaro. In the afternoon they met at the Caffè Biffi; in the evening, the animated conversations continued at the Caffè Savini. This was also the time of Quasimodo's meeting Maria Cumani, a dancer who, after the death of Bice Donetti in 1946, was to become his second wife and mother of their only son, Alessandro. His relationship with Cumani has been preserved in the collection of love letters Quasimodo wrote to her between 1936 and 1959, the year of their legal separation: *Lettere d'amore a Maria Cumani* (1973).

In 1959 Quasimodo won his Nobel Prize. With his new fame Quasimodo, of course, achieved international recognition and received several invitations to speak and to read his works. In 1961 he traveled to Germany, Hungary, Romania, Spain, Mexico, Norway, and Bulgaria. In Spain he was met with great enthusiasm, especially in Barcelona, by leading Catalan writers such as José María Castellet, Carlos Barral, and Juan Goytisolo. In January 1963 at the Freie Universität in West Berlin, Quasimodo gave two lectures: one on the Italian theater and another on contemporary Italian poetry. This was his second visit to West Berlin. In 1960 at the Kongress Halle he had given a reading of his verses. In spring 1963 he was invited by the Istituto Italiano di Cultura to London and Dublin. In London he visited Chiswick to pay homage to Ugo Foscolo's memorial in the church cemetery at Turnham Green. He also was invited to go to Oxford and Cambridge for a lecture at the University Arms Hotel. In the summer of 1963 he returned to Norway. Then in November of the same year he went on an extensive tour of Yugoslavia. In January 1964 he went to Paris, accompanied by his secretary Annamaria Angioletti—who later published a somewhat sensational account of her personal relationship with the poet, *E fu subito sera* (1969)—and Pericle Patocchi, a Swiss writer and Quasimodo's French translator. The Nobel Prize winner was introduced to the Parisian intellectual elite at the prestigious Istituto Italiano di Cultura by André Chamson of the French Academy. This period of travel, according to Angioletti, coincided with Quasimodo's deepest distrust of the media.

Louis Aragon once attributed to ignorance the resentment of the French media, especially the Parisian press, when the Nobel Prize was awarded to Quasimodo ("Hommage à S. Q.," *Lettres Françaises*, 5-11 November 1959). In Italy, the resentment against the adjudication of the Nobel Prize was due more to political reasons than to literary rivalries. Although his critics appeared to regret his departure from hermeticism, they really meant to oppose his political choices. Nevertheless, in the years following the Nobel Prize his name became familiar to millions of Italians. However, following a period of great popularity, which increased abroad steadily, Quasimodo's fame in Italy seemed to diminish. The poet believed, perhaps with some reason, that the old political opposition had succeeded, at least temporarily, in banning his name from the Italian media.

In June 1965 Quasimodo was invited to read at the Spoleto "Festival dei Due Mondi." In January 1966 he was in Grenoble, France, to do another reading of his verses. January 1967 saw him take an extended tour of Switzerland. In June of the same year he took his last trip outside Italy, when he was invited by Oxford University to receive an honorary doctorate. In February 1968 he was invited to a ceremony at the Capitolium in Rome for the celebration of Ungaretti's eightieth birthday. During the banquet Ungaretti exclaimed to Quasimodo, in the presence of leading Italian writers and artists such as Eugenio Montale, Alberto Moravia, Giacomo Manzù, Pier Paolo Pasolini, Libero Bigiaretti, Alfonso Gatto, Libero De Libero, and Piero Piccioni: "Manigoldo, lo sai che ti voglio bene" (Scoundrel, you know I like you). On 14 June 1968, while presiding over the jury for a poetry prize in Amalfi, Quasimodo was taken ill with a brain hemorrhage and died shortly afterward.

His second book, *Oboe sommerso*, is the one that best represents Quasimodo's hermeticism. His ideal island becomes the archetype of a metamorphosed poet-land, in which even human organs are identified with plants or with the mysterious biological process of nature, with a psychological counterpoint of archaic memories. A good example is "Nell'antica luce delle maree" (In the Ancient Light of the Tides):

Città d'isola
sommersa nel mio cuore,
ecco discendo nell'antica luce

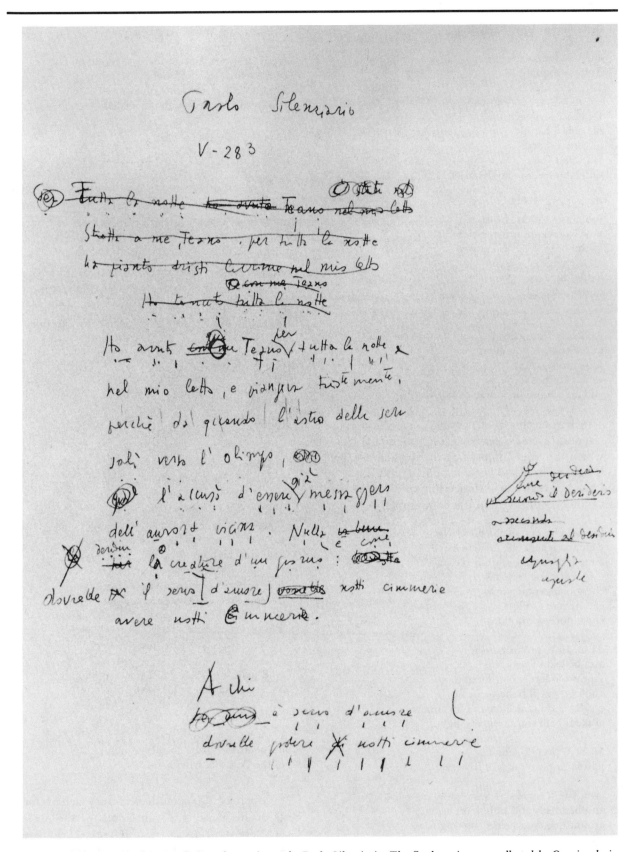

Early draft for Quasimodo's translation of an epigram by Paolo Silenziario. The final version was collected by Quasimodo in 1957 in Fiore dell'antologia Palatina *(from* Storia della letteratura, *volume 7, edited by Luigi Ferrante, 1965).*

delle maree, presso sepolcri
in riva d'acque
che una letizia scioglie
d'alberi sognati.
. . . .

E i tuoi morti sento
nei gelosi battiti
di vene vegetali
fatti men fondi:
un respirare assorto di narici.

(Island city
submerged in my heart,
now I descend in the ancient light
of the tides, near the graves
on the edge of waters
loosed by a joy
of dreamed trees.
. . . .

And I feel your dead
in the jealous pulsations
of plantlike veins
which are not so deep:
and an intense breathing of nostrils.)

An example of what critics have defined as Quasimodo's *parola-mito* (word-myth) is "Parola," in which the poet conjures up an ideal landscape, as if nature itself had become animated as a splendid woman ready to embrace him and yet, at the last moment, elusive and unconquerable:

Tu ridi che per sillabe mi scarno
e curvo cieli e colli, azzurra siepe
a me d'intorno, e stormir d'olmi
e voci d'acque trepide;
che giovinezza inganno
con nuvole e colori
che la luce sprofonda.

Ti so. In te tutta smarrita
alza bellezza i seni,
s'incava ai lombi e in soave moto
s'allarga per il pube timoroso,
e ridiscende in armonia di forme
ai piedi belli con dieci conchiglie.

Ma se ti prendo, ecco:
parola tu pure mi sei e tristezza.

(You laugh because I waste away for syllables
and bend sky and hills, blue hedge
around me, and helms' blowing noise
and voice of quivering waters;
because I deceive youth
with clouds and colors
that the light submerges.

I know you. Wandering beauty
lifts your breasts,
squeezes your hips and with a gentle motion
opens up your timid pubis,
and lowers in harmony of forms
down to your feet with ten shells.

But if I take you, there:
you, too, are word to me, and sadness.)

The intimate religious dimension of Quasimodo's hermeticism is present in "Curva minore" (Lesser Curve), in which recurrent words such as *vento* (wind), *erba* (grass), *ombra* (shade), and *sera* (evening) acquire a haunting connotation, placed as they are in a degrading order from a dynamic allegory to a gradually subdued reality. The poem reveals a kind of pantheistic allusion, not totally new to Quasimodo's archetypal lyricism:

Perdimi, Signore, che non oda
gli anni sommersi taciti spogliarmi,
si che cangi la pena in moto aperto:
curva minore
del vivere m'avanza.

E fammi vento che naviga felice,
o seme d'orzo o lebbra
che sé esprima in pieno divenire.

E sia facile amarti
in erba che accima alla luce,
in piaga che buca la carne.

(Confuse me, Lord, do not let me hear
the quiet secret years emptying me,
so that I can change sorrow for open motion:
a lesser curve
of life is what is left for me.

And make me wind that I may sail happily,
or seed of barley or leprosy
which may express itself in full becoming.

Let it be easy loving you
in the leaf of grass absorbing light,
in the flesh-decaying sore.)

Much of Quasimodo's literary achievement rests on his masterful translations of the ancient Greek poets in *Lirici greci* (Greek Lyric Poets, 1940), which quickly became the center of a long-debated literary question concerning the role of the translator. Not only did the book reveal

Quasimodo circa 1957

Quasimodo's originality as a translator, but many would consider this translation his finest work, due to the "modern" flavor he elicited from texts thousands of years old. Also he revealed a broader register and a more universal spectrum of tonalities than the usual hermetic style of his own previous collections. A case in point is this fragment from Sappho:

> Tramontata è la luna
> e le Pleiadi a mezzo della notte;
> anche giovinezza già dilegua,
> e ora nel mio letto resto sola.
> Scuote l'anima mia Eros,
> come vento sul monte
> che irrompe entro le querce;
> e scioglie le membra e le agita,
> dolce amaro indomabile serpente.
> Ma a me non ape, non miele;
> e soffro e desidero.

> (The moon has waned
> and the Pleiades are gone in the middle of the
>   night;
> even youth is waning,
> and now I am alone in my bed.
> Eros shakes my soul,

> like wind on the mountain
> sweeping through the oak trees;
> and it unties and agitates my limbs,
> sweet bitter indomitable snake.
> But for me no bee, no honey;
> and I suffer and want.)

In a note appended to his translations of the Greek lyrics, Quasimodo asserted, "queste mie traduzioni non sono rapportate a probabili schemi metrici d'origine, ma tentano l'approssimazione più specifica d'un testo: quella poetica" (these translations of mine are not linked to possible metrical schemes in the original, but attempt the most specific textual approximation: a poetic one).

Quasimodo tried to re-create the original feelings. This unusual manner of approach, therefore, has deeper implications for the development of Quasimodo's poetic style than if he had confined himself to the humbler work of a translator. By concentrating more on catching the spirit rather than the letter of the originals he did, in fact, succeed in enlarging vicariously his own experience, especially during those rare moments when he fully identified himself with the inner feelings of others. Cases of such identification, for instance, are to be found in his translations from Sappho and Alcaeus, because the poetry of both left a definite mark on his own work. Other examples of stylistic gains come from the syntactical or rhetorical patterns inherited from a classical text, notably a classical Latin original. In all probability it was through the mediation of these texts that he learned, at least partially, to shake off his hermetic straitjacket and base his themes and melodies on deeper lyrical patterns.

After the hedonistic ideal and the fin de siècle aestheticism of the decadent and crepuscular movements, the new school called hermeticism searched for a new form of expression. The direction seemed to point to "pure poetry," or "poetics of the word," even if the style and language of poetry seemed to have acquired new meaning, due to the unusual analogies and associations. From the vantage point of chronological perspective in relation to that poetic school, one can say that, whereas Ungaretti could qualify as a baroque hermetic, and Montale as an essential hermetic, Quasimodo, the last of the hermetic poets, seems to have been a classical hermetic. Some critics, such as Guillermo de Torre and Angelo Romanó, have stated that, up to a certain point, Quasimodo continues the French Parnassian school of poetry, because of his intimate nostalgia for an ideal, lost land. In the case of Quasimodo this fabulous, mythical land is the land of the orange blossoms, Sicily. The Mediterranean Quasimodo, lost in an ultramodern city, submerged in comfort and technological gadgetry—an alienating universe from the simple world of his childhood—felt intimately related to that past land of his dreams. This attitude can be seen—and for some critics this would mean a limitation of his poetry—in the repetitions of certain key words that become commonplace in his first books, such as *deserti* (deserts), *paradiso* (paradise), *stelle* (stars), *notte* (night), *vento* (wind), and *mare* (sea). According to this interpretation, Quasimodo expressed his nostalgia for a lost paradise with a series of commonplaces.

On the other hand, this could explain the limitations of a critical approach solely concerned with style. That is why it is so important to identify the poetic moment that succeeds the nostalgic longing and actually testifies to a poetic redemption of that Mediterranean paradise of ancient times. With Quasimodo, Italian poetry regained the vigor of the Mediterranean world of the Magna Graecia, which still survives in southern Italy, with her sea, her rocks, and her cities, and mirrors the intimate soul of the poet, its interpreter. That is why it is paramount to assign the proper place to Quasimodo's translations of ancient Greek poets. His translations are more of an interpretation, succeeding in bringing back the ancient text and giving it a present-day tonality and flavor, choosing words and phrases that have kept the original vigor of connotations and analogies.

After romanticism, literary criticism acquired a new dimension of time, from a linguistic point of view. According to this linguistic dimension, the critic can place a given poetic text in its precise historical and cultural context. This quality of modern literary criticism has been applied to the lyrical creative process, which in its turn has acquired a critical dimension of its own, so that the poetic text can and does bring forth the essential character of a cultural phenomenon, chosen as his lyrical target by the poet. In the case of an ancient text, this method worked splendidly for Quasimodo, since his translations aspire to be actually updated versions of the original work: the translator has sought to give new life and relevancy to these works for the benefit of his contemporary reader.

This quality of updating ancient texts, so evident in his translations, was a decisive dimension of his evolution as an original poet. Quasimodo succeeded, perhaps better than anyone else, in expressing for a twentieth-century audience the telluric presence of the Mediterranean world and achieving through it a universal dimension that perhaps was missing. This Quasimodo achieved with his archetypes and myths. What readers still admire today in the work of the Sicilian poet is that feeling of a newly discovered landscape of the world in its primeval vigor, without intermediate reflections, so that one has the impression that the only man alive is Ulysses and the only trip that counts is his interminable journey to the ideal Ithaca.

Modern Italian literature has frequently dealt with the myth of Ulysses because in it one can mirror the alienation of modern man, who has abandoned his native land for a utopian dream but has found himself in the midst of wars and violence, of the denial of permanent values of civilized man, and in the shadow of hatred and tyranny. The myth is still the same, but the man has changed. This man is still looking for his own roots, and instead he finds himself trapped by a way of life he has neither chosen nor can change. For Giovanni Pascoli, Ulysses is the man beloved by the goddess, Calypso, who departs for his last destination in order to see again, at the end of his life, the place of an unknown happiness. For Umberto Saba, Ulysses is a traveler who has not kept a place for the only woman who loved him. For Quasimodo, Ulysses is the symbol of Mediterranean man, whom he conceives as a dimension of every man and, at the same time, as an impossible archetype, gradually and inexorably transformed by the advancing technological society.

Quasimodo's new humanism has been linked to his Marxist sympathies. But one can discount a direct relationship between his outspoken political views and his innermost lyrical vocation. From this point of view, Quasimodo's poetry is better described in terms of a cycle rather than stages, a cycle that begins with the "pure poetry" of *Acque e terre* and culminates with the humanistic poetry of *Giorno dopo giorno* (Day after Day, 1947). The link between the two is the philosophical search for the essence of the Mediterranean man. For Quasimodo the linguistic search of hermeticism was enriched by the philosophical search in his humanistic poetry. Linguistics and philosophy go hand in hand, so the linguistic sign carries a philosophical content. The lesson of Giambattista Vico had been that all language is metaphorical. Behind each word there is an original attitude. For instance, Homer's language amounts to an inventory of a civilization. When linguistics discovers in a word an ontological message, it converges into philosophy. The principle of the search for the deeper meaning of a word is a fundamental method of any translator. Quasimodo is best defined as a poet-translator, as we can see in one of his most popular poems, "Vento a Tindari," the last stanza of which reveals how his work as translator enriched his own poetry:

> Tindari serena torna;
> soave amico mi desta
> che mi sporga nel cielo da una rupe
> e io fingo timore a chi non sa
> che vento profondo m'ha cercato.

> (Serene Tindari come back;
> a sweet friend wakes me up
> so that I can bend over from a rock in the sky
> and I pretend fear to whoever ignores
> what deep wind sought me out.)

Quasimodo believed that Homer's voice preceded Greece. It was Homer who had "formed" Greek civilization. This belief was held, before Quasimodo, by Gian Vincenzo Gravina (1664-1718) and Vico (1668-1744). This is one reason why in a sense the experience of World War II found Quasimodo ready to address the "new" mission of poetry, that of the *rifare l'uomo* (re-making of man).

The war brought about a profound change of style and motives, alluded to in various collections of Quasimodo's poetry and essays, such as *Giorno dopo giorno*, *La vita non è sogno* (Life Is Just a Dream, 1949), *Il falso e vero verde* (The False and True Green, 1954, enlarged 1956), and *La terra impareggiabile* (The Incomparable Earth, 1958). On the war Quasimodo wrote in "Discorso sulla poesia" (published with *Il falso e vero verde* in 1956) that "la guerra muta la vita morale d'un popolo" (war changes the moral life of a nation). He felt that hermeticism was finished by 1945, and he defined this movement as "l'estremo antro fiorentino di fonemi metrici" (the extreme Florentine pastoral cave of metrical phonemes). If one follows Quasimodo's own account of the changes in his poetry brought about by the war, one realizes that he saw correspondence between the events leading up to the war and the end of hermeticism: "La guerra ha sorpreso un linguaggio poetico che maturava una parte-

cipazione con gli oggetti della terra per raggiungere l'universale. Le allegorie si erano dissolte nella solitudine della dittatura" (War had surprised poetic language, [and] that matured a participation with the objects of the earth in order to reach universality. The allegories had vanished in the solitude of the dictatorship).

It is possible that Quasimodo wanted to see it that way because it provided him with a new ideological identity, since his contribution to the anti-Fascist movement was much less decisive than other Italian writers and intellectuals of his own generation, such as Giacomo Matteotti, Ignazio Silone, and Benedetto Croce. The truth was probably much more complex than that. Once Italy lost the world war and the country plunged into a state of virtual civil war, with the North controlled by the Germans and the South by the Allied forces, all the sympathies of the Italian people went to those who had resisted Fascism even at the height of its power. In the postwar era hardly anyone in Italy argued the right of the Communists to be the moral voice of the nation, in spite of fears of the totalitarian nature of the Communist party and its subservient role to the Soviet Union. Therein ensued one of the most fascinating chapters in Italian history. The northern capitalistic bourgeoisie, which had profited and prospered during the Fascist regime but had also supported the war effort, anxious to regain respectability, began to support the leftist intelligentsia, knowing how the literary prizes, academic posts, and prestigious positions would be coveted by the intellectuals, writers, artists, musicians, and poets, who very soon became aware that an ideological realignment was necessary for most of them, since the vast majority had not had the courage and the vision of Matteotti, Silone, or Croce. Communist propaganda made the most of this change, encouraging it and supporting it with a visible campaign in its publications, as well as in the cultural policies it supported, especially within the influential movie industry, soon a milieu totally dominated by the left. The postwar years were decisive in the restructuring and reorganization of the cultural institutions and academies of Italy, including the universities. Totally subservient to the Fascist regime prior to the war, they became the battlefield for what would be known in later years as the *lottizzazione*, the parceling of exclusive influence to a given party, with the three leading parties (Christian Democrat, Communist, and Socialist) receiving the lion's share. It is clear that in

Quasimodo in Stockholm receiving the 1959 Nobel Prize for Literature

such an environment no artist would ever succeed if left to his own devices. Without the support of a visible influential group, no verses would be effective, since their tonality would only be harmonious if and when the leftist siren was heard in it. This explains Quasimodo's repeated forays as a speaker and a writer; it made him appear more "engaged" than he really was. Ultimately this allowed Marxist critics to claim Quasimodo as one of their own, while justifying the moral commitment already implied in the considerations of the Swedish Academy when it decided to award him the Nobel Prize.

This explains why Quasimodo's humanism is none other than a label conceived for the broader consumption of a society romantically in love with the left but solidly anchored to material possessions, aware of its sins and willing to reward the severe poet who, from the height of his underdeveloped, and therefore innocent, island, can freely dispense his musical warnings of doom. The compositions of *Giorno dopo giorno* rep-resent this new humanism, understood as the interpretation of a nation, its moral voice. A case in point is the opening composition of the book, "Alle fronde dei salici" (On the Willow Boughs):

E come potevamo noi cantare
con il piede straniero sopra il cuore,
fra i morti abbandonati nelle piazze
sull'erba dura di ghiaccio, al lamento
d'agnello dei fanciulli, all'urlo nero
della madre che andava incontro al figlio
crocifisso sul palo del telegrafo?
Alle fronde dei salici, per voto,
anche le nostre cetre erano appese,
oscillavano lievi al triste vento.

(And how could we sing
with the foreign foot upon our heart,
among the dead abandoned in the squares
on the frozen grass, amid the lamblike
bleating of the children, amid the black howling
of the mother rushing up to her son
crucified on the telegraph pole?
As an offering, on the willow boughs

our lyres, too, were hung,
quivering slightly in the sad wind.)

There is a sophisticated double level of connotations, both pointing out the renunciation of hermeticism. The first level is a denunciation of the brutality of war in general, and, in particular, the civil war that devastated northern Italy after the armistice of 8 September 1943 between Italy and the Allied nations. The poet is an anguished witness of the carnage and destruction of war, and his usual style is no longer justified; his hermeticism, like the lyre offered by the poet to assuage the sorrow of his countrymen, is buffeted by the sad winds of war. To this first connotative level, one can add a second, which becomes the melodic structure of the new style, hinged on the hendecasyllabic tonality of the whole poem, which is at the same time a classical retreat and a reassuring foray in the consoling harmony of the highest tradition of solemn Italian poetry, demanding a role in the somber, almost funereal landscape of the apocalyptic vision of Quasimodo:

Giorno dopo giorno: parole maledette e il sangue
e l'oro. Vi riconosco, miei simili, o mostri
della terra. Al vostro morso è caduta la pietà,
e la croce gentile ci ha lasciati.
E più non posso tornare nel mio eliso.

(Day after day: unbearable words and the blood
and the gold. I acknowledge our common origin,
    monsters
of the earth. Piety has died torn to pieces by you,
and the gentle cross has abandoned us.
Nor can I ever go back to my Elysium.)

The success of *Giorno dopo giorno* depends on Quasimodo's ability to strike just the right note between admonition and regret, in order to capture the sympathy of the reader. The biblical tone confers on the poems that extra ethicality required to spread a message of solidarity equally pleasing to the left as to progressive Catholics, after the empty rhetoric of Fascism. In fact the book's essential style was something of a novelty, although illustrious models could be found, especially in Dante, Girolamo Savonarola, and Leopardi. It was Quasimodo's ability to revive the best tradition of Italian poetry and combine it with the ever-present classical allusions in dealing with the topic of the war that made the book an instant success, in Italy and abroad. None of his sub-

sequent books would achieve the same popularity.

The following book, *La vita non è sogno*, represents a reconciliation between his Sicilian roots and the adopted Lombard environment, as in "Lamento per il Sud" (Lament for the South):

La luna rossa, il vento, il tuo colore
di donna del Nord, la distesa di neve . . .
Il mio cuore è ormai su queste praterie,
in queste acque annuvolate dalle nebbie.
Ho dimenticato il mare, la grave
conchiglia soffiata dai pastori siciliani,
le cantilene dei carri lungo le strade
dove il carrubo trema nel fumo delle stoppie,
ho dimenticato il passo degli aironi e delle gru
nell'aria dei verdi altipiani
per le terre e i fiumi della Lombardia.
Ma l'uomo grida dovunque la sorte d'una patria.
Più nessuno mi porterà nel Sud.

(The red moon, the wind, your coloring
of woman of the North, the wilderness of snow . . .
My heart is now in these plains,
in these waters clouded by mists.
I have forgotten the sea, the heavy
shell blown by Sicilian shepherds,
the singsong of the carts along the roads
where the carob tree quivers in the smoke of the
    stubble,
I have forgotten the flight of the herons and the
    storks
in the air of the green plateaus
for the lands and rivers of Lombardy.
But man cries everywhere for his country's destiny.
No one will ever take me South again.)

The solemn enumeration reminds one of the nostalgic verses of *Acque e terre*, but there is an almost narrative tonality, which allows for a resigned solution to the conflict that dominated his early poetry. The aftermath of the war still demands the poet's attention. He still has a message of redemption, and his priest is Orpheus, the new archetype, capable of shaking man from the depths of his moral depression:

E tu sporco di guerra, Orfeo
come il tuo cavallo, senza la sferza,
alza il capo, non trema più la terra;
urla d'amore, vinci, se vuoi, il mondo.

(And you, Orpheus, filthy with war,
like your horse, without the whip,
raise your head, the earth no longer shakes;
shout your love, if you want, you can conquer the
    world.)

At this point Quasimodo, having lost the initial enthusiasm of *Giorno dopo giorno*, relapses into conventional phraseology and poetic schemes, so that one can perceive an alternating mood, from an outright propagandistic effort to a pristine neohermeticism, as represented in two different compositions, "Il mio paese è l'Italia" (My Country Is Italy) and "Quasi un madrigale" (Almost a Madrigal):

Là Buchenwald, la mite selva di faggi,
i suoi forni maledetti; là Stalingrado
e Minsk sugli acquitrini e la neve putrefatta.

(There Buchenwald, the gentle wood of beeches,
its cursed ovens; there Stalingrad
and Minsk on the swamps and the putrified snow.)

In contrast with this superficial demagoguery, one sees the example of neohermeticism:

Il girasole piega a occidente
e già precipita il giorno nel suo
occhio in rovina e l'aria dell'estate
s'addensa e già curva le foglie e il fumo
dei cantieri. S'allontana con scorrere
secco di nubi e stridere di fulmini
quest'ultimo gioco del cielo.

(The sunflower turns to the west
while the day already plunges into his
decaying eye and the summer wind
builds up and already is bending the leaves and
  the smoke
of the builders' yards. It vanishes with a dry
rushing of clouds and bursting of thunders
this last play of the sky.)

The last books show a poet in search of social utopia. Alienation and the nuclear threat are dominant themes in his last poems, such as "In questa città" (In This City) and "Ancora dall'inferno" (Still from Hell), collected in *La terra impareggiabile*:

In questa città c'è pure la macchina
che stritola i sogni: con un gettone
vivo, un piccolo disco di dolore
sei subito di là, su questa terra,
ignoto in mezzo ad ombre deliranti
su alghe di fosforo funghi di fumo;
una giostra di mostri
che gira su conchiglie
che si spezzano putride sonando.

(In this city there is even the machine
that grinds the dreams: with a token,

Quasimodo at Gardone, Italy, 1960

a quick, a small disk of sorrow
you are there in no time, on this earth,
unknown amid delirious shadows
upon phosphorous seaweeds and mushrooms of
  smoke:
a merry-go-round of monsters
turning around shells
which crack putrified with a sound.)

The city is like a Dantesque hell, an alienating environment for everyone who happens to be trapped inside:

Non ci direte una notte gridando
dai megafoni, una notte
di zagare, di nascite, d'amori
appena cominciati, che l'idrogeno
in nome del diritto brucia
la terra. Gli animali i boschi fondono
nell'Arca della distruzione, il fuoco
è un vischio sui crani dei cavalli,
negli occhi umani. Poi a noi morti
voi morti direte nuove tavole
della legge. Nell'antico linguaggio
altri segni, profili di pugnali.
Balbetterà qualcuno sulle scorie,
inventerà tutto ancora
o nulla nella sorte uniforme,
il mormorio delle correnti, il crepitare
della luce. Non la speranza
direte voi morti alla nostra morte

220

negli imbuti di fanghiglia bollente,
qui nell'inferno. (*Tutte le poesie*, p. 227)
(From "Ancora dall'inferno")

(You will not announce screaming one night
through the bullhorns, one night
of orange-blossoms, of births, of loves
just begun, that the hydrogen
in the name of the law scorches
the earth. The animals and the woods melt
in the ark of destruction, the fire
is a snare on the horses' skulls,
in human eyes. Then to us dead
you dead will tell us new codes
of the law. In the ancient language
new signs, outlines of daggers.
Someone will babble on the remains,
will again invent everything
or nothing in the identical destiny,
the whispering of streams, the crackling
of the light. Of hope
you dead will not speak to our death
in the funnels of boiling mud,
here in hell.)

This poem expresses well the sentiments of humankind's longing for peace, the horror of the impending nuclear holocaust forever looming on the horizon since the time of Hiroshima and Nagasaki, the obscure forces of history incessantly at work, with the poet imagining a distant day when civilization will start again from scratch in order to repeat the same mistakes. This is a pessimistic viewpoint, one which contrasts with the more civic call to moral regeneration and social commitment of compositions such as "Vàrvara Alexandrovna" and "Solo che amore ti colpisca" (Only if Love Should Pierce You), collected in *Dare e avere* (1966; translated as *To Give and to Have*, 1969). In the first poem, composed during an illness in the Soviet Union in memory of a nurse who took care of him, Quasimodo identifies in her and her solidarity a new spirit of humankind:

sei la Russia, non un paesaggio di neve
riflesso in uno specchio d'ospedale
sei una moltitudine di mani che cercano altre mani.

(you are Russia, not a snowy landscape
reflected in a hospital mirror
you are a crowd of hands searching for other
    hands.)

In the second poem, he identifies love as the new religion, capable of tying every person to the es-

sence of humankind: "ricorda che puoi essere l'essere dell'essere / solo che amore ti colpisca bene alle viscere" (remember that you can be the being of the being / if only love should pierce you deep inside).

In one of the last compositions of *La terra impareggiabile*, "Una risposta" (An Answer), Quasimodo flashes the magic name of Ulysses. Ulysses appears amid the mystical desire of the poet to reach out to God:

Se arde alla mente l'àncora d'Ulisse . . .
Se in riva al mare di Aci, qui fra barche
con l'occhio nero a prua contro la mala
sorte, io potessi dal nulla dell'aria
qui dal nulla che stride di colpo e uncina
come la fiocina del pesce-spada,
dal nulla delle mani che si mutano
come Aci, viva formare dal nulla
una formica e spingerla nel cono
di sabbia del suo labirinto o un virus
che dia continua giovinezza al mio
più fedele nemico,
forse allora sarei simile a Dio—
nell'uguale fermezza della vita
e della morte non contrarie:
onda qui e lava, larve
della luce di questa già futura
chiara mattina d'inverno—risposta
a una domanda di natura e angoscia
che folgora su un numero miliare,
il primo della strada torrida
che s'incunea nell'al di là.

(If Ulysses' anchor is fire to the mind . . .
If by Aci's sea, here amid boats
with the black eye at the bow against bad
luck, I could from the empty air
here from nothing suddenly screaming and hook-
    ing
like the harpoon of the swordfish,
from nothing of hands changing
like Aci, mold alive from nothing
an ant and push it on the cone
of sand of its labyrinth or a virus
that brings unending youth to my
most dedicated enemy,
perhaps then I would be like God—
in the firm sameness of life
and death not opposing each other:
wave here and lava, larvae
of the light of this already future
clear winter morning—answer
to a question of nature and anguish
which bolts a milestone,
the first on the torrid road
which penetrates into the world beyond.)

Always the poet-translator, Quasimodo succeeds in blending all the most diverse materials of his poetic style. The neohermetic technique is alive in this poem, except for a religious tonality, and the classical hero is placed at the beginning with the verb *arde*, signifying a Dantean allusion to the fire that surrounds Ulysses in Canto XXVI of the *Inferno*. One sees the three lyrical ingredients of Quasimodo's poetry: hermeticism, classicism, and biblical mysticism. Furthermore, the hendecasyllabic structure that predominates throughout this composition reinforces the traditional technique of the allusion, which finds a corresponding "allegoric" mode with an authority such as Dante, giving to the word *àncora* of the first verse a referential meaning, confirmed by *arde* and the fact that Quasimodo's text is itself "anchored" on firm hermetic tradition.

It would be difficult to compare Quasimodo with any other Italian poet, except the last three great nineteenth-century poets, Giosuè Carducci, Giovanni Pascoli, and Gabriele D'Annunzio. Probably no other Italian poet, in the first decades of the twentieth century, exercised such a deep and lasting influence as Quasimodo has. However, his lyrical contribution after the war seems to pale when compared to his success as a prewar hermetic poet and translator. After the war his commendable political stance was a detriment to his artistic achievement whenever he committed himself too strongly to prevailing fashions and descended to a documentary kind of poetry. All in all his name and poetry are to be considered at the very center of the latest developments of Italian poetry, making his work the decisive experience for the newest generations of Italian poets.

Letters:

Le lettere d'amore, edited by Guido Le Noci (Milan: Apollinaire, 1969);

Lettere d'amore a Maria Cumani (1936-1959), edited by Davide Lajolo (Milan: Mondadori, 1973);

Salvatore Quasimodo—G. La Pira: Carteggio, edited by Alessandro Quasimodo (Milan: All'Insegna del Pesce d'Oro, 1980);

Lettere d'amore (1936-1959), edited by Alessandro Quasimodo (Milan: Spirali, 1985);

Carteggio, 1929-1966 (Milan: All'Insegna del Pesce d'Oro, 1988).

Interviews:

Gilberto Finzi, "Domande a Quasimodo," *L'Europa Letteraria*, 30-32 (1964): 21-26;

Ferdinando Camon, "Salvatore Quasimodo," in his *Il mestiere di poeta* (Milan: Garzanti, 1982), pp. 15-21.

References:

Luciano Anceschi, Introduction to Quasimodo's *Lirici greci* (Milan: Mondadori, 1951), pp. 7-22;

Anceschi, Introduction and "Per la poesie di Quasimodo," in *Lirici nuovi*, edited by Anchesi (Milan: Mursia, 1964), pp. 3-13, 214-225;

Mirko Bevilacqua, ed., *La critica e Quasimodo* (Bologna: Cappelli, 1976);

Carlo Bo, Preface to Quasimodo's *Giorno dopo giorno*, in *Tutte le poesie* (Milan: Mondadori, 1960), pp. 199-226;

Rosalma Salina Borello, ed., *Per conoscere Quasimodo* (Milan: Mondadori, 1973);

Glauco Cambon, "A Deep Wind: Quasimodo's Tindari," *Italian Quarterly*, 3 (Fall 1959): 16-41;

Stelio Cro, "El sentimiento telúrico del Mediterráneo en Salvatore Quasimodo," *La Nación* (15 June 1969): 2;

Gilberto Finzi, Introduction to Quasimodo's *Tutte le poesie* (Milan: Mondadori, 1986), pp. 5-18;

Finzi, *Invito alla lettura di Salvatore Quasimodo* (Milan: Mursia, 1983);

Marcello Gigante, *L'ultimo Quasimodo e la poesia greca* (Naples: Guida, 1970);

Gianni Grana, ed., "Salvatore Quasimodo," in his *Novecento: I contemporanei*, volume 9 (Milan: Marzorati, 1979), pp. 8103-8147;

F. J. Jones, "Osservazioni sulla simbologia di Quasimodo," *Cenobio*, 3 (May-June 1961): 254-274;

Jones, "The poetry of Salvatore Quasimodo," *Italian Studies*, 16 (1961): 60-77;

Jones, "Quasimodo and the Collapse of Hermeticism," in his *The Modern Italian Lyric* (Cardiff: University of Wales Press, 1986), pp. 512-561;

Oreste Macrí, *La poesia di Quasimodo* (Palermo: Sellerio, 1986);

Gaetano Munafò, *Quasimodo, poeta del nostro tempo* (Florence: Monnier, 1973);

Gioacchino Paparelli, *Da Ariosto a Quasimodo* (Naples: Società Editrice Napoletana, 1978);

Paparelli, "Humanitas e poesia di Quasimodo," *Letterature moderne* (1961): 719-748;

Paparelli, "Poesia e poetica di Quasimodo," *Il Baretti*, 9-10 (1961): 134-139;

Pietro Pelosi, *Presenza e metamorfosi del mito di Orfeo in Salvatore Quasimodo* (Naples: Delfino, 1978);

Bortolo Pento, *Lettura di Quasimodo* (Milan: Marzorati, 1966);

Elena Salibra, *Salvatore Quasimodo* (Rome: Dell'Ateneo, 1985);

Gaetano Salveti, *Salvatore Quasimodo con otto inediti del poeta* (Padua, Italy: Sestante, 1964);

Roberto Sanesi, "La poesia di Quasimodo," *Inventario*, 16 (1961): 107-124;

Sergio Solmi, Preface to Quasimodo's *Ed è subito sera*, in *Tutte le poesie* (Milan: Mondadori, 1960), pp. 15-30;

Mario Stefanile, *Quasimodo* (Padua, Italy: Cedam, 1943);

Orazio Tanelli, "Quasimodo e la sua terra," *Follia di New York*, 92 (March-April 1985): 37;

Natale Tedesco, *L'isola impareggiabile: Significati e forme del mito di Quasimodo* (Florence: Nuova Italia, 1977);

Tedesco, *Quasimodo* (Palermo: Flaccovio, 1959);

Michele Tondo, *Salvatore Quasimodo* (Milan: Mursia, 1970);

Tondo, "Salvatore Quasimodo," in *Letteratura italiana contemporanea*, volume 2, edited by Gaetano Mariani and Mario Petrucciani (Rome: Lucarini, 1980), pp. 241-257;

Giuseppe Zagarrio, *Quasimodo* (Florence: Nuova Italia, 1969).

Clemente Rèbora

(6 January 1885 - 1 November 1957)

Nicolas J. Perella
University of California, Berkeley

BOOKS: *Frammenti lirici* (Florence: Libreria della Voce, 1913);

Canti anonimi (Milan: Convegno, 1922);

Le poesie, edited by Pietro Rèbora (Florence: Vallecchi, 1947); enlarged edition, edited by Vanni Scheiwiller (Milan: All'Insegna del Pesce d'Oro, 1961; enlarged again, 1982);

Curriculum vitae (Milan: All'Insegna del Pesce d'Oro, 1955);

Canti dell'infermità (Milan: All' Insegna del Pesce d'Oro, 1956; enlarged, 1957);

Gesù il fedele (Milan: All'Insegna del Pesce d'Oro, 1956);

Il Natale (Milan: All'Insegna del Pesce d'Oro, 1959);

Iconografia, edited by Scheiwiller (Milan: All'Insegna del Pesce d'Oro, 1959);

Aspirazioni e preghiere, compiled by Scheiwiller (Milan: All'Insegna del Pesce d'Oro, 1963);

Antologia reboriana, edited by Carlo Zapelloni (Stresa, Italy: Istituto E. Maggia, 1963);

Ecco del ciel più grande (Milan: All'Insegna del Pesce d'Oro, 1965);

Mania dell'eterno, edited by Daria Banfi Malaguzzi (Milan: All'Insegna del Pesce d'Oro, 1968);

Antonio Rosmini, asceta e mistico (Vicenza, Italy: Premiá, 1979);

Dammi il tuo Natale (Vicenza, Italy: Locusta, 1986).

OTHER: "Per un Leopardi mal noto," in *Omaggio a Rèbora* (Bologna: Boni, 1971), pp. 69-165.

TRANSLATIONS: Leonid Andreyev, *Lazzaro e altre novelle* (Florence: Voce, 1919);

Nikolay Gògol, *Il cappotto* (Milan: Convegno, 1922);

Anonymous, *Gianardana* (Milan: Bottega di Poesia, 1922);

Leo Tolstoy, *La felicità domestica* (Milan: Bompiano, 1942).

SELECTED PERIODICAL PUBLICATION—
UNCOLLECTED: "G. D. Romagnosi nel pensiero del Risorgimento," *Rivista d'Italia*, 14 (November 1911): 808-840.

Frequently characterized by a violent wrenching of rhythm within a sometimes extreme metrical experimentation, and by an aggressive, eccentric, and cacophonous linguistic expressionism uncommon in the Italian lyric tradition, Clemente Rèbora's difficult verses—in particular

Clemente Rèbora, 1919

those of his first volume of poetry, *Frammenti lirici* (Lyrical Fragments, 1913)—present the reader with perhaps the most intense utterances of twentieth-century Italian poetry. Representing a radical break with Gabriele D'Annunzio's aestheticizing heroism (though D'Annunzian elements are absorbed and transmuted by Rèbora) and the crepuscular renunciatory mode (low-keyed and melancholically self-ironic at its best), as well as differing from the exhibitionistic anarchical vitalism of futurism, Rèbora's tensive new style is thematically linked to a highly charged moral and mystical impulse even in his "secular" phase, that is, before his conversion to Catholicism in 1929. His poetry reflects urgently and persuasively the crisis in values and the desire for renewal and regeneration (with the accompanying swing between hope and despair) felt by many of Italy's intellectuals in the pre–World War I period and even more deeply in its aftermath. But Rèbora's voice, while expressing this general air of crisis, does so from within the context of a personal existentialist drama and thirst for an absolute he struggled to reconcile with, or even subor-

dinate to, a high sense of social responsibility.

In part because of the sheer difficulty of much of his poetry, in part because of strong currents of poetry in a different direction, and in part because of the near silence of Rèbora's muse following his religious conversion, his poetry was largely neglected by critics and anthologists until his death in 1957. Since then, however, he has come to be recognized as one of the country's most essential poets, and one with a hitherto unsuspected presence. For example, in addition to his own distinction as a major poetic voice, he was almost certainly one of the two chief twentieth-century Italian influences (the other being Camillo Sbarbaro) on the early and middle periods of Eugenio Montale's poetry.

Clemente Rèbora was born in Milan on 6 January 1885. The son of Enrico Rèbora (a free-thinker and staunch adherent of the great nineteenth-century republican patriot Giuseppe Mazzini) and Teresa Rinaldi Rèbora (who, though nominally a Catholic, followed her husband's ideas), he was baptized only at the insistence of Catholic relatives. He did not, however, receive a religious upbringing. After attending the schools of Milan through the lyceum, he studied medicine at the University of Pavia, only to quit the program after little more than a year. Back in Milan he enrolled in the Accademia Scientifico-Letteraria and received his degree in 1910, having written as his thesis "G. D. Romagnosi nel pensiero del Risorgimento" (G. D. Romagnosi in the Thought of the Risorgimento, 1911). In the meantime he also completed military service. In this period he established significant friendships with young intellectuals of bright promise. After receiving his degree he attended courses at the university in Milan, attracted above all by the lectures of Piero Martinetti, a professor of theoretical philosophy who was especially concerned with religious and metaphysical questions and whose Plotinian and Spinozistic thinking, in opposition to the currents of positivism and Hegelian idealism, upheld a doctrine of pluralistic spiritualism according to which individual subjects strive to unite with a universal reason. Rèbora also cultivated artistic interests, with a particular passion for music. He was an accomplished pianist with considerable powers of improvisation. This interest in music, coupled with his love of poetry, can be seen in a remarkable essay of some length that he wrote in 1910 dealing with music in the thought and poetics of Giacomo Leopardi: "Per un Leopardi mal noto"

(On a Poorly Known Leopardi), which originally appeared in *Rivista d'Italia* in September 1910, was published in 1971 in *Omaggio a Rèbora*.

A letter to Rèbora's father, dated 22 October 1909, in which Rèbora says he is unable to adapt to the demands of practical life, already suggests a crisis within his early optimistic faith in reason. Having neither the connections nor the temperament to make headway in academe, he taught in technical and public evening schools between 1910 and 1915. But he had a vision of education as something more than the mere imparting of facts, for he felt that school should educate the whole person with a view to a reformation of society. Thus in 1913 he wrote pedagogical articles for *La Voce*, the journal that was at the forefront of a campaign for moral revitalization in Italy. It was under the auspices of *La Voce* that *Frammenti lirici* was published in 1913. In 1914 he entered into a close relationship with the Russian pianist Lidia Natus that lasted until 1919. With her assistance he learned Russian and then produced a few fine translations of works by Russian writers, among them Nikolay Gogol and Leo Tolstoy. In the meantime, Rèbora had been called back to military service on the eve of World War I, and in July 1915 he was sent to a combat zone, where he was seriously traumatized when a grenade exploded near him. Hospitalized, he was diagnosed by a psychiatrist as suffering from a "mania dell'eterno" (mania for eternity) and was finally discharged. Late in 1918 Rèbora returned to teaching, preferring evening school because it allowed him to stay in contact with the working class to which, out of a deep humanitarian sentiment, he felt bound. He also gave private lessons and lectures while continuing to contribute to literary journals, living in poverty all the while. Increasingly drawn to spiritual thought, he read intensely the writings of the world's various religions. By 1922 his second book of poetry—*Canti anonimi* (Anonymous Songs)—had been published. The title bespeaks a wish to efface himself and become the voice of the human condition in a world becoming progressively dehumanized, while he himself yearned for something purer, something higher. In a way, this continues a thematic line already present in *Frammenti lirici*, although the poems are relatively more accessible. Yet the best poem in *Canti anonimi*, "Dall'immagine tesa" (From the Tense Image), suggests a deeply personal experience.

His move toward Catholicism was completed in November 1929 when Rèbora received

Holy Communion, followed soon by confirmation. In May 1931 he became a novice in the Rosminian monastery Monte Calvario, in Domodossola, where in September 1936 he was ordained a priest. Significantly the Rosminian religious order, in which one takes a vow of annulment or self-effacement, has a strong mystic bent. In the spirit of self-sacrifice that was his even before the conversion, Rèbora did a period of pastoral service among the poor, the sick, and the downtrodden. His ministry took him to several locations. Without doubt the best of Rèbora's poetry was written before his conversion. The ensuing silence was intermittently broken by pious poems and prayers he wrote at the request of his superiors. But with the onset of illness in the last six years of his life came the return of a true poetic vein, in a clearly defined Christian context, best exemplified in the intense, if brief, "autobiography" in verse, *Curriculum vitae* (1955) and in the slim volume *Canti dell'infermità* (Songs of Infirmity, 1956). Many of Rèbora's poems (among them the war poems) and lyrical prose pieces that had appeared in various journals between 1913 and 1927 were published as a group under the title "Poesie varie" (Miscellaneous Poems) in the 1947 volume *Le poesie* prepared by the poet's brother, Pietro Rèbora. After twenty-five months throughout which Clemente Rèbora was bedridden and bore his extreme suffering with exemplary patience, he died on 1 November 1957.

The title of Rèbora's first volume, *Frammenti lirici*, should not mislead readers. Each of the seventy-two lyrics, of various lengths, is in fact complete and may be considered a "fragment" only insofar as it contributes to a book that can be said to be an organic whole; indeed, the single lyrics have a way of returning to or recalling others in terms of thematic content, as though not everything had been said, or as though it needed retelling from a different stance or in a different way. In this sense it is the whole book that constitutes the poem. The city, and the opposition between nature and the city, is thematically central to *Frammenti lirici*. Alongside it are the great archetypal images of rain, wind, sun, the mountain, and the existentially keyed motifs of thirst and waiting/expectancy.

In the very first lyric of the collection, "Frammento I," Rèbora recognizes an uncertainty about his own place in the pulsating life around him, but despite his doubts he seeks to enter its flow:

L'egual vita diversa urge intorno;
Cerco e non trovo e m'avvio
Nell'incessante suo moto.

(The equal diverse life urges all about;
I seek and do not find and set forth
In its incessant movement.)

Though he knows that his own propensity is for nature and eternity—"Se a me fusto è l'eterno" (Though eternity is my trunk)—he nonetheless proclaims his desire to have his being, from his roots on up, ripen in the "vivido tutto" (vital whole), suck in the sun, and offer a rich crop of fruit. It is an offer to participate in all of life, including that of the city, to mingle with others and assist them. Yet there is also an awareness of his basic solitariness; already, in "Frammento III," one notes something especially negative in connection with the city. Whereas the storm's violent passage through the countryside remains associated with phenomenal reality, its furious collision with the city is expressionistically internalized and transformed into a cataclysmic psychic reality:

Dall'intensa nuvolaglia
Giù—brunita la corazza,
Con guizzi di lucido giallo,
Con suono che scoppia e si scaglia—
Piomba il turbine e scorrazza
Sul vento proteso a cavallo
Campi e ville, e dà battaglia;
Ma quand'urta una città
Si scàrdina in ogni maglia,
S'inombra come un'occhiaia,
E guizzi e suono e vento
Tramuta in ansietà
D'affollate faccende in tormento:
E senza combattere ammazza.

(From the intense cloud-mass
Downward—its breastplate burnished,
With flashes of brilliant yellow,
With sound that bursts and charges—
The hurricane crashes;
Astride the wind it darts and dashes through
Fields and hamlets, and wages war;
But when it collides with a city
It unhinges all its mail,
It blackens like an eye-socket,
And its flashes and sound and wind
Are changed into anxiety
Of tumultuous bustle in torment:
And without battling it kills.)

The poem exemplifies Rèbora's extraordinary synthesizing power and a characteristic ability to fuse the realm of the abstract and the realm of the concrete. The psychic internalization of natural phenomena, the storm and all the intensity of its threat, probably owes something to the poet Giovanni Pascoli, but Rèbora's language is more expressionistic, laden with rhyming words ending in -aglia and -azza that are harsh and discordant to both ear and eye.

There are times when Rèbora intimates a faith in a *ratio* that is inherent in all things, in the *vivido tutto*, including human activities; but he is restlessly aware of limits, as seen in "Frammento XIV," also called "O pioggia dei cieli distrutti" (O rain of the destroyed skies), which begins with a description of a rain that falls monotonously, "rinsing" everything with a uniform grayness and intoning the great funeral of dreams and light. The rain also intones "il vario contrasto / Della carne e del cuore" (the multifold contrast / Of the flesh and of the heart)—a typical Rèbora-like intuition of negative and positive pulsations in the same situation—in an atmosphere where the footsteps of men drip with mud, the human vortex slips, and human work is closed indoors, "mentre s'incava respinta l'ebbrezza" (while joy repulsed retreats within). Yet reason, says the poet, advances, albeit slowly and in a limited way. It cannot satisfy Rèbora's overriding need to overcome anxiety and to penetrate the great mystery; it cannot appease his aspiration for something beyond. That is left to an intuitive or ecstatic impulse and a higher wisdom that alone can look down serenely from "above" at the cruelty of human life, which, in being metaphysically confined, is like a raging beast in a cage. The high doctrine and immortal beauty that will issue forth from ruin, announced in the poem's last three lines, depend upon this faculty that transcends reason: "Un'eletta dottrina / Un'immortale bellezza / Uscirà dalla nostra rovina" (A precious doctrine, / An immortal beauty / Will come forth from our ruin).

Rèbora's oscillation between faith in industry and progress on the one hand, and impatience and pessimism on the other, is illustrated by the contrastive "twin" lyrics 34 and 35, both of which begin with the line "Scienza vince natura" (Science conquers nature). The lyrics are ambiguous in their language and imagery: concrete and concretely abstract with ideas or concepts taking on a weight and physicality that permit reading the two poems as variations on a celebration of human industry. But in the final analysis they sug-

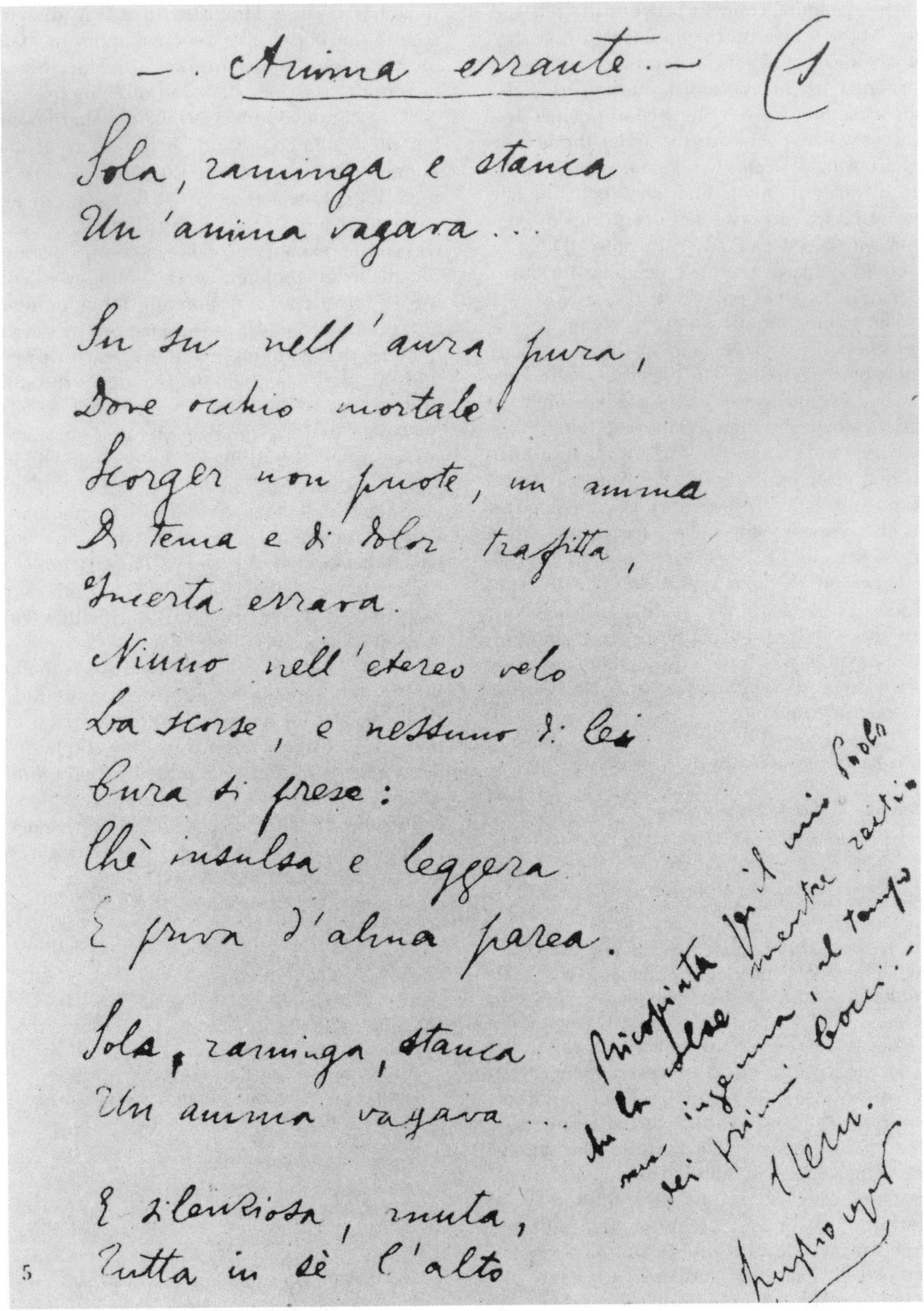

— . Anima errante . —

Sola, raminga e stanca
Un'anima vagava...

In su nell'aura pura,
Dove occhio mortale
Scorger non puote, un'anima
Di tema e di dolor trafitta,
Incerta errava.
Niuno nell'etereo velo
La scorse, e nessuno di lei
Cura si prese:
Chè insulsa e leggera
E priva d'alma parea.

Sola, raminga, stanca
Un'anima vagava...

E silenziosa, muta,
Tutta in sè l'alto

5

Page from the manuscript for Rèbora's "Anima errante," written on 26 May 1900 (from Clemente Rèbora, edited by Vanni Scheiwiller, 1959)

gest a fundamental contrast between the self and reality. At the very least, the optimistic attitude toward rationality and action is in danger of being undermined by an existential yearning that demands something more. The second poem's closing image of the poet-as-carter under the blazing sun, harboring a sleep of dust and thirst, can be found in various authors and painters of the late nineteenth and early twentieth centuries in connection with a sense of reality's aridity. Thirst in this respect is a key existential metaphor for burning desire in Rèbora's poetry.

The ecstatic intuition that transcends reason in the quest for appeasement in the absolute is not necessarily unrelated to physicality, although in the end even physicality (at least individual or subjective physicality) must be transcended. This may be seen in "Frammento IX." Of the four quatrains that make up this lyric, the last two are perhaps too abstractly concerned with expressing the sense of a yearning for purity, for release from the crass banality of the city and modern civilization. However, the first two stanzas (really self-sufficient) evoke an Alpine midday in which the purity and pulsating harmony of the cosmos vibrate in the poet who thus "knows" them in a phenomenal or sensualistic way, as especially seen in the second quatrain:

> Tutta è mia casa la montagna, e sponda
>
> Al desiderio il cielo azzurro porge;
> Ineffabile palpita gioconda
> L'estasi delle cose, e in me si accorge.
>
> (The whole mountain is my abode, and
>
> The blue sky offers a shore to my desire;
> Ineffably, joyfully, the ecstasy of things
> Throbs, and reaches awareness in me.)

The poet is the vehicle through which the absolute or the cosmic life acquires consciousness: what is meant is not just communion but identification with the "all" in the hour of Pan, an identifying pantheistic ecstasy that involves the triumphant experience of self-expansion and self-realization. This is not to be confused with D'Annunzio's mythology of the midday delirium and the advent of joy, because D'Annunzio's experience of self-realization and unity (the unity of all being) is grounded in a naturalistic pantheism—his root metaphor remains the "body" or "matter." In Rèbora's poem the subjective center of experience is the core of being itself with which the

poet has become identified in a way that transcends the body. The root metaphor is "spirit" or, better yet, "consciousness." It is the consciousness not of the poet alone but of being itself.

In "Frammento XXVIII," not the mountain but the whole countryside is the scene of a vast noontide stasis in which the sun appears as a mighty explosion of silent glory. From an initial suspended moment, in which there is a sense of the cosmic expansion of life, Rèbora interiorizes the quality of absoluteness felt in midday, discovering in himself a corresponding inner immensity and infinite potency, and intimations of the same qualities that lie untapped in the hearts of people and things. To a certain degree, this is the sort of midday truth proclaimed earlier by Friedrich Nietzsche and D'Annunzio. In its light Rèbora, no less than they, disdains the ordinary limits to which humans too readily submit. The truth of everyday things that is rightfully humankind's is that of unbounded potentiality, the same as that which belongs to the Deity. Thus Rèbora, too, hails the possibility if not the advent of the superman, but his version is more spiritually charged than the earlier ones.

Certain poems in *Frammenti lirici*, then, reveal in Rèbora, long before his conversion to Catholicism (1929), the yearning for and the intuition of a divine presence or the absolute. But other poems of the same period reveal moments of anxiety, strife, and even a nausea with life—especially city life. The midday experience of "Frammento IX" and the rural noontide revelation of "Frammento XXVIII" have a negative counterpart in the urban midday of "Frammento XXXVI":

> Nell'avvampato sfasciume,
> Tra polvere e péste, al meriggio,
> La fusa scintilla
> D'un dèmone bigio
> Atterga affronta assilla
> L'ignava sloia dei rari passanti,
> La schiavitù croia dei carri pesanti.
>
> (In the blazing ruin,
> Betwixt dust and footsteps at midday,
> The melted spark
> Of a gray demon
> Assails from behind, confronts, goads
> The slothful tedium of the few passersby,
> The vile bondage of the heavy wagons.)

In this mocking vein Rèbora depicts the city as a Dantean *malebolge* (evil pit of hell)—the *bolgia* of the barrators in particular—populated by a *perduta gente* (lost people) moving in the destructive blaze of noon. The ashen-colored demon has Dantean connections, but in the present context he may also be taken as Rèbora's version of the biblical *daemon meridianus*, the destruction that "wasteth" at noon. Yet from this hell the poet emerges untainted because he has accepted the mute sacrifice of humble and pure service: "Nell'ascesi segreta / Del mio nume che s'immola / Al sacrificio muto" (In the secret asceticism / Of my god that immolates himself / In a mute sacrifice).

No less sardonic is the ambiguous and even blasphemous use of the sun as a symbol for an as-yet-uncertain concept of the Deity. In "Frammento XXIV" lines 10-16 picture a cosmic eroticism and the sort of meridian *atroce despota* (fierce despot) that one encounters in D'Annunzio, but transposed by Rèbora into a skeptical key. Rèbora evokes an image of the Deity as a fiercely reigning creative force that remains indifferent to individual suffering while it generates and perpetuates the multiple forms of existence:

Ma sopra, Dio feroce nello spazio
Guizza di luce e si sdraia
Sul nostro patire, e lascivo non sazio
Fra donne d'eternità gaia
Rinnova le estasi libere
Del suo piacere; e inconscio ricrea
Del mondo le specie e l'idea.

(But above, God in space fiercely
Quivers with light and stretches out
Upon our suffering, and lustful, never satiated,
Among women of joyous eternity
He renews the uninhibited ecstasies
Of his pleasure; and unaware re-creates
The species and the idea of the world.)

But in "Frammento XVII" the sexually charged image of the midday sun as an *atroce despota* is placed in the context of a more authentically existentialist drama wherein it figures as a positive rather than a negative value. The poem begins with a hallucinatory vision of the midday sun as a lover enacting a violent, cosmic game with a turgid earth that strains to respond. Verbs and images of this cosmically dithyrambic noon piece indicate a thrust of verticality as toward a superior realm. What is suggested is a call to a higher life with unspecified Nietzschean overtones, a passionate invitation to a "Great Midday": "E scaturiva l'invito bramoso / D'intorno"

(And the yearning invitation gushed / all about). It seems at first that the invitation will be realized by the young couple who have come under the spell of the intoxicating meridian hour: "Ebbra l'ora si smarriva / Nel senso delle voci / Di giovani a diporto / Di giovani cercanti / Dal pensiero la vita" (Drunken the hour was dissolving / into sensations of the voices / Of youths at play / Of youths seeking life / From their thoughts). The glorious "truth" aspired to by the couple is analogically represented in terms of the dazzling vastness of noontide in whose luminosity the couple dreams of realizing new worlds and even, it seems, of attaining the mystical two-in-one existence of lovers and a simultaneous pantheistic reintegration with nature: "Il compagno alla compagna / La compagna al compagno, / Volea ciascuno gridare / Ciò che non era mai detto, / E passar da ogni varco / E popolare la reggia, / E confondersi insieme / Nell'acciecante verità enorme" (He to her / She to him, / Each one wanted to shout / That which was never said, / And pass beyond every limit / And populate the court palace / And merge together / In the enormous dazzling truth).

But Rèbora's couple is not equal to the high intensity of midday; their first élan subsides, and they sink into a lesser, banal reality: "Ma rotolarono sillabe, / Ma ragionarono il mondo" (But they rolled out syllables, / But they reckoned the world). The adversative *ma* (but), found so frequently in Rèbora's poems to indicate a turning or a rebuttal or a reversal, occurs here at the beginning of two successive verses, accentuating the sense of the falling away from the earlier idealistic and intuitive fervor. The poem has a diurnal time structure, and the downward plunge to ordinariness and separateness is emblematized first by the sky whose meridian glory has been extinguished, giving way to an ashen dullness: "S'annidò il cielo corto, / E si fece uno spento bracere" (The sky quickly made its nest, / And turned into a spent brazier). The violent joy of the earth in its upward surge to receive the embrace of the sun has subsided, and the earth takes on the aspect of a corpse. Finally, as the culminating picture of desolation, night falls, and for nature is substituted the negative image of the city—a roaring abyss that swallows all—to which the couple has returned after a rich noon in the country.

The couple in this poem could refer to Rèbora and a female companion, but that there is an emblematic value in the couple and their experience can hardly escape the reader. The sense of exacerbated frustration in not being able to realize the superior life is typical of Rèbora's struggle before his conversion and results in part from the impossibility of specifying what the Great Midday (from Nietzschean mythology) should be in practical terms if it were to be more than solipsistic idealism. The couple's separation from one another is a loss of or renunciation of youth.

If this is a statement of a moment of personal failure, it is also a picture of humankind falling away from the splendor of youthful vision—emblematized by nature's savagely joyous midday—and its submission to the confining, oppressive air of a mediocre reality. It is not nature in the season and hour of a summer noontide that provides the distress and suffocating atmosphere but Rèbora's version of the *city of dreadful night*. The anxious reaching out or the supine passivity (the poles between which the young Rèbora moved) and the sense of the loss or insecurity of the wild desire to possess a superior life were expressed by the tormented poet in words from an early letter (to Daria Banfi Malaguzzi), which helps to explicate the poem and the *Frammenti lirici* in general: "L'ellenica armonia di equilibrio? Io non la conosco. O balzo o giaccio; altro non so. Tendo perennemente verso qualche cosa che non sarà mai; esulto talvolta di creature che si agitano in me e che io non potrò mai scorgere nella realtà degli uomini. Ecco, la fonte regina della mia angoscia perenne; il mio tormento lusingatore e vano! Tutto mi scivola via; anche il volere, che pure mi domina talvolta selvaggio" (The Hellenic harmony of balance? I do not know what it is. Either I leap or I lie prone; I know nothing else. I stretch out perennially toward something that will never be; sometimes I exult with creatures that stir in me and that I shall never succeed in seeing in the real world and in men. This is the main source of my perennial anguish; my flattering and vain torment! Everything slips away from me; even my desire which sometimes possesses me savagely).

In a letter to Angelo Monteverdi dated 28 March 1913, shortly before the printing of *Frammenti lirici*, Rèbora gave another clue to the tensive nature of his verses when he revealed the Dantean title he originally had in mind for the volume: "Anzitutto, ho scovato un titolo alla mia raccolta che per esser ambiguo (non per me) mi piace; eccolo: *I guinzagli del Veltro* (devi sapere che per me quest'ultima parola significa infinite cose: è l'eterno, anzi l'aspirazione all'eterno, e il

presagio dell'essere ossia il divenire: e tante altre faccende)" (Above all, I have hit upon a title for my volume of lyrics that I like because of its ambiguity [not for me]; here it is: *The Leashes of the Greyhound* [you should know that for me this last word signifies an infinity of things: it is the eternal, indeed the aspiration toward the eternal, and the presentiment of being or rather becoming: and so many other things).

But not all the poems of *Frammenti lirici* express Rèbora's yearning in aggressively expressionistic accents and imagery. There are lyrics in which he modulates his voice to an almost melancholy softness while retaining its tensive quality. Among the best in this vein is "Frammento LVII," which tells of a little bird decoyed into a net placed by a hunter whose experienced hands will give it a quick death, the bird emitting its death with a last trill. The poet's wish is that he too may die in an act of love for others:

Stan nel folto gli stami:
L'uccelletto ai richiami
Svola e discende con vispezza e amore;
Pàlpita nelle accorte
Mani un poco, e la morte
Dal becco gli esce in un ultimo trillo.

Cader così vorrei dietro il mio cuore;
Così finir, con generoso squillo.

(The netting is in the thicket:
Toward the lures the little bird
Flits and descends with sprightliness and love;
It throbs in the experienced
Hands a little, and death
Comes forth from its beak with a final trill.

Just so would I fall after my heart;
And finish thus, with a generous blare.)

Behind the pathos or melancholy charm of such lyrics is the same yearning toward something beyond, toward an absolute, and the same sense of *attesa* (tense expectancy) unsatisfied that permeates the *Frammenti lirici* as a whole and which is expressed tersely in two lines (31-32) from "Frammento XLV," one of the volume's longest poems: "Attesa che scocca / Verso un ben ch'è vicino e non tocca" (Expectation that darts / Toward a good that is near and does not touch).

Rèbora's experience in World War I confirmed and exacerbated his disillusionment and disgust with the actions of humankind. Among his few war poems is "Viatico" (Viaticum). Written in 1916 (and collected in *Le poesie*, 1947), it is perhaps the most starkly powerful and existentially dramatic poem to come out of the war:

O ferito laggiù nel valloncello,
. . . .
Pietà di noi rimasti
A rantolarci e non ha fine l'ora,
Affretta l'agonia,
Tu puoi finire,
E conforto ti sia
Nella demenza che non sa impazzire,
Mentre sosta il momento,
Il sonno sul cervello,
Làsciaci in silenzio -

Grazie, fratello.

(O you, wounded there in the gully,
. . . .
Have pity on us who are left
To rattle here in an endless hour,
Hasten your agony,
You are allowed to end,
And be comforted
In the dementia that does not know how to go
    mad,
While the moment pauses,
By the sleep that comes over your brain,
Leave us in silence -

Thanks, brother.)

The wounded soldier, reduced to a legless trunk and a continuous pleading lament that has cost the lives of three companions who tried to reach him, is told to have mercy on the survivors by hastening his agony. It is this reversal of roles in calling for help that is fraught with bitter existential irony. The agony of the dying man will end soon, but the living are condemned to their death rattle for an "hour" whose duration is that of life itself. Because awareness is still intact, the wounded soldier's "dementia"—his excruciating pain—does not become a full-fledged madness, which at least would be a liberating condition. But comfort may come to him in the guise of a loss of consciousness and sensibility, something the poet can wish for the dying man but which a terrible lucidity makes him know is impossible for himself, condemned to go through life in that dementia that will not become madness. The apparent crudity of the imperatives and the starkness of the language may indicate the frayed nerves of the poet, but it is directed as a protest not against the wounded soldier and his anguished lament, but rather against the madness

and horror of war. In this respect, it masks a profound sense of humanity toward the victims of war, a humanity that is made overt in the last line (spoken after a pause during which the soldier has died and the lament has finally ceased) where the poet thanks his "brother."

In 1922 Rèbora published *Canti anonimi*, a slim volume of twenty pages, containing nine poems written between 1920 and 1922. In general the tone and stylistic modes of the poems reveal a relaxation of the extreme expressionistic violence and wrenching rhythms characteristic of much of *Frammenti lirici* and other poems. There is a desire to submerge the assertiveness of the romantic self so pronounced in his earlier period. In part this sentiment derives from a sense of the futility of action, connected, however, as before, with the desire for a superior or purer realm. It is sometimes expressed in aphoristic fashion, as in "Sacchi a terra per gli occhi" (Sacks on the Ground for the Eyes), where one reads that "L'atto è un pretesto" (The act is a pretext), and "La solitudine è vita— / Ma un nodo scorsoio / Agli altri t'impicca" (Solitude is life— / But a slipknot / Hangs you to others). But vertical tension is not absent. "Gira la trottola viva" (The Live Top Spins) makes use of the image of a spinning top and spare, didactically intoned verses to indicate the idea of a divinely drawing force that moves inertness—the top is spiritually anthropomorphized—into a whirl of desire. The top must be "whipped" into its motion; otherwise it remains on its side, "stuck to the ground," whereas its spinning is live tension toward the absolute: "Vive la trottola e gira, / La sferza Iddio, la sferza è il tempo. / Così la trottola aspira / Dentro l'amore, verso l'eterno" (The top lives and spins, / God whips it, the whip is time. / Thus the top aspirates / Love, aspiring toward the eternal). Again, then, readers find the motif of the human being as a prisoner seeking to be released from the earth and time.

"Gira la trottola viva," the eighth poem of *Canti anonimi*, is followed by the volume's last poem, "Dall'immagine tesa" (From the Tense Image), Rèbora's best-known poem, one of the great lyrics of the twentieth century, and surely one of the great religious or mystic lyrics in the annals of European poetry. Though the poem was written in 1920, some years before Rèbora embraced the faith and God taught by Roman Catholics, the mystic yearning is evident enough from the time of the *Frammenti lirici*. In 1920 he was already immersed in the reading of texts of different religions, but the last six lines seem to implement Christian elements. The poem is the culminating point of Rèbora's ever-recurring theme of anxious waiting:

> Verrà a farmi certo
> Del suo e mio tesoro,
> Verrà come ristoro
> Delle mie e sue pene,
> Verrà, forse già viene
> Il suo bisbiglio.

> (He will come to assure me
> Of his and my treasure,
> He will come as a comforter
> Of my and his sufferings,
> He will come, perhaps his whisper
> Already comes.)

After the whirling top of "Gira la trottola viva" in an upward tension, "Dall'immagine tesa" might seem to indicate an absence of motion. But this is not the calm of Buddhistic contemplation. The tension of the subject is all the greater in its being restrained. The intensity of certain *laudi* of Jacopone da Todi is here concentrated in an economy of words unknown to the medieval poet. One thinks more of Michelangelo's non-Platonizing religious poems—in which he turns directly to Christ and the Cross. In the last two lines the visitor's "whisper"—which perhaps is already coming—recuperates, synthesizes, and gives certitude to the sense of presence-in-absence. Who is to come is no human or earthly visitor but a spiritual visitor who, though unnamed, is characterized in salvific and Christological terms: *treasure*, for Christ is the soul's treasure, and a saved soul is Christ's treasure; *comforter*, for Christ is the comforter/redeemer of the soul's pain and comforter of his own pain caused by human sin. Thus if the concluding poem of a volume entitled *Canti anonimi* is one in which the self, the *Io* (I), of the poet is so dramatically present, it is because the encounter or presentiment of the encounter with the divine is necessarily a highly personal one, even if the ultimate aim or desire is to sacrifice or surrender oneself. Thus the apparent Christological character of the "someone" or "something" who is to come is Rèbora's way of expressing the urgent need he felt for being delivered from the self; but it does not mean that he was ready to find that deliverance in Christianity. At the end of *Canti anonimi*, the poet is in the same spiritual condition expressed in the three verses (from an unpublished

"fragment" of 1914) that he used as an epigraphic introduction to the volume: "Urge la scelta tremenda: / Dire sì, dire no / A qualcosa che so" (The awesome choice urges: / To say yes, to say no / To something that I know). At the time of the preparation of *Canti anonimi*, in a letter of 1921 (hence, after the poem "Dall'immagine tesa" was written) Rèbora lucidly and desperately defined his own condition: "sono uno che ubbidisce, incerto e senza speranza, a un dio che non gli si rivela" (I am one who, uncertain and without hope, obeys a god who does not reveal himself to him). The definitive step in the conversion had not yet been taken, but for Rèbora the wait or expectancy, the *attesa*, could not be an acceptable or preferred condition.

Twenty-six years after his actual conversion, in the opening verses he placed as a "Preludio" to the *Canti dell'infermità*, the ailing Rèbora, in returning to poetry, acknowledges that the anguish and sin that had been his were indeed to have "sung" of the self, of the "I":

> Se il sole splende fuor senza Te dentro,
> tutto finisce in cupa nebbia spento.
> Orrore disperato, Gesù mio,
> trovarsi in fin d'aver cantato l'io!

> (If the sun shines outwardly without Thou within,
> everything ends extinguished in dark fog.
> Desperate horror, my Jesus,
> to find in the end one has sung one's I!)

And in the second of the two quatrains of the "Preludio," he announces his readiness to do without poetry if, in his song, the self is not immolated, consumed in Christ. Indeed, Rèbora's late religious poetry often carries the extreme accents of self-abnegation of Jacopone da Todi and other medieval Italian writers (though it is a tone and manner already present in early Rèbora).

And yet, despite the certitude of the awesome choice and of God after the conversion in 1929, and despite Rèbora's willingness to offer himself to others within the context of that certitude, he could still thirst and feel himself a prisoner—an existential sentiment inherent in Christianity. Thus one of the better "fragments" of *Curriculum vitae* returns to the image of the captive bird and its trill found earlier in the *Frammenti lirici*, except that now the bird is one of the captive lures:

> O allodola, a un tenue filo avvinta,
> Schiavo richiamo delle libere in volo,

*Rèbora (right) talking with a priest at the Rosminian monastery in Domodossola, where Rèbora went to study for the priesthood
in May 1931*

Come in un trillo fai per incielarti
Strappato al suolo agiti in vano l'ali!

(O skylark, clasped to a thin wire,
Captive lure for those flying free,
With a trill you strive to go heavenward
Pulled to the ground in vain you beat your wings!)

The poem expresses with deep pathos and concentrated intensity (despite the apparent relaxation of the rhythm) desire and frustration, the tension between the sense of enchainment to the earth and the desire to transcend it.

Similarly, following his conversion Rèbora's desire for the absolute was no less "savage" than before, but its focus was clear and its direction (still "upward" in terms of metaphorical space) unswerving. The image of the implacable sun burning cruelly over a parched, drought-stricken earth that yearns for life-saving rain becomes the emblematic representation of the soul's unquenchable thirst for mystical union with Christ. The "rain" will be God's succor to the burning soul; but God is also the spiritual force of the deity (the midday sun) that sears the soul.

The early poem "Frammento IX" has its counterpart in three lines from *Curriculum vitae* in which Rèbora recounts his conversion in terms of a mystical experience that occurred in the radiant blaze of the sun while he was gently rocking in a boat on a lake:

Tutto era irraggiamento al solleone:
Cullato in barca stavo in mezzo al lago:
Svanì il creato e apparve il Creatore.

(All was a radiance in the torrid light:
Lulled in a boat I was in the middle of the lake:
The world vanished and the Creator appeared.)

In the midday splendor the world (and the self with it) disappears and only the Deity remains.

And finally, in the last months of his life, during which the poet/priest was paralyzed and confined to bed, passing from moments of lucidity to moments of loss of consciousness, Rèbora dictated one of his last lyrics (in *Le poesie*), yet another testimony of his fundamental sense of not being at home on earth, and his lifelong tensive desire to go beyond:

> Terribile ritornare a questo mondo
> quando già tutte le fibre
> erano tese
> a transitare!
> E il corpo mi rifiuta ogni servizio,
> e l'anima non trova più suo inizio.
> Ogni voler divino è sforzo nero.
> Tutto va senza pensiero:
> l'abisso invoca l'abisso.

> (Cruel to return to this world
> when already all my fibers
> were stretched out
> to transit!
> And my body refuses me any service,
> and my soul does not find its beginning.
> Every divine wish is a black struggle.
> Everything goes without thought:
> the abyss invokes the abyss.)

To the last line Rèbora added the following comment: "L'abisso di miseria invoca l'abisso di misericordia" (The abyss of misery invokes the abyss of mercy).

Letters:
Lettere familiari, edited by Piero Rèbora (Milan: All'Insegna del Pesce d'Oro, 1962);

Il primo Rèbora—22 lettere inedite (1905-1913), edited by Daria Banfi Malaguzzi (Milan: All'Insegna del Pesce d'Oro, 1964);

Lettere, 2 volumes, edited by Margherita Marchione (Rome: Storia e Letteratura, 1976, 1982);

Per veemente amore lucente: Lettere a Sibilla Aleramo, edited by Anna Folli (Milan: Scheiwiller, 1986).

Bibliographies:
Margherita Marchione, *L'immagine tesa—La vita e l'opera di Clemente Rèbora* (Rome: Storia e Letteratura, 1976), pp. 263-280, 359-387;

Vincenzo Sala, "Indicazioni bibliografiche su Rèbora," *Rivista Rosminiana*, 4 (October-December 1982): 447-453;

Alberto Frattini, "Clemente Rèbora: Sviluppi della sua fortuna critica," *Cultura e Scuola*, 25 (April-June 1986): 35-43.

Biographies:
Renata Lollo, *La scelta tremenda: Santità e poesia nell'itinerario spirituale di Clemente Rèbora* (Milan: I.P.L., 1967);

Lollo, "Rèbora poeta d'amore," in *Studi sulla cultura lombarda in memoria di Mario Apollonio* (Milan: Vita e Pensiero, 1972), II: 228-241;

Ezio Viola, *Mania dell'eterno: Gli ultimi due anni della vita di Clemente Rèbora nel diario del suo infermiere*, edited by E. Fabiani (Vicenza, Italy: Lacusta, 1980);

Nicolino Sarale, *Dall'ateismo alla mistica: Clemente Rèbora* (Naples: Dehoniane, 1981).

References:
Felicita Audisio, "Rèbora, la tradizione, il ritmo," *Paradigma*, 5 (1983): 127-155;

Fernando Bandini, "Elementi di espressionismo linguistico in Rèbora," in *Ricerche sulla lingua poetica contemporanea* (Padua, Italy: Liviana, 1966), pp. 3-35;

Daria Banfi Malaguzzi, *Il primo Rèbora* (Milan: All'Insegna del Pesce d'Oro, 1961);

Giorgio Bàrberi Squarotti, "Tre note su Clemente Rèbora," in his *Astrazione e realtà* (Milan: Rusconi & Paolazzi, 1960), pp. 197-219;

Glauco Cambon, "Concettismo esistenziale di Rèbora," *Paragone*, 12 (June 1961): 43-51;

Gianfranco Contini, "Due poeti anteguerra: I, Dino Campana; II, Clemente Rèbora," in his *Esercizi di lettura* (Florence: Monnier, 1947), pp. 1-17;

Maura Del Serra, *Clemente Rèbora: Lo specchio e il fuoco* (Milan: Vita e Pensiero, 1976);

Alberto Frattini, "L'esperienza della guerra nella coscienza e nella poesia di Rèbora," *Humanitas*, new series 61 (December 1986): 835-858;

Marziano Guglielminetti, *Clemente Rèbora* (Milan: Mursia, 1961);

F. J. Jones, *The Modern Italian Lyric* (Cardiff: University of Wales Press, 1986), pp. 163-194;

Renée Kingcaid and Charles Klopp, "Coupling and Uncoupling in Rèbora's 'O carro vuoto,'" *Italica*, 56 (Summer 1979): 147-171;

Mario Luzi, "Azione poetica di Rèbora" (1968), in *Letteratura italiana: Novecento. I Contemporanei*, edited by Gianni Grana (Milan: Marzorati, 1979), IV: 3356-3365;

Oreste Macrí, "La poesia di Clemente Rèbora nel secondo tempo o intermezzo (1913-1920) tra i *Frammenti lirici* e le *Poesie religiose*,"

Paradigma, 3 (1980): 279-313; and *Paragone*, 4 (1982): 177-209;

Margherita Marchione, *Clemente Rèbora* (Boston: Twayne, 1979);

Artal Mazzotti, "Clemente Rèbora," in *Letteratura italiana: I Contemporanei*, edited by Grana (Milan: Marzorati, 1963), I: 595-601;

Nicolas J. Perella, *Midday in Italian Literature* (Princeton: Princeton University Press, 1979), pp. 145-155, 298-301;

Silvio Ramat, *Storia della poesia italiana del Novecento* (Milan: Mursia, 1976), pp. 88-100;

Antonio Russi, "L'esperienza lirica di Clemente Rèbora," in his *Poesia e realtà* (Florence: Nuova Italia, 1962), pp. 285-305;

Claudio Scarpati, "Per un'antologia," *Vita e Pensiero*, 68 (November 1985): 17-30;

Donato Valli, "Lingua di Rèbora," *Vita e Pensiero*, 68 (November 1985): 5-16.

Ceccardo Roccatagliata Ceccardi

(6 January 1871 - 3 August 1919)

Mark Pietralunga
Florida State University

BOOKS: *Dai paesi dell'anarchia (impressioni sui moti del 1894)* (Genoa: Operaia, 1894);

Il libro dei frammenti (Milan: Aliprandi, 1895);

In morte di due bimbi innamorati (Genoa: Montorfano, 1901);

Nel primo compleanno del mio bimbo (Carrara, Italy: Picciati, 1903);

Il viandante (Turin & Genoa: Streglio, 1904; revised edition, Naples: Julianis, 1906);

Il principe di Roma (Sarzana, Italy: Costa, 1904);

Apua Mater (Lucca, Italy: Marchi, 1905; revised and enlarged edition, Naples: Julianis, 1906);

Per un brindisi a Guglielmo Imperatore (Turin & Genoa: Streglio, 1906);

Per una nave di battaglia (Genoa: Ebe, 1907);

Quando tornerà Garibaldi?—In morte di mio fratello (Genoa: Podestà, 1908);

Sonetti e poemi (Empoli, Italy: Traversari, 1910);

Per un brindisi di Guglielmo Imperatore ed altre Odi: Il saluto a Costante Garibaldi (Parma, Italy: L'Editrice, 1915);

Don Chisciotte (Genoa: I.G.A.P., 1916);

Sillabe ed ombre, poesie (1910-1919), edited by Pierangelo Baratono (Milan: Treves, 1925);

Antologia ceccardiana, edited by Tito Rosina (Genoa: Orfini, 1938);

Tutte le opere, edited by Pier Antonio Balli (Carrara & Pisa, Italy: Giardini, 1969);

Ultimi inediti, edited by Emma Pistelli Rinaldi (Savona, Italy: Sabatelli, 1981);

Tutte le poesie, edited by Bruno Cicchetti and Eligio Imarisio (Genoa: Sagep, 1982).

PLAY PRODUCTION: *Don Chisciotte*, with music

Ceccardo Roccatagliata Ceccardi

by Guido Dell'Orso, Genoa, Carlo Felice Theater, 4 March 1916.

OTHER: Giovanni Cattanei, ed., *La Liguria e la poesia italiana del novecento*, includes poems and prose by Roccatagliata Ceccardi (Milan: Silva, 1966), pp. 453-634;

Urio Clades, *Roccatagliata Ceccardi*, includes *Il libro dei frammenti* and selections of prose by Roccatagliata Ceccardi (Florence: Sansoni, 1969), pp. 248-362.

Ceccardo Roccatagliata Ceccardi's poetry is a significant testimony to the need for a new expression in Italian poetry at the close of the nineteenth century. He was among the first poets of the twentieth century whose works suggest a sense of disorientation between the prevailing classical poetry of Giosuè Carducci and the more modern verses of Giovanni Pascoli and the French symbolists. Roccatagliata Ceccardi's poetry oscillates from a traditional and, at times, highly artificial verse form to a fragmentary and simple style. Although he remained isolated and was by nature incapable of adhering to any literary movement, he felt the need to adjust his style to a pre-established literary scheme that had its roots in the nineteenth century. This decision was a result of the turbulent historical and cultural situation in Italy at the close of the century, which left many writers confused, disappointed, and in search of some order. One solution was the classical model with its Latin rhetoric and its appeal to heroic endeavors, which seemed to revive the lost spirits of the Roman tradition in order to resolve the disillusionment that followed the Italian Risorgimento. Roccatagliata Ceccardi's desire to adopt this model is reflected in his hope for a return to the idea of the poet as the spokesman for one's country. In the Latin tradition, the poet had this role; however, Roccatagliata Ceccardi was the first to recognize that it was no longer possible for anyone to assume this position. This role was especially difficult for a poet like him, who was more inclined toward humble and simple aspects of life, such as those found in the poetry of Pascoli. It is from this perspective that critics have appreciated Roccatagliata Ceccardi's poetic originality. His poetry reaches new results with its bare and incisive style and delineates for the first time the tormented Ligurian landscape of sea and rocks, of wind and sun that Camillo Sbarbaro's *Pianissimo* (1914) and Eugenio Montale's *Ossi di seppie* (1925; translated as *The Bones of Cuttlefish*, 1983) render emblematic to Italian poetry of the twentieth century.

Roccatagliata Ceccardo Maria Bartolomeo was born in Genoa on 6 January 1871. His parents, Lazzaro Roccatagliata and the former Giovanna Battistina Ceccardi, were both landowners, with his mother boasting an illustrious aristocratic family of military and literary distinction. Shortly after his birth, financial difficulties forced the young Roccatagliata Ceccardi and his mother to leave Genoa and move to the latter's hometown of Ortonovo in the Apuanian Alps (today the town is located in the province of La Spezia). A brother, Luigi, was born soon after their arrival. Subsequently the ties between the poet's parents were severed. Not much is known about his father after his parents' separation. After the loss of the family's wealth, Lazzaro Roccatagliata returned to Genoa, where he lived many years in absolute poverty. The poet never refers to his father in his writings nor to the reasons behind the family's financial downfall. Instead, his mother holds a special place in both his life and poetry. According to the critic Carlo Bo, Roccatagliata Ceccardi's mother represented all that was purity in life. He remained under the close protection of his mother even after he moved to Massa to pursue his secondary education. His decision to add his mother's maiden name of Ceccardi to that of his father's surname demonstrates the love and gratitude he felt toward her as both a maternal and cultural guide. In one of his first poems, "La preghiera" (The Prayer; collected in *Il libro dei frammenti* [The Book of Fragments, 1895]), he addresses his mother, who, like God, interprets the future:

> Madre, se tu lo sai, dillo al tremante
> figlio, che curvo ne la notte aspetta
> —ei te ne prega con le tue più sante
> . . . .
> se mai coglierà bocce di viole:
> e se alfin—dopo aver camminato
> al buio, avrà sul volto un po' di sole!
>
> (Mother, if you know, tell it to your
> trembling son, who awaits, bent in the night
> —he begs you with the most holy prayers
> . . . .
> if ever he gathers violet buds:
> and if at last—after having walked
> in darkness, he will have on his face a touch of
> sun!)

Through the contacts made while at school in Massa, Roccatagliata Ceccardi was encouraged to contribute to the popular student newspaper *Manicomio*, published in Parma. There he placed his first poems. At this time he also fell in love with a young girl he called "L'Emilia Novella."

Tormented by this unrequited love, he shot himself in the chest with a pistol loaded with nails, but recovered. This dramatic gesture was typical of the heroic proportions he placed on every action. He completed only one scholastic year in Massa: his failure to pass a mathematics examination prevented his promotion to the second year. Consequently he dropped out of school and pursued his education privately. It was not until three years later, in October 1892, that he completed his secondary-school examinations and received his diploma, as an external candidate. The following December he enrolled in the faculty of law at the Università di Genova. One month earlier he had received news of his mother's death. He opted to leave the university after a very unsuccessful first year and to pursue a career as a journalist. Meanwhile, in Genoa, he began to meet with a local coterie of young, politically active artists and writers, the "Bohème di Vico Paglia," at whose gatherings, held in taverns and restaurants, he recited his poetry. He also began to contribute to local newspapers and published a pamphlet, *Dai paesi dell'anarchia (impressioni sui moti del 1894)* (From the Land of Anarchy [Impressions of the 1894 Revolts], 1894). He had worked for a Carrara newspaper, *Lo Svegliarino*, and was familiar with the harsh conditions of the marble-quarry workers in the area. The publication of this essay marked the first of several works in prose and the beginning of a long series of battles with the law. The judicial authorities deemed the pamphlet an incitement for anarchic rebellion and confiscated it. The news of the censorship contributed to his already growing popularity as a poet and helped him increase his journalistic activity. His controversial nature and his unfavorable remarks concerning various local personalities, whom he attacked in his articles or at literary gatherings, led to several open duels.

In 1895 he published *Il libro dei frammenti* and dedicated the book to the memory of his deceased mother. In the notes to his second book of poetry, *Sonetti e poemi* (Sonnets and Poems, 1910), Roccatagliata Ceccardi recalls these first verses:

Poca cosa erano, è vero, quei canti; ma, sebben nati tra la rovina di mia casa, e la battaglia aspra di quei miei giovanissimi anni, s'avean pur un vanto: che non erano litanie di querimonie o di bestemmie alla vita, od al caso: tutt'altro! Si pompeggiavan, come meglio sapean, ad un'eco di Pan, L'Eterno, cui, a null'altro badando allor tendevo l'orecchio, come tra un sogno. E s'ebbero qualche lode, tra cui quella ancor oggi carissima di Giovanni Marradi, l'onor di un saggio critico sul "Marzocco," allor al suo primo anno di vita, per la penna acuta e onesta di Pietro Mastri, il quale, poi, lo volle raccolto in un suo volume di critiche: *Su per l'erta*, edito nel 1903 dallo Zanichelli. Ma per un fiore che ronzio di saette, assiduo, dall'ombra alle spalle! Per uno sprazzo di sole quanto intrigo di insidie ai pie' del povero viandante!

(It's true that those poems weren't much; and yet, even though they were born amid the ruin of my household and the harsh battle of my youthful years, they could boast one thing: they were not a volley of laments and curses to life or fortune: not at all! They flaunted themselves, as best they could, like an echo of Pan, the Eternal, who captured my full attention at that time, as if in a dream. And they received some praise: one, by Giovanni Marradi, is still dear to me, and another was the honor of having a critical essay in "Marzocco," then in its first year, written by the sharp and honest pen of Pietro Mastri, who later included it in a book of critical essays: *Su per L'Erta*, published in 1903 by Zanichelli. And yet for one flower what a constant buzzing of arrows from the shadows behind one's back! For a flash of sun what a conspiracy of deceit at the foot of the poor wayfarer!)

Il libro dei frammenti displays close ties to the poetry of the French symbolists. Roccatagliata Ceccardi was among the first promoters in Italy of the symbolist movement—in this first collection, he translates and imitates poems of Paul Verlaine ("Colloque sentimental") and Arthur Rimbaud ("Tête de faune") nearly twenty years before they were officially recognized by Italian critics. These translations and others, of Parnassian poets André Lemoyne and Leconte de Lisle, underline the formal and technical discipline that characterizes much of his poetry. In *Scrittori d'oggi* (Writers of Today, 1946) Pietro Pancrazi cites this collection as one of the few good examples of Italian symbolism. Roccatagliata Ceccardi's symbolism, according to Pancrazi, is, above all, pictorial. These poems represent a detailed, descriptive testimony to a dreamlike communion between the poet's spirit and a familiar natural setting. A fundamental characteristic of these poems is a pervading sense of transiency and melancholy. The dominant motifs, which suggest these sensations, are drawn from the thematics of the French symbolists. Those most common are fallen leaves, dried flowers, the use of gray in its various gradations, seasonal changes, and the interactions among love, death, youth, and decay. The elegiac and rustic elements of these verses also reflect the influence of Pascoli's *Myricae* (Tamarisks, 1892).

In 1896 Roccatagliata Ceccardi accepted the directorship of the Carrara newspaper, *Lo Svegliarino*, and changed its format to a more political and literary orientation. In Carrara he met and fell in love with a young woman, Gemma Catalani, who inspired some of his most beautiful love poems. The relationship abruptly ended when the woman's father discovered she was in love with an unknown, vagrant poet. In the early months of 1898 Roccatagliata Ceccardi left Carrara and returned, depressed and abandoned, to Genoa in search of consolation and employment. In Genoa he found his old friends and the necessary inspiration for his art in the atmosphere of a restaurant, Trattoria dei Mille. In a small room of this restaurant, Roccatagliata Ceccardi met with well-known local poets and artists, such as Angiolo Silvio Novaro, Gian Pietro Lucini, and Adelchi Baratono. Roccatagliata Ceccardi nevertheless had difficulty in securing a job in the journalistic or cultural field that would allow him to earn a living.

In 1898 he began his long collaboration with the literary magazine *La Riviera Ligure*, which was still under the direction of its founder, Angiolo Silvio Novaro. The editorship was passed on to Angiolo's brother, Mario, who published it from 1899 to 1919. It was under Mario Novaro's guidance that the Oneglia-based periodical gained national and international distinction. In these years *La Riviera Ligure* had among its contributors Pascoli, Luigi Pirandello, Grazia Deledda, Dino Campana, Giovanni Boine, Giuseppe Ungaretti, Aldo Palazzeschi, and Giovanni Papini. Novaro recognized Roccatagliata Ceccardi's talent and often provided the poor and homeless poet with financial assistance and shelter. Roccatagliata Ceccardi was the most assiduous contributor to *La Riviera Ligure*, with more than fifty works of poetry and prose published from 1898 to 1917.

On 10 September 1901 he married Francesca Giovanotti in the latter's hometown of Sant'Andrea Pelago, in the Modenese mountains. Francesca seemed to provide him with stability. What was lacking, however, was a sense of reality and the ability to face life. Five years later Roccatagliata Ceccardi wrote his close friend Manfredo Giuliani about his decision to marry Francesca: "Ho creduto di far del bene, e di far

anche un bel gesto. E poi ero nel fiorir di giovinezza e l'amore mi aveva bendato ambedue egli occhi" (I thought I had done a good service and also performed a noble deed. After all I was in the blossoming of youth and love had blindfolded both my eyes). This reaction was typical of his nature. His eyes would always remain somewhat blindfolded, and he always felt the need to perform some noble deed. He returned with his wife to Genoa, where on 11 October 1902 a son was born. The name Tristano was chosen in honor of the French poet Tristan Corbière, with whom Roccatagliata Ceccardi professed an affinity. After a short period, financial conditions forced the poet to send his wife and child to live with her relatives in Sant'Andrea Pelago.

In 1901 Roccatagliata Ceccardi had published a long poem, *In morte di due bimbi innamorati* (On the Death of Two Children in Love), inspired by an actual event that had been reported in a French newspaper in 1898. In his poem he transfers a late-Romantic theme into the world of simple nature, which was most congenial to him. His depiction of nature in flashes of fragmentary images is also a characteristic of this poem.

In 1902 Roccatagliata Ceccardi was involved in another well-publicized dispute. In an article— "L'arte a Genova," in *Vita Nova*—he attacked the administration of Genoa for its inept handling of the restoration of some paintings by Van Dyck in the city's Palazzo Rosso. With the support of artist Plinio Nomellini, he succeeded in the suspension of the restoration project, but it cost him his job with several newspapers. With opportunities for employment drastically reduced, he joined his wife in Sant'Andrea Pelago. There he published in 1904 what many critics consider his masterpiece, *Il viandante* (The Wayfarer). The title of the poem highlights a major theme of his writings: the recurrent motif of the free individual, the wayfarer, who is an example of freedom, independence, and total contact with nature, outside the artificial constraints imposed by society and civilization. Roccatagliata Ceccardi's wayfarer has a tragic sense of life. This view of life as a harsh and painful journey under open skies was intimately felt by the poet, whose existence was characterized by continuous instability without obtaining peace. Nothing is more significant than the request in his will that the epigraph "Hic constitit viator" (Here lies the wayfarer) be inscribed on his urn. Through a poetry intimately linked to the countryside, he found a poetic means to establish a close identity between the wayfarer and nature. His readings of Walt Whitman were particularly influential in his realization of this union:

> Cosi' viandante
> nel cuor mi crebbi, ed un amor de l'aspra
> mia terra azzurra ingentilia quel primo
> desio vago di errori, con pensose
> illusioni di ricordi.
>
> (So wayfarer
> in the heart I grew, and a love of my harsh
> blue land refined that first
> vague desire of errors, with thoughtful
> illusions of memories.)

In 1905 Roccatagliata Ceccardi gained some recognition among the people of the Apuanian mountains with the publication of twelve sonnets entitled *Apua Mater*. These patriotic poems are historical and celebrate the proud tradition of the Apuanian land.

Roccatagliata Ceccardi's heroic passion and strong nationalistic spirit reappear in the civic poetry of his odes. In the Val di Magra, near Pontremoli, in 1905 he read publicly one of these poems, *Per un brindisi a Guglielmo Imperatore* (For a Toast to Emperor William, 1906), a fiery protest of Latin pride directed at the German monarch. With his civic poems Roccatagliata Ceccardi saw himself as a perpetuator of a long tradition in Italian letters, whose most recent spokesmen were Carducci and Gabriele D'Annunzio. Instead of pursuing a direction that conformed more naturally to his elegiac, contemplative instinct, Roccatagliata Ceccardi was intent on asserting the nineteenth-century Romantic concept of the poet's place in history as intellectual leader. This attitude explains his idea to form in the fall of 1906 the "Repubblica di Apua," a circle of intellectuals and artists. Its members were given anachronistic, chivalric-sounding titles. The more prominent names of the group were Lorenzo Viani, "Grande Aiutante" (Great Adjutant); Giuseppe Ungaretti, "Console d'Egitto" (Egyptian Consul); and Enrico Pea, "Sacerdote degli Scongiuri" (Priest of Exorcism). According to the intentions of its founder, the Repubblica di Apua represented the need to live heroically in an ideal world, which contrasted sharply with real events. The group professed a desire for action, together with a vindication of the role of culture and art; the group took rather crass positions on political, civil, and cultural issues. Many of the

group's disputes and demonstrations were primarily relegated to provincial news. It was not a period in history that readily accommodated the poetic resurrection of ideals and titanic actions similar to those promoted by Roccatagliata Ceccardi's beloved Percy Bysshe Shelley.

The founding and meetings of the Repubblica di Apua were some of the few joyous events in Roccatagliata Ceccardi's life. He had separated from his wife in spring 1906 and was without a fixed residence. In January 1907 he was in Florence as art critic for a short-lived political newspaper, the *Popolo*. Later in the year he won a much-contested competition sponsored by the Commune of La Spezia to write an inscription for the plaque honoring the residence in which Shelley had lived.

In spring 1910 Roccatagliata Ceccardi's friends rallied around him once again and published his poems written between 1898 and 1909. Many of the works in this collection, *Sonetti e poemi*, had already appeared in print. He had entertained the project for some time, but financial reasons had prohibited him from realizing it. He showed his appreciation to his friends by dedicating the book to them. *Sonetti e poemi* contains thirty-five sonnets and ballads; the poem *In morte di due bimbi innamorati*; twenty poems under the title "Cantilene e ritmi" (Lullabies and Rhythms); the elegy "In morte di mio fratello" (On the Death of My Brother); the thirteen sonnets of *Apua Mater*; the poem *Il viandante*; six odes; the "Congedo" (Envoi); and two epigraphs, for Dante and Shelley. Several of the poems in the collection are notably rhetorical and heavily influenced by Carducci, as in the volume's opening sonnet, "Genova":

> Un dì le torri, aeree, giganti
> munirono le tue darsene fiere
> com'ira e libertà tra lor balzanti
> armate, il cor del tuo popolo artiere.
>
> (One day the giant, lofty towers
> fortified your proud docks
> like wrath and freedom amidst their bounding
> fleets, the heart of your ardent people.)

Many of the themes from Roccatagliata Ceccardi's earlier works of poetry and prose reappear. Descriptive details of landscapes occupy a great amount of space. His language becomes more sober and essential when he describes in vivid terms the familiar and simple world of the Ligurian seaside, as is the case in "La vita dei marinai" (Life of the Sailors):

> Oh vecchi marinai!
> A dì tardi, fumando
> entro pipe di creta
> un torpido pensier tra il dubbio e il sogno,
> convengono su le soglie
> di lor umili case
> contemplano le nuvole e le vele

> (Oh old sailors!
> At day's end, smoking
> within the clay pipes
> a torpid thought between doubt and dream,
> converge on the doorways
> of their humble homes
> they contemplate the clouds and the sails).

Roccatagliata Ceccardi dedicated the most effective, and least rhetorical, of these poems with seaside settings, "Piccolo porto di Liguria" (Small Port in Liguria), to Mario Novaro. This natural depiction of a small port was to become a recurrent motif among the poets of Liguria:

> E tra i riflessi
> di aeree finestre
> che perdono fuor da un lembo
> di oliveti occheggiando,
> sonnecchiano in un grembo
> di azzurra acqua i velier, con un perenne
> lamentìo di carene,
> e uno sbatter di vele
> levate ad asciugare in su le antenne
> o in sui bompressi.

> (And amid the reflections
> of airy windows
> that fall from a strip
> of olive groves casting glances,
> the sailing ships doze in the lap
> of blue water, with a perennial
> wailing of keels,
> and a flapping of sails
> raised to dry in the lateen yards
> or in the bowsprits.)

Roccatagliata Ceccardi's scenic poems, like his elegiac verses, express a sense of intimacy and communion with nature. His elegiac style develops from reflections of childhood and the sad remorse of something that has been irremediably lost. The title of the section "Cantilene e ritmi" suggests, through the rhythmic voice of a children's lullaby, the incessant reminder of this perpetual remorse. The opening poem of this section, "Quando ci rivedremo" (When We'll See Each Other Again), was inspired by the painful loss of his youthful love, Gemma, a loss partly eased by his creation of a nostalgic dreamworld:

> Quando ci rivedremo
> il tempo avrà nevicato
> sul nostro capo, o amore;
> avremo quasi passato
> il mare, e sarà il cuore
> più sincero e pacato.
> Ma non avremo più remo:
> io ne l'onda infinita
> del sogno, tu, de la vita,
> lo avremo infranto, o amore!

> (When we'll see each other again
> time will have snowed
> on our head, o love;
> we shall have nearly crossed
> the sea, and our heart will be
> more sincere and calm.
> But we shall no longer have an oar:
> I in the infinite wave
> of dream, you, of life,
> shall have shattered it, o love!)

Roccatagliata Ceccardi reveals his genuine poetic vein when he depicts a real and naturalistic setting in a nostalgic, melancholic tone. In 1927 Montale recognized in this naturalistic, elegiac expression a model for a tradition of poets from the region of Liguria: "Ceccardo mi ha interessato anche perché egli è un pò come il padre dei cantori della terra ligure. E' questo il Ceccardo che amiamo" (Ceccardo interested me also because he was a bit like the father of the poets of the Ligurian land. This is the Ceccardo we love). A poem from *Sonetti e poemi*, "In un cimitero di monti" (In a Mountain Cemetery), illustrates those characteristics indicated by Montale. This short poem, inspired by the memory of Roccatagliata Ceccardi's mother, displays many features that are associated with the Ligurian tradition of poetry and, in turn, with modern poetry of the first fifty years of the twentieth century:

> Tarda il sentiero in un silenzio d'erba
> che ingialla di rammarico, e rinverde
> non mietuta, tra un vel d'aridi gambi.
> Una rosa selvatica, una stella
> di iride azzurra, affacciansi talora
> da quel deserto come un sogno . . . ; un sogno
> che intende con le pallide pupille
> a un altro sogno, lungi, interminato.

> (The path delays in a silence of grass
> that yellows from regret, and unreaped

grows green again, amid a veil of dry stems.
A wild rose, a row
of blue irises, sometimes appear
from that desert like a dream . . . ; a dream
that views with pale eyes
another distant, boundless, dream.)

The novelty of Roccatagliata Ceccardi's poetry consists not only in the sobriety of a language that aims at capturing the austere landscape of Liguria, but also in his ability to mesh physical elements with his state of mind. It is precisely this relationship between the self and the elements that was to evoke Montale's lapidary expression "il male di vivere" (the pain of living).

On 2 January 1914 Roccatagliata Ceccardi, while in Genoa, developed a serious case of arthritis and was hospitalized. Unbeknownst to him, a Genovese newspaper, the *Lavoro*, promoted a national subscription campaign to assist him and his family. This humanitarian act was soon copied in kind by the country's major newspaper, *Corriere della sera*. At the same time, many friends and admirers, including D'Annunzio and Giuseppe Borgese, joined together in a project to publish a new edition of Roccatagliata Ceccardi's poems. Interpreting the gesture as merely an act of charity, he immediately declined.

The events on the eve of World War I became an obsession for him. He traveled throughout the country and delivered speeches in support of the interventionist cause. He also composed and republished several works of poetry and prose that exalted a nationalistic spirit, including *Per un brindisi a Guglielmo Imperatore* and *Quando tornerà Garibaldi?* (When Will Garibaldi Return?, 1908).

On 4 March 1916 his three-act poetic drama *Don Chisciotte* (Don Quixote), with music by Guido Dell'Orso, was performed in Genoa and then published later that year. The performance proved to be unsuccessful. What is significant in this theatrical work is the reproposal of the myth of the wayfarer within the fable of the knight-errant. Roccatagliata Ceccardi's personal experiences had taught him that certain heroic ideals and endeavors were impossible within a historical context; therefore, he relegated them to the world of myth:

O fortunata
età, secolo grande, allor che al sole
fuor da volumi alieran con grido
epico le mie gesta, e misurate
in canti di battaglia risonanti
fiammeran nel crepuscolo de' miti.

(O fortunate
age, great epoch, when toward the sun
out of tomes will fly with an epic
cry my actions, and measured
in resounding songs of battle
they will blaze in the twilight of myths.)

On 24 January 1918 Roccatagliata Ceccardi's wife died, leaving him in a state of despair. In a letter to Lorenzo Viani, he expressed his willingness to exchange his few small treasures in order to have her return: "Ti giuro, Lorenzo, anche se potessi far ritornare anche così, un po' malata, come fu sempre, quella mia cara morta ne darei al prezzo il volume di *Sonetti e poemi* e quell'esile rametto di alloro che dicono io mi abbia" (I swear to you, Lorenzo, even if my dearest departed should return a bit sickly, like she always was, I'd give up my *Sonetti e poemi* and the frail laurel branch they say I deserve).

While in Carrara in the fall of 1918 Roccatagliata Ceccardi met a young teacher named Sidonia Serponia. The passion of the prematurely aged poet was not shared by the young woman; however, this final illusion was the inspiration for the poems in "Elegie del demonio meridiano" (Elegies of the Midday Demon), which are among his last. They are collected in *Sillabe ed ombre, poesie (1910-1919)* (Syllables and Shadows), published in 1925. Roccatagliata Ceccardi spent his final months in Genoa, where he died on 3 August 1919 of a cerebral hemorrhage.

Sillabe ed ombre reveals Roccatagliata Ceccardi's unyielding attempt to declare himself the poet of the glories and myths of Italy; consequently these compositions bear much of the anachronistic rhetoric of nineteenth-century civic poetry. The "Poemi eroici" (Heroic Poems) and "In morte di Leone Delagrange, guidatore di carri alati" (On the Death of Leone Delagrange, Driver of Winged Chariots) are examples of a triumphal and bombastic tendency inherent in much of his poetry. Within the distinctly literary structures of tomb inscriptions inspired by classical Latin poetry, however, he expresses his more natural idyllic vein. In "Epigrafe tombale: Per i bimbi Maria e Marco Carbonaro" (Tomb Epigraph: For the Children Maria and Marco Carbonaro), for example, he returns to the motif of childhood within an elegiac context. The presence of death permeates these lines:

La primavera in cuore ci bisbigliava: eravamo
come rondini, e in nido ci sorprese l'autunno.

Ma vano nome non crederci e cenere: ancor da
   quel breve
ambito noi torniamo come rondini a un cuore.

(Springtime whispered in our hearts: we were
like swallows, and autumn surprised us in our nest.
But do not think we are an empty name and ashes:
   still from that brief
sphere we return like swallows to a heart.)

    In this lapidary poem Roccatagliata
Ceccardi highlights characteristic features of his
poetry. The sharpness of images and the bareness of language combine to instill the natural setting with the poet's melancholic feelings. His use
of the poetic fragment in several poems of *Sillabe
ed ombre*, which evoke similar naturalistic impressions, recalls his comments in his notes to the
first edition of *Il viandante*: "Solo di frammenti
mi par che lo potessi comporre, lasciando allo
spirito, che unico li informi, il debito e il vanto
pur di congiungerli in una ideale armonia" (It
seems that I could have only composed it in fragments, leaving to the spirit, which alone shapes
it, the duty and pride if only to unite them in an
ideal harmony). The main innovation of his poetry is his employment of the fragment. Although
his verses still maintain the formal features of a
long classical tradition, his fragments manifest a
restlessness with these inherited characteristics, insofar as they are no longer appropriate to the
poet's humble condition. He anticipates, with the
fragment, a form of expression that was to be
the foundation for a new poetic discourse among
Italian poets.

    Roccatagliata Ceccardi represents a cross-
roads in Italian poetry. It is a point where the
old and new meet and, thus, mix their respective
forms and styles. The figure of the wayfarer, and
particularly Roccatagliata Ceccardi's treatment of
him, is exemplary of this transitional point. On
one hand, Roccatagliata Ceccardi continues the
tradition of the *viator*, who has as his distant ances-
tor Dante and who is also the heir to the romantic force of rebellion against history; on the other
hand, his failure to find a personal justification
in reality makes him a precursor of modern Italian poetry.

Letters:

Lettere a "La Riviera Ligure," volume 2 (of 2), edited by Pino Boero (Milan: Meynier, 1986).

Biographies:

Lorenzo Viani, *Ceccardo* (Milan: Alpes, 1922);

Pierangelo Baratono, Preface to *Sillabe ed ombre*,
   edited by Baratono (Milan: Treves, 1925);

Tito Rosina, *Ceccardo Roccatagliata Ceccardi*
   (Genoa: Orfini, 1937);

Urio Clades, *Roccatagliata Ceccardi* (Florence:
   Sansoni, 1969);

Eligio Imarisio, "Un bohemien maudit," in *Tutte
   le poesie*, edited by Imarisio and Bruno
   Cicchetti (Genoa: Sagep, 1982), pp. 59-78.

References:

Rita Baldassarri, *Ceccardo Roccatagliata Ceccardi*
   (Rome: Ateneo, 1984);

Pierangelo Baratono, *Genova a lume di naso*
   (Genoa: Libreria Moderna, 1925);

Carlo Bo, "Lavoro per Roccatagliata Ceccardi,"
   L'Italia, 3 March 1937, p. 3;

Bo, "Ripensando a Ceccardo," *L'Approdo Letterario*, 59-60 (December 1972): 3-22;

Bo, "Verso la nuova poesia," in *Storia della
   letteratura italiana*, 9 volumes (Milan: Garzanti, 1976), IV: 240-242;

Giorgio Caproni, "La corrente ligustica della nostra poesia: Ceccardo Roccatagliata Ceccardi
   e Mario Novaro," *La Fiera Letteraria*, 11 (11
   November 1956): 3;

Caproni, "La corrente ligustica nella nostra
   poesia: Boine, Sbarbaro, Montale," *La Fiera
   Letteraria*, 20 (11 November 1965): 1;

Sandro Cassone, "Ceccardo il viandante tragico,"
   Arte Stampa, 20 (July-August 1970): 3-8;

Giovanni Cattanei, "Ceccardo Roccatagliata Ceccardi," in his *La liguria e la poesia italiana del
   novecento* (Milan: Silva, 1966), pp. 108-139;

Mario G. Celle, "Poesia ed arte in Ceccardo
   Roccatagliata Ceccardi," *Giornale storico e
   letterario della Liguria*, 3 (January-March
   1927): 56-67;

Bruno Cicchetti, "Uno 'scapigliato' nel novecento," in *Tutte le poesie*, edited by Cicchetti and Eligio Imarisio (Genoa: Sagep,
   1982), pp. 9-57;

Vittorio Coletti, "La lingua irrequieta di Ceccardi," in his *Momenti del linguaggio poetico
   novecentesco* (Genoa, San Salvatore &
   Monferrato: Melangolo, 1978), pp. 15-46;

Giuseppe Conte, "Il peccato della parola," *Persona*, 3-4 (March-April 1971): 10-11;

Rodolfo Della Felice, "Ceccardo Roccatagliata
   Ceccardi inquieto viandante della poesia,"
   Telegrafo, 15 (25 March 1937): 3;

Francesco De Nicola, *L'ulivo e la parola: Studi sui poeti e la poesia in Liguria nel Novecento* (Savona, Italy: Sabatelli, 1986);

Ruggero Jacobbi, "Il primo Ceccardo," *L'Albero*, 56 (1976): 17-26;

Ettore Janni, *Poeti minori dell'ottocento*, 4 volumes (Milan: Rizzoli, 1958), IV: 206-216;

Gina Lagorio, "Ceccardo: Il 'domestico titano' della poesia ligure," *Nuova Rivista Europea*, 33 (February 1983): 65-68;

Lagorio, *Cultura e letteratura ligure del '900* (Savona, Italy: Sabatelli, 1972);

Gaetano Mariani, "Ceccardo Roccatagliata Ceccardi," in his *Poesia e tecnica nella lirica del '900* (Padua, Italy: Liviana, 1983), pp. 73-96;

Eugenio Montale, "Poeti e paesaggi di Liguria," *Atlas* (January 1927): 46;

Montale, "Primasera di Angelo Barile," *Pan*, 2 (June 1934): 288;

Montale, "Variazioni," in his *Sulla Poesia* (Milan: Mondadori, 1976), pp. 348-351;

Pietro Pancrazi, "La poesia di Ceccardo Roccatagliata Ceccardi," in his *Scrittori d'oggi* (Bari, Italy: Laterza, 1946), pp. 212-222;

Giovanni Petronilli, "Ceccardi Roccatagliata Ceccardi," *Persona*, 3-4 (March-April 1971): 12-13;

Emma Pistelli Rinaldi, *Ceccardo Roccatagliata Ceccardi tra ottocento e novecento* (Savona, Italy: Sabatelli, 1978);

Giovanni Raboni, "Dai maestri in ombra nasce la nuova poesia italiana," *Tuttolibri*, 9 (14 May 1983);

Eduardo Villa, "Ceccardo Roccatagliata Ceccardi," in his *I poeti liguri e Leopardi* (Padua, Italy: Liviana, 1979), pp. 53-82.

Umberto Saba
(9 March 1883 - 25 August 1957)

Stelio Cro
McMaster University

BOOKS: *Poesie* (Florence: Italiana, 1911);

Coi miei occhi (Florence: Libreria della Voce, 1912);

La serena disperazione (Trieste: Libreria Antica e Moderna, 1920);

Cose leggere e vaganti (Trieste: Libreria Antica e Moderna, 1920);

L'amorosa spina (Trieste: Libreria Antica e Moderna, 1920);

Il canzoniere (Trieste: Libreria Antica e Moderna, 1921; revised and enlarged edition, Rome: Einaudi, 1945; revised and enlarged again, 1948; further enlarged, 1961);

Preludio e canzonette (Turin: Primo Tempo, 1923);

Autobiografia (Turin: Primo Tempo, 1924);

I Prigioni (Turin: Primo Tempo, 1924);

Figure e canti (Milan: Treves, 1926);

L'Uomo (Trieste: Libreria Antica e Moderna, 1926);

Preludio e fughe (Florence: Solaria, 1928);

Tre poesie alla mia balia (Trieste: Antica e Moderna, 1929);

Ammonizione ed altre poesie, 1900-1910 (Trieste: Libreria Antica e Moderna, 1932);

Tre composizioni (Milan: Treves, 1933);

Parole (Lanciano, Italy: Carabba, 1934);

Ultime cose (Lugano, 1944);

Scorciatoie e raccontini (Milan: Mondadori, 1946);

Mediterranee (Milan: Mondadori, 1946);

Storia e cronistoria del Canzoniere (Milan: Mondadori, 1948);

Poesie dell'adolescenza e giovanili (Milan: Mondadori, 1949);

Tutte le opere, 8 volumes (Milan: Mondadori, 1949-1959);

Uccelli (Trieste: Zibaldone, 1951);

Uccelli; e, Quasi un racconto (Milan: Mondadori, 1951);

Ricordi—racconti, 1910-1947, edited by Guido Piovene (Milan: Mondadori, 1956);

Cuor morituro, e altre poesie (Milan: Mondadori, 1959);

Epigrafe; Ultime prose (Milan: Saggiatore, 1959);

Quello che resta da fare ai poeti (Trieste: Zibaldone, 1959);

Il piccolo Berto (Milan: Mondadori, 1961);

Antologia del "Canzoniere," edited by Carlo Muscetta (Turin: Einaudi, 1963);

Prose, edited by Linuccia Saba (Milan: Mondadori, 1964);

Il vecchio e il giovane, edited by Linuccia Saba (Milan: Mondadori, 1965);

L'adolescenza del Canzoniere e undici lettere (Turin: Fògola, 1975);

Ernesto (Turin: Einaudi, 1975); translated by Mark Thompson (New York: Carcanet, 1987);

Amicizia, edited by Carlo Levi (Milan: Mondadori, 1976);

Poesie; Prose scelte, 2 volumes, edited by Giovanni Giudici (Milan: Mondadori, 1976);

Tutte le poesie (Milan: Mondadori, 1988).

Edition in English: *Umberto Saba: Thirty-One Poems*, translated by Felix Stefanile (New Rochelle, N.Y.: Elizabeth, 1978; Manchester: Carcanet New Press, 1987).

Ambiguity or duality could be the dominant character of Umberto Saba's life and poetry. Even in his concept of a poet (stated in *Scorciatoie e raccontini* [Shortcuts and Small Tales, 1946]) Saba posits a duality of child/man, ever present at the moment of artistic creation:

Solo là dove il bambino e l'uomo coesistono, in forme il più possibile estreme, nella stessa persona, nasce—molte altre circostanze aiutando—il miracolo: nasce Dante. Dante è un piccolo bambino, continuamente stupito di quello che avviene a un uomo grandissimo; sono veramente "due in uno."

(Only when the child and the adult coexist in the most extreme forms, in the same person, can we say that the miracle happens: Dante is born. Dante is a small child, constantly surprised by what happens to a very great man; they are really "two in one.")

Umberto Saba

More important than a judgment on Dante, this observation reveals the duality of Saba's own perception of his life and poetry. Other elements also show that dualism is a kind of general attitude of Saba: his desire for fame and his pretended humility; his *dannunzianesimo* (adherence to the ideas of Gabriele D'Annunzio) and his sympathy for the Left; his admiration for Sigmund Freud and his nostalgia for an innocent, pre-Freudian world. In Saba's poetry one finds narrative, lyricism, Freudianism, and realistic descriptions of people and places.

Characteristic of his later writings in prose is his judgment of the modern era as a period of crisis and transition, a new Middle Ages, preceding a new era that in his opinion will be dominated by Freud, his great forerunner Friedrich Nietzsche, and their disciples, as Saba outlines in *Scorciatoie e raccontini*:

Troppi anni dovranno adesso passare (un intero Medio Evo) prima che gli uomini cessino di fraintendere, cioè maledire, il primo; e disarmino, davanti al secondo, le loro resistenze inevitabili e assurde.

(Too many years will now have to go by [a whole Middle Ages] before men cease to misunderstand, that is to condemn, the first [Nietzsche] and desist, for the second [Freud], from their absurd and inevitable resistance.)

Born on 9 March 1883 in Trieste, to a Jewish mother and an Aryan, Christian father who abandoned the family before Saba's birth, Umberto Saba did not follow regular studies. He read avidly and started writing poetry at the age of seventeen. His childhood was not easy. He was raised by a Slavic wet nurse, Peppa, who, being a Christian, made him recite the Lord's Prayer in Slovak every night and took him to the Church of the Rosary every Sunday. When he was old enough, he gave up his family name, Poli, and chose instead a Jewish one, Saba, which means "bread." Poverty and misery dominated his childhood in the Jewish ghetto in Trieste. He recalls vivid memories of the ghetto in "Gli ebrei" (The Jews), collected in *Prose* (1964) but originally dated 1910-1912. An aunt of his, Regina, took him and his mother into her home. Saba interrupted his schooling in order to work as a clerk in a store, but then he discovered the adventure of the sea, working as a cabin boy on a coastline passenger vessel in the Adriatic Sea. For two years (1907-1908) he served in the Italian army and was stationed in Florence and Salerno. His readings were not systematic.

Saba's poetry betrays a certain naiveté of themes and style, which paradoxically may be part of his originality. Personal autobiography became the single, innermost motivation for all his writings in verse and prose. Saba's work is admirable because of his ability to see great meanings in small events.

His first book of poetry, *Poesie*, was published in 1911. Other small books followed—*Coi miei occhi* (With My Eyes, 1912), *La serena disperazione* (The Serene Desperation, 1920), *L'amorosa spina* (The Amorous Thorn, 1920)—up to the 1921 publication of *Il canzoniere* (literally, The Collection of Poems—the title is borrowed from Petrach's book of the same name), which contains Saba's poetry from 1900 to 1921 and is an invaluable tool in reconstructing the stages of development of his artistic vocation and poetic achievements.

Saba's poetry shows all the important events, people, and places of his life: the fatherless home; the ghetto in Trieste; the people of Trieste; his friends; his wife, Lina (whom he married in 1908); his only daughter, Linuccia; and the racial persecutions during World War II. Critics began to acknowledge him late, with the publication of *Preludio e fughe* (Prelude and Fugues, 1928), still considered by many to be his best book. Saba never belonged to any literary circle. Even though present-day criticism tends to appreciate the fact that he wrote without visible adherence to any current school of poetry, and certainly not to the predominant hermetic school of his day, his isolation brought a sense of frustration and solitude, which in turn became a considerable part of his poetry.

Saba's life was not an eventful one from the point of view of external events. This does not mean that it was not a rich one, since he gave poetic wings to his state of mind, sometimes triggered by memory, or a flower, or a familiar face, or the need to recount a love experience. The Fascist racial laws of 1938 must have been deeply troubling to the fifty-five-year-old Saba. Always a good patriot, having served in World War I in the Italian army, he was horrified by the empty nationalistic policies and speeches of Benito Mussolini. Saba fled and tried to settle in Paris, but to no avail. He soon returned to Italy and spent the darkest war years in hiding. After the war he rejoined his family and reopened his bookstore, the Libreria Antica e Moderna, in Trieste. (He had bought the store in 1918 with the aid of his aunt.)

In *Storia e cronistoria del Canzoniere* (History and Chronicle of the *Canzoniere*, 1948) Saba reconstructed in detail the origin and development of his *Canzoniere*. One can detect, in several apologetic passages, a naive desire to be recognized, perhaps a compensation for all the years during which he saw more fortunate poets of his own generation getting awards and recognition. At any rate the book shows his desire for honor and glory. Another important work in prose is his *Scorciatoie e raccontini*, a series of brief annotations on contemporary literature, politics, and culture, some of which were originally published in the leading Italian newspapers and magazines of the day. His judgments sometimes have a haunting quality, as if Saba had anticipated later times. For example, his understanding of Friedrich Nietzsche and Sigmund Freud was fundamentally intuitive: he felt that both were symbols, representing the end of one culture and the beginning of a new one. He insists on the same message contained in his poetry: love, care, understanding, piety, and tolerance. He opposed the pure intelligence and reason behind some contemporary literature.

Critics have often indicated that Saba's classicism consists of a conscious effort to assimilate, in his autobiographical poetry, the best of the Italian tradition. The names of Petrarch, Giacomo Leopardi, Gabriele D'Annunzio, Giovanni Pascoli, Giacomo Zanella, and Eugenio Montale have been mentioned in connection with his poetry. Saba's works remind one of Petrarch and Leopardi. However, the study of his sources places D'Annunzio, followed by Giosuè Carducci, at the top of the list of those from whose work Saba has more frequently taken or adapted a verse, a metaphor, or a simple image during his formative years between 1900 and 1921. Saba himself must have realized the problem caused by his habit of borrowing, which might explain some of the changes he made to the subsequent editions of *Il canzoniere*. This revising or excluding of previous compositions indicates a search for his own identity, which in turn becomes a main theme of *Il canzoniere*.

The first two books Saba wrote were not published until their inclusion in *Il canzoniere*. "Casa e campagna" (House and Country, 1909-1910)

Come il mio amico si è consolato di
Lissa.   Lissa

Tu non sai - mi diceva il mio amico - quanto io abbia sofferto di quella ventura. Ne ò sofferto da bambino fino a qualche anno fa, con un'intimità di sofferenza sempre più acuta: ormai sentivo Lissa come una vergogna della mia vita privata, e neppure sconfitta mi amareggiava più di questa ricevuta sul mare, per marina... in vista alle coste dalmate, con tante e così belle navi che avevamo. Che Lissa! esclamavo, quando volevo significare un accaduto particolarmente disastroso, un gioco perduto fuori d'ogni previsione... le carte migliori. Ricordo le liti a scuola coi condiscepoli di parte contraria (il mio amico, suddito italiano, era nato ed aveva studiato a Trieste), le discussioni acri fino alle lacrime e ai pugni coi pochi ragazzi austriacanti del ginnasio Comunale, ai quali, non so per quale profondità o morbosità del mio temperamento, mi accompagnavo più volentieri che agli altri. E quando mi affannavo a dimostrare la superiorità dell'Italia sull'Austria, per terra certo (bastavano i bersaglieri) e per mare certissimo (bastava la Duilio), ricevevo sempre questa risposta annientante, questa torpedine esplosa a tempo nel del mio entusiasmo... filante via a tutte bandiere spiegate;
"E Lissa?"

Page from the manuscript for Saba's 1913 autobiographical essay that was first published in the March 1950 issue of Europa Letteraria *(from* Storia della Letteratura, *volume 7, edited by Luigi Ferrante, 1965)* and "Trieste e una donna" (Trieste and a Woman, 1910-1912) were inspired by his wife, Lina, called "Laura" in the poems. He became interested in Lina after a friend, who liked her younger sister, talked to him about her. He went to visit her; they became friends and fell in love. A few years later, in 1908, they were married. They had one daughter, Linuccia. Saba loved Lina very much and, after her death, he often thought of her as a saint. After she died in 1956, Saba managed to survive only nine months.

The first book, "Casa e campagna," evokes the feeling of a countryside environment, near Trieste, the typical farming community. The collection includes some of the best and best-known compositions of Saba, such as "A mia moglie" (To My Wife) and "La capra" (The Goat). The first conveys a genuine feeling of love:

> Tu sei come una giovane,
> una bianca pollastra.
> Le si arruffano al vento
> le piume, il collo china
> per bere, e in terra raspa;
> ma, nell'andare, ha il lento
> tuo passo di regina,
> ed incede sull'erba
> pettoruta e superba.
> E' migliore del maschio.
> . . . .
> E così nella pecchia
> ti ritrovo, ed in tutte
> le femmine di tutti
> i sereni animali
> che avvicinano a Dio . . .

> (You are like a young,
> white chicken.
> The wind ruffles
> her feathers, while she bends her neck
> to drink and scratches the dirt;
> but when she moves slowly
> she reminds me of your majestic steps,
> as she advances on the grass
> proudly strutting and thrusting out her chest.
> She is better than the male.
> . . . .
> And I find you in the bee
> and in every other
> female animal
> who quietly brings us
> closer to the Lord . . .).

Saba considered this his most famous poem. "A mia moglie" has been linked to a biblical inspiration, in part after a suggestion by Saba himself, be-

cause of the indirect, psalmlike praise of the Lord through the female creatures.

A good example of Saba's humanization of animals can be seen in "La capra," the goat being a symbol of sorrow and, more precisely, of the pain associated with the Jewish people:

> Ho parlato a una capra.
> Era sola sul prato, era legata.
> Sazia d'erba, bagnata
> dalla pioggia, belava.

> Quell'uguale belato era fraterno
> al mio dolore. Ed io risposi, prima
> per celia, poi perché il dolore è eterno,
> ha una voce e non varia.
> Questa voce sentiva
> gemere in una capra solitaria.

> In una capra dal viso semita
> sentiva querelarsi ogni altro male,
> ogni altra vita.

> (I have spoken to a goat.
> She was alone in the field, she was tied up.
> Filled with grass, soaked
> by the rain, she was bleating.

> The sameness of her bleating meant
> brotherly sorrow to me. And I answered, first
> as if teasing her, then because pain is everlasting,
> has one voice with no variations.
> I felt this voice crying
> in a lonely goat.

> In a goat with a Semitic face,
> I felt the suffering
> of everyone's life.)

Saba's humanization sometimes projects objects into an unusual but effective metaphoric dimension, such as in "Trieste," from the "Trieste e una donna" collection:

> Trieste ha una scontrosa
> grazia. Se piace,
> è come un ragazzaccio aspro e vorace,
> con gli occhi azzurri e mani troppo grandi
> per regalare un fiore;
> come un amore
> con gelosia.

> (Trieste has a shy
> appeal. If you like it,
> it is like a rough and hungry boy,
> with blue eyes and hands too big
> to give away a flower;
> like a love
> with jealousy.)

The duality in much of Saba's poetry is confirmed in *La serena disperazione*, which even in the title seems to express an intrinsic ambiguity. In no other collection of poems can one perceive so readily the extent of Leopardi's influence on Saba. A characteristic of Leopardi's poetry is also duality: he reached an awareness of sorrow, yet insisted on the beauty of the images conjured up by his pessimistic state of mind. Likewise, Saba presents a series of images that, on one hand, bring reality into focus and, on the other, interpret a subjective state of mind, the prevailing mood of which is pessimistic and decidedly Leopardian, even in the choice of words, as in "Il patriarca":

Nella collina che splende in faccia
seguo d'un vecchio l'operosa traccia.
Nella mia mente di fantasmi carca,
non è un agricoltore, è un patriarca.
La sua forza al peccato non s'estingue;
tien le radici nella zolla pingue,
nel forte figlio, nella bella nuora,
in lui stesso; e con questo non ignora,
lo scaltro vecchio, che la vita è un male,
che la vita è il peccato originale.
Fin giù all'ultimo campo, per divino
volere, dato ai suoi, tolto al vicino,
un mondo nuovo ha di sè fecondato.
Ne gode, e pensa: Felice il non nato!

(On the hill in front of me
I observe the labor of an old man.
In my mind full of fantasies,
he is not a farmer, he is a patriarch.
His strength does not finish with sin;
it has deep roots in the fertile soil,
in the strong son, in the beautiful daughter-in-law,
in himself, and with this he does not ignore,
the wise old man, that life is evil,
that life is the original sin.
Down to the last field, which, taken, for an act
of God, from his neighbor, he has given to his
    family
He enjoys a new world, populated by him,
and thinks: lucky the unborn!)

Commenting on this poem in *Storia e cronistoria*, Saba seems to justify this pessimism as limited to a certain period, what he deems as being the first part of his life and poetry.

"Caffè Tergeste" is perhaps the most renowned poem of *La serena disperazione*, in part because of its political reference to the coexistence of the Italian and the Slavic populations in Trieste:

Caffè di plebe, dove un dì celavo
la mia faccia, con gioia oggi ti guardo.

E tu concili l'italo e lo slavo,
a tarda notte, lungo il tuo bigliardo.

(Café of the populace, where one day I was hiding
my face, today I look at you with joy.
And you reconcile the Italian and the Slavic,
late at night, at the pool table.)

Saba's next book, *Cose leggere e vaganti* (Light and Wandering Things, 1920), includes several poems dedicated to Paolina, a character who symbolizes the joy of life:

Paolina, dolce
Paolina,
che tieni in cuore? Io non lo chiedo. È pura
la tua bellezza;
vi farebbe un pensiero quel che un alito
sullo specchio, che subito s'appanna.

(Paolina, sweet
Paolina,
I do not ask you what is hidden in your heart.
Your beauty is pure;
a thought would veil it
like a breath on a mirror.)

Paolina arouses the poet's sensuality, albeit fantasized; she is a Lolita figure, a girl capable of releasing the basest needs of the male character.

Saba's next collection, *L'amorosa spina*, also treats the theme of love but reveals a more passionate experience than the previous love poetry. The woman who inspired this collection, and others, was Chiaretta, Saba's assistant in his bookstore. The poet clearly speaks of her in terms of a love affair, amid sensual connotations that strongly resemble those used in connection with Paolina. Whether this love affair was real or imagined is not known. However, Saba claimed that Chiaretta was, after Lina, the most important female character mentioned in *Il canzoniere*.

In *L'amorosa spina* Saba deals with Eros, without abstractions. It is this direct, simple, humane treatment of the theme of love that places him in a different category than most modern and contemporary Italian poets. The musicality of this collection allows one to appreciate even more the simplicity of the poetry:

Guarda là quella vezzosa,
guarda là quella smorfiosa.
Si restringe nelle spalle,
tiene il viso sullo scialle.

Saba in his Italian army uniform during World War I

O qual mai castigo ha avuto?
Nulla. Un bacio ha ricevuto.

(Look at that charming girl,
look at that coquette.
She flirts with her shoulders,
while hiding her face in the scarf.
What punishment has she received?
None. Just a kiss.)

A stage of Saba's poetry seems to have concluded with *L'amorosa spina*, the last collection to be included in *Il canzoniere* of 1921. This stage can be considered the formative period of Saba's poetry and can be retraced only by studying the 1921 edition of *Il canzoniere* itself. Too often critics have followed Saba's own criticism contained in *Storia e cronistoria*.

Almost all the compositions of *Preludio e canzonette* (1923), comprising a "Preludio," twelve "Canzonette" (songs) and a "Finale," were in-

spired by Chiaretta, but the poet seems to have distinguished different stages in his love: the innocent, natural spontaneous beginning of two unsuspecting lovers, in "Chiaretta in villeggiatura" (Chiaretta on Vacation); the idealization of true love, which can never be vulgar, embarrassing, or offensive, in "L'incisore" (The Engraver); and the stable relation of a love affair in "Chiaretta." The first composition has a narrative frame, consisting of the story of a man in love with a young lady and their first kiss:

Era il tempo in cui piace
con l'amata fanciulla passar l'ore;
e godono gli occhi e tace il cuore.
Assai, bella Chiaretta, assai godere
si può con gli occhi; ma più dolce è avere
chi s'ama, sola a solo.
Dietro ad un muricciolo
per man ti trassi, e sulla bocca ardente
ti baciai, ti baciai sì lungamente.

(It was the time when it is pleasant
to spend hours with the beloved girl;
the eyes enjoy while the heart is silent.
Much one can enjoy, beautiful Chiaretta,
with one's eyes, but so much sweeter it is
to have the beloved one, to be alone with her.
Behind a wall
I held you by the hand, and I gave you a kiss
on your ardent lips, a very long kiss.)

The sudden erotic twist of the last three lines—prepared for by the flirting of Chiaretta, the poet's awareness of her physical beauty, and, finally, the culminating act of kissing—seems a confession. It is because of this evident change in Saba's poetry, which now shows a more psychological interest, that one could place *Preludio e canzonette* at the beginning of the second, and more important, period in Saba's poetry, that of his psychological poetry.

The second composition, "L'incisore," tells of a dream of the poet: to be an engraver, in order to reach that stage of purifying sensual love through aesthetic beauty—a familiar process, not only to Italian classical poets but to the visual artists, especially Titian with his nudes. Saba, in his poem, imagines a scene in an engraving: the weather, a tree, a wall, a road full of people, the detail of a blacksmith shoeing a horse and finally an interior, where he sees a naked girl:

Là senza un pentimento
(o non sa ch'altri spia?)
giace fanciulla ignuda.

Nella luce che cruda
entra dalla finestra
scopre il dorso gentile.
E quel che ha un nome vile
è un'assai gentil cosa
nelle mie stampe accolta.

(There, without fears
[doesn't she know that there is a Peeping Tom?]
a naked girl is lying down.
She uncovers her gentle back
to the stark light
entering from the window.
And what has a coarse name
it is a very fine thing
placed in my engraving.)

The third composition, "Chiaretta," is a reminiscence of his love for this young girl, of the time they initially met in the bookstore, the necessary force of nature, and the consolation that, once the impulse of passion is gone, with Eros subdued, a consoling feeling still remains; the experience of love has left a positive balance, and a reassuring sense of a meaningful relationship still binds the two lovers together:

Quanto dolce all'amara
vita hai mesciuto, cara
tenera delicata
onesta ispiratrice
Chiaretta! Oh me felice
se pur posso ancor dire:
Male non feci io a lei.

(How much sweetness you have mixed
in the sourness of life, dear
tender delicate
honest inspiring
Chiaretta! How happy I am
if I can still say:
I did not harm her.)

All his life Saba felt he was excluded, especially by the official cultural circles of Italy, as if his poetry did not belong anywhere, for the simple reason that it could not be classified with a fashionable or acceptable label. In the first of the fifteen sonnets of *Autobiografia* (1924) he acknowledges his disillusionment:

A viver senza il molto ambito alloro
fui forse il solo poeta italiano;
nè questo ancor mi fa un'anima amara.

(I was perhaps the only Italian poet
to live without the much coveted laurel;
and not even this makes my heart resentful.)

The duality of his roots is the theme of sonnet 3:

Mio padre è stato per me l' "assassino,"
fino ai vent'anni che l'ho conosciuto.
Allora ho visto ch'egli era un bambino,
e che il dono ch'io ho da lui l'ho avuto.
Aveva in volto il mio sguardo azzurrino,
un sorriso, in miseria, dolce e astuto.
Andò sempre pel mondo pellegrino;
più d'una donna l'ha amato e pasciuto.
Egli era gaio e leggero; mia madre
tutti sentiva della vita i pesi.

(My father was for me the "assassin,"
up to the time I met him, at twenty years of age.
Then I realized that he was a child,
and my gift I received from him.
He had my bluish eyes,
a smile, in his misery, sweet and sharp.
He always wandered as a pilgrim;
more than one woman loved him and fed him.
He was happy and lighthearted; my mother
always felt the weight of life.)

I Prigioni (The Prisoners, 1924) and *Fanciulle* (Girls, 1925) have a similar structure and artistic conception. They are composed of brief sketches of human types, young men in the first book and young women in the second. In "L'appassionato" (The Passionate Man) Saba reveals a rare eclectic view of religion:

Ero Mosè che ti trasse d'Egitto,
ed ho sofferto per te sulla croce.
Mi chiamo in Arabia Maometto.

(I was Moses leading you away from Egypt,
and I suffered for you on the cross.
In Arabia they call me Mohammed.)

More earthly and realistic is the gallery of *Fanciulle*. Of a girl named Maria, the poet says:

E mezza
bambina e mezza bestia. Eppure l'ami.
La sai ladra e bugiarda, una nemica
dei tuoi intimi pregi;
ma quanto più la spregi
più la vorresti alle tue voglie amica.

(She is half
little girl and half beast. And yet you love her.
You know that she is a thief and a liar, an enemy
of your most inner qualities;
but the more you despise her

the more you would want her submissive to your wishes.)

In *Cuor morituro* (Heart Meant to Die)—written between 1925 and 1930, published in 1959—Saba collected memories of his childhood, focusing on places and people dear to him, such as his nanny's house and Glauco, a friend. The delicate reminiscences also indicate how the poet has conquered the fears of his childhood. Therefore one sees the therapeutic benefit of poetry.

L'Uomo (Man, 1926) is relevant as a document of Saba's place in the Italian literary landscape of his time, beginning with the dedication to Giacomo Debenedetti, a personal friend and a renowned literary critic and professor of Italian literature at the Università di Roma. Saba and Debenedetti were both victims of the racial persecutions of the Fascist regime. They also shared a fierce anti-Crocianism and a profound admiration for Freud and Italo Svevo. Debenedetti was instrumental in the attention Saba's poetry elicited at the end of World War II. *L'Uomo* is Saba's longest poem and contains several autobiographical allusions, within a narrative structure, interspersed with biblical connotations that give the impression of an ancient fable of the life of every man:

Uscì per lei dalla dolente casa
del padre,
e la disse sua moglie, e fu la madre
dei figli suoi. D'ogni altra dolce cosa
parve l'anima sua fatta obliosa,
per sempre.

(For her he ran away from the sad house
of his father,
and he took her for his wife, and she was the
    mother
of his children. Everything else, even the sweetest,
he seemed to have forgotten,
forever.)

In *Storia e cronistoria* Saba acknowledges the autobiographical elements in this poem and presents a clear psychoanalytical interpretation, both of his poem and of the reaction of the Italian reader, which he believed was unjustifiably cool:

abbiamo pensato che l'odio per *L'Uomo* possa essere derivato dal fatto (dal lettore inconsciamente avvertito) che Saba ha voluto creare con esso una figura "paterna," il padre che mancò alla sua infanzia, e del quale egli portò sempre la nostalgia.

(we thought that the hatred for *L'Uomo* must have come from the fact [which the reader must have perceived subconsciously] that with it Saba wanted to create a "paternal" character, the father whom he missed in his childhood, and for whom he always longed.)

Curiously Saba posits as the artistic inspiration for this poem the work of Michelangelo, especially the frescoes in the Sistine Chapel, and, for the style, Saba refers to the Holy Scriptures.

Preludio e fughe is one of the most successful collections of Saba's poems. The inspiration for this book was clearly lyrical. He seems aware that he is experiencing an exceptional lyrical vein and urges his "voices" to give out his inner feelings, again speaking of the duality of his origins:

Come i parenti m'han dato due vite,
e di fonderle in una io fui capace,
in pace
vi componete negli estremi accordi,
voci invano discordi.
La luce e l'ombra, la gioia e il dolore
s'amano in voi.
Oh, ritornate a noi
care voci d'un tempo!

(Like my relatives who have given me two lives,
which I have been able to fuse into one,
at peace
you, voices quarreling in vain,
find harmony in these last notes.
Light and shadow, joy and sorrow
love each other in you.
Alas, come back to me
dear voices of one time!)

The lyricism is intensified in the "Fughe," often achieved through a polyphonic structure of two or more voices.

Il piccolo Berto (Little Berto)—written between 1929 and 1931, published in 1961—perhaps best shows the profound difference between Saba and Italian decadentism. The book stands in the poetic scenario of the *Novecento* (Twentieth Century) as the verse equivalent to Svevo's *La coscienza di Zeno* (1923), and, like this novel, was also inspired by a friendship with a psychoanalyst—in Saba's case, Dr. Edoardo Weiss. Saba is, like his older contemporary Svevo, antiliterary, a poet of intimate daily experiences and of psychological introspection. Like a psychoanalyst, the poet must first come to grips with his subconscious past, buried in the experiences of his childhood, looking for the key to

Self-portrait by Saba (from Dizionario universale della letteratura contemporanea, *volume 4, edited by Alberto Mondadori, 1960)*

unravel the mysteries of his existence. Through association, the poet, while cuddling his own daughter, remembers his nanny:

> Mia figlia
> mi tiene il braccio intorno al collo ignudo;
> ed io alla sua carezza m'addormento.
> . . . .
> Al seno
> approdo di colei che Berto ancora
> mi chiama, al primo, all'amoroso seno,
> ai verdi paradisi dell'infanzia.

> (My daughter
> embraces my naked neck with her arm;
> while she caresses me I fall asleep.
> . . . .
> I reach
> the breast of the one who still calls me
> Berto, to that first, loving breast,
> to the green paradise of childhood.)

After this psychoanalytical search, the poet can now account for the time elapsed. He has recovered that intangible good his childhood gave him:

> E ora addio,
> ma non per sempre, amata infanzia. Il fiore

della mia vita a te lo devo; ad essere
io rimasto un fanciullo, uno che reggere
ben sa gli umani pesi, e ha, in più, il dolore
che di tra i gravi e tetri uomini appena
può far la cosa che non far gli è pena
grande: giocare.

(And now farewell,
but not forever, beloved childhood. I owe
to you the flower of my life; to have
remained a child, someone who can
carry human burdens and, moreover, has
the pain of being able to do the only
thing allowed without great sorrow among
deadly serious men: to play.)

Saba exhibits consistent antihistoricism, a refusal to deal with political or ideological issues in a time that saw, as few others, political and ideological upheavals. He also shunned all established traditions including realism and avant-gardism, between the end of the nineteenth century and the first decades of the twentieth century. Perhaps because he considered his time one of crisis and transition, and believed that Freud was its prophet, Saba decided that the only true, original contribution could come from attentively listening to and spontaneously rendering his inner voice.

Therefore, from this point of view, one could argue that Saba does belong to the general ambience of decadentism, in terms of the emphasis on the inner conscience of the poet; however, he did not agree with the anarchist tendencies of the movement. Saba also had a profound dislike for any bombastic, empty rhetoric that confused patriotism with exterior manifestations of nationalism and, of course, xenophobia. It was the defeat in World War II that spurred Saba to abandon his usual silence and seeming lack of interest in political matters. This national tragedy added to his own personal drama of racial persecutions. He found the strength to write an unusually forceful poem—"Avevo," written in 1944 and included in the 1945 edition of *Il canzoniere*:

> Avevo una famiglia, una compagna;
> la buona, la meravigliosa Lina
> . . . .
> Avevo una bambina. Oggi una donna.
> . . . .
> Avevo una città bella tra i monti
> . . . .
> Avevo un cimitero ove mia madre
> riposa, e i vecchi di mia madre.
> . . . .
> Tutto mi portò via il fascista abbietto
> —anche la tomba—ed il tedesco lurco.

> (I had a family, a companion,
> the good, marvelous Lina[.]
> . . . .
> I had a little girl, now a woman.
> . . . .
> I had a beautiful city among the mountains[.]
> . . . .
> I had a cemetery where my mother
> is resting, and her parents.
> . . . .
> The hateful Fascist and the revolting German
> took everything away from me, even the tomb.)

With this kind of poetry Saba shifted to a newly found "neorealistic" style, but it never left a deep impression on readers or critics. So his last books return to an exploration of the subconscious.

In *Parole* (Words, 1934) Saba evokes the myth of Ulysses—a recurrent theme charged with symbolism in the works of other poets, such as Pascoli and Salvatore Quasimodo—in order to express the intimate dimension of his own search and solitude. The myth reappears again with autobiographical connotations in *Mediterranee* (1946):

> Nella mia giovanezza ho navigato
> lungo le coste dalmate. Isolotti
> a fior d'onda emergevano, ove raro
> un uccello sostava intento a prede,
> coperti d'alghe, scivolosi, al sole
> belli come smeraldi. Quando l'alta
> marea e la notte li annullava, vele
> sottovento sbandavano più al largo,
> per fuggirne l'insidia. Oggi il mio regno
> è quella terra di nessuno. Il porto
> accende ad altri i suoi lumi; me al largo
> sospinge ancora il non domato spirito,
> e della vita il doloroso amore.

> (In my youth I have explored
> the Dalmatian coasts.
> Covered with algae, slippery, beautiful
> like emeralds in the sun, islands
> emerged over the crest of the waves and rarely
> you'd see a bird there foraging. When the high tide
> and the night covered them, the sails
> avoided them, turning towards the sea,
> in order to escape their danger. Today my kingdom
> is that land of nobody. The harbor
> lights up for others its lights; my indomitable spirit
> and the painful love of life
> still push me away on the high seas.)

In the same collection one finds "Tre poesie a Telemaco" (Three Poems to Telemachus), charged with psychoanalytical connotations pointing to Saba himself, the perennial fatherless son in search of his ideal father, like Telemachus in the *Odyssey*, searching for his father, Ulysses.

In his conclusion to *Storia e cronistoria del Canzoniere*, Saba states:

> Il *Canzoniere* è la storia (non avremmo nulla in contrario a dire il "romanzo," e ad aggiungere, se si vuole, "psicologico") di una vita, povera (relativamente) di avvenimenti esterni; ricca, a volte, fino allo spasimo, di moti e di risonanze interne, e delle persone che il poeta amò nel corso di quella lunga vita, e delle quali fece le sue "figure."

> (The *Canzoniere* is the story [I would not object to the name of "novel," and to add, if you like, "psychological"] of a life, poor [relatively] of external events; rich, sometimes, heartbreaking even, of emotions, and of people loved by the poet during his long life, the people who are his "characters.")

Saba's mixed origin and difficult yet rewarding childhood impressed a seal on his life and his poetry; the lyrical character of his verses and the narrative elements in them; the attachment to his

Umberto Saba

beloved Trieste and his love for Italy; his common sense and his blind faith in psychoanalysis as the key to a "new world"; his feeling of being provincial, relegated away from the cultural mainstream of Italy; the intimate tone of his *Canzoniere*; and his ability to deal with the most important cultural issues of the day in several of his prose writings—racial persecutions, fascism, communism, psychoanalysis, the two world wars, and the literary avant-garde—in a fashion that includes a surprising openness and plurality of suggestions. All these elements make Saba an unusual voice in the literary landscape of the Italian *Novecento*. His influence and success were certainly minimized by the success of his "antagonists": hermeticism in poetry and Crocianism in literary and art criticism. Nevertheless he was a forerunner of postwar dissatisfaction with both schools, and, therefore, he could legitimately consider himself a kind of visionary and enjoy a period of reasonable popularity, spearheaded by his longtime friend Debenedetti. Above all, Saba's life and poetry stand out in the varied panorama of contemporary Italian poetry as examples of artistic courage and dedication, and his prose is a sobering reminder of a world in crisis.

Letters:

Lettere a un'amica (Turin: Einaudi, 1966);

Saba, Svevo, Comisso (Lettere inedite), edited by Mario Sutor (Padua, Italy: Gruppo di Lettere Moderne, 1968);

Lettere a un amico vescovo (Venice: Locusta, 1980);

La spada d'amore: Lettere scelte, 1902-1957, edited by Aldo Marcovecchio (Milan: Mondadori, 1983).

Biographies:

Folco Portinari, *Umberto Saba* (Milan: Mursia, 1967);

Giorgio Baroni, *Umberto Saba e dintorni* (Milan: Istituto Propaganda Libraria, 1984).

References:

Luciano Anceschi, "Umberto Saba," in his *Lirici Nuovi* (Milan: Mursia, 1964), pp. 105-132;

Atti del Convegno Internazionale "Il punto su Saba" (Università di Trieste, 25-27 marzo 1984) (Trieste: Lint, 1985);

Giuseppe Antonio Borgese, *La vita e il libro* (Turin: Bocca, 1913), pp. 148-152;

Aldo Borlenghi, "Su Umberto Saba," in his *Fra Ottocento e Novecento* (Pisa: Nistri-Lischi, 1955), pp. 197-209;

Giuseppe Antonio Camerino, "Nietzsche e la poetica rinnovata di Saba," *Scrittura e Società* (Rome: Herder, 1985), pp. 135-151;

Joseph Cary, "Umberto Saba," in his *Three Modern Italian Poets: Saba, Ungaretti, Montale* (New York: New York University Press, 1969), pp. 31-133;

Stelio Cro, "Un poeta del dolor: Umberto Saba," *Nación*, 15 September 1968, p. 3;

Giuseppe De Robertis, "Saba (Il Canzoniere)," in his *Scrittori italiani del '900* (Florence: Monnier, 1940), pp. 26-37;

Teresa Ferri, *Poetica e stile di Umberto Saba* (Urbino, Italy: Quattroventi, 1984);

Francesco Flora, " 'Ultime Cose' di Saba," in his *Saggi di poetica moderna* (Messina, Italy: D'Anna, 1949), pp. 199-202;

Alberto Frattini, "Umberto Saba," in his *Poeti e critici italiani dell'Otto e del Novecento* (Milan: Marzorati, 1966), pp. 97-118;

Alfredo Gargiulo, "Umberto Saba," in his *Letteratura Italiana del '900* (Florence: Monnier, 1940, pp. 155-163;

Giovanni Getto, "Saba," in his *Poeti, critici e cose varie del Novecento* (Florence: Sansoni, 1953), pp. 91-101;

Ann H. Hallock, "Umberto Saba's Reply to Chaos," *Canadian Journal of Italian Studies*, 9, no. 32 (1986): 10-20;

F. J. Jones, "The Development of Saba's Lyricism," in his *The Modern Italian Lyric* (Cardiff: University of Wales Press, 1986), pp. 259-297;

Mario Lavagetto, *Per conoscere Saba* (Milan: Mondadori, 1981);

Francesco Muzzioli, *La critica e Saba* (Bologna: Cappelli, 1976);

Muzzioli, "La critica e Saba: contributi e problemi dell'ultimo decennio (1975-1984)," *Metodi e ricerche*, new series 4 (January-June 1985): 25-34;

"Omaggio a Umberto Saba," *Galleria*, 10 (January-April 1960);

Pietro Pancrazi, "Classicità di Saba," in his *Scrittori d'oggi* (Bari, Italy: Laterza, 1946), pp. 163-171;

Giuseppe Petronio, "Umberto Saba," in his *Guida al Novecento letterario italiano* (Palermo: Palumbo, 1971), pp. 120-122;

Lorenzo Polato, "Rassegna di studi sabiani," *Lettere italiane*, 35 (October-December 1983): 530-549;

Gianni Pozzi, "Umberto Saba," in his *La poetica italiana del Novecento* (Turin: Einaudi, 1965), pp. 53-69;

Giuseppe Ravegnani, "La poesia di Umberto Saba," in his *Dal tramonto dell '800, all'alba del '900* (Turin: Bocca, 1930), pp. 363-371;

Franco Rella, *La cognizione del male: Saba e Montale* (Rome: Riuniti, 1985);

Natalino Sapegno "Umberto Saba," in his *Compendio di storia della letteratura italiana*, 3 volumes (Florence: Nuova Italia, 1947), III: 464-465;

Rosita Tordi, ed., *Umberto Saba, Trieste e la cultura mitteleuropea. Atti del Convegno (Roma, 29-30 marzo 1984)* (Milan: Mondadori, 1986).

Camillo Sbarbaro
(12 January 1888 - 31 October 1967)

Rosetta Di Pace-Jordan
University of Oklahoma

BOOKS: *Rèsine* (Genoa: Caimo, 1911);

Pianissimo (Florence: La Voce, 1914; revised edition, Venice: Neri Pozza, 1954);

Trucioli (Florence: Vallecchi, 1920; enlarged edition, Milan: Mondadori, 1948);

Liquidazione (Turin: Ribet, 1928);

Rimanenze (Milan: All'Insegna del Pesce d'Oro, 1955);

Fuochi fatui (Milan: All'Insegna del Pesce d'Oro, 1956; enlarged, 1958);

Primizie, edited by Vanni Scheiwiller (Milan: All'Insegna del Pesce d'Oro, 1958);

Scampoli (Florence: Vallecchi, 1960);

Poesie (Milan: All'Insegna del Pesce d'Oro, 1961; revised and enlarged, 1971);

Autoritratto (involontario) di Elena De Bosis Vivante da sue lettere (Verona: Stamperia Valdonega, 1963);

Gocce, edited by Scheiwiller (Milan: All'Insegna della Baita van Gogh, 1963);

Il "Nostro" e nuove Gocce, edited by Scheiwiller (Milan: All'Insegna del Pesce d'Oro, 1964);

Contagocce (Milan: All'Insegna del Pesce d'Oro, 1965);

Bolle di sapone (Milan: All'Insegna del Pesce d'Oro, 1966);

Vedute di Genova 1921 (Milan: All'Insegna del Pesce d'Oro, 1966);

Quisquilie, edited by Scheiwiller (Milan: All'Insegna del Pesce d'Oro, 1967);

Licheni: Un campionario del mondo (Florence: Vallecchi, 1967);

Ricordo di Giorgio Labò (Milan: All'Insegna del Pesce d'Oro, 1969);

Poesie e prosa, edited by Scheiwiller (Milan: Mondadori, 1979);

L'opera in versi e in prosa (Milan: Garzanti, 1985).

Editions in English: *Camillo Sbarbaro: Poesie*, translated by Diana Wormuth (Stockholm: Italica, 1979);

The Poetry and Selected Prose of Camillo Sbarbaro, edited and translated by Vittorio Felaco (Potomac, Md.: Scripta Humanistica, 1985).

Camillo Sbarbaro

OTHER: Pierangelo Baratono, *Il beato Macario*, introduction by Sbarbaro (Rome: Formiggini, 1929);

Raffaello Franchi, *L'equilibrista*, includes a note about the author by Sbarbaro (Florence: Vallecchi, 1934).

TRANSLATIONS: Gustave Flaubert, *Salambò* (Turin: Einaudi, 1943);

Sophocles, *Antigone* (Milan: Bompiani, 1943);

Joris-Karl Huysmans, *Controcorrente* (Milan: Gentile, 1944);

Stendhal (Marie-Henri Beyle), *La certosa di Parma* (Turin: Einaudi, 1944);

Jules Supervielle, *La figlia del mare aperto* (Milan: Gentile, 1945);

Jules Barbey d'Aurevilly, *Le diaboliche* (Milan: Bompiani, 1945);

Guy de Maupassant, *Il porto ed altri racconti* (Milan: Bompiani, 1945);

Flaubert, *Tre racconti* (Milan: Bompiani, 1945);

Auguste Villiers de L'Isle-Adam, *Storie insolite e racconti crudeli* (Milan: Bompiani, 1945);

Euripides, *Il Ciclope* (Genoa: Genovese Lettere e Arti, 1945);

Honoré de Balzac, *La pelle di zigrino* (Turin: Einaudi, 1947);

Henri Poulaille, *Il pane quotidiano* (Milan: Mondadori, 1949);

Aeschylus, *Prometeo incatenato* (Milan: Bompiani, 1949);

Henry de Montherlant, *Quelle che prendiamo fra le braccia*, *Sipario*, 63 (July 1951);

Roger Martin du Gard, *I Thibault* (Milan: Mondadori, 1951);

Emile Zola, *Germinale* (Turin: Einaudi, 1951);

Euripides, *Alcesti*; *Il Ciclope* (Milan: Bompiani, 1952);

De Montherlant, *Malatesta* (Milan: Bompiani, 1952);

Julien Green, *Varuna* (Milan: Mondadori, 1953);

Fernand Commenlynck, *Teatro* (Milan: Bompiani, 1957);

Pythagoras, *I versi d'oro* (Milan: All'Insegna del Pesce d'Oro, 1958);

De Montherlant, *Il cardinale di Spagna - Port Royal* (Milan: Bompiani, 1961);

Flaubert, *Bouvard e Pécuchet* (Turin: Einaudi, 1964);

Huysmans, *A rovescio* (Milan: All'Insegna del Pesce d'Oro, 1968).

With the publication of *Pianissimo* in 1914, Camillo Sbarbaro's position in twentieth-century Italian poetry was assured. As Gianni Pozzi says (in his *La poesia italiana del Novecento*, 1967), Sbarbaro expressed "un interiorità poetica che era nell'aria" (the lyrical self of his time). And *Pianissimo* is still eloquent. It is also what sets him apart from his fellow Ligurian poets and what makes him Eugenio Montale's true contemporary. Giovanni Boine, a poet himself, was one of the few critics who saw the importance of this small book of poems when it first appeared. In his review of *Pianissimo* for the *Riviera Ligure* (October 1914) he prophetically called Sbarbaro's poet-ry "una di quelle poesie su cui i letterati non sanno ne possono dissertare a lungo, ma di cui si ricorderanno gli uomini nella vita per i millenni" (a kind of poetry about which "literati" know and can say little, but which ordinary men will remember for millennia).

When Sbarbaro, barely out of adolescence, began to publish, the Italian cultural and literary scene was divided into two camps: the passive *crepuscolari* (twilight) poets and the hyperactive futurists. Gabriele D'Annunzio, somewhere in the middle, still ruled as the arbiter of literary taste, but there were already signs, even in D'Annunzio's work, that a new poetic mood was in the making. Closer in spirit to the *crepuscolari*, as were in general all the Ligurian poets that gathered around the literary journal *Riviera Ligure*, Sbarbaro shared their introversion and their low-key style, if not their somewhat overlanguid posture.

In *Pianissimo* Sbarbaro carries his confession to a point the *crespuscolari* never did. He never blunts his emotions and is deliberate and self-accusatory in a way they never were. His lucid, ruthless self-analysis, his violent dislocation and displacement of self totally distances him from the position of the *crepuscolari*. Furthermore, the decadent tendencies in Sbarbaro's poetry have to be seen in relation to his naturalistic ones. His insistence on dispassionate and accurate observation, his description of inner and outer states of reality, and his respect for the factual over and above any abstract principle all adhere to the realistic tenets of naturalism. In spite of his rebellious heart, he bowed to what he considered to be life's inevitable deterministic forces, to what he saw as the mechanistic workings of necessity in human behavior. Unlike the naturalists and closer to the decadents he so admired, he placed the source of such determinism not in biological but in psychological factors.

Sbarbaro was a botanist with an international reputation. His collections of lichens were sold all over Europe. Both Harvard and the University of Chicago bought herbariums from him. But the poetic process by its very nature always succeeded in subverting his intentional aim of dispassionate objectivity. The originality of his poetry lies in that special blend of naturalistic and expressionistic elements; in his concept and treatment of the self freed from romantic self-idealization and crepuscular self-complacency; in his adherence to the immediate content of his consciousness; and in his ability to express it lyrically without idealistic or rhetorical mystification.

Given Sbarbaro's profound skepticism toward life and history, and his refusal to adhere to any form of dogma, system, or abstract idealism in general, and given his temperamental disinclination to generate any positive pattern of consciousness, he was the perfect candidate to portray the condition of the contemporary, marginal, alienated self and its psychological and aesthetic space in Italian poetry. He does this by carving a large empty space that turns the world into a desert and by establishing rigid boundary lines between the self and all reality external to it. In Sbarbaro's case this separation is marked by his conviction of the inability of human beings to communicate fully. This severe degree of detachment remains in all his writing. It constitutes one of the basic characteristics of his poetry, and it creates one of its major tensions. Even later, when he found a measure of comfort in contact with nature, his way of experiencing relatedness did not vary. As early as *Rèsine* (1911), the small book of poems he wrote in his teens and that his school friends had published for him in Genoa at their expense, the existential theme of alienation is present. Sbarbaro was to reject *Rèsine*, refusing its reissuing and always considering it his apprenticeship work. He did not even keep a copy. Its twenty-one poems comprised mostly sonnets, a closed form that he was to reject for the freer forms in *Pianissimo* and of all his subsequent poems. When *Rèsine* appeared, the poet had already begun his employment as a clerk at Siderurgica of Savona. A more troubled period of his life had begun, and he felt that with *Rèsine* he had left his youth behind him. The period of *Pianissimo* had started.

Born on 12 January 1888 in Santa Margherita Ligure, Camillo Sbarbaro had known tragedy early in life with the death of his mother from tuberculosis when he was only five years old. His father, Carlo Sbarbaro, an engineer and an architect, had joined the army under Giuseppe Garibaldi and had remained as a career officer until an accident deprived him of his hearing. Partially blind and in poor health, he spent the last years of his life in Savona, where his son was attending the Liceo Chiabrera and was beginning to write. Refusing to go on with his formal education, the young Sbarbaro began work in 1910 with the firm in Savona, transferring to Genoa the following year, when his company was absorbed into the Ilva conglomerate. At this same time another obscure clerk by the name of Franz

Kafka was undergoing the same experience in the gray fog of Prague, finding it as unrewarding as Sbarbaro did and obviously sharing the same dark vision of life, the same burden of isolation, guilt, and anxiety. It was during these years of employment that Sbarbaro completed *Pianissimo*.

These were also the years during which he was most involved with the leading journals of the day. But although he was an active contributor to the prestigious Florentine journal *La Voce*, he remained quite apart from its polemical atmosphere, fostered mostly by the two literary lion cubs Giuseppe Prezzolini and Giovanni Papini. Sbarbaro shied away from literary and artistic circles in general, preferring the company of his few lifelong friends, of which the poet Angelo Barile was one. It was through Barile's effort that both *Rèsine* and *Pianissimo* were published. Later, again through Barile's effort, Sbarbaro and Montale would meet. Sbarbaro always remained closer to the *Riviera Ligure*, the literary journal founded in 1895 by Angelo Silvio Novaro of the Sasso Oil family. In 1899 the direction of the journal passed from the D'Annunzian, flamboyant Angelo to his more withdrawn brother Mario, who had studied philosophy in Berlin. Prominent on the Italian literary scene and open to the major cultural and philosophical European currents, the *Riviera Ligure* attracted to this important provincial corner of Italy many leading talents. Sbarbaro's contribution consisted of prose pieces, but the two celebrated poems dedicated to his father (*Pianissimo* poems 7 and 17) first appeared in the *Riviera Ligure* in 1912 (the year of his father's death) and in 1913 respectively.

The period of *Pianissimo* was a stressful one for Sbarbaro. His form of employment had not been freely chosen but was needed to help support his sick father, his sister, and the old aunt who had raised the two siblings. While willing to accept this responsibility, Sbarbaro was not resigned to his fate and resented the choices that had been made for him, the restrictions that had been imposed on his life. His poems, his prose writings, and his correspondence leave no doubt that he could hardly tolerate some aspects of the life-style of his environment, nor subscribe to some of its values. At a time when the family as an institution was idealized, and devotion to it was considered a duty, he continually and secretly lashed out at some of the illusions that had clustered around this superassimilated social nucleus. He was constantly escaping, venturing into taverns and brothels in order to find relief and oblivion. Freedom for Sbarbaro was always outside the home.

Forced into apathy since childhood by tragedy and circumstances, yet weighed down by a sense of obligation, resentment, and remorse, Sbarbaro responded by refusing any kind of emotional or social commitment. But he felt the urge to unburden his conscience of the guilt he felt, especially toward his father, as can be seen in poem 17 of *Pianissimo* when the speaker says he wants to express to everyone his cowardice toward his father. In this poem the excessive amount of guilt and the urge to confess it point to the fact that his anger has an element of repression in it, something other than the acknowledged reason of the father's age and infirmity. The same form of repression that underlies his attitude toward his father underlies his anger toward women, an attitude that can be traced in all his writing. In gathering the material to write the poem that deals with his relationship to his father, he has to look into himself. In pausing to confront his own feelings, he immediately turns this piece of self-knowledge into self-accusation, typical on Sbarbaro's part. He uses guilt, this most subtle, most silent, most internalized of all human emotions, to torment himself. In Sbarbaro's world guilt energizes many psychological states, above all his need to suffer.

Pain and loneliness, in Sbarbaro's poetic world, have their roots in his profound skepticism concerning the capacity of human beings to communicate on an emotional level. His reiterated belief that humankind is locked in this condition, that nothing can change it, not even the experience of love, is what separates him the most from Montale. There are no visiting angels in Sbarbaro's world bringing encoded, mysterious messages from another realm. Sbarbaro had the painful awareness that one's consciousness is an island, that apart from the consciousness of one's own being all else is otherness. He perceives this reality as a gap, essentially the same as Charles-Pierre Baudelaire's "insurmountable abyss." This core view of life constituted Sbarbaro's torment and conditioned all his writing. Many of the descriptive passages in *Pianissimo* reflect this problematic essence of human unrelatedness. Most of them focus on his night walks through the city streets, a fitting setting, in its indifference and estrangement, for the alienated, marginal self. The literary topos of the city, a constant in Western literature since the Industrial Revolution, becomes Sbarbaro's dark labyrinth, the symbolic space for the restless modern consciousness, much as the medieval castle had been for the Gothic imagination.

The definite proof of Sbarbaro's isolation is found in his relationships with women, which are all defined in terms of rejection, separation, and absence. All his poems that deal with women are either about sexual encounters with prostitutes or of bereavement for an absent, idealized woman. In his inability to combine erotic and tender feelings, he treats women either as presences he negates or as absences he mourns for. All his life Sbarbaro resisted long-term commitments of any kind. He had a string of short-lived romances with women of whom he soon grew tired, but no lasting relationship. The sexual encounters that appear in his poetry are all with prostitutes. They are all brief, isolated episodes in which he seeks most of all to inflict and to suffer pain. As always, he holds on to his need to suffer more firmly than anything else in life. Pain is the only thing that Sbarbaro is unwilling or unable to let go of, as can be seen in poem 8 from *Pianissimo*:

> Poiché son rassegnato a viver, voglio
> che ogni ora del dì mi pesi sopra
> mi tocchi nella mia carne vitale.
> Voglio il Dolore che m'abbranchi forte
> e collochi nel centro della vita.
>
> (Since I am resigned to live, I want
> every hour of the day to weigh on me,
> to touch my living flesh.
> I want Pain to grab me tight
> and place me in the center of life.)

Sbarbaro induces and provokes the negative emotional charge of pain to feel rooted in life.

Sex has a limited escape value in Sbarbaro's poetry; aside from providing the obvious release of physiological tension, it fails to alleviate his frustration, the real cause of which clearly exists at a deeper level. The poet has either repressed this cause or is unwilling to reveal it. One can venture the hypothesis that the trauma suffered as a child at the death of his mother might have had a conditioning effect on his relationships with others, and with women in particular. Perhaps he unconsciously assumed guilt for her death, as any child might at such an early age. He might have also felt angry at being abandoned by her, and anxious because of the void that her absence had caused in his world. At a certain level this determinism of the past cannot be avoided. But it may be significant to notice that in Sbarbaro's poetry

> * Mi piove in mente, tutto il giorno
> m'accompagna il verso: Nos parva
> gracili modulamus avena. Un ver-
> so fatto per me su misura.
>
> "Il y a tel écrivain dont on dirait
> qu'il écrit à petits plis„ Sarei
> di questi?
>
> Scrittore? se il più della vita spre-
> mere da me una riga sarebbe
> stato spremer sugo da pomice?
>
> La volta che constatai: nel de-
> serto, io guardo con asciutti
> occhi me stesso, parevo comin-
> ciare e finivo. Senza voce m'ero
> fatto l'epitaffio.

Fair copy of four "Gocce," published the next year in Sbarbaro's Il "Nostro" e nuove Gocce *(from* Storia della letteratura: Italiana, *volume 6, edited by Luigi Ferrante, 1965)*

it is the father, the surviving parent, who is present; his mother never appears, per se, in his poems. While the behavior he displays toward the women in his poems may be a form of transference, the induced pain sustains his need to be cruel, to feel guilty, and to feel bereaved.

The condition of mourning prevails in the celebrated "Versi a Dina" (Poems to Dina)—collected in *Rimanenze* (Remnants, 1955)—Sbarbaro's elegy to a lover and his eulogy to the myth of happiness. The five poems in the series are written through the distancing dimension of memory, an unusual stance in Sbarbaro's work, as is the direct form of address *tu*, a form famous in Montale. Dina is not just the memory of a past love, since she is experienced as an absence, a loss that is mourned in the present.

The woman in this series of poems is not only the lost love; she is, in the biographical sense, the woman that cannot be found.

Sbarbaro's main biographers have not found or provided her identity. So Dina remains both a memory and a mystery. Although Sbarbaro's reticence in revealing her identity is puzzling in a poet as overtly autobiographical as he was, such silence does not detract from the poems' relevance to his overall aesthetic world. The important fact remains that Dina is represented as what is lost forever, which in Sbarbaro's psychological makeup is identical to what is most longed for. Her physical presence in the poems is hardly felt. She fades in and out of their aesthetic space—the fleeting image of a woman seen at a distance as she crosses the street to meet her lover; at closer range as she reaches to hold his wrist; in the indeterminate space of the lovers embracing in the dark:

> Estrema delusione degli amanti!
> invano mescolarono le vite
> s'anche il bene superstite, i ricordi,
> son mani che non giungono a toccarsi.

> (Extreme lovers' delusion!
> in vain they mixed their lives
> if even the best that is left, the memories,
> are hands that fail to join and touch.)

"Versi a Dina" first appeared in the January-February 1931 issue of *Circoli*, the journal directed by Adriano Grande. *Rimanenze* includes "Versi a Dina" and all the poems written by Sbarbaro during the 1920s and the 1930s. After this time he no longer published poetry. For the rest of his life he wrote lyrical prose pieces that came to be known as *trucioli* (wood shavings). They belong to the literary form that in Italy is called the *frammento* (fragment). In Sbarbaro's *frammenti*, autobiography, observation, and description prevail, with the narrative element remaining minimal.

After the publication of *Pianissimo* Sbarbaro joined the Red Cross and later served as an infantryman and as an officer in the Italian army during World War I. Upon his return to civilian life he suffered the first in a series of severe depressions. He managed, however, to complete the first edition of *Trucioli* (1920), which Montale favorably reviewed in Genoa's *L'Azione* on 16 November 1920. *Liquidazione* followed in 1928, containing Sbarbaro's prose written between 1920 and 1928. In 1938 another volume of *trucioli* was denied publication by the Fascist censors. Sbarbaro's refusal to carry a party card also cost him a teaching position at the Jesuit Istituto

Arecco in Genoa, where Carlo Bo had been one of his students. Sbarbaro spent most of the period of the Fascist regime and of World War II in relative seclusion, doing translations, tutoring, and dedicating himself to scientific study. In 1951 he retired to Sportorno, where he spent the rest of his life.

Central to his postwar writing is the volume *Fuochi fatui* (Will o' the Wisp, 1956), which was followed by a series of prose collections, all essentially in the style of the *trucioli*. In *Fuochi fatui* his tragic vision remains the same, but the book shows how his rejection of the world of men—the world of history—never meant a rejection of nature, especially of nature in the botanical sense. While nature does not provide him with a cosmic or mystical experience, it does give him moments of pristine perception, as in his well-known poem "Voze":

> Se l'occhio che restò duro per l'uomo
> s'inteneriva ai volti della terra,
> nella casa di allora che inchiodato
> reca sull'uscio il ferro di cavallo
> portafortuna,
> serbagli sopra i tetti la finestra
> che beve al lapislazzulo laggiù
> del mare, si disseta
> alla polla perenne dell'ulivo,
> Voze, soave nome che si scioglie
> in bocca . . .

> (If the eye that remained hard for man
> used to become tender when in front of the faces
>   of the earth
> in that house that has nailed on
> its threshold the horseshoe as a
> lucky charm,
> save him the rooftop window
> that drinks from the lapis lazuli
> of the sea down there, quenching
> its thirst at the perennial spring of the olive tree.
> Voze, sweet name that melts
> in the mouth . . .).

Done in impressionistic strokes, the scene welcomes the sensations of sunlight and color that fill all its spaces. Through the act of seeing, the poet passes with extreme ease from outer to inner states, creating the impression that his fusion fantasy has found an outlet in Voze, the other. The sensual connection of the images of taste and touch creates this feeling. Here sight is anything but cold. Contact with nature brings for Sbarbaro a relaxation of tension, reinforces his sensual connection to life, and satisfies his instinctive curiosity, which was immense.

The 1954 Neri Pozza edition of *Pianissimo* marked a milestone in Sbarbaro's career as a poet. In the postwar political and literary climate, the crucial, existential problem of alienation, with which Sbarbaro had dealt early on, as a young man, became a major concern. Sbarbaro's stark message, as stark as his style, was heard all over again in a voice that had not become at all dated. This still holds true in reading *Pianissimo* today. Alluding to the semipeace he had found in nature, Sbarbaro wrote in his introduction to the Neri Pozza edition:

> *Pianissimo* è la mia voce di quando ero vivo; da allora—e cioè da quando imparai a appagarmi d'un colore del cielo—una voce che mi scotta ogni volta che la riodo.
>
> (*Pianissimo* is my voice from when I was alive; since then—that is to say since I learned to be satisfied with a color of the sky—it is a voice that, each time I hear it again, burns me.)

Letters:

Cartoline in franchigia (Florence: Vallechi, 1966);

"Le ultime lettere di Camillo Sbarbaro," *L'Osservatore politico letterario* (October 1971);

"Lettere a Diogene," *Resine* (June 1972);

"Lettere inedite di Carlo Emilio Gadda e di Camillo Sbarbaro ad Aldo Camerino," *Strumenti critici*, 27 (1975);

La trama delle lucciole, edited by Domenico Astengo and Franco Contorbia (Genoa: Marco dei Giustiniani, 1979).

Interview:

Ferdinando Camon, *Il mestiere di poeta* (Milan: Garzanti, 1965), pp. 31-38.

Biographies:

Giacinto Spagnoletti, *Sbarbaro* (Padua, Italy: Cedam, 1943);

Giorgio Barberi Squarotti, *Camillo Sbarbaro* (Milan: Mursia, 1971).

References:

Atti del Congresso Nazionale di Studi su Camillo Sbarbaro, edited by Adriano Guerrini (Genoa: Resine, 1974);

Giorgio Barberi Squarotti, "Camillo Sbarbaro," in his *Letteratura italiana: I contemporanei*, volume 1 (Milan: Marzorati, 1975), pp. 843-867;

Piero Bigongiari, "Sbarbaro alle origini del Novecento," in his *Poesia italiana del Novecento* (Florence: Vallecchi, 1965), pp. 117-132;

Emilio Cecchi, "Libri di poesia: Enrico Pea e Camillo Sbarbaro," *Letteratura italiana del Novecento*, volume 2, edited by Pietro Citati (Milan: Mondadori, 1972), pp. 605-610;

Corrado Federici, "Il grottesco nei *Trucioli* di Sbarbaro," *Italica*, 58 (Winter 1981): 301-306;

Federici, "Indifference in Camillo Sbarbaro's *Pianissimo*," *Canadian Journal of Italian Studies*, 2 (Fall-Winter 1978-1979): 92-104;

Vittorio Felaco, Introduction to *The Poetry and Selected Prose of Camillo Sbarbaro*, edited by Felaco (Potomac, Md.: Scripta Humanistica, 1985);

Franco Fortini, "Premesse alla poesia del nostro secolo: linee di sviluppo e problemi di periodizzamento," in his *I poeti del Novecento* (Rome & Bari: Laterza, 1977), pp. 3-7;

Adriano Guerrini, *Il significato di Sbarbaro* (Genoa: Sabatelli, 1968);

Gina Lagorio, *Sbarbaro: Un modo spoglio d'esistere* (Milan: Garzanti, 1981);

Pier Vincenzo Mengaldo, "Camillo Sbarbaro," in his *Poeti italiani del Novecento* (Milan: Mondadori, 1981), pp. 317-328;

Luciano Nanni, *L'idea di oggettivazione artistica in Camillo Sbarbaro* (Naples: Guida, 1973);

Gianni Pozzi, "Camillo Sbarbaro," in his *La poesia italiana del Novecento* (Turin: Einaudi, 1967), pp. 84-95;

Silvio Ramat, "I passi del vagabondo e l'immobilità del libro (*Pianissimo*)," in his *Storia della poesia italiana del Novecento* (Milan: Mursia, 1976), pp. 73-104;

Adriano Seroni, "Immagini di Sbarbaro," in his *Ragioni critiche* (Florence: Vallecchi, 1944), pp. 85-94;

Giacinto Spagnoletti, "Camillo Sbarbaro," in his *Poeti del Novecento* (Milan: Mondadori, 1965), pp. 114-119.

Leonardo Sinisgalli

(9 March 1908 - 30 January 1981)

Jack Shreve
Allegany Community College

BOOKS: *18 poesie*, edited by Giovanni Scheiwiller (Milan: Vera, 1936);

Poesie, edited by Carlo Cardazzo (Venice: Cavallino, 1938);

Campi Elisi, edited by Scheiwiller (Milan: Vera, 1939); enlarged and edited by Artidoro Benedetti (Rome: Cometa, 1941);

Vidi le Muse (Milan: Mondadori, 1943);

Furor mathematicus, edited by Vero Roberti, Guglielmo Santangelo, and Orfeo Tamburi (Rome: Urbinati, 1944; enlarged edition, Milan: Mondadori, 1950);

Horror vacui (Rome: OET, 1945);

Fiori pari, fiori dispari (Milan: Mondadori, 1945);

L'indovino (Rome: Astrolabio, 1946);

I nuovi Campi Elisi (Milan: Mondadori, 1947);

Belliboschi (Milan: Mondadori, 1948);

Quadernetto alla polvere (Milan: Meridiana, 1948);

La vigna vecchia (Milan: Meridiana, 1952; enlarged edition, Milan: Mondadori, 1956);

Cinque poesie (Verona: Stella Alpina, 1955);

Banchetti (Milan: All'Insegna del Pesce d'Oro, 1956);

Tu sarai poeta (Verona: Riva, 1957);

La musa decrepita (Rome: Marsia, 1959);

L'immobilità dello scriba (Rome: Castaldi, 1960);

Cineraccio (Venice: Neri Pozza, 1961);

L'età della luna (Milan: Mondadori, 1962);

Prose di memoria e d'invenzione (Bari, Italy: Leonardo da Vinci, 1964);

Poesie de ieri (Milan: Mondadori, 1966);

I martedì colorati (Genoa: Immordino, 1967);

Archimede, i tuoi lumi, i tuoi lemmi! (Alpignano, Italy: Tallone, 1968); republished as *Càlcoli e fandonie* (Milan: Mondadori, 1970);

La rosa di Gerico, edited by Filiberto Mazzoleni (Milan: Mondadori, 1969);

Il passero e il lebbroso (Milan: Mondadori, 1970);

Il tempietto (Rome: Castaldi, 1971);

L'ellisse: Poesie 1932-1972, edited by Giovanni Pontiggia (Milan: Mondadori, 1974);

Mosche in bottiglia (Milan: Mondadori, 1975);

Un disegno di Scipione e altri racconti (Milan: Mondadori, 1975);

Leonardo Sinisgalli

Dimenticatoio, 1975-1978 (Milan: Mondadori, 1978);

Più vicino ai morti, edited by Mario Gorini (Padua, Italy: Panda, 1980);

Imitazioni dall'antologia palatina (Rome: Cometa, 1980);

Ventiquattro prose d'arte (Rome: Cometa, 1983);

Promenades architecturales (Bergamo, Italy: Lubrina, 1987).

Editions in English: *The Ellipse: Selected Poems of Leonardo Sinisgalli*, translated by W. S. Di Piero (Princeton, N.J.: Princeton University Press, 1982);

Where the Age of the Rose Burned Proudly: Poems by Leonardo Sinisgalli [chapbook], translated by

Rina Ferrarelli (Bowling Green, Ohio: Bowling Green University Press, 1988).

Early poetry by Leonardo Sinisgalli seems typical of the hermetic school of Italian poetry, and in view of his characteristic commitment to free verse, his emphasis on metaphor, and his tendency to objectify and to avoid adjectives, he has been seen as one of the more extreme of that group. The delicate interplay of his images and his delight in epigrammatic situations bring to mind Greek and Oriental poetry; and he shares important similarities with his more immediate antecedents as well—demonstrating the sensitivity of Giovanni Pascoli and the *crepuscolari* (twilight poets) on one hand, and the elliptical and evocative tendencies of Stéphane Mallarmé and Paul Valéry on the other. Sinisgalli's canny ability to forage in his rural southern past for the seeds of poetry; his technical training, which allowed him to use mathematics as a source of fantasy; and his remarkable capacity to adapt to changing literary tastes all contributed to his style, both within and beyond the hermetic tradition.

The third of seven children and the elder of two sons, Sinisgalli was born on 9 March 1908 in Montemurro, in the province of Potenza, near enough to the old Roman city of Venosa for Giuseppe Ungaretti to have dubbed him a modern Horace. To escape the poverty of Basilicata, several of Sinisgalli's uncles emigrated. His father, Vito Sinisgalli, left twice, once before the turn of the century for New York and again in 1911 for Barranquilla, Colombia. As an immigrant, he was a tailor, but upon his return to Italy in 1923 he became a farmer and vinedresser.

The poet's deep attachment to his mother, Carmela Lacorazza Sinisgalli, whom he strongly resembled, is everywhere evident in his poetry. In "Caldo com'ero nel tuo alvo" (How Warm I Was in Your Womb; in *18 Poesie*, 1936), he speaks of himself as the fruit of her womb and states his desire to return to her every night and at the hour of death, with the soles of his feet pressed against her heart. The date of her death, 16 September 1943, he enshrined as the title of a narrative poem in *I nuovi Campi Elisi* (The New Elysian Fields, 1947). The poem minutely details the event. Sinisgalli saw his own childhood as an Elysian experience, and although he did not write so much about the sentimental joys of that childhood, he liked to write about watching children in the ecstasy of play, always careful to describe their playthings, such as a rag ball, or a ram bone, or red coins for pitching.

After attending local elementary schools, he transferred to secondary schools in Caserta, Benevento, and finally Naples, where he graduated with an outstanding record in 1926. Attracted by the sciences, he claimed that between the age of fifteen and twenty the contemplation of mathematics provided him with great joy. While studying mathematics in Rome, he was invited by Enrico Fermi to join his Physics Research Institute in 1928, but Sinisgalli refused, preferring instead to seek the company of poets and painters. Nonetheless he continued his allegiance to his technical studies, and in the early 1930s he obtained a degree in electrical and industrial engineering.

To nourish his growing interest in poetry, Sinisgalli read not only the newest Italian poets, such as Umberto Saba, Giuseppe Ungaretti, Vincenzo Cardarelli, Camillo Sbarbaro, Dino Campana, and Clemente Rèbora, but also the older *crepuscolari*, such as Sergio Corazzini, Guido Gozzano, Corrado Govoni, and Marino Moretti. As an antidote to the crepuscular melancholy, it was Jules Laforgue who infused in Sinisgalli a love of playfulness. Of all the French poets, however, it was Charles-Pierre Baudelaire who affected him most deeply, and whenever he was in Paris, he searched out places associated with this beloved poet.

In addition to his admiration for poets, Sinisgalli had great respect for the technical prose of Galileo, Francesco Algarotti, Francesco Redi, and Lorenzo Magalotti, and he developed a taste for the naturalism of Bernardino Telesio and Tommaso Campanella. Later he wrote poems about such great thinkers as René Descartes, Blaise Pascal, Arthur Schopenhauer, and Johann Wolfgang von Goethe.

While Sinisgalli was completing his degree, he made friends with Arnaldo Beccaria, Mario Mafai, Libero De Libero, and Ungaretti. Sinisgalli spent his military training at the Caserma San Romano in Lucca from 1930 to 1932 as an officer of artillery. By 1933 he was living in Milan, where eventually he worked for the Olivetti Company from 1936 to 1940 as an advertising technician.

In 1936 he published a collection of his finest poems, *18 Poesie*. Ungaretti in 1934 had already written praise of the young poet, and this was followed by a long, favorable review by Giuseppe De Robertis in *Letteratura* (1937). This in turn was followed by Emilio Cecchi's solemn and authoritative linking of Sinisgalli's name with Ungaretti and Montale (in *Corriere della Sera*, 19 October 1938).

With the onset of World War II Sinisgalli returned to service and was sent to Sardinia. Discharged in 1942, he returned to Rome, and in the Monte Parioli quarter he met Giorgia De Cousandier, the blond baroness, author, poet, and translator who was to become his wife. The details of Giorgia's background were incorporated into his story "Il chierichetto" (The Little Cleric), in *Belliboschi* (Lovely Wood, 1948). In 1947 *I nuovi Campi Elisi* was dedicated to Giorgia and her youngest son, Filippo, whom Sinisgalli came to regard as his own son. The poem "Crepuscolo di febbraio a Monte P." (February Twilight in Monte P.; in *I nuovi Campi Elisi*) is about their courtship: they lament the years lost before they knew each other, she notices his slanting eyes and tells him of her past unhappy loves, and they take the symbol of a spider spinning a thread in the twilight as an omen of good fortune. Because Giorgia was only separated and not yet divorced from her husband, she and Sinisgalli were not able to marry until 1969.

Monte Parioli remained for Sinisgalli one of the most beautiful places on earth, having as an additional advantage its proximity to the Valle Giulia and Rome's famous museum of pre-Roman and Etruscan antiquities, the Villa Giulia. Sinisgalli was fascinated by Etruscan vestiges and made frequent allusions to them in his poems. The title "Il cacciatore indifferente" (The Indifferent Hunter), a subdivision of *Vidi le Muse* (I Saw the Muses, 1943), is from a painted figure glimpsed on one of the walls of an Etruscan hypogeum.

Sinisgalli remained in Rome until 1947, working for RAI (Italian Public Radio) and writing the epigrammatic and theoretical prose of *Horror vacui* (Empty Horror, 1945). He was briefly involved in making animated film shorts, two of which—*Lezione di geometria* (Geometry Lesson) and *Un millesimo di millimetro* (One Thousandth of a Millimeter)—won prizes at the Venice Film Festival in 1948 and 1950, respectively. In 1948 he returned to Milan to work as a publicity consultant for Pirelli, a transportation products company. The enlarged edition of *Furor mathematicus* (1950) is a compilation of all his polemical writings on mathematics, technology, history, science, art, and architecture. It includes the contents of *Horror vacui*. In 1952 Sinisgalli moved back to Rome to found *Civiltà delle Macchine*, a sumptuous re-

view of the mechanical arts and crafts, illustrated by paintings to express the culture of the machine age. Under his direction until 1959, it became perhaps the most influential journal of design arts in the world. In 1954 Sinisgalli made an ocean crossing to New York to make the acquaintance of various cousins and to see his father's brother, who made artificial flowers and had been away from Italy for sixty years.

Five years later, at the invitation of Enrico Mattei, Sinisgalli became director of advertising for ENI (Ente Nazionale Idrocarburi), the national energy council, and in 1961 he won the esteemed Etna-Taormina prize (which he shared with Tristan Tzara) for his poetry book *Cineraccio*, published that year.

In the early 1960s he also worked as a consultant for Alitalia and founded the magazine *La Botte e il Violino*. He retired in the early 1970s but continued to write, paint, and draw, exhibiting his graphics and watercolors at several galleries.

By the time *Dimenticatoio, 1975-1978* (Oblivion, 1975-1978), was published in 1978, Sinisgalli wrote that poor circulation had robbed him of the use of his arms and legs. He had suffered a heart attack in 1967, and although he stopped smoking, Sinisgalli was unable to slow his extremely active pace. In addition, his wife, Giorgia, who had undergone a laryngectomy in 1970, died in 1978. He survived for another two years, succumbing to heart failure on 30 January 1981.

There are two noteworthy primary components of Sinisgalli's poetry. One is his "southernness"—his rampant imagination and subtle sensuality. From this stems his appreciation for the mythic quality of his ancient, impoverished homeland of Basilicata (or Lucania, as he consistently calls it). The second is his respect for intellectual rigor and the clean unequivocal purity of geometric lines, as well as his openness to mechanical innovations. These two attitudes of lush imagination and scientific precision, polarized as they are, have been seen by some critics as complementary. Indeed Sinisgalli himself observed that whenever he wanted to check an overpowering emotion, all he needed to do was to concentrate on an abstruse geometric axiom.

Despite the personal and often nostalgic quality of much of his poetry, Sinisgalli has a knack for objectifying sentimental emotions. He distances himself admirably from emotional stickiness and carefully monitors the expression of his grief.

On the other hand, his commitment to the bare *disegno delle cose* (outline of things) yields a kind of geometric poetry that some readers find cold and unappealing. Aridity is the accusation most often leveled against him by hostile critics. Giorgio Bàrberi-Squarotti calls his poetic catalogue of bones, skulls, and tools a museum of charred and useless things that Sinisgalli only sporadically manages to endow with the wonder of life.

Yet such ideas as the poet's inability to reach others with his message, the cruel delusion that seizes the poet that he alone is capable of gathering truths indecipherable to others, and the loneliness implicit in the life of any poet had long been accepted by Sinisgalli. He wrote in *Quadernetto alla polvere* (Notebook for the Dust, 1948), "Le donne, anche le più affettuose, si disamorano di lui che ha consumato tutta la sua energia per scrivere qualche buon verso. Gli amici lo lasciano ormai solo a passare le Pasque in trattoria, rassegnati a non sentir mai sulle sue labbra una parola di lode o di biasimo" (Women, even the most devoted, lose interest in a man who spends all his energy writing a few good lines. His friends, tired of hearing him praise or criticize, leave him to spend his Easters alone in a restaurant). Sinisgalli's lot in life was mostly to enjoy being alone.

Sinisgalli felt a strong desire to seek himself in all places. He returns to his native land in every one of his books of poetry, as if to the center of his existence. Throughout his work the names of streets, piazzas, rivers, and cities reflect his reverence for terrestrial space. Since every place is also a point in time, Sinisgalli sometimes links time and place in his titles.

Neatness and concision are a trademark of Sinisgalli's verse. Alluding to the utter simplicity of Albert Einstein's Theory of Relativity, as well as the chemical formulae for such essentials as water and salt, Sinisgalli dared to deduce that God himself is laconic. Truth should not be hidden in unnecessary wordiness, nor should one be obstreperous about one's search for it. Sinisgalli observed that truth flees the sweeping broom, and thus, in order to observe it, one must remain quite still.

The impressions and sensations in his poetry are taken directly from reality and are scientifically precise. His style is always spare, deliberately devoid of eloquence, and often unusually noun-heavy. The metaphor, which Sinisgalli felt was gradually and inevitably losing its cutting

Drawing of Sinisgalli by Domenico Cantatore (from Sinisgalli's Quadernetto alla polvere, *1948)*

edge, is nonetheless typical of both his poetry and prose. The poet writes in *Quadernetto alla polvere* that poetry itself, which cannot be decanted, fixed, or separated, escapes filters of any kind, like certain colloidal gold solutions. The poet is like a rabbit in a hutch, for every morning he finds—under his paws, before his eyes, near his nose—his syllables and signs. And many traditional poets are like hens because they love to show off their talent for producing perfect forms. Sinisgalli's own childhood, lost behind him, is like a shadow in the dust.

Like the Spanish surrealist poet Federico García Lorca, Sinisgalli was fascinated by the moon, savoring the incantatory repetition of the very word *luna* and indulging in surrealistic images. Sinisgalli maintained that the poet belongs to the same race as the humble creatures of the earth. Like Antonio Machado, he cherished a special sympathy for the lowly, obnoxious fly, which he characterized as being similar to poetry because it buzzes around roses and dung indiscriminately, and it sniffs the living and the dead alike. In his poem "La corte," he speaks of the "cortege" of flies that follows the poet wherever he goes, and in another, "Autunno" (Autumn), he affectionately gives flies names such as Fantina, Filomena, and Felicetta. In mock humility he even pretends that his flies (like poems) beat a hasty retreat whenever the poet bends over his notebooks, because they are sick of literature and repulsed by its very smell.

Like Giovanni Pascoli, Sinisgalli delights in the presence of birds. In "La strada del Carmine" (The Road to the Carmelite Chapel) he lists the names of seven birds for the sheer joy of enumeration. As a naturalist he was never careless about the precise designations of birds, flowers, trees, or insects. Also like Pascoli, Sinisgalli writes often of dogs, as in "Il cane di Lazzaro" (Lazarus's Dog; in *Vidi le Muse*), where the poet assumes the dog's voice: "Ti portavo all'aurora / Il primo saluto del giorno, / L'odore di timo sul muso" (I was always the first / to greet you at dawn, / muzzle smelling of thyme).

True to the hermetic tradition, the frozen moment of an impression caught in an epigram is highly characteristic of Sinisgalli's work. The epigrams are simple and unadorned, but not as pathos-laden as those of Sandro Penna, with whom Sinisgalli was on friendly terms. The two poets differed with respect to the need for formal rhyme in poetry (Sinisgalli wrote in free verse), but the two did seem to share a wistful, idealistic reverence for youth.

Sometimes Sinisgalli extracts an aphorism from his epigrammatic poems, and this is what critics refer to as the "gnomic quality" of his verse. Still the aphorisms are gentle, never didactic or reprobative, for Sinisgalli disapproved of didactic rhetoric (according to Sinisgalli poets should not be prophets or entertainers but rather sharers of experience).

Fandonia (Tall Tale) is one of Sinisgalli's favorite words, the plural of which is used in the title of his book of aphorisms *Càlcoli e fandonie* (Calculations and Tall Tales, 1970; originally published as *Archimede* in 1968), and is stated in a poem as the object of his recidivism—"Torno alle mie storture, / alle mie fandonie" (I go back to my crooked ways, my tall tales). As Sinisgalli wrote in the preface to *Dimenticatoio, 1975-1978*, life in its disorder is more like a dream than the perfection of a geometric construct. Faced with the confusion of daily existence, he found comfort in imagination and the poetry it produced.

Although he began his career as a poet in the footsteps of Ungaretti, with the setting of the hermetic sun after World War II, at a time when Sinisgalli was still in his mid thirties, he realized the need for change. Without losing the characteristics of his origins, he became more open to de-

tail, less committed to the effect of enigma, and more accessible generally to readers.

F. J. Jones selects "Pianto antico" (Old Grief), from *Cineraccio*, as typical of the unsentimentalized changeover from the prewar to the postwar Sinisgalli. Despite a lingering touch of hermetic mystery, the poem reveals a deeper and far more open commitment to life than is evident in his earlier work:

I vecchi hanno il pianto facile.
In pieno meriggio
in un nascondiglio della casa vuota
scoppiano in lacrime seduti.
Li coglie di sorpresa
una disperazione infinita.
Portano alle labbra uno spicchio
secco di pera, la polpa
di un fico cotto sulle tegole.
Anche un sorso d'acqua
può spegnere una crisi
e la visita di una lumachina.

(Grief comes easily to old people.
At midday
sitting in a corner of an empty house
they burst into tears.
Infinite despair
catches them by surprise.
They lift a withered slice of pear
to their lips, or the pulp of a fig
baked on the roof tiles.
Even a sip of water
or a visit by a snail
helps to ease a crisis.)
—Translation by Jones

The change is already apparent in *I nuovi Campi Elisi*, where Sinisgalli demonstrates a new freedom from the straitjacket of symbolic surrealism and allows himself to develop some longer poems, which are among his most anthologized. These include "Lucania," with its powerful geographic metaphors:

a chi torna dai santuari o dall'esilio, . . .
la Lucania apre le sue lande,
le sue valli dove i fiumi scorrono lenti
come fiumi di polvere.

(to whoever comes back from refuge or exile, . . .
Lucania opens its barren plains,
its valleys where rivers crawl
like rivers of dust.)

In "Elegia romana" the poet exults:

So quando fioriscono al Pincio
le mimose, quando gelano i carrubi,

conosco la forma delle tue rose,
delle tue nubi.

(I know when the mimosas on the Pincio
bloom, when the locusts freeze,
I know the shape of your roses
and of your clouds.)

In 1952 Sinisgalli incorporated the following confession in his poem "Pasqua 1952" (Easter 1952):

Tutto quello che io so non mi giova
a cancellare tutto quello che ho visto.

(All I know can never help me
to efface all I've seen.)

According to Giuliano Manacorda, it is precisely Sinisgalli's long-gestating conviction that reason and knowledge cannot alleviate human suffering and cannot displace or modify the experiences of childhood that allowed him to renew himself and permitted his poetry to survive the changing tastes of Italian readership during the postwar period. The incumbency of old age, his sense of inescapable death, and a vague religious nostalgia give his later poetry an authentic measure of apprehension that serves to neutralize the suspicion of erudition that had haunted his prewar poetry.

Sinisgalli wrote in *Quadernetto alla polvere* that poetic form is an anachronism and that the boundaries separating prose and poetry have been dissolved. In the modern age, Sinisgalli asserts, the structure of words and sounds is less regular, and the geometric perfection of formal literary models, which for centuries led poets to trust completely in the incorruptibility of standardized style, is no longer the object of idolatry. Unable to believe in the ephemeral value of academic formulae and traditional poetic language, the modern poet has had to seek truth "tra gli sterpi e i lugubri arredi delle camere mobiliate" (among thorn bushes and the dismal furnishings of rented rooms), articulating it in slang and other nonstandard modes of linguistic expression.

As poets of the postwar era tried to initiate a colloquium with the public, there was greater interest in the popular *cantari* (folk songs), with their lyrical immediacy and their ingenuous motifs. Since dialect literature had been anathema to the Fascists, this new emphasis on folkloric literature helped abjure the errors of the past. So Sinisgalli assembled fifteen indigenous poems from Lucania, including love poems, yarns, and lullabies, refurbished them into acceptable Italian, and published them as part of *Quadernetto alla polvere*. Later this selection of indigenous poetry was augmented, given the title "L'albero di rose" (The Tree of Roses) and included in the poetry collection *La vigna vecchia* (The Old Vine, 1952).

For all the loyalty Sinisgalli felt for his roots in sun-drenched and shadow-draped Lucania, he could hardly have disdained the dialect that nourished those roots. In *Horror vacui* he defined *dialect* as synonymous with inspiration, and citing Sappho as a dialect poet par excellence, he praised dialect poets as those most attentive to the Muses.

Leonardo Sinisgalli was one of the most genuinely cultured men of his generation. He gave up what could have been a brilliant career as a physicist in order to devote his intellectual powers to the metaphysical uncertainties of poetry and art. Although writing was not his sole, nor even primary, vocation, the impressive body of work he produced stands as a monument to his commitment to poetry. His career as a poet spanned a half century, he associated with some of the greatest artistic talents of the Italian *Novecento* (twentieth century) and was greatly praised by critics for his capacity to adapt to literary tastes as they evolved from hermetic standards to straightforward, neorealistic styles in the wake of Italy's tragic experience in World War II.

Interview:
Ferdinando Camon, *Il mestiere di poeta* (Milan: Garzanti, 1982), pp. 73-79.

Biography:
Giuseppe Appella, Ida Borra, and Vincenzo Sinisgalli, *Iconografia, biografia e bibliografia di Leonardo Sinisgalli* (Rome: Cometa, 1982).

References:
Giorgio Bàrberi-Squarotti, *Poesia e narrativa del secondo Novecento* (Milan: Mursia, 1961);
Giovanni Battista De Sanctis, *Cinque poeti (Gatto, Sinisgalli, Montale, Quasimodo, Ruffato)* (Padua, Italy: Rebellato, 1971), pp. 27-35;
W. S. Di Piero, Introduction to *The Ellipse: Selected Poems of Leonardo Sinisgalli*, translated by Di Piero (Princeton, N.J.: Princeton University Press, 1982), pp. 3-8;

F. J. Jones, *The Modern Italian Lyric* (Cardiff: University of Wales Press, 1986), pp. 85-91;

Giuliano Manacorda, *Storia della letteratura italiana contemporanea, 1940-1965* (Rome: Riuniti, 1967), pp. 145-149;

Gaetano Mariani, *L'Orologio del Pincio: Leonardo*

Sinisgalli tra certezze e illusioni (Rome: Bonacci, 1981);

Gianni Pozzi, *La poesia italiana del Novecento da Gozzano agli Ermetici* (Turin: Einaudi, 1965), pp. 233-242.

Ardengo Soffici
(7 April 1879 - 19 August 1964)

Joseph Perricone
Fordham University

BOOKS: *Ignoto toscano* (Florence: Seeber, 1909);

Il caso Medardo Rosso (Florence: Seeber, 1909);

Arthur Rimbaud (Florence: Italiana/Quaderni della Voce, 1911);

Lemmonio Boreo (Florence: Libreria della Voce, 1911);

Cubismo e oltre (Florence: Libreria della Voce, 1913);

Cubismo e futurismo (Florence: Libreria della Voce, 1914);

Arlecchino (Florence: Vallecchi, 1914);

Giornale di bordo (Florence: La Voce, 1915);

Bïf &zf+18: Simultaneità e chimismi lirici (Florence: Vallecchi, 1915);

Kobilek: Giornale di battaglia (Florence: Vallecchi, 1918);

La giostra dei sensi (Florence: Vallecchi, 1919);

Scoperte e massacri (Florence: Vallecchi, 1919; enlarged, 1929);

La ritirata del Friuli (Florence: Vallecchi, 1919);

Statue e fantocci (Florence: Vallecchi, 1919);

Primi principi di una estetica futurista (Florence: Vallecchi, 1920);

Rete Mediterranea (Florence: Vallecchi, 1920);

Giovanni Fattori (Rome: Valori Plastici, 1921);

Battaglia fra due vittorie (Florence: La Voce, 1923);

Armando Spadini (Rome: Valori Plastici, 1925);

Elegia dell'Ambra (Florence: Vallecchi, 1927);

Periplo dell'arte: Richiamo all'ordine (Florence: Vallecchi, 1928);

Carlo Carrà (Milan: Hoepli, 1928);

Medardo Rosso (Florence: Vallecchi, 1929);

Ardengo Soffici in Camaiore, Italy, 1956

Ricordi di vita artistica e letteraria (Florence: Vallecchi, 1931; enlarged, 1942);

Taccuino d'Arno Borghi (Florence: Vallecchi, 1933);

Ardengo Soffici: 30 tavole, edited by Giovanni Papini (Milan: Hoepli, 1933);

Ritratto delle cose di Francia (Rome: Selvaggio, 1934);

Ugo Bernasconi (Milan: Hoepli, 1934);

L'adunata (Florence: Vallecchi, 1936);

Thrène pour Guillaume Apollinaire (Milan: Esemplare, 1937);

Fior fiore, edited by Giuseppe De Robertis (Florence: Vallecchi, 1937; abridged, 1938);

Marsia e Apollo (Florence: Vallecchi, 1938);

Salti nel tempo (Florence: Vallecchi, 1939);

Selva, arte (Florence: Vallecchi, 1943);

Itinerario inglese (Florence: L'Arco, 1948);

Trenta artisti moderni italiani e stranieri (Florence: Vallecchi, 1950);

Autoritratto d'artista italiano nel quadro del suo tempo, 4 volumes: volume 1, *L'uva e la croce* (Florence: Vallecchi, 1951); volume 2, *Passi tra le rovine* (Florence: Vallecchi, 1952); volume 3, *Il salto vitale* (Florence: Vallecchi, 1954); volume 4, *Fine di un mondo* (Florence: Vallecchi, 1955);

D'ogni erba un fascio: Racconti e fantasie (Florence: Vallecchi, 1958);

Opere, 7 volumes (Florence: Vallecchi, 1959-1968);

Diari, 1939-1945, by Soffici and Giuseppe Prezzolini (Milan: Borghese, 1962);

L'opera incisa (Reggio Emilia, Italy: Prandi, 1972);

I diari della Grande Guerra (Florence: Vallecchi, 1986).

OTHER: Mario Richter, ed., *La formazione francese di Ardengo Soffici, 1900-1914*, includes poems by Soffici (Milan: Università Cattolica del Sacro Cuore/Vita e Pensiero, 1969).

Ardengo Soffici's significant contribution to Italian letters is attributed almost exclusively to the innovative works in which the author moved away from traditional literary forms and evolved a freer and more original style of his own. His role as innovator of poetic language was most pronounced between 1908 and 1915, the years during which writers, philosophers, and literary critics were fashioning modern conceptions of life and of artistic expressive modes in Italy. The epochal journals *Leonardo, La Voce*, and *Lacerba*, which succeeded one another during those years, testify to the engaging socioethical, philosophical, and artistic principles discussed during the first quarter of the twentieth century. Toward the end

of this period, in 1915, Soffici produced his most avant-garde works. After 1915, however, he reverted to a conservative ideology. Consequently, in some of his later works, he returned to the closed, traditional forms that characterized his earliest writings. The antinomies of the twentieth century are reflected in Soffici's existential and ethical preoccupations and in the mutable character of his works.

Soffici, novelist, literary and art critic, essayist, and biographer, was a prolific writer who, at the age of thirty-four, had attained such recognition among his peers that in an entry in his quasi-autobiographical diary *Giornale di bordo* (Logbook, 1915) he could legitimately boast of being "pittore fra i pittori, e poeta fra i poeti" (a painter among painters and a poet among poets). He spent the early part of his youth at the beginning of the new century in the wake of the impressionist and symbolist movements, but in the middle years of his life he witnessed the unfolding of diverse artistic and literary movements such as cubism, fauvism, expressionism, and futurism, which in different measures exercised their influence on his sensibilities. To the promptings of these artistic developments he responded with his own individual blend of vision and innovative stylistic techniques.

Circumstances as well as a genial, engaging personality favored his influential participation in the momentous changes taking place in Italy, particularly during the euphoric years around the turn of the century, which were full of fervor and promise, as the recently unified nation was again playing an important role. within the context of European culture.

Soffici's longevity permitted him to view from the vantage point of serene old age the events, both artistic and political, that shaped indelibly the character of the nation. His venturesome and affable qualities made him privy to the experiences of many artists, which he recorded in his writings in a vivacious style. To know Soffici well is to become acquainted with most of the artists and writers who, at the turn of the century, formed the cultural physiognomy of southern Europe. Soffici's memory returned with nostalgia and contentment to the enthusiastic years leading up to World War I in the last work of his life, the four-volume autobiography entitled *Autoritratto d'artista italiano nel quadro del suo tempo* (Self-Portrait of an Artist in the Frame of His Times, 1951-1955). Almost two entire volumes of *Autoritratto* are devoted to his Parisian experience and to the prewar years in Florence, whereas there is considerable reticence concerning the later years of his life. This reticence, as Giuseppe Prezzolini maintains in his introduction to Soffici's *Opere* (Works, 1959-1968), is attributable to Soffici's inability to deal with the latter part of his life "con la stessa franchezza distaccata" (with the same detached frankness). After reading his *Autoritratto* one is left with the impression that Soffici always regarded as especially gratifying the years that he spent in Paris in the company of Guillaume Apollinaire, Blaise Cendrars, Jean Moréas, and Pablo Picasso, and in Florence with Giovanni Papini, Prezzolini, Giuseppe Ungaretti, Gianpietro Campana, Umberto Boccioni, Carlo Carrà, and Filippo Tommaso Marinetti, to name only a few of the artists and writers with whom he associated between 1900 and 1915.

Ardengo Soffici was born on 7 April 1879 in the heart of the Tuscan countryside near Rignano sull'Arno in a rural area nicknamed Il Bombone, a term of onomatopoeic origin, associated with *bombo* (bumble bee) as well as with *bombone*, a Tuscan colloquial expression for a local alcoholic beverage. The term, which can also indicate a jovial, playful individual, befittingly designates the colorful rustic ambience in which Soffici spent the idyllic years of his childhood.

Soffici was engaged from the start in the elaboration of his own spiritual biography in accordance with a poetics grounded in the Platonic belief that self-knowledge is the worthiest of all human pursuits. This precept is embodied in several alter egos encountered in his works. The first of these, the protagonist of *Ignoto toscano* (An Unknown Tuscan, 1909), is so described as to underline that Platonic belief: "Aggiungeva che vivere non vuol dir altro che riconoscer se stessi, e paragonava la vita umana a un gomitolo che si svolge a poco a poco: ma il cui filo esiste già" (He would add that to live means no more than to know again one's own self. He would compare man's life to a skein that unrolls little by little, but the thread is already all there). In keeping with this idea, the persona in *Giornale di bordo* provocatively asserts that: "Il romanzo, la novella, il dramma sono forme d'arte ibride, transitorie destinate a sparire per lasciar libero il campo al puro lirismo—e all'autobiografia" (The novel, the short story, the drama are all hybrid art forms, momentary, destined to disappear in order to leave the field free for pure lyricism— and for autobiography). The lyrical and the auto-

biographical forms are indeed the most congenial for the extrication of his complex personality.

A true child of his times, Soffici derived the preferential status accorded to pure lyricism from symbolist poetics and particularly from Crocean aesthetic theories. As for the biographical and introspective tendencies, these found supportive correlation in the temperament of the writers who gravitated toward Prezzolini's journal *La Voce*, which was concerned with discussing socioethical, pedagogical, and didactic issues. For Soffici and other contributors to *La Voce*, truth meant a novel way of looking at reality and the use of a language that transcribed it in a direct, plain style unencumbered by rhetorical pomposity or superfluous adornments. The pursuit of this ethical, artistic ideal is evident in all of Soffici's literary works that display the existential doubts, the conflicts, and the contradictions inherent in his personality and in the times in which he lived.

His personality was characterized by a cluster of conflicts whose genesis Soffici attributed to the general circumstances of his birth and upbringing. In *L'uva e la croce* (The Grapes and the Cross, 1951), the first volume of his *Autoritratto*, he recollects his childhood and focuses on the contrastive natures of his parents. He describes his father as generous, rubicund, expansive, jovial, and of rural stock, and his mother as taciturn, religious, guileless, and of aristocratic background. The conflictual nature of the mature artist was polarized symbolically by two emblematic birthmarks. The impression that appeared on his forehead looked like a bunch of grapes, and as time passed, it disappeared almost completely. The other sign, a cross on his abdomen, however, proved indelible and remained on his body throughout his life. Soffici thus interprets the significance of these signs:

Non so se sia il caso di trarre qualche auspicio da questa singolarità. Volendo si potrebbe veder simboleggiata nel grappolo d'uva la gioia di vivere, nella croce la pena, il sacrificio; e nella loro unione sopra il mio corpo una doppia caratteristica e disposizione del mio spirito, con la loro duplice contrastante influenza sul corso della mia vita.

(I am not certain whether it is appropriate to draw any augurs from this singular event. If one wanted to, one could see symbolized in the bunch of grapes the joy of living, in the cross suffering and sacrifice; in their union on my body a double characteristic and disposition of my mind, and their conflicting influence on the course of my life.)

Soffici's life falls neatly into two periods, having World War I as their pivotal moment. The first of these was characterized by a carefree, iconoclastic, artistic experimentalism, and the second was dominated by conservatism, traditional literary forms, and Christian religiosity. The binomials that epitomize his character: innovation and tradition, the avant-garde and classicism, iconoclasm and conformity, and intuition and rationalism, among the most salient ones, are not dissimilar from those that characterized the temperament of the age in which he lived, particularly the Florentine ambience of the first fifteen years of the twentieth century. Soffici's own indefatigable dedication to recording the lives of the artists and cultural movements of his times points to the need to catalogue and discriminate among the many models that the era in which he lived presented to him.

When he was still in his teens, Soffici's family relocated for economic reasons from Il Bombone to Prato, a city near Florence. Soon after settling in Prato, Soffici's father died, and Soffici found work in the office of a Florentine lawyer as an apprentice. Fortunately the employer supported young Soffici's interests in art and helped him attend the Scuola Libera del Nudo (Independent School of the Nude) at the Accademia. This constituted Soffici's initiation into the cultural life of the city, because it was at the Scuola Libera that he met the most prominent representative of the "Macchiaioli" school—as the Italian impressionists were called—Giovanni Fattori, Soffici's mentor. Soffici also became acquainted with the works of the divisionist, art-nouveau painter Giovanni Segantini.

As is evident from an early (1890s) poem now found in Mario Richter's *La formazione francese di Ardengo Soffici, 1900-1914* (Ardengo Soffici: The French Formative Years, 1900-1914 [1969]), Soffici's literary apprenticeship was influenced by writers such as Giosuè Carducci, Giovanni Pascoli, Gabriele D'Annunzio, and other canonical authors of Italian letters. Although the poem is little more than a mere exercise in meter, it does reveal a subtle analogical ability and a mastery of melodic orchestration, which effects the melancholy atmosphere that permeates the work. Beyond these stylistic attributes,

the composition reveals an author alert to the concrete aspects of objects in the landscape, of the familiar "olivi" (olive trees) and "melo" (apple tree), for instance, which will be permanent emblems in Soffici's naturescapes:

Io voglio questa sera (è festa in cielo
Hanno le stelle fremiti più vivi)
Io vo' salir la costa degli olivi
Tutta ricordi ond'è lo spirto anelo.

Rosee quivi'l fior del melo,
Sboccian intorno le memorie; a rivi
Scendono le dolcezze onde rivivi
Giorni che il tempo già coprì di un velo.

(I want this evening [the sky is festive
The stars twinkle more lively]
I want to climb up the slope of the olive groves
Full of memories for which the heart is still yearning.

Here blossom the pink memories
All around the blooming apple tree; like rivulets
Sweet thoughts descend and you relive
The days that time already covered by a veil.)

Judging from this youthful accomplishment, it would seem that Soffici was not as naive as Prezzolini implied when he stated that the poet went to Paris "senza visiera di cultura" (without the visor of culture).

In 1900 Soffici moved to Paris, where he was to make his debut as a painter, all the while continuing to write poetry in Italian and contributing prose pieces in French to various journals. Although the French experience was fundamental in the evolution of Soffici's poetics during the first decade of the new century, his poetic character was essentially already formed when he decided to undertake the voyage to Paris. After the first difficult year, he made his way into the Parisian milieu, gaining the respect and often the admiration of everyone he met. The first official praise came in October 1901, when the art critic Tristan Klingsor, in his review *Les Salons*, wrote enthusiastically about Soffici's painting *Mathilda Gathering Flowers*. Thereafter Soffici was asked by Karl Boas to write articles about Italy and Italian art for his journal *La Plume*. Consequently the Tuscan artist became an assiduous participant at the eventful meetings of the Soirées de la Plume, where he met Moréas, Cendrars, Picasso, Apollinaire, and many other artists and intellectuals. Soffici's participation in the cultural life of the French capital increased in intensity as he be-

Giovanni Papini and Soffici, founders of the journal
Lacerba *in 1913*

came a regular and welcomed member of the group, which met at the Causerie des Lilas.

Equally significant were Soffici's readings of French authors; traces of their influence are present in his Paris writings. Among the writers he assimilated were Charles-Pierre Baudelaire, Paul Verlaine, and more important, Arthur Rimbaud, whose life-style and myth of the "poète maudit" (damned poet) inspired Soffici's admiration. His monograph on this French poet, which he published in Italy in 1911, introduced Rimbaud to Italian readers for the first time. While Richter's assertion that, for Soffici, "Rimbaud diventa un ideale artistico, un motivo di rottura" (Rimbaud becomes a [symbol of] an artistic ideal, a cause for breaking [with tradition]), is essentially accurate, a closer study reveals that the influence of the French poet is relatively superficial. Edoardo Sanguineti's opinion that there is no convincing presence of Rimbaud's poetry in Soffici's own poetics is textually more accurate. Rimbaud remained for Soffici a significant symbol of freedom and revolt, not a specific literary model to emulate.

Clearly more significant for Soffici's stylistic evolution are the works and the friendship of Moréas, whereas in the case of Cendrars, who at that time was not yet a published author, the friendship with Soffici must have been reciprocally influential. What is evident in Soffici's French writings is the gradual development of a modern style free of academic and classical encumbrances; with a simplified, almost colloquial syntax; and with a current vocabulary—a style that was congenial to Soffici's character and artistic orientation.

During his residence in France, as well as when he returned to Italy, Soffici, whose ties with Florence never waned as the years passed, played an important role as cultural mediator and innovator. Perhaps no one has stated Soffici's role as initiator of new poetic diction and its importance for later generations more succinctly and completely than Giuseppe Ungaretti, in his letter of 1914 to Giuseppe Prezzolini: "Soffici ci ha avviati nei dedali dell'arte moderna" (Soffici started us off in the labyrinth of modern art). In this role Soffici in some ways anticipated for Italian letters what Gertrude Stein was to accomplish later for American writers.

After 1908 Soffici's direct participation in the cultural life of Florence was decisive in shaping the literary character of that period. With Giovanni Papini he changed the identity of Prezzolini's *La Voce*, which in Soffici's opinion had remained impervious to the artistic experimentation taking place during those years. The journal had barred from its pages writings of a literary nature and retained only essays dealing mainly with ethical concerns. Soffici brought to *La Voce* the experiences he had accumulated while in France. By 1913 his and Papini's often vehement insistence that new poetics and ideologies be given full expression in the journal so collided with Prezzolini's conception of *La Voce* that Prezzolini resigned. Soffici and Papini then proceeded to found *Lacerba*, a journal of extreme literary and artistic iconoclasm and social anticonformism. It hosted the works of the futurists, whose movement, however, Soffici had criticized in 1909, the year of Marinetti's *Futurist Manifesto*. But by 1914 continuous contact with avant-garde writers and ideological-political interest in the Italian irredentist cause contributed to Soffici's brief adherence to Marinetti's movement. *Lacerba* thus hosted writings by Apollinaire, Max Jacob, Aldo Palazzeschi, Luciano Folgore, and Marinetti himself. By 1915, the year in which *Lacerba* ceased publication, the journal had become essentially a forum for nationalist ideologies and an exaltation of war. This was Soffici's most vociferous period, during which he published his most rebellious, avant-garde works. However, as might be expected, this period of maximum stylistic revolt had a gradual and lengthy evolution, traceable through a group of poems, "Poesie giovanili 1901-1908" (Juvenilia 1901-1908), collected in 1938 in a volume containing all his lyrical production to date, *Marsia e Apollo*.

It is evident that the works in "Poesie giovanili" developed out of the lyric poetry of Pascoli and D'Annunzio, as well as out of a broader European symbolist poetics filtered through the rhythms of Verlaine. Soffici's "Autunno" (Autumn) illustrates the translation in subtle melancholic musicality of a sentiment of languid weariness, manifested in the carefully orchestrated alliterations and in the keen selection of adjectives and in the insistent, rhythmic cadences of the rhyming words, all accented on the antepenultimate syllable, an unusual occurrence in normal Italian prosody that reveals Soffici's interest in experimenting with new disruptive accentual patterns:

Lungo i canali sonnolenti e fumidi
Gli allineati pioppi abbrividiscono
. . . .
Il vento svola fra le fronde, e all'anima
Reca uno sciame di ricordi teneri . . .

(Alongside the canals somnolent and misty
The poplars are shuddering in their rows
. . . .
The wind flits among the leaves, and to the mind
Brings a swarm of fragile memories . . .).

It is evident from this poem that novel stylistic procedures such as the analogical association of disparate sensations and ideas are making their way into Soffici's poetic language.

In "Doppio" (Tolling Knell) the mournful bell that is a typical motif in Pascoli's poetry becomes in Soffici's a mere pretext for the agile prestigious description of sound floating through the air, embracing in its movement the entire countryside. Noteworthy is the increased break with tradition underlined by the use of seemingly unpoetic words (mainly the verbs), unsanctioned by the elevated canon of classical vocabulary:

Svolazza pe' campi, lambisce gli ulivi,
Riempie le case, investe, circonda i cipressi;

Si lancia pe' cieli fioriti di nubi,
S'avvolge, s'intreccia, si snoda,
Si squaglia, si perde
Nell'aria profonda.
. . . .
E anche il mio cuore è come una campana
Che suona, che suona, che suona
A festa o a morto, e non si queta mai.

(It flutters over the fields, it laps the olive trees,
It fills the houses, it hits and surrounds the cypresses;
It hurls itself to the sky blossoming with clouds,
It winds itself, braids itself, unwinds,
It melts and vanishes
Deep in the sky.
. . . .
My heart is also like a bell
That tolls, tolls and tolls
For a holiday or a funeral and is never at rest.)

The distended rhythms of this poem constitute the essential element in the development of that masterful poetic prose achieved in his later works. Also of particular interest in the poem "Doppio" are such verbs as *svolazza, squaglia*, and *sfrulla* (flutters, melts, and whirs), onomatopoeic words that stress the sensorial adherence of the subject to the object observed. Unlike Pascoli's onomatopoeias, which are descriptive and static, Soffici's emphasize the dynamic aspect of the imagery.

However, not all the poems of "Poesie giovanili" demonstrate this innovative trend. Rather, some compositions of this period manifest Soffici's continued fondness for classical forms, even while he was moving toward avant-garde poetics. "I miei amori" (My Loves), for instance, is from the same group of poems but is written in distichs of a canonical, fifteen-syllable verse (or hemistichs of seven syllables) and therefore is a poem relevant only insofar as it displays what can be loosely labeled as Soffici's mystical pantheism, his intense love of nature and of the Tuscan countryside, which are such dominant themes in his art. Nonetheless, on the whole, Soffici in this phase is resolutely making his way toward a freer diction uncluttered by cumbersome syntactical structures, archaic words, and canonical prosodic constructions.

When Soffici returned to Italy in 1908 to join in the debate centering on the various new aspects of Italian national culture, he began to contribute articles to *La Voce*. Soffici disseminated the artistic and literary ideas that he had been developing while in France. Prose, which became for a while his exclusive expressive medium, can be, however, melodic, alliterative, and figurative—characteristics of poetry. He elaborated between 1908 and 1915 his conception of a lyrical prose composition, brief and complete in itself, that was to be labeled *frammentismo*, or fragment writing. This new literary form developed gradually and reached a peak of rebellious and even abrasive language in *Giornale di bordo* and *Bïf&zf+18: Simultaneità e chimismi lirici* (Bïf &zf+18; Simultaneity and Lyrical Chemisms, 1915).

Soffici began to elaborate this new prose in *Ignoto toscano*, the first work he published after his 1908 return from Paris. Although ostensibly a succinct biography of a poet in his prime who recently died prematurely, the pamphlet is really a portrait of the artist as a young man. The following description from the book provides a clue as to how Soffici envisioned himself as a poet-artist:

> In tutto il suo aspetto portava un non so che di sacerdotale e guerriero che lo rendeva poco gradito ai più; ma singolare e riconoscibile da lontano. —Era piuttosto riservato e severo, ma non si peritava di ridere e non disprezzava sempre la baldoria e la buffoneria. Impiegava spesso, quando ce n'era bisogno per esprimere bene il suo sentimento, le parole più crude, con una specie di voluttà, e a chi se ne scandalizzava, cercava di spiegare come lo spirito scoppia sempre fuori dalle forme più reali, rudi ed anche triviali, come un fiore dal concio.... Poneva la vita spirituale sopra ogni grandezza umana; né cessò mai di considerarsi come uno dei rarissimi uomini del suo tempo che avesse una fede sincera.

> (In his whole appearance there was something of the priest and of the warrior which made him unappealing to most people, but unique and recognizable from afar. He was rather reserved and serious, but he did not shun laughter and did not always disparage carousing and jesting. He often employed harsher words even with a sort of indulgence when it was necessary to express his feelings well. To those who were shocked he tried to explain that wit bursts forth always out of the more real, rude, and even trivial forms, as a flower from manure.... He valued the life of the mind above any other human achievement; nor did he ever cease to consider himself one of the few men of his times who possessed a sincere faith.)

Ignoto toscano was intended to be provoking. Its supple syntax and frequent use of Tuscan colloquialisms inserted among erudite Italian lexemes give the prose the vivacity of then-current spoken language, thereby shattering ostentatiously the archaic standards of rigid academism. The pamphlet, which the narrator is supposedly publishing to preserve the memory of his deceased poet friend, is being submitted for evaluation (in the fictional plot) to a professor whom the narrator warns of the inadequacies of the text so insistently and apologetically as to effect a tone of irony and sarcasm, which results in lampooning the rigidly academic and traditionalist professor.

Soffici's next stage in the evolution of his prose style is exemplified by *Lemmonio Boreo* (1911), his only attempt at writing a novel. It is structured as a series of picaresque vignettes whose predecessors may include Miguel de Cervantes' *Don Quixote* (two parts, 1605, 1615), Ugo Foscolo's *Notizie intorno a Didimo Chierico* (News About Didimo Chierico), and *Jean Christophe* (1931-1933), by the contemporary French writer Romain Rolland. Soffici's protagonist, Lemmonio Boreo, is a brooding, idealistic intellectual who enlists the complicity of a rogue and a prankster to roam the Tuscan countryside and impart to one and all their lessons in proper civil conduct. The lessons include subverting social complacency, unmasking the hypocrisy of religious and civil servants, and curbing the abuses of power. The language is essentially similar to that of *Ignoto toscano*—perhaps sporadically more scurrilous—but the intention to shock and provoke the traditional, conservative, well-mannered, but hypocritical and egotistical sector of the dominant bourgeois class is more pronounced. After this uneven attempt at using the novel as an artistic medium, Soffici abandoned this form and veered off toward a genre and a style much more consonant with his artistic personality: autobiographical lyrical prose.

Arlecchino (Harlequin, 1914), "A nimble work of motley colors" in the felicitous definition of critic Gina Trovato Dapper, embodies several characteristics of Soffici's new style, the *frammento*. As varied as the patches of Harlequin's costume, the well-known style of the homonymous character of the commedia dell'arte, the nine parts of the book are held together mainly by the single narrator, who records episodes, recollections, reflections, brief dialogues, and descriptions of fleeting scenes. The structuring of experience by the rules of traditional logic is abandoned because it is viewed as false since reality, according to Soffici's precepts, is constituted of the free-flowing impressions that only an immediate, colloquial, at times even grammatically incomplete language can transcribe. Consequently, the orderly distinctions normally existing among the different literary genres are obliterated, and what triumphs is the immediate, rapid, notational writing down of fleeting experiences in a form that oscillates from the nominal sentence to the brief dramatic dialogue, from lyrical sublime effusiveness to quotidian narrative. Stripped of all philosophical systems because of an innate inability to accept any metaphysics, Soffici had already donned the disguise of "un baladin" (a buffoon), an image that made its first appearance in "Masque," an early poem written in French. The speaker rejects all systematic organization of reality and sees himself as a "ramassis de nerfs et de néant / confits dans le bleu du jour, je voltige léger, je danse / Aux carrefour / Comme un clair reflet sur le vent" (bundle of nerves and of nothing / nailed in the blue of the day, weightless I twirl, I dance / At the crossroads / Like a clear reflection on the wind). In this poem, as well as in *Arlecchino*, Soffici's alter ego assumes the tragic aspect of a tearful clown. However, the main persona in *Arlecchino* epitomizes Soffici's celebration of the apotheosis of the senses, especially that of sight, according to him the noblest of them. Menalio, the narrator, who is apostrophized as "il disgraziato dalle tre tragedie—filosofica, sentimentale e finanziaria" (the wretch of a threefold tragedy—philosophical, sentimental, and financial), discovers in nature, in the bright light of the sun the only true reality. The phenomenon itself, free of any burdensome metaphysics, is all there is.

In *Giornale di bordo*, stylistically very similar to *Arlecchino*, Soffici enacts fully his poetics of the *frammento*, in which he so excelled as to be thought its inventor, so congenial it is to his particular artistic vision. It is a poetics he shared, though, with other writers of the prewar period, such as Piero Jahier. However, Soffici's intent is clearly more caustic than that of his contemporaries, defiant as it is and scurrilously shocking in parts. The language he uses is the same spontaneous, direct language he had been elaborating in earlier works, although intentionally less lyrical, as the literary sublime ideal is banished from these pages in favor of a writing that ought to be instinctive, like the style in a letter to a friend or lover. The conception of art as the rhetorical elaboration of feeling is equated with artifice, and therefore is considered insincere and false. The result in *Giornale di bordo* is the crisp, colloquial,

frank, and unabashed style of a diarist, unprecedented in Italian literature. Vignettes, aphorisms, effusive moments, vivid descriptions of nature, and descriptions of meetings in cafés with the futurists Carrà, Boccioni, Palazzeschi, and Marinetti are all rendered in playful, antibourgeois rhetoric. The graceful levity, so characteristic of Soffici's art, prompted Renato Serra to define him as a "gift": "Soffici non è né un genere né un'opera è un dono" (Soffici is neither a genre nor a work, he is a gift).

Soffici's art is instinctively balanced and harmonious in its use of adjectives, similes, and comparisons that transcribe and capture the essential properties of an object or an aspect of nature. Soffici himself often formulated definitions of his ideal conception of art, such as the following one in *Giornale di bordo*: "Posar le parole come il pittore i colori e vedere il mondo spiegarsi nel suo splendore!" (To place words as the painter his colors and watch the world unfold in all its splendor!). Even more suggestive is this other concrete, palpable formulation characteristic of Soffici's poetical ideal during this period (also from *Giornale di bordo*): "Ah! poter avere uno stile che sbucciasse il mondo sensibile come un'arancia che io metterei davanti col suo profumo e il suo sugo colante!" (Ah! to possess a style that would peel the sensible world as an orange that I would place before you with its scent and its flowing juice!). This style, developed in *Giornale di bordo*, is an aspect of the poetics most often associated with Soffici's art.

Giornale di bordo and the compositions of *Bïf &zf+18* reflect Soffici's extreme iconoclasm during 1914 and 1915, the period in which he and Papini founded *Lacerba*, which hosted the works of Apollinaire and Jacob, as well as Marinetti's and those of other Italian futurists. Neither Papini nor Soffici ever wrote truly futurist works, and both undermined their participation in the movement later in their lives. Soffici had repeatedly criticized the facile, flamboyant, superficial qualities of some aspects of Marinetti's movement since its inception in 1909, but, during the years of *Lacerba*, because of interventionist political reasons and the sharing of certain artistic motives, he joined hands with the futurists.

Coeval with *Giornale di bordo* but somewhat different because of a more lyrical tone inspired by daring analogical and synaesthetic techniques, *Bïf &zf+18* displays Soffici's expert use of the art of the fragment. The imagination is given full rein as it defies traditional laws of versification

Cover for Soffici's first collection of fragmentary poetry (1915)

and accepted logic, and abandons altogether customary punctuation, obeying only the powers of intuition and free association, annulling all boundaries of time and space, while asserting the contemporaneity of all experience in the flow of the poet's consciousness. However, Soffici never really subscribed to the more evident aspects of futurist poetics, such as the total reduction of language to a phonetic/graphic signifier. Only in very few compositions of *Bïf &zf+18*, such as "Buffet di stazione" (Train Station Buffet), does Soffici actually approximate a sort of cubofuturist style, as Willard Bohn chose to define it in his 1976 study in *Pacific Coast Philology*.

The main persona in *Bïf &zf+18*, who bears many similarities to the ones presented in earlier works, from *Ignoto toscano* to *Giornale di bordo*, is a melancholy Pierrot, who rejects customary traditions, rigid philosophical systems, and traditional logic by donning the rebellious costume of the circus clown, a metaphor for freedom and anticonformism. In the poem "Arcobaleno" (Rainbow) he exclaims: "Ci sarebbe da fare un carnevale / Di tutti i dolori / Dimenticati con

l'ombrello nei caffè d'Europa" (One could make a carnival / Of all the suffering / Forgotten with the umbrella in the cafés of Europe), verses marked by a jovial irony generated from the startling association of *suffering* with *umbrella*. The book is rich in synaesthesia and captivating images: "Oh! nuotare come un pesce innamorato che beve smeraldi / Fra questa rete di profumi e di bengala" (Oh! to swim like a fish in love who drinks emeralds / In this net of perfumes and fireworks). All of *Bïf &zf+18* holds unexpected, captivating descriptions, but this section of "Luci di Roma" (Roman Lights) concisely renders the tone and quality of the book: "Notti! Come una smisurata rosa la notte romana pendeva dalle stelle Soffregata di profumi la seta calda del firmamento oscillava sulle palme dei giardini intorno alla fronte accesa de' palazzi inzuppata d'oriente e di mare" (Nights! Like a rose without dimensions the Roman night hung from the stars Suffused lightly with perfumes the warm silk of the firmament oscillated over the palm trees in the gardens around the glowing forehead of the palaces soaked with orient and sea).

In 1915 Soffici was sent to the war front as a lieutenant in the Italian army. His grueling experience in the trenches is recorded in *Kobilek: Giornale di battaglia* (Kobilek: Battle Journal, 1918) in an energetic prose as naturally eloquent as any fragment of *Giornale di bordo*. In the midst of death and suffering, notwithstanding a leg wound, Soffici found the strength to praise life, to describe the beauty of dawns and sunsets, and of the goodness of his fellow soldiers. The spirit that imbues the book is reminiscent of Ungaretti's war poems in *Allegria di naufragi* (Joy of Shipwrecks, 1919).

During the years in the trenches Soffici's *ritorno all'ordine* (return to order) consciousness began to mature. After the war his socioethical views changed slowly but decisively. As his ideology shifted, the classical measures of traditional diction gradually returned to Soffici's work. The conversion experienced by the Tuscan poet during the decade after World War I was by no means limited to him alone. Long before him, his friend Jean Moréas had reverted from avantgarde to traditional writing in his desire to emulate classical beauty and harmony. Similarly Ungaretti and Clemente Rèbora, Soffici's peers, also converted to traditional poetics after the war. As the years passed, the admiration for previous Italian literary achievements, which Soffici had expressed in the poetry of his youth, returned with renewed vigor. The changes occurred over a period of years, but they are evident and at times appear to be even drastic in comparison with his previous, experimental achievements. However, certain characteristics of his innovative style continue to be present, scattered throughout his later works.

A few long poems written in the 1930s, inspired by the political goals and euphoric ambience of the times, are the least accomplished of Soffici's postwar writings. There are moments in these works when the rhetoric may seem bombastic, as is the case in *L'adunata* (The Assembly, 1936) or "Ode a Mussolini" (Ode to Mussolini, 1931). However, the enthusiasm expressed by these poems is grounded in a genuine feeling of fraternal sentiment and sharing of pristine ideals with the common man. Industriousness, justice, dignity, love of the past, and love of the Tuscan countryside are sentiments that inspire these works and ones which the poet champions for the masses. He is the self-proclaimed interpreter of the people's hopes and aspirations, as in these lines from "Ode a Mussolini": "Ti saluta la gente tutta / Col poeta, che n'è la voce" (All the people salute you / Through the poet who is their voice). Although the language is archaic and the cadence traditional, nonetheless the authenticity of the inspiration is manifest in the celebration of grassroots values and sentiments, of the productivity of the land, and of the beauty of nature. The poet never engages in any abject adulation of Il Duce. Instead Soffici's clear intention is to praise the people, their work ethic, and the land, which he urges Mussolini himself to admire and respect. There transpires in these verses a truthfulness and sincerity that might be overlooked were one to focus merely on the archaic vocabulary and syntax, which confer to the poem its elevated tone.

Similar motives inspire *L'adunata*, whose verses are sustained by heartfelt participation in the activities and aspirations of the people. In addition there occurs in this poem a certain lexicon characteristic of Soffici, such as the verb *c'inzuppava* ([the light] soaked us) carried over from earlier expressive modes. *L'adunata* epitomizes the poet's new ideology:

Ero sul ponte della nuova casa
Tra i muratori, anch'io lavoratore,
Esercitando intonachi e tinteggi;
Sotto ondeggiava il mar nell'ampia luce
Che tutti c'inzuppava: il due d'ottobre.

(I was on the bridge of my new house
Among the carpenters, myself a laborer,
Applying plaster and paint;
Below were the waves of the sea in the vast light
That soaked us all: October second.)

Most of Soffici's works published soon after the war retain the vital originality customarily associated with his style. Because these works are chronologically closer to *Arlecchino* and *Bïf&zf+18*, they keep the tenor of the poet's prewar diction, with the predilection for synaesthesia, free verse, and the innovative lexical and rhythmic choices. These stylistic elements are found in the poem "Ospedale da campo 026" (Camp Hospital 026), in *Kobilek: Giornale di battaglia*. Indeed, the continuity of Soffici's literary personality appears obvious in any of the following works: *La giostra dei sensi* (The Merry-Go-Round of the Senses, 1919), *La ritirata del friuli* (The Retreat from Friuli, 1919), and *Taccuino d'Arno Borghi* (Arno Borghi's Notebook, 1933). In the last of these Soffici returns to the style of the self-contained fragment with renewed success. The prose of *Taccuino d'Arno Borghi*, however, is inspired by the stately cadence of traditional Italian prose and not by the eruptive, colloquial prose of *Giornale di bordo*. It is perhaps burdened at times by an overabundance of aphorisms, but nothing in it is superfluous; the vivid limpidity of Soffici's poetic prose flourishes, as always, with typical gracefulness.

Soffici pursued the rhythms of classical Italian verse as his poetic ideals after the 1920s. He aspired to capture the ubiquitous music in the high tradition of Italian poetry but not identifiable with any one author. He is searching for the balance of measure and harmony, "musica e misura" (music and measure), as he puts it in the poem "Resurrezione" (Resurrection), an ideal that also inspired Ungaretti during the same period.

Soffici obtains remarkable results in some later verses, as, for instance, in *Elegia dell'Ambra* (The Ambra Elegy, 1927). The full measure of the music he longed for is also palpably evident in certain very brief compositions, some of which are only one verse, as in the paradigmatic "La fine di Troia" (The End of Troy).

To clarify the relationship that the earlier 1908-1915 phase of Soffici's poetry bears to the later mid-1930s classic style, one might rely on Soffici's own statement in the epigraph preceding his poems in *Marsia e Apollo*:

Marsia non era un insolente rivale di Apollo: era una parte del Nume stesso. Marsia era la giovinezza d'Apollo. Arrivato Apollo alla virilità dello spirito, i canti giovanili, sfrenati di Marsia gli sturbavano dentro la nuova serena musica sorgente dalla maturità del suo cuore poetico. Volle liberarsi da quella disarmonia; e scuoiò Marsia. Ma della sua pelle divina si fece un florido manto, e se ne ornò poi per sempre.

(Marsias was not an insolent rival of Apollo: he was a part of the god himself. Marsias was the youth of Apollo. Apollo having reached full manhood, the youthful unfettered songs of Marsias disturbed the new serene music rising from the maturity of his poetic heart. He wanted to free himself of that disharmony; he flayed Marsias. But afterward with his [Marsias's] divine skin he [Apollo] decorated himself forever.)

Soffici's later works, particularly the ones written during the *ritorno all'ordine* period, are deserving of attention, as they are often refuted on mere ideological grounds and usually misconstrued and misunderstood. Ultimately, though, it is his earlier phase, the 1908-1915 period, that may prove the most fruitful with respect to Soffici's contribution to the renewal of Italian literary language.

The cluster of conflicts manifested throughout Soffici's works can be reduced to a schematic duality, as the poet himself did in the symbolic episode of the grapes and the cross that he narrated in his *Autoritratto*. Stylistically that dualism is seen in the shifting between traditional prosody and the poetics of free verse, characterized by the alogical association of spatially and temporally distant objects and ideas. Such a stylistic polarization reflects the greater European crisis present from Friedrich Nietzsche's work onward, arising from the awareness that reason cannot comprehend the nature of reality. This failing of reason is frequently encountered in Soffici's writings in images revealing his concept of life as a continuous flux, an ever-incessant flow of sensations that rationality attempts in vain to order through rational discourse. Consequently art and intuition are posited as early as *Ignoto toscano* as the only means to apprehend reality. Perhaps Soffici deduced this idea from Henri Bergson's *L'Evolution Créatrice* (Creative Evolution, 1907). However, Bergson, surprisingly enough, is never mentioned in Soffici's work. The Tuscan poet elevates art, particularly poetic art, above all other human activities, as the speaker in *Ignoto toscano*, *Arlecchino*, *Giornale di bordo*, and *Taccuino d'Arno*

Borghi so frequently asserts, and as is so clearly evident in these verses that celebrate poetry, in a poem from *Bif &zf+18*, "Poesia":

Un solo squillo della tua voce senza
epoca e tutte le gioiellerie di questo
crepuscolo rassegnato in pantofole si
mettono a lampeggiare creando
un giorno nuovo

(One ring only of your timeless voice
and all the jewelry shops
of this resigned dusk wearing
slippers will begin to flash
creating a new day).

But Soffici wavered between a conception of poetry that is rationally constructed, therefore rigid and traditional, and a poetics based on irrational, analogical principles of association, although the latter is dominant in his work, not only from a quantitative point of view but also from the presence of irrationalist vestiges that appear even in his traditional period. From linguistic and stylistic points of view, Soffici's dualism, the grapes and the cross, is emblematic of most poetry of the twentieth century. It is even at the basis of the life/art dichotomy represented in the stylistic elaboration of more recent poets very different from Soffici, such as Eugenio Montale and Andrea Zanzotto, among others.

During most of his mature life, Ardengo Soffici lived a retiring, quiet existence spent in part at Forte dei Marmi by the Tyrrhenian Sea, and in part at Poggio a Caiano, his rural residence not far from his beloved Florence, where he continued to paint and write until his death on 19 August 1964. He was buried in the small country cemetery near Poggio a Caiano.

Letters:

Carlo Carrà, Ardengo Soffici, edited by Massimo Carrà and Vittorio Fagone (Milan: Feltrinelli, 1983);

Lettere a Prezzolini, 1908-1920, edited by Annamaria Manetti Piccinini (Florence: Vallecchi, 1988).

Biography:

Giuseppe Marchetti, *Ardengo Soffici* (Florence: Nuova Italia, 1979).

References:

Ardengo Soffici: l'artista e lo scrittore nella cultura del '900 (Florence: Centro Di, 1976);

Zygmunt G. Baranski, "Italian Literature and the Great War: Soffici, Jahier and Rèbora," *Journal of European Studies*, 10 (1980): 155-177;

Carlo Bo, "Ardengo Soffici," *L'approdo letterario*, 10 (1964): 21-25;

Arnaldo Bocelli, "Frammentismo," in *Letteratura del Novecento*, volume 2, edited by Salvatore Sciascia (Rome: Caltanissetta, 1975), pp. 121-131;

Willard Bohn, "Ardengo Soffici, parole in libertà," *Pacific Coast Philology*, 2 (1976): 23-29;

Luigi Cavallo, *Soffici: Immagini e documenti, 1879-1964*, edited by Oretta Nicolini (Florence: Vallecchi, 1986);

Emilio Cecchi, "Ricordi d'infanzia di Soffici," in his *Di giorno in giorno: Note di letteratura contemporanea (1945-1954)* (Milan: Garzanti, 1977), pp. 302-305;

N. F. Cimmino, "Ricordo di Ardengo Soffici," *L'Italia che Scrive*, 47 (1964): 121-127;

Gina Trovato Dapper, "The Enchanted World of Arlecchino," *Italica*, 40 (1963): 339-345;

Domenico De Robertis, ed., *Almanacco della Voce* (Milan: Mondadori, 1980);

Giuseppe De Robertis, "L'artista Ardengo Soffici," in his *Saggi* (Florence: Monnier, 1953), pp. 173-196;

Enrico Falqui, "Ardengo Soffici," in his *Novecento letterario italiano*, volume 2 (Florence: Vallecchi, 1954-1963), pp. 205-238;

Alfredo Gargiulo, "Ardengo Soffici," in his *Letteratura italiana del Novecento* (Florence: Monnier, 1958), pp. 133-141;

Gianni Grana, ed., *Letteratura italiana: Novecento: I contemporanei* (Milan: Marzorati, 1963), pp. 1346-1396;

Giuseppe Marchetti, "Appunti per una rilettura del Soffici poeta," *Paragone*, 27, no. 322 (1976): 148-152;

Carlo Martini, "Lettere ad Ardengo Soffici," *Nuova Antologia*, 492 (1964): 333-340;

Pier Vincenzo Mengaldo, "Ardengo Soffici," in his *Poeti italiani del Novecento* (Milan: Mondadori, 1978), pp. 337-351;

Armando Meoni, "Ardengo Soffici sul piede di casa," *L'osservatore Politico Letterario*, 21 (1975): 33-40;

Meoni, "L'opera di Soffici," *Nuova Antologia*, 494 (1964): 458-467;

Leone Piccioni, ed., *Giuseppe Ungaretti: Lettere a Soffici, 1917-1930* (Florence: Sansone, 1981);

Giuseppe Prezzolini, Introduction to Soffici's *Opere*, 7 volumes (Florence: Vallecchi, 1959-1968);

Edoardo Sanguineti, "Poetica e poesia di Soffici," *Aut-Aut*, 24 (November 1954): 491-502;

Renato Serra, *Scritti letterari, morali e politici* (Turin: Einaudi, 1974), pp. 446-451;

Vittorio Vettori, "Scrittori vociani: Papini, Prezzolini, Soffici," *Cultura e Scuola*, 2 (1962-1963): 28-35.

Sergio Solmi

(16 December 1899 - 7 October 1981)

Patricia Lyn Richards
Kenyon College

BOOKS: *Il pensiero di Alain* (Milan: Scheiwiller, 1930; enlarged edition, Pisa: Nistri-Lischi, 1976);

Fine di stagione (Lanciano, Italy: Carabba, 1933; abridged, 1939);

La salute di Montaigne (Florence: Monnier, 1942; enlarged edition, Milan & Naples: Ricciardi, 1952);

Poesie (Milan: Mondadori, 1950);

Levania e altre poesie (Milan: Mantovani, 1956);

Modernità di Zanini (Alpignano, Italy: Tallone, 1961);

Scrittori negli anni: Saggi e note sulla letteratura italiana del '900 (Milan: Saggiatore, 1963);

Dal balcone (Milan: Mondadori, 1968);

Scritti leopardiani (Milan: All'Insegna del Pesce d'Oro, 1969); republished as *Studi e nuovi studi leopardiani* (Milan & Naples: Ricciardi, 1975);

Della favola, del viaggio e di altre cose: Saggi sul fantastico (Milan & Naples: Ricciardi, 1971); republished as *Saggi sul fantastico: Dall'antichità alle prospettive del futuro* (Turin: Einaudi, 1978);

Meditazioni sullo scorpione e altre prose (Milan: Adelphi, 1972);

Poesie complete (Milan: Adelphi, 1974);

Saggio su Rimbaud (Turin: Einaudi, 1974);

La luna di Laforgue e altri scritti di letteratura francese (Milan: Mondadori, 1976);

Poesie (1924-1972), edited by Lanfranco Caretti (Milan: Mondadori, 1978);

Quadernetto di letture e ricordi (Cremona, Italy: Polifilo, 1979);

Il giardino del tempo (Turin: Einaudi, 1983);

Opere, 2 volumes, edited by Giovanni Pacchiano: volume 1, *Poesie, meditazioni, e ricordi* (Milan: Adelphi, 1983); volume 2, *Studi leopardiani: Note su autori classici, italiani e stranieri* (Milan: Adelphi, 1987).

OTHER: *Filippo de Pisis*, introduction by Solmi (Milan: Hoepli, 1931), pp. 5-16;

Salvatore Quasimodo, *Ed è subito sera*, includes an essay by Solmi (Milan: Mondadori, 1944);

Marco Polo, *Il milione*, preface by Solmi (Turin: Einaudi, 1954);

Giacomo Leopardi, *Opere*, 2 volumes, edited by Solmi (Milan & Naples: Ricciardi, 1956, 1966);

Sergio Corazzini, *Liriche*, includes an essay by Solmi (Milan & Naples: Ricciardi, 1959);

Le meraviglie del possibile: Antologia della fantascienza, 2 volumes, edited by Solmi and Carlo Fruttero (Turin: Einaudi, 1959, 1961);

Leopardi, *Pensieri, memorie del primo amore, Elegia I, Elegia II*, introduction by Solmi (Alpignano, Italy: Tallone, 1970);

Leopardi, *Operette morali*, edited by Solmi (Turin: Einaudi, 1976);

Leopardi, *Lettere*, selected, with commentary, by Sergio and Raffaella Solmi (Turin: Einaudi, 1977);

Leopardi, *Zibaldone di pensieri: Scelta*, edited by Sergio and Raffaella Solmi and Fruttero (Turin: Einaudi, 1977);

Il giardino del tempo, edited by Solmi and Fruttero (Turin: Einaudi, 1983).

TRANSLATIONS: Pedro Calderón de la Barca, "L'alcalde di Zalamea," in *Teatro spagnolo*, edited by Elio Vittorini (Milan: Bompiani, 1942);

José Ortega y Gasset, *Il tema del nostro tempo* (Milan: Rosa & Ballo, 1946);

Alain (Emile-Auguste Chartier), *Cento e un ragionamenti* (Turin: Einaudi, 1960);

Versioni poetiche da contemporanei (Milan: All'Insegna del Pesce d'Oro, 1963);

Jules Laforgue, *Poesie* (Rome: Ateneo, 1966);

Alfred Jarry, *Opere*, 3 volumes (Milan: Adelphi, 1969);

Quaderno di traduzioni, 2 volumes (Turin: Einaudi, 1969, 1977);

Raymond Queneau, *Piccola cosmogonía portatile* (Turin: Einaudi, 1982).

Frontispiece and title page for the 1979 publication of some of Solmi's notes on literature and life

Sergio Solmi's poetry, though contemporaneous with both the crepuscular and hermetic tendencies of the first half of the twentieth century, remained apart from any movement. He was, however, influenced by the poetry of Giacomo Leopardi and Eugenio Montale. Often melancholic and even ironic, Solmi's verses record the spiritual essence of events and feelings both momentous and intimate, alternating an enthusiasm for life with a sense of life's lacerating toll. Memory plays an important role, as a source of enchantment and unexpected revelation and as a source of painful nostalgia. Solmi's poetry is occasionally marked by an expressionistic element, yet remains controlled by his skeptical intelligence.

In addition to his poetry, Solmi produced a large corpus of essays and literary criticism. The poetry itself has something of an expository tendency: it attests his desire to bear witness to his time by revealing the experience of one man subject to the century's vitality, the illusions it fostered, and the doubts it engendered. Yet despite

disenchantment with his own era, Solmi did hold out hope for a future that might offer new solutions to seemingly insoluble problems. From an initial attitude of isolation, as seen in *Fine di stagione* (End of Season, 1933), Solmi moved toward a feeling of solidarity with others in *Poesie* (1950), and then to a meditative acceptance of alienation and separation in *Levania e altre poesie* (The Moon and Other Poems, 1956), ending in a retrospection of the twentieth century in *Dal balcone* (From the Balcony, 1968).

Born at the end of the nineteenth century (16 December 1899) and living through the greater part of the twentieth (he died in Milan on 7 October 1981), Solmi in his poetry meditates on cultural and personal matters, determined to come to grips with the more disquieting aspects of his era. From his youth onward Solmi engaged in varied literary endeavors: founding, directing, and contributing to periodicals; publishing essays on the works of Italian and foreign authors; translating from several languages; and writing his poems. He participated in both world wars and led a responsible life as a middle-class bank lawyer; he married and was the father of two children, Renato and Raffaella, born to Solmi and his wife, Dora. He once said in jest that if he had not been precocious as a child and an insomniac as an adult, he never would have had time for literature.

Solmi was born in Rieti (in the Lazio region) to a bourgeois Modenese family, well-educated in the humanities. His mother was Clelia Lollis Solmi. His father, Edmondo, known for an important study of Leonardo da Vinci (*Leonardo*, 1900) used by Sigmund Freud, was a professor of philosophy whose professional assignments caused the family to move often while Sergio was young. Sergio Solmi lived much of his youth in Turin, which figures as an important childhood landscape in his poems, as does the Emilian countryside, where he spent summers at his grandparents' villa. In 1912 his father died, acquainting the poet early with the experience of loss. He completed his preparatory studies in Turin, studying under Attilio Momigliano, and was drafted into the army in 1917. While a student at officer's training school in Parma, Solmi met Eugenio Montale, and they began a lasting friendship. Solmi fought in the war in 1918 and afterward studied at the Università di Torino (Turin), graduating with his law degree in 1923. He then joined (and later became head of) the legal department of the Banca Commerciale in Milan, where he spent his entire career. During World War II, opposed to the Fascist regime, Solmi joined the Action party and took the name Mario Rossetti (which he also gave to a section of his poems). In 1944 he was captured by Fascists, but daringly escaped; they seized him again in 1945, imprisoning him in San Vittore in Milan. After the war Solmi, freed, continued writing, collaborating with noted men of letters. Among his friends were Giacomo Debenedetti, Marion Fubini, and Natalino Sapegno.

After his first adolescent experience with *Cronache Latine*, Solmi worked on other journals, such as *Primo tempo, Baretti, La Cultura, Lettere e Arti*, and *La Rassegna d'Italia*. He received several prestigious prizes, including the 1948 Saint Vincent Prize for poetry (shared with Alfonso Gatto); the 1949 Montparnasse for his French studies; the 1963 Viareggio Prize for *Scrittori negli anni: Saggi e note sulla letteratura italiana del '900* (Writers through the Years: Essays and Notes on Italian Literature of the Twentieth Century, 1963); the 1968 Fiuggi Prize for *Dal balcone*;

the 1973 Bagutta Prize for *Meditazioni sullo scorpione* (Meditations on the Scorpion, 1972); and the 1976 Viareggio Prize for *La luna di Laforgue e altri scritti di letteratura francese* (Laforgue's Moon and Other Writings on French Literature, 1976).

Several elements contributed to Solmi's formation as a writer. The beginning of his serious commitment to literature coincides with Benito Mussolini's rise to power. During the twenty-year Fascist regime, Solmi dedicated himself to French studies, developing a lifelong interest in French thought and poetry, including that of Arthur Rimbaud, Michel Montaigne, and the symbolists. Another key to Solmi's formation as poet and critic was the work of the contemporaneous French thinker and moralist, Alain (pseudonym for Emile-Auguste Chartier). For Solmi, Alain's work offered a corrective to the systematization of thought of another writer who influenced him, the philosopher Benedetto Croce (who tended to lose sight of the particular for the universal, something Solmi rarely did). As Alberto Frattini noted in 1969—when writing of the Solmi-Alain connection—for Alain, "verità non può essere chequella vissuta integralmente dall'essere, che non separa, nella sua intenzione, conoscenza da sostanza, necessità da volontà" (truth cannot be other than that lived integrally by the human being, who doesn't separate, in his intention, knowledge from substance, necessity from will). Solmi's *Il pensiero di Alain* (The Thought of Alain, 1930) remains exemplary for its acuity and rigor. The book shows Solmi's independence of mind and intellectual curiosity (as well as his commitment to cultural discourse) in looking beyond Italy's heritage for understanding and enrichment at a time when few writers were doing so. Solmi's interest in Alain continued with his translation of Alain's *Cento e un ragionamenti* (One Hundred and One Reasonings) in 1960. The same open-minded quality that Solmi brought to Alain is also found in his *La salute di Montaigne* (1942), which also treats such authors as André Gide, Paul Valéry, Jean Cocteau, and the surrealists. Other French authors who interested him are indicated by the titles of later books, including *Saggio su Rimbaud* (Essay on Rimbaud, 1974) and *La luna di Laforgue*.

In addition to French literature, science fiction occupied Solmi throughout his later life. With Carlo Fruttero, Solmi edited the first Italian science-fiction anthology series, beginning with *Le meraviglie del possibile* (The Wonders of the Possible, 1959, 1961) and ending with *Il giardino del tempo* (The Garden of Time, 1983). Such Solmi poems as "Levania" (in the book of that name) and "Lamento del vecchio astronauta" (The Lament of the Old Astronaut)—in *Dal balcone*—also reflect his fascination with science fiction.

Beginning at least as early as 1926, Solmi translated the poetry of others. In 1963 he published *Versioni poetiche da contemporanei* (Poetic Versions of Contemporaries), a diverse collection ranging from the work of Valéry to that of Rafael Alberti, Cocteau, W. H. Auden, Antonio Machado, Stephen Spender, and Ezra Pound. He also edited and introduced the work of many other artists and authors. Solmi's lifelong interest in Italian writers, especially Leopardi, manifested itself in critical works as well as in excellent editions of Leopardi's works. Solmi's knowledge of other authors exerted a subtle but significant influence on his own writing.

Solmi's first important book of poetry, *Fine di stagione*, consists of twelve lyrics composed between 1924 and 1932, accompanied by prose pieces that were deleted in subsequent editions. These poems have lightness and strength, with references to Petrarch and, more especially, to Leopardi. According to Frattini (1969), "al mito dell'angoscia corrisponde il mito dell'infanzia perduta, simbolo di un irreversibile eliso" (the myth of anguish is developed alongside the myth of lost childhood, symbol of a never-to-be-regained Elysium). According to Giovanni Pacchiano, Solmi's poetry testifies to a life condemned to alienation, a life that swings between progression toward everyday existence and regression toward a prenatal state. Giacinto Spagnoletti, writing in 1985, sees an element of childlike wonder: Solmi mixes trust and irony in his verses and examines the interdependence of dream and reality. He moves between the real and the surreal, between the everyday and the cosmic.

Some of these elements are seen in the 1930 poem "Aeroplano." The location of the poet in space and the sense of his distance from earth (which the poem projects) prefigure aspects of "Levania" and "Lamento del vecchio astronauta." The speaker, immersed in routine work, is suddenly roused by the sound of an airplane; the sound draws his imagination upward, shifting his perspective to the sky. Like the plane, he is buoyed by the air, feeling embraced by it. He flies to the clouds and sees the earth anew

from above. The sky becomes a sea of space, and the poet remakes himself:

> Nell'ora sorda che i sogni preclude
> nella mia oscura agonia quotidiana,
> il tuo ronzare d'organo
> d'un balzo mi ridesta
> angelo di metallo a vele tese.
> All'alta tua dimora mi protendo
> alla tua solitudine librata
> oggi mi riassumi,
> dove, d'ogni suo peso denudata
> e d'ogni suo pensiero, ormai soltanto
> scandito spazio, vibrazione pura,
> fulmineo slancio immoto
> fatta è la vita, e la morte uno schianto.

> (In the deaf hour that precludes dream
> in my obscure daily agony,
> your organ droning
> reawakens me in one bound
> angel of metal with wings taut.
> To your high dwelling I stretch
> to your soaring solitude
> today you bring me once again,
> where, denuded of all weight
> and of every thought, now only
> scanned space, pure vibration,
> flashing immobile impulse
> this is life, and death a sudden great blow.)

"Sera al parco" (Evening at the Park, 1932) reflects the more frequent early crespuscular tone of Solmi's lyrics and registers his acceptance of failure:

> Sotto il vento deluso della sera
> che l'ora già densa schiarisce
> anche la fame con cui sono nato
> —oscuro vagheggiare di desii—
> morirà insoddisfatta.

> (Under the deluded evening wind
> which the hour already dense lightens
> even the hunger with which I was born
> —obscure yearning of desires—
> will die unsatisfied.)

Also in this poem the theme of disappointed waiting—a leitmotiv in Solmi's work—appears:

> Troppo mi sono illuso d'aspettarti
> o fiume smemorato della vita
> o selva adolescente, prodigiosa
> notte che sbianchi e t'allontani, e nulla,
> solo il tuo gelo estremo, in cuor mi lasci.

> (Too much have I been deceived waiting for you
> o forgetful river of life

o adolescent forest, prodigious
night that pales and withdraws, and nothing,
only your extreme chill, do you leave in my heart.)

In his second poetry collection, *Poesie*,
"Bagni popolari" (Public Baths, 1933) records a
shift, however tentative, away from abstraction
and isolation toward awareness of others and of
a shared human experience. The speaker expresses a sense of incommunicable otherness,
made painful by his desire for reconciliation:

Uomo che sfioro per la via col braccio
e sempre a me così paurosamente
estraneo, ti ritrovo
in questa bigia caserma, che grava
l'oscura sera di dicembre.
Tra gli scrosci dell'acqua, a mezza voce
un motivo tu accenni, ti fa eco,
invisibile, un altro.

Dal finestrino in sé raccolti tremano
gli alberi scarni del cortile.

(Man whom I graze on the street with my arm
and always to me so fearfully
extraneous, I meet you again
in these gray barracks, which weigh upon
the darkening evening of December.
Amid the sound of pouring water, in a half voice
you hum a tune, and to you echoes back,
invisible, another.

Outside the little window, assembled together,
the bare trees tremble in the courtyard.)

Here Solmi touches a theme he develops as
his poetry matures, that of humankind's destiny
to share an unknown fate, in "Bagni popolari"
an imprisoning one:

Dalla dura ubbidienza quotidiana
sciolte alfine le membra dentro il lene
bagno domenicale, prigionieri
rassegnati, la timida
libertà nostra in musica s'esala.

A mezza voce, finalmente insieme,
miei fratelli, cantiamo.

(From the hard daily obedience
the limbs are finally loosened in the gentle
Sunday bath, resigned
prisoners, our timid
liberty issues in music.

In a half voice, finally together,
my brothers, we sing.)

Cover for the 1974 collection of Solmi's poems

The sense of fraternity reappears in his
group of poems "Dal quaderno di Mario Rossetti" (From the Notebook of Mario Rossetti), especially in the title poem, written in 1945, the year
Solmi was jailed by the Fascists:

L'avvenimento ci somiglia. Traccia
un segno inconfondibile. Firmiamo
noi stessi la sentenza che temiamo.
E il destino ha l'eguale nostra faccia.

(The event resembles us. It traces
an unmistakable mark. We ourselves
sign the sentence that we fear.
And destiny has our same face.)

Other poems, such as "Ricordo" (Recollection, 1939) and "Aprile a San Vittore" (April in
Saint Victor Prison, 1945), develop the themes of
war, destruction, and solidarity. With World War
II impending, "Ricordo" recalls Solmi's youthful
traumatic experience in World War I:

A braccia aperte giacciono nel grano
verde i compagni, usciti di soppiatto

dal sogno, la terra
irta di fumi s'approssima, trema
la collina, crèpita
dai fossati la morte. Su un cratere
calvo, dove il mondo finisce
sventola un lembo di mascheramento
come lacera vela su un relitto.

(With open arms the companions lie in the green
grain, stealthily having left
the dream, the earth
bristling with smoke draws near, the hill
trembles, from the ditches
crackles death. On a bald
crater, where the world ends
flutters a strip of camouflage
like a tattered sail on a shipwreck.)

Even in the throes of war, however, the other
side of Solmi's spirit, a delight in life, appears in
"Aprile a San Vittore":

Grazie sien rese ai ciechi
iddii ridenti, che il poeta trassero
di morte e dalla nera muda al gaio
giorno del camerone dove cantano
i giovinetti partigiani.

(Thanks be given to the blind,
smiling gods, who delivered the poet
from death and the black prison to the joyous
day of the dormitory where
the young partisans sing.)

Solmi has moved stylistically from preciosity
to a more colloquial tone. But the fraternal experience of the war paradoxically left him afterward
with a clear, bitter awareness of his own difference and inevitable exile from his fellow man. In
"Giardini di Vercelli" (Vercelli Gardens, 1947),
set against the crystal noon hour, the poet's relationship to the objects of an unyielding world
threatens to undo itself because of his weakness.
The world stubbornly resists his desire to participate in that world. The speaker underscores his
sense of exclusion as he addresses not human beings, but things:

Per non sommergere
mi sforzo a nominarvi, cose: panca,
giornale, cattedrale. . . . Colorita
esistenza terrestre, a cui m'affaccio
di soppiatto, fugace testimone:
ma tu non fai che stare, t'allontani
dal diorama fiorito m'escludi.

(So as not to submerge
I force myself to name you, things: bench,
newspaper, cathedral. . . . Colored
terrestrial existence, to which I show myself
stealthily, fleeting witness:
but you do nothing but exist, you withdraw
from the flowering diorama you exclude me.)

In the final strophe of "Giardini di Vercelli" the
poet supposes a lost existence, in a warmer, more
restful land, to which it would take years to return:

Quale, di là di questo vago schermo,
quale terra perduta, quale nido
toccar di caldo sonno? Forse anni,
anni varcare, farmi
a una sepolta origine, fasciata
dalla notte. Al principio, ove una bianca
mano, nel quieto cerchio della lampada,
sfoglia le belle pagine del libro.

(Which, beyond this vague screen,
which lost world, which nest
to touch in warm sleep? Years, perhaps
years to cross, to return to a buried origin wrapped
by the night. To the beginning, where a white
hand, in the quiet circle of the lamp,
leafs through the beautiful pages of the book.)

This sense of distance from the objective
world and the notion of a preexistence elsewhere
take on epic dimensions in the title poem of
Levania, where the poet imagines a lunar arrival
in some "sepolta esistenza anteriore" (buried ante-
rior existence). He does not see the moon in
mythic or trusting terms, but as a remote sentinel
at the threshold of space. And his imagined early
journey there has left him with the desire to return to its silent light as hippogriph, rocket
("proiettile"), or spaceship. This moon is an absolute of existence:

il punto fermo apposto alla insensata
fantasia delle forme. Era lo zero
che ogni calcolo spiega, era il concreto,
bianco, forato calcinato fondo
dell'essere.

(the fixed point opposed to the insensate
fantasy of the forms. It was the zero
that every calculation explains, it was the concrete,
white, pierced limed bottom
of being.)

From this distanced vantage point the poet contemplates the green planet Earth, so far away, so
full of fleeting life.

In *Dal balcone* Solmi's poetry bears witness to the crisis of basic elements in his own formation and that of his generation: scientific positivism, critical idealism, and a "neo-Enlightenment" buttressing modern technology. Solmi's attitude ranges from perplexity to dismay. Modern emblems (seen earlier in his work as almost demonic forces) reveal themselves as signs of redemption from the mediocre and confused routine of daily events. Or these emblems become his new landscape of familiar existence, as Solmi attempts to decide between rejection and acceptance of a technocratic pride and myths of consumerism.

Within history's long reach backward and into the future, how does the poet see himself and his task? In "Dal balcone" he lives out his existence, one among a multitude, part of some unknown pattern:

E me, tra questi esseri
biforcuti a me simili, mandragore
affacendate all'orlo del lentissimo
verificarsi d'uno tra i miliardi
di possibili, ansante, faticoso
geroglifico, storia, che tracciamo
su questo duro quaderno di spazio
e di tempo, carattere incompiuto
di quale testo interminato?

(And me, among these forked
beings similar to me, mandrakes
busy on the edge of the very slow
coming to pass of one among the billions
of possibilities, breathless, exhausting
hieroglyph, history, which we outline
on this hard notebook of space
and time, unfinished character
of what incomplete text?)

The poet sees himself as:

la semiconsunta
puntina d'un esistere che stride
rauca, sul microsolco.

(the nearly worn out
needle of an existence that shrieks
hoarsely, on the microgroove.)

As he grew older, Solmi came closer to the world he observed, and he tried to express his relationship to that world. His openness toward new solutions extends to current cultural manifestations, with images and phrasing from advertising,

as in two 1962 poems in *Dal balcone*: "Letteratura e industria" (Literature and Industry) and "L'età dei semidei" (The Age of the Demigods). In "Letteratura e industria" Solmi uses striking images of modern times, such as the Condor petroleum refinery. His landscape is that of his times. No longer so alienated from the emblems of his age, he considers the Condor:

Un emblema
del paesaggio mio, del paesaggio
che ha cominciato a crescere
con me dentro i miei anni, in cui vivo,
in cui muoio.

(An emblem
of my landscape, of the landscape
that began to grow
with me in my years, in which I live,
in which I die.)

The integration with his environment, however, is not lasting. He oscillates between acceptance and alienation. In "L'età dei semidei" he recapitulates the emblems of his life and his century, from infancy to adulthood, to find himself lost among the new wonders of his waning years:

M'aggiro
sperso, sopravvissuto,
sordo tra i nuovi miracoli . . .

(I wander
lost, surviving,
deaf among the new miracles . . .).

The poet as astronaut in "Lamento del vecchio astronauta," intent upon rendering his interior experience of life, necessarily remains apart from much of daily living. The poem also suggests the scientific, mechanistic, engineering mentality of the astronaut, who leaves earth for long, lonely voyages, to return to face briefly his alienation from the simple joys of nature and human relations:

Che ho mai conosciuto
degli uomini, delle loro storie? Dicevano
che in un'ora del mio volo
sfiorivano, rinascevano
le ere, le civiltà. Ma non me sono mai accorto.

(What have I ever known
of men, of their stories? They used to say
that in an hour of my flight
withered and revived
eras, civilizations. But I was never aware of it.)

This lack of awareness about fundamental questions is developed further in "La scuola serale" (Evening School, 1963), a prose poem that quietly voices acceptance of ignorance about the meaning of life and shows solidarity with unknown, anonymous others who, like the poet, persist in the tasks assigned by an invisible authority. The poem, perhaps the culmination of Solmi's work, conveys a wearying inability to become independent and gain knowledge of life's ends:

>   Ma noi
> che sbagliammo tutti i sentieri, fino a che ci colse
> all'improvviso la sera, ci sforziamo di rimediare,
> anche se la luce discende, l'aritmetica ci propone
> calcoli sempre più astrusi, e non possiamo
> fare più assegnamento su manuali e prontuari.

>   (But we
> who took all the wrong paths, until evening
> suddenly caught us, we strive to make up lost time,
> even if the light fails, arithmetic presents us
> always more abstruse calculations, and we can
> no longer rely upon manuals and handbooks.)

"La scuola serale" shows the reversal of Solmi's sense of alienation from the human and objective world, an individual sense now canceled within the larger alienation of an entire age, to which all are subject. He sees himself as sitting with others, equally mystified as to the purposes of life's "curriculum." He is united with others in common subjection to "the (absent) teachers" who require that over and over again men attempt impossible tasks, while the enigmas of existence remain unanswered. Solmi sees himself as no longer alone in his ignorance and exclusion. Modern man, not simply an individual, has been isolated and excluded by the invisible operations of the forces he has unleashed.

Speaking of his varied prose pieces in his introduction to *Meditazioni sullo scorpione*, Solmi attributes to them the same quality he used to describe his poems:

> Se non vado errato, vi si può riconoscere un filo unitario proprio nel loro carattere ambiguo, bifronte, oscillante tra l'asciuttezza dell'aforisma ed il pieno abbandono al colore. Una tale duplicità è forse inerente al carattere-destino di chi le scrisse, e ad un grafologo—o ad una chiromante—che le leggessero in filigrana, denoterebbero probabilmente perplessità, esitazione e divisione interiore.

(If I am not mistaken, one can recognize a unifying thread here precisely in their ambiguous character, oscillating between the aphorism's dryness and a full abandon to color. Such a double nature is perhaps inherent in the character-destiny of him who wrote them, and to a graphologist—or to a fortune-teller—who would read them with utmost care by holding them up against a light the way one looks at a paper watermark, they would probably denote perplexity, hesitation and internal division.)

Solmi also offers insight into his poetry while distinguishing it from science fiction, saying that poetry "pone la condizione che il sogno abbia ad essere un sogno autentico, con radici reali, e che l'astrazione dell'ipotesi abbia ad imbeversi ed a colorisi del sentimento da cui germina" (posits the condition that the dream be an authentic one, with roots in reality, and that the abstraction of the hypothesis be imbued with and colored by the feeling from which it germinates). For Solmi the aspirations of the mind had to measure themselves against the integrity of the lived experience.

References:

Giorgio Bàrberi-Squarotti, *Poesia e narrativa del secondo Novecento* (Milan: Mursia, 1978), pp. 98-106;

Lanfranco Caretti, *Antichi e moderni* (Turin: Einaudi, 1976), pp. 425-452;

Caretti, "Lettura di Solmi," in *Novecento: I contemporanei: Gli scrittori e la cultura letteraria nella società italiana*, 11 volumes, edited by Gianni Grana (Milan: Marzorati, 1979-1982), VI: 5092-5107;

Giuseppe De Robertis, *Altro Novecento* (Florence: Monnier, 1962), pp. 349-353;

De Robertis, *Scrittori del Novecento* (Florence: Monnier, 1958), pp. 274-280;

Marco Forti, *Le proposte della poesia e nuove proposte* (Milan: Mursia, 1971), pp. 186-192;

Franco Fortini, "Da Ungaretti agli ermetici (I 'moderni' e l'eclettismo lirico)," in *Il Novecento: Dal decadentismo alla crisi dei modelli*, 10 volumes, edited by Fortini and others (Rome & Bari: Laterza, 1976), IX: 317-323;

Alberto Frattini, "Sergio Solmi: Classicismo stilistico, inquietudine esistenziale, stoicismo laico," in *La letteratura italiana: I contemporanei*, 6 volumes (Milan: Marzorati, 1969), III: 349-360;

Giovanni Pacchiano, "Ricordo di Solmi," in Solmi's *Poesie, meditazioni e ricordi* (volume 1 of

Opere), edited by Pacchiano (Milan: Adelphi, 1983), pp. 305-322;

Silvio Ramat, *Storia della poesia italiana del Novecento* (Milan: Mursia, 1976), pp. 435-438;

Giacinto Spagnoletti, *La letteratura italiana del nostro secolo*, 3 volumes (Milan: Mondadori, 1985), II: 542-546;

Spagnoletti, *Scrittori di un secolo*, 2 volumes (Milan: Marzorati, 1974), II: 731-742;

Donato Valli, "Sergio Solmi," in *Letteratura italiana contemporanea*, 4 volumes, edited by Gaetano Mariani and Mario Petrucciani (Rome: Lucarini, 1980), II: 319-325.

Delio Tessa

(18 November 1886 - 21 September 1939)

Elena Urgnani
Wheaton College

BOOKS: *L'è el dì di mort, alegher!* (Milan: Mondadori, 1932); enlarged and edited by Fortunato Rosti (Milan: All'Insegna del Pesce d'Oro, 1960); enlarged again and edited by Dante Isella (Turin: Einaudi, 1985);

Poesie nuove ed ultime, edited by Franco Antonicelli and Rosti (Turin: De Silva, 1947);

Scritti (Turin: De Silva, 1947; enlarged edition, 2 volumes, Turin: Einaudi, 1988);

Alalà al pellerossa: Satire antifasciste e altre poesie disperse, edited by Isella (Milan: All'Insegna del Pesce d'Oro, 1979);

Vecchia Europa, edited by Cristina Sacchi (Milan: Bompiani, 1986).

Delio Tessa, one of Italy's best-known dialect poets, was born in Milan on 18 November 1886 to Senio and Clara Besozzi Tessa. Senio Tessa was a bookkeeper. The young Delio attended the classical high school that was the most prestigious among middle-class, well-to-do families: the Liceo Beccaria. Subsequently he obtained a degree in law from the Università di Padova (Padua), was a lawyer without enthusiasm, and even became a justice of the peace.

During the 1920s Milan was still the official focal point of Italian culture and the cradle of almost every novelty. Arrigo Boito represented the heritage of the *scapigliatura* (free and easy) movement; the Italian theater had artists such as Marco Praga, Gabriele D'Annunzio, and Luigi Pirandello. Futurism was organizing its most provoc-

ative meetings and raising its popularity, despite the indignant reaction of much of the public.

Tessa lived detached from everything; he did not attend any particular meetings; he did not belong to any particular intellectual or political group. He was mostly a spectator, for his aristocratic haughtiness kept him away from those chaotic movements.

Since he had poor eyesight, he was able to avoid military service in World War I. At the end of the war there was an additional reason for his aloofness: his strong anti-Fascist feelings. He resented the vulgar methods of the regime's propaganda and rebelled against it on the basis of that common sense he liked to think he had inherited from his principal model, the writer Carlo Porta. Tessa was skeptical, sarcastic, and an enemy of intolerance. Those who were in contact with him would later recall that he was a very good reader of Porta's verses. He also started to attend some private meetings and was admitted to a few cultural circles. As a journalist, he contributed to newspapers and magazines of minor importance and made some radio broadcasts. He also wrote a movie script in the Milanese dialect, entitled *Vecchia Europa* (Old Europe), published in 1986.

In 1932, after many hesitations and much encouragement from his friends, he published his first collection of verses: *L'è el dì di mort, alegher!* (It's All Souls Day, Let's Be Happy!). It comprises nine Milanese-dialect lyrics. He had to be urged and encouraged to make this decision, but most of the fifteen hundred copies remained un-cal characteristics of the Milanese dialect is the dropping of all the final vowels except *a*, so that the consonants remain exposed and the syllabic volume is reduced.

Tessa's Milanese words are not found in the dictionary. It was the people's dialect he used and not the dialect of the social class to which he belonged. He collected about five hundred entries in his unpublished manuscript "Frasi e modi di dire del dialetto milanese" (Phrases and Idiomatic Expressions in Milanese Dialect), and most of the terms he employed will not be found in nineteenth-century dictionaries. It was neither the crystallized dialect used in the literary tradition nor the Milanese of the bourgeoisie.

Porta's work was usually influential in Tessa's writing, not only as a linguistic model but also as a stylistic one. Tessa even dedicated one of his poems to Porta—"A Carlo Porta" (in *Poesie nuove*):

> Contra i melanconij, contra i magon
> rezipe, el me zion,
> rezipe i rimm del Porta; el pà Carloeu
> dopo la gran pacciada
> per el Santo Natal . . . (e ravioeu,
> pollin, torron, mostarda) . . . in cà Marianna
> ultem piatt de portada—varda, varda
> l'è chì, largo, l'è chì!—pas e legria!!

> (Against melancholy, against sadness
> take, my dear uncle,
> take Porta's rhymes; papa Carlo
> after the big Christmas meal . . . [ravioli,
> chicken, torrone, mustard] . . . at the Mariannas' house
> last course—have a look
> it is here, make room, it is here
> grand and big!—peace and joy!!)

There is a point where Porta's and Tessa's lyrical techniques differ substantially: Porta has a methodology of narration that is linear, stretched out, and enriched by a cultured, middle-class, humorous comment. On the other hand, Tessa dissociates himself from Porta, that is from the Milanese tradition, because of the modernity of his narrative taste, which has little to do with linearity. When he tells a story, as for instance that of the prostitute in the "Poesia della Olga" (Olga's Poem; in *Poesie nuove*), he does so in an allusive way, with foreshortened sight, and he adopts a narrative mode of presupposing that the reader already knows the facts and is now able to understand the background and the intrigues—causing

Delio Tessa (drawing by an unknown artist; from Dizionario universale della letteratura contemporanea, *volume 4, edited by Alberto Mondadori, 1960)*

sold. From the publisher's point of view it was a failure, and the opposition of the state cultural organizations to his experiments with dialect significantly contributed to that result.

His second book, *Poesie nuove ed ultime* (New and Latest Poems, 1947), was published posthumously by his friends. Only five out of the twenty-one poems it contains had been approved by Tessa for publication. They were meant to be sent to a Swiss publisher; the others were added by his friends.

To be a Milanese poet, using the Milanese dialect, meant choosing to follow a literary tradition that is commonly recognized as dating back to the end of the seventeenth century and to Carlo Maria Maggi; it is a highly cultured tradition that flourishes on a parallel with the regular lyric tradition in the Italian language, but in vivacious confrontation with it. One of the phonologi-

the story to be told in a disordered manner, fusing comments and facts.

Pier Paolo Pasolini's opinion in analyzing Tessa's poetry is that his violence and desperation are much more influenced by G. G. Belli's poetry than by Porta's. Tessa's images, like Belli's, have their equivalent in the grandiose Roman baroque. It is an expressionistic vision: a reality continuously violated, dilated, and dramatized. The best label for Tessa is expressionist, the same one used for Oskar Kokoschka's portraits.

However, Tessa's sense of death is taken directly from the *scapigliatura* movement, as in the first poem in *L'è el dì di mort, alegher!*—"La pobbia de ca Colonnetta" (The Colonnettas' Poplar):

> L'è creppada la pobbia de cà
> Colonnetta: té chì: la tormenta
> in sto Luj se Dio voeur l'à incriccada
> e crich crach, pataslonfeta—la
> me l'à trada chì longa e tirenta,
> dopo ben dusent ann che la gh'era!
> L'è finida! eppur . . . bell' e inciodada
> lì, la cascia ancamò, la voeur nò
> morì, adess che gh' chì Primavera . . .
> andemm . . . nà . . . la fa sens . . . guardegh nò!

> (The poplar has died
> at the Colonnettas': here it is: the storm
> this July by God's will split it
> and crash, bang, gallumph
> brought it straight down,
> after it had been there for more than two hundred
>   years!
> It is all over! but . . . even stuck
> there, it's still sad, it doesn't want
> to die, now that Spring is here . . .
> let's go . . . away . . . it
> makes me feel bad . . . don't look at it!)

At other times death is present among living creatures, as in the poem "Caporetto 1917," written in 1919 and collected in his first book. The poem was defined by Tessa as "a nightmare from the past." It is All Souls' Day, and while it is getting dark the speaker returns to the city from the cemetery. An excited and thoughtless crowd is in the streets, unaware of the recent defeat of the Italian army at Caporetto. But suddenly the crowd's attitude changes: the Austrians are almost in Milan. Defeat and chaos are about to degenerate into an outburst of social hatred. The middle class is closing bank accounts. The vision of what is happening is almost physical:

> Torni da vial Certosa,
> torni di Cimiteri

> . . . .
> L'è el dì di Mort, alegher!
> Sotta ai topiett se balla,
> se rid e se bacalla;
> . . . .
> . . . a furia de batost
> tirom là . . . "Caldarost!"
> . . . e giò vers porta Volta,
> . . . .
> umed e nebbia . . . Ottober,
> cocober . . . pover nun!
> vun per vun, vun per vun,
> me perteghen i rogher!
> Oh Gesù, che sbiottada
> de piant! che pertegada
> là sù! Ottober . . . cocober! . . .

> (I'm coming back from Viale Certosa,
> I'm coming back from the cemetery
> . . . .
> It's All Souls' Day, let's be happy!
> People are dancing underneath the bowers,
> they are laughing and drinking;
> . . . .
> . . . blow after blow
> we go ahead . . . "Roasted chestnuts!"
> . . . and down on the way to Porta Volta,
> . . . .
> wet and fog . . . October,
> blockhead . . . poor us!
> one by one, one by one,
> my oak trees are beaten down!
> Oh Jesus, how naked
> are the trees! what a beating
> over there! October . . . blockhead! . . .).

This excerpt is more comprehensible if readers remember the popular Milanese proverb "Settember Ottober l'e el mes che se pertega i rogher" (September and October are the months that the oak trees are beaten down). Here it signifies the many human lives that are "harvested" by the war, among general indifference.

In the poem "La mort della Gussona" (Mrs. Gussoni's Death)—also in his first book—death is personified:

> dormiva fors
> quand l'oo vista quella vacca
> con la soa pedana stracca
> slontanà giò per el cors?

> No dormiva on crist . . . oh giusta . . .
> si . . . l'andava a tend el lazz
> a tant alter per i piazz,
> per i strad a batt la frusta . . .

(maybe she was sleeping
when I saw her, that bitch [Death]
with that tired pace of hers
going down the avenue?

No, the hell she was sleeping . . . oh, right . . .
yes . . . she was going to lay a snare
to many others on the squares,
on the roads cracking her whip . . .).

Death is represented as wandering around in the crowd and molesting passersby. Later the informal speech focuses on the image of poor Mrs. Gussoni, very old (almost ninety), but nevertheless still attached to life:

la Gussona, per esempi!
Quella povera veggetta
ghe n'à miss a fà spazzetta,
l'à patii pur anca! on scempi
. . . .
sorda pesg dell'avvocatt
Verga i dì che pieuv, e in fond,
orba, crincio, de sconfond
la Livietta cont el gatt!

Corno acustic, lavativ,
perucchina, caij, dentera,
cint erniari e ona filera
de quaresem maladiv!

(Mrs. Gussoni, for example!
That poor little old woman
took a long time before she passed away,
she was even suffering! What a slaughter
. . . .
more deaf than the lawyer
Verga when it rains, and after all,
blind, hell, so blind that she confused
little Livia with the cat!

Acoustic horn, enema,
wig, corns, denture,
truss, and a long list
of sickly Lents!)

It is a devastating and moving description of Mrs. Antonietta Gussoni, a neighbor for whom Tessa's father used to administer her few properties, collect her income, and pay the bills, since she could not leave her house anymore.

When Tessa writes about death, he does not only mean personal death but sometimes the death of hope, the death of moral values, or a generic putrescent atmosphere. In the second volume of his lyrics there is a strong focus on a particular Milanese neighborhood that was also well known to the *scapigliati*: the *naviglio*, an urban channel whose waters, once used to transport barges of sand from the suburbs into the city, were partially covered shortly before World War II. It still is one of the most characteristic areas of the "Old City." In Tessa's poetry the picture of those muddy city waters includes a surrounding crowd of drunkards and potential suicides, who become the epicenter of Milanese desperation. Thus death is not only physical—it could be moral, or it could simply be the death of a milieu: "Old Milan."

"La canzone della Olga" (Olga's Song) is emblematic of a sense of decadence. Olga is a successful procuress in charge of a renowned brothel. She has to send away a poor prostitute, who has now become too old to stay in the brothel. With sarcastic images Tessa presents a sense of the ineluctability of her departure. Later in the poem Olga herself is in her old age and can barely walk to go shopping. She is alone, and the children in the streets pull at her legs. She is an old bigot who walks close to the church walls. The poet assumes a playful attitude so as to avoid the pathetic tone that would otherwise come naturally out of a similar situation. A childish lullaby intermittently interrupts the description:

Dan—daran—dan Luzia . . .
sott a quell cassinott
ghe sta la veggia stria
che fa ballà i pigott . . .
dan—daran—dan Luzia!

la Cicì l'è malada, la po pu
fa qui basej di trenta volt al dì . . .
l'e quasi in sul finì . . . i pee la gh'à
che sdoloren . . . ghe tocca tegnij su
alt a la sira per podé requià!

(Dan—daran—dan Lucia . . .
underneath that hovel
stands the old witch
that makes the puppets dance . . .
dan—daran—dan Lucia!

Cici is sick, she can no more
climb those stairs thirty times a day . . .
she is almost at the end . . . her feet
hurt . . . she has to lift them
up in the evening so that she can rest!)

Tessa's use of Milanese dialect is extremely particular; he was so free in his use of the language as to make a parody of the "cultured" use of French among middle-class bourgeoisie, as in the poem "I cà" (The Houses), where he uses the juxtaposition of two voices: one is coming from the streets and is the terrible, desperate, and anguished scream of an unemployed laborer, while from the closed windows he is reached by voices from a middle-class family having dinner in the living-room:

"Demm de mangià.a.a!"
vosen . . . chi l'è?
"Demm de mangià.a.a! . . ."
vosen . . . la giò . . .

Fra on tram e on car
semper quell sgar! . . .
L'è on operari,
mi disi, "Demm
de lavorà.a.a! . . ."
on operari
chì della fabbrica,
de quij, magari,
ch'an lassaa a cà . . .

on desperaa!
. . . .
Vedritt . . . tendinn . . .
mauves ai finester . . .
a quella lus
d'ora—soo no
perché—
te disariet
che l'è ona sala . . .
Parlen: . . . *buffet* . . .
contrabuffet . . .
Sala-manger
della famiglia
polida . . . [emphasis added]

("Give me something to e.e.eat!"
someone's screaming . . . who's there?
"Give me something to e.e.eat!"
someone's screaming . . . down there . . .

Between a tram and a truck
always that scream! . . .
It is a workman,
I tell myself, "Give me
some wo.o.ork! . . ."
a workman
of the factory here,
one of those, maybe,
that have been left at home . . .

I am desperate! . . .
. . . .
crystals . . . *mauve*
curtains at the windows . . .
underneath that golden
light—I don't know

why—you would say
it is a dining room . . .
They are speaking: . . . *buffet* . . .
counterbuffet . . .
dining room
of the neat
family . . .).

Like a cinematographic procedure, the camera focuses first on the exterior, the streets, and then comes close to the internal scenario of the house, with the dinner table. The French terms accentuate the pretentious tone of the room.

Tessa's taste for colorful, onomatopoeic words is drawn from a symbolist, decadent tradition, with its implicit mistrust of the communicative power of denotative language. Though Pasolini refuses to call Tessa a *poète maudit* (damned poet), he does not deny the presence of some decadent influences, and it is easy to be reminded of Giovanni Pascoli's ornithological onomatopoeic words. However, what brings Tessa particularly close to the decadent movement is the prevalence in his poetry of the theme of death. He was also extremely concerned with musicality, and he even developed the habit of writing musical reading suggestions on the margin of his manuscripts, such as "pianissimo," or "allegro," stating exactly when and how the voice had to rise or fall.

Tessa died at the age of fifty-two, on 21 September 1939, with a premonition of the tragedy and horrors that World War II was about to bring. He could have escaped to Switzerland, where he had some friends, but he was tired and unmotivated. On 6 September he wrote to a friend that he had the feeling he had lived enough. A few days later he died of a tooth abscess—at that time there were no antibiotics or sulphamides available. He was surrounded by his friends: the painter Elisabetta Keller, Fortunato Rosti (with whom he had shared his office as a lawyer), and others. He had no family. The Fascist regime's opposition to any sort of dialectal culture, which was considered dangerous to national cohesion, prevented any major funeral, so that it was only ten years later that the municipality gave permission to transfer his tomb from the Cimitero di Musocco in the suburbs to the Famedio, in the cemetery of Milan. Today there is also a Milan street that bears his name.

References:
Benedetto Croce, "Poesia dialettale," *Critica* (20

March 1933): 249-250;

Franco Fortini, "Delio Tessa," in his *I poeti del Novecento* (Bari, Italy: Laterza, 1977), pp. 109-112;

Ferdinando Giannessi, "Delio Tessa," in his *Novecento*, 10 volumes (Milan: Marzorati, 1979), VI: 3672-3698;

Dante Isella, Introduction to *L'è el dì di mort,*

alegher! (Turin: Einaudi, 1985), pp. vii-xiii;

Giorgio Luti, "Delio Tessa," in his *Poeti italiani del Novecento* (Rome: Nuova Italia Scientifica, 1985), pp. 238-239;

Pier Paolo Pasolini, "La poesia dialettale del Novecento," in his *Passione e ideologia* (Milan: Garzanti, 1960), pp. 76-86.

Trilussa
(Carlo Alberto Salustri)
(16 October 1871 - 21 December 1950)

Antonio Vitti
Wake Forest University

BOOKS: *Le stelle de Roma* (Rome: Cerroni & Solaro, 1889); republished with *Poesie varie (1887-1889)* (Rome: Carra & Bellini, 1913);

Er mago de borgo; Lunario pe' 'r 1890 (Rome: Cicerone, 1890);

Er mago de borgo; Lunario romanesco pe' 'r 1891 (Rome: Lovesio, 1891);

Quaranta sonetti romaneschi (Rome: Voghera, 1895);

Altri sonetti (Rome: Folchetto, 1898);

Favole romanesche (Rome: Voghera, 1901; enlarged, 1904);

Caffè concerto (Rome: Voghera, 1901);

Er serrajo (Rome: Voghera, 1903);

Le favole (Rome: Voghera, 1908);

Sonetti romaneschi (Rome: Voghera, 1909);

I sonetti (Rome: Voghera, 1909);

Le storie (Rome: Voghera, 1913; revised edition, Milan: Mondadori, 1948);

. . . a tozzi e bocconi (Rome: Carra & Bellini, 1913);

Ommini e bestie (Rome: Voghera, 1914); republished with *Libro muto* and *Acqua e vino* (Milan: Mondadori, 1950);

La vispa Teresa (Rome: Voghera, 1917);

Le finzioni della vita (Rocca San Casciano & Bologna: Cappelli, 1918);

Lupi e agnelli (Rome: Voghera, 1919; revised edition, Milan: Mondadori, 1940);

Favole (Rome: Novissima, 1920);

Nove poesie (Rome: Voghera, 1920);

Le cose (Rome & Milan: Mondadori, 1922; enlarged, 1922);

Le favole fasciste (Rome: Giovanile, 1927);

Picchiabbò ossia la moje der ciambellano (Rome: Fauno, 1927);

La gente (Milan: Mondadori, 1927);

Libro no. 9 (Milan: Mondadori, 1930);

La porchetta bianca (Milan: Mondadori, 1930);

Er segreto der mago (Rome: Grafia, 1930);

Il buffone di Re Pipino (Picchiabbò) (Naples: Tirrena, 1930);

Campionario (Rome: Formiggini, 1931); abridged as *Campionario delle favole* (Rome: Colombo, 1943);

Pulviscolo (Rome: Formiggini, 1931);

Giove e le bestie (Milan: Mondadori, 1932; revised, 1940);

Cento favole (Verona & Milan: Mondadori, 1934);

Libro muto (Milan: Mondadori, 1935); republished with *Ommini e bestie* and *Acqua e vino* (Milan: Mondadori, 1950);

Cento apologhi (Verona & Milan: Mondadori, 1935);

Trilussa (Carlo Alberto Salustri)

Duecento sonetti (Verona & Milan: Mondadori, 1936);

Lo specchio; Altre poesie (Milan: Mondadori, 1938);

La sincerità e altre fiabe nove e antiche (Milan: Mondadori, 1939);

Trilussa, poeta di popolo (Rome: Mondini, 1945);

Acqua e vino (Milan: Mondadori, 1945); republished with *Ommini e bestie* and *Libro muto* (Milan: Mondadori, 1950);

Trilussa e la libertà, edited by Gustavo Brigante Colonna (Rome: O. E. T., 1947);

Tutte le poesie, edited by Pietro Pancrazi (Milan: Mondadori, 1951; enlarged, 1955);

Il castello dei sogni, edited and translated [into standard Italian] by Maria Arcangeli (Orvieto, Italy: Marsili, 1960);

Poesie scelte, 2 volumes, edited by Pietro Gibellini (Milan: Mondadori, 1970);

Disegni inediti, edited by Cecilia Pericoli Ridolfini (Rome: Galleria L'agostiniana, 1974).

Editions in English: *Roman Satirical Poems and Their Translation*, translated by Grant Showerman (New York: Vanni, 1945);

Fables from Trastevere, translated by Blossom Kirschenbaum (Woods Hole, Mass.: Pouboire, 1976).

Trilussa's dialect poetry shows the human comedy of everyday life of the Roman streets, filled with lower-middle-class people. The protagonists of his best poems are clerks, waiters, porters, maids, barbers, seamstresses, or aristocrats fallen from their social status. Large families inhabit filthy dwellings among the squalid sections of Rome; self-interest and the effort to survive make them resentful and hypocritical. Trilussa keeps an ironic distance from this world, depicting its essential outline without penetrating below its surface. His poetic investigation is photographic; it anticipates by fifty years the humor and tone of the cinematic sequences found in the Italian comedy of Cinecittà in the 1950s.

Carlo Alberto Salustri (who used the nom de plume Trilussa) grew up in what was then a predominantly agrarian city, dominated by the clergy and the landed aristocracy. After Rome became the new capital, the aristocracy got involved in construction, land development, and speculation. The lower classes who first lived on the land or in the outskirts of the city were exploited as manual labor for the new constructions. The middle class, involved in the appropriation of governmental public funds, competed for jobs in the new bureaucracy. The dominant classes were reinvesting the money earned from agriculture into building, while trying to prevent workers from forming political alliances as alternatives to existing problems. This process was undermined by speculation, corruption, and bank scandals, all of which had reduced the local people to mere spectators of events over which they had no control.

Because Trilussa grew up in this environment, he understood the political games and the manipulation by the dominant classes. He learned to tolerate these adverse conditions, and he confronted them sagaciously, without illusions. His poetic descriptiveness unveils the violation of all human respect and conduct, while his ideas on life mirror the everyday mentality of a cynical, lower-middle-class person, without any clear political ideology, as depicted in the poem "Ministro" (Minister) in *Ommini e bestie* (Man and Beasts, 1914):

Se sa: l'omo politico italiano
procura d'annà appresso a la corrente;

si lui nun ciriolava, certamente,
mica finiva cór potere in mano!

Perche da socialista intransiggente
un giorno diventò repubbricano,
poi doppo radicale e, piano piano,
sortì dar gruppo le fece er dissidente.

Adesso? E ricevuto ar Quirinale!
E, siccome è Ministro, non te nego
che sia 'na conseguensa naturale:

però non so capì co' che criterio
chiacchieri cór Sovrano, e nun me spiego
come faccia er Sovrano a restà serio!

(It is well known: the Italian politician
makes sure to follow the general trend;
if he were not so unreliable, surely he
would never hold any power!

Because from intransigent Socialist
he became one day Republican,
then later Radical and, little by little,
broke from the party and became a dissident.

And now? He is received at the Quirinal Palace!
And since he is a Minister, I can't deny
that it is a normal procedure:

nevertheless, I don't understand by what criterion
he can hold a meeting with the King; and I can't
    explain
how the King can keep a straight face!)

Trilussa's poetry has nothing in common with some of the major poetic trends of his time, such as the neoclassicism of Giosuè Carducci or the poetics of the *crepuscolari* (twilight poets). This fact as well as his use of Roman dialect contributed to the lack of critical attention given his poetry. It was not until 1936 that Trilussa was recognized nationally—when Arturo Galletti included him in his book *Il Novecento* (The Twentieth Century). Before this time the well-known literary critics had either completely disregarded his work or had harshly attacked him, as Giuseppe Antonio Borgese did in his *La vita e il libro* (1913). Trilussa's work represents a historicizing of a specific sociopolitical period and was intended to destroy any form of classicism, linguistic purism, or lyricism. Through the voices of his characters, Trilussa tries to celebrate the spirit and wit of the petite bourgeoisie. He remains attached to and attracted by the astuteness, the impudence, the wickedness, and the capacity to compromise of the Roman lower middle class. While his poetry never reaches the tone of the great mor-

e touches on sarcasm and cynicism but maintains a loving relationship with his characters. At times, Trilussa makes philosophical, pessimistic statements on human interaction in a playful manner, as in "L'amicizzia" (Friendship), from *Libro Muto* (Silent Book, 1935):

La Tartaruga aveva chiesto a Giove:
—Vojo una casa piccola, in maniera
che c'entri solo quarche amica vera,
che sia sincera e me ne dia le prove.
—Te lo prometto e basta la parola:
—rispose Giove—ma sarai costretta
a vive in una casa così stretta
che c'entrerai tu sola.

(A turtle asked Jupiter:
—I want a small house, so that
I can entertain only a few true friends
who are sincere and can prove it.
—I promise you and you can count on my word:
—answered Jupiter—but you will
be forced to live in such a small house
that only you yourself will be able to get in.)

Born on 16 October 1871, Trilussa was the son of a Roman waiter, Vincenzo Salustri, and a Bolognese seamstress, Carlotta Poldi Salustri. Trilussa's father died when the poet was only three, and Trilussa grew up in the aristocratic home of his godfather, Marquis Ermenegildo dei Cinque Quintili. After the death of Trilussa's little sister, Isabella, he moved with his mother into a small apartment on the fifth floor of his godfather's palace. He attended elementary school at Collegio San Giuseppe in Rome and then went on to the secondary school of Angelo Mai, where he failed twice. After dropping out of the Fratelli delle Scuole Cristiane at the age of sixteen, Trilussa published his first sonnet, "L'invenzione della stampa" (The Invention of Printing), which was published in the *Rugantino*, under the direction of the poet Giggi Zanazzo, with whom he began a long collaboration. Between the end of the nineteenth century and the first decade of the twentieth century, he wrote for almost all the satirical and humorist magazines of the capital, beginning to use the pseudonym Trilussa, which is an anagram of Salustri.

In 1889 he published his first collection of poetry, which was written in madrigals and titled *Le stelle de Roma* (Stars of Rome), in honor of twenty beautiful Roman women, and dedicated to his mentor, Zanazzo. The volume was reviewed by Filippo Chiappini, a follower of Gioacchino Belli, and a distinguished student of

A group of bohemian writers in 1900: seated are Romeo Carugati, Trilussa, and Alfredo Testoni.

Roman dialect, who accused Trilussa of not knowing the true Roman dialect spoken in the Trastevere section of the city. Although one year later Trilussa also repudiated his first book, it was for stylistic rather than linguistic reasons. Trilussa's language is that used by the petite bourgeoisie who live in small apartments in the Prati quarters or in Piazza Vittorio.

Trilussa's work resembles more closely that of his contemporary Cesare Pascarella than it does Belli's. Pascarella had concluded, in writing *La scoperta de L'America* (The Discovery of America, 1894), that, given the new historical situation, it was impossible to imitate Belli's Roman dialect. Rome had completely changed since the days of Belli, when it was under the papacy of Pope Gregory XVI. In the late nineteenth century Rome was the capital of the newly founded Italian state. The Roman middle class wanted to learn how to speak standard Italian, hoping to gain positions in the state bureaucracy. Trilussa's linguistic interest lies with this class, of which he was a member. Thus, the stylistic differences between Pascarella and Trilussa are mainly linked to the linguistic stratification of their social classes, the latter being more popular than the former. Belli,

on the other hand, lived in a different historical context and also had a different poetic temperament and personality. His Roman dialect can be understood only with the help of a special Roman vernacular dictionary. Trilussa's language is basically southern Italian lightly coated with Roman dialect. Because of these particular linguistic characteristics, Trilussa can be considered and read as the only major Italian poet attempting to write on an intellectual level from a lower-middle-class perspective without assuming an anti-bourgeois stance. Trilussa's poetry is included in the long tradition of Italian dialect poetry, and specifically within the Roman dialect mode. The Roman dialect also has a long written tradition, which started in the sixteenth century, reaching its apogee with Belli's sonnets. Trilussa's poetry, before being accepted for its own merit, was compared to Belli's poetry. Although it is true that Trilussa does not have the poetic impetus of Belli, he can be appreciated as the poet of events that become current at any reading. The modernity of Trilussa lies in his undeniable ability to catch the hidden merits and vices of humanity. Trilussa describes human nature without moral judgment or glorification, as he observes it in "Chiaroscuro," collected in *Acqua e Vino* (Water and Wine, 1945):

Giustizia, Fratellanza, Libbertà . . .
Quanta gente ridice 'ste parole!
Ma chi le vede chiare? Iddio lo sa!

Er Gallo canta quanno sponta er sole
er Gufo canta ne l'oscurità.

(Justice, Brotherhood, Liberty . . .
How many people say these words over and over!
But who really understands them? God only knows!

The Cock crows at dawn,
the Owl hoots in the darkness.)

Trilussa's poetic corpus developed into two different stylistic forms: that of the allegorical fable exemplified by *Ommini e bestie, Lupi e agnelli* (Wolves and Lambs, 1919), and *Favole* (Fables, 1920); and that of the more photographic and vignette-like form of his *I sonetti* (The Sonnets, 1909), *La gente* (The People, 1927), and *Libro no. 9* (Ninth Book, 1930). Regardless of form, Trilussa's work was a continuous effort to point out political cover-ups. With the exception of a few poems, written or dedicated to his family, friends, or specific situations, most of his poetry was inspired by the events of his lifetime and is set in Rome. He left Rome only twice, going to Egypt in 1914 with his friend the actress Leda Gys, and traveling to Brazil in 1924.

Trilussa's work is never cerebral, reflective, or speculative. Unlike that of his Roman contemporaries, such as Giggi Zanazzo, Giovanni Monaldi, and Luigi Chiarelli, Trilussa's art lies in his capacity to go beyond stereotypes and sketches of a typical street situation. His greatest strength is the perfect re-creation and understanding of the humor of his class, tinged with pessimism and skepticism. Trilussa does not believe in the human ability to change reality radically, but he views humankind as prone to compromises and mere acceptance of the status quo. During his youth he saw the newly formed state inherit the cultural stagnation of the former papal state. The new political leaders simply labeled the problems differently without making changes to the social conditions. This view is expounded in Trilussa's "Giordano Bruno," included in *I sonetti*:

In oggi, co' lo spirito moderno,
se a un Papa je criccasse d'abbruciallo
pijerebbe l'accordi cór Governo.

(In these modern times,
if a Pope wishes to burn someone at the stake,
the government must concur.)

One of Trilussa's first targets was Giovanni Giolitti, and when this subject became redundant, Benito Mussolini's Fascist state provided Trilussa an impetus to renew his biting and pungent sarcasm. Under fascism Trilussa reached the peak of his popularity and fame. Although Trilussa always claimed that he was not a Fascist, his opposition to the dictatorship was never based on deep political convictions, but rather on a strong protest against abusive power that utilized fear as a controlling force. Thus, Trilussa, despite his sarcastic tone toward Fascist policies, was allowed to publish, because his criticism was light and could be used by the regime's propaganda to show that freedom of expression was preserved in Italy.

In 1922 Mondadori started a systematic publication of all Trilussa's works. During the same year, he was selected to join the Arcadia under the pseudonym previously given to Belli: Tibrindo Plateo. Trilussa's simple and unpresumptuous manners did not change. He preferred to stay with his old friends in the Roman taverns rather than become a member of the Roman circle of intellectuals, which included Gabriele D'Annunzio and Luigi Pirandello, habitués of Caffè Aragno. Trilussa never visited Grazia Deledda or even Pascarella.

The newly imposed Fascist censorship worked to Trilussa's advantage. Even though, in 1927, twenty-three fables by Trilussa were published under the title *Le favole fasciste* (Fascist Fables), Trilussa was never a Fascist, and, unlike so many other intellectuals of the time, he refused the party membership card. Forced to mock the new regime subtly, his verses became increasingly mordacious and his popularity increased. His jibes at fascism were taken up by the common people, who looked on him as the spokesman for their personal frustrations. Having been the chronicler of Umbertine Rome, he facily put on the mantle of acerbic commentator on fascism. Commenting on the regime and on the innovations promised by Mussolini, Trilussa wrote in "Tinte" (Colors), collected in *Acqua e vino*:

Un Sorcio, che correva a più nun posso
pe' nun fasse acchiappà da un Micio rosso,
s'intrufolò de dietro a un cassabbanco
dove c'era accucciato un Micio bianco.
Lì pure la scampò; ma verso sera
cascò fra l'ogne d'una Micia nera.

Caricature of Trilussa (from Dizionario universale della letteratura contemporanea, volume 4, edited by Alberto Mondadori, 1960)

—Purtroppo—disse allora—o brutta o bella,
la tinta cambia, ma la fine è quella.

(A Mouse, that was running as hard as he could
to escape from a red Cat,
hid behind a chest
where a white Cat was sleeping.
There he was safe, too; but toward evening
a black Cat pounced on him.
—Unfortunately—said he—whatever the color,
ugly, or beautiful, the outcome is the same.)

Trilussa's sarcasm became increasingly bitter and resentful during the Ethiopian campaign (1935) and after the 1938 racial laws were passed, under the direct influence of Germany. In defense of black Ethiopians he wrote "Questione de Razza" (On the Race Question)—in the collection *Libro muto*—in which he affirms

that color is not as important as the good will of people. In regard to the racial laws, he wrote "L'affare della Razza" (The Race Question) in *Acqua e vino*. In this poem a cat named Ajò is taken to a high police official to find out if it is secure from racial persecution. The owner is willing to change its name to Ajù and is also prepared to show that its mother is an Angora cat and its father is a Siamese. The difficulty is that the cat's mother used to visit the ghetto too often and that he was born only three months after his parents mated. After listening to the story, the high police official concludes that the cat is a true Aryan, but, to be more certain, he recommends having its name changed to Ajà. The last word is a subtle pun on fascism: "Ajà" is what the *squadristi's* shouted to reaffirm their faith, at the end of a hymn in honor of Il Duce.

Perhaps the sonnet that exemplifies more closely what life was like in Italy under fascism is "Difetto de pronunzia" (Mispronunciation)—also contained in the collection *Acqua e vino*. In this poem the king, after making the rounds of his palace, asks what happened to the parrot that used to yell "Long live liberty." One of the servants replies that the bird has broken its beak trying to break the chain on his claw:

Mó sta avvilito, povera bestiola,
e ogni vorta che chiacchiera, s'ingrifa:
invece de di "viva" dice "fifa" . . .
e 'r rimanente je s'incastra in gola.

(The poor little animal is disheartened now,
every time he tries to talk, he gets mixed up:
instead of saying "viva" he says "fear". . .
and the rest gets caught in his throat.)

In 1945 Trilussa published *Acqua e vino*. Most of the poems were written in the mid 1930s. Their tone reflects the destitute state in which Trilussa was living. Asthma had forced him to stop drinking his beloved Frascati wine. Rosa Tomei was the last person and companion left at his side. He lived a life away from all the public and political events reshaping the new Italian republic. On 21 December 1950 Trilussa died in Rome, only twenty days after he had been appointed senator for life by President Luigi Einaudi.

Trilussa was an excellent dialect poet who was a chronicler of his period and his social class. He saw reality in a Machiavellian sense: self-interest and self-preservation triumph over any higher sense of morality or values. Trilussa's characters embrace this sense of philosophy in fulfilling their immediate gratification. Life becomes a comedy in which everyone knows his role and plays it with a cynicism that springs from the knowledge that circumstances are immutable. To these characters progress is seen as a form of deceitful illusion. Trilussa believed that historical changes would never transform human nature. Humans will go on, driven by their survival instincts and their sexual drives. Justice and honesty are merely constructs for self-serving purposes. Humankind is a will-o'-the-wisp, poised to adapt ideals, convictions, or morality itself at any time for personal gain. Humans conceal their different interpretation of social events through the manipulation of refined language and euphemisms. For Trilussa life was a stage for marionettes, and only when the strings are not pulled do people appear as equals. "La strada mia" (My Street), in *Acqua e vino*, succinctly presents the essence of Trilussa:

> La strada è lunga, ma er deppiù l'ho fatto;
> so dov'arrivo e nun me pijo pena.
> Ciò er core in pace e l'anima serena
> der savio che s'ammaschera da matto.
>
> Se me frulla un pensiero che me scoccia
> me fermo e bevo e chiedo ajuto ar vino:
> poi me la canto e seguito er cammino
> cor destino in saccoccia.

> (The road is long, but I have traveled most of it;
> I know what awaits me and I don't worry about it.
> My heart is at peace and my soul is serene
> like the wise man who passes himself off as a fool.

> If a disturbing thought crosses my mind,
> I stop for a drink and I console myself with wine:
> then I go happily on my way
> with destiny in my hand.)

Biographies:

Silvio D'Amico, *Trilussa* (Rome: Formiggini, 1925);

Mauro De Falco, *Trilussa e la sua opera poetica* (Naples: Chiurazzi, 1935);

Mario Dell'Arco, *Lunga vita di Trilussa* (Rome: Bardi, 1951);

Giuseppe D'Arrigo, *Trilussa: Il tempo, i luoghi, l'opera* (Rome: Tipolitografia Spada, 1968);

Ettore Paratore, *Trilussa nel centenario della nascita* (Rome: Istituto di Studi Romani, 1972);

Gaetano Mariani, *Trilussa: Storia di un poeta* (Rome: Bonacci, 1974).

References:

Giovanni Orioli, *Letteratura italiana: I contemporanei* (Milan: Marzorati, 1963), I: 159-171;

Pietro Pancrazi, Preface to *Tutte le poesie di Trilussa*, edited by Pancrazi (Milan: Mondadori, 1951), pp. xvii-xxxiii;

Ettore Paratore, "Trilussa," in *Novecento: I contemporanei*, edited by Gianni Grana (Milan: Marzorati, 1979), IV: 3619-3654;

Pier Paolo Pasolini, *Passione e ideologia* (Milan: Garzanti, 1960), pp. 59-84;

Leonetta Cecchi Pieraccini, *Visti da vicino* (Florence: Vallecchi, 1952), pp. 109-115;

Leonardo Sciascia, *Il fiore della poesia romanesca* (Caltanissetta & Rome: Sciascia, 1952), pp. 77-99;

Pietro Paolo Trompeo, *Il lettore vagabondo* (Rome: Tumminelli, 1942), pp. 251-257.

Giuseppe Ungaretti

(8 February 1888 - 2 June 1970)

Douglas Radcliff-Umstead

BOOKS: *Il porto sepolto* (Udine, Italy: Stabilimento Tipografico Friulano, 1916);

La guerre (Paris: Etablissements Lux, 1919);

Allegria di naufragi (Florence: Vallecchi, 1919);

Il porto sepolto (La Spezia, Italy: Apuana/Serra, 1923);

L'Allegria (Milan: Preda, 1931; revised edition, Rome: Novissima, 1936); enlarged as *Allegria di Ungaretti*, edited by Annalisa Cima (Milan: Scheiwiller, 1969);

Sentimento del tempo (Florence: Vallecchi, 1933);

Vita d'un uomo: part 1, 6 volumes (Milan: Mondadori, 1942-1954); part 2, 3 volumes (1946-1950); part 3, 3 volumes (1961-1974); selections translated by Allen Mandelbaum as *Life of a Man* (London: Hamilton/New York: New Directions, 1958); enlarged as *Selected Poems* (Ithaca, N.Y.: Cornell University Press, 1975);

Frammenti per la terra promessa (Rome: Concilium Lithographicum, 1945);

Derniers jours: 1919 (Milan: Garzanti, 1947);

Il povero nella città (Milan: Meridiana, 1949);

La terra promessa (Verona & Milan: Mondadori, 1950);

Pittori italiani contemporanei, trilingual edition [Italian, French, and English] (Bologna: Cappelli, 1950);

Gridasti soffoco (Milan: Fiumara, 1951);

Un grido e paesaggi (Milan: Schwarz, 1952);

Il taccuino del vecchio, edited by Leone Piccioni (Milan: Mondadori, 1960);

Il deserto e dopo (Milan: Mondadori, 1961);

75° compleanno: Il taccuino del vecchio; Apocalissi (Milan: Le Noci, 1963);

Ungaretti: Poesie, edited by Elio Filippo Accrocca [includes recording] (Milan: Nuova Accademia, 1964);

Viaggetto in Etruria (Rome: ALUT, 1965);

Il Carso non è più un inferno (Milan: All'Insegna del Pesce d'Oro, 1966);

Fontane d'Italia (Rome: Editalia, 1967);

Morte delle stagioni (Turin: Fógola, 1967);

Giuseppe Ungaretti

Dialogo, by Ungaretti and Bruna Bianco (Turin: Fógola, 1968);

Innocence et mémoire, translated [into French] by Philippe Jaccottet (Paris: Gallimard, 1969);

Croazia segreta (Milan: M'arte, 1970);

302

L'impietrito e il velluto (Rome: Grafica Romero, 1970);

Per conoscere Ungaretti, edited by Piccioni (Milan: Mondadori, 1971);

Lettere a un fenomenologo (Milan: All'Insegna del Pesce d'Oro, 1972);

Saggi e interventi, edited by Mario Diacono and Luciano Rebay (Milan: Mondadori, 1974);

Invenzione della poesia moderna (Naples: Scientifiche Italiane, 1984).

Edition in English: *Selected Poems*, translated and edited by Patrick Creagh (Harmondsworth, U.K.: Penguin, 1971).

TRANSLATIONS: *Traduzioni* (Rome: Novissima, 1936);

XXII Sonetti di Shakespeare (Rome: Documento Editore Libraio, 1944);

Stéphane Mallarmé, *L'Après-Midi et le Monologue d'un Faune* (Milan: Balcone, 1947);

"*Andromaca* di Jean Racine, Atto III," *L'Approdo Letterario*, 4 (January-March, 1958): 40-62;

Murilo Mendes, *Finestra del caos* (Milan: Scheiwiller, 1961);

Visioni di William Blake (Milan: Mondadori, 1965);

Saint-John Perse, *Anabase*, translated by Ungaretti and T. S. Eliot (Verona: Le Rame, 1967);

"*Frammenti dall'Odissea* di Omero," *L'Approdo Letterario*, 42 (1968);

"Il prato e nuove note su Fautrier di Francis Ponge," *L'Approdo Letterario*, 43 (1968);

Ezra Pound tradotto (Milan: Scheiwiller, 1968).

When the soldier Giuseppe Ungaretti saw his first volume of poetry, *Il porto sepolto* (The Buried Port), published in 1916, Italian writers and artists were in the process of restoring their nation to cultural prominence. Creative young Italians were reviving an appreciation for Italy's artistic and literary traditions. After World War I that appreciation influenced the founding of the Roman cultural journal *La Ronda*—issued from April 1919 to November 1922 and then in a special number in December 1923—with its goal of preserving past glories amid modernity. Vincenzo Cardarelli, editor in chief of *La Ronda*, looked back to a classical model for Italian poetry and prose before the time of the nation's unification, rejecting post-1860 writers such as Giosuè Carducci, Giovanni Pascoli, and Gabriele D'Annunzio in favor of Giacomo Leopardi. Ungaretti was to be one of the contributors to *La Ronda*, and he would exalt the works of Leopardi as a poetry of eternal remembrance and a prose of infinite discovery. Throughout Ungaretti's career as a poet he would move from the metrical and syntactical radicalism of futurists and modernists to the lyrical traditions of Leopardi and Petrarch in order to transform the modern into the eternally classical.

In mediating between modernists and traditionalists Ungaretti initially sought a verbal reductionism that stripped away the rhetorical excess of lyricists such as D'Annunzio to produce a laconic style of verse brought to pristine purity. It is as if the poet acted like a sculptor, a modern Michelangelo, to chisel away at the granite and marble of language to liberate images from static imprisonment. Ungaretti describes his early method as one of excavating, as stated in his poem "Commiato" (in *Il porto sepolto*):

Quando trovo
in questo mio silenzio
una parola
scavata è nella mia vita
come un abisso

(When I find
in this silence of mine
a word
it is dug into my life
like an abyss).

Ungaretti originally aspired toward a poetry of intense condensation, a telegraphic style of concision. He aimed at concentrating on an object to free all its lyrical reverberations and carry it to its fullest philosophical dimensions. From the primitivism of his first poems Ungaretti would turn in time to complex syntax and traditional meters. Frequently focusing on isolation, Ungaretti's poetry marks an attempt to overcome the alienation of humankind in the twentieth century as it points out the tension between the self and the world in the void of existential identity. The abyss represents a failure of willpower and the surrender to oblivion. Ungaretti's mythopoetic process becomes a unifying act of cognition, a synthesis of a multitude of recurring patterns in the universe captured in flashing dreams, intuitions, or insights. With an ideal of self-creation his works pursue a quest for a *paese innocente* (innocent land) or promised homeland. Progressing from the modernism of his earliest verse, Ungaretti would seek inspiration from cultural ancestors such as Virgil, Petrarch, and Leopardi to follow that spiritual journey.

Critics have customarily labeled Ungaretti's poetry as being hermetic. The Crocean literary critic Francesco Flora in his *La poesia ermetica* (1936) attacked Ungaretti's verse as being esoteric, obscurantist, born of strained analogies, and closed to genuine lyrical experience. To Flora, the impressionism of the poet's works reflects a gulf between art and life in the breakdown between sign and referent as it corresponds to an escape of the individual into himself; Ungaretti's elliptical style seems suffused with artificiality. As has often happened with labels, in time they lose their derogatory force and instead continue on to indicate a major school or trend in literature and art, such as impressionism in painting. Consequently the term *hermetic* stands for the poetry of Ungaretti, Eugenio Montale, the early Salvatore Quasimodo, and some others in their attempt to create "pure," naked verse free of false rhetoric. Ungaretti's hermeticism consists of expressing poetic substance through the fulminations of lightning-flash imagery, a poetry of allusions forever escaping the banality of simplistic statement.

Ungaretti was born on 8 February 1888 in Alexandria, Egypt, of Italian parents from Lucca, Tuscany. The father, Antonio Ungaretti, a construction worker, died in an accident in 1900, and his widow, Maria Lunardini Ungaretti, was left alone to rear the two children. Alexandria during the fin-de-siècle era was a cosmopolitan center, the major naval base for the British in the Mediterranean, and an outpost of French culture. Ungaretti, living in the Arab quarter, where his mother operated a bakery, was torn between attraction to his exotic native city and recognition of his Italian heritage. From 1904 to 1905 he attended the Ecole Suisse Jacot, an elitist French upper school, where he became acquainted with the main currents of contemporary European culture. Throughout Ungaretti's life French remained his second language. In Alexandria's anarchist circle he made the acquaintance of the novelist and political radical Enrico Pea. Despite Ungaretti's fascination with Alexandria's colorful Middle Eastern atmosphere, he longed to discover his European identity while forever considering himself a bedouin nomad at heart.

Finally in 1912 the future poet traveled to Paris by way of Italy. Studying at the Sorbonne brought him in contact with the philosopher Henri Bergson. Above all the young Ungaretti passionately studied writers such as Charles-Pierre Baudelaire, Stéphane Mallarmé, and Arthur Rimbaud for their revolutionary attempt to transform language into a magical alchemy of poetic discoveries. From the works of André Gide he learned the doctrine of active availability or receptivity (*disponibilité*) to powerful sensations of experience. As a personal friend of the poet Guillaume Apollinaire, Ungaretti shared the appreciation for constant experimentation with verse form. The period of his education in Paris coincided with the explosion of the modernistic "isms" in the fine arts: cubism with Georges Braque and Pablo Picasso; fauvism with Henri Matisse; and futurism with Carlo Carrà. Because of Ungaretti's immersion in French culture he composed his earliest poems in French. But Paris also brought him the opportunity to meet the Italian avant-gardists Giovanni Papini and Ardengo Soffici, who invited him to have his poems published in their futurist journal *Lacerba*. Even in Egypt, Ungaretti had become aware of the currents of experimentalism in Italian literature through reading Giuseppe Prezzolini's journal *La Voce*. While in Paris, Ungaretti definitively established his European artistic character; military service in World War I was to determine the depth of his devotion to the cause of Italian culture.

With Italy's entry into hostilities in May 1915 on the side of the Western Allies, Ungaretti volunteered to fight in the Italian army. He spent most of his active service on the rugged Carso plateau on the front line against the Austrian forces. In moments of leisure he would jot down poems on backs of envelopes and other slips of paper. A friend, Lt. Ettore Serra, arranged for the limited-edition publication of Ungaretti's collected poems in *Il porto sepolto*. Despite all the confusion and the devastation brought on by the war Italians still persisted in affirming their nation's tradition of artistic creativity. As many of Ungaretti's poems of that period testify, out of the horror of combat arose illuminating moments of human solidarity.

Shortly before the war's end Ungaretti's regiment moved to France. By the time of the Armistice he reached Paris hoping to greet Apollinaire, only to learn of his friend's death. As a survivor Ungaretti acknowledged his responsibility to voice not only the pain of his generation but also its hopes. However, like most Italians following the end of the war and the signing of the Treaty of Versailles, he shared a sense of disillusionment. Italy failed to received all the unredeemed territories for which it had fought.

Frequently soldiers returning home to cities in northern and central Italian industrial-commercial regions met a hostile reception from socialist agitators intent on gaining political control of the nation. In the midst of the deteriorating social and political situation Benito Mussolini and the Fascist party seemed to offer a way to reestablish order and bring about justice for the tormented country. By 1919 Ungaretti became the Paris correspondent for Mussolini's newspaper *Popolo d'Italia*. That same year saw the publication of Ungaretti's volume of Italian poems titled *Allegria di naufragi* (Joy of Shipwrecks), and the printing of his book of French verse called *La guerre* (The War). In 1920 he married a Frenchwoman, Jeanne Dupoix. They eventually had a daughter, Anna Maria, and a son, Antonietto.

In 1921 the couple settled in Rome, where Ungaretti found employment in the press division of the foreign ministry. The opportunity to visit monuments of baroque architecture left a powerful impression on him; he recognized the sense of apocalyptic catastrophe that had oppressed artists such as Michelangelo at the end of the optimism and confidence in human ability characteristic of the Renaissance. Living in Rome also permitted Ungaretti to meet members of the *La Ronda* editorial staff such as Emilio Cecchi. After the Fascist coup d'état of late 1922, the suppression of all other political parties in 1925 (thus ending parliamentary democracy but also eliminating the political chaos of splinter group coalitions), and the return to dynamic stability, which brought Italy international respect, Ungaretti expressed the euphoria felt by many of his compatriots in the essay "Originalità del fascismo" (*Popolo d'Italia*, June 1927) celebrating the exciting era of restoration inaugurated by Il Duce. In the atmosphere of increasing accord between church and state in Italy, Ungaretti abandoned his free-thinking sentiments to become a convert to Catholicism in 1928. While continuing to write and publish poems, Ungaretti persisted in his journalistic endeavors, and by 1930 he assumed the duties of foreign correspondent for the Turinese newspaper *Gazzetta del Popolo*.

During the 1930s many of Italy's most gifted and sensitive writers made themselves voluntary exiles to escape the growing spirit of mediocre conformity under the Fascist dictatorship. Alberto Moravia, for example, spent a great deal of the decade in journalistic travels to France, England, Greece, the United States, Mexico, and China. Even Luigi Pirandello, who had joined

Drawing of Ungaretti by Luigi Bonichi, known as Scipione (Collezione Enrico Falqui, Rome; from Storia della letteratura: Italiana, *volume 6, edited by Luigi Ferrante, 1965)*

the Fascist party at one of its most difficult political moments and had at first enjoyed Mussolini's favor, kept moving from country to country for premieres of his plays as he felt his innovative dramas coming under increasingly bitter attacks by the official Fascist press. But Ungaretti's travels as a foreign correspondent and a lecturer on Italian literary tradition, to countries such as Belgium, Holland, Spain, Switzerland, Czechoslovakia, and Argentina, reflected professional pursuits rather than dissatisfaction with the political and cultural milieu in Italy. A year after the publication of his *L'Allegria* (1931) he received Venice's Premio Gondoliere, the beginning of a long list of awards for his contributions to literature.

From 1936 to 1942 Ungaretti held the Chair of Italian Literature at the Universidade do Saõ Paulo in Brazil. The controversy stirred by the publication of his volume of poems *Sentimento del tempo* in 1933, with accusations of hermetic obscurantism, had catapulted him to the forefront of Italian poets, a role he did his utmost to promote through his selection of publishers and editors to advance his cause. Because of his sojourn in Brazil he avoided living through the ugly phase of Fascism during its alliance with Nazi Germany following Italy's conquest of Ethiopia in 1935 and 1936. But his years in Brazil proved to be unhappy. In 1937 his brother, Costantino, who had remained in Alexandria, died. Then in 1939 Ungaretti suffered the loss of his nine-year-old son, Antonietto, to a poorly diagnosed case of appendicitis. The desolation of that period is expressed in the poems of *Il Dolore* (Grief), published in 1947—volume four of part 1 of *Vita d'un uomo* (1942-1974; translated in part as *Life of a Man*, 1958). Ungaretti's exile ended in 1942 after the Italian government named him to the Academy of Italy and invited him to assume the Chair of Modern Italian Literature "per chiara fama" (for bright fame) at the University of Rome. He returned to a country on the brink of collapse after losing its East African empire. He was there during the period that saw the 1943 coup, which ended Mussolini's first reign with Marshal Pietro Badoglio's provisional government, and then the German occupation of Rome until its liberation by the Allies in June 1944. An era that had started with the brash self-confidence of renewal ended in the violence of warfare and political treachery.

After the war, Ungaretti struggled to reach an understanding of his physical limitations as he was growing older and facing death. His previously uncollected poems were published in the 1945 volume *Poesie disperse*—volume three of the first part of *Vita d'un uomo*. Two years later he managed to survive that time of intolerance when various professors accused of Fascist loyalty lost their university posts, retaining his chair by exonerating himself of complicity with the dictatorship. His poetic vision of Italy found partial realization in 1950 with *La terra promessa* (The Promised Land).

Despite failing health he persisted in his nomadic travels throughout the final two decades of his life. Many of his earlier travel sketches for newspapers were gathered in the 1961 book *Il deserto e dopo* (The Desert and Afterward). The death of his wife in 1958 led him to the frenetic journeys, such as a round-the-world trip in 1960, that were an effort to distract him from his loneliness. His lyrical productivity remained uninterrupted, albeit less insightful and original than in

the period prior to 1950, and included *Un grido e paesaggi* (An Outcry and Passages, 1952) and *Il taccuino del vecchio* (The Old Man's Notebook, 1960).

During that final season of his life Ungaretti more and more identified with the Virgilian hero Aeneas, the mythic figure driven from burning Troy on the perilous sea voyage to a new promised land in Italy but delayed by a sentimental sojourn in northern Africa. Friendship with the Brazilian poet Bruna Bianco brought Ungaretti a rejuvenated sense of solace. Ungaretti continued to translate the works of writers whose poetic styles and attitudes toward existence paralleled his own, producing in 1965 a version of William Blake's poems. Recognition of his lifelong contributions to twentieth-century literature came with such honors as his election in 1962 as president of the European Writers' Community and in 1966 his winning the Etna-Taormina International Poetry Prize. Ungaretti's intimate feeling for Leopardi's works became evident in a series of lectures at Columbia University. His final trip to the United States occurred early in 1970 to accept the Books Abroad award of the University of Oklahoma. But bronchitis, brought on by the rigors of that winter journey, so weakened him that on 2 June 1970 Ungaretti died in Milan.

Spontaneity never characterized Ungaretti's poetry, as he would return again and again to revise his lyrics. That method of composition resulted in the charge that his works were painfully belabored. In truth he was endeavoring to refine his expression, to arrive at the quintessence of meaning and poetic utterance by removing unnecessary elements or rearranging word order to convey in the most concise manner possible the content of his verses. Consequently, across the different editions of the individual collections, there often exist numerous variants of the same poem. Sometimes he would take a long poem and divide it into two separate lyrics, always aiming at perfection and away from sentimentality and period-style phrasing that might date a particular work. Ungaretti saw those different revisions as variants of his soul, so that human substance always prevailed over formalistic considerations. The definitive collected edition, *Tutte le poesie*, was first published in 1969, as volume two in part 3 of *Vita d'un uomo*, which is a sort of poetic biography, where individual experiences are elevated mythically to represent all of humankind throughout time. The variants mark the progression from the youthful poet's early free-verse experimentations to the mature mastery of classical discipline in diction and meter.

Ungaretti's collected poems begin with the volume *L'Allegria*. Most of the *L'Allegria* lyrics come from the earlier volumes *Il porto sepolto* and *Allegria di naufragi*, with publication of the assembled version in 1931 and inclusion in *Vita d'un uomo* in 1942. The title *Il porto sepolto* refers to a submerged harbor of pre-Hellenistic times (beyond the promontory of Pharos) that Ungaretti as a youth in Alexandria "explored" with his imagination. Echoes of the concluding line from Leopardi's poem "L'Infinito" (1819) inspired the title of *Allegria di naufragi*—"e il naufragar m'è dolce in questo mare" (and to be shipwrecked in this sea is sweet to me)—as Ungaretti, like his nineteenth-century predecessor, envisions a gentle annihilation or immediatization in the ecstasy of the infinite. A rapturous exultancy when life and death face each other arises in the Ungarettian shipwreck of the soul experiencing a love stronger than all-consuming time. Both the deserts of Egypt and the no-man's-land of the war front form the background for the poems of *L'Allegria*. From the buried port that annihilates itself from moment to moment the poet moves to the spiritual shipwreck of self-awareness.

Ungaretti divided his volumes of verse into chapters so that each separate part would constitute a distinct song made up of dialogues, dramas, and choruses that altogether advance the unifying theme of the entire book. *L'Allegria* opens with the section "Ultime" (Last Poems): those were the verses from which he was moving away. Then there follow the poems of the section "Il porto sepolto," which express the submerged mysteries of his soul. In "Naufragi" he reveals moments of shattering intensity and illumination. Ungaretti's receptivity to new places and experiences is described in "Girovago" (Wanderer). In "Prime" (First Poems) the collection concludes with poems written after the Armistice, in Paris and Milan when he was taking his first steps toward a different stage of his life. Following the example of avant-garde French poets of the period, he frequently notes the place and the date of the original composition of many of these poems as he marks the instants of an interior biography.

Like an emblem, "Eterno," the first poem of "Ultime," proclaims the writer's exploration of the void:

Tra un fiore colto e l'altro donato
l'inesprimibile nulla

(Between one flower plucked and the other given
the inexpressible nothingness).

Eternity is the escape into a moment outside of time. The writer's quest is to abolish continuous temporal flow to achieve the harmony of timelessness. It is with a baroque sensitivity that Ungaretti initiates his collection of poems as he points to the ineffable abyss. Flowers recall Baudelaire's *Les Fleurs du Mal* (1857) with its greenhouse atmosphere that reinforces the idea of cultivation as in an artificial paradise. Life provides the "plucked flower" of the everyday event that the poet transforms into the gift ("the given flower") of his creations.

Present and past face each other in the poem "Levante," in which Ungaretti sees himself standing on the deck of the ship bringing him to Brindisi in 1912 upon his arrival in Europe. The very construction of each verse evokes images of the ship's wake through the sea:

La linea
vaporosa muore
al lontano cerchio del cielo

(The line
vaporously dies
at the distant circle of the sky).

Ungaretti's musicality becomes apparent in the internal rhymes and the effect of onomatopoeia employed to recapture the dancing (of Syrian immigrants) on the stern:

Picchi di tacchi picchi di mani
e il clarino ghirigori striduli
e il mare è cenerino
trema dolce inquieto
come un piccione

(Clicks of heels claps of hands
and the clarinet shrill flourishes
and the sea is ashen
quivers sweet restless
like a pigeon).

At the sound of the exotic Middle Eastern music accompanying the dancing the thoughts of the solitary young man on the prow return to Saturday evenings in his native Alexandria when the town's Hebrew community would conduct funerals in the wavering chiaroscuro of the alleylike streets of their quarter. As in other poems of *L'Allegria*, such as "Fase" (Phase), the poet develops his persona as the nomad wandering away from the "Arabian Nights" atmosphere of Alexandria. Memory, instead of formal syntax, serves to link faraway places and severed moments in time.

In the section titled "Il porto sepolto" Ungaretti reaches one of the high points of his poetic production with the elegy "In memoria." Originally this was a rather long poem that he divided into two: "In memoria" and the verse "Chiaroscuro" that appears in the section "Ultime," where the poet speaks of the ghost of a suicidal Arab friend coming to visit him in the night. That friend from Alexandria was Moammed Sceab, Ungaretti's schoolmate who also went to study in Paris and lived in the same hotel at No. 5 rue des Carmes. The shattering desperation of being a rootless exile drove Sceab to self-destruction. Through "In memoria" the poet recounts the circumstances leading to suicide:

> Si chiamava
> Moammed Sceab
>
> Discendente
> di emiri di nomadi
> suicida
> perché non aveva più
> Patria
>
> Amò la Francia
> e mutò nome
>
> Fu Marcel
> ma non era Francese
> e non sapeva più
> vivere
> nella tenda dei suoi
>
> (He was named
> Moammed Sceab
>
> Descendant
> of emirs of nomads
> suicide
> for he no longer had
> a Fatherland
>
> He loved France
> and changed his name
>
> He was Marcel
> but was not French
> and he no longer knew how
> to live
> in the tents of his people).

While this poem does supply details such as the exact address of their hotel and the name of

the cemetery where Sceab was buried in exile, in this final version Ungaretti avoids sensationalistic description of the suicide itself, unlike the treatment in his earlier French poem "Roman cinéma" with its vivid picture of the corpse stretched out in bed. Sceab's pathetic homelessness is emphasized by the isolation of the capitalized word *Patria* as a line unto itself. For the first time Ungaretti starts to define his task as a poet who must rescue his friend from isolating oblivion through composing this elegy, as made explicit in the final stanza:

> E forse io solo
> so ancora
> che visse
>
> (And perhaps I alone
> still know
> that he lived).

This work is no esoteric exercise in obscurant imagery or tour-de-force modernist technique. Ungaretti is confronting the reality of death; the poet must go on living to awaken his readers to the destiny of individuals such as Sceab, to make them acquainted with the youth's royal lineage, and to share in his fate as an exile without life-sustaining identity.

Traditionally in literature rivers have represented the flow of time. The enduring self of the river can also stand for the stream of consciousness within the self, an accumulation as well as a continuum, merging memory and the present. Through their flow rivers symbolize the impulse toward fulfillment. Ungaretti's poem "I fiumi" (Rivers) honors the four rivers that formed epochs of his family past and his present reality: the Serchio of the farming area near the Lucca of his parents' ancestry; the Nile, by which he was born; the Seine, where he discovered his literary vocation and established his European identity; and at the present moment of the poem itself the Isonzo on the war front, where out of the horror of carnage he is creating eternal beauty. He finds in the Isonzo a purifying baptism into a new life where he is spiritually cleansed "like a pebble." At the lyric's opening the Ungarettian persona is clinging to a shattered tree, which, in hermetic poetry, usually represents human suffering. Through a startling analogy the gully where he has taken shelter resembles a languorous circus before or after a performance, since the confusion of the war arena suggests the chaos of a circus. He is watch-

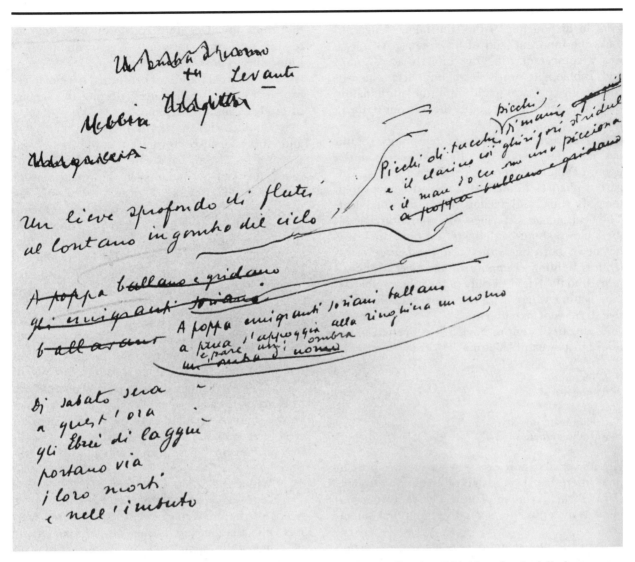

Excerpt from the manuscript for Ungaretti's "Levante," a poem collected in L'Allegria, *1931 (from* Storia della letteratura: Italiana, *volume 6, edited by Luigi Ferrante, 1965)*

ing clouds pass across the moon, a Leopardian reference (in Leopardi's poetry the moon is placidly indifferent to the anguish of earthbound mortals). As the poet bathes in the Isonzo's waters, he envisions himself stretched out in an urn resting like a relic, as if life had already left him. But this is a poem of rebirth where the writer achieves harmony with nature by recognizing himself floating on the Isonzo as "a docile fiber / of the universe." Islamic and Christian sacred imagery fuse here, for the poetic persona who divests himself of his war-soiled garments is like a bedouin repeatedly bowing to pray toward the direction of Mecca. And as he treads water, the soldier-poet resembles Christ walking on waves. While his greatest torture would be to fall away from harmony with the universe, as a pliant fiber

he can be kneaded back to a state of grace. For although combat may be raging around him, the Ungarettian persona has discovered in the Isonzo a site of redeeming serenity. At the poem's close a corolla of nocturnal darkness is settling around the soldier who has, in meditating on his four rivers, succeeded in becoming one with that natural world that will always renew itself after the violation of warfare.

Throughout "Il porto sepolto" Ungaretti endeavors to define himself. In the poem "Pellegrinaggio" (Pilgrimage) he names himself and sets the terms for his nomadic existence: "Ungaretti / uomo di pena / ti basta un'illusione / per farti coraggio" (Ungaretti / man of pain / you need but an illusion / to give you courage). Like the bedouin in the desert, like the Christian pilgrim in his journey to the true home, Ungaretti seeks the innocent land of his dreams. As a war-weary combatant dragging himself across mud and rubble, he nearly loses himself in his all-consuming physical pain until the illuminating flash of poetic illusion points the way out of darkness.

That search for a state of deliverance continues into the section "Naufragi," where in the poem "Dolina notturna" (Nocturnal Gully) Ungaretti pictures himself as a nomad bent over in the soft snow and feeling like a shriveled leaf. The leaf image describes the condition of soldiers blown about battlefields, but here the leaf is not newly born but withered in the fatigue of relentless fighting. Temporarily the poet abandons himself to the frigid sterility of the inhospitable Alpine setting where nighttime possesses the abrasive dryness of parchment.

Ungaretti's entire poetics is expressed in the brief but powerful "Mattina" (Morning):

M'illumino
d'immenso

(I illuminate myself
with the immense).

His universal vision exists in an eternal present time where his "I" scans all of creation that gains clarity from his contemplation. This rapturous moment transcends any spatial or temporal limitation.

In the title poem of the "Girovago" section Ungaretti has to acknowledge his rootlessness: "In nessuna / parte / di terra / mi posso / accasare" (In no / part / of the world / can I / find a home). This homeless wanderer may occasionally discover an oasis, whether in the desert of burning sands or in the desert of the war zone; but the Promised Land eludes him except as a self-sustaining hope. Every time he visits a new setting he dreams of finding a mythic homeland, but he has to depart as a stranger. That land of dreams is not so much a real place as a state of mind, a realm of cherished childhood memories, a psychological "inscape" sheltering him from alienation. Despite his unrelenting condition of estrangement, in being a poet blessed with a gift of insight and verbal enchantment he can overcome the travail of his temporal existence: "Godere un solo / minuto di vita / iniziale" (To enjoy a single / minute of original / life). The failings and the lack of fulfillment of any one moment in life's journey yield to the ecstatic vision

of primal life. Ungaretti concludes by admitting to his unceasing mission: "Cerco un paese / innocente" (I am searching for an innocent / country). The eternal wanderer continued to remain receptive to novel experiences, despite the feeling of grief because of his exile.

Contact with the world of human endeavors and necessary compromises produces what Ungaretti calls a "barbaglio della promiscuità" (dazzlement of promiscuity) in the final poem of *L'Allegria*: "Preghiera" (Prayer). Free of the weight of involvement with historical circumstances he longs to follow a clear path away from the finite into the infinite's liberation of the spirit. Throughout *L'Allegria* the movement toward mythic time and the innocent land has arisen from an aspiration to experience harmony and a sense of completeness with the cosmos: a prayer that can never be fully granted. This first volume presents instants of flashing insight where poignant memory and intense emotion have permitted the often startling linking of vastly distinct realities in dazzling images that are as exact as they are unexpected in their rapport. In the succeeding volumes of his verses Ungaretti struggled to master a feeling for time by reconciling his personal past with Latin cultural tradition.

With the volume *Sentimento del tempo* Ungaretti was attempting to blend the expressive needs of the modern era with conventional metrics. Punctuation and use of the definite article in syntactically complete phrases also signal an effort at formal restoration. Through the use of the hendecasyllable and the septenarius he hoped to create a twentieth-century *canto italiano* in full accord with the national literary heritage, especially as represented by Petrarch and the Petrarchists in poetry of melodic introspection. Memory and dream carry the writer back to the innocence of the past in his desire to convey the substance of words through their musical power. Once again Ungaretti, as indicated by the volume's title, was seeking to explore time not as an objective fact but as an emotional quality of experience. As a resident of the Roman metropolitan zone he frequently concentrated on key landscapes in the countryside outside the capital and also focused on the physical appearance of its baroque buildings. Along with the return to traditional meters, he restored mythical classical deities to modern poetry by evoking their original condition as cosmic forces: Chronos as the lord of a temporal domain that must fall; Diana with her luminous chastity; Juno as the supreme woman in her full sensual being; Apollo as the solar overlord; and Venus-Aphrodite bringing forth love and beauty from the waves of the eternal sea. Recognizing that the age of ancient divinities was long dead, Ungaretti consciously worked with sweet illusions to recall with a sadly hopeless piety the longing for grace and beauty that those gods once incarnated for all humankind.

Once again he structured his collection into chapters: "Prime" includes the poems of his early days in Rome; "Fine di Crono" (The End of Chronos) is a fantasy about the end of the world; "Sogni e accordi" (Dreams and Accords) concerns oneiric experiences and the search to renew ancient harmonies; "Leggende" is an attempt to fashion modern myths out of death and destruction; "Inni" ("Hymns") expresses not only Ungaretti's religious crisis but that of his entire postwar generation; "La Morte meditata" ("The Meditated Death") envisions death as a challenging otherness and the result of the fall from paradise; and in "L'Amore" love inspires the modern Italian song. Decline and renascence appear as a cosmic rhythm that the poet has to reproduce by reviving the cultural tradition of his ancestral homeland.

Among the transitional poems of "Prime" a Mallarmesque atmosphere of lexical filters prevails in "Le Stagioni" (The Seasons). The notion of seasonal cycles reflects human awareness of universal vicissitudes such as birth and death, success and failure, victory and defeat, peace and war, a desert and an oasis. This four-part poem on nature's dynamic process builds toward a conclusion of static perseverance in the deathlike winter: "Ora anche il sogno tace. / È nuda anche la quercia, / Ma abbarbicata sempre al suo macigno" (Now even the dream is silent. / Naked too is the oak, / but always firmly rooted in its rock). The bare tree represents the will to resist time's onslaught.

A Petrarchistic obsession with the memory of a loved one predominates in the poem "Alla noia" (To Ennui). A temptation for oblivion derives from ennui, a cardinal symptom of spiritual decadence that deprives the poet not of desire but of the ability to act. Like a phantom, the beloved lady of this poem takes away the glowing touch of her hand from her admirer who in frustration loses himself in vain attempts at pursuit. She is a mirage. Vacillating between active and passive moods the poet acknowledges that such loving pursuit might lead to insanity, since ennui is

the handmaiden of madness. The faculty of memory that can recall the vision of feminine loveliness ends by enticing and tormenting the poet, for memory merely brings forth sham images. Like a fountain in the refreshing shade of ancient olive trees, memory may soothe the troubled soul into a state of peacefulness. Remembrance, however, also surges through his being with the dark tormenting force of blood. Whenever the poet reawakens to the stillness of morning, memory compels him to desire his beloved's lips with an intensity of emotion that at the lyric's close he hopes will abate: "Non le conosca più!" (Let me know them no longer!). A poem such as this one reminds readers of Petrarch's infatuation with Laura, remembered as an angel but also as the fierce beast refusing to respond to his yearning. Similarly the Ungarettian persona discovers momentary relief but also abiding pain in the cherished image of the recalcitrant lady.

Ungaretti initiates part 2 of *Sentimento del tempo* with another of his elliptical, emblematic statements: "D'altri diluvi una colomba ascolto" (I listen to a dove of other floods). The fluttering of a dove's wings forms one of those mysterious harmonies that comfort the poet as he hears the bird's actual flight. The sound of wings also attracts a shepherd to a wooded shore in the lyric "L'Isola" (The Island), a poem whose gently nuanced eroticism definitely recalls with irony Mallarmé's pastoral "L'Après-midi d'un faune" (1865). A succession of lengthy and short verses over two stanzas in Ungaretti's poem re-creates the shepherd's sighting of a phantomlike nymph at sleep and his wandering through thickets of olive trees to a gleaming pasture. The summertime heat of the Latium countryside intensifies the shepherd's movements through a somnolent setting. Here, as with the goddess Diana, the nymph represents the dream of pagan beauty in a sylvan landscape. In the perennial evening of the island the wanderer finds a human reflection of that divine loveliness in the eyes of maidens resting in the groves. This is the dream-poet's innocent land where he pursues the phantom of his yearnings. Whereas Mallarmé's faun is a creature of bold lust, Ungaretti's shepherd appears as a docile dreamer passing through an enchanted island. Movement in the poem is from the darkness of elm and olive trees to luminous fields. A gentle fever of desire has led the explorer over hills, through woods where arrows seemed to be falling in showers from branches, and then to the shining fields. As a figure of eternal longing the shepherd becomes a creature of evanescence with glasslike hands seeking the illusion of perfect beauty.

Any confrontation with time must result in the facing of death. Ungaretti's "Inno alla morte" (Hymn to Death) is a coming to terms with death by the poet, who begins by addressing "Amore, mio giovine emblema" (Love, my young emblem), recognizing that the hopeful glow of youth is dimming and the future is weighing down upon him. He calls death "an arid river" or an "unremembering sister." But the poet acknowledges that death can give him the still heart of a god; in full innocence he will exist beyond thoughts and beyond goodness in a state of oblivion. Death's kiss plunges him into a perpetual dream condition where he will serve as the guide to the happiness of others. In his godlike innocence the poet explores in the following parts of this collection his promised realm.

Analogies carried to nearly surrealistic effect characterize the section "Sogni e accordi," where a brilliant palette of sense impressions and musical overtones express the poet's insights. That cosmic visualization is evident in the verses of "Stelle" (Stars):

Tornano in alto ad ardere le favole.

Cadranno colle foglie al primo vento.
Mi venga un altro soffio.
Ritornerà scintillamento nuovo.

(Fables are returning to blaze on high.

They will fall at the first wind with the leaves.
But let another gust come.
There will return a new sparkling.)

What the poet accomplishes here, and throughout the entire volume, is to restore the fabled time of myths, for once again the flaming stars embody pagan divinities and the heroic figures of ancient mythology. As in "Fine di Crono" the age of gods does end, like leaves falling in the first autumn breeze, but cyclic time renews itself as the stars sparkle again with the brilliance of a legendary eon. From visual impressionism the lyric moves to a quivering mood of meditation on the eternal.

Dramatic objectivity is Ungaretti's goal in the "Leggende" section, as he evokes perennial emblems of human significance. The opening poem, "Il capitano," recalls an actual victim of war: Nazzareno Cremona, whose destiny comes to symbolize the death of an entire generation whose hopes perished on the Carso. Here, the poet is continuing a task similar to that of "In memoria," except that the individual military officer becomes a mythic figure. Speaking of himself in the past tense, the narrator affirms his spiritual readiness for new experiences and adventures: "Fui pronto a tutte le partenze" (I was prepared for every departure). Then he addresses the night as a source of mystery and compassion: "Quando hai segreti, notte hai pietà" (When you have secrets, night you have pity). Ungaretti's orphic power arises in his probing into archetypal emotions such as the childhood dread of nocturnal darkness and the lifelong desire to wander empty roads. The child's loneliness in the night is that of everyone who needs to search for the consolation of company. Once again, in the fifth stanza, the narrator addresses the night, which has become harsh, with its face naked.

Typography and punctuation serve to advance the drama: verses referring to the fallen figure of military authority are italicized—"*Il Capitano era sereno*" (*The Captain was serene*). Three Leopardian verses describing nature's indifference to wartime carnage are enclosed in parentheses. The tall captain has fallen to his death unobserved, like thousands of other casualties of combat with no one to listen to their death rattle. When his corpse was found in a furrow, it lay already as in state with hands held upon his breast. The narrator intervenes directly by paying final respect to the dead warrior, commenting (in the first person) that he closed the captain's eyes. While the moon casts its veil over the final ceremony of reverence, the officer's body appears to lose its deadly weightiness, becoming as light as feathers. As the symbol of military authority has vanished into sheer nothingness, there remains the modern myth of conquering aloneness in childhood and adulthood, where metaphorical fear of the night's darkness yields to the moon's illumination. Throughout all these legends Ungaretti attempts to join his role as poet to immortal figures of inspiration. This section closes with the poem "Epigrafe per un caduto della rivoluzione" (Epigraph for a Man Fallen in the Revolution), in which the writer's young heart is seen as immortal because his individual destiny has been lovingly touched by his fatherland.

Through his hymns Ungaretti tries to discover some meaning to his life beyond his private circumstances. These are poems of anguished questioning about his value as a lyricist. Out of this torment of doubt came his return to Roman Catholic faith. After a sojourn during Holy Week in 1928 at a monastery in Subiaco, Ungaretti underwent the conversion whose ordeal by faith he celebrates in the hymn "La pietà." Feeling wounded and exiled among men, the speaker wonders about his self-worth, for although he has attempted to defeat the devouring void of silence with the names of legendary, mythic characters whom he rescued from oblivion, he may have been only the slave of empty words that produced mere phantoms. As in the earlier piece "Pellegrinaggio" the controlling word here is *pena*: the pain suffered by the sensitive creator whose pride may be born of arrogance. Like Dante's sinners in the second circle of Hell who in eternally being punished for erotic passion are tossed about like leaves by ferocious winds, the poet's soul is swept away in every direction. These verses strike with the agony of penetrating arrows.

Ungaretti structures "La pietà" in four divisions. In the opening section the poet questions why God has banished him from life and perhaps from death. His unbearable torment is to stay walled-off within desire but without love. The lack of any certainty festers in his soul like a throbbing wound. Having lost the sense of sin it is no longer possible to express remorse and obtain salvation. The Lord appears as a God of cruelty who has not made his law manifest to humankind. Only a divine lightning blast can free the sufferer's disquiet. The writer here demonstrates that his religious turmoil is directly linked to his self-doubts as an artist.

Hope emerges in the second division through death's liberating the soul from its burden of flesh. The dead are the source of redemption for the living. This poem explodes with baroque images of torrents of ghostly shadows that burst like seeds in our dreams. The dead provide the substance to the names of the living. But doubt once again assails the poet who wonders if God is only a dream, yet a necessary illusion to sustain our folly. With extravagant analogy the shining madness of faith in God is briefly but negatively compared to branches quivering from morning sparrows. What could degenerate into a tour de force of technical artifice instead represents how through poetic imagery of the most unbounded nature the writer is seeking to confirm his faith by acknowledging his task as a Christian poet who invokes the dead to console the living.

Portrait of Ungaretti by Carlo Carrà, 1947 (Collezione Carrà, Milan)

While the longing to know a remote God remains the "mysterious wound" that closes the second division, the poet's hope springs forward in the third section as the dazzling but piercing light that is God. As in Gian Lorenzo Bernini's representation of the angel holding the golden arrow before an ecstatic St. Teresa of Avila, the poet ends the third division by entreating the Lord to give him the "supreme joy" of that slender-thread penetration of divine fulmination. In the absence of that crushing illumination mankind, as asserted in the final stanza, is the creature of a monotonous world where having rather than being leads to accumulating self-limiting goods. Earthly existence is imagined as a spider's web to which the living are attached amid the outcry of their fears and desires. Ungaretti recalls the early nineteenth-century poet Ugo Foscolo who in his hymn "Dei sepolcri" (Of Tombs) suggested that while tombs were only a burial place for the dead, they could serve to establish an affectionate communion between the departed and their surviving admirers. At the end, however, only blasphemy is left. For "La pietà" is not a poem of triumph but of spiritual struggle and weariness in which with searing candor the author admits that his religious crisis reflects his artistry founded on a linguistic attempt to enfold the entire cosmos across the ages.

Six songs comprise "La Morte meditata," as the poet's meditations on sin and the possibility of remorse lead naturally to considerations of death, to be seen not as a surrender to stasis but as a dynamic renewal of life's significant events through the force of memory. Chiaroscuro effects start the initial song in which death is the sister of shadow that, even as night's darkness yields to dawn's light, persists in pursuing the narrator. Ungaretti views death as the consequence of humankind's exclusion from Paradise, "un giardino puro" (a pure garden) from which Eve's ingenuous lusting exiled us. Many of the first song's attributes of death could easily be applied to Eve: "Madre velenosa degli evi" (Venomous mother of the ages); "Bellezza punita e ridente" (Beauty punished and laughing); "Sognatrice fuggente" (Fugitive dreamer). The poet also dreams of that prelapsarian time when Eve was totally innocent in all her yearnings, and his poetry is an endeavor to return to that pure garden of Edenic serenity. To close his opening song the writer addresses death as a sleepless athlete, asking her how long his shade will be permitted to fly among the living who might remember his lyrical accomplishments. Even after the confessions of egotism in "La pietà," Ungaretti still sees eternity as lasting fame.

Cantos 2 and 3 echo each other in pondering on death as an intensified state of mind that conquers the void of time. The second verse of each song reads "Della nostra infelice maschera" (Of our unhappy mask) in a nearly Pirandellian vision of life as a mask worn before society. Toward the close of each song death sings like a locust, the angry insect that strips away every vestige of vitality. The second song's opening stanza is a five-line sentence employing the principle of suspension holding the subject to the final verse: "La buia veglia dei padri" (The dark vigil of the fathers). Ungaretti acknowledges that he founds his poetry on a long tradition of his predecessors: Virgil, Petrarch, Leopardi, the fathers of that time-subduing vigil that he intends to continue. While death paradoxically resounds like the cruel cicada over the blood-streaked sands of time, its voice is a mute word before the eternal tradition of great poets. But the third song ironically recognizes that those very same vigilant fa-

thers of poetry are playing an infinite jest that cuts deeply into the masklike visage of the modern lyricist. Death's deep night is the darkness of confused silence that threatens to confound the aspirations of the contemporary poet to join the vigil of his forbears. All that is left is the mockery of the hissing locusts through whom death drowns out the poetic song of the ages.

Ungaretti overcomes the despairing doubts of the third canto to reach a baroque apotheosis in the following song where clouds have taken him by the hands atop a hill (note that he uses the word *colle* in remembrance of Leopardi's "ermo colle"—the "solitary hill" of the major poem "L'Infinito"). From his height the speaker in Ungaretti's poem possesses the metaphysical powers to burn time and space. That annihilating might has come to him as a messenger, as a fabricator of dreams for "divine" death. Indeed in the fifth canto, after death has closed the poet's eyes, in his fatal sleep he envisions the domain of death as a realm of nocturnal darkness, a marine kingdom of deceptive hollows, unechoing sounds, and corks floating from lowered nets. Death as the deep sea of drowning is an archetypal image of the watery grave that has seized its victims with invisible hands. An ambivalent Leopardian sequence of moonlight follows in an aura of the most gently swaying sensation that, if death were kind, would touch the poet's soul to console him. Then, a reminiscence of Baudelaire's lyric "A une passante" occurs in the last two stanzas, in which death is compared to an enigmatic lady who passes by like a leaf firing autumn trees with brilliant colors. While trees usually represent anguish, here the fire of fall colors completes the poem's dynamic progress through the void of the deep, dark sea to the soft passage of the moon and finally the fleeting feminine presence that remains eternally elusive.

Just as the initial canto evoked the oxymoron of the darkest moment before dawn, the final song will close this section of meditations on death by building to the last verse's "Quando fa giorno" (When day breaks). The night of fatal dreaming is drawing to a close in the feverish mind of the poet who has been heeding its spectral voice. Through memory, especially when it is deranged in flights of fantasy, death has become a category of intensified awareness in time that the poet, a disciple of dreams, can free from the captivity of destructive change by participating in the creative traditions of his literary predecessors. Here, as in "La pietà," the narrator regrets his limitations that prevent him from liberating the phantom shades of death from the dread weight of their sins. Like a baroque cathedral constructed with dark zones and apertures, the chapter of "La Morte meditata" dramatically moves from fatal gloom to the uplifting brilliance of the dawn.

To conclude *Sentimento del tempo* Ungaretti seeks in the grouping titled "L'Amore" to fathom the nature of love, seen now as the handmaiden of death. Earlier writers such as Petrarch serve as Ungaretti's guide to comprehend the sweetness and pain of love. Two quatrains, one with verses of eight syllables and the second with verses of six syllables in a rhyme scheme of *aabbccdd* make up the opening "Canto beduino," where the writer remembers his first awakening to love in Egypt. The chief terms are *donna* (woman), *vento* (wind), *terra* (earth), and *sogno* (dream), weaving through the quatrains to evoke the woman's arising, singing, walking in the enchantment of the wind, stretching upon the earth to be overtaken by a dream. This loving woman on the naked earth swept by the strong wind is caught up in the dream which is death. Although some critics have identified the woman with Eve at the moment of her first intimacy with Adam, she is more likely the primal woman of the desert who initiated the poet to love. As in the fifth canto of the *Divine Comedy*, wind represents the force of erotic passion. Eve does appear in a "Canto" of 1932, where she sets a loom of lost paradises on the dreaming eyes of the poet. Throughout these poems Ungaretti traditionally identifies Eros with Thanatos. The poet's telegraphic style characterizes the last lyric, "Silenzio stellato" (Starry Silence), with typical symbols of anguished trees, the night of unshaped existence, when nothing stirs except for nests. Although in this chapter Ungaretti acknowledges, as in a poem celebrating his fifty-seventh birthday, that time is catching up with him, he pleads to retain that suffering openness to love which is the sign of continuing vitality. This entire volume, *Sentimento del tempo*, has shown human time to be a chronicle of inner experience through a single day, the seasons of the heart, and the cycles of the ages. Ungaretti's return to traditional meter and occasional rhyme is expressive of that desire to renew the past of his poetic fathers who have sought to defeat the anonymity of death. By recalling figures of pagan mythology or creating his own legendary characters like Captain Cremona the poet endeavored to abolish destructive time. With his next book of poetry, he confronts a destruction whose agony he can never quiet.

Until the deaths of his brother Costantino and his son, Antonietto, Ungaretti knew death merely as a source of poetic meditation, not as a totally crushing catastrophe. The devastation of those losses compelled him to face a reality that he could never fully transform or transcend in poetry. The passing of persons close to himself seemed like the death of parts of his own being. In the 1947 text *Il Dolore*, Ungaretti touches the depths of authentic sadness and bereavement without any recourse to verbal pyrotechnics. Structured into chapters like his other books of poetry, *Il Dolore* opens with laments for his brother in the section "Tutto ho perduto" (I Have Lost Everything, 1937); it then moves in "Giorno per giorno" (Day by Day) to relate Antonietto's sickness and death. Poems of despair make up part 3: "Il tempo è muto" (Time Is Mute). Tree symbolism reappears in the section "Incontro a un pino" (Against a Pine). At last in "Roma occupata" the poet overcomes personal grief to lament the occupation of Rome by the Germans from fall 1943 to early summer 1944. With "I ricordi" Ungaretti reviews memories of crisis and hope. Throughout this book, he succeeds in joining private grief to universal suffering.

Absolute desperation pervades the poem "Tutto ho perduto." His brother's death marks the loss of his childhood. Time resembles an invisible sword cutting the poet off from the most precious memories of his youth, when existence was fully spontaneous for the writer before maturity inhibited his receptivity to life's vibrant experiences. Nocturnal darkness has swallowed up the images of brightness associated with his brother. Here and throughout this volume a key word is *grido* along with its plural *gridi* to mark the outcry of excruciating pain that nothing can alleviate. Through the figure of Costantino it was once possible for Giuseppe to relive the sharpness of sensations as a child; now nothing remains but a "rock of outcries" in the depth of his throat. His brother's death has left the poet spiritually petrified. As Ungaretti recognizes in the first section's other poem "Se tu mio fratello" (If You My Brother), he is now only the "annihilating nothingness of thought."

Seventeen outcries of anguish mark the piercing moments of "Giorno per giorno," where the father witnesses but cannot prevent his son's dying. Even at the start, the poet has scattered crumbs to lure sparrows into Antonietto's room, and the boy's eyes and face show unmistakable signs of his fatal suffering. Already at the second lament Ungaretti admits to his loss and comments that only in dreaming can he still have his son with him. Once again the image of night occurs to indicate the realm of darkness and irreparable separation. Now the only consolation that the poet can experience is the memory of his child uplifting him through moments of hopelessness. Just as Leopardi looked back in his poem "A Silvia" to a lost image of maidenly beauty, Ungaretti relives the time of joyfulness when a little boy running from room to room could distract him from disquieting thought. Both the modern poet and the nineteenth-century lyricist weave their elegies from scenes of modest everyday settings; both grieve for the creatures of happiness that death cut short. Ungaretti employs the *ubi est* device, common to elegiac poetry since Boethius and best expressed by François Villon, to wonder where that incarnation of spontaneous mirth has gone. By this section's midpoint, the eighth outcry is a single screaming line: "E t'amo, t'amo, ed è continuo schianto! . . ." (And I love you, I love you, and it is a continuing pang! . . .). All of the poet's efforts to exercise control over his emotions apparently break down under the strain of his suffering.

Even the isolating distance of land and sea after Ungaretti returned from Brazil to Italy could not quiet his anguish at the thought of the boy's final agony: the "ferocious" land and the "immense" sea became like so many vast unfeeling spaces separating the writer from his son's grave. Antonietto's voice continues to cry out to him across the thousands of miles and the passing of years with the force of an ever-haunting presence. Even the otherwise comforting sight of the hills of Latium with their beloved pine trees could not truly console the writer since he was unable to share the joy of return with his son.

Ungaretti draws a parallel between the flight of a swallow to mark summer's end and his own passing into the autumn of life with its feeling of decay. His prayer by the end of the eleventh outcry is for a sign of his finally rising from the hell of his suffering to some quietude of soul. Antonietto's death summons up images of an axe felling a tree or a leaf in autumn falling at the gentle touch of a breeze: life's fury (expressed with the past definite tense of no possible recall) cut down the defenseless child. Neither summer with its rages, spring with its promises, nor fall with its pompous glory can stir the poet in the winter-

time desperation of his soul. In his baroque chiaroscuro art Ungaretti envisions a mad splendor coming as the secret torture of twilight to illuminate the deep abyss of his spirit that has become empty of all happiness. His present torment derives from a feeling of guilt that he survives while his son has perished in a state of purity. By the sixteenth outcry a flashback occurs, as in a surrealistic film, of a sultry summer afternoon in the garden of their home in São Paulo: synaesthetically the brilliant sunlight through the windowpanes resounds like a bell; a hydrangea plant suggests the tropical setting while skyscrapers in the background remind readers of the modern metropolis under blazing, merciless clouds; and the boy (called "bimbetto" in the pathetic, vulnerable diminutive) plays on the limbs of a tree. Then, in the concluding stanza, Antonietto's voice rings out in ghostly power to declare that his presence will be felt in the sunlight and air to console his father. This poem closes with the child's promise to act as dawn and wholesome day to sustain his parent's hope.

Although "Giorno per giorno" through the intensity of its naked emotions seems about to explode from the limits of art to be a form of therapeutic catharsis, it is actually a thoroughly disciplined poem inspired by both Leopardi and also Petrarch (in his lyrics after the death of his beloved Laura). Ungaretti controls the length of each single verse from five syllables, to express the all-devouring void, to noble hendecasyllables that succeed in renewing literary tradition in a modern sense. This poem begins with a heart-rending outcry by the dying child: "Nessuno, mamma, ha mai sofferto tanto . . . " (No one, mamma, has ever suffered so much . . .). It ends with Antonietto's whispering a message of comfort on the wind.

Death can mark a complete stop in the lives of surviving loved ones, as Ungaretti demonstrates in the three poems of the section "Il tempo è muto." The title poem starts its initial verse in the present tense to describe the stillness of time in a deadening seashore setting. Away from the motionless reed beds of the shore a canoe used to wander (*errava*: the imperfect tense) carrying its inert, exhausted oarsman. After his son's death Ungaretti became that lifeless boatman being transported passively away from life's mooring. The skies have fallen into chasms of smoke where the poet's hopes were buried upon the loss of Antonietto. On the rim of those abysses, a loving survivor is stretched out in

Caricature of Ungaretti by Mario Vellani Marchi (from Storia della letteratura: Italiana, *volume 6, edited by Luigi Ferrante, 1965)*

memories, so that to fall in the void was a merciful act. World and mind, the subject and the object, are both recognized by the poet to be an illusion, a fact he did not find out before the trauma of his son's passing. The two concluding verses recall the Leopardian language of "Naufragi" but with a bitterness that never oppressed the earlier poems: "Che nel mistero delle proprie onde / Ogni terrena voce fa naufragio" (That in the mystery of its own waves / Every earthly voice experiences shipwreck). Sweetness is lacking in this dead sea. The poet's whole being has drowned in the despair caused by the shock of his child's death. From a writer who always stressed the power of memory to defeat time and death this opening poem appears all the more devastating in its flight away from memory into the abyss of oblivion. Memory also strikes a harsh accord in the bitter second poem, "Amaro accordo," where the poet relives the move from Italian skies with constellations of the northern hemisphere to Brazil under its southern stars. The flora and the fauna of the tropical country arise in his memory

as monstrous apparitions: shadowy banana trees, gigantic tortoises traveling in hordes, strange seagulls. His little boy playing in the sand of a foreign beach is a ghostly figure illumined in the rain and wind by fierce lightning. Then Ungaretti sees death clearly as independent of place or local tradition: "Ma la morte è incolore e senza sensi" (But death is colorless and without feelings). As the child played, death like a monster with fangs was about to devour him.

That helpless, defenseless child against the pitiless, rugged Brazilian landscape is the subject of the concluding poem, "Tu ti spezzasti" (You Shattered), where Petrarchistic and Leopardian strains contribute toward a musicality of inevitable surrender to the alien country. A grandiose baroque style characterizes the first strophe with its evocation of the Brazilian coastline of gigantic gray cliffs, virgin torrents, and dazzling beaches. But Ungaretti deliberately deflates his Petrarchistic manner of accumulating impressive lists of adjectives when in the opening strophe's final line he writes, "In un vuoto orizzonte, non rammenti?" (On an empty horizon, don't you remember?); the interrogative in the present singular familiar strips the description of its forcefulness. Deeply classical, Latinate expressive devices are employed to construct a numbing effect before the starkness of the landscape.

It is Antonietto that the father asks to remember a tree, which comes to symbolize the whole, fatal experience of merciless Brazil: the araucaria (the monkey-puzzle tree) defiantly arising in the shadow of rocks from roots tearing into barely yielding flintstone. The description of the stubborn and yet magical tree brings to mind Leopardi's final canto, "La Ginestra," on the broom plant that grows out of hardened lava on the slope of Mt. Vesuvius. But whereas the plant in Leopardi's poem optimistically symbolizes fragile humankind struggling against volatile forces, here the Brazilian tree is an integral part of nature that crushes delicate creatures like Antonietto. Throughout the third strophe the child, like the tiny firecrest bird on the branches of a gigantic tree, is remembered scaling the araucaria in order to look down to the ocean's shoreline to watch large tortoises. But the boy's victory is ephemeral when death does not respect his defenselessness against the alien climate. Ungaretti reproduces the enormous physical effort of climbing, through his use of hendecasyllables, and then changes to shorter verses after the child reaches the tip. A funereal mood develops as the boy gazes down on the procession of turtles, where the poem anticipates his death in the final tension of the marine spectacle. Although the lyric's second section is a dance of joy performed by the supple lad, the tenses are imperfect and past definite to note that the moment of ecstatic victory celebration is decidedly part of lost time. For, in the third and final division, that creature of lightness and happy musical gracefulness cannot endure against the hardened blindness of the Brazilian setting where the naked sun synaesthetically roars in the savage fury of its pitilessly cruel shining that shatters the crystalline glow of the frail child. Ungaretti constructs this entire poem on the contrast between the nearly ethereal boy and the destructively ferocious landscape. As in the four adjectives that describe the sun's roar—*empio* (pitiless), *selvoso* (savage), *accanito* (relentless) and *ronzante*, (droning)—the writer builds to the final explosion of light and heat that annihilate his son. While North Africa showed Ungaretti the sun-streaked desert that could lead to the refreshing oasis, Brazil's jungle coast acquainted him with infernal violence that claimed its innocent victim.

Italy's familiar landscapes enabled Ungaretti to regain a sense of human proportion in the midst of a gentle nature, as suggested in the solitary poem of the section "Incontro a un pino," where the Italian pine welcomes him back to its memory-laden solitude. But the time of Ungaretti's return to Italy was of course a time of war's desolation, as recounted in "Roma occupata." The eternal city, caught in the grip of a merciless occupying force, is another victim for whom the poet utters his lament. Having ended his Brazilian exile, Ungaretti recognizes Rome as his own city, the home of civilized Latin tradition now menaced by barbarism. The monuments of the capital city at a moment of universal threat inspire the poet to meditate on the faith needed to live through the time of crisis. In the opening poem, "Folli i miei passi" (Wild My Steps), the writer pictures himself numbed by the war, walking down those customary Roman streets with all the mechanical unawareness of an automaton, since it is a natural defense mechanism in a period of wartime danger to close oneself to outside stimuli. Although the streets are rich with time's heritage, they no longer serve as measures of human accomplishment. The dark, war-torn city can find no "allegria" in the synaesthetic resounding of sunset on windowpanes. But by the third stanza a miracle occurs as the poet opens his arms and his physical being to the humble hope that Michelangelo created with the dome of St. Peter's. The baroque artist succeeded in walling in space as in a lightning flash, denying the soul the opportunity to shatter itself. In contemplation of this architectural wonder Ungaretti ceases to be an automaton or zombie, for he sees and makes his readers see how Michelangelo gave wing to the city's collective imagination with his monument born of a desolate shudder from an outstretched body. Although a profoundly Roman Catholic faith lies at the heart of this poem and the monument which inspired it, it centers on the aesthetic experience that reanimates the war-wearied human spirit. The vision of the cupola brings the silent, ghostly city back to life.

Just as Ungaretti's open arms and Michelangelo's outstretched figure suggest the Crucifixion in the poem "Folli i miei passi," a painting of the Crucifixion at the Roman church of San Clemente, usually attributed to Masaccio, lifts the narrator out of the deadly gloom of the oppressed city in the poem "Defunti su montagne"

(The Dead on the Mountains). The great mass of the Colosseum dominates the opening stanza; it is foreboding with its blind sockets under an azure sky that stirs no emotion. Ironically Ungaretti refers to *azzurro*, the favorite color of the French symbolists. On that tense day crowds of people passing by the ancient Roman stadium appear as spectral points lost in the desert of the city. The poet inserts himself into the scene by the third stanza when he speaks of answering a "strano tamburo" (strange drum): this deeply echoing sound was the drum roll of Radio London that during the war years broadcast its call of the Victory-sign all across the occupied continent as a promise of eventual liberation. In this lyric, the poet combines recondite symbolist imagery with events of everyday life under the German occupation. In the fourth stanza the narrator recounts entering San Clemente to view Masaccio's painting. The perspective here begins from the floor level with the spectator looking up to the lofty painting whose figures welcome him, then up to the fresco's lower level with its commotion of angry mounted Roman centurions, then upward beyond Christ and two thieves to a vision in clouds and mountains of the triumphant dead resurrected from their tombs. Movement throughout the entire poem is from the anonymous passersby dwarfed by the Colosseum to the joyous, stirring flight through clouds by the eternally rewarded faithful. In the most emphatic position of the lyric there rings the final word: *speranza*, hope for all those who hold onto faith during times of oppression.

Rome's occupation by the Germans was a period of continuing atrocities when all citizens had to fear for their safety. On 16 October 1943 a Black Sabbath occurred for the Jews of Rome when SS teams swept through the old ghetto and rounded up victims for deportation to Auschwitz. Gentiles, too, had to beware of deportation to Nazi labor camps and war industry factories. In retaliation for the murder by partisans of 33 German soldiers in the spring of 1944, Nazi authorities ordered the execution of 335 Romans at the Ardeatine Caves outside of town. Ungaretti cries out in anguish for his suffering fellow citizens in the poem "Mio fiume anche tu" (My River even You), where he adds the Tiber (here the "fatal" Tiber) to the list of rivers that have influenced his life. This song of agony resounds with all the pain of offended pride as in the Lamentations of Jeremiah on the fall of Jerusalem to the Babylonians. That Old Testament sense of collective in-

jury is apparent in rhetorical devices such as the eleven repetitions of the verse opening "Ora che . . . " (Now that . . .) to point out the horrifying depths to which the city has declined. Equally powerful is the repetition of *notte* with variants in the adjectives (frequently past participles) to express the torment of nocturnal hours: *turbata* (troubled), *straziata* (anguish-stricken), *sconvolta* (convulsed), and *triste* (sad). In three verses in the first stanza there is a play on *male, mali,* and *male* to stress the terror of a reign of unceasing and unforeseeable acts of evil. Similarly, the noun *gemito* (wailing) and the verb *geme* (moans) indicate the tortured outcry from the intimidated citizens who are reduced to being *agnelli* (lambs) and *pecorelle* (sheep) that are led to slaughter along *strade esterrefatte* (terrified streets). At one time the people turned to emigration to seek a better life; now the city is depopulated by forced deportations from which there might be no return.

While part one of "Mio fiume anche tu" is an unrelieved portrait of the pitiless hell occurring in the capital city, in the second division Christ appears as the loving and suffering redeemer who forever sacrifices himself to rebuild man in a humane way. Seven times the attribute *Santo* rings out to emphasize the holiness of the Master and Brother who sustains people in their moral weaknesses. Part two is Ungaretti's first-person prayer in the tradition of the medieval *lauda* of poets such as Jacopone da Todi, who praised the Savior for enduring his passion to rescue for eternity an errant humanity. Through Christ humanity will regain the divine image that the horrors of occupation have torn away from human features.

Transition to the final section of *Il Dolore*, "I ricordi," comes in the initial poem, "L'Angelo del povero" (Angel of the Poor), through the twice-repeated phrase "Ora che" in the first stanza, where the silence of numerous unjust deaths weighs oppressively in expectation of the liberating arrival of a heavenly angel. Those war dead with their imperceptible whisper are recalled in the two elliptical quatrains of "Non gridate più" (Do Not Cry Out Anymore), when the poet warns the living to save themselves by heeding those victims with reverence. Ungaretti's characteristic analogical style returns when in "Non gridate più" he compares the sound made by the dead to the growing of untrodden grass. Reflections in a Leopardian key on the role of memories take up the chapter's title poem, which begins: "I ricordi, un inutile infinito, / Ma soli e

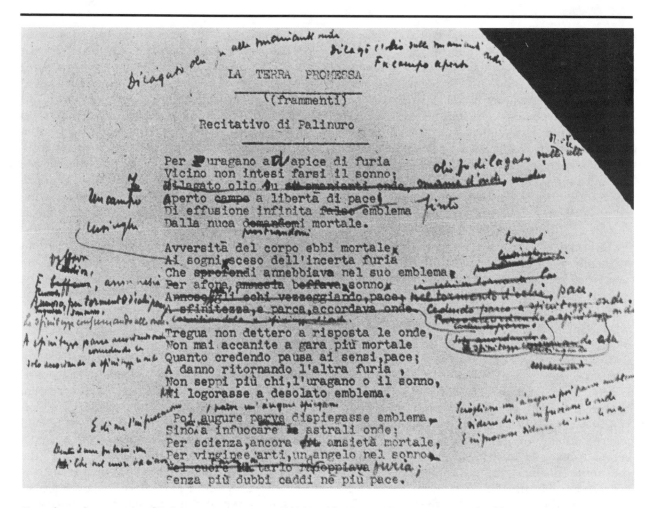

Page from the typescript for La terra promessa (1950) with Ungaretti's corrections and additions (from Storia della letteratura, volume 15, edited by Luciano Bertolini and Goffredo Dotti, 1965)

uniti contro il mare, intatto / In mezzo a rantoli infiniti ... " (Memories, a useless infinity, / But alone and united against the sea, intact / In the midst of infinite death-rattles ...). Stanzas two and three of the poem "I ricordi" start with "Il mare," where the sea symbolizes time forever renewing itself as it eliminates the traces of memories. Like grains of sand shifting across a shore, memories in the concluding stanza seem but mute echoes of farewell to happy moments. Here the anguish of Il Dolore is growing calm as the poet surmounts personal loss and patriotic lamentation to reflect on the power of time to wear away at precious memories. This entire volume has been an appeal to listen to the dead, whether members of immediate families or the anonymous crowds driven sheeplike away on deportation trains. The concluding poem, "Terra" (Earth), closes by asserting that the cry of the dead is stronger than any force of physical nature. Ungaretti loved Il Dolore more than any of

his other collections since it bore testimony to the grief and pain of death that would always stay with him. As the title of the volume's last lyric suggests, this poet who has always revered the dead (Moammed Sceab, Captain Cremona, Costantino, Antonietto) is prepared to resume his quest for the Promised Land.

An autumnal melancholy over the last signs of earthly youth pervades the penultimate season in La terra promessa (1950). In the symbolist tradition Ungaretti envisages that lost paradise of harmonious forms to be recollected and reconstituted in the poetic act. Through the figure of pious Aeneas, the incarnation of handsomeness, youth, and innocence, the writer takes up the drama of the vigilant voyager at the moment when upon touching the Promised Land he looks back in memory to past experiences and ponders on the future in an attempt to comprehend the significance of his quest. For Ungaretti, the eternal exile of Egyptian birth, French education, and the deadening Brazilian sojourn, the Promised Land represented a coming home to his cultural origins, to forever-inspiring traditions. Along with Aeneas as the searcher for civilization and aesthetic form, this collection focuses on Dido as the autumnal character of self-defeating carnal passion and Aeneas's faithful pilot Palinurus as the doomed activist incapable of fathoming the reason for his deeds. By taking Virgil and Ovid as his sources of inspiration, Ungaretti follows those poetic "fathers" who have endeavored to restrain death's annihilation. Once again that return to tradition will be reflected in the poetic form: the hendecasyllable, the canzone, and the sestina. The aged modernist poet acknowledges that like Aeneas he must assess the purpose of his existence or perish like Dido and Palinurus. At first, intending to compose a poetic drama with choruses and recitative in the style of Robinson Jeffers, Ungaretti produced a fragmentary volume (in 1945) where Aeneas recedes before the two condemned figures. Again, throughout the poet's works what sustains his inspiration is his preoccupation with the dying.

The opening "Canzone" of the full, 1950 version of *La terra promessa* describes Ungaretti's state of mind. Petrarch influences the language, structure, and oblivion-steeped imagery of this poem. The stately hendecasyllables end with the intricate rhyme scheme of this medieval metric form. Anguish over the effects of growing old and the continuing strength of desire alternate as the thrusts of the canzone with the recognition that sources of inspiration must shift from the realm of the senses to that of the intellect. From that recognition will come a rebirth. Now that the poet is in the autumn of his life, he sees that he must turn to the past to re-create intense experiences. The poem begins powerfully with the word *Nude* to describe the naked arms that, despite having been heavy from the secrets they once bore, have succeeded in swimming to the depths of Lethe (the river of oblivion) to free the alluring charms and the fatiguing labors that used to illuminate the world with life's experiences. A sense of weariness pervades the opening quatrain with its plunge into forgetfulness. Images of the void predominate in the second quatrain, where old age resembles a mute street barren of trees (where consequently leaves never change and fall), a time equally barren of sensations of pain or pleasure, of waking or sleeping. With the octave, however, there emerges the primeval dawning of love in roseate luster to be recol-

lected in memory if not experienced in immediate carnal sensation; verbs such as *si sporse* (emerged) and *trasalì* (leapt forward) convey the rainbow force of this moment of renewal.

That plunge into the depths of nothingness and forgetfulness and the subsequent rising to the sight of the dawn conquering the darkness mark a breakthrough in the following quatrain to a primal image that bursts in lightning flashes through icy barriers of old age. By the fourth quatrain the image of love appears as life's obsessive goal of truth and beauty made incarnate, a pure idea capable of arousing wrath and of opposing the devouring void. In the couplet that links the canzone's first half to the second part that primal image of love, beauty, and truth prophetically divines the shores of the promised land with palm trees that indicate the oasis of the bedouin-poet, who like every artist has the fingers of a Daedalus to open up the land's mysterious labyrinths. The poet in the first-person intervenes in the first sestet to declare that although the primal image bears a metaphorical blade (stressed by three verses ending with *lama*), which devastates, imprisons, and makes desolate the human spirit, he will persist in beholding it at the very depth of the frightening void as he aspires to the eternal fame promised to writers. Here Ungaretti follows the tradition of Petrarch seeking the laurel crown of the great poet. By the second sestet the writer undergoes a metamorphosis into Ulysses, the eternal wanderer seeking new adventures whose outcome might be death, which Ungaretti in old age is forced to acknowledge as near at hand. The closing tercet presents that forever fresh, final road of fatality untouched by light or darkness to which the human odyssey moves inexorably. Before Ungaretti could portray the self-destructive passion of Dido or the deadly stubbornness of Palinurus, he had to assess his own emotions in this canzone with its first downward, then upward movement toward the innocent land and death.

Nineteen choruses describe Dido's radically shifting states of mind. Focus falls on the mental condition of this queen of Carthage facing the fading of her beauty and the desertion by her lover Aeneas, who, unlike her, is impelled to follow a destiny of duty rather than yield to his emotional drives. The opening chorus starts at the present time of tormenting anguish to return through memory to Dido's adolescence and the awakening of her body to physical desire. But the sensual idyll cannot persist as the derisive awareness of present despair agitates the mature woman and makes her hope to quiet her heart in the somnolence of the night. Dido represents not merely a woman but an entire civilization reaching the state of its inner dissolution. Standing at night by the seashore the queen recalls the moonlit birth of Echo before the shimmering waves; that delicate nymph also perished before the scorn of her lover, Narcissus. In chorus 3, readers first feel the silence of outward nature in the still sea and wind until Dido's inner emotions explode in the repetition of the word *grido* five times: twice as the first-person verb "I cry out" and three times as the noun "outcry" to express the anger, shame, and burning pain caused since she and Aeneas originally looked at each other and she lost her autonomy before him. Her inner emotions are like a tropical jungle of stifled and twisted rage and yearning. In the delirium of her sleep the queen wishes only that she had never been born. Neither memories of adolescent awakenings to beauty nor mythic self-identification can assuage the hysteria corroding Dido's heart.

A schizoid barrenness of effect afflicts her, as she can merely remember the ripening of erotic desire in her being from which she presently feels absolutely divorced in the engulfment of abandonment by her beloved Aeneas. Like a Leopardian pessimist she has lost the capacity to sustain herself with precious illusions of reciprocated affection. Her present image of Aeneas is of a solitary and arrogant creature wandering through a wasteland while deciding to embark on the sea journey to his destiny in Italy away from Dido. Their mutual gaze becomes a mirror to reflect their contrasting desires: his to sail to the promised land; hers to hold on to his love. But bearing the dark night of desperation in her heart, the queen rationally knows that dawn and sea can promise her no hope. By the tenth chorus Dido is already contemplating her self-immolation upon a flaming pyre as she speaks of the crackling leaves of a plane tree and a roselike gleaming of dry leaves in the evening. Dido contends that her meeting with Aeneas was fated to occur since theirs were twin souls; the storm at sea that brought his ship to the safe harbor of Carthage was no accident but a predestined event. Dido consequently can reject responsibility for her original infatuation.

By the fourteenth chorus the imagery of eyes gazing at each other has ceased to represent any reciprocated feelings. All that remains is the queen's imploring an impassive Aeneas for a pite-

Ungaretti circa 1963

ous response. Now she views herself only as a deserted woman, capable merely of remembering verdant, roseate, and golden moments of a loving past while the present is without color. While she can still imagine her spirit taking wing at sunset—the hour of decadence—to soar over the shores, her flight exists only in fantasy. Total desolation prevails in the eighteenth chorus—without and within—since the fields are bereft of crops and the city lies in ruins, all the result of the queen's neglect of her royal duties because of her preoccupation with Aeneas. The sole color of the present moment is the deadening ashen hue of herons (figured by Virgil in book 4 of the *Aeneid* as symbols of Dido's furious passion) howling out in marshes and thickets. Ungaretti's language deliberately reaches a depth of crudeness to express the woman's deterioration as she speaks of the feces of the herons' fledglings and the stench that extends to Aeneas's fame now that he is abandoning her without leaving even the consolation of a child born of their former love. Dido's emotions have moved from the blush of an adolescent girl remarking on the wondrous changes in her physical being, to the enchantment of her first beholding Aeneas's eyes that answered hers in desire, to devastating scorn and despair at the decline of her beauty, to this last fecal anger toward her paramour. Ungaretti portrays here the possessiveness of a love that constantly demands reciprocation without ever recognizing the independent will of the beloved, who is committed to a sense of duty away from the needs of his mistress. Then in two shrieking verses (a hendecasyllable and a septenarius) the final chorus closes with the fall of queenly pride in horrors and moral errors. Ungaretti has produced here a fragmentary but deeply condensed "melodrama" in the Italian operatic tradition with his customary hermetic concision. While the language does degenerate to an excremental level, this poem is one of his most musical, with its liquid alternation of voiced consonants and harsh unvoiced gutturals and plosives. Expansive verses contrast in their *legato* flow of emotion and melodiousness with the explosive brevity of fierce outcries of anger and suffering. These choruses have graphically portrayed the devastating outcome of an obsession that results from the moral failure to follow duty.

To develop the recitative of Palinurus, Aeneas's trustworthy but ill-fated helmsman, the poet chose the complex metrical form of the sestina: six sestets of hendecasyllabic verses with lines ending in the key words *furia* (fury), *sonno* (sleep), *onde* (waves), *pace* (peace), *emblema* (emblem), and *mortale* (mortal), followed by a closing tercet whose lines finish with *sonno, pace,* and *mortale.* Each stanza is linked to the next one by the end-line repetition of one of these key words in the final verse of the first stanza and the opening line of the following stanza. Ungaretti intended far more than technical virtuosity by employing the sestina pattern: to present the death struggle of Aeneas's navigator against sleep, intellectual doubts, and the furious waves, a poetic structure that turns back and forth upon itself ideally serves the writer's purpose.

This poem opens with a hurricane, which is not only the physical storm that shattered the rudder of Palinurus's ship, as recounted in the *Aeneid,* but also here the tempest of the navigator's inner emotions, since Ungaretti focuses upon a psychological struggle. The enemy that Palinurus faces is sleep, an emblem of his spiritual weaknesses, rather than the god Somnus, who is his adversary in Virgil's poem. In commenting on the first sestina, Ungaretti speaks of a drowsy indo-lence that delights (but here has fatal results). Recoiling from the shock of the storm the pilot of this first-person recitative lulls himself into a deceptive sense of sleep-induced peacefulness, so that the second sestina is the narrative of his body's unsuccessfully trying to resist the gentle coaxing of sleep. Already by the third sestina confusion reigns in Palinurus in his inability to distinguish the greater threat: the ever-increasing tempest or sleep. While the storm is a call to action, sleep calms his spirit to cause him to ignore the danger about to bring about his destruction. In the fourth sestina readers see Palinurus's role as an intellectual—a facet wholly original in his portrayal by Ungaretti—who has mastered the science of navigation with its charts and astral reckonings, but the pilot succumbs to dreaming as brought on by sleep in the guise of an angel, who delivers the kiss of death as the helmsman falls into the sea.

The final verse of the fourth sestina recalls the close of the Francesca da Rimini episode at the end of Dante's *Inferno,* canto 5. Throughout Ungaretti's fifth sestina Palinurus is struggling in the waves, trying to pursue his ship in its course to the Promised Land while sleep still clings to him with its offer of deep rest. That pursuit ends in the sixth sestina as it links without any syntactical break to the concluding tercet, where a growing fury petrifies and kills the defeated pilot. Ungaretti refers to the mythic metamorphosis of Palinurus into Cape Palinurus, the great rock formation near Elea after Paestum. The human spirit obdurate in its intellectual and physical pursuits but lacking the liberating goal that inspired Aeneas finds its eternal but ironical emblem in the rocky cape, to symbolize the emptiness of Palinurus's blind devotion to his quest. Aeneas's faithful helmsman, like Moses, was fated to glimpse the Promised Land but never to cross into it.

Three brief poems complete *La terra promessa.* In "Variazioni su nulla" (Variations on Nothing) Ungaretti uses the image of an hourglass as the symbol of temporal duration that will continue to mark time's passing even during a future void of the presence of humankind. Ungaretti's intimate hope for love reappears in the verses of "Segreto del poeta" (The Poet's Secret), where night is his unfailing friend that casts its magical light on the undying memory-image of his beloved. But hope reaches its limit in the oppressively haunting "Finale" with the hypnotic repetition twelve times of the refrain "il mare" (the sea). Although emblematic of death, the sea here does not resemble Walt Whitman's sea of delicious death in "Out of the cradle endlessly rocking" but is a dismal, deadened sea that sets bounds to human aspirations. As a volume written in the autumn of the poet's life, *La terra promessa* explores human limitations. The "Canzone," Dido's choruses, and Palinurus's recitative all point to death, as Ungaretti recognizes that the Promised Land must remain a dream.

With the volume *Un grido e paesaggi*, he hoped to reflect on certain epiphanic moments of his life in settings of heightened significance. The Italian state radio had asked Ungaretti to deliver a broadcast for New Years's Day 1952 about a month of special meaning to him. That prose broadcast became the poem "Monologhetto" (Brief Monologue) centering on the month of February: the time of the writer's birth, the month also of Antonietto's birth and dying. The Italian *febbraio* brings to mind *febbre* (fever), for in the sites depicted throughout the poem—Corsica, Brazil, North Africa—February is a period of feverish celebration in Christian carnivals of pagan rejoicing in the flesh before the self-sacrifices of Lent and also in the Moslem moon of the amulets that Ungaretti as a boy in the company of his mother in Alexandria would watch with the ironical detachment of sophisticated Europeans. The poet confesses that at those festive occasions as well as throughout life he and his fellow lyricists have all engaged in a Pirandellian game of donning masks to cover the one true self. All the poets (and every sensitive person has the touch of the poet within his soul) have guided their lives on illusions, that are properly the domain of naive children. Life's tragedy is that childhood far too soon becomes a distant memory, a feverish reaching out in the dusty void across mirages to a glimmer of truth. Through "Monologhetto" Ungaretti has dared to cast aside the professional masks of poets even at the cost of revealing disillusionment.

Recall to the agony of *Il Dolore* occupies the lyric "Gridasti: soffoco" (You Cried Out: I Am Suffocating) on Antonietto's death throes and the father's consoling memories of the child's presence in his life. Ungaretti describes the boy's face with his eyes dilated in pain after the sleepless child cried out that he was suffocating. His mouth, once the expression of joyous gracefulness, is twisted in the last struggle of death. Two levels of experience operate here: the boy's painful demise and the father's desperate attempt to sur-

vive his anguish by grasping illusions of comforting past images. Like Dante in *La Vita Nova* the poet tries to develop a magic of the number nine for the years Antonietto shared his life with his father, who will always search for traces of his son's brief existence. But in the twentieth century one does not have the medieval science of numerology to sustain belief in the powers of numbers. Even as Ungaretti imagines he is clasping the boy's hands in his own, reality dispels the dream with the image of the withering of Antonietto's hands. Yet, although the child will be buried, his spirit will live on to free his father from total despair. Ungaretti fervently longs in spite of rationalistic doubts for some hope to sustain him in his loss—this is the pathos of the poem, which is rescued from morbid sentimentality because the corrosive doubt of reason pervades the attempts by the poet to delude himself. But the father admits that he is crazed by remorse in surviving his son. Ungaretti's sense of guilt is compounded by his having taken the boy away from Italy to alien Brazil, where the sky was too blue and the numerous southern hemisphere stars too unfamiliar for the family to feel at home. The poem closes with images of that deaf sky of the southern climes that falls without a breath and whose oppressiveness will always weigh upon the writer. While much of *Un grido e paesaggi* consists of vivid impressionistic sketches, as in the section "Svaghi" (Amusements), with "Gridasti: soffoco" one hears the authentic heart-rending outcry of the poet, who employs language to combat the pain of death and remorse.

In *Il taccuino del vecchio* Ungaretti at first thought to include a series of choruses for Aeneas as the triumphant builder of a new kingdom. Instead he produced "Ultimi cori per la terra promessa" (Last Choruses for the Promised Land), where in twenty-seven divisions of hendecasyllabic and septenarius verses he endeavors to assess his own existence as a poet of memory-images within the context of an age of artificial satellites and jet travel. The first three divisions serve as a prelude to meditation on time, seen as a concatenation of days succeeding one another in which the poet, like everyone else, is but a refugee. Once again Ungaretti returns to the image of the exile, now one who is nearing the end of his wearisome wanderings. He reaches an understanding of his persona as a lifetime accumulation of events, individuals encountered, objects acquired or lost, places visited, and emotions experienced. Eventually the promise of every new

Drawing of Ungaretti by an unknown artist (from Frederic J. Jones, Giuseppe Ungaretti, Poet and Critic, *1977)*

day becomes, in passing, merely wayward smoke. With the fourth division, the lyric questions where the goal of life's quest lies: the dream is not of Ithaca (not the longing to return home) but of Sinai for the glimpse of the Promised Land. Yet in the fifth division the poet confesses that throughout one's traveling in the desert of life what is known of the Promised Land (what one can only know) is an archetypal image. While Mt. Sinai may offer the promise of a new kind of Mosaic law, in the meanwhile one must accept prevailing laws that cruelly demolish illusions. In his disillusionment the poet, in the seventh division, wonders if memory can defeat oblivion, a belief in tradition that was always central to Ungaretti's poetic creed. The unity of preexistence and existence has been lost in the bewilderment of fragmentation. All the Italian poet has left is tatters of memories.

By the eighth division a feminine presence accompanies the speaker: perhaps his wife at the time close to her death. Ungaretti wonders if the two of them passed through life as sleepwalkers; admits defeat here since as a poet he should have looked at life with intensified sensitivity and awareness. Divisions 9 through 13 form the birthday sequence, once published separately in 1958 as a poem in itself: here in the month of February hope in continuity can be renewed just as mimosa suddenly springs forth in golden blossoming. Death then exerts control merely over appearances. Although the poet commemorates his wife's passing by referring to her absence, his suffering reveals his capacity for love. As typical with Ungaretti, private grief takes on universal dimensions in the twelfth division, where the color of the sunset suggests the waning of the West in violence when blood will streak the sun. But this section closes optimistically in the thirteenth division with the image of a red rose blooming over abysses to console with its sudden fragrance the poet's lament. Despite personal loss and dread for the future of civilization, Ungaretti succeeds in overcoming his despair.

Throughout the fourteenth and fifteenth divisions the poem examines the nature of love, understood in its primeval erotic force as between Adam and Eve just before the Fall from Eden when they yielded to curiosity and the delirium of passion. The spirit of the poem leaps upward in the sixteenth and seventeenth sections, inspired by the launching of artificial satellites, but Ungaretti does not celebrate that triumph of modern scientific technology, for he sees the satellites as merely connecting from star to star, in the measureless swirling void of outer space, the solitude of humankind. The whole idea of solitude preoccupies the elderly writer cut off from his wife and his son, so that by the nineteenth division he cries out for an end to waking and sleeping. But thoughts of the beloved dead and of the few survivors that are dear to him can, as expressed in the twenty-second division, come to him in the eventide of his life to calm his spirit with their affectionate presence.

Transglobal jet travel inspires the twenty-third and twenty-fourth divisions as Ungaretti looks down upon the earth from the precarious cocoon of his high-velocity air carrier to behold the sweet morning and the fiery sunset in a world that has lost the sense of human proportions. Flying over the Egyptian desert compels the poet to envision his death: a kite-bird seizes him in its talons and feeds him to the ravens and jackals of the wasteland; in the end all that remains of the wanderer is a pile of the whitest bones to be discovered by the passing bedouin. Dissonance between the self and the world will terminate when the fleshed-out image of human existence has been stripped away. After the presentiment of his near demise the writer recognizes that he is no longer a creature of inner passions and chiaroscuro moods. His ultimate transfiguration, as stated in the poem's concluding verse, is as "the old captain," a commander of the seas rather than of the infantry on the Carso of decades before, sailing calmly toward the gleaming of a lighthouse. How appropriate a close for the last major poem of Ungaretti's *Vita d'un uomo*, with the term *faro* (lighthouse), derived from the Greek *pharos* for the lighthouse of ancient Alexandria, one of the seven wonders of the world. Close to dying, the poet of the buried port is finally coming home to end his odyssey. Unlike Aeneas who could travel from burning Troy to found his new realm on Italian shores, Ungaretti perceives that the Promised Land is not an earthly place but a state of mind to be reached after the tempest-driven voyage of life.

His collected lyrics illustrate how a crisis of poetry gives rise to the poetry of crisis. Ungaretti's early ties to the symbolists and the futurists reflected the concern at the start of this century over the possibility of poetic creation in an atmosphere of ennui and artistic impotence, where a writer might very well yield to impressionism and the atrophy of moral values to record the passive collision of his psyche with random stimuli. Although *L'Allegria* holds numerous examples of Ungaretti's lightning-flash opening of his being to the world, his was never a passive surrender to phenomena. Similarly, his hermeticism never brought about a flight from outer reality, only its transformation through purified language and imagery removed from the Italian rhetorical excesses prevailing from the time of national unification through the eras of Carducci, Pascoli, and D'Annunzio. Even the extremely personal agony of *Il Dolore* does not constitute an escape into oneself, for the poet's grief rises to encompass the torment of his nation under enemy occupation. But while always aware of particular historical circumstances, as on the battlefront of World War I, Ungaretti aimed at evoking the hidden universal life beneath surface conditions, whether in the enigmatic and telegrammatic verses of his early collections, in the baroque illuminations of his midcareer, or in the increasingly traditional songs and choruses of his later years. Constantly revising his texts, he sought to achieve a dazzling

stage of absolute condensation and limpidity. Guided by Italian models such as Petrarch and Leopardi, this poet strove to reach the essential through minimalist techniques while upholding literary traditions of individual introspection and the cherishing of precious illusions.

As a poet of radiant yet nocturnal memory-images, Ungaretti concentrated on the power of time that annihilates transient realities except when the poetic fathers of the past speak out with their eternal voices. His personal task throughout his poems was to rescue certain of life's victims from that temporal annihilation: a suicidal Egyptian student succumbing to alienation in Paris, a captain fallen in a furrow on the war front, a nine-year-old boy agonizing far away from his Italian homeland. As a poet of metaphysical divination, Ungaretti abolishes time to make eternal such vulnerable victims, who then become mythic figures in his verses alongside ancient characters including Aeneas, Dido, and Palinurus. He could move with equal ease in the contemporary period and antiquity, since for him all time was of psychological duration. Similarly Ungaretti transformed the places of his life into mythic spaces of universal significance: Alexandria between the shifting sands of the desert and the engulfing waves of the sea; the rivers that witnessed the poet's artistic and intellectual development along with his introduction to the destructiveness of war and brutal military occupation; the savage coastline of Brazil that crushed a defenseless child; and the baroque monuments and works of Roman art that lifted the writer out of the dismal depression of a time of menacing atrocities. As persons, times, and places undergo mythic transfiguration, Giuseppe Ungaretti's *Vita d'un uomo* attests to the perpetual artistic unity of fabled poetic illumination.

Letters:

Lettere dal fronte a Gherardo Marone: 1916-1918, edited by Armando Marone (Milan: Mondadori, 1978);

Giuseppe Ungaretti: Lettere a Soffici, 1917-1930, edited by Leone Piccioni (Florence: Sansoni, 1981);

Carteggio, 1931-1962, edited by Piccioni (Milan: Saggiatore, 1984).

Interview:

Ferdinando Camon, "Ungaretti," in his *Il mestiere di poeta* (Milan: Lerici, 1965), pp. 25-30.

Bibliography:

Giorgio Baroni, *Giuseppe Ungaretti: Introduzione e guida allo studio dell'opera ungarettiana* (Florence: Monnier, 1981).

Biography:

Leone Piccioni, *Vita di un poeta: Giuseppe Ungaretti* (Milan: Rizzoli, 1970).

References:

Luciano Anceschi, *Da Ungaretti a D'Annunzio* (Milan: Saggiatore, 1976);

L'Approdo Letterario, special Ungaretti issue, 18 (March 1972);

Piero Bigongiari, "Struttura dell'*Allegria* di Ungaretti," *L'Albero*, 52 (January 1974): 3-35;

Carlo Bo, *Otto studi* (Florence: Vallecchi, 1939);

Bo, ed., *Convegno internazionale su Giuseppe Ungaretti, Urbino, 3-6 ottobre 1979* (Urbino, Italy: 4 Venti, 1981);

Armando Brissoni, *Due saggi di poesia: Ungaretti e Foscolo* (Padua, Italy: Rebellato, 1969);

Glauco Cambon, *Giuseppe Ungaretti* (New York: Columbia University Press, 1967);

Cambon, *La poesia di Ungaretti* (Turin: Einaudi, 1976);

Joseph Cary, *Three Modern Italian Poets: Saba, Ungaretti, Montale* (New York: New York University Press, 1969);

Gigi Cavalli, *Ungaretti* (Milan: Fabbri, 1958);

Giovanni Cecchetti, "Giuseppe Ungaretti," *Italica*, 26, no. 4 (1949): 269-279;

Maura Del Serra, *Giuseppe Ungaretti* (Florence: Nuova Italia, 1977);

Silvano Demarchi, *Guido allo studio di Ungaretti* (Bolzano, Italy: Edinord, 1976);

Giuseppe De Robertis, *Scrittori del Novecento* (Florence: Monnier, 1946);

Franco Di Carlo, *Ungaretti e Leopardi: Il sistema della memoria dall'assenza all'innocenza* (Rome: Bulzoni, 1979);

Giuseppe Faso, *La Critica e Ungaretti* (Bologna: Cappelli, 1977);

Francesco Flora, *La poesia ermetica* (Bari, Italy: Laterza, 1936);

Alberto Frattini, *Da Tommaseo a Ungaretti* (Rocca San Casciano, Italy: Cappelli, 1959);

Gérard Genot, *Sémantique du discontinu dans 'L'Allegoria' d'Ungaretti* (Paris: Klincksieck, 1972);

Emerico Giachery, *Civiltà e parola: Studi ungarettiani* (Rome: Argireto, 1974);

Giachery, *Nostro Ungaretti* (Rome: Studium, 1988);

Ioan Gutia, *Linguaggio di Ungaretti* (Florence: Monnier, 1959);

Michael Hanne, "Ungaretti's *La terra promessa* and the *Aeneid*," *Italica*, 50 (March 1973): 3-25;

Ivar Ivask, ed., *Books Abroad*, special Ungaretti issue, 44, no. 4 (1970);

Frederic J. Jones, *Giuseppe Ungaretti, Poet and Critic* (Edinburgh: Edinburgh University Press, 1977);

Jones, *The Modern Italian Lyric* (Cardiff: University of Wales Press, 1986);

Romeo Lucchese, ed., *Letteratura*, special Ungaretti double issue, 35-36 (September-December 1958);

Giorgio Luti, *Invito alla lettura di Ungaretti* (Milan: Mursia, 1974);

Carmine A. Mezzacappa, *Noia e inquietudine nella "Vita d'un uomo" di G. Ungaretti* (Padua, Italy: Rebellato, 1970);

José Minervini, *Temi e motivi nell'opera di Ungaretti* (Rome: Baroni, 1972);

Nila Noto, *La spazialità poetica in Ungaretti* (Palermo: Celebes, 1976);

Tom O'Neill, "The Problem of Formalism in Ungaretti's Poetry," *Italian Quarterly*, 14 (March 1970): 59-73;

Carlo Ossola, *Giuseppe Ungaretti* (Milan: Mursia, 1975);

Mario Petrucciani, *Il condizionale di Didone: Studi su Ungaretti* (Naples: Scientifiche Italiane, 1985);

Folco Portinari, *Giuseppe Ungaretti* (Turin: Borla, 1967);

Luciano Rebay, *Le origini della poesia di Giuseppe Ungaretti* (Rome: Storia e Letteratura, 1962);

Michele Ricciardelli, ed., *Forum Italicum*, special Ungaretti issue, 6, no. 2 (June 1972);

Linda Samson-Talleur, "Ungaretti, Leopardi and the Shipwreck of the Soul," *Chimères*, 16 (January 1982): 5-19;

Piero Sanavio, ed., *Herne*, special Ungaretti issue, 69 (1969);

André Sempoux, "Le premier Ungaretti et la France," *Revue de Littérature Comparée*, 37 (July-September 1963): 360-367;

Ghan Singh, "The Poetry of Giuseppe Ungaretti," *Italian Studies*, 28 (1973): 64-82;

Ornella Sobrero, ed., *Galleria*, special Ungaretti issue, 18 (July-December 1968);

Carlo Torchio, "Analisi della struttura di una lirica di Ungaretti: 'Gridasti: soffoco,'"

L'Arte dell'interpretare: Studi critici offerti a Giovanni Getto (Cuneo: Arciere, 1984), pp. 745-756;

Rosita Tordi, ed., Ungaretti e la cultura romana: Atti del convegno 13-14 novembre 1980 (Rome: Bulzoni, 1983);

Alvaro Valentini, Semantica dei poeti Ungaretti e Montale (Rome: Bulzoni, 1970);

Tobias Wyss, Dialog und Stille: Max Jacob, Giuseppe Ungaretti, Fernando Pessoa (Zurich: Juris, 1969).

Giorgio Vigolo

(3 December 1894 - January 1983)

Alberto Frattini
University of Rome II

La città dell'anima (Rome: Romano, 1923);

Canto fermo (Rome: Formiggini, 1931);

Il silenzio creato (Rome: Novissima, 1934);

Conclave dei sogni (Rome: Novissima, 1935);

Linea della vita (Milan: Mondadori, 1949);

Canto del destino (Venice: Neri Pozza, 1959);

Le notti romane (Milan: Bompiani, 1960);

Il genio del Belli, 2 volumes (Milan: Saggiatore, 1963);

La luce ricorda (Milan: Mondadori, 1967);

Mille e una sera all'opera e al concerto (Florence: Sansoni, 1971);

Spettro solare (Milan: Bompiani, 1973);

Poesie scelte, edited by Marco Ariani (Milan: Mondadori, 1976);

I fantasmi di pietra (Milan: Mondadori, 1977);

Il canocchiale metafisico (Rome: Cometa, 1982);

La Virgilia (Milan: Nuova, 1982);

La fame degli occhi (Rome: Florida, 1982);

La vita del beato Pirolèo (Milan: Nuova, 1983).

OTHER: Giuseppe Belli, I sonetti, edited by Vigolo (Rome: Formiggini, 1931; revised edition, with an essay by Vigolo, Milan: Mondadori, 1952);

E. T. A. Hoffmann, Maestro Pulce, translated by Vigolo (Rome: Petrella, 1945);

Belli, Er giorno der giudizzio, edited by Vigolo (Milan: Mondadori, 1957);

Friedrich Hölderlin, Poesie, translated, with an introduction, by Vigolo (Turin: Einaudi, 1958).

SELECTED PERIODICAL PUBLICATIONS—
UNCOLLECTED: "Della poesia come fondamento," Bollettino del centro-studi di poesia italiana e straniera, 1 (March 1962): 5-32;

"Inediti di estetica e di poetica," Segnacolo, 2 (1962): 25-47.

Giorgio Vigolo was above all a poet and novelist, but he was also a capable philologist, critic, and musicologist. In the context of a tradition that is as much European as it is Italian, his work represents a rich fusion of the values of the Italian North and those of the South: his work collates the dramatic, spellbinding, existential restlessness, derived from romantic notions, proper to the writers of the North, and the ecstasy of meditation proper to the writers of the South—in effect a classical tone.

Vigolo was born on 3 December 1894 in Rome, where he lived his entire life—a life marked by few exceptional events, other than the two periods that brought him considerable pain: the times of his involvement in World Wars I and II. Vigolo's artistic temperament was inherited from his parents, both musicians. His mother, Bettina Venturi Vigolo, was also a singer, the

Giorgio Vigolo

niece of Rome's mayor Pietro Venturi, and the family was friendly with the well-known poet Giuseppe Belli. Vigolo's father, Umberto, took him for long walks in the city and introduced him to the works of Johann Wolfgang von Goethe, Friedrich von Schiller, and Immanuel Kant. Another of the young Vigolo's favorite authors was Arthur Rimbaud. After receiving a humanistic education in literature, music, and philosophy, Vigolo began to devote more and more time to his writing.

Following the 1923 publication of his first book, *La città dell'anima* (The City of the Soul)—a penetrating exploration of Rome, where echoes of the ancient world are interspersed with vivid naturalist vistas and Vigolo's sense of cosmic memory—he outlined his poetics in definite terms in his essay "Della poesia come fondamento" (On Poetry as Foundation). The work was written in 1929 but published many years later in Rome in the journal *Bollettino del centro-*

studi di poesia italiana e straniera (March 1962). Vigolo articulates his central themes, which are especially visible in works published after the death of his parents; it was an event that left a deep, tragic scar on his psyche.

"Della poesia come fondamento" clarifies the nature of the conflict between the aesthetics of Vigolo and those of his contemporaries. Primarily Vigolo was reacting to Benedetto Croce's *Estetica* (Aesthetics) and its subordination of poetry. He was also responding to Hegelian panlogism and Johann Gottlieb Fichte's *Wissenschaftslehre* (1794-1795), translated into Italian in 1910 as *Dottrina della scienza* (Doctrine of Science), in which the poetic nature of the spirit was displaced by a rational-activistic nature. Finally Vigolo opposed Giovanni Gentile's *Filosofia dell'arte* (Philosophy of Art). In the Weltanschauung of "Della poesia come fondamento" poetry is at the base of all profound knowledge of humanity and the universe by virtue of the fact that it constitutes the "assoluta unità dello spirito nella sua convergente totalità" (absolute unity of the spirit in its convergent totality) and functions autonomously with respect to Saint John's notion of the word as exclusive principle and vehicle of the creative act (at least as it pertains to the formulation of poetic discourse). Young Vigolo tried to accomplish a unique eschatological and symbolic interpretation of history as the projection of human destiny. In the process, he proposed his own theory on the maieutic properties of poetry:

> Oggi l'opera della poesia è ricuperare il valore violento delle antitesi, enucleare gli elementi puri ed originari di sotto il tegumento, la testuggine pietrosa. Disciogliere nel fossile le primigenie correnti della vita è opera di poesia non meno che stringere in pietra la nube. Il diamante è anche il fossile della luce.

> (Today the function of poetry is to recover the violent value of antitheses and enucleate the pure and original elements beneath the hard, tortoise-shell exterior of things. Releasing from fossils the primordial flow of life is no less a function of poetry than encasing a cloud in stone. The diamond is also a fossil of light.)

Vigolo was able to construct his ars poetica, in which he stressed the role of the poet who reconciles extremes and is capable of transforming fire into ice or of turning "in visione l'intero suo mondo fantastico" (into vision his entire imaginative world). In the light of these observations, the reader can interpret Vigolo's poetry more appropriately, beginning with *Conclave dei sogni* (Conclave of Dreams, 1935); in the introduction, Vigolo attempts to identify, with figurative language, the most important aspect of the volume's orientation as the anticipation of dawn, when nature stirs to life. Vigolo's symbolic and existential vision of cosmic metamorphoses softens the dramatic component of *Conclave dei sogni* by means of idyllic textures, but the poem "Conclave dei sogni," strangely omitted from the volume of the same title (it is collected in *Linea della vita* [Lifeline, 1949]), permits better access to Vigolo's tragic imagination:

> Io m'esiliai vivente
> in archi di mortale ombra, né sole
> più vidi, né di donna un caro viso.
> Letto di pietra al doloroso corpo
> m'ebbi e dementi sogni; angeli e mostri
> s'azzuffavan nel mio sangue le febbri.
> In cane, in lupo ero mutato. Strane

alghe e rossi funghi
mi gremivano il petto e foglioline
purpuree m'accendevano nel buio.
Luce fecero immensa
dentro la notte, e un sole
mio faticoso su dai rami sorse
d'un bosco oscuro. Le mie vene incendio
ebbero e lume d'universa aurora,
diafane tutte e diramate in mille
alberi e faune ardenti.

> (I went into exile living
> among the arches of mortal shade, no sun
> did I then see, nor sweet woman's face.
> A bed of stone for my aching body
> I had, and mad dreams; the fevers,
> angels and monsters, waged war in my blood.
> Into a dog, a wolf, I was changed. Strange
> algae and red mushrooms
> covered my chest and small purple
> leaves set me on fire in the darkness.
> Immense light they made
> in the night, a weary sun
> of mine rose over the branches
> of a shrouded wood. My veins were afire
> with the light of earth's dawning;
> all diaphanous they stretched over
> a thousand flaming trees and fauna.)

The oneiric-visionary component of Vigolo's work is extended in his subsequent publications. The last section of *La luce ricorda* (The Light Remembers), published in 1967, constitutes a summa of Vigolo's writing. In the poem "Giona" (Jonah) one reads:

> O sogno, o immagine di destino,
> senso della mia vita
> scagliata da una fionda,
> balestrata da altezze inenarrabili,
> o sogno, o segno, sei rimasto immobile:
> il Giona rovescio, inghiottito dal pesce
> è sopra me, costellazione fissa,
> su me che in fondo al gorgo
> dell'esistenza mi trovo supino.
> Forse nell'ultimo istante, un vasto
> cielo di notte si aprirà sul mio letto
> e vedrò scintillare invece dell'Orsa
> il gran Giona rovescio tra le stelle.

> (Oh dream, image of destiny,
> meaning of my existence,
> hurled by a sling,
> fired from incalculable heights,
> oh dream, oh sign, you've remained constant:
> a supine Jonah, swallowed by the fish,
> is above me, a fixed constellation,
> as I lie supine on the bottom

of the gorge of existence.
Perhaps at the last moment,
a vast night sky will open up over my bed
and instead of Ursa I will see the
great supine Jonah among the stars.)

However, one can trace the strong tendency to oneiric representation in Vigolo's poetry of the 1960s back to the visionary tension of the poems he composed in the 1930s.

In order to gain a fuller grasp of the dialectic (in Vigolo's poetry) between immersion in the tragic concreteness of reality and lived experience on the one hand, and the inclination to fantasize or conjure up dreamy visions on the other, one needs to consider his encounters with Belli in the 1930s, as well as his meetings with Friedrich Hölderlin, occurring at approximately the same time. Vigolo was then busy translating Hölderlin's *Poesie*, which he eventually published in 1958 with an introductory note. The work is important not only because of the quality of the translation but also because of the vast spiritual horizon within which Vigolo interpreted the great romantic poet.

But counterpoised against the fire of Hölderlin's *Begeisterung* (inspiration) is Vigolo's own interlacement of light and shadow, ecstasy and dread. At the root of such a technique one sees the influence of Charles-Pierre Baudelaire, Franz Kafka, Edgar Allan Poe, and, especially, E. T. A. Hoffmann, with his haunting, magical, and dreamlike scenarios. Nor can one exclude the possibility of even more esoteric sources for Vigolo's art—sources such as Giovanni Pico della Mirandola and Goethe. Vigolo took these literary sources in a direction that led beyond the attractions and objectives of the currents or models of his day.

His is an unmistakable poetics in which the oneiric and the visionary merge. For instance, in "Cerchio di memoria" (Circle of Memory), in *Conclave dei sogni*, dreaming and wakefulness exchange places:

ma ti sei addormentato
dalla parte del cuore
e sogni di sognare
la tua camera e ti pare
d'essere sveglio.

(but you fell asleep
on the side of your heart
and dream of dreaming

about your bedroom and you feel
you are awake.)

One could also point to a composition in *La luce ricorda*, "Al centro delle visioni" (At the Center of Visions):

Donde s'irraggiano i paesi ammirabili
risali al punto vivo ch'è dentro te nel cuore,
ove il tuo guizzo primo s'innestò
e il filo gittato s'avvolse
a quel minimo uncino
che fu la tua presa alla vita.

(From where the marvelous lands irradiate
you return to the bright point in your heart,
where the first spark of life ignited
and the tossed thread wound itself
around that microscopic hook
by which you cling to life.)

Meanwhile, in the same book, in "I secoli poeti" (The Poet Centuries) visions and dreams undergo magnification in a sort of religious epic with an expressly Dantesque quality. "Coro di spiriti nel cielo di una città" (Chorus of Souls in a City's Sky) revives a Leopardian archetype in which the song of the dead, who hover above their homeland, is transposed to a dream of life, which, to the amazement and anguish of the speaker, is rediscovered as "anelito breve" (brief yearning) or a "notturno guado d'ambascia" (nocturnal passage of anguish). In "Miraggio" (Mirage) oneiric epiphany is coincident with an affectionate and astonishing "contatto" [contact] with childhood memories: "Un sogno / d'un'altra vita oggi mi sembra quello" (that seems / the dream of another life). In fact the entire volume can be read as a passionate "caccia ai ricordi" (memory hunt), or a search conducted to the deepest recesses of the soul and of Rome's "prime apparizioni" (first apparitions).

In the 1940s a new condition took hold in Vigolo's poetry and combined with the oneiric and the surreal, which were dominant factors in the first phase of the poet's career. This new condition was born of the unsettling correlation between the extreme ephemerality of life and the inescapable constancy of death. Where the finite and the infinite, stasis and motion, appearance and essence intersect, a new meaning of the poetic *evento* emerges. Vigolo defines that "event" as: "quell'incrocio di relazioni viventi e il loro fissarsi nella parola, come qualche cosa di 'avvenuto' spontaneamente in una prima 'sintesi vitale' di forze interne ed esterne" (that intersection of living relations and their acquisition of form within the word, like something which "occurs" spontaneously in an original "vital synthesis" of internal and external forces).

In *Canto del destino* (Song of Destiny), published in 1959, the spiritual and stylistic features of *Linea della vita* recur. However, Vigolo expands and enriches his style, as a result of maturation. The painful series of disappointments, uncertainties, and humiliations suffered during and after World War II had prepared him for a more gratifying experience of reality or a more enthusiastic receptivity with respect to the *evento*. These same forces, though, seem to push him once more (in *Canto del destino*) into a closely guarded and hermetic world of private memories, regrets, insights, and fears. It is a dialectic confirmed by the contrast between the closed metrical forms, the refined, and at times aulic, syntax on the one hand, and a more versatile or open meter, a more fluid syntax (even if it can occasionally be broken or dissonant)—as well as vocabulary taken directly from daily conversations—on the other. In *Canto del destino* the serenely evocative atmosphere of "Quando il cielo s'illumina" (When the Sky Glows) is followed by a bitter and sometimes desperate sinking into tragedy, which occurs in "Enchiridion" (Manuscript) and "Canto del destino." In "L'istante di pace" (The Instant of Peace) one notices a renewed aspiration toward "l'alta pace dell'essenza" (the deep peace of essence), suffused with the poet's anxious wonder and fearful premonitions.

A critical profile of Vigolo cannot overlook his activity as a music critic. He wrote professionally for a thirty-year period after World War II, contributing pieces to various newspapers and periodicals, such as *Epoca, Risorgimento Liberale*, and *Il Mondo*, as well as to the programs of RAI radio. In his work as a music critic Vigolo developed a style characterized by moods and whimsical observations of a cultural, philosophical, and artistic nature, while resisting the temptation to go off on literary tangents. An ample selection of his "cronache musicali" (music reports), from the period 1945-1966, are collected in *Mille e una sera all'opera e al concerto* (A Thousand and One Evenings at the Opera and the Concert), published in 1971. The large volume documents a critique that avoids all tendency to excess in praising tradition and its values, as well as in defending the importance of every form of experimentation.

Vigolo was well aware of the vagaries of caprice and fashion. The poetics he finds most attractive is that of intimacy, not opportunistic mimicry or gratuitous experimentation that often ends up confusing *rictus*—"una sorta di tetano della musica" (a kind of musical lockjaw)—with rhythm, "l'anima delle arti" (the soul of the arts). The work of Vigolo the musicologist (some of which is still scattered in a variety of dailies and magazines) represents not only important material that prepares the reader to enter the labyrinth of modern and contemporary music; it also provides useful information to the reader who wishes to penetrate the complex artistic, literary, historical, and existential phenomenology of present civilization. Finally, Vigolo's criticism is a source that cannot be ignored by the reader who wants to study Vigolo the fiction writer and poet.

Vigolo's reception by critics has been substantial. However, during the 1970s the interest of scholars decreased somewhat, and Vigolo began to bemoan the fact that he was being neglected or boycotted by members of the critical establishment (as indicated in his 1977 interview with Luigi Vaccari). Vigolo's concerns were only partly justified. If Vigolo's work was seen as belonging to the history of Italian literature in the 1930s, with the support of Italy's most prestigious critics, such as Alfredo Gargiulo, Giuseppe De Robertis, Gianfranco Contini, and Giacomo Debenedetti, even in the 1960s and 1970s Vigolo's work was being monitored by several well-qualified, astute critics, such as Enrico Falqui, Arnaldo Bocelli, Carlo Bo, Giacinto Spagnoletti, Geno Pampaloni, Giuliano Manacorda, and Giorgio Barberi Squarotti. Even if some reservations were expressed about the validity of Vigolo's work, the Marco Ariani monographic study in 1976 made reparation to the elderly poet. In that same year Vigolo's *Poesie scelte* (Selected Poems) was published by Mondadori.

Even at the age of eighty Vigolo did not cease to amaze his readers with a seemingly inexhaustible lyrical vein. In his *I fantasmi di pietra* (Stone Ghosts, 1977) one rediscovers the poet's somewhat bitter but always luminous fantasy, infused with elements of morbidity and delirium. A *gelo surreale* (surreal iciness) seems to echo the power of Belli's realist verses, with their meaning overturned, as in the title poem:

> Roma, questi fantasmi pietrificati
> fra i quali io m'aggiro da sempre
> e che si disciolgono la notte

e si rovesciano nei miei sogni
come un Tevere
che nel mio sangue s'insala . . .

    ma poi di giorno, eccoli di nuovo diritti
agli angoli delle strade,
sugli sfondi del cielo o fra le nuvole,
i fantasmi di pietra
mi guardano, mi aspettano
che diventi uno di loro.

(Rome, these petrified ghosts
among which I've always roamed
disperse in the night
and collapse into my dreams
like a Tiber
that becomes salty in my blood . . .

    then, by day, they are again standing
on the street corners
against a backdrop of sky and clouds,
the stone ghosts
watch me, they wait for me
to become one of them.)

But the receptivity to innocence and splendor is not interrupted, as seen in "Luce immensa degli angeli" (Immense Light of Angels):

Luce immensa degli angeli, ti vedo
sopra di me come frumento al sole
e io, formicola, in fondo agli alti steli,
il due di ottobre, autunnale splendore:

    quante volte ho sentito
la vostra ala coprirmi
nella mia folle temeraria vita
e guidare i miei passi e trattenermi
sul ciglio dei pericoli.
           Ora vi prego
guidatemi la mano anche sul foglio,
che come attento fanciullo al dettato,
la vostra lingua impari.

(Immense light of angels, I see you
above me like wheat in the sun
and I am an ant at the base of tall stalks,
on October second, in autumnal splendor:

    how often I've felt,
in my foolish fearful life,
your wing cover me
and guide my steps and hold me
on the precipice of danger.
           Now I pray you,
guide my hand on the page too,
so that, like a child attentive to dictation,
I may learn your language.)

In 1982, the year before Vigolo's death, there was an extraordinary revival of interest in his work, ushered in by the publication that year of the poems of *La fame degli occhi* (The Hunger of the Eyes), the prose fiction of *Il canocchiale metafisico* (The Metaphysical Telescope), and the novel *La Virgilia* (Virgilia)—a novel written as early as 1921. These three publications confirm Vigolo's rightful position within the context of modern Italian literature. This is particularly true of the poems in which one finds the unmodified basis of his worldview condensed and emerging in striking ways out of the friction between the reverie of the soul and the lucidity of reason—the most dramatic distancing of the self from the contingent. The entire process implies desolate immersion in pain and the awareness of existential defeat—even in Vigolo's last works.

Il canocchiale metafisico, which is almost an "addition" to the two volumes *Le notti romane* (Roman Nights, 1960) and *Spettro solare* (Solar Spectrum, 1973), constitutes a valuable enrichment of the prose writings of Vigolo, representing a new spectrum of narrative style, which alternates between the intense, baroque, visionary qualities of "Le beatricine" (The Inspirations) and the taste for a profound analysis of the relationships connecting sense, imagination, nature, and culture, as in "Ogni libro un vino" (Every Book a Wine). In these short stories, Vigolo is also attentive to the patterns of popular speech and manages to suggest the literary, ethical, and cultural connotations inherent in the musical rhythm of that speech, as occurs in "La morra cantata" (The Sung Mora).

The essence and premises of *La Virgilia* appear in condensed form in a short story of the same title, included in *Spettro solare*. Written more than fifty years before it was published in any form, the novel's plot unfolds as the diary of a young German musician and paleotologist who comes to Rome in the early 1700s in search of Renaissance musical texts preserved in the city's convents and palaces. At the very heart of Vigolo's "città dell'anima" there takes place an adventure that turns out to be a search for the tomb of a beautiful adolescent girl, Virgilia, loved by the cardinal Galeazzo Guidi. After her death, the cardinal composes a musical piece dedicated to her memory. At his request, Regiomontano, a well-known astronomer and mathematician, but also a technological wizard, constructs a tomb that is also an organ—which can be opened only by playing a specific tune on the keyboard; the tune, of course, is the piece composed by the cardinal. The tomb is discovered by the young musicologist, who, with the aid of his Roman friend Monseigneur Gualdi, succeeds in entering the tomb.

La Virgilia gives ample evidence of Vigolo's extraordinary descriptive power as well as of the dangers of excess his oneiric-visionary fantasizing tends to incur. One need only look at the final pages of the novel, where the epiphany occurs. The entombed Virgilia is described as an "usignolo della fantasia" (nightingale of the imagination), whose voice is "sigillata sotto gli spessori del diamante" (sealed within the density of the diamond). Elémire Zolla, who reviewed this *incantato* (enchanted) novel for *Corriere della Sera* (16 January 1983), underscores Vigolo's ability to transform actual situations, to the point where he extracts "per virtù di stile, tutto ciò che Roma barocca può far sogno alla vista" (by the force of style, everything which the baroque city of Rome has to make the eyes dream).

La Virgilia is suffused with romantic elements, coincident with Vigolo's oneiric, baroque reverie, whereas the pseudonymous tales of Pirolèo Vasario, whose "gioconde fantasie" (merry fantasies) were written early on in Vigolo's career but published posthumously as *La vita del beato Pirolèo* (The Life of Saintly Pirolèo, 1983), are characterized primarily by a quality that is more "visual" than "visionary." Together with the novel *La Virgilia*, this work places Vigolo in a context that can best be described as essentially neoclassical.

In Vigolo's last collection of poems, *La fame degli occhi*, previous tensions crystallize to form a kind of oneiric tragedy:

Mi crolla addosso
il peso del mio scheletro
con la frana d'un secolo
sul decrepito infante
ancora vivo.

(The weight of my skeleton
collapses on me
with the landslide of a century
on the decrepit child
who still breathes.)

Vigolo's baroque imagination reverts to its roots of horror and pain, derived from the unresolved conflict between the "irruzione" (irruption) of reality, here transfigured to nightmare, and the "essenzione" (escape) into the ideal, which can ele-

vate the anguished soul to a place where it can obtain consolation. It is a dream that keeps hope alive, as one can see in the closing poem, "Le madri" (The Mothers):

Dopo passati di là
ci si deve sentire
come convalescenti della vita.
Con incerto passo ci si leva
da un letto di lunghe pene,
vacillando tentiamo la nuova strada.
Ma dolci madri forse ci sorreggono
nell'altra nascita, ci aiutano a uscire
la prima volta dal funebre chiuso
per le vie della città celeste.

Sulle scale d'immense
cattedrali d'azzurro ci conducono
a prendere il nuovo sole
accanto al loro sorriso.

(After passing that way
we must feel
like life's convalescents.
With an unsteady step we rise
from a bed of enduring pain,
shaking we set off on a new road.
But sweet mothers perhaps support
us in the next birth, help us to emerge
for the first time from the funereal enclosure
along the streets of the celestial city.

On the steps of immense
cathedrals of blue they lead us
to take in the new sun
beside their smiles.)

This is Vigolo's visualized destiny and the meaning of his poetry: to go from the "città dell'anima" to the infinity of the sky and dreams.

Interview:
Luigi Vaccari, *Messaggero*, 3 April 1977.

Bibliographies:
Marco Ariani, *Vigolo* (Florence: Nuova Italia, 1976), pp. 137-143;
Alberto Frattini, *Introduzione a Giorgio Vigolo* (Milan: Marzorati, 1984), pp. 96-103.

Biography:
Marco Ariani, *Vigolo* (Florence: Nuova Italia, 1976).

References:
Giorgio Bàrberi Squarotti, "Vigolo (*Canto del de-*

stino)," *Paragone Letteratura* (April 1960): 123-136;

Pietro Cimatti, "Il sogno, il mito, il carcere," *Messaggero*, 27 January 1982, p. 7;

Gianfranco Contini, "Giorgio Vigolo *à la musique*" and "Giorgio Vigolo—*Conclave dei sogni*," in his *Esercizi di lettura* (Florence: Parenti, 1939), pp. 127-143;

Giacomo Debenedetti, "Un poeta Nuovo," in his *Saggi critici* (Rome: O.E.T., 1945), pp. 127-137;

Giuseppe De Robertis, "*Canto fermo*," in his *Scrittori del Novecento* (Florence: Monnier, 1958), pp. 281-286;

Enrico Falqui, *Prosatori e narratori del Novecento italiano* (Turin: Einaudi, 1950), pp. 191-196;

Lucio Felici, "Giorgio Vigolo," *Rivista di studi romani* (January-March 1982): 4;

Alberto Frattini, "Giorgio Vigolo," *Letteratura italiana—I contemporanei* (Milan: Marzorati, 1963), II: 1071-1092; later published in *Letteratura italiana—900* (Milan: Marzorati, 1979), IV: 3527-3548;

Frattini, *Introduzione a Giorgio Vigolo* (Milan: Marzorati, 1984);

Frattini, "Vigolo o della poesia come itinerario dello spirito," *Humanitas*, 5 (November 1950): 1151-1153;

Alfredo Gargiulo, "A proposito di *Canto fermo*" and "A proposito di *Silenzio creato*," in his *Letteratura italiana del Novecento* (Florence: Monnier, 1943), pp. 545-568;

Giacinto Spagnoletti, "Giorgio Vigolo e altri poeti," *Messaggero*, 13 August 1968, p. 3;

Donato Valli, "Giorgio Vigolo," in *Letteratura italiana contemporanea*, edited by G. Mariani and M. Petrucciani (Rome: Lucarini, 1980), II: 297-303.

Books for Further Reading

Anceschi, Luciano. *Lirici nuovi*. Milan: Mursia, 1964.

Anceschi. *Le poetiche del Novecento in Italia*. Turin: Paravia, 1972.

Antonielli, Sergio. *Aspetti e figure del Novecento*. Parma: Guanda, 1955.

Bàrberi Squarotti, Giorgio. *Il codice di Babele*. Milan: Rizzoli, 1972.

Bàrberi Squarotti. *La cultura e la poesia italiana del dopoguerra*. Bologna: Cappelli, 1966.

Bàrberi Squarotti and Stefano Jacomuzzi, eds. *La poesia italiana contemporanea, dal Carducci ai giorni nostri*. Florence: D'Anna, 1970.

Bigongiari, Piero. *Poesia italiana del Novecento*. Milan: Saggiatore, 1978.

Binni, Walter. *La poetica del decadentismo italiano*. Florence: Sansoni, 1962.

Bo, Carlo. *Otto studi*. Florence: Vallecchi, 1939.

Cary, Joseph. *Three Modern Italian Poets: Saba, Ungaretti, Montale*. New York: New York University Press, 1969.

Cecchi, Emilio. *Letteratura italiana del Novecento*. Milan: Mondadori, 1972.

Cecchi and Natalino Sapegno, eds. *Storia della letteratura italiana*, volume 9: *Il Novecento*. Milan: Garzanti, 1969.

Contini, Gianfranco. *Esercizi di lettura*. Florence: Parenti, 1939.

Contini, ed. *Storia della letteratura dell'Italia Unita, 1861-1968*. Florence: Sansoni, 1968.

Debenedetti, Giacomo. *Poesia italiana del Novecento*. Milan: Garzanti, 1988.

De Robertis, Giuseppe. *Scrittori del Novecento*. Florence: Monnier, 1940.

De Sanctis, Francesco. *History of Italian Literature*, 2 volumes. Translated by Joan Redfern. New York: Harcourt, Brace, 1931.

Flora, Francesco. *La poesia ermetica*. Bari, Italy: Laterza, 1936.

Folena, Gianfranco, and others. *Ricerche sulla lingua poetica contemporanea*. Padua, Italy: Liviana, 1966.

Fortini, Franco. *I poeti del Novecento*. Bari, Italy: Laterza, 1978.

Frattini, Alberto. *Poeti italiani del Novecento*. Alcamo, Italy: Cielo d'Alcamo, 1953.

Frattini, ed. *Poeti italiani del XX secolo*. Brescia, Italy: La Scuola, 1974.

Friedrich, Hugo. *La lirica moderna*. Milan: Garzanti, 1958.

Friedrich. *The Structure of Modern Poetry*. Evanston: Northwestern Illinois University Press, 1974.

Getto, Giovanni, and Folco Portinari, eds. *Dal Carducci ai crepuscolari*. Bologna: Zanichelli, 1971.

Gioanola, Elio. *Storia letteraria del Novecento in Italia*. Turin: SEI, 1976.

Golino, Carlo, ed. and trans. *Contemporary Italian Poetry: An Anthology*. Berkeley: University of California Press, 1962.

Grana, Gianni, ed. *Letteratura italiana. Novecento: I contemporanei*. Milan: Marzorati, 1979.

Jones, Frederic J. *La poesia italiana contemporanea: Da Gozzano a Quasimodo*. Florence: D'Anna, 1975.

Livi, François. *Dai simbolisti ai crepuscolari*. Milan: Istituto di Propaganda Libraria, 1974.

Livi. *La parola crepuscolare*. Milan: Istituto di Propaganda Libraria, 1986.

Luti, Giorgio, ed. *Poeti italiani del Novecento*. Milan: Mondadori, 1978.

Macrì, Oreste. *Caratteri e figure della poesia italiana contemporanea*. Florence: Vallecchi, 1956.

Macrì. *Realtà del simbolo*. Florence: Vallecchi, 1968.

Manacorda, Giuliano. *Storia della letteratura italiana contemporanea: 1940-1965*, third edition. Rome: Riuniti, 1967.

Marchione, Margherita, ed. and trans. *Twentieth-Century Italian Poetry*. Rutherford, N.J.: Fairleigh Dickinson University Press, 1974.

Mariani, Gaetano. *Letteratura italiana: I contemporanei*. Milan: Marzorati, 1969.

Mariani. *Poesia e tecnica nella lirica del Novecento*. Padua, Italy: Liviana, 1958.

Mariani and Mario Petrucciani, eds. *Letteratura italiana contemporanea*. Rome: Lucarini, 1979.

Marzot, Giulio. *Il decadentismo italiano*. Bologna: Cappelli, 1970.

Mazzotti, Artal. *Letteratura italiana. Orientamenti culturali: I contemporanei*, 3 volumes. Milan: Marzorati, 1963-1969.

Mengaldo, Pier Vincenzo. *Poeti italiani del Novecento*. Milan: Mondadori, 1981.

Noferi, Adelia. *Le poetiche critiche novecentesche*. Florence: Monnier, 1970.

Pancrazi, Pietro. *Scittori d'oggi*. Bari, Italy: Laterza, 1946.

Pasolini, Pier Paolo. *Passione e ideologia: 1948-1958*. Milan: Garzanti, 1960.

Pellegrinetti, G. A., ed. *Un secolo di poesia*. Turin: Petrini, 1957.

Petrocchi, Giorgio. *Poesia e tecnica narrativa*. Milan: Mursia, 1962.

Petronio, Giuseppe. *Poeti del nostro secolo: I crepuscolari*. Florence: Sansoni, 1937.

Petrucciani, Mario. *Poesia pura e poesia esistenziale*. Turin: Loescher, 1957.

Petrucciani. *La poetica dell'ermetismo italiano*. Turin: Loescher, 1955.

Pieri, Marzio. *Biografia della poesia: Sul paesaggio mentale della poesia italiana del Novecento*. Parma: Pilotta, 1979.

Pozzi, Gianni. *La poesia italiana del Novecento*. Turin: Einaudi, 1965.

Prezzolini, Giuseppe. *Il tempo della Voce*. Milan & Florence: Longanesi/Vallecchi, 1960.

Ramat, Silvio. *L'ermetismo*. Florence: Nuova Italia, 1969.

Ramat. *Storia della poesia italiana del Novecento*. Milan: Mursia, 1976.

Ravegnani, Giuseppe, and Giovanni Titta Rosa, eds. *L'antologia dei poeti italiani dell'ultimo secolo*. Milan: Martello, 1972.

Sanguineti, Edoardo. *Tra libertà e crepuscolarismo*. Milan: Mursia, 1961.

Sanguineti, ed. *Poesia italiana del Novecento*. Turin: Einaudi, 1970.

Sewell, Elizabeth. *The Orphic Voice*. New Haven: Yale University Press, 1960.

Solmi, Sergio. *Scrittori negli anni*. Milan: Saggiatore, 1963.

Spagnoletti, Giacinto. *Tre poeti italiani del Novecento*. Rome: ERI, 1956.

Spagnoletti, ed. *Poesia italiana contemporanea*. Parma: Guanda, 1959.

Spagnoletti, ed. *Poeti del Novecento*. Milan: Mondadori, 1973.

Tedesco, Natale. *La condizione crepuscolare*. Florence: Nuova Italia, 1970.

Valli, Donato. *Anarchia e misticismo nella poesia italiana del primo Novecento*. Lecce, Italy: Milella, 1973.

Vallone, Aldo. *I crepuscolari*. Palermo: Palumbo, 1973.

Viazzi, Glauco, ed. *I poeti del futurismo*. Milan: Longanesi, 1978.

Viazzi and Vanni Scheiwiller, eds. *Poeti simbolisti e libertà in Italia*. Milan: Scheiwiller, 1973.

Contributors

Paolo Barlera ....*New York University*
Fiora A. Bassanese...*University of Massachusetts—Boston*
Luigi Bonaffini...*Brooklyn College*
Romana Capek-Habeković ....*University of Michigan*
Natalia Costa-Zalessow ....*San Francisco State University*
Stelio Cro ....*McMaster University*
Rosetta Di Pace-Jordan ....*University of Oklahoma*
Pietro Frassica...*Princeton University*
Alberto Frattini...*University of Rome II*
Joseph E. Germano...*Buffalo State College*
Andrea Guiati ....*Buffalo State College*
Emanuele Licastro..............................*State University of New York at Buffalo*
Clara Orban ....*De Paul University*
Nicolas J. Perella...............................*University of California, Berkeley*
Joseph Perricone ....*Fordham University*
Massimo Mandolini Pesaresi.......................................*Columbia University*
Mark Pietralunga...*Florida State University*
Douglas Radcliff-Umstead ....*Kent, Ohio*
Patricia Lyn Richards...*Kenyon College*
Jack Shreve ....*Allegany Community College*
Giovanni Sinicropi...*University of Connecticut*
Anthony Julian Tamburri...*Purdue University*
Elena Urgnani ....*Wheaton College*
Antonio Vitti...*Wake Forest University*
Maria Rosaria Vitti-Alexander ....*Nazareth College of Rochester*
Rebecca West ....*University of Chicago*

Cumulative Index

Dictionary of Literary Biography, Volumes 1-114
Dictionary of Literary Biography Yearbook, 1980-1990
Dictionary of Literary Biography Documentary Series, Volumes 1-9

Cumulative Index

DLB before number: *Dictionary of Literary Biography*, Volumes 1-114
Y before number: *Dictionary of Literary Biography Yearbook*, 1980-1990
DS before number: *Dictionary of Literary Biography Documentary Series*, Volumes 1-9

A

C

E

F

G

I

J

N

Q

Y

Z

ISBN 0-8103-7591-5

90000>

(Continued from front endsheets)

80: *Restoration and Eighteenth-Century Dramatists,* First Series, edited by Paula R. Backscheider (1989)

81: *Austrian Fiction Writers, 1875-1913,* edited by James Hardin and Donald G. Daviau (1989)

82: *Chicano Writers,* First Series, edited by Francisco A. Lomelí and Carl R. Shirley (1989)

83: *French Novelists Since 1960,* edited by Catharine Savage Brosman (1989)

84: *Restoration and Eighteenth-Century Dramatists,* Second Series, edited by Paula R. Backscheider (1989)

85: *Austrian Fiction Writers After 1914,* edited by James Hardin and Donald G. Daviau (1989)

86: *American Short-Story Writers, 1910-1945,* First Series, edited by Bobby Ellen Kimbel (1989)

87: *British Mystery and Thriller Writers Since 1940,* First Series, edited by Bernard Benstock and Thomas F. Staley (1989)

88: *Canadian Writers, 1920-1959,* Second Series, edited by W. H. New (1989)

89: *Restoration and Eighteenth-Century Dramatists,* Third Series, edited by Paula R. Backscheider (1989)

90: *German Writers in the Age of Goethe, 1789-1832,* edited by James Hardin and Christoph E. Schweitzer (1989)

91: *American Magazine Journalists, 1900-1960,* First Series, edited by Sam G. Riley (1990)

92: *Canadian Writers, 1890-1920,* edited by W. H. New (1990)

93: *British Romantic Poets, 1789-1832,* First Series, edited by John R. Greenfield (1990)

94: *German Writers in the Age of Goethe: Sturm und Drang to Classicism,* edited by James Hardin and Christoph E. Schweitzer (1990)

95: *Eighteenth-Century British Poets,* First Series, edited by John Sitter (1990)

96: *British Romantic Poets, 1789-1832,* Second Series, edited by John R. Greenfield (1990)

97: *German Writers from the Enlightenment to Sturm und Drang, 1720-1764,* edited by James Hardin and Christoph E. Schweitzer (1990)

98: *Modern British Essayists,* First Series, edited by Robert Beum (1990)

99: *Canadian Writers Before 1890,* edited by W. H. New (1990)

100: *Modern British Essayists,* Second Series, edited by Robert Beum (1990)

101: *British Prose Writers, 1660-1800,* First Series, edited by Donald T. Siebert (1991)

102: *American Short-Story Writers, 1910-1945,* Second Series, edited by Bobby Ellen Kimbel (1991)

103: *American Literary Biographers,* First Series, edited by Steven Serafin (1991)

104: *British Prose Writers, 1660-1800,* Second Series, edited by Donald T. Siebert (1991)

105: *American Poets Since World War II,* Second Series, edited by R. S. Gwynn (1991)

106: *British Literary Publishing Houses, 1820-1880,* edited by Patricia J. Anderson and Jonathan Rose (1991)

107: *British Romantic Prose Writers, 1789-1832,* First Series, edited by John R. Greenfield (1991)

108: *Twentieth-Century Spanish Poets,* First Series, edited by Michael L. Perna (1991)

109: *Eighteenth-Century British Poets,* Second Series, edited by John Sitter (1991)

110: *British Romantic Prose Writers, 1789-1832,* Second Series, edited by John R. Greenfield (1991)

111: *American Literary Biographers,* Second Series, edited by Steven Serafin (1991)

112: *British Literary Publishing Houses, 1881-1965,* edited by Jonathan Rose and Patricia J. Anderson (1991)

113: *Modern Latin-American Fiction Writers,* First Series, edited by William Luis (1992)

114: *Twentieth-Century Italian Poets,* First Series, edited by Giovanna Wedel De Stasio, Glauco Cambon, and Antonio Illiano (1992)

Documentary Series

1: *Sherwood Anderson, Willa Cather, John Dos Passos, Theodore Dreiser, F. Scott Fitzgerald, Ernest Hemingway, Sinclair Lewis,* edited by Margaret A. Van Antwerp (1982)